MW01629284

EAST INDIA
Publishing Company

THE HISTORY of ENGLAND:
From the Earliest Times to the Norman Conquest
Thomas Hodgkin

Published by the
EAST INDIA PUBLISHING COMPANY
Ottawa, Canada

9781778943201

www.eastindiapublishing.com

Contents

I. The Prehistoric Foreworld ... 1
II. Caesar in Briton ... 8
III. The Century of Suspense ... 24
IV. The Roman Conquest of Britain ... 28
V. The Roman Occupation ... 49
VI. The Anglo-Saxon Conquest ... 73
VII. The Coming of Augustine ... 103
VIII. Edwin of Deira ... 119
IX. Oswald of Bernicia ... 134
X. Oswy and Penda ... 147
XI. Territorial Changes—The Conference at Whitby—
The Great Plague ... 157
XII. King Egfrid and Three Great Churchmen:
Wilfrid, Theodore, Cuthbert ... 175
XIII. The Legislation of King Ine ... 196
XIV. The Eighth Century ... 217
XV. Early Danish Invasions—Egbert and Ethelwulf ... 236
XVI. Ethelwulf's Sons—Danish Invasions to the
Baptism of Guthrum ... 250
XVII. Alfred at Peace ... 263
XVIII. Alfred's Last Days ... 281
XIX. Edward and his Sons ... 292
XX. Edgar and Dunstan ... 316
XXI. Edward the Martyr—Old Age of Dunstan—
Normans and Northmen ... 331
XXII. Ethelred the Redeless ... 344
XXIII. Canute and his Sons ... 368
XXIV. Legislation of the Later Kings ... 390
XXV. Edward the Confessor ... 407
XXVI. Stamford Bridge and Hastings ... 436
Appendix—Authorities ... 453

I.

THE PREHISTORIC FOREWORLD

The history of England if we wish to take it in its narrowest sense begins with the migrations of the Angles, Jutes and Saxons in the fifth century after Christ. Yet, remembering that we have dwelling close beside us and mingling their blood with ours a gallant little people who own no descent from the Anglo-Saxon invaders, and remembering also how magical was the effect on all the barbarian races, of contact with the all-transmuting civilisation of Rome, we cannot surely leave altogether untold the story of those five centuries during which our country was known to the rest of Europe not as Anglia but as Britannia. Can we absolutely stop even there? It is true that the conscious history of Britain, the history that was written by chroniclers and enshrined in libraries, begins, as do the histories of all the nations of Western Europe, with the day when they came first in contact with the Genius of Rome. But is it possible to avoid trying to peer a little further into the infinite, dim and misty ages that lie beyond that great historic landmark? This is what our teachers of natural science have endeavoured to do on our behalf, labouring with the spade of the excavator and the collected specimens of the comparative anatomist to read a few of those faded pages of the history of Britain which had already been long illegible when Julius Cæsar landed on our shores.

And first we listen to the voice of Geology. After toiling through the all-but eternities of the Primary and Secondary systems of rock-formation, she seems to heave a sigh of relief as she enters the vestibule of the Tertiary system. New heavens and a new earth, an earth not utterly unlike that upon which we now dwell, seem to lie before her, and she names the four vast halls through which she leads her disciples "the Dawn of the New," "the Less New," "the More New," and "the Most New" (Eocene, Miocene, Pliocene and Pleistocene). In the last of these halls, which is represented by a mere line on the geological ground plan, yet which may easily have had a duration of 200,000 years, we at last find our fellow-countryman, the first human inhabitant, as far as we know, of the British Isles. In certain well-known caves on the south coast of Devonshire (Kent's Cavern and Brixham) there were found some sixty years ago flint implements undoubtedly fashioned by human hands, along with the remains of hyenas and other animals long since extinct in the British Islands, and these were lying under a stalagmite floor which must have taken at least 12,000 years, and may well have taken 100,000 years, for its formation. It was thus conclusively proved that Palæolithic man whose handiwork has been found in many other European countries, especially in the wonderfully interesting caves of Aquitaine, lived also, how many millenniums ago none can say, in the limestone caves of Britain. Besides these dwellers in caves and probably of an even earlier period than they, were the other Palæolithic men who have left abundant traces of their presence in the spear-heads, flints, scrapers and other large stone implements which are often found in the gravel deposits of ancient rivers.

The Old Stone-workers, as this earliest known race of men is called to distinguish them from Neolithic men, their immeasurably remote descendants or representatives, knew, of course, nothing of the use of metals, and generally fashioned their flint implements or their bone needles in a somewhat rough and unworkmanlike manner. They knew nothing of the art of the weaver, and can therefore have had no other clothing than the skins of beasts. Neither did they ever manufacture anything in the nature of pottery; so that shells and the skulls of animals must have been their only drinking cups. But the relics of their primeval feasts show that they were in all probability not cannibals, and the very few Palæolithic skulls which have been preserved show a type decidedly nobler than some of the backward races of the present day. Curiously enough the men who had made so little advance in the homely industries of life had nevertheless a distinct feeling for graphic art. "By far the most noteworthy objects" in the Palæolithic caves "are the fragments of bone, horn, ivory and stone, which exhibit outlined and even shaded sketches of various animals. These engravings have been made with a sharp-pointed implement, and are often wonderfully characteristic representations of the creatures they portray. The figures are sometimes single; in other cases they are drawn in groups. We find representations of a fish, a seal, an ox, an ibex, the red-deer, the great Irish elk or deer, the bison, the horse, the cave-bear, the rein-deer and the mammoth or woolly elephant."*

Whatever may have been the precise relation of the Pleistocene period to the Great Ice Age—a point as to which there is some difference of opinion—it is admitted that at some time or other after that when the hyena howled in the Brixham Cave, and when Palæolithic man left there his rudely worked flint implements, the conditions of life in Northern Europe changed. The Arctic zone invaded the larger part of the Temperate zone, and a great cap of ice covered not only the Scandinavian countries and the greater part of Russia but Ireland, Scotland and England, at least as far south as the valley of the Thames. Now were our chalk hills rounded into smoothness, now were many of our river beds hollowed out, and untidy heaps of "terminal moraine" deposited where the glaciers debouched into the valleys. This dismal change, destructive of all the higher organic life and continuing possibly over a period of thousands of years, makes, in our island at any rate, an impassable barrier between two races of mankind. When the great ice deluge subsided, when the winter-tyrant returned to his true Arctic home, when the oak and the pine began again to appear upon the hills, and flowers like our own bloomed in the valleys, then the Neolithic man, the "New Stone-worker," came upon the scene and scattered abundant evidences of his presence over the land. From that period—date we cannot call it, for we have no evidence which would justify us in making the roughest approximation to a date—man has been continuously a dweller in this island, Neolithic man at length yielding ground to the immigrant Celt, the Celt to the Saxon, the Saxon to the Dane and the Norman.

At this point Ethnology must intervene and take up the story of the ages which has thus far been told by her sister Geology. Of what race were the men who after the retreat of the great desolating glaciers came to inhabit this our island? We know that on the one hand they were in a decidedly more advanced state of civilisation than their Palæolithic predecessors. Instead of the rough unshapely pyramids of flint which the Old Stone men used for axes and chisels, Neolithic man went on shaping and polishing his implements till scarcely a fault could be found in the symmetry of their curves. He continued, of course, to hunt and fish as his predecessor had done, but he had also some knowledge of agriculture, he was a breeder of cattle and he knew how to weave cloth and to bake

* Geikie, Prehistoric Europe, p. 13.

pottery. He no longer lived principally in caves, but sometimes in a fairly constructed house, often, for security, built on the edge of a lake. But, strange to say, with all these great advances towards civilisation, he does not seem to have felt any of that passion for picture-drawing which distinguished his predecessor "the artistic hunter of the Reindeer period."* The physiological characteristics which differentiate Neolithic man from the Celt, his conqueror, will be more fully dwelt on when we come to the next act in the drama; but meanwhile it may be stated that the race was not a tall one. Professor Rolleston says: "I have never found the stature to exceed 5 feet 9 inches in any skeleton from a barrow which was undoubtedly of the 'stone and bone' [i.e., Neolithic] period." There is some reason to think that they were dark complexioned with black and curly hair, but it must be admitted that the evidence for this statement is not very conclusive.

On the whole Ethnology decides that these earliest inhabitants of our island after the Great Ice Age were a non-Aryan race, strangers therefore to that great and widely scattered family to which, as far as language is concerned, all the great European peoples save the Turks, the Hungarians and the Finns, ultimately belong. Of course since no vestige of language survives to indicate their nationality, even this universally accepted classification, or rather refusal to classify, must be considered as purely conjectural. In the words of Professor Rolleston: "The race which used stone and bone implements, may, so far as the naturalist's investigations lead him, have spoken either a Turanian or an Aryan tongue: what he sees in their skulls and their surroundings impresses him with the notion of an antiquity which may have given time enough and to spare for the more or less complete disappearance of more than one unwritten language." The important fact to lay hold of is that the whole of the long period of Stone-workers in this country is pre-Celtic. Any name which we may for purposes of convenience give to these aborigines of Britain, whether the now nearly discarded word Turanians, to mark their exclusion from the Aryan family; or Iberians, to indicate a possible connexion with the mysterious Basques of the Pyrenees; or Silurians, in order to show a possible survival of their type in the countrymen of Caractacus; is only like an algebraical symbol, a label affixed to a locked box, denoting our ignorance of its contents.

Perhaps the most important fact known in connexion with the Neolithic

* Geikie, p. 119.

inhabitants of Britain is that recent discoveries show that they were the builders of Stonehenge. That a race of men using no implements of iron should have succeeded in rearing those huge blocks into position on the plain of Wiltshire is a stupendous marvel, equalling in its way the erection of the pyramids of Ghizeh, the placing of the great stones in the temple at Baalbek, or the superposition of the 300-ton block of Istrian marble on the tomb of Theodoric, at Ravenna. This discovery seems to throw some doubt on the generally received notion that Stonehenge was connected with Druidical worship, since that was probably of Celtic origin. It is possible that Stonehenge may be the "magnificent circular temple to Apollo" which, according to Diodorus Siculus, existed in an island which may be identified with Britain.

*****

To the age of stone succeeded the age of bronze, and to the age of bronze succeeded that of iron. Both in our island belong to the domination of the Celts, except in so far as the age of iron may be said to have lasted through Roman, Saxon and Norman domination down to our own day. It is admitted by all that the Celtic immigrants came in two successive waves, the distinction between which may be seen to this day, or if not always seen in physical type, at least always heard in the language of their descendants. The first wave, which is generally known as the Gaelic, eventually rolled to the Highlands and islands of Scotland and to the shores of Ireland, and is represented philologically by the kindred dialects of Gaelic and Erse. The second wave, popularly known as the Cymric, overspread the whole east and centre of Britain, the Gaels being probably forced to retire before their Cymric conquerors. To this race belong the Welsh and the Bretons of France; and Cumberland and Cornwall once spoke their language. Some of our most recent authorities on British ethnology, believing the term Cymri to be of late origin and the term Gaelic to have some misleading associations, prefer to speak of Goidels and Brythons (early national names) instead of Gaels and Cymri; but the distinction between the two races and the main lines of their geographical distribution are generally accepted, and are not affected by this question of nomenclature.

It is probable, then, that at some period whose date cannot yet be even approximately conjectured, and from some quarter which we may guess, but can only guess, to have been the north of Germany, a bronze-using race of warriors and hunters, ancestors of the modern Highlander and Irishman, crossed the sea and established themselves in the island of Britain, or, as it was, perhaps, then called, Albion. Later on, but how many centuries later none can say, another race, kindred but probably hostile, invaded our shores, drove the Gaels or Goidels before them, established themselves in the best parts of the southern portion of the island, and, being themselves called Brythons, gave to the whole land the name by which the Romans called it, Britannia. As we know that iron had been introduced into the country before the arrival of the Romans, we may conjecture that this second Celtic wave consisted of the wielders of weapons of iron, and that this was one cause of their victory over the Goidels. The Brythons, thus settled in the valley of the Thames and above the chalk cliffs of Sussex, were the enemies whom Cæsar encountered when he invaded Britain.

A word may be said as to the relation of these Aryan invaders to the presumably non-Aryan aborigines, the Neolithic men to whom allusion was previously made. It used to be supposed that these aborigines disappeared before the men of bronze and iron as completely as the aborigines of Tasmania have disappeared before the Anglo-Saxon immigrant. More careful investigation has led our recent ethnologists to deny this conclusion. In the first place, there are features in the rude polity of the historic Celts which suggest a doubt whether they really constituted the whole population of the country. Their chiefs are warlike leaders, their rank and file are themselves owners of slaves. Everything about them seems to show that they were, like the Spartans, a comparatively small ruling race surrounded by a subject population, which they perhaps needed to keep severely in check. Then the testimony of the tombs—and it is after all to the tombs that we must chiefly resort for information as to the fate of these buried peoples—decidedly confirms the theory of the survival of the aborigines and of their blending to a considerable extent with their Celtic conquerors. The stone-using people buried their dead in oblong mounds technically known as "long barrows" generally some one hundred to two hundred feet long by forty or fifty feet wide. The skulls found in these long barrows, lying side by side with implements of stone, are uniformly of the type known as Dolicho-cephalic, that is, the width from ear to ear is very considerably less than the length from the eyes to the back of the head. With the introduction of bronze we at once find a noticeable difference both in the shape of the tomb and the appearance of its occupant. The mound is now circular, generally from forty to sixty feet in diameter, the "round barrow" of the archæologist; and the skulls found in it are at first uniformly of the Brachy-cephalic type, square and strong, the width generally about four-fifths of the length. The important point to observe for our present purpose is that as we pass from the early Celtic to the late Celtic type of barrow—a transition of which we are assured by the gradual introduction of iron as well as by other signs known to archæologists—the character of the skulls undergoes a certain modification towards the Dolicho-cephalic type. The conclusion arrived at by the greatest investigator of British barrows, Dr. Greenwell, is that "ultimately the two races became so mixed up and connected as to form one people. If this was the case, by a natural process the more numerous race would in the end absorb the other, until at length, with some exceptions to be accounted for by well-known laws, the whole population would become one, not only in the accidents of civilisation and government, but practically in blood also."

II.

CÆSAR IN BRITAIN

Down to the middle of the first century before Christ the British Isles were scarcely more known to the civilised nations of southern Europe than the North Pole is to the men of our own day. The trade which had probably long existed in the tin of Cornish mines had been purposely kept in mysterious darkness by the Phœnicians who profited thereby, so that Herodotus, the much inquiring, only mentions the Tin-islands (Cassiterides) to say that he knows naught concerning them. That trade had now probably become, save for the short passage of the channel, an overland one, and enriched the merchants of Marseilles. A citizen of that busy port, Pytheas by name, who seems to have been contemporary with Alexander the Great, professed to have travelled over the greater part of Britain, and afterwards to have sailed to a great distance along the northern coast of Germany. It was the fashion of later authors, such as Polybius and Strabo, to sneer at his alleged voyage of discovery and to doubt his veracity, but the tendency of modern inquiry is in some degree to restore the credit of this Marco Polo of pre-Christian times, to show that in some points he had a more correct knowledge of geography than his critics, and to deepen our regret that his work is known to us only in a few passages selected and perhaps distorted by his hostile reviewers. It must be admitted that if he reported that the circumference of Britain was 40,000 stadia (about 5,000 of our miles), and that he had traversed the whole of it on foot,* his statement was not altogether consistent with fact.

Such, however, was all the information that the Greeks and Romans possessed concerning our island near the middle of the first century B.C., at the time when Cicero was thundering against Catiline, and Pompey

* Bunbury (History of Ancient Geography, i., 591) disputes this translation, and contends that Pytheas only said that he travelled (not necessarily on foot) over such parts of the island as were accessible.

was forcing his way into the temple at Jerusalem. Her time, however, for entrance on the great theatre of the world was near at hand, and it was for her a fortunate circumstance, and one not inconsistent with the part which she has played thereon in later ages, that the man who brought her on to the stage should have been himself the central figure in the world's political history—Gaius Julius Cæsar.

Sprung from one of the oldest and proudest families of Rome, yet nephew by marriage of the peasant-soldier Marius, Cæsar, the high-born democrat, possessed in his own person that combination of qualities which has ever been found most dangerous to the rule of a narrow and selfish oligarchy. The outworn machine which men still called the Roman republic was obviously creaking towards an utter breakdown, and must soon, if the provinces were not to be bled to death by greedy senators, be replaced by the government of a single man, whether that man were called king, or general, or dictator. The only question was who that single man should be. Cæsar felt that he was the man of destiny, foreordained to stand on that awful eminence. He flung out of the Roman forum and senate-house, teeming as they were with squalid intrigues and echoing to the cries of ignoble factions, and at the age of forty set himself to a ten years' apprenticeship to empire on the banks of the Loire and the Saône, amid the vast forests of Britain or of Gaul. The French historian, Michelet, has finely said: "I would that I could have seen that pale countenance, aged before its time by the revelries of Rome: that delicate and epileptic man, walking at the head of his legions under the rains of Gaul, swimming across our rivers or riding on horseback among the litters in which his secretaries were carried, and dictating five or six letters at once: agitating Rome from the furthest corners of Belgium: sweeping two millions of men from his path and in the space of ten years subduing Gaul, the Rhine and the northern ocean."

At the end of the first three years of Cæsar's proconsulship (58–56 B.C.) having apparently almost completed the conquest of Gaul, he stood a conqueror on the southern shore of the Straits of Dover, looked across at the white cliffs of Albion, and dreamed of bringing that mysterious island within the circle of Roman dominion. Pretexts for invasion were never lacking to an adventurous proconsul. There were close ties of affinity between many of the northern tribes of Gaul and their British neighbours. Some tribes even bore the same name. The Atrebates of Arras were reflected in the Atrebates of Berkshire; there were Belgæ in Somerset and Wiltshire as well as in Belgium; even men call Parisii were found, strangely enough, in the East Riding of Yorkshire. Then there was also the connexion, whatever may have been its value, between the religion of the continental and the insular Celts. Our information concerning the Druids (chiefly derived from Cæsar himself) is somewhat vague and unsatisfactory, but there is no reason to doubt his statement that the Druidic "discipline" had originated in Britain and had been carried thence into Gaul, and thus any religious element that there may have been in the resistance of the Gallic tribes to Roman domination would look across the channel for sympathy and inspiration.

There was already a certain amount of commercial intercourse between Britain and Gaul, and Cæsar endeavoured to ascertain by questioning the merchants engaged in that trade what was the size of the island, what were its best harbours, and what the customs and warlike usages of the natives. On none of these points, however, could he obtain satisfactory information. The proconsul therefore sent a lieutenant named Volusenus with a swift ship to reconnoitre the nearer coast, but he returned in five days without having ventured to land. Meanwhile, as the object of the general's prolonged stay in the territory of the Morini became more and more evident, messengers from certain of the British tribes began to cross the channel, charged—so Cæsar says—with a commission to promise "obedience to the rule of the Roman people," and to give hostages as a pledge of their fidelity. The arrival of the ambassadors and their attempt to turn the proconsul from his purpose by fair speech and unmeaning promises we may well believe. How much the Regni and the Cantii knew about the rule of the Roman people, and what intention they had of loyally submitting to it, may be left uncertain. Cæsar, however, availed himself of the opportunity to send over with these returning envoys a certain Celtic chieftain named Commius, whom he had himself made king of the continental Atrebates, and on whose fidelity he thought that he could rely, to exhort the native tribes peacefully to accept the dominion of the Roman people, as the representative of whom Cæsar himself would shortly make his appearance among them. This mission of Commius proved quite fruitless. As soon as he landed—so he said—the Britons arrested him and loaded him with chains, and it was only after the defeat which will shortly be described that they sent him back to Cæsar. As we find Commius only four years later taking a leading part in the insurrection of the tribes in the north of Gaul, and professing an especial hostility to all who bore the name of Roman, we may, perhaps, doubt whether, even at this time, his pleas for subjection were as earnest, or the chains imposed upon him by the Britons as heavy, as Cæsar's narrative would seem to imply.

Cæsar had determined to make his exploratory voyage with two legions, the Seventh and the Tenth. He perhaps hoped that actual war would not be necessary to bring about the formal submission of the tribes on the coast, and he therefore did not take with him more than the 8,000 to 10,000 men, which were probably the actual muster of two legions, and a body of cavalry whose precise number is not stated. As fighting, however, might, after all, prove to be necessary, he took care that one of the legions which accompanied him should be the famous Tenth on whose courage and devotion he often relied, not in vain. To transport the legions he had collected about eighty cargo ships (naves onerariæ), many of which had been employed the year before in his naval campaign off the coast of Brittany. He had also a certain number of galleys (naves longæ) capable of being rowed much faster than the heavy transport ships could sail. On these latter his staff of officers, quæstors, legates and prefects were embarked, and no doubt the proconsul himself was their companion.

The fleet set sail about midnight on August 26, B.C. 55, or on some day very near to that date. The port of embarkation was probably near to Cape Gris Nez and at the narrowest part of the channel, but almost every sentence of the following narrative has been the subject of an animated topographical discussion, and Cæsar himself mentions no names of places that can be certainly identified.* Whatever may have been the harbour from which the legions embarked it was not the same which had been appointed as a rendezvous for the cavalry. These latter were to be borne upon a little fleet of eighteen transports which were detained by a contrary wind at a port eight miles farther up the channel. As we shall see, their ill fortune in the matter of weather continued throughout the expedition, and their consequent inability to co-operate with the legions may have been the chief cause of the expedition's failure.

As for the main body of the fleet, it must have made an extremely slow voyage, for it was not till the fourth hour of the day (about 8.30 A.M.) that the foremost ships caught sight of the shores of Britain. The landing was evidently not to be unopposed: on all the hills armed bodies of the

* See Note at the end of this chapter.

enemy were drawn up. The word used by Cæsar signifies properly "hills," but as he goes on to say that "the sea was commanded by such steep mountains that a weapon could easily be hurled from the higher ground to the shore," we are probably right in understanding these "hills" to be the well-known chalk cliffs of Kent. Seeing therefore no suitable place for landing, Cæsar signalled for his fleet to gather round him, and lay quietly at anchor for five hours. Summoning his staff he imparted to them such information concerning the nature of the country as he had been able to gather from Volusenus, and explained that in maritime warfare such as that in which they were now engaged, liable to be affected by rapid changes of the weather and the sea, it was pre-eminently necessary that they should give prompt obedience to his orders. At about 3 P.M., apparently, the fleet weighed anchor, and, wind and tide having become favourable, moved forward about seven miles and there halted opposite a level and open shore which seemed well adapted for landing.

The barbarians, however, who were of course watching Cæsar's movements, sent forward their chariots and their cavalry, and following themselves with rapid movements were on the spot to oppose the Romans' disembarkation. It seemed for some time as if their opposition would be effectual. The ships drawing many feet of water could not approach near to the land, and the soldiers, with their hands encumbered by the pilum or the sword and their bodies weighted with the heavy armour of the Roman legionary, found it no easy matter to jump from the ships, to stagger through the slippery ooze, to defend themselves against the attacks of the nimble and lightly armed barbarians. Seeing this, Cæsar ordered up the galleys, which were rowed rapidly backwards and forwards between the transports and the shore, and from the decks of which slings, bows and balistae freely employed worked havoc among the barbarians, already disposed to terror by the unwonted sight of the triremes. But as the soldiers still hesitated, chiefly on account of the depth of the water into which it was necessary to plunge, the standard-bearer of the Tenth legion, after a short prayer to the gods for good luck to his legion, leapt into the sea, shouting with a loud voice: "Jump! comrades! unless you would see your eagle fall into the enemy's hands. I at any rate will do my duty to the Republic and our general." His example was contagious. All the soldiers leapt from the ships and were soon engaged in a hand-to-hand struggle with the Britons, each man rallying to the standard that was nearest to him as it was hopeless in such a mêlée to form regular rank by legions and cohorts. The barbarians, charging with their horses into deep water, were sometimes able to surround smaller parties of the invaders or to harass them from a distance with their darts. Hereupon, Cæsar filled the boats of the long ships and some of the lighter skiffs with soldiers, who rowing rapidly backwards and forwards carried help where it was most needed.

It was probably at this stage of the encounter that an incident took place which is recorded not by Cæsar himself but by Valerius Maximus, an anecdote-collector of a later date. He tells us that a legionary named Scæva with four comrades rowed to a rock surrounded by the sea and from thence dealt destruction with their arrows among the Britons. Before long the ebbing tide made their rock accessible from the shore and the other soldiers thought it was time to row back to their ship. Scæva, refusing to accompany them, was soon surrounded by the barbarians, with whom he fought single-handed. Many he killed, but he himself suffered fearfully. His thigh was pierced by an arrow, his face smashed by a stone, his shield broken. At last he threw himself into the sea and swam to his vessel. Cæsar and the officers began to applaud him for his bravery, but he flung himself at the proconsul's feet and with tears implored forgiveness for the military crime of the loss of his shield.

When the great body of the soldiers had at last struggled to the shore and could fight on firm land, Roman discipline soon prevailed over barbarian ardour. The Britons took to flight, but the absence of cavalry, bitterly regretted by Cæsar, checked pursuit. Next day there came ambassadors from the dispirited Britons praying for pardon, bringing the liberated Commius and promising to obey all Cæsar's orders. After a grave rebuke for having violated the laws of nations by imprisoning his messengers, the proconsul granted his forgiveness and ordered the natives to hand over hostages for their good faith. A few were given, the rest who were to be sent by the more distant tribes were promised but never came. The reason of this failure of the negotiations (if they had ever had a chance of success) was the catastrophe which befel the lingering squadron with its freight of cavalry. On the fourth day after Cæsar's landing, the eighteen ships with the horsemen on board drew nigh to Britain. Already they were descried by their comrades on shore when so violent a storm arose that they were hopelessly beaten off their course. Some were driven straight back to the harbour which they had quitted, others with imminent danger of shipwreck drifted down channel and at last, waterlogged and nearly helpless, regained some port in Gaul.

On the night which followed this disastrous day, a night of full moon, the unusually high tide, a marvel and a mystery to these children of the Mediterranean, surrounded the Roman ships which had been drawn up, as they hoped, high and dry on the beach. Cables were broken, anchors lost, some of the ships probably dashed against one another; it seemed as though Cæsar would be stranded without ships and without supplies on the inhospitable shore of Britain. He at once sent out some of his soldiers to collect supplies from the Kentish harvest fields, and set others to repair those ships, whose repair was yet possible, at the expense of their hopelessly ruined companions. He admits an entire loss of twelve, but leaves us to infer that the remainder were patched into some sort of seaworthiness. By this time undoubtedly the one thought of both general and army was how to get safe back to Gaul; and naturally the one thought of the Britons, who knew all that had occurred, was how to prevent that return. The promised hostages of course never appeared; and a troop of barbarians ambushed in a neighbouring forest watched for a favourable opportunity of attacking the Romans. That opportunity came one day when the soldiers of the Seventh legion were out foraging in the harvest fields. The sentinels in the Roman camp descried a cloud of dust rising in the direction whither their comrades had gone, and brought word to the general, who at once suspected that the precarious peace was broken and that mischief was abroad. Sallying forth with four cohorts he found that it was even so. The barbarians had emerged from their ambush, had fallen upon the unsuspecting legionaries, quietly engaged in reaping the British harvest, had slain a few of them and were harassing the rest with "alarums and excursions" by their cavalry and their charioteers.

At this point Cæsar interrupts his narrative to describe the British custom of using chariots in war, a custom which was evidently strange and disconcerting to the Roman soldiery. "This," he says, "is their manner of fighting. First they drive their horses about in all directions, hurling darts, and by the very terror of their horses and clashing of their wheels often throw the ranks [of their enemies] into confusion. Then when they have insinuated themselves between the squadrons of the [hostile] cavalry they leap from their chariots and fight on foot. The charioteers meanwhile gradually draw out of the fray and so place the cars that if their friends should be overborne by the multitude of the enemy they may easily take refuge with them. In this way they combine the rapid movements of cavalry with the steadiness of infantry, and have acquired such a degree of dexterity by daily practice that they can hold up their galloping horses in the steepest descents, check and turn them in a moment, run along the pole or sit on the yoke, and then as quickly as possible fly back into the car." It will be observed that Cæsar says nothing about the famous scythe-armed chariots of the Britons which, as has been often suggested, would surely on a battlefield be as dangerous to friends as to foes.

Cæsar's arrival rescued his troops from their perilous position, and he was able to lead them back in safety to the camp. Many stormy days followed, during which warlike operations were necessarily suspended on both sides, but the barbarians employed the interval in beating up recruits from all quarters, attracted by the hope of plunder and of making an end at one blow of the army of invasion, whose scanty numbers moved them to contempt. When fighting was resumed the legions easily repelled the British attack, and some horsemen who had been brought by Commius, though only thirty in number, enabled Cæsar to pursue the flying foe for some distance, to kill many of them and to lay waste a wide extent of country with fire and sword. The usual group of penitent ambassadors appeared the same day in Cæsar's camp; the usual excuses were offered; were accepted as a matter of necessity; and twice the number of hostages was ordered to be surrendered. It did not greatly matter how many were demanded, for Cæsar had no intention of awaiting their delivery. Soon after midnight the Roman fleet set sail, and the whole army returned eventually safe to Gaul, though two of the ships bearing 300 men drifted down the coast of Picardy, and the soldiers, attacked by no fewer than 6,000 of the Morini, had much ado to defend themselves till the general sent a force of cavalry to their succour.

On the arrival of Cæsar's despatches in Rome the senate ordered a solemn supplicatio or thanksgiving to the gods, which was to last for twenty days. The British expedition had been a daring and a showy exploit, but no one knew better than Cæsar himself that it had been an entire failure, and that nothing had really been done towards bringing a single British tribe under "the rule of the Roman people." If this island was to be conquered, it was plain that a much larger force than two legions would be needed for the work. This Cæsar recognised, and accordingly he determined to make another attempt next year (B.C. 54) with five legions (perhaps about 21,000 men) and 2,000 cavalry. The previous campaign had evidently convinced the general of the importance of mounted men for this kind of warfare. He was also determined to have a longer interval before the autumnal equinox for the conduct of his campaign than he had allowed himself in the previous year, and accordingly somewhere about July 23 he set sail from the Portus Itius. He would, in fact, have started at least three weeks earlier, but the wind had been blowing persistently from a point a long way to the north of west. As soon as it shifted to the south-west, the fleet (which with all its companions consisted of 800 ships) started at sunset. In the night, however, the wind fell and the tide (which probably neither Cæsar nor any of his officers understood) carried the ships far out of their course. When the sun arose they saw that Britain was far behind them, on their left hand. Dropping their sails, they took to the oars, and Cæsar has words of well-deserved praise for his sturdy soldiers, who rowed so well that they made the heavy transport ships keep up with the lighter galleys which, as before, accompanied them. By a little after noon they reached the coast of Britain, apparently at their old landing-place. Their disembarkation was not now opposed; the Britons having, as it seems, lost heart when they saw so vast a flotilla approaching their shores.

Notwithstanding his larger armament, Cæsar's second invasion was in many respects a mere replica of the first, and it is hardly worth while to describe it in equal detail. There was again a violent tempest which swept the fleet from its anchorage, destroyed forty of the ships, and obliged Cæsar to waste ten precious days in repairing the remainder. Toilsome as the task must be, he judged it advisable to draw all his ships up on land and surround them with a wall of circumvallation. When we remember that this was the precaution adopted by the Greeks who warred in Troy, we see how little essential change had been wrought in naval warfare in the course of 1,000 years. Meanwhile the Britons had assembled in large numbers in order to oppose the progress of the invaders, and had entrusted the national defence to a chief named Cassivellaunus who ruled over some of the tribes north of the Thames. Hitherto he had made himself apparently more feared than loved by his dealings with neighbouring tribes: the Trinobantes, especially, who dwelt in the district now known as Essex, had seen their king murdered and their king's son made a fugitive by his orders; but now in the supreme hour of danger the hard, unscrupulous soldier was by general consent chosen as a kind of dictator.

After some preliminary skirmishes in which the heavily armed Roman legionaries suffered severely from the dashing onslaught and rapid retreat of the British chariots and cavalry, Cæsar determined to cross the Thames and beard the lion Cassivellaunus in his den. He was stationed on the north bank of the river which was fordable, but defended by sharp stakes placed in the bed of the stream. It is not quite clear from Cæsar's account how this obstacle of the stakes was dealt with by his soldiers. Possibly they may have been partly removed by the cavalry whom he says that he sent first into the water. They were followed by the legionaries, who went, he says, so swiftly and with such a dash, though only their heads were out of water, that the enemy, unable to stand before the combined rush of horsemen and foot soldiers, left their stations on the bank and scattered in flight.

As was so often the case with these Celtic tribes, domestic discord in some degree lightened the labours of the invader. We have seen that Cassivellaunus had obtained by violence the sovereignty of the Trinobantes of Essex. Mandubracius, the son of the dead king, had fled to Gaul and cast himself on the protection of Cæsar, in whose train he returned to Britain. There was still probably a party in favour of the dethroned family, and it was not a mere formality when Cæsar ordered the tribe to accept Mandubracius for their chief, to supply his troops with corn, and to deliver forty hostages into his hands. Five other tribes whose unimportant names are given by Cæsar came in and made their submission; and from them the general learned that not far distant was the town (oppidum) of Cassivellaunus, filled with a multitude of men and cattle, and defended by forests and marshes. "Now the Britons," says Cæsar, perhaps with a sneer, "call any place a town" (oppidum) "when they have chosen a position entangled with forests and strengthened it with rampart and ditch, so that they may gather into it for shelter from hostile incursion." Thither then marched Cæsar with his legions. He found a place splendidly strong by nature and art, but he determined to attack it from two sides at once. After a brief defence, the natives collapsed before the headlong rush of the Romans, and streamed out of the camp on the opposite side. Many were slain, many taken prisoners, and a great number of cattle fell into the hands of the Romans.

In order probably to divert the forces of his enemy from his own oppidum, the generalissimo Cassivellaunus had sent orders to the four kings of Kent to collect their forces and make a sudden attack on the naval camp of the Romans. The attack was repulsed by a vigorous sortie: many of the Britons were slain and one of their noblest leaders taken prisoner. Hereupon Cassivellaunus, recognising that the fortune of war was turning against him and that his own confederates were falling away, sent messengers to offer his submission and obtain peace through the mediation of his friend, perhaps his fellow-tribesman, Commius. Cæsar, who had his own reasons for desiring a speedy return to Gaul and who doubtless considered that enough had been done for his glory, accepted the proffered submission. He "ordered hostages to be delivered, and fixed the amount of tribute which was to be yearly paid by Britannia to the Roman people. He forbade Cassivellaunus to do any injury to Mandubracius or the Trinobantes," and with these high-sounding phrases he departed. As he carried back many captives and not a few of his ships had perished in the storm, he had to make two crossings with his fleet, but both were accomplished without disaster. Of Cassivellaunus himself no further information is vouchsafed us, nor do we know what was the fate of the abandoned allies of Rome.

The great general in this instance "had come and had seen" but had not "conquered." Most valuable, however, to us is the information which he has given us concerning our sequestered island, though in some cases it is evidently inaccurate. We need not linger over Cæsar's geographical statements, though it is curious to see how certain errors of earlier geographers still lingered on even into the Augustan age of Roman literature. Thus he thinks that, of the three sides of Britain's triangle one looks towards Gaul and the east, another towards Spain and the west, while the third, which has no land opposite it, faces north. Besides Ireland, which is half the size of Britain, there are other islands, apparently on the west, concerning which certain writers have said that they have continual night during thirty days of winter. As to this Cæsar was not able to obtain any definite information, but his own clepsydræ (water clocks) showed him that the nights in July were shorter in Britain than on the continent.

"Of all the natives far the most civilised are those who inhabit the district of Kent, which is all situated on the coast: nor do these differ greatly in their manners from the inhabitants of Gaul. Those who live farther inland sow no corn, but live on milk and flesh, and are clothed in skins. All the Britons however dye themselves with woad, which gives them a blue colour and makes them look more terrible in battle. They wear long hair and shave every part of the body except the head and the upper lip. Ten or a dozen men have their wives in common, especially brothers with brothers, fathers with their sons, the woman's offspring being reckoned to him who first cohabited with her." This ghastly statement is probably a mere traveller's tale, utterly untrue of the Celts of Britain or of any other Aryan tribe. It has been thought that it may possibly have been derived from an institution something like the Sclavonic mir, which caused all the descendants of one married couple for two or three generations to herd together in a single household. "The interior of Britain is inhabited by tribes which are, according to their own tradition, aboriginal: the sea-coast by those which for the sake of plunder have crossed over from Belgic Gaul, and after carrying on war have settled there and begun to cultivate the land. It is in consequence of this that nearly all of them have the same tribal names as those of the states from which they came. There is an infinite number of inhabitants, and one constantly meets with buildings almost like those of Gaul, as well as a great number of cattle."

"They use either golden money or thin bars of iron of a certain weight which pass for money." Thus (according to the best reading of a much-disputed passage) does Cæsar speak as to the numismatic attainments of the Britons. We shall probably never know more than this as to the iron currency or quasi-currency of our predecessors; but the statement as to their gold currency has been entirely confirmed by modern discoveries. The most curious fact, however, in connexion with the pre-Roman gold coinage of Britain is that it is evidently an imitation, though a most barbarous imitation, of the coinage of Philip II. of Macedon, the father of Alexander the Great. In the British imitations the fine classical features of the Macedonian monarch are twisted into the ignoble profile of a savage, while the curls of the hair and the leaves of the laurel crown, mechanically repeated and magnified, fill up the greater part of the coin. The effigy of a charioteer on the reverse of the coin is attempted to be copied in the same grotesque fashion with rather less success than the drawing of a child upon its slate. The charioteer himself is gradually resolved into a cluster of atoms, and though the likeness of the horse is for some time preserved, he is furnished with eight legs and gradually dwindles away into the spectre of a rocking-horse. Yet these queer pieces of money which occasionally turn up in English soil are intensely interesting, as showing how the influence of Greek art penetrated even into our world-forgotten island three centuries before the birth of Christ, travelling possibly by the same commercial route between the Euxine and the Baltic by which the Runes passed up from Thrace to Scandinavia, and the highly prized amber descended from Stralsund to Odessa.

Cæsar proceeds to inform us that "tin (plumbum album) is found in the midland parts of the country [as to this he was of course misinformed]; iron in the maritime regions, but in small quantities; all the bronze used is imported. There is timber of all kinds, as in Gaul, save the fir and the beech. They do not think it right to eat hares, geese or poultry, but keep these animals as pets. The climate is more temperate than that of Gaul, the cold less intense." One regrets to learn from Strabo, who wrote half a century after Cæsar, that though "the climate is rainy rather than snowy, even in clear weather mists prevail so long that through the whole day the sun is visible only for three or four hours about noon."

In reviewing the history of Cæsar's invasions of Britain we naturally inquire what was his object in fitting out those expeditions, why did they fail and why did he acquiesce in their failure. Whatever may have been the motive of the first (which, according to him, was chiefly the assistance given by the Britons to the cause of his Gaulish enemies), the second expedition at any rate, on which from 20,000 to 30,000 men were employed, cannot have been a mere reconnaissance, undertaken in the interests of scientific discovery. It was no doubt politic to stimulate the zeal of his partisans in Rome by voyages and marches which appeared to be

Beyond the utmost bounds of human thought,

but the general would hardly have spent so much treasure and risked the lives of so many of his legionaries without some hope of substantial advantage to himself, his soldiers, or the republic. Evidently the Britons fought better than he expected. Probably also, the forests and the marshes of the country made the movements of his troops exceptionally difficult. We can perceive also that the country was not so rich as he had hoped to find it—an important consideration for a general who had to reward his soldiers by frequent opportunities of "loot." "We already know," wrote Cicero to his brother Quintus, "that there is not an ounce of silver in that island nor any hope of booty except slaves, among whom I do not think you will expect to find any skilled in literature or music." The only spoil that we hear of Cæsar's carrying back from Britain was a breastplate adorned with precious pearls, which he dedicated in the Temple of Victory at Rome.

One argument which doubtless influenced Cæsar against attempting a third expedition was derived from the peculiarly stormy and baffling character of the sea at the Straits of Dover. Each of his expeditions had been endangered and all but ruined by these unaccountable tides, these suddenly rising gales. He had to learn by bitter experience how different was that strange chopping sea from the peaceful waters of the Mediterranean. Had he been able to survey the channel more thoroughly, he would probably have found it worth while to make his passage at a broader part of it, like that which now separates Newhaven from Dieppe; perhaps even to anticipate the Saxon chieftains of the fifth century, to occupy the Isle of Wight, or to seek for his fleet the shelter of Southampton Water. After all, however, a sufficient reason for not renewing the attempt to conquer Britain was to be found in the precarious state of Roman dominion in Gaul. Cæsar evidently thought that his work in that country was practically finished in B.C. 55, when he first set his face towards Britain. Far otherwise: the hardest part of that work was yet to come. Five months after Cæsar's return from his second expedition he heard the terrible tidings of the utter destruction of fifteen Roman cohorts by the Eburones. Then followed the revolt of Vercingetorix, bravest and most successful of Gaulish champions; the unsuccessful siege of Gergovia; the siege, successful but terribly hard to accomplish, of Alesia. Certainly we may say that the two years and a half which followed his return from Britain were among the most anxious, and seemed sometimes the most desperate stages in all that wonderful career which ended when, ten years after he had sailed away from Britain, he fell pierced by more than twenty dagger wounds—

E'en at the base of Pompey's statua,
Which all the while ran blood.

NOTE ON CÆSAR'S POINTS OF ARRIVAL AND DEPARTURE IN HIS EXPEDITIONS TO BRITAIN

I. As to the point of embarkation from Gaul, the controversy lies principally between Boulogne and Wissant, Sir George Airy's suggestion that Cæsar sailed from the estuary of the Somme being not easy to reconcile with his own statement that he went to the country of the Morini, "because thence was the shortest transit to Britain."

Boulogne, which was called by the Romans first Gesoriacum and then Bononia, was undoubtedly the regular harbour for passengers to Britain under the empire, and there would be little doubt that Cæsar started thence if he had not told us that the second expedition (presumably also the first) sailed from Portus Itius. It is not clear why Cæsar should have called Gesoriacum by any other name.

The advocates of Wissant identify the Itian promontory with Cape Gris Nez, well known to all passengers from Dover to Calais, and think that its name would be naturally shared with the neighbouring village of Wissant, which was probably at one time nearer to the sea than it is now. On the whole, though the arguments on both sides are pretty evenly balanced, those in favour of Wissant seem slightly to preponderate.

II. Sailing, then, from some port in Picardy (either Boulogne or Wissant), Cæsar reached a part of the British coast which from his description looks like the chalk cliffs west of Dover. So far there is not much difference between the commentators, but what happened in the afternoon when, after his long halt, he found the wind and tide both in his favour, gave the signal to weigh anchor, and "having advanced (progressus) about eight miles from that place, brought his ships to a stand at a level and open beach"? Certainly the natural rendering of these words would seem to be that he went seven English miles up channel, and so if he had really anchored off Dover he would reach Deal, and that port would be, as it has been generally supposed to be, the scene of the world-historical landing of the first Roman soldiers in Britain. It must be admitted, however, that there are great difficulties in this hypothesis. The most careful and minute inquiries that have been made seem to show that on that day (the fourth before the full moon) and at that hour (3 P.M.), the tide, if it ebbed and flowed as it does now, would be setting down, not up, the channel: and accordingly many authors have come to the conclusion that Cæsar sailed westward for those seven miles and landed either at Hythe or Lymne (well known afterwards to the Romans as Portus Lemanis), or possibly at some such place as Appledore, now inland but then at the head of a very sheltered bay.

The discussion is much complicated by the undoubted fact of the great changes which have taken place in that part of the coastline, and Dr. Guest is perhaps entitled to argue that these changes may have so altered the set of the tides as to allow him to postulate an eastward flowing tide when Cæsar weighed anchor in the afternoon. It must, however, remain for the present a disputed question: Cæsar's word, "progressus," on the one side, the present course of the tides on the other. On the whole it seems to me that the balance of probability is slightly in favour of Deal.

Among the authors who have written on this question may be mentioned Airy, Lewin, Appach, in favour of some port west of Dover; Long, Merivale, Guest, in favour of Deal. Guest's arguments are perhaps the most satisfactory, but justice should be done to the extremely painstaking little treatise of Appach (Caius Julius Cæsar's British Expeditions, etc., 1868), who, however, surely attempts the impossible in his elaborate back-calculations of the winds and tides of two thousand years ago.

On the question of the point of departure from Gaul, reference may be made to T. R. Holmes's Conquest of Gaul (London, 1899) and to F. Haverfield's review of that book in English Historical Review, xviii., 334–6.

III.

THE CENTURY OF SUSPENSE

The second invasion of Britain by Cæsar took place, according to Roman reckoning, in the year 700 from the foundation of the City. The next, the successful invasion which was ordered by his collateral descendant in the fourth generation, the Emperor Claudius, took place in the year 797 of the same reckoning. There was thus all but a century between the two events; that century which more powerfully than any other, before or after, has influenced the course of human history; yet which for that very reason, because in our chronology the years change from B.C. to A.D., the historical student sometimes finds it hard to recognise in its true perspective.

As far as the work of the literary historian goes, Britain is almost a blank page during the whole of this century. It may be said that to the eyes of the Romans, her own mists closed round her when Cæsar left her shores, B.C. 54, and did not rise till Aulus Plautius approached them, A.D. 43. But the patient toil of the numismatist* has discovered the names of some British kings and enabled us to say something as to their mutual relations; a few brief notices of Roman historians have faintly illumined the scene; and it is now just possible to discern the actual lineaments of one who is not entirely a creature of romance—the royal Cymbeline.

As has been already mentioned, a certain Commius, king of the continental Atrebates, was sent on an unsuccessful mission to Britain before Cæsar's first invasion. In the mighty refluent wave of the Gaulish revolt against Rome, Commius either was actually swept away from his former fidelity or was suspected of being thus disloyal. However this might be, a foul attempt at his assassination, planned by Cæsar's lieutenant, Labienus, converted him into an embittered enemy of Rome.

* Pre-eminently of Sir John Evans, on whose great work on ancient British coins this chapter is founded.

He took part in the great campaigns of Vercingetorix; when they failed he sought succour from the other side of the Rhine; as captain of a band of freebooters he preyed on the subjects of Rome. At length (B.C. 51), seeing that further resistance was hopeless, he made his submission to Mark Antony, his only stipulation being that he might be allowed to go and dwell in some land where he would never again be offended by the sight of a Roman. With these words he vanishes from the pages of the historian of the Gallic war. As we find about the same time, or a little later, a certain Commius coining money in Britain, it is, at least, a tempting theory that the Roman-hating Gaulish refugee came to our island and reigned here over his kindred Atrebates and other tribes besides.

Actual coins of Commius are, it must be admitted, not too certainly extant, but the large number of coins struck by three British kings who are proud to proclaim themselves his sons, clearly attest his existence and justify us in attributing to him considerable importance. These three British kings were Tincommius, Verica and Eppillus, and their dominions stretched from Hampshire to Kent. Their reigns probably occupied the last thirty years before the Christian era, and their coins exhibit an increasing tendency towards Roman manners and Roman art. The old barbaric survivals of the Macedonian effigies gradually disappear; classical profiles are introduced and the cornucopiæ, the eagle and the lion sometimes make their appearance.

A British prince who was apparently a contemporary and a neighbour, possibly a rival of the family of Commius, was named Dubnovellaunus. The obverse of his coins shows a remarkable similarity to some of those of the just-mentioned King Eppillus. But the interesting fact in connexion with this otherwise unknown British chieftain is that a monument in the heart of Asia Minor preserves his name and records his dealings with the Roman Imperator. In the Turkish town of Angora on the side of a desolate Galatian hill stand the ruins of the marble temple of Augustus and Rome: and on the walls of the porch of that temple is a long bilingual inscription, recording in Latin and Greek the most memorable events of the fifty-eight years' reign of the fortunate Augustus. Towards the end we find this passage: "To me fled as suppliant the Kings of the Parthians Tiridates and afterwards Phraates, Artaxares, son of Phraates, King of the Medes: the Kings of the Britons Dumnobellaunus and Tim ..." (the end of the last name being obliterated). It is not likely that if there had been many similar instances of British princes imploring the protection of Augustus they would have been left unrecorded in the monument of Angora; and it is therefore probably with some little courtly exaggeration that the contemporary geographer Strabo says: "Certain of the rulers of that country [Britain] by embassies and flattering attentions have gained the friendship of Cæsar Augustus and made votive offerings in the capital and have now rendered almost the whole island subject to the Romans." This is certainly untrue. "The taxes which they bear are in no wise heavy and are levied on imports and exports between Britain and Gaul. The articles of this commerce are ivory rings and necklaces, and amber and vessels of glass and all such trumpery. It is not therefore desirable to put a garrison in the island, for it would require at least one legion and some cavalry in order to ensure the collection of the tribute, and the expense of keeping up such a force would equal the revenue received, since it would be necessary to lessen the customs duties if you were also levying tribute and there would be always a certain amount of danger attending the employment of force." A very clear and sensible statement surely of the reasons which induced the cautious Augustus finally to abandon his thrice contemplated* scheme for the conquest of Britain.

The British kings whom we have lately been describing reigned chiefly south of the Thames. North of that river in Middlesex, Herts and Essex (the district occupied by Cassivellaunus at the time of Cæsar's invasion) there was reigning, probably from about B.C. 35 to A.D. 5, a chief named Tasciovanus, practically unknown in literary history but abundantly made known to us by his coins, which, though still for the most part barbarous, show some signs of Roman influence. His capital was Verulamium, the little Hertfordshire town which now bears the name of the martyred Saint Alban. On his death, which probably occurred about A.D. 5, he was succeeded by his two sons, one of whom, Cunobelinus, reigned at Camulodunum (the modern Colchester) over the Trinobantes and probably other tribes. Of him not only are the coins numerous and well known, but as the Cymbeline of Shakespeare's drama, his name will be in the mouths of men as long as English literature endures. Of course the Cymbeline of the play has very little in common with the faintly outlined Cunobelinus of history. The lovely Imogen, faithful to her husband unto seeming death; the clownish Cloten, the wicked queen, the selfish boaster Leonatus; all these are mere creatures of the poet's brain, of whom neither the romancer Geoffrey of Monmouth nor his copyist Holinshed had ever

* In B.C. 34, 27 and 25 (Dion Cassius, xlix., 38; liii., 22 and 25).

spoken. Yet in the conception of Cymbeline's character, as an old king who rules his family and his court with little wisdom, there is nothing which clashes with historic truth; and the way in which Shakespeare has described the attitude of these little British princes towards the great, distant, dreadful power of Rome is surely one of the many evidences of his power of realising by instinct rather than by reason the political condition of a by-gone age. It may be noted in passing that Geoffrey of Monmouth informs us, whatever his information may be worth, that Kymbelinus, as he calls this king, "was a great soldier and had been brought up by Augustus Cæsar. He had contracted so great a friendship with the Romans that he freely paid them tribute when he might very well have refused it. In his days our Lord Jesus Christ was born."

A certain Adminius, who seems to have been a son of Cunobelinus, being expelled by his father, fled to the Roman camp in Germany with a small band of followers, and their humble supplications to the Emperor Caligula (37–41) caused that insane egotist to vaunt himself as the conqueror of Britain. A pompous epistle conveyed to the Senate the news of this great triumph, and the bearers thereof were especially charged to enter the city in a state-chariot and to deliver their important communication only in the Temple of Mars and to a crowded assembly. But the buffoonery of the nephew was to be followed by the serious labour of the uncle. The conquest of Britain was now nigh at hand.

IV.

THE ROMAN CONQUEST OF BRITAIN

In the year 41 after Christ's birth the short madness of Caligula's dominion over the world was ended by his assassination in one of the long corridors of the Palatine. His uncle Claudius, the despised weakling of the imperial family, dragged forth trembling from his hiding-place behind a curtain, and to his intense surprise acclaimed as Augustus by the mutinous Prætorians: this was the man for whom by a strange destiny was reserved the glory of adding Britain to the Roman Empire. Yet Claudius, for all his odd ways, his shambling gait, his shaking head, his stammering speech, was by no means the mere fool whom his relatives, ashamed of his physical deficiencies, had affected to consider him. He wrote in countless books the story of his imperial ancestors and his own; he knew the old Etruscan tongue, a knowledge, alas! now lost to the world, and translated treatises written therein; he cleared out the harbour of Ostia; he planted flourishing colonies; he brought water to Rome from the Æquian hills by the aqueduct which bears his name. Could the poor timorous old man have ventured to rely on himself, and to act on his own initiative, his name had perhaps been revered as that of one of the best emperors of Rome. It was his reliance on his wives and his freedmen, the government of the boudoir and the servants' hall, which ruined his reputation with posterity.

It was probably in the same year in which Claudius succeeded to the empire, or it may have been a year later, that old King Cunobelinus died in Britain and was succeeded by his two sons, Caratacus* and Togodumnus. There was, as usual, an exiled prince (whose name was

* The popular form of this prince's name, Caractacus, is not justified by the MSS., but one would not think it necessary to restore the true form by the omission of one letter, were it not that the correct spelling brings us nearer to the Welsh equivalent, Caradoc.

Bericus) claiming Roman assistance for his restoration to his country, but whether he was one of the sons of Cunobelinus or not, neither history nor the coins inform us. The petition of the exiled Bericus was granted by Claudius, and an expedition was resolved on, nominally for his restoration (from this point onwards his name disappears from history), in reality for the conquest of Britain (A.D. 43). The command of the expedition was entrusted to Aulus Plautius, a senator of high rank—he had been consul fourteen years before with the Emperor Tiberius—and was possibly a kinsman of Claudius by marriage. Under his orders marched four legions*:—

The Second: Augusta.

The Ninth: Hispana.

The Fourteenth: Gemina Martia; and

The Twentieth: Valeria Victrix.

All of these but the Ninth were withdrawn from service in Germany, and that legion came from Pannonia, in modern language Hungary west of the Danube. The Second and the Twentieth legions found a permanent home in our island; the Ninth, a grave; the Fourteenth after a brilliant career was withdrawn to Italy after about twenty-five years of British service. We have no exact statement of the number of the army of Plautius. The legions, if at their full complement, should stand for 20,000 men: the cavalry and cohorts of the allies should at least double that number. We are probably not far wrong in putting the invading force at 50,000, but the difficulty of forming an exact estimate is shown by the divergence between the calculations of two such experts as Mommsen and Hübner, the former of whom reckons the total at 40,000, and the latter at 70,000 men.

Not without great difficulty (says our sole authority, Dion Cassius) was the army induced to depart from Gaul. The soldiers grumbled sorely at being called to do military service "outside of the habitable world," and Claudius deemed it advisable to send to them his freedman-minister Narcissus to overcome their reluctance. The glib-tongued Greek mounted

* That these four legions took part in the Plautian conquest of Britain is undoubted. It may perhaps, however, be questioned whether all sailed with Aulus Plautius at the very outset of the expedition. The fact that the army was divided for the purpose of the crossing into three portions looks rather as if it consisted of three legions: and the fourth might form the nucleus of the reinforcements which came with the Emperor Claudius.

the general's rostrum and began to harangue them greatly to his own satisfaction. But it was too much for the patience of the veteran legionaries to hear this imperial lackey, this liberated slave, preaching to them about their military duty. They shouted him down with a well-concerted cry of Io Saturnalia (Hurrah for the slaves' holiday), and then with the curious illogicality of soldiers they turned to Plautius and said that for his sake they would willingly follow wherever he led them. All this hesitation had caused considerable delay, but at last the flotilla bearing the soldiers embarked in three divisions, in order that the whole expedition might not be put to the hazard of a single landing. The soldiers were much disheartened when they found the winds or the tides apparently drifting them back to the port from which they had started, but then a meteor flashing from east to west seemed to indicate that their voyage would be prosperous and encouraged them to proceed. Their landing, or, more properly speaking, their three landings, were accomplished without difficulty, for the Britons, believing that the expedition was postponed on account of the mutiny, had made no preparations, and now fled to the forests and the marshes, hoping that the experience of the great Julius would be repeated and that this expedition also might soon return empty-handed.

Plautius had therefore hard work to discover his foe, but he did at last come to close quarters, first with Caratacus and then with Togodumnus, both of whom he overcame. Either now or in the following operations, Togodumnus perished, but his brother survived to be for many years a thorn in the side of the Roman general. A British tribe named the Boduni, of whose geographical position we are ignorant, but who were subjects of the Catuvellauni, came in and offered their submission. Plautius left a garrison among them and marching forward arrived at the banks of a river, possibly the Medway, which the barbarians fondly hoped could not be traversed without a bridge. The Roman general, however, had in his army many Gaulish soldiers, probably those dwelling near the mouths of the Rhine and the Waal, who were accustomed to swim with all their armour on across the swiftest streams. These men, at the word of command, plunged into the river, swam across, attacked the dismayed and carelessly encamped barbarians, and directing their weapons especially against the horses harnessed to the chariots made the usual cavalry tactics of the Britons impossible. The young Vespasian (future emperor, and conqueror of the Jews) and his brother Sabinus were ordered to lead some more troops across the stream and complete the victory, which they did, slaying multitudes of the barbarians. Still the Britons made a stubborn resistance, till at last an officer named Cnæus Hosidius Geta, a kind of Roman paladin who had before this done knightly deeds in fighting against the Moors, almost single-handed and at the imminent risk of capture, achieved a victory which compelled them to retire, and for which he received the honours of a triumph.

Hereupon the Britons withdrew behind the Thames, at that time and place a broad and shallow stream flowing wide over the marshes of Essex. The barbarians knew well its deeps and its shallows, and could find their way across it in safety. Not so the Romans, who suffered severe loss in attempting to follow them. As a mere question of strategy Plautius could probably have marched up the stream and crossed it at some narrower part of its course. He determined, however, to reserve this achievement for the emperor who had apparently already arranged to visit Britain and pluck the laurels planted for him by his general. Claudius prepared reinforcements, including, we are told, a number of elephants (not very serviceable, one would have thought, in the Essex marshes), sailed from his own port of Ostia to Marseilles, then travelled, chiefly by water, up and down the great rivers of Gaul, arrived at the camp of Plautius, crossed the Thames, the proper appliances having no doubt been prepared by the loyal general, and then marched on Camulodunum, which he took, making the palace of Cunobelinus his own. The fall of the powerful kingdom of the Catuvellauni brought with it the submission, voluntary or forced, of many neighbouring tribes.

Claudius was saluted not once but many times as Imperator by his soldiers, and returning to Rome after a six months' absence he was hailed by the Senate with the appellation of Britannicus, an honour which was also bestowed on his six-year-old son. He rode in his triumphal chariot up to the capitol, and he erected some years later in honour of this conquest a triumphal arch which spanned the Via Lata (now the Corso), and which was still standing almost perfect till the seventeenth century, when it was destroyed (1662) by Pope Alexander VII. Some fine sculptured slabs from this arch are still preserved in the Villa Borghese at Rome, along with fragments of an inscription which record that "Tiberius Claudius Augustus, Germanicus and Pious, tamed the Kings of Britain without any loss [to the republic], and was the first to bring her barbarous races under the control of Rome."

*****

The capture of Camulodunum involved the downfall of the house of Cymbeline, and the acceptance, at any rate the temporary acceptance, of Roman domination in all the south-eastern part of Britain. While Caratacus escaped to South Wales and there organised a desperate resistance to the Roman arms among the Silures, most of the smaller British chieftains seem to have bowed their necks beneath the yoke. An inscribed stone still standing in Goodwood Park, but originally found at Chichester, seems to record the building of a temple to Neptune and Minerva for the safety of the imperial house, at the command of King Tiberius Claudius Cogidubnus, "legate of Augustus in Britain." This inscription is an interesting confirmation of the statement made by Tacitus that "certain cities were handed over to King Cogidubnus who remained till our own day most faithful to the emperor, according to the old and long-established custom of the Roman people to make even kings the instruments of their dominion."*

It was probably about the same time that Prasutagus, King of the Iceni, who inhabited Norfolk, Suffolk and a part of Cambridgeshire, became a subject ally of Rome. Farther south the invaders were making less peaceful progress, if it be true, as we are told by the biographer of the future Emperor Vespasian, that he in these early years of the conquest "fought thirty battles as commander of the Second legion, subdued two powerful nations, took more than twenty towns and brought into subjection the Isle of Wight." We learn from another source that he was once, when surrounded by the barbarians and in imminent peril of his life, rescued by his brave son Titus, and further that it was the elder soldier's distinguished successes in this British war which won him the favour of the Roman people, and led to his being eventually clad in the imperial purple. An interesting evidence of the rapid development of this first act of the Roman conquest is afforded by the fact that a pig of lead mined in the Mendip Hills has been discovered, bearing the name of Claudius and his son with a date equivalent to A.D. 49, only six years after the landing of the legions. In the year 47, Aulus Plautius left Britain to receive the honour of an ovation, then almost exclusively reserved for the imperial family, and to find his wife Pomponia (a woman of gentle nature but touched with sadness) tending towards "a

* Agricola, xiv.

foreign religion" which, there is good reason to believe, was none other than Christianity. He probably left the frontier of the Roman dominion nearly coincident with a line drawn diagonally from the Bristol Channel to the Wash, though outlying districts like Cornwall and Devonshire were not yet assimilated by the new lords of Britain. But even so the fairest and most fertile half of Brythonic Britain was now apparently won for the empire.

To the new Roman legatus, Ostorius Scapula, fell the hard labour of fighting the Goidelic nation of the Silures who occupied the hills and valleys of South Wales and were nerved to desperate resistance by the counsels of their willingly adopted leader Caratacus. Wales must therefore undoubtedly have been the main objective of the general, but meanwhile even the part of the country already conquered was not too secure. The lands of the friendly tribes were being overrun by the still unsubdued Britons beyond the border, who thought that winter and the change of commander would both be in their favour. Ostorius, who knew the importance of first impressions, hurriedly collected a sufficient number of troops to repel and harass these marauders, but the stern measures which he took for the defence of the line between Severn and Trent so angered the Iceni (proud of their unconquered condition, "the allies not the subjects" of Rome) that they took up arms, gathered round them a confederacy of the neighbouring tribes and drew themselves up in battle array in a position difficult of access and protected by an embankment, probably of turf. Without much difficulty, Ostorius stormed this rude fort, using only the irregular allied troops and without moving the legions from their quarters. As these irregulars were mostly cavalry and the Icenian camp was impervious to horsemen, the riders had to fight on foot, but nevertheless they won. Deeds of great valour were performed on both sides, and the son of Ostorius won the civic crown for saving the life of a Roman citizen. With the Iceni forced back into sullen tranquillity, and with the wavering tribes round them now siding with the victors, Ostorius was free to turn his attention to the difficult problem of Wales. He led his army into the territory of the Decangi,* who probably inhabited what is now Flintshire; he ravaged their fields; he gazed on the sea which separated him from Ireland; he would perhaps have anticipated the conquest of Anglesey had not some hostile movements among the Brigantes of Yorkshire, threatening his communications with the Midlands, warned him against a further advance. When the Brigantes were chastised and

* The name of this tribe is doubtful.

in a manner reconciled, he turned again to the work which he probably ought never to have delayed—the vanquishing of the Silures.

This war against the Silures evidently occupied many years, and it is almost admitted by the Roman historian that Caratacus won many victories. Gliding rapidly, however, over this unpleasant interval, Tacitus brings us to the final battle—decisive so far as Caratacus was concerned—which, as a result of the strategy of Caratacus, was fought not in the territory of the Silures but in that of their northern neighbours the Ordovices. On the border of three counties, Shropshire, Hereford and Radnor, is the district in which tradition or the conjecture of learned men has placed the battlefield. High up soars Caer Caradoc, commanding a splendid view of the distant Wrekin. Not far off are the strongly marked lines of Brandon Camp (possibly the work of the soldiers of Ostorius); the quiet little village of Leintwardine, encircled by the rapid waters of the Teme, sleeps at the foot of hills, any one of which may have been the chosen position of the British king. Tacitus describes to us the way in which that position, already strong by the steepness of the hill and the treacherous deeps and shallows of the river, was further strengthened by a barrier of stones where approach seemed least difficult. Caratacus flew from rank to rank, exhorting his countrymen, descendants of the men who had repulsed the great Julius, to do their utmost on that eventful day which would decide their freedom or their slavery for ever. Ostorius, on the other hand, awed by the strength of the British position, was almost inclined to evade the encounter, but the legionaries loudly demanded battle and the officers backed their ardent entreaties. Ostorius thereupon moved forward and crossed the river without great difficulty. At the stone wall matters for a time went ill with the Romans and death was busy in their ranks, but after they had formed a testudo, with their locked shields held on high, they succeeded under its shelter in pulling out the stones of the roughly compacted wall. Once inside the camp, the well-drilled ranks of the Romans soon pierced the disorderly crowd of the barbarians, who had neither helmet nor breastplate to protect them from the sword and the pilum of the legionary, from the rapier and the spear of the auxiliary cohorts. The victory was a brilliant one, and though Caratacus himself escaped, his wife, his daughter and his brethren fell into the hands of the Romans. The liberty of the fugitive prince was of short duration. Having escaped to the court of Cartimandua, Queen of the Brigantes, he was by her basely surrendered, in chains, to the victorious general. This event which may possibly have taken place some time after the battle, happened, as Tacitus remarks, in the ninth year after the commencement of the British war. This probably means A.D. 51 or 52, the same year in which the inscription was engraved on the triumphal arch of Claudius.

The exhibition of the captive British king who had for so many years defied the power of Rome, was made the occasion of a splendid Roman holiday. The prætorian cohorts were drawn up in the meadows outside their camp (near where now stands the Villa Torlonia), and through the lane formed by their glittering spears passed first the train of the followers of Caratacus, bearing the golden torques, the embossed breastplates and other ornaments which he himself had won in former wars from vanquished kings, then his brothers, his wife and his daughter, and last of all Caratacus himself. He did not crouch or fawn, but looked boldly in the emperor's face, and (if the speech recorded by Tacitus be not a mere rhetorical exercise) with quiet dignity reminded his conqueror that but for adverse fortune he might have entered Rome in very different guise as an ally, not as a captive. "I had horses, men, arms, wealth. Do you wonder that I was reluctant to lose them? If you wish to lord it over all the world, must others at once accept slavery? Slay me if you will, and I shall soon be forgotten. Preserve my life and I shall be an eternal memorial of your clemency." The courageous and manly address touched the not ignoble nature of Claudius, who granted pardon to the British king and all his family. He was required, however, to offer thanks for his preservation to the emperor's wife, Agrippina, mother of Nero, who sat haughtily on a tribunal of her own, not far from that of her husband: "a new and strange sight," says Tacitus, for Roman soldiers to behold. Far better known than the speech thus recorded by Tacitus is the remark of the British king, preserved by the Greek historian Dion. After his liberation, when he was taken round through the streets of Rome, and saw all the wonders of the city, he said: "And yet you who possess all these things, and many others like them, actually covet the shanties of Britain." With the capture and pardon of Caratacus, the house of Cymbeline disappears from history. It is implied that he and his family spent the rest of their days in Italy.

*****

For the next seven years (A.D. 52–59), under Didius Gallus and Veranius, the history of Roman conquest was void of striking events. Didius was elderly and disinclined to risk his already great reputation by distant operations against the natives. Veranius, who was probably younger, certainly more adventurous, promised his master Nero (who succeeded Claudius in 54) that in two years the province should be at his feet, but died in his first year of office, with his high hopes unrealised. However, these two governors had apparently succeeded in pushing the Roman frontier northward as far as Chester and Lincoln: they had checked, though not subdued, the Silures, and had rescued their ally Cartimandua from the perilous position in which she had been placed by her indignant subjects, as a punishment for summarily dismissing her husband and handing herself over to his armour-bearer. Probably these seven years of rest were really useful to the cause of the empire. The more civilised tribes in the south and east were adopting Roman ways, and some of them, at any rate, were growing fat on Roman commerce, and if the subordinate officials of the empire would have used their power with moderation Britain might have become Roman without more blood-spilling. Unfortunately, these conditions were not observed, and a day of vengeance was at hand.

In the year 59 Suetonius Paulinus, one of the two greatest generals that obeyed the orders of Nero (Corbulo, conqueror of Armenia, being the other), was appointed legatus of Britain, and began his short but memorable career. Believing that he had a tranquil and easily governed province behind him, and desiring to rival the fame of Corbulo, he determined to attempt the conquest of Anglesey, which was invested with a mysterious awe as the high place of Druidism. After all, the difficulties of the enterprise were spiritual rather than material. A flotilla of flat-bottomed boats transported the legionaries across the Menai Straits; of the cavalry some swam, and some, we are told, forded the channel. But there on the other side stood not only a dense mass of armed men, but women, dressed like Furies with their hair hanging down and with lighted torches in their hands, were rushing about through the ranks, and Druid priests, with their hands upraised to Heaven, in terrible voices called down vengeance on the foe. At the unaccustomed sight the awed legionaries hung back; then the cheering speech of the general and their own reflection—"We must never let ourselves be frightened by a parcel of women and priests"—revived their fainting courage. They carried the eagles forward, hewed down the armed Britons, and used the terrible torches to burn the hostile camp. A fort and garrison were placed in the island in order to maintain the conquest, and the woods in which human sacrifices had been offered and cruel auguries practised with the bleeding limbs of men, were by Roman axes cleared from the face of the earth.

All seemed going splendidly for Roman dominion in Britain when a breathless messenger brought to the tent of Suetonius (A.D. 60)* a tale not unlike that with which we were thrilled half a century ago at the outbreak of the Indian mutiny. The outburst of the flame of British discontent was in the country of the Iceni, and the exciting cause was the shameless and heartless greed of the Roman officials. The capital of the new province at this time seems to have been Cymbeline's old city, Camulodunum (the modern Colchester), which had been turned into a Roman colony, a place in which the time-expired veterans might spend their old age, surrounded by their families, and lording it with no gentle mastership over their British slaves. High in this town, which took its name from Camulus, the Celtic war-god, rose the great temple dedicated to Claudius and Rome, a temple which was almost a fortress; but the town itself was surrounded by no walls, a piece of improvidence for which Tacitus justly blames the generals, who were thinking more of pleasurable ease than of military utility. In the chief house of the colony resided Catus Decianus, the procurator, who represented the emperor in all civil and financial matters, as Suetonius, the legatus, represented him in military affairs. Of all the grasping and unjust officials who made the name of the empire hated, this Catus seems to have been one of the worst. While oppressing the peasants by rigorous exaction of tribute, he demanded from the chiefs the return of the property (probably the result of confiscations from their own fellow-countrymen) which Claudius had bestowed upon them, saying that gifts such as this, of course, reverted to the giver. The financial distress of the unhappy province was aggravated, according to Dion, by the selfish timidity of the philosopher Seneca, Nero's minister, who chose this opportunity suddenly and harshly to call in loans to the amount of 10,000,000 sesterces (about £90,000 sterling), which he had lent at usurious rates of interest to the natives or the settlers in Britain.

Thus all was ready in Essex for revolt, when Norfolk and Suffolk, the country of the Iceni, were the scenes of outrages which set fire to the gathered fuel. King Prasutagus, the old and apparently loyal ally of Rome, who had long been famous for his wealth, died leaving the emperor and

* For the reasons in favour of the date 60 instead of 61 (given by Tacitus), see Henderson, Life and Principate of Emperor Nero, p. 477.

his own two daughters his joint heirs. There were old examples of this testamentary liberality in Roman history, both Pergamum and Cyprus having been bequeathed by their kings to the Roman people. Prasutagus hoped, we are told, by this display of confidence in the honour of the emperor that he would, at least, safeguard his kingdom and his family from violence. Bitterly was this hope disappointed. At the bidding of the legatus, centurions tramped across his kingdom; at the bidding of the procurator, clerks of servile condition swept bare the palace of its treasures, just as if all had been lawful prize of war. Nor did they even stop there. With incredible stupidity, as well as wickedness, the governor ordered or permitted the widow of Prasutagus, herself daughter as well as spouse of kings, to be beaten with rods, and gave over her two daughters to be violated. The chiefs of the Icenian nation were banished from their ancestral homes, and the kinsmen of the royal family were treated as slaves. At this all the manhood of the nation rose in rebellion; the widowed queen, who is known to posterity as Boadicea,* put herself at the head of the maddened confederates (for the Iceni were at once joined by the Trinobantes, possibly also by some of the other neighbouring tribes), and the numbers of the insurgent army are said to have reached 120,000.

Of the long harangue which Dion represents Boadicea as having delivered to her army "from a tribunal made after the Roman fashion of peat-turves," it is not necessary to quote anything here, as it is obviously but a literary exercise by a Greek rhetorician. The most interesting things which it contains are the description of the grievances endured under the Roman rule, as the rhetorician imagines her to have painted them, and her invocation of the Celtic goddess, Andraste,† whom she seems to invoke as the special protectress of her nation. The description which the same author gives of the appearance of the warrior-queen is life-like, and we must hope that it is trustworthy. "Tall in stature, hard-visaged and with fiercest eye: with a rough voice: with an abundance of bright yellow hair reaching down to her girdle: wearing a great collar of gold: with a tunic of divers colours drawn close round her bosom and a thick mantle over

* Her name seems to have been really Boudicca, meaning the Victorious. The form Boadicea rests on no authority and conveys no meaning, but it is now too late to change it.

† Several names of British gods begin like Andraste. A little farther on Dion speaks of the sacred grove of Andate or Victory; and we find dedications to Ancasta, Anociticus, and Antenociticus.

it, fastened with a clasp. So she was always dressed, but now she bore a lance in her hand to make her harangue more terrible."

The first onset of the barbarian army was directed against the hated colony, and thus there were soon a hundred thousand or more enraged Britons howling round, not the walls, but the unwalled enclosure of Camulodunum. Help for the defenceless city there was none or next to none. The four brave legions were far away: one in quarters at Caerleon upon Usk, two fighting with Druids in Anglesey or quartered at Chester, one, the nearest, at Lincoln. The greedy procurator, Catus, when appealed to for help, sent two hundred imperfectly armed soldiers to reinforce the scanty garrison, and then began to arrange for his own speedy flight to Gaul. Within the city there were treachery and the paralysis of despair. No ditch was dug nor even the hastiest rampart reared: the non-combatants, the old men and the women, were not sent away; as passive as if in profound peace they awaited the approach of the multitude of the barbarians. The city was stormed at once: the great temple-citadel, in which the few soldiers were collected, stood a two days' siege and then likewise fell. Both here and in the two Roman cities which were yet to fall, indescribable horrors of murder, rape, ghastly and insulting mutilations are reported to have been practised by the barbarians. The Ninth legion under its commander (Petillius Cerialis), marching southward to the rescue, was met by the exultant conquerors, routed and almost destroyed. All the foot soldiers perished in the battlefield or in the flight; only Cerialis himself with his cavalry escaped to his former camp and was sheltered behind its fortifications.

Some part of these dismal tidings must have been brought to Suetonius on the shore of the Menai Straits. "With marvellous constancy," says Tacitus, "he marched through the midst of enemies to Londinium, a place which is not indeed dignified with the name of colony, but which is greatly celebrated for the number of its merchants and the abundance of its supplies." This is the first mention of London in history. At this time it had not apparently attained anything like the dimensions of which even Roman London could boast in later times. It formed an oblong which measured probably about 800 yards from east to west and 500 from north to south, and covered a little more than 600 acres. The northern boundary was almost certainly the line of Cheapside and Cornhill, the southern that of Upper and Lower Thames Street. The eastern and western frontiers of the city are still obscure, but it is generally admitted that neither St.

Paul's on the west nor the Tower on the east would have been included within it. Such was the little busy city which Suetonius reached at the end of his daring march. He heard there, if he had not heard before, the terrible news of the loss of the Ninth legion. He probably also learned at the same time that the officer in charge of the Second legion, daring to disobey his general's orders, was lingering at Caerleon, instead of marching to join him in the defence of the eastern portion of the province. The double ill-tidings upset all his plans for the defence of London. His army, which consisted of the Fourteenth legion and a detachment of the Twentieth, amounted only to about 10,000 men; provisions were running short, and the perpetual raids of the enemy made foraging difficult. It was too late to save Verulam, once a British capital, now a Roman municipium, which Boadicea had taken and where the bloody scenes of Camulodunum had been only too faithfully repeated. Now, with a heavy heart, notwithstanding the prayers and the tears of the citizens, Suetonius decided that London also must be left to its fate; by the loss of that one city all the rest of the province might haply be saved. Only this much he could grant, that those of the male inhabitants who could march with his troops might do so. Those whom the weakness of their sex or the weariness of age, or even their attachment to their homes, retained in the city were left, and were soon massacred by the barbarians, who took no captives and had no desire for ransoms, feeling that now was their day of vengeance, and foreboding that that day would be short. The Roman historians compute the loss of life in the three cities at 70,000 persons, by no means all Romans, but including many of British, perhaps also of Gaulish extraction, who in the years of peace had become peaceable and trade-loving subjects of the empire.

The movements of Suetonius, after he had decided to abandon Londinium to its fate, are not clearly indicated by Tacitus, but it seems probable that he retraced his steps northward in order to effect a junction with the troops which he had left at Chester and with the wreck of the Ninth legion still bravely defending itself at Lincoln. Boadicea with her vast horde of exultant Britons was probably hanging on his rear. Battle was inevitable, but the Roman general had some power of choosing the ground, and he chose it in a place protected on each side by the steep hills of a narrow defile and on the rear by a forest. The enemy could only move towards him across the open plain in front and there could be no lurking in ambush. The line was not too long to prevent the legionary soldiers from being drawn up in close ranks; on each side of them were the more lightly armed cohorts of the allies, and the cavalry were massed upon the wings. In great disorderly squadrons the Britons prepared to charge, full of fierce exultation at their past successes and so certain of their impending triumph that they had brought their wives, in waggons drawn up at the farther side of the plain, to behold their victory.

The barbarians came on with loud clamour and menacing war-songs; the Romans awaited them in silence and perfect order till they were within reach of a javelin's throw. Then at the signal given, raising the battle-cry, they hurled the pilum and rushed at the double against the slow-marching barbarians, broke their ranks, and pierced through the dense mass like a wedge. After a desperate hand-to-hand struggle, the barbarians, whose lack of defensive armour had caused them to suffer terribly from the arrows and the pila of the Romans, fled in disorder before them. The fugitives reached and were stopped by the waggons. The pursuers, maddened probably by the remembrance of the horrors of the sack of the three Roman cities, hewed down not only the fugitive combatants but the women, and even the horses that drew the chariots. So the victory was won. The Romans admitted a loss of some 800 killed and wounded, and claimed to have slaughtered a little less than 80,000 Britons. The apparent accuracy of these words, "a little less," need not deceive us as to the general untrustworthiness of such estimates as these, but the victory was undoubtedly decisive, and, as such things are reckoned, glorious. Boadicea is said by Tacitus to have ended her life by poison. Dion Cassius, with less probability, says that she died of disease.

Far away in Monmouthshire there was another suicide, the result of this great encounter. "Poenius Postumus, prefect of the camp of the Second legion" (who had presumably held the command in the temporary absence of the legatus), "when he heard how well things had gone with the Fourteenth and the Twentieth, enraged with himself because he had cheated his own legion of like glory, and had, contrary to military rule, disobeyed the orders of his superior, pierced himself through with his own sword." Possibly he was neither a coward nor a mutineer, but a man suddenly called to assume a crushing load of responsibility in a terrible crisis, who had failed to read aright the signs of the times. The Fourteenth legion, which had borne the greatest part of the work in the suppression of the rebellion, was called, when its officers would stimulate its military pride, the "Tamers of Britain" (Domitores Britanniæ). The renown which it had acquired caused its services to be eagerly sought for in the great game of Cæsar-making which followed upon the death of Nero. It was transferred to Belgic Gaul in A.D. 70, helped to quell the insurrection of Civilis, and never afterwards returned to Britain.

The tenure of office by Suetonius Paulinus was a very short one. He had indeed shown himself

A daring pilot in extremity;

but Nero, who with all his viciousness was not destitute of statesmanlike ability, probably considered that the pilot ought not to have taken his ship into such dangerous channels. After replacing the losses of the Ninth legion by the transfer of some 7,000 soldiers from Germany, the emperor sent a certain Julius Classicianus as successor to the detested procurator Catus. Suetonius seems to have been in favour of stern repression, laying waste with fire and sword the territories of all the tribes of doubtful loyalty. Classicianus, on the other hand, held that the real foe that had now to be fought was famine, especially since the insurgents, intent on the plunder of the Roman warehouses, had neglected the sowing of their spring corn. Differences soon arose between the merciful procurator and the stern legatus. To settle the quarrel Nero sent one of his freedmen, named Polyclitus, who travelled with great pomp and a long train of attendants, burdensome to the provinces through which he passed, but calculated to impress the Roman soldiery with a sense of his importance. The barbarians, on the other hand, who had heard from what a low and servile condition Polyclitus had risen, marvelled that so great a general and so brave an army should tamely submit to the arbitrament of a slave. They profited, however, by that docility; for Polyclitus, though, as his after career showed, not averse from plundering on his own account, made a report to the emperor in favour of the lenient policy of the procurator, and Suetonius, after an eventful lieutenancy of not more than two years, was recalled to Rome (A.D. 61).

In the ten years that followed the recall of Suetonius (A.D. 61–71), years which witnessed the downfall of Nero and the terrible civil war which shook the empire after his death, no great commotion disturbed the much-needed repose of the exhausted province. In the career of Trebellius Maximus, the governor who held nominal power for the greater part of this time, we have a typical instance of the bickerings, sometimes between the civil and military authorities, sometimes, as in this case, between the chief legatus and his military subordinates, which varied the monotony of existence in a conquered province. Tacitus tells us that Trebellius, who was an indolent man, with no experience of camp life, endeavoured to hold the province by mere good nature; a policy not altogether impracticable, because the barbarians had now begun to look more favourably on the pleasant vices of civilisation. The army, however, despised and hated the governor for his avarice and meanness, and their discontent was fomented and forcibly expressed by Roscius Coelius, the legatus of the Twentieth legion. "It is your fault," said the governor to him, "that discipline is relaxed and the troops are on the verge of mutiny." "It is yours," replied Coelius, "that the soldiers are kept poor and defrauded of their pay." Soon not the legionaries only, but the humbler auxiliaries, dared to hurl their taunts at the governor, who, at last alarmed for his safety, fled to some obscure hiding-place. Drawn out from thence, he prolonged, apparently for a little while, the precarious tenure of his rule; the implied bargain between him and the army being: "To you licence to do as you please; to me unthreatened life." Then the situation again became desperate. The miserable Trebellius escaped to Germany, took refuge in the camp of the insurgent Emperor Vitellius, did not share his transient success, and never returned to Britain.

When the civil war was ended by the triumph of the strong, sensible, common-place emperor Vespasian, a new impulse was given to Roman conquest in Britain. Petillius Cerialis, a near relative of the new emperor, a capable if somewhat rash soldier, the same who, at the head of the Ninth legion, had vainly sought to stem the torrent of Boadicea's rebellion, held office for four years (A.D. 71–75), during which time he humbled and perhaps subdued the Brigantes, who ever since Cartimandua's marital troubles had been more or less at enmity with the empire. This conquest, if really made at this time, involved the addition of Yorkshire to the empire, perhaps the foundation of Eburacum (York), once the capital of Roman Britain. Julius Frontinus (A.D. 75–78) followed Cerialis, and completed the long-delayed subjugation of the Silures in South Wales, who at this time, twenty-four years after Caratacus had been led in triumph through the streets of Rome, were still unreconciled to the Roman dominion. An interesting point in connexion with the name of Julius Frontinus is the fact that nearly twenty years after his return from Britain (A.D. 97) he was appointed by the Emperor Nerva Curator Aquarum, and in that capacity, though he was already advanced in years, carried great reforms and corrected many abuses which had grown up in connexion with the water-supply of the Eternal City. His treatise on the subject is still the source from which we derive almost all our information concerning the splendid aqueducts of Rome.

In the year 78, the Emperor Vespasian appointed as his legatus the most celebrated and probably the greatest of the governors of Britain, Gnæus Julius Agricola. Verging as he was upon his fortieth year he was in the very prime of his matured and disciplined strength. He knew Britain well, having served when quite a young man as tribune (a rank nearly corresponding to our lieutenant) under Suetonius Paulinus, and having probably heard the clamour of the barbarian multitude who crowded round the chariot of Boadicea. Again, ten years later, he had been sent over to Britain to confirm the doubtful loyalty of the Twentieth legion. Since then he had been governor of the important province of Aquitaine, afterwards consul, and he was actually holding the distinguished and well-paid office of Pontifex Maximus when he was appointed to the British command. What was more important for his future fame and for our knowledge of the history of Britain, he had given his daughter in marriage to that master of grave historic style, shot with indignant epigram, Cornelius Tacitus. When the new governor landed in Britain, both soldiers and natives thought that, the summer being now nearly ended, there would be no more fighting that year. Not so, decided Agricola. The Ordovices, dwellers in North Wales, had lately almost destroyed an ala (squadron) of cavalry stationed within their borders. This insolence, it was felt, must be chastised, and the might of Rome speedily displayed by the new legatus, who at once marched against them with a moderate force of legionaries and allies. The Ordovices refused to descend into the plain and fight there on equal terms. Agricola having climbed the hills of Denbighshire at the head of his troops, defeated and all but destroyed that clan of mountaineers. He looked westwards to the sacred Isle of Anglesey, once conquered by his old general Suetonius, but almost immediately abandoned on account of the terrible tidings from Camulodunum. He had no ships in which to cross the Menai Straits, but he had among his auxiliary troops men, probably from the mouths of the Rhine and the Waal, expert swimmers and skilled in finding possible fords, and these men laying aside the cumbrous loads which the Roman soldier was accustomed to carry, dashed into the stream, appeared on the shore of Mona and received the submission of the surprised and terrified islanders, who thought that till ships appeared in the straits they at least were safe from conquest. Having thus displayed his power, the governor now set himself to win the hearts of the natives by reforms in the administration, especially the financial administration, and redress of grievances. The burdens which rested upon the provincials of Britain were of two kinds, the tributum and the annona: the former a payment in money which was, it may be presumed, remitted by the revenue officers direct to Rome; the latter a payment in kind of the various stores needed for the sustenance of the army—fodder, lard, fish, firewood, but pre-eminently corn; and these things would of course not be sent out of the country but consumed in the various camps and cities where the soldiers were quartered. There was some good work to be done by Agricola in equalising the assessments to tributum, or rendering them proportionate to the ability of the British town or village responsible for its payment. But the chief abuses seem to have arisen in connexion with the annona. Fraudulent revenue officers would probably contract for the harvest on low terms before it was reaped, would gather it into the granaries, close the doors and laugh in the faces of the unhappy natives who were ordered to furnish so many bushels of corn and could only comply with the order by buying it from them at their own extortionate price. Then they would purposely fix the place where the annona had to be delivered, as far off as possible, in districts traversed by the poorest of roads. All these various abuses were, we are told, at once removed or greatly mitigated by the firm hand of Agricola.

It was not enough to remove causes of complaint. He would also win over the natives to positive affection for the Roman rule. He was constantly urging all the wealthier Britons to come into the towns and to take part in building operations. Everywhere temples, market-places, well-built houses were rising, reared by British natives, and pledges for their future loyalty. He gathered round him the sons of the chiefs, had them instructed in liberal arts, praised their aptness to learn at the expense of their Gaulish contemporaries, listened before long to eloquent declamations, delivered, of course, in the Latin tongue, by young Britons, gracefully clad in the Roman toga. The bath and the luxurious banquet offered their attractions not in vain to the late hunter of the forests, and as Tacitus sarcastically observes "the simple folk called that civilisation (humanitas) which was really the beginning of slavery."

The summer of A.D. 79, the second year of Agricola's command, seems to have been chiefly occupied in measures for completing the military occupation of the recently conquered territory, that is, probably, Yorkshire, Lancashire and Northumberland, the country of the Brigantes. "He himself chose the site of the camps; he himself reconnoitred the forests and the estuaries" (probably of the Tees, the Wear and the Tyne, and perhaps also Solway Firth), "and meanwhile he gave the enemy no rest, but was for ever harassing them by sudden excursions, and when he had terrified them sufficiently, then by holding his hand he gave them an inducement to desire peace. In consequence hereof many native states which up to that time had treated the empire on a footing of equality now gave hostages and laid aside their animosity. They found themselves surrounded with forts and garrisons, and all was done with so much science and system as had never before been applied to any newly conquered part of Britain." It is possible that Eburacum, which at this time, or very soon after, became the headquarters of the Ninth legion, was one of the strong places thus founded or fortified by Agricola.

The record of the year 80, the third year of Agricola's command, is one of the most interesting to all north-country Englishmen, but it is unfortunately also one of the most obscure. It will be well to quote the words of Tacitus as they stand, without attempting conjectural amplification. "The third year of expeditions opened up to us new tribes, all the nations up to the estuary called Tanaus having their lands laid waste. The enemy cowed by these operations did not dare to harass the army, though it was buffeted by fierce tempests, and thus a respite was afforded which was employed in building more forts. It was observed by military experts that no general ever showed greater ability in his choice of suitable sites for such defences. No fort founded by Agricola was ever stormed by hostile violence, or surrendered, or abandoned by its fugitive garrison: yet frequent sallies were made from them, for they were fortified against a tedious siege by a yearly renewed stock of provisions. This gave the defenders courage for the winter; each garrison relied on itself for its safety, and the enemy were driven to despair by the uselessness of their attacks. For aforetime they had been wont to recoup themselves for the losses of the summer by the successes of winter, but now they found themselves repelled in both seasons alike." We have here evidently to deal with an extensive system of fortification; but we are provoked by being unable precisely to identify the region in which it took place. What is the meaning of the estuary called Tanaus "up to which Agricola ravaged the land"? It is certainly not the Tay (which was indicated by the corrupt reading Taum); it may be the Firth of Forth; only that estuary is immediately after called Bodotria. The little Scottish river Tyne near North Berwick has a kind of estuary, and Mommsen's conjecture that this is the Tanaus of Tacitus would have much probability, were it not so near to the far mightier estuary of the Forth that it is difficult to imagine any one choosing it as a landmark. The better known Tyne of Newcastle would be clearly the strongest claimant if the course of the narrative did not seem to have already carried us to the north of it. No piece of water would meet the geographical condition better than the splendid estuary of the Tweed, so well fitted by nature for a limitary stream, but no other passage of any author has been found in which any name resembling Tanaus has been applied to that river. In the next year (A.D. 81) Agricola undoubtedly reached and fortified the narrow neck of land between Clyde and Forth (Clota and Bodotria); but the point practically at issue is this: "May we understand that we have in this passage of Tacitus a description of the building by Agricola of some at least of the forts between Tyne and Solway on the line which was afterwards marked by the Roman wall?" It has been often suggested, and in the opinion of the present writer with some probability, that we may. In that case great additional interest attaches to Chesters, Housesteads and others of the ruined Roman stations in Northumberland, when we think that they may have been planned by the exceptional military genius of Agricola.

With the three remaining campaigns of this general (A.D. 82–84) we have no special concern, as they were all fought beyond the limits of England. We must not follow him as he cruises about the Kyles of Bute and the Mull of Cantire, gazes across to Ireland (an island, Tacitus thinks, with better harbours and more frequented by merchants than England), nor discuss his opinion, often expressed to his son-in-law, that with one legion and a moderate supply of auxiliaries he could have added Hibernia to the empire. Nor must we linger over Tacitus' celebrated description of the great fight on the Mons Graupius,* and the spirited war-speech of the Caledonian hero Galgacus, which according to Tacitus preceded the encounter. Almost immediately after this victory—perhaps more dearly bought and less decisive than would appear on the surface of the Tacitean narrative—Agricola, whose term of command was already of exceptional length, was recalled to Rome. The Emperor Domitian's jealousy of a soldier whose admiring legions might insist on proclaiming

* From a misreading of this name is derived the modern Grampian.

him as a candidate for the empire, may have been, as Tacitus suggests, the sole reason for his recall; but nearer danger was also threatening Rome from the region of the Danube, and, as Mommsen has pointed out, one of the British legions was actually recalled for service in Pannonia. True statesmanship as well as mean personal jealousy may have prompted the recall of so adventurous a general from the scene of his triumphs. Agricola made no attempt to resist his supersession, but returned to Rome, lived there as a private but harassed citizen, declining the governorship of Syria (which was offered to him with a hint that it would be dangerous to accept it), and died at Rome in the fifty-fourth year of his age on August 23, A.D. 93. The suggestions of foul play and of poison stealthily administered by order of Domitian are mentioned, but hardly endorsed, even by the suspicious pen of his son-in-law. That son-in-law was absent from Rome at the time of his death, but describes the deathbed scene from the reports of the bystanders; and his farewell to the departed spirit of the beloved one, the celebrated peroration of the Life of Agricola, is one of the most beautiful things in Roman literature.

V.

THE ROMAN OCCUPATION

With the departure of Agricola the literary history of Roman Britain comes to an end. For three centuries longer the legions were to remain in our island, and the buildings which they reared, the altars which they inscribed, the roads which they constructed, tell us something of the life which they led during that long space of time, as long as the whole period that has elapsed from Elizabeth's days to ours. Archæology has much to tell us concerning it, but history is almost altogether silent. A few sections of Dion Cassius, some confused notices in the Historia Augusta, a page or two of Ammianus Marcellinus, are practically all that is left to us of the written history of our country from Agricola to Stilicho. We need not here discuss the causes of a silence so tantalising and so irremediable; how far it may have sprung from Roman contempt of a distant and mist-enveloped island, how far from a decay of courage and hopefulness in the Romans themselves, symptoms of the impending ruin of their empire; it is enough that the pages are for us left blank and can now never be filled.

The greatest monument of Roman power in Britain and that which has yielded the most fruitful results to archæology is the Roman Wall between the two estuaries of Tyne and Solway. Almost all that we know of Roman life in Britain during the second century centres round this one great work. Towards the end of the first century a change took place in the organisation of the defence of the empire on the frontiers. Hitherto the republic, and after it the empire, had been satisfied to keep a strong body of troops in all the imperfectly conquered provinces, and to plant well-garrisoned castles near the river or the range of mountains on the other side of which were the barbarians of Europe or Africa, or the hostile monarchies of Asia. Soon after the death of Nero a different system was adopted, involving the formation of a definitely marked boundary which when not protected by very strong natural barriers was guarded by an actual wall of stone or earth upon which the garrisoned fortresses were strung, like beads on a chain. Not only in Britain are traces of these limiting walls to be found, but also in Germany, between the Lower Rhine and the Danube, and in the Dobrudscha on the western shore of the Black Sea: and there is reason to believe that a similar wall of defence shut out the barbarians of Mount Aures who threatened the provincials of Roman Africa.

"The real authors of the frontier system were the Flavian and Antonine Emperors, and the period extending from the accession of Vespasian to the death of Marcus Aurelius, or, roughly, from 70 A.D. to 180 A.D., witnessed its complete organisation. The interest of these emperors in the matter was no doubt quickened by the growing anxiety, an anxiety unknown to the Augustan age, but perceptible in Tacitus, as to the increasing pressure from without upon the empire.... It is well for students of the British frontier to remember that the emperor with whose name the organisation of the imperial frontier system is most closely connected is Hadrian."*

There has been much discussion about this matter. As we shall see, there is good reason for connecting the name of a later emperor, Severus, with the building of the wall, but, on the whole, the testimony of inscriptions and the labours of archæologists tend to confirm the clear statement of the biographer Spartianus (writing, it is true, a century and a half after the event): "Hadrian visited Britain, in which island he corrected many things that were amiss, and was the first to draw a wall across for eighty miles, in order to divide the barbarians and the Romans." In all the long list of Roman emperors it would be hard to find a more fascinating figure than that of this great wall-builder. By no means the best of his class, far surpassed in moral excellence by Trajan, Antoninus and Marcus, but removed by an immeasurable distance from the worst, from such men as Nero, Domitian and Commodus; architect, artist, author, and, above all things, indefatigable traveller, Publius Ælius Hadrianus united a truly Greek versatility and brilliancy of intellect to all the Roman's strong sense of duty towards the great Res Publica, and willingness for Rome's sake to sacrifice many of the sensual gratifications in which his soul only

* These sentences are quoted from Prof. Pelham's paper on "The Roman Frontier System" (Transactions of Cumberland and Westmorland Antiquarian Society, xiv., 170–84), in which the reader will find an admirable statement of the object of the Roman frontier defences and the manner of their construction.

too clearly delighted. The traveller who wanders for hours through the ruins of the vast collection of luxurious palaces which is called the Villa Hadriani, or who, in sunny Athens, sees the arch which bears the proud inscription, "On this side the city of Theseus, on that the city of Hadrian," can in some measure realise the self-denial which must have been involved in Hadrian's presence with the legions during the setting out of eighty Roman miles of wall* across the misty moors of Northumberland and Cumberland.

It was probably in the year 120, three years after his accession to the empire, that Hadrian visited Britain. The journey may have been only part of his pre-arranged tour through the western portion of his dominions, but it is also possible that it was the result of some recent and special disaster in Britain to the Roman arms. Some forty or fifty years afterwards the orator Fronto alluded to "the great number of soldiers slain by the Britons during the reign of Hadrian," and it is allowable at least as a matter of conjecture to couple these words with the ominous disappearance of one of the legions stationed in Britain from the army list of the empire. The unlucky Ninth legion, once quartered at Lincoln, afterwards at York, had been, as we have seen, nearly destroyed in the insurrection headed by Boadicea. It had again suffered most severely, under Agricola, from a night attack made by the Caledonians before the battle of Mons Graupius. And now, just about this time, either in the later years of Trajan or the earlier years of Hadrian, it vanishes clean out of the lists of the Roman army and is replaced by the Sixth legion, surnamed the Victorious, which was brought over to Britain and stationed at Eburacum. There is some discussion as to the earlier cantonment of the legions, whether four or three, that had been quartered in Britain, but as to the general question of their allocation during, at least, the second and third centuries of our era there can be no doubt. The Second legion (Augusta) at Isca (Caerleon-upon-Usk); the Sixth (Victrix) at Eburacum (York), and the Twentieth (Valeria Victrix) at Deva (Chester), have left abundant tokens of their long-continued presence.

From all these legions, however, considerable drafts were taken to assist in the building of the wall from Tyne to Solway, the existing remains of which must now be described. At the two ends of its course, where it has had the ill-fortune either to meet with the fierce industrial

* Equivalent to seventy-three and a half English miles: the distance from Wallsend to Bowness.

energy of the dwellers by the estuary of the Tyne, or to attract the envious glances of the farmers of fertile Cumberland, the wall has practically ceased to exist, though it has seldom passed that way for more than two or three miles without leaving some traces, however faint, of its presence to reward the quest of the earnest antiquary. But in the central part of its course, where it has left the busy haunts of men and climbed the bleak moorlands and the steep basaltic cliffs of Western Northumberland and Eastern Cumberland, it still exists in what its great historian, Dr. Bruce, used to call "an encouraging state of preservation." For twenty miles or more it goes striding over mountain and moor, religiously climbing every cliff and dipping down into every hollow of the sharply outlined, serrated, whinstone range. Sometimes we see only the rough rubble-work which formed the core of the wall, but more often the well-hewn square blocks which faced its northern and southern sides are still visible. The height attained by it is in one or two places as much as nine feet, but its more usual altitude is four to five feet. It was probably when perfect about seventeen feet high; and its width, as we know from the existing remains, varied from six to eight feet. The line of the wall once fixed, its builders seem to have pursued a nearly uniform plan, regardless of the help which they might have derived from natural defences. Thus in one place it crowns the heights of some steep basaltic cliffs at whose feet lies a small Northumbrian lake. No desperation of bravery would ever have caused a Brigantian chief to dash across that lake and climb those pinnacles of columnar basalt: still even here the wall pursues its undeviating course, and, so far as we know, retained its undiminished height. It is possible, however, that in such a case as this it was meant as a defence, not against barbarians, but against the weather. Snowstorms sometimes sweep violently across these bleak moorlands, and it may have been thought desirable to provide the Roman sentinel, pacing backwards and forwards between camp and camp, with some shelter from their fury.

Along the line of the wall are situated fortified enclosures of three kinds which now go by the names of camps, mile-castles and turrets. The camps, of which there were seventeen, between Tyne and Solway, and which were probably called by the Romans Prætenturæ or Stationes, vary in size from three to six acres. They were destined for the housing of one cohort—a body of men varying in size from 600 to 1,000—with, no doubt, a certain number of camp-followers, and in some cases a considerable troop of horses. Public buildings, known by antiquaries as the prætorium, the forum and the like, are to be found generally in the centre of the camp, sometimes on the side most exposed to the enemy's attacks: and the quarters of the officers may generally be distinguished from those of the common soldiers by the elaborate arrangements for warming them, known as hypocausts. In these the floor of the room is supported on ranges of short pillars (generally about eight or nine inches high), between which the hot air circulated, being brought by flues from the furnace at a corner of the camp, in which it is evident that the fuel used was often the coal of Northumberland. The great number of oyster-shells, the beef-bones and mutton-bones found near many of the camps give us an indication of the food supplied to the officers, perhaps also to some of the privates. Many interesting illustrations of the immense length of time that the Roman occupation of Britain endured may be derived from these Prætenturæ. Thus we have several inscriptions recording the repair of a granary or a temple ruined by age (vetustate conlapsum): and in the sacred well of the nymph Coventina, just outside the camp of Procolitia, there were found 16,000 coins ranging over a period from A.D. 100 to 300 which had been thrown into the well by generations of Roman soldiers as votive offerings to the goddess.

Besides the larger camps, there were, as has been said, also smaller forts, erected at regular intervals of a thousand Roman paces, which are now known by the designation mile-castles; and other still smaller enclosures, hardly more than sentry boxes, about three to the mile, which are called, not very aptly, turrets, and of which very few specimens still remain.

The soldiers by whom the line of the wall was defended did not belong to the legions, though legionaries had been employed in its construction. They belonged to various auxiliary corps recruited in the outlying provinces of the empire, and they were theoretically less Roman, less Italian, than their comrades enlisted in the legions, though this distinction was practically to a large extent breaking down in the second and third centuries of the empire. While Britons were being enlisted for service abroad, Asturians from Spain, Frisians and Batavians from Holland, Tungrians from Belgium, Lingones from Gaul, even Dalmatians and Dacians from the distant provinces which bore their names, were tramping from station to station along the mighty wall of Hadrian, bathing in the chilly waters of the Tyne, or hunting the deer on the misty slopes of Cross Fell. Most gladly would we learn how these detachments of soldiers, which for something like three centuries guarded the British Limes Imperii, were recruited; whether fresh drafts came, for instance, from Spain and from Dalmatia to replace the veterans who had earned their discharge, or whether the sons of the barracks kept the barracks full, in which case there would be probably an ever-increasing strain of British blood in the limitary garrisons. But on this point we lack definite information, which may possibly be supplied to us by the spade and the pick-axe of future excavators.

The total number of actual soldiers on the line of the wall has been computed at 10,000. In addition to these there would undoubtedly be a certain number of domestic servants, grooms, camp-followers of various kinds, besides the wives and concubines of the soldiers, so that we may probably conjecture the population of the Limes at not less than 20,000, a much larger number of persons than is to be found in that beautiful but solitary region to-day. Not only the numbers but the nationality of these vanished dwellers by the Tyne and Irthing strike us by their strange contrast with the present. Besides the Asturian and Dalmatian soldiers there must have been merchants and money-lenders and camp-followers of all kinds, speaking many tongues, upon these wind-swept moorlands. In the museum at South Shields is a sepulchral monument representing a woman seated, holding in her right hand a jewel-box, in her left implements of needlework. Underneath is a bilingual inscription, telling us in Latin that the figure represents "Regina, freedwoman and wife of Barate the Palmyrene, herself of the [British] nation of the Catuallauni, who died at the age of thirty." In characters akin to Hebrew the Oriental part of the inscription says simply, "Regina, the freedwoman of Barate. Alas!" The blended nationality, the British girl bought, enfranchised, loved and too soon lost by the Syrian,—merchant perchance or usurer,—who followed the flight of the eagles of Rome, are all brought before us by these few roughly carved lines, and they tell a story of world-wide empire, in which, perhaps, the Britain of our own day could offer the closest parallel to Rome.

Under the Emperor Antoninus Pius (138–161), the successor of Hadrian, another wall was built, some fifty or sixty miles north of the first, between the Firths of Forth and of Clyde. There were no stones in this wall, which was made of layers of turf, and, moreover, it has suffered cruelly (from an archæological point of view) through the operations necessary first for the cutting of a canal and afterwards for the building of a railroad between the two seas; but an abundance of inscribed stones tell us much concerning the names and occupations of the soldiers by whom it was garrisoned, and abundantly confirm the testimony of historians who attribute its erection to Antoninus Pius (138–161), one of the best and noblest of Roman emperors. Doubtless, at the time of its building, the country between the two walls (comprising the county of Northumberland and the whole south of Scotland) was subject to Roman rule. The precise period when that district was finally lost to the empire is still unknown to us. The philosopher emperor, Marcus Aurelius (161–180), was closely occupied with the defence of the empire against the barbarians of the Middle Danube, and his name is scarcely mentioned in connexion with the history of Britain. We are told, however, that "the Britannic war pressed heavily on his mind," and that he sent a second Agricola to settle it. This general of Marcus, Calpurnius Agricola, was not, as far as we know, descended from his great namesake, the general of Domitian.

With the accession of Commodus (180–192), son of Marcus, the long and glorious period of the patriot emperors came to an end, and the ruin of the empire began. The foolish and headstrong boy, who was now lord of the Roman world, sacrificed some of the best generals in his service to his jealous and cowardly suspicions, and while he was devoting himself to the bloody pastimes of the amphitheatre, allowed the necessary work of the defence of the frontier to fall behind. "The tribes in the island of Britain," we are told by Dion Cassius, "over-passed the wall which separated them from the Roman armies, committed widespread ravages, and cut to pieces a Roman general with the troops under his command." Which of the two walls is here referred to is not easy to say. It may be conjectured, however, that the wall of Antoninus had been already broken down in the reign of Marcus, during the "heavily pressing" Britannic war, and that we have here a description of one of those barbaric demolitions of which we find such abundant traces in the wall of Hadrian. To chastise the barbarians and to restore the broken Limes Commodus sent probably his best general, the sturdy old soldier, Ulpius Marcellus. If discipline were relaxed in the legions on the British frontier, here was certainly the man to restore it. St. Paul himself was not more resolute to "buffet his body and bring it into subjection" than this chief of many legions. A scanty sleeper himself, he framed ingenious plans to keep his centurions and officers at night harassed and awake. An old man with toothless and tender gums, he would eat only the stale hard bread which he had brought from Rome, in order that he might not fall into gluttony and excess. Such was the man who restored for a time the honour of the Roman arms, and who chastised the barbarians so thoroughly that all men marvelled that he was not, on his return to Rome, condemned to death by the jealous Commodus.

The assassination of Commodus (192), followed in less than three months by the murder of his excellent successor, Pertinax, and by the sale of the imperial dignity to the highest bidder, introduced a dreadful period of civil war in which the whole empire had nearly fallen asunder in ruin. Of the three candidates for the purple, Pescennius Niger in Syria, Albinus in Britain, and Septimius Severus on the Middle Danube, Severus, who had the advantage of being nearest to the capital and was therefore first acclaimed as emperor, was also at last the victorious one, but he had a hard fight, especially with Albinus, who led the three legions which still composed the army of Britain to a bloody battle in the plains of Lyons. The confusion of the times and the absence of the Roman legions were undoubtedly favourable to the restless barbarians. The wall of Hadrian was broken through; the Mæatæ, who lived immediately to the north of it, burst into the province, and the governor, Virius Lupus, purchased a precarious peace by paying a large sum to the invaders. It may be easily imagined that the condition of Britain after such an ignominious conclusion of a campaign, and even after the return of the disaffected legions of Albinus, was far from satisfactory, but it was apparently not till 208 that Septimius Severus set forth from Rome to bring the affairs of the province into order. He was already more than sixty years of age, his joints were racked by gout and his heart was sore through the fierce dissensions of his two sons, Caracalla and Geta, and the evils which these foreboded for the empire. Yet even these dissensions urged him the more to undertake the expedition, for he hoped that common labours and common dangers might in some degree tend to draw the two hostile brothers together, and that the necessary hardships of a camp life under our northern skies might restore some of the moral tone which had been lost amid the vicious indulgences of Rome. In this hope, it is true, he was completely disappointed. The hatred of Caracalla, especially for his brother, waxed fiercer and fiercer, and included also his father, for whose death he longed with scarcely concealed eagerness. Borne in his litter, on account of his sufferings from gout, the brave old soldier traversed the greater part of

Caledonia, hewing down forests and throwing causeways across marshes; slaying, of course, multitudes of barbarians, but losing also 50,000 of his own troops (so we are told, but the estimate is probably exaggerated) by hostile ambuscades, severities of weather, even by the swords of his own soldiers, who often killed their own comrades to prevent their falling into the hands of the barbarians. He had a mind, too, to explore the secrets of Nature, and compared with wonder the all-but perpetual day of midsummer and the scanty measure of light at midwinter in northern Scotland.

The dates of Severus' campaign are only obscurely indicated, but it seems probable that by the year 210 the subjection of the Caledonians had been apparently completed. Severus, accompanied by Caracalla and his staff, was riding on horseback, notwithstanding his physical infirmity, towards a certain place of meeting which had been appointed for the barbarians, that they might surrender their swords and swear fidelity to the empire. Caracalla, riding behind him, drew his sword and made his horse rear and prance, intending, apparently, to be brought into collision with his father and thus to kill him by apparent misadventure. A warning shout from some member of the staff caused the emperor to look round and the parricidal design was foiled. Severus said nothing, but rode calmly on, took his place on the tribunal and went through the ceremony that had been arranged. He then sent for his son and two of his chief ministers (one of them the great lawyer Papinian), having ordered that a naked sword should be placed in the middle of the tent. He sternly rebuked his son for the impious deed which he had meditated in the sight of the allies and the enemies of Rome, and then, changing his tone, said: "If you still desire to slay me, here is the sword, draw it and destroy me. Or, since I have associated you with me in the empire, give your orders to Papinian and let him be my executioner. You are young and strong: I am old and shall lay me down to rest without a sigh." The invitation was not accepted, for Caracalla shrank now from the guilt of manifest parricide. But the father's words revealed too plainly the bitterness of his soul. Many cruelties and much needless bloodshed had marked his own ascent to power, but they were surely all avenged by the misery of that day in the land of the Caledonians.

It was possibly in this same year 210, at any rate during his stay in Britain, that Severus completed a great and necessary work—the repair of the wall of Hadrian. So grievously had this long barrier suffered at the hands of the barbarians that reconstruction seemed to the soldiers engaged in it like an actual fresh construction. It is only thus that we can explain the language of the careless, inaccurate authors of the Historia Augusta, who, forgetful apparently of the fact that they have already assigned the credit of the work to Hadrian, now say of Severus: "The greatest glory of his reign is that he fortified Britain by a wall drawn across the island and ending on both sides with the ocean, for which achievement he received the name of Britannicus." Attempts have been made to explain the apparent discrepancy between the two accounts by assigning part of the fortification to Hadrian and part to Severus—for instance, the earthen mounds to the former and the stone wall to the latter; but a careful study of the existing remains does not favour these theories. It seems better to admit that the writer was careless and forgetful, and that British affairs and the story of the Roman wall were of infinitely less importance to him than they are now to us, dwellers in Britain.

Severus was doomed to discover, like Edward Plantagenet a thousand years later, how deceptive were victories over the Northern mountaineers. Next year (211) the Mæatæ were again up in arms and were joined by the Caledonians. Filled with wrath he ordered his troops again to invade their land, repeating often the lines of Homer:—

Let not one of the race escape the steepness of ruin,
None, your avenging hands, not e'en the babe at the bosom.

He was preparing himself once more to set forth in his litter in the short dark winter days for the northern moorlands, when sickness attacked him, aided, some men thought, by Caracalla and the physicians, and on February 4, 211, the old man died at Eburacum. He had lived sixty-five years and reigned seventeen, and he was the last Roman emperor of whose doings in our land we have any detailed description. Scarcely had Severus died when his sons, renouncing apparently all thoughts of vengeance on the Caledonians, left the wintry north and returned to the delights of Rome. The hardly suppressed enmity of the brothers now broke out into open flame; and after various ineffectual attempts, always foiled by the younger man's vigilance, Caracalla's centurions slew Geta in his mother's arms. Wheresoever the name of his victim occurred on the monuments, it was erased by order of the murderer. This strange manifestation of posthumous vindictiveness has left traces in our own country (for instance on a monument in the abbey-church of Hexham) as well as on the Arch of Severus in Rome, and in an inscription near the Second Cataract of the Nile.

Caracalla himself was assassinated in 217, but emperors of his kindred wore the imperial purple down to the year 235, and thus the dynasty of Severus may be said to have lasted for more than forty years. Both in coins and inscriptions the princes of this house have left an exceptionally full record in the British province. From 235, the date of the murder of Severus Alexander (an excellent young emperor, last of his line), down to 284, a period of almost half a century, the Roman empire was in a state of absolute disintegration. The barbarians were pressing fiercely on its frontiers. This was the era of the first and terrible invasion of the Goths (244–270), an invasion which after awful losses on both sides, and the death of a Roman emperor from the pestilence caused by the war, ended in the abandonment to the barbarians of the great province of Dacia, won for the empire by the victories of Trajan. It was the era, too, of a most humiliating defeat by the Persians, and the conversion of a Roman emperor into a footstool for the Persian king. But more dangerous, if possible, than the external foes of the empire, was its internal disorganisation. In these forty-nine years no fewer than fifteen emperors were recognised at Rome, besides a multitude of obscure competitors (commonly known as the thirty tyrants) in the provinces. It is needless to say that the reigns, which thus lasted on an average little more than three years, were generally terminated by mutiny and murder; needless to dilate on the miserable collapse of law and order which inevitably followed from such continual changes in the depositary of supreme power in the state. Of this dismal period there is, naturally enough, no written record in the annals of Britain. Undoubtedly the wave of Roman influence ebbed; we can hardly be wrong in thinking that now, at any rate, if not before, the country between the two walls was permanently abandoned to the barbarians. The Northumbrian camps were probably also sacked, and we may, if we will, read some pages of that long unwritten chapter in the ruined walls of the camps erected by Hadrian and Severus, in the places where fire has evidently passed upon the corridors of a Roman villa, destroying the elaborate bathing arrangements of tribune or centurion.

For the empire as a whole this interregnum of anarchy came to an end in the year 284 when Diocletian, the second Augustus, ascended the throne. This man, of obscure, even of servile origin, showed statesmanship of a rare order, rescuing the water-logged and all-but foundering vessel of the state from destruction, and steering it into a harbour in which it rode safely for a hundred years. His chief expedient was the division of the imperial power, in recognition of the fact that the vast fabric of the empire could no longer be upheld by a single ruler, and that if the supreme Augustus would not have rivals he must have partners. Dividing the empire into four great sections called prefectures, he chose for himself the prefecture of the East, including Egypt, Syria, Asia Minor and Thrace. His contemporary and colleague, the stout old soldier Maximian, who, like himself, bore the title of Augustus, ruled Italy, southern Germany and the greater part of Roman Africa. After Diocletian had reigned seven years he associated with himself in addition two junior partners, not Augusti but merely Cæsars; Galerius who governed the Illyrian lands, which in the meaning then given to the name stretched from Cape Matapan to the Danube. To the youngest of all, Constantius Chlorus, was assigned the prefecture of the west, stretching from Tangier to Hexham, and including three great "Dioceses" as the divisions intermediate between prefectures and provinces were called: Western Africa and Spain, Gaul and Britain. A noble portion was this, for the junior partner of the imperial firm, and one which might have satisfied the ambition even of a Napoleon. But there was one annoying drawback to the greatness of the western Cæsar. After all the rest of the empire had been restored to tranquillity the island of Britain still remained outside the imperial orbit, and what made this circumstance the more exasperating was the remembrance that it was due to the treachery of an officer chosen by the emperors themselves. Desiring to check the piratical expeditions of the Franks and Saxons who were already beginning to infest both coasts of the British channel, Maximian, who was at that time ruling and warring in Gaul, had entrusted the command of a naval squadron to a certain Carausius, a man of mean extraction, born either in Flanders or Ireland,* who had already distinguished himself by his bravery and his skill in naval warfare. From his strong place of arms at Gesoriacum (Boulogne), Carausius soon made his power felt by the barbarians, but before long Maximian had reason to suspect that the officer of the empire was himself in secret league with at least some of the pirates and shared their plunder. He summoned Carausius to appear before him, but that astute personage, suspecting the motive for the summons, hastily quitted Boulogne and sailed for Britain, which in the disorganised condition of Roman affairs he had not much difficulty in making his own.

Having declared himself emperor and having even constrained the two

* The term "Menapian" may apply to either country.

legitimate Augusti to recognise him as a quasi-partner of their dignity, Carausius actually succeeded in maintaining his position for six years (287–293), perhaps the only time in the history of our island when there has been a veritable "Emperor of Britain." Of the character of his government we have unfortunately no information except some sentences of invective from professional rhetoricians; but at least the numismatist has reason to remember his reign which has supplied our museums with a multitude of coins. In these, while the obverse represents the head of the self-made emperor, a middle-aged common-place man who looks like a self-made manufacturer, the reverse bears sometimes the well-known Roman emblems of the wolf and the twins; or a lion with a thunderbolt in his mouth symbolises the valour of Augustus; or a female milking a cow the fertility of his kingdom; while in some of them the association with Jovius and Herculius (the titles of the two legitimate Augusti) attests his share in the imperial partnership.

Notwithstanding this interchange of compliments it was felt at headquarters that it was time that this separatist empire should come to an end, and it was in fact chiefly to accomplish this that Constantius had been created Cæsar of the west. The history of the campaign has to be gathered with difficulty from the rhetoric of Mamertinus and Eumenius, two professional panegyrists of the conqueror, but we seem to perceive that Carausius or his pirate allies still held the harbour of Boulogne, and that it was necessary to seal up the channel with beams of timber and cargoes of stone to prevent their exit. Stormy weather then delayed for some time the operations of Constantius, and meanwhile Carausius had been assassinated by one of his officers named Allectus, who at once assumed the purple and struck coins describing himself as Pious, Fortunate and August.

For nearly three years Allectus reigned. At last, in 296, Constantius set forth for the overthrow of this new usurper. "Other emperors," cries his flatterer, "have received the credit of victories won under their auspices though they themselves were tarrying in Rome. You, unconquered Cæsar! put yourself at the head of your troops; you gave the signal to start, when sea and sky were alike turbid, notwithstanding the hesitation of the other leaders. The wind struck obliquely on your sail: you made your vessel tack. All the soldiers, enraptured, cried: 'Let us follow Cæsar wherever he leads us'. Fortune did indeed favour you. We have heard from the companions of your voyage how the mists hung low over the back of the sea so that the hostile fleet stationed in ambush round the Isle of Wight never saw you pass. As soon as they touched the shore of Britain your unconquered army set fire to all their ships, urged surely, by some warning voice of your divinity, to seek their safety only in fight and victory." And so, with more of these pompous periods, the orator describes how the usurper Allectus fled as soon as he saw the imperial fleet, and fleeing fell into the hands of the soldiers of Constantius, how half dead with terror he thus hastened to his death, and by his neglect of all military precautions handed over an easy victory to the imperial troops. "Scarcely one Roman was killed while all the hills and plains around were covered with the ugly bodies of the slain. Those dresses worn in barbarian fashion, those locks of bright red hue were now all defiled with dust and gore. That standard bearer of rebellion himself [Allectus], having in the hope of concealment stripped off the purple robe which he had degraded by wearing it, now lay with scarce a rag to cover his nakedness."* The orator then goes on to describe in words of turgid obscurity how some of the soldiers of Constantius, parted from the main body of the fleet in the fog which had baffled the look-out of Allectus, wandered to the "oppidum Londiniense," and there were fortunate enough to meet and defeat the remains of the "mercenary multitude" of the usurper's forces which had taken refuge in that town. We thank even the bombastic orator for some slight indication of what was passing in the streets of the little Roman London at the end of the third century.

It was, as we have seen, in the year 296 that Britain was recovered for the empire by Constantius. Ten years afterwards that emperor, in failing health and knowing that he had not long to live, was looking anxiously eastwards for the arrival of his favourite son, the offspring of his concubine Helena, the brave and brilliant soldier Constantine. Diocletian and Maximian had both abdicated the empire. Constantius Chlorus was now raised from the rank of Cæsar to the higher rank of Augustus, but he shared that dignity with a jealous colleague, Galerius, who had been allowed to name the two new Cæsars. Of those two junior partners Constantine was not one. Worse than that, he was retained as a kind of

* Notwithstanding the positive statement of the panegyrist that the victory over Allectus was won by Constantius in person, the merit of it is assigned by some of the historians to the Prætorian Prefect Asclepiodotus. It is, perhaps, impossible to frame a satisfactory narrative out of the very fragmentary materials at our disposal.

hostage at the Bithynian palace of Galerius, and it was doubtful whether father and son would ever be allowed to meet again. But in a moment of irresolution or of alarm Galerius gave the desired permission, and Constantine, not risking the chance of its withdrawal, departed from the court without formal leave-taking and hurried across Europe to Boulogne where his father was then residing. It was currently reported two centuries later that in order to prevent the possibility of pursuit he ordered the post-horses at each imperial mutatio, which he did not himself require, to be either killed or so mutilated as to make them unfit for travel. Gibbon derides this "very foolish story," but it is not easy to understand why, if untrue, it should have obtained such general acceptance.

However this may be, it is certain that Constantine arrived safely at his father's headquarters at Boulogne, shared with him the labours of a short campaign against the Picts, and was present in his chamber, in the Prætorian palace at Eburacum, when, worn out with toil and disease, Constantius Chlorus breathed his last (July 25, 306). His own elevation to the imperial dignity by the soldiers, who enthusiastically hailed him as Augustus, followed immediately after, and we may fairly suppose that the same place which had witnessed the death of the father witnessed also the accession of the son. He speedily quitted Britain in order to take part in that desperate game of empire, with partners constantly changing and occasionally putting one another to death, from which after eighteen years he finally arose sole emperor. With all this later life of his, with his adoption of Christianity, with his choice of a new capital by the Bosphorus, with his convocation of the Nicene council, we have here no concern; but it is worth while to emphasise the fact that a reign so immensely important for all the after-history of Europe and of the world began in our island by the slow, wide-wandering river Ouse. Thus in a certain sense York is the mother-city of Constantinople.

We come now to another blank half century in the history of Roman Britain. Save for an obscure hint of the presence of the Emperor Constans, son of Constantine, at some time between 337 and 350, we have scarcely any information as to British affairs from the proclamation of Constantine in 306 to the despatch of the elder Theodosius to Britain in 367. This general, father of the more celebrated emperor of the same name, was sent by the Emperor Valentinian to restore some degree of order in the unhappy island, which had suffered from rapacious governors, from accusations of disloyalty cruelly avenged, and more recently from bloody inroads of the Picts and Scots with whom were now joined a tribe who are called "the most valiant nation of the Attacotti," but who, if we may believe the extraordinary statement of St. Jerome, were actually addicted to the practice of cannibalism. In the three years of Theodosius' command, the northern invaders were driven back to their mountains, the inhabitants of "that ancient town which was formerly called Londinium but which (in the fourth century) "more often bore the name Augusta" were relieved from their terrors: a new province, the geographical position of which is not made known to us, was staked out and received the name Valentia, in compliment to the emperor. For the time, but probably not for a long time, the blessings of "the Roman peace" were restored to Britain. The general who had achieved this result was shortly after executed at Carthage, a victim to the cowardly suspicion and jealousy of the Emperor Valens, brother of Valentinian. Soon, however, the whirligig of Time brought about a strange revenge. Valens himself perished in the awful catastrophe of Hadrianople, the battle in which the Visigoths utterly routed a great Roman army, the battle which first brought home to the minds of men the possibility of the collapse of the Roman empire. The nephew of Valens, the young and generous Gratian, looking round for some man who as partner of his throne might avert the menaced ruin, found none more suitable than the son and namesake of the murdered pacifier of Britain, and accordingly, in the year 379, Theodosius (whom historians have surnamed the Great) was hailed as Augustus at Constantinople.

But now did Britain begin to rear that crop of rival emperors who were the curse of Europe during some of the dying days of the western empire. In 383 a general named Maximus, of whom an unfavourable witness, the ecclesiastic Orosius, testifies that he was "vigorous and honest and would have been worthy of the diadem if he had not, to obtain it, broken his oath of loyalty" was almost against his will declared emperor by the army. He crossed over into Gaul, carrying with him no doubt the bulk of his army. He skilfully played on the disaffection of Gratian's legions, offended at the partiality which he had showed for his barbarian auxiliaries; a general mutiny was organised; Gratian fled for his life, was pursued and murdered near the city of Vienne. For five years Theodosius had to endure the enforced partnership in the empire of his benefactor's murderer: then in 388 the smouldering hatred broke out into a flame, and after a hard struggle Maximus was defeated and slain at Aquileia, on the northern shore of the Adriatic (388). According to traditions current two centuries later, this usurpation of Maximus and his consequent withdrawal of the British legions in order to vindicate his claims to the empire, were most important factors in the overthrow of Roman power in Britain.

A large army, on paper, still existed in the island. It was probably about the year 402 that the last edition of the Notitia Imperii, that edition which has been handed down to posterity, was issued from the imperial chancery. In this most valuable document—an army list and official directory of both the eastern and western portions of the empire—we still find cohorts of infantry and wings of cavalry stationed per lineam valli (along the line of the Wall) as they had been for three centuries. We may, however, doubt whether any Roman soldiers were actually keeping the line of the Wall so late as 402. It is remarkable that very few coins have been found in the ruins of the camps of a later date than the reign of Gratian (375–83). If there were any such military units still there, they were probably but the ghosts of their former selves.

To understand the political condition of our island at this time we must have recourse to the pages of the Notitia, which elaborately sets forth the various degrees of the civil and military hierarchy of the empire. On one page we find:—

THE ILLUSTRIOUS PRÆTORIAN PREFECT OF THE GAULS.

"Under his disposition are the Vicarii of Spain, of the Seven Provinces of Gaul and of Britain."

On a later page:—

"The Spectabilis VICARIUS BRITANNIARUM."

Under his disposition were five (civil) governors:—

The Consularis of	Maxima Cæsariensis.
"	Valentia.
The Præses of	Britannia Prima.
"	Britannia Secunda.
"	Flavia Cæsariensis.

The limits and geographical position of these five districts (we are not entitled to call them provinces) have not yet been ascertained, though they have been often conjectured. It may be hoped that the discovery of further inscriptions may enable us to fix them decisively.*

* It has been shown by Mr. Haverfield that Britannia Prima included Cirencester (Arch. Oxon., p. 220).

Besides these civil officers there were, according to the rearrangement of offices made by Diocletian, certain military commandants, called comites and duces, of whom the count was, contrary to medieval usage, generally of higher rank than the duke.

The Notitia introduces us to three of these officers:—

1. The Comes Britanniæ.
2. The Comes Litoris Saxonici per Britanniam.
3. The Dux Britanniarum.

As to the first it gives us no information beyond the simple fact that the Provincia Britannia was "under his disposition." The obvious conjecture is that numbers 2 and 3 were subject to him, but this is not asserted, and it perhaps militates against this theory that they, like him, belonged to the second grade in the official hierarchy, the spectabiles. It is possible that his special duty was the defence of Mid-Britain against the imperfectly subdued tribes of the Welsh mountains, and that the Second legion at Caerleon and the Twentieth at Chester were for a time under his orders for this purpose. The more interesting title for us is that of "The Count of the Saxon Shore in Britain." He had under his command the garrisons of seven fortified places dotted around the eastern and south-eastern coast of England, from the Wash to Beachy Head.* He had also at his bidding the prefect of the Second "Augustan" legion, which had been moved from the quarters it had so long occupied at Caerleon-upon-Usk to Rutupiæ, or Richborough, close to the Isle of Thanet. The meaning of this arrangement is obvious. Like the Martello towers, which were reared along the same coasts last century, these fortresses were raised and garrisoned in order to defend that part of the projecting coast of Britain which was most exposed to the attacks of the Saxon pirates, already no doubt swarming in these seas in the fourth century, and to become far more formidable in the fifth century. The words, "per Britanniam," added to the title of the spectabilis comes, are used because, as the Notitia informs us, there was another Saxon shore which needed to be guarded on the other side of the channel; and, taken in this connexion, there is a special interest for us in the words of Apollinaris Sidonius, bishop of Clermont,† which show that

* They were Branodunum (Brancaster in Norfolk), Gariannonum (Caistor, near Yarmouth), Othona (at the mouth of the Blackwater in Essex?), Regulbium (Reculver in Essex), Rutupiæ (Richborough), Dubræ (Dover), Lemannæ (Lymne), Anderida (close to Beachy Head), Portus Adurni (not yet identified).

† Epist. viii. 6.

in the succeeding century the coasts of Gaul, as well as of Britain, were kept in constant alarm by the Saxon sea-rovers.

3. Of the Duke of the Britains we have only here to remark that he appears to have had under his disposition the Sixth legion, stationed at York, and numerous detachments of auxiliary troops in Yorkshire, Westmorland and Lancashire, and item per lineam valli (also along the line of the wall) the various auxiliary cohorts raised in Spain, Gaul and Germany, to whom reference has already been made, and who are to all students of the literature of the Roman wall among the most interesting elements of the army of the empire.

Meanwhile events were rapidly ripening towards the catastrophe which was to make the solemn Notitia Imperii a mere hunting-ground for the archæologist. In 395 died the great Emperor Theodosius, who had for a generation staved off the ruin which seemed inevitable at the death of Valens. He was succeeded by his two sons, Arcadius and Honorius, who, with about equal incapacity, presided over the collapse of the eastern and the western half of the empire. For the first thirteen years, however, of the reign of Honorius his incapacity was somewhat veiled by the courage and ability of the Vandal soldier Stilicho, whom Theodosius had left as the guardian of his son. When in the year 400 Alaric, the far-famed King of the Goths, entered Italy, Stilicho undertook the long and wearisome campaigns, partly, as it would seem, north of the Alps, but chiefly in what we now call Piedmont and Lombardy, by which Alaric's designs on Rome were foiled, and at last in the year 403 the Goths were driven forth from Italy. But in order to avert the danger which thus threatened the heart of the empire, it was necessary seriously to weaken the defence of its extremities. One of the three Roman legions quartered in Britain (probably the Twentieth) was recalled to Italy and apparently never returned. Three years after the repulse of Alaric came in 406 the great cataclysm of the irruption of barbarian hordes, Vandals, Sueves, Burgundians and Alans into Gaul, which led, though not immediately, to the severance of Gaul and Spain from the empire. The inrush of the barbarians spread terror even into Britain, and caused the soldiers, weary of the inept government which was manifestly ruining the empire, to elect an emperor on their own account, and set up, as it were, a "government of national defence." But revolutionary rulers of this kind are more easily proclaimed than established. First a certain Marcus was proclaimed: then as they found that "he did not suit their tempers" he was slain, and a

British citizen named Gratian was invested with the purple, crowned with the diadem and surrounded with a bodyguard. After four months Gratian also was deposed and murdered, and thereupon a private soldier of the meanest rank, named Constantine, who had nothing but that great historic name to recommend him, was robed in the imperial purple. He at once crossed over into Gaul, where he maintained himself with varying fortune for three or four years, being even once, in 409, for a short time recognised as a legitimate partner in the empire by Honorius. With his later fortunes, however, and with the whole story of the fall of the Roman empire in the west we have no further concern. We have heard of the exit of the legions, but we never hear of their return, and we are probably justified in fixing on the date 407, the period of the usurper Constantine's departure from our island, as the end of the Roman occupation of Britain.

Writers and readers must alike lament the extremely jejune character of the history of that occupation. Since we lost the guidance of Tacitus, we have had scarcely anything that could be called a continuous and intelligible narrative of events; nor, unless some happy fortune could restore to us the lost books of Ammianus, is such literary assistance now to be expected. We are thus thrown back on such information as inscriptions, buried ruins, finds of coins may afford to the patient archæologist. And these have done something for us, though we may reasonably hope that the judicious use of the spade and pickaxe, guided by science and not by mere capricious quest for curiosities, may do much more.

We may here notice very briefly some of the chief contributions which archæological research has thus made to history.

1. Of all the marks made by our imperial conquerors in this island, the most distinct and ineffaceable was that made by them as road-makers. Often indeed their works survive only as boundaries between parishes or counties, but sometimes we can see the track still going straight to its mark over hill and dale, and we say instinctively, "That must be a Roman road." It was certainly not mere unskilfulness or ignorance of the science of road-making which led the stratores viarum to draw their lines across the country with this uncompromising directness. The prime object of the officer charged with the work was essentially military, and for watching the movements of barbarian insurgents or preventing the ravages of marauders, the crests of the hills successively surmounted by the marching legions were invaluable posts of observation.

The chief highways of the Romans, known to us for the most part by the names given to them by our Anglo-Saxon forefathers, converging, as most of them do, towards "the town anciently named Londinium," coincide in a remarkable manner with the main lines of our modern railroad communication. The Watling Street, running from the neighbourhood of London to Etocetum (a little north of Birmingham) and thence to Deva (Chester) and so on into Lancashire, corresponds with the London and North-Western Railway; while another road which generally bears the same name and which traverses Yorkshire and Northumberland is less accurately represented by the North-Eastern. Erming Street, from London to Doncaster, is often not far from the line of the Great Northern; and Abona (on the Avon near Bristol) and Isca Damnoniorum (Exeter) were reached by roads bearing now no special names, but imitating in their general course the Great Western and South-Western Railways. One great artery, the Fosse Way, may be clearly traced between Axminster (in Devonshire) and the great colony which now bears the name of Lincoln; but this road has no representative in our railway system. The imperfect character of the Roman conquest of the district which we now call Wales is evidenced by the feeble and fragmentary traces of Roman roads now to be found in the principality. There was, however, a road traversing the country from north to south, from Carnarvon to Carmarthen, and thence by a somewhat circuitous course to Caerleon-upon-Usk, and part of this road is still known by the name of Sarn Helen. Is it possible that there is in this name some vague and inaccurate remembrance of the mother of Constantine?

2. The sepulchral inscriptions which have been discovered in large numbers in various parts of the island give us a little insight into the domestic relations of the Roman garrison, as the votive altars do into their sentiments concerning religion. The former class of inscriptions always begin in the usual Roman style with a dedication to the Dii Manes, the shade-gods, or, as we should say, the spirit of the departed one, and often add some endearing epithet to the name, such as "a well-deserving husband," "a most religious wife who lived for thirty-three years an unspotted life." Where the age is mentioned it is most frequently that either of a child or a person in middle life, the numbers between thirty and forty being of frequent occurrence. This is probably accounted for by the fact that veterans, whether officers or privates, would generally return to their native land to spend the last years of their lives. The religious inscriptions bring before us some interesting phenomena, but are so far characterised

by one memorable omission, that of the new religion which was destined to supplant the old. The ordinary Olympian deities, Jupiter, Mars, Bellona, Neptune, are of course commemorated, though in a somewhat perfunctory fashion; and the official divinity of the emperors, living and dead, is duly recognised. But we have also a number of altars to gods bearing uncouth Celtic names: Belatucader, Anociticus, Cocidius and the like, plainly showing that the Roman soldiers, like the Assyrian settlers in Palestine,[*] wished to keep on good terms with the gods of the land. Even more conspicuous is the devotion of the Roman soldiers to "the unconquered Mithras." The strange Oriental cult called Mithraism, probably a form of sun-worship, spread rapidly through the Roman empire in the second and third centuries, and seemed likely at one time to be a successful rival to Christianity. It is marvellous to see in the palace of the Roman emperors at Ostia a chapel with all the emblems of Mithraic worship, and then to find the remains of a similar chapel with precisely similar emblems, though broken and mutilated, on the bare hillside of Housesteads in Northumberland. The favourite symbol of this strange dead religion is a young man, crowned with a tiara, bestriding a bull, into whose side he is driving deep a short sword or dagger. Whatever this curious bas-relief may represent—and some have seen in it a symbol of the sun, the unconquered hero entering the constellation Taurus—it was no doubt faithfully reproduced in that little chapel on our northern moorlands, and it is perfectly figured on a small marble tablet lately discovered under the pavement of a London street while the workmen were repairing a sewer.

Thus, of so many strange pagan superstitions we have abundant vestiges, but of Christianity in Roman Britain we have singularly few traces. It is true that here and there among undoubtedly Roman remains the Christian monogram (X P) or Christian formulæ such as Vivas in Deo or Spes in Deo have been met with.[†] In the recent excavations at Silchester a small building which is almost certainly a Christian basilica has also been discovered, but these are slight evidences for the existence of a faith which was certainly professed by multitudes ere the legions quitted Britain. As to the actual date of the introduction of Christianity into our island we must be contented to confess our ignorance. The story contained in the book of Papal Lives, which was reproduced by Bede, that

* 2 Kings xvii. 27.

† See English Historical Review, xi., 420, for a list of these evidences of Christianity in Britain, drawn up by Mr. Haverfield.

a certain King Lucius of Britain, about the year 180, sent over to Pope Eleutherus, asking for missionaries to instruct his people in the Christian faith, must be dismissed as the fable of a later age; nor can we speak with much certainty concerning the so-called proto-martyr, St. Alban, who is said to have suffered for the faith in the persecution of Diocletian. There can be no doubt, however, that there were some converts to Christianity in Britain during the second century, and in the third century it must have become the dominant religion here as in the rest of the empire. Towards the end of that century our island, which produced so many rival Cæsars, produced also one of the most famous of heretics, Pelagius, and, of course, the existence of his heterodoxy implies also the existence of the orthodoxy out of which it sprang. Thus, though we cannot help sometimes relying on the "argument from silence," the present condition of our archæological information concerning the existence of Christianity in Roman Britain shows us how untrustworthy may sometimes be that very argument.

3. It is, however, partly in reliance on such negative evidence that we venture to assert that the Roman occupation of Britain was before all things a military occupation, and that they either did not attempt, or did not succeed in the attempt, largely to win over the inhabitants to their own ways and to accustom them to that civic life which had been the cradle of their own civilisation. In Italy itself, in Gaul and in most of the provinces of western Europe we find abundant evidence of the municipalisation of the conquered tribes. "Decurio" and "Duumvir," which we may represent by town councillor and mayor, are indications of rank which we meet with continually on provincial tombstones in those countries; but in Britain amid the crowd of inscriptions to centurions, tribunes and other military officers who served here we meet with only one here and there to civic dignitaries. "The highest form of town life known to the Romans was naturally rare in Britain. The coloniæ and municipia, the privileged municipalities, with institutions on the Italian model, which mark the supreme development of Roman political civilisation in the provinces, were not common in Britain. We know only of five: Colchester, Lincoln, Gloucester, and York were coloniæ, Verulam probably a municipium, and despite their legal rank none of these could count among the greater cities of the empire. Four of them, indeed, probably owed their existence not to any development of Britain but to the need of providing for time-expired soldiers discharged from the army."* There was, of course, a

* Quotation from Haverfield, Victoria History of Norfolk, i., 282.

certain number of towns such as Londinium which had sprung out of pre-Roman settlements, some of which no doubt grew and prospered exceedingly with the growth of commerce due to the prevalence of "the Roman peace," but these towns were apparently not modelled on the Roman pattern, and what may have been the nature of their institutions can only be a matter of conjecture.

It seems probable that the prevailing type of social organisation during the Roman period was the villa or great estate owned by a Roman proprietor and dotted over with the cottages of British serfs or slaves, whose labour was directed for his lord's benefit by a villicus or farm bailiff, sometimes himself a slave. Whether or no this system lasted on to any great extent after the Saxon invasion (the barbarian invader seating himself in the place of power and claiming all his ousted predecessor's rights), and whether it thus passed in the course of centuries into the feudal manor, is one of the most interesting questions now debated by our archæologists. Mr. Seebohm is the most conspicuous advocate of this Roman-villa theory, which cuts right across the theories of Kemble and Freeman, who held that the Teutonic invaders brought with them to our island and everywhere established a system of free but co-operative land-ownership, resembling that described in the Germania of Tacitus. The discussion, as has been said, is one of great interest to all who desire to get below the surface in the history of the past ages of Britain, but many positions will probably be won and lost before the battle is finally decided.

The same may be said of the larger question, how far the influence exerted by our Roman conquerors during the four centuries of their stay lasted on after the departure of the legions. That Britain was not assimilated as Gaul was, is admitted by all, the mere fact that Welsh is not, like French, an offshoot from Latin, being in itself a sufficient proof of the difference between the two conquests; but why the Romanisation of Britain was so much less thorough; how far it did after all extend; and what influences modified or destroyed it; these are all questions still unsolved, to which, however, we may, perhaps, some day get an answer from a more thorough and scientific study of Celtic literature, and of Romano-British antiquities.

VI.

THE ANGLO-SAXON CONQUEST.

With the departure of the Roman legions from Britain we enter upon a period of even denser darkness than those which we have been lately traversing, nor is the veil lifted till by the mission of St. Augustine (596) our island is again brought into the family of the Christian nations of Europe. The two centuries during which the voice of authentic history is thus silent, from 407 to 596, were the period of the fall of the Roman empire in the west and the establishment in its stead of the great Teutonic kingdoms, Frankish, Burgundian, Visigothic, from which the states of modern Europe are descended.

Owing to the extremely imperfect character of our information concerning the Anglo-Saxon conquest, which was for us the chief event of these two centuries, and the fact that scarcely any of it is contemporary, some of it obviously legendary and fabulous, it is impossible to speak with any confidence as to its details. Almost every date may be challenged: "probably" or "to the best of our knowledge" are qualifying clauses which should be prefixed to almost every statement. It may be well, however, first to set forth in broad outlines the main facts which are beyond the reach of controversy. No one doubts that about the middle of the fifth century, if not before, the Romano-Celtic inhabitants of Britain were invaded by Teutonic tribes from the shores of the German Ocean and the Baltic. The tribes chiefly concerned in the invasion were the Saxons and the Angles, but the smaller nation of the Jutes are said to have been the first to undertake a definite scheme of conquest, and it is asserted with much positiveness that they came at first as auxiliaries to help the Britons against the Picts of Caledonia and the Scots of Ireland, who were ravaging the undefended land. To the Jutes is attributed the foundation of the kingdom of Kent and a settlement in the Isle of Wight. The far more numerous Saxons who followed them established the two kingdoms of the South Saxons and East Saxons, which are represented by the modern counties of Sussex and Essex; and after the lapse of two generations the West Saxons, invading Hampshire, laid there the foundation of the great kingdom of Wessex, which gradually included almost all the country south of the Thames. Their kings eventually became lords of the whole of Britain, and were ancestors through females of the sovereign who now sits upon the throne. The Angles, who were apparently the latest comers of all, founded the kingdoms of East Anglia (Norfolk and Suffolk), Mercia (the midland counties), Deira (Yorkshire), and Bernicia (Durham, Northumberland, and East Scotland as far as the Firth of Forth).

A few words must be said as to the ethnological relations of these three tribes. It is not disputed that they all belonged to the great Low German family of nations, to which the Goths probably belonged and from which the Dutch and most of the inhabitants of northern Germany are descended. As to the little nation of the Jutes we require further information. They were once said to be identical with the Goths, and more recently they have been connected with the inhabitants of Jutland. The first identification is certainly wrong, the second, for philological reasons, is doubtful.* It seems that at present the question must be left in suspense.†

The Saxons were placed by the geographer, Ptolemy (who wrote early in the second century), in the country now known as Holstein, but in the fourth century the name seems to have been applied to a much wider range of people. The Saxons with whom Charlemagne waged his stubborn wars at the close of the eighth century, inhabited the whole of Westphalia, Hanover and Brunswick and other lands beside. From any part of that country our Saxon ancestors may have come.

Of the Angles, who in the first century after Christ were living on the right bank of the Elbe, near its mouth, Tacitus gives us an interesting account. He tells us that they, together with the kindred tribes between Elbe and Oder, worshipped the great goddess Nerthus, whose image, ordinarily kept in the dark recesses of a sacred island, at certain seasons paraded the lands of her votaries in a chariot drawn by kine. Wherever the image of the goddess came, mirth reigned and war ceased; but when her pilgrimage was ended, the image and the chariot, returning to the

* See Stevenson's Asser, p. 166, for reasons against it.

† Possibly their name may be connected with that of the Eudoces, a tribe mentioned by Tacitus as neighbours of the Angli. But that identification, if confirmed, would not add much to our knowledge.

dark island, were washed in a sacred lake, beneath whose waters all the slaves who had taken part in the ceremony were at once engulfed, in order to ensure their silence as to the mysteries which they had beheld. A more interesting fact for us is the close relation which, according to Tacitus, existed between the Angli and the Longobardi, the tribe by whom, after long wanderings through central Europe, the conquest of Italy was at last achieved in 568, possibly at the very time when some of their old Anglian neighbours were beginning to fit out their barks for the invasion of England. This ethnological connexion is confirmed by the similarity of names to be found among the two nations, a similarity which is but slightly veiled by the changes which in the course of five centuries turned the Lombards from a people speaking Low German to one with a High German language. Thus the Adelperga of the Lombards corresponds to the Ethelberga of the Anglo-Saxons; Sisibert to Sigeberht, Alipert to Alberht, Rotopert to Rodberht, Adelbert to Ethelberht, and Audoin to Edwin. Moreover, the great historian of the Lombards, Paulus Diaconus, who wrote towards the end of the eighth century, tells us that their queen, Theodelinda, adorned her palace at Pavia with pictures representing the Lombard invaders of Italy in the very garb which they then wore, and which had become antiquated in the two centuries that had elapsed before his own time. "Their garments," he says, "were loose and for the most part made of linen, such as the Anglo-Saxons are wont to wear, adorned with wide borders woven in various colours." This is a valuable note of costume, for its own sake, and a striking confirmation of the close relationship once existing between the ancestors of two great nations now joined in friendly alliance.

*****

After this sketch of the antecedents of the three new actors on the stage of British history, it remains for us to examine the evidence—the slender evidence, as has been already said—as to their proceedings during the conquest. It will be well to consider this evidence under three heads:—

(1) The slight notices contained in the works of contemporary or nearly contemporary Latin authors.

(2) The story of the conquest as given to us by the descendants of the invaders, that is, especially by Bede and the authors of the Anglo-Saxon Chronicle.

(3) The same story as told by the descendants of the conquered, that is, especially by Gildas and Nennius.

1. In the fifth century the writing of history in the Roman empire had practically dwindled down to the composition of short books of chronicles, generally by ecclesiastics. As literary compositions they have no merit: they are generally very short, giving only three or four lines to each year, and they have no sense of the proportionate importance of the events which they record. But they give us for the most part absolutely contemporary evidence, and the historian, therefore, accepts them gratefully, with all their defects. One such chronicle, by no means the best of its kind, is generally known by the name of Prosper Tiro (a friend and correspondent of St. Augustine), though it is certain that it was not written by him but by some ecclesiastic of the period, with semi-Pelagian views. This dull and second-rate writer gives us the two following precious entries, the only contemporary evidence that we possess as to the Saxon invasions: "The fifteenth year of Arcadius and Honorius [A.D. 409]: at this time the strength of the Romans was utterly wasted by sickness; and the provinces of Britain were laid waste by the incursion of the Saxons." "The eighteenth year of Theodosius II. [A.D. 441]: the provinces of Britain which up to this time had been torn by various slaughters and disasters, are brought under the dominion of the Saxons."

There are two points in these entries to which the reader's attention should be particularly directed: the first, that the Saxon invasions are represented as beginning in 409, almost immediately after the departure of the usurper Constantine with the legions; the second, that the subjugation of Britain by the Saxons is assigned by the chronicler to 441, not 449, the date usually current on the authority of Bede. It should be remarked, in passing, that if the chronicler supposed that the whole of Roman Britain (which he calls Britanniæ, in the plural) came under the dominion of the Saxons (or Saxons, Angles, and Jutes) in that year, he was certainly mistaken. But some important stage in the conquest, if we may trust this, our only contemporary authority, was evidently reached in the year 441, and it was the climax of a series of aggressions which had apparently been going on for thirty-two years.

It should be mentioned that one other nearly contemporary authority, the Greek historian Zosimus, alludes to the collapse of Roman rule in Britain, which he attributes to a revolt of the natives, following on the departure of the usurper Constantine with the legions. His language, however, is obscure and even self-contradictory, and he throws little light on the situation.

The authority which we have next to consider is the Life of St. Germanus, written by the presbyter Constantius about the year 480. It will be seen that this document is not strictly contemporary, the writer being separated by an interval of about half a century from the chief events recorded by him: and, moreover, there is throughout the Life a tendency to glorify the saint by attributing to him various manifestations of a miraculous or semi-miraculous kind, which does not increase our confidence in his trustworthiness as a historian. But all students of early medieval history are accustomed to this kind of document, in which every remarkable event in the life of the subject of the biography is invested with a halo of thaumaturgic sanctity, and though they are not the sort of historic materials which we prefer, we must accept them (while making our own private reservations as to the amount of faith which we repose in all their details) or give up writing the story of the Middle Ages altogether.

In the case before us, the missionary Germanus, whose adventures in Britain are related by the biographer, was a great and well-known historical personage. He had held, under the empire, the high military dignity of duke of the Armorican shore (Normandy and Brittany), had been consecrated Bishop of Auxerre against his will, had thereupon said farewell to the delights of sportsmanship, and entered earnestly on the duties of his new calling. He had as a fellow-missionary, Lupus, who many years after, as Bishop of Troyes, earned great renown by dissuading the savage warrior, Attila, from an attack on his cathedral city. It is a striking testimony to the character of both men that their contemporary, Apollinaris Sidonius, when he wishes to celebrate the virtues of another eminent prelate, Anianus, Bishop of Orleans, can find no higher term of praise than this: "He was equal to Lupus and not unequal to Germanus." Such were the two men who in the year 429 were sent at the bidding of Pope Celestine, and in conformity with the resolutions of a synod of Gaulish bishops, "to purge the minds of the people of Britain from the Pelagian heresy and bring them back to the Catholic faith," that is, to the Augustinian teaching on free-will and the Divine grace. Their zealous preaching won over the multitude to their side, but the Pelagians, who seem to have been found chiefly among the wealthier Britons, challenged them to a public discussion, in which their simple earnestness prevailed over the elaborate rhetoric of the gaily clothed orators on the other side. A miracle followed: the restoration of sight to a little girl of ten years old, the daughter of "a certain man of tribunician rank." After visiting the tomb of the martyred Saint Alban and exchanging relics with the keepers of the shrine, they resumed their journey, but, unfortunately, Germanus was for several days confined by a sprained ankle to a humble cottage in the country. The cottage itself and all the little hovels round it were thatched with reeds from the marsh, and fire having broken out in the little settlement, the saint's life seemed to be in jeopardy, but he refused to stir, and his cottage alone remained unconsumed.

Then followed the celebrated incident of the Hallelujah battle which is the chief reason for referring to the mission. The scene of the encounter is not made known to us, but it evidently took place in a mountainous country, possibly in Wales.* The first sentence of the biographer, describing the campaign, is so important that it must be translated literally: "In the meanwhile the Saxons and the Picts, driven into one camp by the same necessity, with conjoined force undertook war against the Britons, and, when the latter deemed their strength unequal to the contest, they sought the aid of the holy bishops, who, hastening their arrival, brought with them such an accession of confidence as was equivalent to a mighty host." The biographer then describes the baptism of the larger part of the army on Easter day; their eagerness for battle while they were still moist with the baptismal water; the choice of the battle-field by the veteran officer Germanus; that battle-field a valley surrounded by mountains; the placing of an ambuscade whose duty it was to signal to him the approach of the foe. At the signal given the bishops gave the word "Hallelujah," which was repeated in a tremendous shout by the multitudes carefully posted out of sight, and was repeated from peak to peak of the surrounding mountains. Hereat the terror-stricken foes imagined not only rocks hurled down upon them, but the very artillery of heaven let loose for their destruction. Casting away their arms they fled in all directions, and the larger number of them were swallowed up in the river which they had just crossed; the Hallelujah victory was complete, a victory like that of Gideon over the Midianites, won by moral means alone.

This narrative when we remember its nearly contemporary character has an important bearing on the history of Britain in the fifth century. It

* It is conjectured, but only conjectured, that it took place at Maes Garmon (the field of Germanus?), near Mold in Flintshire.

seems to show that, twenty years after the withdrawal of the legions, the condition of the Britons was not absolutely desperate. There were still among them wealthy men and eloquent ecclesiastics dressed in costly garments, and the people were not too much engrossed by the mere struggle for existence to have leisure to listen to the elaborate arguments about original sin, free will and assisting grace which formed the staple of the Pelagian controversy. Moreover the union of the Saxons with the Picts in the hostile army is surely a point of no small importance. If we connect it with the previously quoted entry of Tiro, assigning to the year 409 the beginning of a series of Saxon devastations, we may suspect that the commonly received story which attributes the Teutonic invasions entirely to the folly of the Britons who called in the Saxons to help them against the Picts, is, if not altogether false, at any rate an exaggeration of one not very important incident in the contest.

*****

2. For the story told by the invaders, our chief authorities are Bede and the Anglo-Saxon Chronicle. (a) It must be confessed that for this part of the history we do not get much assistance from the monk of Jarrow, the Venerable Bede. He was probably the most learned man of his time in Europe; his conception of the duty of a historian is a high and noble one, and when we reach the seventh century, the golden age of Northumbrian Christianity, we shall find his assistance invaluable; but, writing as he did in 731, he was separated by nearly three centuries from the great Saxon invasions, and it seems clear that he had little or nothing derived from the genuine traditions of his race to say concerning them. The first book of his Ecclesiastical History is therefore little more than a mosaic of passages from Orosius, Eutropius, and, pre-eminently, the Briton Gildas (hereafter to be described), from whom he derives almost the whole history of the Caledonian invasion, and of the calling in of the Saxons as defenders against the attacks of the Picts. It is, however, to Bede that we owe the first mention of the British king Vortigern as well as of the names of Hengest and Horsa. It must remain an unsolved question from what source Bede derived the name of Vortigern, the inviter of the Saxons into Britain. Gildas, who is his main authority for this part of the story, while hinting at the personality of Vortigern, hides his name. After describing the three invading nations, the Jutes, the Saxons and the Angles, Bede

continues: “Their generals” (according to strict grammatical construction this should refer not to the Jutes but to the Angles) “are said to have been two brothers, Hengest and Horsa, of whom Horsa was afterwards slain in war by the Britons. To this day a monument inscribed by his name exists in the eastern parts of Kent. These two were sons of Wictgils, the son of Witta, the son of Wecta, the son of Woden, from whose stock the royal families of many provinces derived their origin.” Bede then goes on to describe how the bands of the three nations already named began to pour into the island, how they made a treaty with the Picts whom they had previously conquered and driven far away, and how they then turned their arms against their British allies. From this point he merely copies Gildas, describing in lamentable tones the ravage wrought by his countrymen. It is pointed out by Bede’s latest editor, Plummer, that such information as the Northumbrian monk possessed concerning Kent would be naturally derived by him from his Kentish friends, Albinus, abbot of Canterbury, and Nothelm, priest of the church of London, to both of whom he expressly refers in his preface. But apparently even their traditions could not carry him very far. Save for such information as the conquered race could supply, Bede’s mind was little more than a blank as to events in England between the ages of Honorius and Gregory the Great.

The Anglo-Saxon Chronicle is the great historical monument of our race in its youthful days, and probably owes its original inception to the wise encouragement of Alfred. As that great prince ruled in the later years of the ninth century it is plain that the interval between the historian and the events recorded is even greater in the case of the Chronicle than in that of Bede. To a considerable extent the early annals in the Chronicle are founded upon Bede’s history, and so far we may safely neglect them since they add nothing to the evidence already before the court; but there is also a certain amount of information, especially relating to the kingdom of Wessex, to which we find nothing that corresponds in Bede; and this part of the Chronicle—whatever it may be worth—must of course be treated as a primary authority. What is the real historical value of the statements which we find in it concerning yet heathen England? There is evidently in them some admixture of the fabulous. When we find, as we shall do, a Saxon chieftain, Port, described as the founder of Portsmouth, the Portus Magnus of the Romans, and Wihtgar made the name-giver to the Isle of Wight, which had been known as Vectis for centuries before he was born, we feel that we are in the presence of traditions, not genuine but manufactured out of etymology. Moreover the dates so elaborately given by the Chronicle seem to have been arranged (as was pointed out by Lappenberg) on an artificial system with recurring periods of eight and four years; which looks like the work of men with slender materials trying to make the bricks of history without the straw of genuine chronology. There is a good deal of distrust of the earlier portions of the Chronicle in the minds of historical students, side by side with a high appreciation of its general fairness, and gratitude to the scribes who have preserved for us so much of the records of the past, even though their narrative is often somewhat arid. On the whole it seems the wisest, in fact the only possible course, to take thankfully the information which the Chronicle gives us as to these two mist-enshrouded centuries, not absolutely maintaining its accuracy in every particular, but yielding to it a provisional assent, until either by internal or external evidence it shall be proved to be legendary or impossible.

It may be as well to state here that there are various manuscripts of the Chronicle hailing from different ecclesiastical centres, the divergences of which in the later centuries of Anglo-Saxon history are sometimes of great importance. For the present, however, this question does not arise. Save for a few not very important Northumbrian interpolations, the manuscripts of the Chronicle may be considered as one, and their source of origin may be considered to have been Winchester, the focus of all West Saxon government and culture.

The allusions made in the Chronicle to the departure of the Romans from Britain are naturally very scanty: "In 409 the Goths broke up the city of Rome, and never after that did the Romans rule in Britain." "In 418 the Romans gathered together all the gold-hoards that were in Britain and hid some in the earth, so that no man thenceforth should ever find them, and some they took with them into Gaul." Let us proceed therefore to examine the evidence furnished from this source as to the foundation of the kingdoms of Kent, Sussex, Wessex, and Northumbria. As to the early history of East Anglia, Essex and Mercia the Chronicle is altogether silent.

Kent.—A.D. 449.* Wyrtgeorn [Vortigern] invites the Angles to Britain. They come over in three "keels" and land at Heopwines-fleet [Ebbs-fleet

* It will be observed that this date is eight years later than that given by Tiro. It is probably derived from Bede (i., 15), who, however, does not seem to have had any definite information as to the exact year of the first invasion, though he certainly places it in the reigns of the Emperors Marcian and Valentinian III., that is (according to his inaccurate reckoning) somewhere between 449 and 455.

in the Isle of Thanet], and he gives them lands in the south-east of the country on condition of their fighting the Picts. This they do successfully, but they send home for more of their countrymen, telling them of the worthlessness of the Britons and the goodness of the land. Their generals were two brothers, Hengest and Horsa, sons of Wictgils with the pedigree as given by Bede.

A.D. 455. Hengest and Horsa fight with Vortigern at Aegeles-threp [Aylesford on the Medway]. Horsa is slain. Hengest assumes the title of king, and associates with himself his son Aesc.

A.D. 456. Hengest and Aesc fight with the Britons at Crecgan-ford [Crayford, about six miles south-east of Woolwich], and slay 4,000 of them. The Britons evacuate Kent and with much fear flee to London-borough.

A.D. 465. Hengest and Aesc fight with the "Welshmen" [Britons] near Wippedes-fleote, and there slay twelve Welsh nobles, themselves losing one thane, whose name was Wipped.

A.D. 473. Hengest and Aesc fight with the "Welshmen," and take booty past counting. The Welsh flee "as a man fleeth fire."

That is all the information vouchsafed us as to the conquest of Kent, which was evidently not an easy matter, taking as it did nearly thirty years to finish. Possibly ere the strife was ended the invaders somewhat modified their views as to the military worthlessness of the Britons. London, which is transiently mentioned here in the annal for 456 is not mentioned again in the Chronicle till 851. We hear of it, however, in Bede's Ecclesiastical History in 604. The history of Kent is a blank from the year 473 till 565 when Ethelbert, who afterwards embraced Christianity, began his long reign of fifty-three years.

Sussex.—We know from other sources that, far on into the Middle Ages, Sussex was divided from Kent by the dense forest of the Andredesweald or Andredesleag, and accordingly the conquest of one country by no means necessitated the conquest of the other, which is assigned to a considerably later date than that given for the landing of Hengest and Horsa.

A.D. 477. Aelle with three sons and three keels come to the place called Cymenes ora. He slays many "Welshmen," and drives others to take refuge in the wood that is called Andredesleag.

A.D. 485. He fights with "Welshmen" near Mearcredesburn.

A.D. 491. "Aelle and Cissa begirt Andredesceaster and slay all who dwell therein, nor was there for that reason one Briton left alive."

This wholesale butchery of the British defenders of the Roman fortress of Anderida, overlooking Pevensey Bay, has naturally attracted much attention, and is constantly appealed to by those who maintain that the earlier stages of the Saxon conquest were an absolute war of extermination. It is to be observed that Aelle, who founded an exceptionally short-lived dynasty, is not credited with any long line of ancestors reaching back to the mythic Woden. Chichester, capital of the South Saxon kingdom, founded probably on the site of the Roman city of Regnum, is said to have derived its name from Cissa, son of Aelle.

Wessex.—As might naturally be expected in a chronicle having its birth-place in Winchester, the historical details as to Wessex are much fuller than for the other kingdoms; so full that it is possible to relinquish the mere annalistic form and to weave them into a continuous narrative. In 495 (more than half a century after Tiro's date of the Saxon conquest) two chieftains, Cerdic and Cynric his son, came with five ships to a place called Cerdices ora, and on the very day of their landing fought a battle with the "Welshmen." The scene of the landing was probably somewhere in the noble harbour of Southampton Water. The two chieftains were not as yet spoken of as kings, but bore the lower title of ealdormen. Of Cerdic, however, the Chronicle recites the usual half-legendary pedigree, reaching back through eight intervening links to Woden, from whom (of course under later Christian influences) the line is traced back to Noah and Adam. These pedigrees, or at least the genuine Teutonic portion of them, may very probably have been preserved in the songs of minstrels, and obviously belong to that element of the Chronicle which is independent of Bede. We may look upon the divine ancestor Woden as marking the limit of the minstrel's memory or knowledge, and we shall therefore probably be justified in concluding that the West Saxon tribe possessed some sort of continuous historical tradition reaching back for eight generations behind Cerdic (himself a middle-aged man in 495), or about to the beginning of the third century. No wonder that kings whose very flatterers could not trace back their lineage to an earlier date than that of the Emperor Severus, felt their dynasties new and short-lived in presence of the immemorial antiquity of Rome.

In 508, the two chiefs slew a British king named Natanleod and 5,000 men with him. Evidently by this time they must have been at the head of a large number of followers. We are told that "the land"—apparently the scene of the battle—was named after the slain king; and it is generally supposed that this gives us the origin of the name Netley, well known for its ruined abbey and its military hospital. Eleven years later (in 519) they assumed the title of kings, being no longer contented with the humbler designation of ealdormen, and fought the Britons at Cerdicesford, a place identified with Charford on the Avon, about six miles south of Salisbury. Meanwhile, however, there had been other Saxon invasions of the same region. In 501 is placed the visit of the legendary Port with his two sons to Portsmouth, and the death of a young Briton of very high birth who vainly tried to defend his land from their invasion. In 514 certain West Saxon reinforcements are represented as arriving (perhaps in the Isle of Wight) under the leadership of another eponymous hero, Wihtgar, and his brother Stuf, nephews of Cerdic; and, probably with their help, in 530 Cerdic and Cynric took possession of the Isle of Wight, after slaying many Britons at Wihtgaræsbyrg or Carisbrooke. The statements in the Chronicle about the conquest of the Isle of Wight, obscure and confused in themselves, become yet more so when we compare them with an earlier passage interpolated from Bede, in which the Jutes, not the West Saxons, are represented as the conquerors of the Isle of Wight. Of course two tides of Teutonic conquest may have passed over the island, but it is difficult to bring the two lines of tradition into their proper relation to one another.

In 534, Cerdic, who must now have been an old man, ended his life and his near forty years of British warfare, and Cynric his son reigned alone. We may sum up the total of Cerdic's achievements by saying that he seems to have completed the conquest of Hampshire and the Isle of Wight, and that he probably fixed his royal residence at the Romano-British city of Venta Belgarum, thereafter to be known as Winchester. The fact that it required the labour of a lifetime to achieve the conquest of a moderate-sized English county, sufficiently shows that the Britons were not the mere Nithings (men of naught) whom Hengest and some of Hengest's Teutonic countrymen have represented them to have been.

Of the reign of Cynric, which, according to the Chronicle, lasted from 534 to 560, we have but little told us in that work. We hear of a battle at Old Sarum in 552 and of another four years later at Beranbyrig which is identified with Barbury in the north of Wiltshire. Apparently the achievement of his reign was the addition of the greater part of Wiltshire to the West Saxon kingdom. We may so far anticipate the evidence of the British writers as to say that the twenty-six years of Cynric probably coincide with part of the forty-four years of comparative peace which they describe as following the British victory of Mount Badon.

Far fuller of decisive events was the memorable reign of Ceawlin, son of Cynric, which is assigned to the years between 560 and 592. He was the eldest of a gallant band of brothers whose mutually resembling names, Cutha and Cuthwine and Ceol and Ceolric, have given no small trouble to the genealogists. The eighth year of his reign was signalised by an event, unprecedented as far as we know in the history of Anglo-Saxon England, namely, war between the invaders themselves. The object of the West Saxon attack in 568 was Kent, whose young king Ethelbert, after but three years of kingship, saw his land invaded by Ceawlin and his brother Cutha. The battle-place was Wibbandune, possibly Wimbledon in Surrey, and there two of Ethelbert's ealdormen were slain and himself put to flight. What terms he may have made with the victors we know not, but he was not permanently dethroned, since twenty-eight years afterwards we find him welcoming to his palace in Canterbury the missionaries from Rome.

Three years later (571) a vigorous attack was made by Cutha on the Britons, north of the Thames. A battle was fought at Bedford in which Cutha himself was slain, but victory crowned the Saxon arms in the general campaign, and four towns in Oxfordshire and Bucks (of which Aylesbury alone has retained its importance till the present day) were added to the kingdom of Wessex. The year 577 was of immense importance in the history of the Saxon progress. In that year a great battle was fought at Deorham, in Gloucestershire, about ten miles east of Bristol. There were arrayed on the one side Ceawlin and his brother Cuthwine, on the other three British kings, Coinmail and Condidan and Farinmail, all of whom were slain. Three great cities of Roman foundation ("ceastra" as the Chronicle calls them) were the price of victory: they were Gloucester, Cirencester and Bathanceaster or Bath. All historians are agreed as to the importance of this victory, which not only added Gloucester and (probably) part of Somerset to the West-Saxon kingdom, but by cutting off the Cymry of "West Wales" (Devon and Cornwall) from their brethren north of the Bristol Channel practically ensured their eventual if slow submission.

"In 584 Ceawlin and Cutha fought with the Britons in the place that is called Fethan-lea,* and Cutha was slain, and Ceawlin took many 'towns'

* The site of Fethan-lea is not ascertained. Dr. Guest's identification of it with Faddiley in Cheshire, and the large consequences thence deduced by him (Origines Celticæ, ii., 287–309), can hardly survive the strenuous attack made on them by Mr. Stevenson in the Eng. Hist. Rev., xvii., 637.

and innumerable quantities of booty and departed in anger to his own land." The chronicler seems to be here telling us of a Saxon reverse. Though Ceawlin captured many towns and took vast heaps of spoil he lost his son in the great battle and departed in wrath, assuredly in effect defeated, to his own land. After defeat came apparently domestic treason and civil broils. The entries for 591 to 593 show us the proclamation of a certain Ceolric, brother or nephew of Ceawlin, and a battle in 592 evidently not with the Britons, but between Saxon and Saxon, fought at Wodnesbeorge,* which resulted in the "driving out" of Ceawlin. Next year (593) Ceawlin with two others, probably princes of his house, named Cuichelm and Crida "perished."† The wording of the annal shows pretty plainly that they all died a violent death, whether on the battlefield or by assassination, whether as friends or foes, it is impossible to say; but there can be no doubt that the sun of Ceawlin's fortunes, which had at one time shone so splendidly, set in clouds and storms.

In 597 (apparently on the death of Ceolric) Ceolwulf, nephew of Ceawlin, "began to reign over the West Saxons, and he fought continually and successfully either with Englishmen or with Welshmen or with Picts or with Scots." He was, however, reigning at the time of Augustine's mission, and with that event the historical interest which has been slightly stirred by the story of the West Saxons' advance is transferred to another quarter. Throughout the seventh century Kent and Mercia and pre-eminently Northumbria claim our attention so absorbingly that we cannot spare much thought for the obscure annals of Wessex.

Concerning the two Northumbrian kingdoms, Deira and Bernicia, we have no information in the Chronicle for the first hundred years after the landing of Hengest and Horsa. We are then under the year told that Ida (descended in the ninth generation from Woden) was the founder of the royal line of Northumbria; that he built Bebbanburh (Bamburgh) and that this celebrated fortress was in the first instance surrounded with a fence and afterwards with a wall. The chronicler then tells us that in 560, on the death of Ida, Aelle (eleventh in descent from Woden) began to reign over Northumbria and reigned for [nearly] thirty years. The chronicler here either wilfully or inadvertently has suppressed something of the truth. From his language one might have conjectured that Aelle was of the lineage of Ida, and had succeeded peaceably to his ancestor. Instead

* Probably in Wiltshire (ibid., 638).

† "Forwurdon," not the usual peaceful and beautiful "forth-ferdon" (fared forth).

of this peaceable succession, however, we know from other sources that we have here to deal with two rival kingly lines, whose feuds and reconciliations make an important chapter in Northumbrian history. The true situation was this: essentially the kings of Ida's line were rulers of Bernicia, while Aelle and his descendants ruled Deira. That is to say: from their steep rock-palace of Bamburgh the sons of Ida reigned by ancestral right over all the eastern portion of the lands between Tyne and Forth, between the wall of Hadrian and the wall of Antoninus. Similarly Aelle and his sons, firmly settled in the great Roman city of Eburacum, governed the country between Tyne and Humber; but each king ever aspired to extend his sway over the other kingdom and often succeeded for a while in doing so. Thus we have constant vicissitudes but a general tendency towards the union of the two kingdoms into one Northumbria, which obeys now an "Iding," now an "Aelling" ruler. What strifes and commotions may have attended the transition from one line to another we can only in part discern. We are only obscurely told that in 588 Aelle's line was ousted, and that Ethelric the son, and after him Ethelfrith the grandson of Ida reigned over all Northumbria.

*****

3. We now come to the British version of the conquest. Though a nation is naturally reluctant to tell the story of its own defeat, we might have expected to receive from a comparatively civilised and Christianised people, such as the Romano-Britons of the fifth century, some intelligible literary history of so important an event as the Teutonic conquest of their island. This expectation, however, is dismally disappointed. We have practically nothing from the vanquished people, but the lamentations of the sixth century author Gildas, and the obviously fable-tainted narratives of the puzzle-headed Nennius of the eighth century.

Gildas, who obtained from after ages the surname of "the Wise," seems to have been a native of Scottish Strathclyde and was born early in the sixth century; he became a monk and at the age of forty-four wrote what Bede truly calls "a tearful discourse concerning the ruin of Britain." His object in this discourse was to rebuke the ungodliness of his countrymen and to remind them of the tokens of the Divine wrath which they had already received. He is consequently, for our purpose, a most disappointing writer. We go to him for history and we get a sermon, but we ought in fairness to remember that he never proposed to give us anything else. A large part of his treatise consists of reproductions of the denunciatory passages of the old Hebrew prophets: a more interesting section, but one outside our present purpose, consists of fierce invectives against five wicked, or at least unfriendly, kings of Wales. But there are a few chapters, the only ones that now concern us, in which, in pathetic tones, he tells us something as to the circumstances of the invasion of his country. He harks back to the departure from Britain of the usurper Maximus (383), to which, rather than to the later usurpation of Constantine, he traces her defenceless condition. Stripped of the multitude of brave young men who followed the fortunes of Maximus and never returned, and being themselves ignorant of war, the Britons were "trampled under foot by two savage nations from beyond seas, namely the Scots from the north-west and the Picts from the north." The description of the invaders as coming from beyond the seas is important. The term "Scots" at this time and for four centuries afterwards means primarily the inhabitants of the north of Ireland, and only secondarily the offshoot from that race who settled in Argyll and the Isles. These invaders, of course, were as Gildas calls them "transmarini": but it is possible that the Picts also, some of whom we know to have been settled in Wigtonshire, came across the shallow land-girdled waters of Solway Firth, instead of attacking the yet undemolished wall, and thus that they too seemed to the dwellers in North-west Britain to be coming from "beyond the seas."

According to Gildas the Britons sent an embassy to Rome, piteously imploring help against the invaders. The Romans came, drove out the barbarians and exhorted the inhabitants to build a wall between the two seas, which they accordingly did, from Forth to Clyde, building it only of turf. A fresh invasion followed, a second embassy, again utter rout and slaughter of the enemy, but, alas! there came also a solemn warning from the Romans that they could not wear out their strength in these constant expeditions for the deliverance of Britain, and that its inhabitants must henceforth look to their own right arms for safety; but nevertheless before they abandoned them they would help them to build a wall, this time of stone not of turf, on the line between Tyne and Solway. Moreover, they built a line of towers along the coast right down to the southern shore where their ships were wont to be stationed, and then they said farewell to their allies, as men who expected never to see them again.

All this part of Gildas's story is quite untrustworthy. No one who has carefully studied the architecture of the two walls and the inscriptions along their course will attribute their origin or even any important restorations of them, to those troublous years of dying Rome, the years between 390 and 440. Gildas is here evidently retailing the legend which had sprung up among an ignorant and half-barbarised people as to the great works of the foreigner in their land, and he has not only in this matter "darkened counsel by words without knowledge," but he has grievously misled his worthy follower Bede, who is brought into hopeless perplexity by his attempt to reconcile his own more correct information about the Roman walls with the unsound Welsh traditions or conjectures which he found in Gildas. The tearful narrative proceeds: There is more misery in Britain: civil war is added to barbarian invasion, and food, save such as can be procured by hunting, vanishes out of the land. In 446 the poor remnants of the Britons send their celebrated letter to that Roman general whose name was at the time most famous among men: the letter which began, "To Aetius,* thrice consul, the groans of the Britons," and went on to say, "The barbarians drive us to the sea: the sea drives us back on the barbarians: we have but a choice between two modes of dying, either to have our throats cut or to be drowned." But not even this piteous request brought help, for Aetius was too busily occupied with his wars against Attila and the Huns to be able to spare thought or men for the defence of Britain. However, pressed by the pangs of hunger, the Britons grew bolder and even achieved some small measure of success against their enemies. The impudent Hibernian robbers returned to their homes; the Picts at their end of the island remained quiet for a time, though both nations soon began again their plundering forays. But with success came luxury, drunkenness, envy, quarrelsomeness, falsehood, all the signs of a demoralised people. And then for the punishment of the nation came first a pestilence so terrible that the living scarcely sufficed to bury the dead, and then, direst plague of all, the fatal resolution to call in foreign aid.

"A rumour was spread that their inveterate enemies were moving for their utter extermination. A council was called to consider the best means of repelling their fatal and oft-repeated invasions and ravages. Then all the councillors, together with the proud tyrant,† with blinded souls, devised this defence (say rather ruin) for their country, that those most

* Or Agitius, as Gildas calls him.

† The name of Vortigern, inserted here in Gale's edition, is absent from the best, though found in a few manuscripts.

ferocious and ill-famed Saxons—a race hateful to God and man—should be invited into the island (as one might 'invite' a wolf into the sheepfold) in order to beat back the northern natives. Never was a step taken more ruinous or more bitter than this. Oh, the depth of these men's blindness! Oh, the desperate and foolish dulness of their minds! 'Foolish are the princes of Zoan, giving unto Pharaoh senseless counsel.'* Then that horde of cubs burst forth from the den of their mother, the lioness, in three cyuls (keels), as their language calls them, or as we should say, 'long-ships'. They relied on favourable omens and on a certain prophecy which had been made to them, in which it was predicted that for 300 years they should occupy the land towards which their prows were pointed, and for half of that time they should lay it waste by frequent ravages. Thus, at the bidding of that unlucky tyrant did they first fix their terrible claws into the eastern part of the island, pretending that they were going to fight for the deliverance of the country, but in truth intending to capture it for themselves. Then the aforesaid mother-lioness, learning how the first brood had prospered, sent another and more numerous array of her cubs, who, borne hither in barks, joined themselves to these treacherous allies."

Space fails us to repeat in his own words the whole of the author's pitiful story. Somewhat condensed it amounts to this: The strangers claimed that liberal rations should be given them in consideration of the great dangers which they ran. The request was granted and "shut the dog's mouth" for a time. But soon they began to complain of the insufficiency of these rations: they invented all sorts of grievances against their hosts, and used these as a justification for breaking their covenant with the British king, and roaming with ravage all over the island. "The flame kindled by that sacrilegious band spread desolation over nearly all the land till at last its red and savage tongue licked the coasts of the western sea." The towns [coloniæ] were levelled to the ground with battering rams; the farmers [coloni], with the rulers of the Church, with the priests and people, were laid low by the flashing swords of the barbarians or perished in the devouring flames. Coping-stone and battlement, altars and columns, fragments of corpses covered with clots of gore, were all piled together in the middle of the ruined towns, as in a horrible wine-press. Burial there was none, save under the ruins of the houses or in the maw of some beast of prey or ravenous bird. Some of the miserable remnant who had escaped to the mountains were caught there and slain

* Isaiah xix. 11.

in heaps. Others, pressed by hunger, submitted and became slaves of the conquerors; others fled beyond the sea. A very few who had fled to the mountains, there on the tops of precipitous cliffs or in the depths of impenetrable forests succeeded in dragging out a life, precarious truly and full of terrors, but still a life in their fatherland.

At last the tide turned. Some of the invaders returned to their own homes, and the unsubdued mountaineers saw the remnant of their countrymen flocking to them from every quarter and beseeching them to save them from extermination. A little band of patriots was thus formed, under the leadership of Ambrosius Aurelianus, a man of modest temper but of high descent, and in fact the only Roman sprung from the wearers of the purple who had survived the storm of the invasion. Under this leader the patriots dared to challenge the invaders to a pitched battle, which, by the favour of the Lord, resulted in their victory. From that time the struggle went on with varying fortune, now the citizens, now the enemy triumphing, till the year of the siege of Mount Badon, which was also the year of the birth of Gildas, and from which forty-four years had elapsed to the time of his present writing. That was the last and greatest slaughter of "the scoundrels." From that time onwards external war had ceased, and for a space the hearts of all men, delivered from despair and chastened by adversity, turned to the Lord, and all men, whether kings or private persons, whether bishops or simple ecclesiastics, kept their proper ranks and orders in the state. Of late, however, on the decease of the men of that generation, morals had again declined, anarchy had begun to prevail, and owing to the frequent occurrence of civil wars, the cities were no longer inhabited as securely as of old.

Gildas then proceeds to describe further the demoralisation of his countrymen, and especially the outrageous vices of the five contemporary British kings, Constantine, Caninus, Vortipor, Cuneglas, and Maglocunus (or Maelgwn), upon all of whom he pours forth the vials of his righteous indignation; but into this part of his discourse there is no need for us to follow him. However little to our taste may be the somewhat inflated rhetoric of this author, it is important always to remember that he lived about two centuries nearer to the Saxon conquest than our next authority on the subject, Bede, and we must gratefully acknowledge that he does give us a few valuable facts of which we should otherwise be ignorant. His description of the horrors of the invasion, though highly coloured, is sufficiently paralleled by the well-attested events of the later Danish conquest to be not altogether improbable. His mention of Ambrosius Aurelianus, the modest descendant of emperors (perhaps of Maximus or the usurper Constantine), and the brave leader of revolt against the invaders, looks like historical fact, and the story of the British triumph at Mount Badon is not made a whit less probable by the patriotic silence of the Chronicle concerning a Saxon disaster. Both the place and the date of that great battle have been the subjects of long debate. Mons Badonicus used to be thought to represent Bath, and after a good deal of discussion this identification seems again to be coming into favour.

The sentence in which Gildas appears to connect the date of the battle with his own birth is almost hopelessly obscure and the text is probably corrupt; but on the whole it seems most probable that he meant to say, as above suggested: "The battle of Mount Badon was fought forty-four years ago, and in that year I was born." The Annales Cambriæ (a compilation of the tenth century) give 516 for the year of the battle, a date which would fix the composition of the tearful discourse to 560. Mommsen prefers 500 for the date of the birth of Gildas. In any event there is a strong inducement to connect at least a part of the long period of comparative peace which, according to Gildas, followed the battle of Mount Badon with the confessedly uneventful reign of Cynric, the West Saxon.

*****

We now pass on to the other writer of British origin who dealt with the history of the Anglo-Saxon conquest—namely, Nennius. If one has to speak in rather severe terms of the literary quality of this writer's work and of the value of his testimony as a historian, it must be remembered in extenuation of his many faults that he lived at a time and in a nation in which literary excellence and the acquisition of accurate knowledge of the past were made well-nigh impossible by the hard pressure of daily life, brutalised and barbarised as it was by perpetual wars both from without and from within. We shall have again to notice the same phenomenon of the utter decay of the historical and literary faculty in a highly cultured people when the Danes ravaged the monasteries of Northumbria, and it is but justice to these poor stammerers of a vanished age to remember how much more easily a nation might then be deprived of its whole literary heritage than can ever now be the case since the invention of printing.

There have been long and sharp discussions as to the age, the country, and even the personality of the author who is generally known as Nennius. The following pages represent the chief conclusions arrived at by a German student of Celtic literature, Professor Zimmer, who in his book, Nennius Vindicatus, has surely vindicated his client's right to exist, though he admits as fully as any one that client's terrible deficiencies as a historian. We may now, then, venture to assert that Nennius, the author of the Historia Brittonum, was born about the middle of the eighth century, that he lived in South-East Wales, probably near the borders of Brecon and Radnor, that he wrote his book in or about the year 796, and that it was subjected, about 810, to a very early revision by a scribe who calls himself Samuel, and who lived in North Wales. For some reason or other the book had considerable popularity both in England and on the continent, especially in Brittany, but it suffered much at the hands of ignorant transcribers, and a narrative, not originally very lucid, has in some places been made almost unintelligible, owing to the transposition of some of the leaves of manuscript which have fallen out and been replaced in a wrong order. The restoration of these wrongly sorted chapters to their proper place in the book is one of Professor Zimmer's greatest achievements. The work of an ill-informed and uncritical scribe such as Nennius evidently was,* subject also to all these adversities in the course of its transmission to us, and originally written three centuries and a half after the events recorded, might be considered so poor an authority as to be unworthy of our further notice. But, in the first place, we have practically no other British authority save Gildas for the events which interest us so deeply; and, secondly, the author has at one point incorporated in his work a document much earlier and much more valuable than his own. This is the so-called "Genealogies of the Kings," which occupy sections 57 to 65 of the Historia Brittonum, and which, though they consist chiefly of strings of names, the ancestors of Anglian kings, are of a comparatively early date, since they bring the history down only to 679 (being thus slightly earlier even than Bede), and have this especial interest for us that we have here, imbedded in a passionately Celtic work, information otherwise lacking as to the rulers of the Anglian kingdoms of Northumbria and Mercia in the sixth century.

....

* Nennius makes such a muddle of his chronology that he virtually asserts that Christ was born A.D. 183; and he accepts the idle tales about Brutus, ancestor of the Britons, and descendant of Aeneas, which had been apparently fabricated by Irish students of Virgil two centuries before he wrote.

Probably the most valuable piece of information conveyed to us by Nennius, relating, it is true, rather to the history of Wales than to that of England, is derived from these same Genealogiæ Regum. It is to the effect that Maelgwn, King of Gwynedd (North Wales), was descended in the fifth degree from a certain Cunedag, who with eight sons marched southward from Manau Guotodin (which is identified with the district of Lothian), and drove "the Scots" from the region of Gwynedd, to which they never returned. This southward march took place, he says, 146 years before Maelgwn reigned. Now, Maelgwn, who was one of the five kings so fiercely denounced by Gildas, is a historical personage who certainly reigned in North Wales and whose death is dated in 547. He is also a link in the chain of Welsh kings who continued to reign so long as Wales had any independent rulers. The statement, therefore, amounts to this, that a little before 400, say in 380, or about the date of the usurpation of Maximus, a chieftain named Cunedag with his eight sons, and, doubtless, a large army, marched right across Britain from the Firth of Forth to the Menai Straits, drove out the "Scots," that is the Irish invaders who were in possession of the country, and established a dynasty which endured for nine centuries (380–1283), till Llewelyn and David, the last royal descendants of Cunedag, were slain by the order of Edward Plantagenet. This is a fact unrelated to any other that has been handed down to us, but which suggests the reflection how many great movements of population, all memory of which has perished, may have been going forward in our island during these mist-covered fifth and sixth centuries of our era. Moreover, the fact that we have here apparently an instance of a Pictish king conducting a campaign of extermination against the "Scots," though these Scots were in Wales, throws some doubt on the conventional theory that all the calamities of undefended Britain were due to a war in which the Picts and the Scots were acting in concert.

As to the actual events of the Anglo-Saxon conquest Nennius leads us into a perfect jungle-growth of legend and fable, but adds very little to our real information. He repeats the name of the unhappy Vortigern and blackens it with all sorts of foul crimes, such as murder and incest. He blends his narrative with alleged scandals, not only untrue but historically impossible, against the saintly Germanus. He hints that there was rivalry and discord between Vortigern and Ambrosius; and here we can neither confirm nor refute his statement, though certainly the story as told by Gildas does not give us the impression that they were contemporaries.

He tells us that when Hengest sent for the second draft of his followers they came over in sixteen keels, and that in one of those keels was "a girl fair of face and very stately in person, the daughter of Hengest" (the name Rowena is not mentioned till a much later age). The damsel serves the king with strong drink. "Satan enters into the heart of Vortigern, and through an interpreter whose name was Ceretic [this little detail looks like genuine tradition] he asks for the maiden in marriage, promising to give half his kingdom in exchange, and he does in fact give her the district of Kent, though a prince named Guoyrancgon was then reigning there and knew not that he was being thus handed over into the power of the pagans." Hengest then proceeded to give his new son-in-law fatherly advice, which he assured him would effectually secure his kingdom: "I will invite my son and his nephew, for they are warlike men, that they may fight against the Scots, and do thou give unto them those regions which are in the north, next to the wall which is called Guaul." Obeying this recommendation, Vortigern invited them and they came, "to wit Octha and Ebissa with forty keels; but whilst they were sailing round the Picts they laid waste the Orkney islands, and came and occupied many countries beyond the Frisian Sea [the Firth of Forth?] as far as the boundary of the Picts." A dark and difficult passage truly; but there is some reason to think that there may be in it a germ of historical truth, and that there was really a Jutish settlement in Scotland.

After this the story relapses into mere romance. We hear of enchanted towers, of a wonder-working child who was afterwards known as the enchanter Merlin, and who apparently calls up the spirit of the dead Ambrosius. Then we are introduced to Vortimer, the brave son of Vortigern, who defeats the barbarians in four great battles; but, dying soon after, he desires to be buried on a hill above the place where they had first landed, since he has a prophetic intimation that they shall not dwell in the land for ever, but shall one day be driven forth; a prophecy the fulfilment of which still lingers. Discouraged by the victories of Vortimer, Hengest now resorts to stratagem, and calls for a conference to which both Britons and Saxons are to come unarmed, and at which they shall establish a league of lasting friendship. Privately, however, he orders his followers to hide each man a small knife under his foot in the middle of his boot, and when he calls out "Eu Saxones nimmath tha saxas" (Ye Saxons grasp the daggers), out flash the deadly weapons; the 300 senators of Vortigern are slain, and he himself is taken prisoner and loaded with chains till he consents to give Hengest Essex and Sussex for his ransom. The story ends with the death of Vortigern. "Some say that he died a broken-hearted wanderer, hated by all his people, and others that the earth opened and swallowed him up on the night on which the enchanted citadel was burned."

The traitorous conference and Hengest's cry to his followers seem to have about them a slight savour of probability, but it will probably be the opinion of any one who carefully peruses the chapters of Nennius of which a slight outline has here been traced, that they are for the most part of as much historical value as the Arabian Nights' Entertainments. But the elements of which this strange work is composed are of various value. After a sketch of the life of St. Patrick which is taken from a well-known source and which need not here detain us, Nennius gives an important paragraph which seems to be taken from his earlier Northumbrian authority, and, if so, is entitled to more respectful attention: "On the death of Hengest, his son Octha crossed from the northern region of Britain to the kingdom of Kent. From him are descended the present kings of that country. Then did Arthur fight against the Saxons in those days along with the leaders of the Britons, but he himself was leader in the wars."* The author then proceeds to give us the sites of twelve great battles fought by Arthur. Of the eighth, he says it was "in the castle of Guinnion, whereat Arthur carried on his shoulders the image of the holy Mary, ever a Virgin, and the pagans were turned to flight in that day, and a great slaughter was made among them by the power of Christ and his Virgin Mother. The ninth battle was fought in the city of the legion (Castra Legionis).† ... The twelfth was fought at Mount Badon, at which 960 men fell in one day at one onslaught by Arthur, and no one felled them but he alone, and in all the wars he stood forth as conqueror."

The scenes of the twelve battles fought by Arthur have been variously identified, some authors placing them in South Wales and some in the Scottish lowlands. Except as regards Castra Legionis and Mons Badonis, there is something to be said for the latter set of identifications, which seem to agree with the Northumbrian origin of the document quoted by Nennius.

Is there any historical truth in the personality of Arthur, or is he a mere creature of romance? The answer to that much-debated question depends

* Sed ipse erat dux bellorum.

† This may be either Chester or Leicester.

on the degree of credit which, upon a review of the whole case, we may consider ourselves at liberty to attach to these few sentences of Nennius. All the rest that has been said concerning him, whether by pseudo-historians, such as Geoffrey of Monmouth, by avowed romancers like Sir Thomas Malory, or by poets like Tennyson, is confessedly but the product of imagination, some of it very beautiful, some of it rather foolish; but Nennius, and he alone, can answer for us the question whether Arthur ever really was.

It is believed that the reader has now been introduced to all the authentic information which has been handed down to us concerning the great revolution or rather series of revolutions which changed Britannia into Engla-land. The chroniclers of the twelfth century, William of Malmesbury, Henry of Huntingdon, Florence of Worcester, for the most part honourable and truth-seeking men, have dealt with these historical materials, each after his own fashion, seeking to weave them into a connected and harmonious narrative; but it is generally agreed by those who have carefully studied their works that they knew no more than we as to the events of the fifth and sixth centuries, and that historical science can gain little or nothing, for this part of the history of England, from a study of their chronicles. Much less, of course, does it behove us to give any attention to the mere romances which Geoffrey of Monmouth and the storytellers of his school imagined about the fictitious kings of England, from Brut to Lud. Already in the seventeenth century these sports of fancy were beginning to be appraised at their true value by scholars like Milton, who rehearsed but evidently did not believe them. Now, happily, no English historian thinks it necessary to waste his time and the time of his readers by proving their utter unreality. Still, no doubt the mind of every historical student longs for a continuous and rightly co-ordinated narrative of events, and dislikes to see the evidence presented in such disjointed fashion as that in which it has been here submitted to the reader. This however appears to be for the present a disagreeable necessity. Great danger seems to attend every attempt to make one plain story out of the various materials supplied to us by Bede, the Chronicle, Gildas and Nennius. It may be that the labours of future investigators may enable them to achieve this result; but the time is not yet.

One or two great landmarks may perhaps be accurately discerned through the mist. The united testimony of Prosper Tiro and the biographer of Germanus seems to justify us in asserting that the Saxon assaults upon

Britain were contemporaneous with those of the Picts, and never really ceased throughout the first half of the fifth century. The allusion in the Chronicle to a burial of treasure and flight of the Romans in 418 perhaps refers to some otherwise unrecorded invasion of the Saxons and to a consequent emigration of the Romanised Britons to Gaul. That such an emigration on a large scale must have taken place somewhat early in the century seems to follow as a necessary consequence from the fact that the Armorican peninsula received then that name of Britannia, Bretagne or Brittany which in one shape or other it has ever since retained, and that already in 469 we find Apollinaris Sidonius speaking, as a matter of course, of the inhabitants of that region as Britons.*

There was probably an invasion of Kent in 441 by a Teutonic tribe, whom we may perhaps call Jutes, and this invasion was less of a mere piratical raid and more of an abiding conquest than the previous expeditions. We notice the same difference three centuries later in the Danish invasions. Vortigern is probably an historical character, and his marriage with the daughter of the Teutonic chief was the sort of event which might well strike the minds of contemporaries and linger long in the songs of later generations. Probably, however, he was not a "king"—Roman institutions would hardly have allowed of the formation so early of a regal dynasty—but a great and powerful landowner who armed his dependants and wielded practically something like kingly power. His invocation of Jutish aid to repel a Pictish invasion may be historically true, but far too much has doubtless been made of the whole affair by British fabulists, anxious to excuse the failure of their countrymen and determined to make the luckless Vortigern the scapegoat of their nation. "We were betrayed!" is the natural exclamation of every vanquished people.

Ambrosius Aurelianus, the descendant of Roman wearers of the purple,

* Ep. i., 7. This is a very important passage, as showing at what an early date British refugees were settled near the mouth of the Loire in such numbers as to be an important element in Gaulish politics. Arvandus, once Prætorian prefect of Gaul, was accused before the Emperor of high treason because he had corresponded with the King of the Visigoths, inviting him to attack "the Britons situated on the Loire," who were evidently loyal to the empire. In another letter of the same writer (Ep. iii., 9) we find him pleading with his friend Riothamus, a Breton chief (or king), for the restoration of some slaves who have been coaxed away from a friend of his by "Britannis clam sollicitantibus". This same Riothamus, described by Jordanes as "rex Brittonum," fought with Euric, King of the Visigoths, on behalf of the empire (Jord. de rebus Geticis, xlv.).

is almost certainly a historical personage, though it is impossible to fix the time and place of his operations. So, too, with a shade less of probability is Arthur, or Artorius, whom we may fairly credit with having stayed for a time the torrent of the Saxon advance by the great victory of the Mons Badonicus won at some time between 500 and 516. In both these British champions, however, we ought probably to see not Cymric kings, but Romano-British generals, wielding a power like that of the Roman duces and comites, and perhaps even commanding bodies of men trained in some of the traditions of the Roman legion. Most important, on this view of the case, are the words of Nennius himself: "Arthur fought against the Saxons along with the kings of the Britons, but he himself was Dux Bellorum."

The short and business-like entries of the Chronicle as to the successive victories which marked the extension of the West Saxon kingdom seem in the main worthy of belief, though we cannot rely with much confidence on the dates attached to every entry. It does not surprise us to find no record of the Saxon defeat at the Mons Badonicus, nor, as has been said, does such silence lessen the probability of its having actually occurred. Ceawlin, the hero of the West Saxons, is undoubtedly a real figure in history, and we may in the main accept with confidence the history of his battles, especially of his crowning victory at Deorham, which undid the work of Mount Badon, and, by giving the command of the Severn Valley and the Bristol Channel to the Saxons, finally separated "West Wales" from Wales. The domestic strife which disastrously ended his career and hurled him from his throne is pretty clearly hinted at in the Chronicle, and we may be allowed to conjecture that it was the continuance of this internal discord which prevented for a long while the further development of Wessex; which made the rising power of Mercia instead of the West Saxon state the protagonist in the conflict with Wales; and which struck the annals of the latter kingdom in the seventh century with barrenness. When Ceawlin died, in 593, already the great pope who was to reunite Britain to Christian Europe was presiding over the Roman Church, and we may be said now at last to see land, the terra firma of authentic and continuous history.

On reviewing the whole course of the Teutonic conquest of our island we cannot fail to be struck by the different rates of speed at which that conquest proceeded at different times. By about the middle of the sixth century the invaders seem to have possessed themselves of nearly all the country lying to the east of a line drawn from Berwick-on-Tweed through Lichfield to Salisbury. After that period, however, their advance, never very rapid, becomes extremely slow. Wales the Saxons never conquered. "West Wales," as Devon and Cornwall were called, were not subdued till the ninth century. Cumberland, which formed part of the Celtic kingdom of Strathclyde, does not seem to have become English till the close of the seventh century, and even then was very loosely joined to the Anglian kingdom of Northumbria. It is to be hoped that we may one day obtain some clearer light on the reason for this great difference in the rate of conquest between the eastern and western halves of the island; how far it may have been due to the different resisting powers of two Celtic races, the "Brythonic" and "Goidelic"; whether earlier Saxon settlements along the shore of the German Ocean facilitated the work of the new invaders; or whether the flat alluvial lands of the east, more easily overrun by mounted bands of freebooters than the rough mountainous country of the west, were the chief factors in the problem.

A question which has been often and fiercely discussed and on which probably the last word has not yet been said is: "How far did the great movements of invasion which we have been discussing amount to an actual replacement of one population by another?" or, in other words: "Are the Englishmen of to-day pure Saxons and Angles or partly Celts?" In considering this question two factors have to be considered: (1) the amount of new population imported into the country; and (2) the degree to which the invaders carried the process of extermination of the older inhabitants. As to the first point we are furnished with extremely scanty information by all our authorities. The mythical "three keels" and "five keels," which the chroniclers speak of as containing the whole forces of the invaders, point only to a scanty number of warriors, accompanied probably by their horses, but certainly not by their wives and children. The story of the legendary Rowena, on the other hand, suggests—what is doubtless the truth—that the invaders, once established in the land, sent speedily for the wives and daughters whom they had left by the Elbe or the Baltic. One late authority speaks of the Saxons as inviting over so many of their kith and kin that an island which they had previously inhabited was left almost void of people. Undoubtedly every indication of language and of later social state points to the conclusion that the invasions were not mere raids of freebooting warriors, but great national migrations such as were the fashion in the fourth and fifth centuries after Christ, such as

Claudian describes as headed by Alaric and such as Ennodius paints in his laudation of Theodoric.

Moreover, even for such a great national displacement we may find a sufficient cause in the condition of central Europe between 432 and 452. During all these years the fear of the mighty Hunnish war-lord Attila lay like a nightmare upon Europe; not upon the Romanised men of the southern cities only, but quite as much upon the Teuton in his forests, for the Teuton loathed the very smell of the Hun, and, when forced to submit to him for a time, chafed under his yoke and as soon as possible escaped from his abhorred neighbourhood. Now when we find it stated by the Roman ambassadors to his court* that Attila had by the year 448 made "all the islands in the ocean" subject to him, we who know that the coasts of the Baltic, of Denmark and the Scandinavian peninsula were all looked upon as islands by the classical geographers, may not improbably conjecture that the pressure of the Hun was felt by the Angle and the Saxon as it had been felt before by his kinsmen the Goth and the Burgundian. We have every reason therefore to conjecture, if we cannot hold it for proved, that there was an immense transference of Teutonic family life from the lands bordering on the Elbe to the banks of the Thames, the Humber and the Tyne.

But it is on the second factor of the equation, on the extent of denudation of the older, the Celtic stratum of the people, that the controversy chiefly turns. The theory of the virtual extermination of the Britons from at least the eastern half of the island is thus stated by its most illustrious champion, Freeman: "Though the literal extirpation of a nation is an impossibility, there is every reason to believe that the Celtic inhabitants of these parts of Britain which had become English at the end of the sixth century had been as nearly extirpated as a nation can be." In support of this theory Freeman appeals to the absolutely Teutonic type of the language spoken by Englishmen before the Norman conquest, to the Teutonic character of their institutions and to the terrible entry in the Chronicle concerning the capture of Anderida: "491. Now Aella and Cissa encompassed Andredes-ceaster and slew off all that dwelt therein: nor was there afterward a single Briton left there."

It cannot be said that the tendency of recent inquirers is in favour of so strong an assertion as this of the entire obliteration of the British element in any part of our island. Physiological investigations, the measurement

* Excerpta e Prisci historia, p. 199 (ed. Bonn).

of skulls and the examination of graves, do not confirm the hypothesis of the absolute disappearance anywhere of the pre-Saxon races. The study of institutions does not confirm it: the more closely these are examined the more does the conviction grow that some Roman or Celtic elements are imbedded in the generally Teutonic character of the Anglo-Saxon state. And even the celebrated passage concerning the slaughter at Anderida is not, perhaps, so conclusive an argument as it appears at first sight. Nothing is said there which necessarily implies a determination to destroy a whole people. We may see in it only the cruel action of assailants maddened by the stubborn defence of a fortress which may have long held the Saxons at bay; and even the fact of the emphatic mention in the Chronicle of this one bloody deed seems to imply that it was not the usual accompaniment of Saxon conquest.

When we examine carefully the pleadings on both sides we see that the disputants are not so far apart as they suppose themselves to be. No one denies that the general framework of society in Anglo-Saxon Britain, like the language, was Teutonic, or that the masters of the land were English and looked upon the Romanised Celts whom they called Wealas as an alien and inferior race. But, on the other hand, Freeman himself admits, though reluctantly, that the majority of the British women would be spared to be the wives or concubines of the invaders, and nearly all the slaves to be their thralls. This admission is fatal to the claim of the ordinary Englishman of to-day, after all the upheavings and down-sinkings of the various social strata, to be a pure-blooded Teuton. The evidence of language tends in the same direction. It is certainly surprising—and the advocates of the extirpation-theory have a right to point triumphantly to the fact—how small a number of Romano-Celtic words crept into the language spoken here before the Norman Conquest. But the words which did thus survive are, for the most part, such words as women would use in connexion with the affairs of the household, words like rasher and rug. When we thus review the circumstances of the Saxon conquest, and especially when we remember the immense influx of Celtic blood which we have received in later centuries from the Gael and the Erse folk, we may perhaps conclude that we should accept and glory in the term Anglo-Celt, rather than Anglo-Saxon, as the fitting designation of our race.

VII.

THE COMING OF AUGUSTINE

During the two centuries in which Britain had been forgotten by the rest of Europe, great events, most of them disastrous events, had been happening in the world. The imperial city, Rome, had been four times captured and plundered by barbarian armies. After the third of these captures (that by Totila in 546), we are told that the mighty city remained for six weeks absolutely empty of inhabitants, neither man nor beast being left therein. During these two centuries the vast empire of Attila the Hun which seemed likely at one time to be a universal monarchy had risen into greatness and had fallen into ruin; so, too, had risen and fallen the fair fabric raised in Italy by the converted barbarian Theodoric; Clovis the Frank had become, from chief of a petty principality, lord of a mighty realm, which under his sons had spread over the greater part of the two countries which we now call France and Germany; Justinian had framed his imperishable code, and the Bishop of Rome had become the unquestioned patriarch of the west.

Two references to our island made by the greatest historian of the period serve to emphasise its utter seclusion from the world of civilisation and culture. Procopius in his immortal history of the Gothic siege of Rome,* tells us that at a certain period of the blockade (537) when the Gothic leaders began to despair of taking the city they opened negotiations with Belisarius, the imperial general, and endeavoured to persuade him to retire from Italy on condition of receiving a formal cession of the island of Sicily. The absurdity of the suggestion consisted in this, that Sicily, which was the natural prize of the greatest sea power in the Mediterranean, was already hopelessly lost to the Gothic kingdom; and this fact gave point to the sarcastic reply of Belisarius: "And we, too, will allow the Goths to possess the whole island of Britain which is much larger than Sicily and

* De Bello Gothico, ii., 6.

which once belonged to the Romans, as Sicily once belonged to you. For when any one has received a favour it is fitting that he should repay it in kind." So utterly had Britain fallen out of the orbit of the empire that a heroic Roman general could even afford to joke over its disappearance.

Again, towards the end of his history,* Procopius, who evidently wishes to follow the example of Herodotus in supplying his readers with the best information in his power about strange and savage lands, gives a detailed description of Britain. "It is divided into two parts by a wall built by 'the men of old'. On the eastern side of that wall all is fresh and fair; neither heat nor cold excessive; fruits, harvests, men abound; a fertile soil is blessed with abundance of water. But on the western side things are altogether different, so that no man can live there even for half an hour. Numberless vipers and serpents and other venomous beasts abound there, and so pestilent is the air that the moment a man crosses the wall he dies." Furthermore, a strange story was told concerning this island, for the truth of which Procopius does not vouch, but which he repeats lest he should be thought to be ignorant of a matter of common notoriety. "On the shore of the Channel opposite to Britain are many villages inhabited by fishermen who are exempt from the usual tribute 'payable to the Kings of the Franks' on condition of their undertaking in rotation the duty of rowing over to Britain the spirits of the dead. The boatman whose turn it is to undertake this duty lies down at nightfall to snatch a brief slumber. At dead of night a knock is heard at the door of his hut and a muffled voice calls him and his fellows forth to their duty. They see ships, not their own, anchored in the harbour. Embarking on these they seize the oars and push off from land; at once the ships, though apparently empty, are pressed down to the water's edge by an unseen cargo. When they reach the shore of Britain a disembarkation as invisible as the embarkation takes place. They see no man; only a voice proclaims the names of the invisible passengers, the offices they held in life, the husbands of the dead wives, if any such should be among the number. Quickly do they return to the Gaulish shore, and now the ship is not sunk deeper than her keel." Gladly would we learn in whose interest and at what period of the great struggle this wild story was put in circulation concerning a country which had been for at least three centuries in the full prosaic daylight of Roman civilisation.

It was probably about the year 553 that Procopius of Cæsarea wrote

* De Bello Gothico, iv., 20.

this strange story, worthy of the age of Orpheus and the Argonauts, concerning our ghostly island. Some twenty years later, the celebrated scene between Gregory and the fair-haired Yorkshire lads was enacted in the Roman forum.* We cannot avoid listening once more to the thousand times quoted words of Bede:—†

"I may not pass by in silence the event which according to the tradition of the elders was the cause of Gregory's abiding interest in the salvation of our people. They say that on a certain day the news of the arrival of some merchants caused a concourse of intending purchasers to assemble in the forum where their goods were displayed. Among the rest came Gregory who saw there, beside the other market wares, certain boys set up for sale, with fair skins and beautiful faces, noticeable for their golden hair and comely shapes. When he beheld them, he asked from what part of the world they came. The merchant told him that they came from the island of Britain, whose inhabitants all presented the same appearance. Again he asked whether they were Christians, or still involved in the errors of Paganism. 'They are Pagans,' was the reply. Hereupon he heaved a sigh from his inmost heart, and said: 'Alas! the pity of it! that the Prince of Darkness should own as his subjects men of such shining countenance, and that such grace of outward form should veil minds destitute of heavenly grace within'. Again he asked what was the name of that nation. The merchant answered: 'They are called Angles'. 'Well named,' said he, 'for they have angelic faces and ought to be co-heirs with the angels in heaven. What is the name of that province from which they have been brought?' 'The inhabitants of that province are called Deiri.' 'Well again: rescued de ira and called out of wrath into the mercy of Christ. How is their king named?' 'Aelle.' Playing on the name he said: 'Alleluia. It must needs be that the praises of God the Creator resound in those regions.'"

It has been conjectured that the lads who stood on that fateful morning for sale in the Roman forum had lost their liberty owing to the wars waged between their lord, Aelle of Deira, and Ethelfrith of Bernicia. The

* Between 575 and 578, or possibly between 585 and 590.

† This story is told in similar but by no means identical words in an early life of Pope Gregory, probably written by a monk of Whitby who was a contemporary of Bede's, and discovered by Paul Ewald: Hist. Aufsätze an G. Waitz gewidmet. It has been suggested that Bede copied from this biography. To me it seems more probable that Bede and the biographer, independently of one another, repeated the common traditio majorum.

grave and reverend ecclesiastic who spoke to them in that historic forum which still doubtless showed the senate-house and rostra of the republic, and was overlooked by the palaces of the empire, was a man who himself was sprung of a senatorial family and had worn the purple of the prefect of the city. A year or two, however, before the dialogue in the forum, about 575, he had laid aside that splendid robe and donned the coarse scapular of a Benedictine monk. His stately palace on the Cælian he had turned into a monastery, which still exists and bears his name, though originally dedicated to St. Andrew. Such was the man who, intensely Roman at heart as well as Christian, brought Britain once again within the attraction of Rome.

In the first fervour of his missionary zeal, Gregory himself started on the northward road, but was recalled by the command of the pope.* Then came the years which he spent as papal nuncio (apocrisiarius) at the splendid but not altogether friendly court of Constantinople; his return to Rome; his rule as abbot in his monastery; and lastly his election in 590 by the enthusiastic and unanimous voices of the people to the office of pope, vacant by the death of Pelagius II. Still the vision of the conversion of Britain remained dear to his heart; but in the distracted state of Italy, living, as he said, "between the swords of the Lombards,"† he was for some time unable to take any steps towards its fulfilment. In September, 595, he wrote to the steward of the papal estates in Gaul, directing him to buy as many English slaves as he could, of the age of seventeen or eighteen, that they might be distributed to various monasteries and there taught the elements of the Christian faith. The terms of this commission give us a strong impression of the regularity of the export of slaves from Britain to Gaul. And where such a regular slave-trade exists we may generally infer the prevalence of a chronic state of war.

At last, in 596, he sent forth his friend Augustine, prior of his monastery of St. Andrew's, with a company of monks, upon the great enterprise. Augustine himself, a somewhat timorous and small-souled man, who lacked the great qualities of his patron, when he had reached the south of

* Benedict I., if the earlier date is correct; otherwise Pelagius II. On the fourth day of Gregory's journey a grasshopper alighted on the page of the Bible which he was reading during the noontide halt. "Ecce locusta," he said, and interpreted the sign as meaning Loco sta, "Stay where you are". In that hour arrived the papal emissary commanding him to return to Rome.

† "Inter Langobardorum gladios": a favourite expression of Gregory's.

Gaul and heard from the bishops of that province dire stories of Saxon barbarism, turned faint-hearted, and conversation with his companions increased rather than allayed his fears. At last they came to the inglorious conclusion "that it would be safer to return home than to visit a barbarous, fierce and unbelieving nation, of whose very language they were ignorant." Augustine himself started on the return journey, bearer of the unanimous request that they might be excused from undertaking so perilous and laborious a mission, and one of such doubtful issue. Probably he had not reached Rome when he received a letter (dated July 23, 596) in which the pope informed the whole company that it would have been better never to have begun a good work than to turn back disheartened from its accomplishment. He exhorted them not to be daunted by the difficulties of the journey, nor discouraged by the words of evil-speaking men, but to press on with zeal to finish the work which God had given them to do; knowing that the greater the labour the richer would be the eternal recompense of reward. At the same time a letter of commendation to Etherius, Archbishop of Arles, probably smoothed their labours and did something to allay their fears.

In truth the mission upon which the trembling monks were despatched, though of immense importance, was one of no great danger, and it would probably be safe to say that the missionaries of all the Christian Churches have in the last two centuries cheerfully faced greater perils and undergone greater hardships in the service of the Gospel of Christ, than were the portion of Augustine and his friends. Ethelbert, the king of Kent, whose court was the objective of their campaign, was far the most powerful of the English kings, and in his reign, which had now lasted more than thirty years, he had, we are told, "stretched the bounds of his empire as far as the river Humber."* His wife, Bertha, daughter of Charibert, king of the Franks, and grand-daughter of Clovis, was allowed to worship after the Christian manner without let or hindrance, having her own private chaplain, Bishop Liudhard, and we may fairly suppose that the messengers who came to preach the same faith, bringing introductions from Frankish kings and prelates as well as from the great Bishop of Rome, were safe from insult or molestation in the wide region included in the over-lordship of her husband, the limits of which they probably never overstepped.

....

* Bede, Hist. Eccl., i., 25. Evidently the defeat sustained (according to the Chronicle) in 568 at the hands of Ceawlin, king of Wessex, had been more than made good.

At last after long and leisurely journeyings, visits to the courts of Frankish kings, and the formation of a staff of interpreters, Augustine and his companions, forty in number, landed, apparently in the spring of 597, on the shores of Britain. Their landing-place was in that extreme north-eastern corner of Kent which still bears the name of the Isle of Thanet, though it has lost its insular character. In the seventh century the little stream of the Stour, which flows round this region and which then emptied itself into the channel called the Wantsum, was a considerable river, probably tidal, 600 yards broad and fordable only in two places. Thus Thanet was then a genuine island, and here Augustine and his little band took up their temporary quarters. Sending some of their Frankish interpreters to Ethelbert they informed him that they had come from Rome, the bearers of the best of all good news, and that if he would hearken to their counsels they could without any doubt promise him eternal happiness in heaven and a future kingdom without end in the presence of the living and true God. The king replied with words courteous but cautious: "Remain in that island in which you now are, while I consider what I shall do with you. Meanwhile I will supply you with the necessaries of life." After certain days Ethelbert crossed the Wantsum and held a conference with the strangers. The place of meeting was fixed in the open air, for the old king, notwithstanding his life-long intercourse with Christians, feared that he should be fascinated by magical arts if he met the missionaries within doors. Soon Augustine and his forty companions were seen to approach, bearing on high a silver cross by way of banner and a painted picture of the Saviour, and chanting litanies, in which they prayed the Lord to grant eternal life to themselves and to those for whose sake they had come from far. At the king's command they took their seats, and then one of their number, probably Augustine himself, through the medium of an interpreter, set forth to the king "how the mild-hearted Saviour by His own throes of suffering redeemed this guilty world and opened the kingdom of heaven to believing men." The king replied: "Fair are the words which you speak and the promises which you make to me, but since they are new and vague I cannot give my assent to them, nor leave those rites which I, together with the whole English nation, have so long practised. But since you have come from so far, and, as I perceive, desire to share with us that which you hold to be best and truest, we will not be grievous unto you, but rather receive you with friendly hospitality and make it our business to supply you with needful food; nor will we forbid you to attach to yourselves all whom you can, by your preaching, win over to your faith."

Herewith, permitting them to leave the Isle of Thanet, he assigned them quarters in the capital of his kingdom. This was the once insignificant town of Durovernis, situated at the point where the Roman road to Richborough diverged from the road between London and Dover. As the capital of the Jutish kingdom this roadside station had already attained to some importance under the name of Cantwaraburh, but showed little promise of the world-wide fame which it was to achieve under its more modern name of Canterbury. As the missionary band approached their destined home they raised aloft the silver crucifix and the picture, chanting with one accord a litany which may be thus translated:—

From this city, Lord! we pray
May Thy wrath be turned away.
We have sinned: but let Thy pity
Spare Thy house in yonder city.
Alleluia! Alleluia!

This litany was one which had been sung for more than a century on Rogation days in the churches of Gaul, and we must not, therefore, seek in its words for any special application to the little Saxon city towards which the missionaries were gazing. As it happened, however, there was already in that city a Christian church, erected probably in the very last years of the Roman occupation of Britain,* and dedicated to St. Martin of Tours. Here Ethelbert's queen had since her marriage been allowed to attend a Christian service, celebrated by her Frankish chaplain, Liudhard. It was the opinion of Pope Gregory that the Frankish ecclesiastics of Gaul had been somewhat neglectful of their duties in reference to their heathen neighbours of Britain, and probably the court chaplain Liudhard was not altogether exempt from this reproach. However this may be, the church of St. Martin, now handed over to the Roman mission, became a centre of religious activity. The preaching and the prayers, the vigils and the fasts of the white-robed strangers, their patient and self-denying life, their professed willingness to suffer death itself on behalf of the Christian faith, produced a great impression on the minds of the men of Kent, rough doubtless and barbarous, but able to appreciate that which they beheld of noble and godlike. They began to flock to the church and crave the administration of baptism; and at last even the king presented himself at

* This follows from the date of St. Martin's death, which was about 402.

the sacred font and received baptism at the hands of Augustine. From that day the process of conversion went on rapidly, but we are assured that no pressure was put by the king on his subjects to compel them to follow his example, "since he had learned from his teachers that the service of Christ must be a voluntary matter and not a thing of compulsion." He at once, however, provided the missionaries with a residence in Canterbury suitable to their dignity, and notwithstanding their life of abstinence and renunciation he made to them grants of lands in various districts, thus beginning that series of donations to the Church by Anglo-Saxon kings which was continued by them for near five centuries with splendid liberality, and the carefully preserved records of which constitute one of our most valuable sources of information on the social condition of England before the Norman conquest.

The mission having thus far met with such marvellous success Augustine felt that the time was come for him to assume a regular ecclesiastical position, and accordingly he journeyed to Arles, where the archbishop of that see, in accordance with orders received from Gregory, consecrated him as archbishop of the English nation.* Divers doubts and questionings having occurred to the soul of the new metropolitan he despatched, about 600, two of his brethren, Laurentius and Peter, to lay his difficulties before his Roman patron. The questions asked are of an extraordinary kind, and startle us by their strange juxtaposition of things momentous and things indifferent. Thus a question whether it is permissible for two brothers to marry two sisters, to whom they themselves stand in no kind of relationship, is followed by another, whether a man may be permitted to many his father's widow. It is difficult to believe that the framer of such a question can have even read St. Paul's letters to the Christians of Corinth. However, if the archbishop's questions seem to us rather surprising, the pope's answers are noble and statesmanlike. Especially memorable is his answer to the inquiry: "The faith being one, what can I say as to the diverse customs of the Churches, as, for instance, where the mass is celebrated in one way in the Holy Roman Church and in another way in the Churches of Gaul?" Pope Gregory replied, "You, my brother, know well the custom of the Roman Church in which you were reared. But my pleasure is that you should anxiously select whatever custom you

* Archiepiscopus genti Anglorum ordinatus est (Hist. Eccl., i., 27). Observe that Bede without hesitation uses the word Angli to denote the whole Anglo-Saxon-Jutish nationality.

may find, whether in the Roman or in the Gaulish or any other Church, which is pleasing to Almighty God, and teach the customs which you have thus gathered from many Churches to the Church of the Angles, which is yet new to the faith. For things are not to be prized according to the places from which they originate, but places are to be loved according to the good things to which they give birth."

The letter containing these answers was carried, not by the returning messengers of Augustine, but by a fresh mission from Rome, consisting of Mellitus, Justus, Paulinus, and Rufinianus. They brought with them also a woollen pallium for Augustine, the symbol of his archiepiscopal dignity, many relics of saints and ornaments for the churches and the precious gift of a large number of manuscripts. While entrusting Augustine with the precious pallium, a gift which he was somewhat chary of bestowing, Pope Gregory at the same time provided for the erection of an archiepiscopal see at Eburacum. In future, after Augustine's own death, the archiepiscopate of the south was to be placed at Lundonia; and thereafter London and York, the two archiepiscopal centres of their respective provinces, were to have equal power, priority of dignity being assigned to whichever prelate might happen to have been first ordained. The messengers brought also letters specially directed to the King and Queen of Kent. In the letter to Ethelbert, Gregory struck a note which was often heard in his correspondence: "Moreover, we wish your Glory to know that, as we are assured in Holy Scripture by the words of Almighty God, the end of this present world is nigh at hand and the unending reign of the Saints is about to begin. Before that day comes many things must come to pass such as have not yet been seen: changes in the air, terrors in the sky, tempests out of season, wars, famines, pestilences, earthquakes. All these things, it is true, will not happen in our own day, but after our days they will follow." In the letter to Bertha, the pope, while gently hinting that one so well grounded in the true faith ought long ago to have effected the conversion of her husband, praises her for what she has done in protecting and befriending the missionaries; exhorts her to use all her influence in order to keep her husband steadfast in the faith. He assures her that her memory will be revered like that of Helena who turned her son Constantine to Christianity, and that the fame of her great work has reached not only to Rome but even to Constantinople (delightful thought for the daughter of barbarian kings), and that its completion will bring joy to the angels in heaven.

In a letter addressed to the messenger Mellitus, containing some thoughts which had come into the pope's mind during his long musings after the departure of his legation, Gregory desires him to direct Augustine on no account to destroy the temples of the idols, but to sprinkle them with holy water, construct altars and enrich them with relics. The old pagan sacrifices of animals to their false gods are, of course, to cease, but as a sort of concession to the festive propensities of the converts, on the day of the dedication of the church or on the birthday of the martyr whose relics were there deposited, the people were to be encouraged to make little huts of boughs all round the newly consecrated church, and therein, after slaying animals for feasting, not for sacrifice, to express with joy and gladness of heart their gratitude to the Giver of every good gift. A remembrance of the Jewish feast of tabernacles seems to cross the mind of the pontiff as he thus ordains the conversion of pagan sacrifices into Christian festivities.

The story of the conversion of the English nation to Christianity is an interesting one, and if at this point of our narrative religious topics seem to claim too large a share of our attention, it must be remembered that our chief, almost our only authority for this period is the Historia Ecclesiastica of Bede, a splendid piece of historical work, but still one which, by the law of its being, concerns itself rather with the Church than with the State. Church affairs, however, sometimes throw an important light on political changes. We should be in entire ignorance as to the time and manner of the conquest of London by the invaders but for Bede's information that: "Augustine ordained Mellitus as bishop (604), and sent him to preach in the province of the East Saxons, who are separated from Kent by the river Thames and are close to the eastern sea. Their metropolis is the city of Lundonia, situated on the banks of the aforesaid river and itself the mart of many nations flocking thither by land and sea: over which people [the East Saxons] at that time Saberct reigned, nephew of Ethelbert through his sister Ricula. He was, however, in a subordinate position to Ethelbert, who, as has been already said, ruled all the races of the English up to the river Humber. When, therefore, that province [Essex] had received the word of truth from the preaching of Mellitus, Ethelbert built in the city of Lundonia a church to the holy apostle Paul, in which was fixed the episcopal seat of Mellitus and his successors."

At the same time Augustine consecrated Justus, who, as we have seen, was a colleague of Mellitus in the Roman legation, Bishop of Dorubrevi, "which from an old chieftain of theirs named Hrof the English nation calls Hrofaescaestre" (Rochester). These two bishoprics, Canterbury and Rochester, both founded in the one kingdom of Kent, seem to represent a certain political duality in that region,* as if it were the normal state of affairs that East and West Kent should have separate rulers. However this may be, it is well for us to bear in mind that the title of king was one of rather vague significance. Besides the great and powerful kings of the eight chief provinces there was many a cluster of petty princes dignified with the name of kings, of whom the national history can take no notice, but whose names figure royally in charters and testamentary documents.

It was probably soon after the arrival of the messengers from Rome, and to some extent in compliance with Gregory's wishes, that some important but, unhappily, resultless overtures were made by Augustine to the rulers of the Welsh Church. Using the powerful advocacy of Ethelbert, he invited the doctors and bishops of the British province to meet him about the year 602 at a place in the west of England which was known long after as "Augustine's oak." There Augustine addressed the Welsh ecclesiastics and besought them to enter into the Catholic peace, and undertake with him a common labour for the conversion of the heathen. The chief point on which he insisted was the necessity of their conforming to the Roman practice in the calculation of Easter, a wearisome matter of debate as to which we shall hear more than enough in the century of Anglian history that now lies before us. When argument failed, the Roman advocate proposed to have recourse to miracle: "Let some sick man be brought into our midst, and the party whose prayers avail to heal him shall be deemed to be the advocates of the cause approved by God." Unwillingly the Britons consented. A blind Englishman was introduced into the assembly. The prayers of the Welshmen failed to restore him to sight, but the prayers of Augustine, we are told, succeeded. Then, it is said, the Britons professed to be convinced that the course recommended by Augustine was the way of righteousness, but declared that they could not, without the consent of their countrymen, abandon their ancient customs. They therefore pleaded for a second conference, which was to be held at some place which is not named, and was to be attended by a much larger body of clergy.

To this second conference came seven bishops from Wales, possibly including some from Cornwall, and a whole troop of learned doctors,

* See Kemble, The Saxons in England, i., 148.

most of whom hailed from the great and noble monastery of Bangor.* On their way to the council they turned aside to ask the advice of a certain holy hermit, whether they should hold fast their old traditions or accept the teaching of Augustine. "If he is a man of God," said he, "of course you must follow him." "But how can we prove whether he be or no?" The answer showed a rare insight into the true spirit of Christianity: "The Lord said: Take my yoke upon you and learn of Me, for I am meek and lowly of heart. If, therefore, this Augustine is meek and lowly of heart, it is probable that he bears the yoke of Christ himself and offers it to you to share it with him. But if he is proud and discourteous, he is not of God and we need not care for his words.... Arrange therefore, that he shall first reach the place of meeting, and if, when you draw near, he rises to receive you, be assured that he is a servant of Christ and listen to him with deference, but if he despises you and does not choose to rise to you who are the larger party, then let him be despised by you." So it came to pass. The Britons when they arrived found Augustine seated on a chair of state, and he made no motion to arise therefrom. His demeanour may have been the result of shyness or absence of mind, but they set it down to pride, and being filled with wrath they made a point of contradicting everything that he said. Soon doubtless the dispute waxed warm, and cries of "Quarto-deciman," "The last quarter of the waning moon," "The cycle of eighty-four years," "The cycle of eighteen years," "The blessed apostle John," "The prince of the apostles, Peter," with every variety of intonation, from the sharp notes of the Italian cleric to the gruff voices of the Celtic mountaineer, resounded through the air. Augustine seems to have done his best, too late, to calm the ruffled spirits of his hearers. "Ye do many things," he said, "contrary to our custom: nay, contrary to the custom of the universal Church, but if on three points ye will hearken to me we will patiently bear your divergence on all others. These three points are, that ye shall celebrate Easter at its own right time: that ye shall administer baptism according to the usage of the Apostolical Roman Church,† and that ye shall join with us in preaching the word of the Lord to the English nation." The Cambrians, however, refused to comply with any of these conditions or to accept Augustine as their archbishop, muttering one to

* In the county of Flint about ten miles south of Chester: not to be confounded with Bangor on the Menai Straits or with the Irish monastery of Bangor in County Down.

† See H. A. Wilson in Mason's Mission of St. Augustine, pp. 248–52.

another: "He would not even rise to receive us when we were strangers: if we once submit ourselves to his authority he will treat us as the dust under his feet." Before the disputants parted from one another, Augustine raised his voice in threatening prophecy: "If you will not accept peace with your brethren, you will have to accept war with your enemies: and if you will not preach the way of life to the English nation, you shall suffer from their hands the requital of death." A prophecy which Bede considered to have afterwards received its fulfilment in the bloody battle of Chester.

It certainly must raise our opinion of the absolute honesty of Bede as a historian to find him, whose sympathies are all on the side of Roman as against British Christianity, thus faithfully describing a scene in which his hero Augustine certainly plays an unattractive part. The Welshmen may have erred in attributing his conduct to pride, but his most ardent champions must admit that he showed a grievous want of tact in this important interview. It was a golden opportunity that was offered for the reconciliation of two great hostile races at the feet of one Saviour, and that opportunity once lost never returned. The wound which the Saxon invasions had caused, still comparatively fresh, might possibly have been then healed by first intention. Unhealed then, it went festering on for centuries; and more than once or twice since the days of Augustine, Christianity, which ought to be the great reconciler of men, has proved itself the great divider between Celt and Saxon. Soon probably after this fatal interview, Augustine died (May 26, 605?), and was succeeded in his archiepiscopal see by his friend Laurentius, a companion of his labours from the beginning, and the man whom he had himself in his lifetime ordained to be his successor.

The death of Ethelbert of Kent, which occurred in February 24, 616, about eleven years after that of Augustine, serves as the occasion to our one most trusted authority for giving us some valuable information as to the political condition of our island. It will be well therefore to translate in full a few sentences from the Ecclesiastical History.

"In the year of our Lord's Incarnation, 616, Aedilberct [Ethelbert], King of the Cantwaras, after a glorious reign on earth of fifty-six years, entered the eternal joys of the heavenly kingdom. He was the third among the kings of the English nation who ruled over all their southern provinces which are separated from the northern ones by the river Humber, and the boundaries adjoining: but he was the first of all to mount to the Kingdom of Heaven. [He came, as I have said, third in the other list.] For the first to wield dominion of this kind was Aelle, King of the South Saxons; the second Caelin, King of the West Saxons, who was called Ceawlin in their language; the third, as we have said, Aedilberct, King of the Cantwaras; the fourth who possessed it was Redwald, King of the East Angles, who even in the lifetime of Aedilberct won the leadership for that same nation of his." Bede then proceeds to give us the names of three more leader-kings—names which will figure largely in the following chapters of this history—Aeduini (Edwin), Oswald and Oswiu (Oswy), all kings of Northumbria.

The Chronicle when it has to speak of Egbert the West Saxon and his acquisition of supreme power over the English people, remarks that "he was the eighth king that was Bretwalda" (or according to a better attested reading Brytenwealda), and then repeats the above list as given by Bede, adding Egbert's name at its close. On the strength of this passage historians have concluded, no doubt rightly, that Bretwalda or some similar word was the title given to these exceptionally powerful English kings whom we find from time to time during the period of the so-called Heptarchy wielding practically the whole power of English Britain, and this idea of a "Britain-wielder" seems to be now generally accepted as explanatory of the name. There has been much discussion as to the attributes of this Bretwalda sovereignty of Britain, but it cannot be said that any very definite conclusion has yet been arrived at. It was probably what the Greeks called a "hegemony," rather than a formal and constituted sovereignty: a leadership and preponderating influence such as the King of Prussia possessed in Germany even before he was formally proclaimed emperor. It will be observed that during Ethelbert's reign his nephew, the East Anglian Redwald, won the leadership from him. Evidently there were some unrecorded vicissitudes in the life of Ethelbert.

The death of Ethelbert (who had married a second wife after the decease of Frankish Bertha) seems to have been shortly followed by that of his nephew, Saberct the East Saxon. Now was it too plainly seen how slight a hold the new religion, promoted as it had been by royal favour and the fashion of a court, had upon the hearts of the people. The hegemony of Kent, sapped as it had apparently been in the lifetime of Ethelbert, entirely disappeared at his death. Moreover his son Eadbald, who had set his heart on wedding his widowed stepmother, and who could by no means induce Archbishop Laurentius to sanction such an incestuous union, openly revolted from the Church and went back to paganism. In the frequent fits of insanity by which he was afterwards afflicted, the faithful saw the work of unclean spirits and the permitted chastisement of his sin.

Nor did affairs go better for Christianity in the neighbouring kingdom of Essex. King Saberct had left three sons, joint-successors to his kingdom, who during their father's lifetime had yielded a sort of fitful adherence to Christianity, but had not submitted to the rite of baptism and remained apparently pagans at heart. Their quarrel with Mellitus, Bishop of London, arose out of his refusal to permit them to partake of the communion. They saw the bishop standing at the altar administering the eucharist to the people; and "Why," demanded they in angry tones, "do you not give us some of that pure white bread which you used to give to our father, and which we see you still handing forth to the people?" Mellitus explained that it was not permitted to give the bread except to those who had undergone the rite of baptism; but they persisted that they had no need of baptismal purification, yet meant to have a share of the consecrated bread. When Mellitus still refused they said: "If you will not gratify us in so small a matter you shall not stay in our province," and drove him forth from their kingdom. Mellitus, arriving in Kent, conferred with his brethren, Laurentius and Justus, as to what should be done in the face of the gathering storm-clouds. They unanimously came to the conclusion that the better course was to return to their own country, and there serve God with unharassed minds, rather than abide in that barbarous land and carry on their fruitless labours among a population rebellious to the faith. Mellitus and Justus accordingly left their respective sees and betook themselves to Gaul, meaning there to abide till the hourly expected end of the world, of which Gregory had so often warned them, should be revealed. Shortly after their departure the three arrogant East Saxon kings who had expelled Mellitus fell in battle against the Gewissas or men of Wessex. But though the idolatrous rulers were gone, their influence upon the people remained, and it was long before the city of London could be persuaded to tolerate in its midst the votaries of the new faith.

Thus it seemed that the seed sown by Augustine, which had sprung up so quickly, having no deepness of earth, was about to wither away as quickly before the parching blasts of persecution. A dream, or a trance, or a mysterious mental struggle through which Archbishop Laurentius passed, prevented the utter abandonment of the great enterprise. In the night before his intended departure from Britain, having laid him down to rest in a chamber of the monastery dedicated by Augustine to St. Peter and St. Paul, Laurentius saw in a vision the Apostle Peter who indignantly rebuked him for his faint-hearted desertion of the flock committed to his care. With every sentence came a blow from the apostolic scourge on the shoulders of the faint-hearted archbishop, and this chastisement endured through many hours of the secret and solitary night. In the morning Laurentius found that his back was covered with wales from St. Peter's lash, and going straight to the palace he showed his wounds to the king. Eadbald asked in wrath who had dared thus to chastise so eminent a man, and being told that it was the long dead apostle of Christ, he was stricken with fear, abandoned his idolatrous rites, put away his forbidden wife, received baptism, and thenceforward promoted to the utmost of his power the cause of the new religion.*

Thus then Laurentius did not take his hand from the plough. His brethren, Mellitus and Justus, were recalled by Eadbald from Gaul, but the newly converted king, less powerful than his father, availed not to persuade the stubborn Londoners to receive Mellitus into their midst. Not long after (February 2, 619) Laurentius himself died, and was succeeded in the archiepiscopal see by Mellitus. He too died (April 24, 624) after a five years' tenure of office, and was succeeded by Justus. Thus, one after another, Pope Gregory's missionaries were passing away, and their bodies were laid in the portico which, like the great atrium of the church of St. Ambrose at Milan, stood in front of the slowly reared church of St. Peter and St. Paul. But the Christianity of the Saxons in the south was still but a sickly and shallow-rooted plant. It was left for the Angles of Northumbria to show a genuine, hearty, popular conversion to the new faith, and to produce that splendid series of saintly kings, bishops and princesses who have made the seventh century for ever memorable in the history of English Christianity.

* As in the case of the stigmata of St. Francis, modern science has shown that it is possible to accept the historic truth of this narrative without admitting the hypothesis, either of miracle or of fraud.

VIII.

EDWIN OF DEIRA

As our attention in dealing with the history of the seventh century will now be fixed chiefly on Northumbria, that being the region where Christianity won its most glorious victories and as it was at this time undoubtedly the predominant state in Britain, it is necessary at the cost of a little repetition to describe the course of the English settlements in that northern land. And first, a word as to its geographical limits. The district which was popularly called Northhymbraland, and which consisted politically of the two kingdoms of Beornice (Bernicia) and Dearnerice (Deira), stretched from the Firth of Forth to the river Humber. It is important to remember that we have here no concern with the medieval and modern boundary between England and Scotland, in which Tweed and Cheviot are the principal factors. St. Cuthbert, born on the slopes of the Lammermoor Hills, was no Scot but an Englishman; and Edinburgh, which is to us the very type and symbol of Scotticism, was in all probability founded by the English prince whose name stands at the head of this chapter. Between these two great natural frontiers, the Forth and the Humber, the bounding lines ran—as they still do, more than is generally recognised—north and south rather than east and west. The western half of the lowlands of Scotland, together with Westmorland and the greater part of Cumberland, formed the British kingdom of Strathclyde, and was—with the exception of some intervals of subjection to its Anglian neighbours—under the rule of kings of Celtic race, whose capital was the strong rock-fortress of Alclyde or Dumbarton. South of the kingdom of Strathclyde the high land which now sunders Yorkshire from Lancashire probably formed for some generations the boundary between the Angles and the Britons; yet not even up to that boundary was the Anglian dominion pushed in the first invasion, for we hear indistinctly of a British kingdom of Elmet, otherwise called Loidis, which probably included at any rate the upper part of the valleys of the Wharfe, the Aire and the Calder, all Yorkshire streams. As to the boundary between the two Anglian kingdoms of Bernicia and Deira we cannot speak with absolute certainty, but we are told on trustworthy authority* that it was the River Tees. The fact that both kingdoms were so often united under one sovereign perhaps made the assignment of precise boundaries less needful. Thus, to recapitulate these facts in terms of modern geography, Bernicia included probably all the three Lothians, the counties of Berwick, Peebles and Roxburgh, the eastern half of Northumberland and the county of Durham; while Deira claimed the North and East Ridings of Yorkshire.

Surveying the ethnological condition of this region during the fifth and sixth centuries we can dimly discern a few important changes. There are some indications of a settlement of Frisians in that which we now call the Border country, and it is thought that they gave their name to the town of Dumfries. The time of their migration, however, is altogether uncertain, and as they were a Low German tribe, nearly allied in blood to both Angles and Saxons, we may conjecture that in the course of generations they so melted into the great Anglian population by which Bernicia was overrun as to be indistinguishable therefrom. Another national movement, about which we have more certain information, was that migration of the Pictic chief Cunedag from Lothian to Anglesey, about 380, to which attention has already been called, and which gave to Wales a line of sovereigns that endured for nine centuries. Then followed, about the middle of the fifth century, that settlement of the Jutes on the east coast of Scotland to which reference was made in our sixth chapter, and of which Hengest's son and nephew, Octha and Ebissa, were leaders. This settlement is mentioned only by Nennius, but as we meet with it in that part of his history which is borrowed from an earlier Northumbrian annalist, we may probably accept it as historic fact that the Jutes thus bore a part in the migrations which Teutonised the eastern half of Caledonia as well as Britannia. Octha is spoken of in a later chapter of Nennius as having passed over from the northern part of Britain into Kent on the death of his father Hengest, and become the ancestor of the kings of Kent who were reigning in the historian's lifetime.

....

* That of Richard of Hexham (circa 1141. Prologue to his History). Simeon of Durham (circa 1104) says that "all the country between Tees and Tyne was then [in the seventh century] a waste wilderness, the habitation of wild animals, and therefore subject to no man's sway" (Vita Oswaldi, cap. i.).

In the shadowy traditions of the Welsh bards we hear of a certain Ossa Cyllelawr or Ossa the Knife-man, who is spoken of as a great antagonist of Arthur, and who appears to be a genuine progenitor of the Bernician kings. It is apparently his son Eobba who bears the terrible title, "The Great Burner of Towns," which is generally given to the next link in the pedigree, Ida, King of Bernicia. Here, at last, we are on firmer historical ground, for this is that Ida of whom we read in the Chronicle (here quoting Bede) that "he began to reign in 547, and that from him sprang the royal line of Northumbria," that "he reigned twelve years, and that he built Bebbanburh [Bamburgh], which was at first surrounded by a hedge and thereafter with a wall."* Notwithstanding the comparative shortness of his reign, Bernician Ida from his rock-fortress of Bamburgh evidently wielded a mighty power, and we are probably right in attributing to him the first great extension and consolidation of the Anglian power between the Tees and the Firth of Forth. He had twelve sons, six of whom followed him in rather quick succession during the last half of the sixth century. We have no hint of civil war or domestic treason, and it is therefore reasonable to suppose that many of these warlike kings fell in battle with their Celtic neighbours in the west. This is indeed hinted by the scanty notices in Nennius's history.

We appear to be justified in speaking of Ida as king of Northumbria, though that may not have been the title given to him by his contemporaries, for it seems to be the outcome of the very confused notices in Nennius's Historia Brittonum that Deira as well as Bernicia was subject to his sway. But on the death of Ida (560), if we may trust the Chronicle, a prince of another line claiming descent from Woden through eleven generations of mortal men, Aelle or Ella, began to reign over the southern kingdom, Deira, and reigned for twenty-eight years. Were the relations between the two dissevered kingdoms friendly or hostile? It is impossible to say. The presence of the Deiran slave boys in the Roman forum suggests the latter hypothesis; the fact that Acha, the daughter of Aelle, was married to Ethelfrid of Bernicia suggests the former. Possibly a war between the two Anglian kingdoms had been followed by peace and a matrimonial

....

* "Ond rixode twelf gear, ond he timbrode Bebbanburh, seo waes aerost mid hegge betyned, ond aefter mid wealle." Mr. Bates, whose History of Northumberland is a most helpful guide to this part of our history, reminds us that this "hackneyed passage is an interpolation of a Kentish scribe in the eleventh century". Still, though we may not quote it as a first-rate authority, there seems no reason for rejecting it altogether.

alliance. However this may be, on the death of Aelle in 588, Ethelric of Bernicia, son of Ida, succeeded—assuredly not peaceably—to the throne of Deira, which, after five years of reigning, he handed on together with his ancestral kingdom to his son Ethelfrid.

The reign of Ethelfrid which lasted for twenty-four years, from 593 to 617, was undoubtedly an important period in the history of Northumbria. We are apt to think of him only in connexion with that relentless persecution of his young brother-in-law, Edwin, which we shall soon have to consider; but he was certainly a powerful ruler, this fierce pagan sovereign of Northumbria. Read what Bede the Northumbrian, who had often heard his name mentioned with reluctant admiration in the cloisters of Jarrow and Wearmouth, says concerning him: "In these days the kingdom of the Northumbrians was governed by Ethelfrid, a most valiant king and most covetous of glory, who, more than all the chiefs of the Angles, harassed the nation of the Britons, so that it would seem fitting to compare him to Saul, King of Israel, except for this one point that he was ignorant of the Divine religion. For no ealdorman or king made wider tracts of land, after destroying or subduing their inhabitants, either tributary to the English nation or open to their occupation, than this king. So that the blessing which the patriarch, anticipating the deeds of Saul, bestowed on his own son might fittingly be applied to Ethelfrid: 'Benjamin shall ravin as a wolf. In the morning he shall devour the prey: in the evening he shall divide the spoils.'"

In the year 603, when Ethelfrid had been ten years on the throne, "Aidan, King of the Scots who inhabit Britain,"* resenting the Anglian king's encroachments, prepared to invade Bernicia. Here at last we have the word Scots clearly used not of our western but of our northern neighbours. For these are the Scots who crossed over the straits between Ulster and Cantyre and founded in Argyll and the Isles that kingdom of Dalriada which was one day to give a monarch, Kenneth MacAlpine, to the whole of North Britain and impose on Caledonia the name of Scotland. It is important also to observe that by this time all the dwellers in what we now call Scotland professed the Christian faith, the great mission of St. Columba to the Northern Picts and his settlement in Iona having taken place in 565, thirty-eight years before the events with which we are now concerned. The invasion of King Aidan, the friend and in a certain sense the nominee of St. Columba, though made by him at the head of a huge

* Hist. Eccl., i., 34.

host, proved unsuccessful. He was met (says the patriotic Englishman Bede) by Ethelfrid with but few men. The two armies joined battle at Degsastan, probably the high moorland which forms the watershed between Liddesdale and Upper Tynedale, and which by one little stream, the Dawston Burn, still preserves the name of that old battlefield of the nations. Ethelfrid's brother, Theodbald, with all the division of the army which he commanded, fell before the Scottish onslaught, but in another part of the field Aidan suffered so severe a defeat that he was forced to fly ignominiously from the bleak moorland, covered with the corpses of his followers. The battle of Dawston Rig seems to have been in truth the Flodden of the seventh century. Bede, writing 128 years afterwards, says: "Never from that day to this, hath any king of the Scots dared to join battle in Britain with the nation of the Angles."

Some years after this victory over the Scots, Ethelfrid won another of equal importance over the Cambrian Britons (613?). The Archbishop Augustine, as we have seen, in his last conference with the Welsh ecclesiastics, warned them that if they were unwilling to preach the way of life to the English nation they should suffer a bloody requital at their hands.* And now Ethelfrid, having all the hosts of Deira and Bernicia at his disposal, collecting a large army, marched, probably by a branch of the Watling Street,† from York across Yorkshire to Manchester, and appeared full of the menace of battle before the walls of the city on the Dee, which, once known as Deva, now, 200 years after the last Roman soldiers had quitted Britain, still bore the name of the Camp of the Legions. In later times this name—Caerlegion in Welsh, Legacaestir in the English tongue—has been shortened to Chester, and thus this picturesque old city, which still keeps its medieval walls and is crowded with interesting relics both of Roman and of Norman domination, claims not unworthily the right to be the Chester among all the many Chesters in our land, the representative of all the cities which have arisen on the site of the camps of the legions.

....

* Or as the Saxon chronicler quaintly puts it, "that if Welshmen would not be kith and kin (sibbe) with us they should by Saxon hands perish".

† We may probably conjecture that the rapid far-reaching campaigns of early English kings, such as Ethelfrid, were rendered possible by the still solid condition of the great Roman roads, which in the Middle Ages fell grievously into decay. Thus even the civilisation of the Roman empire fought for the barbarians.

On the eve of the battle, Ethelfrid descried a number of men clad in priestly garb who occupied what they deemed to be a place of safe shelter at a little distance from the British army. They were in fact a large deputation from the monastery of Bangor (which contained not fewer than 2,100 inmates), and they had come, sanctified by a three days' fast, to aid the British king Brochmail by their prayers. "Who are those men?" cried Ethelfrid, "and what do they there?" Learning the reason of their presence, he exclaimed, "If they are calling on their God against us, they also are fighting against us, though it be not with arms but with curses," and he directed the first movements of his army against them. This unexpected opening of the game seems to have confounded Brochmail, who is accused by Bede of having in cowardly panic forsaken the holy men whom he was especially bound to protect. However this may be, 1,200 of the Bangor monks were slain and only fifty escaped. The British king and his men fled in disgraceful rout; Ethelfrid's victory was complete; the city of the legions was taken and sacked and remained apparently "a waste Chester" for near 300 years.

Thus for more than twenty years had Ethelfrid of Bamburgh marched from victory to victory. Meanwhile his foe and brother-in-law, Edwin, son of Ella, the rightful heir of Deira, was leading the life of a hunted fugitive, "an ascender of the stairs of other men," hearing perchance of the victories of the enemy of his house, as Charles Stuart in his places of refuge in Holland or France heard of the triumphant campaigns of Cromwell. There is, indeed, a tradition that Edwin, when a boy, had sought shelter at the court of Cadvan, the British king of North-West Wales, and that this was the cause of Ethelfrid's vigorous assault on the British confederacy; but this story seems hardly consistent with the pagan character of Edwin's upbringing. For some time he seems to have sought shelter with a sovereign of the new and rising state of Mercia, whose daughter he married; but probably on her death he wandered forth again into exile. And thus after long and various experiences of the sad life of a fugitive in different kingdoms of the land, he found his way to the court of Redwald, King of the East Angles, and received a promise of protection from that powerful monarch. When Ethelfrid, however, heard that his hated rival was harboured at the East Anglian court, he sent messenger upon messenger to Redwald, offering him large bribes to take the life of his youthful guest. Long did Redwald refuse to do anything that would bring so dark a stain upon his kingly honour, but at last the third messenger, who brought not only more magnificent bribes, but the threat of war in the event of refusal, prevailed. In the first watch of the night an East Anglian noble, friendly to Edwin, entered the fugitive's bedroom, called him forth outside the palace, told him his danger, counselled him to flee, and promised to lead him to a safe hiding-place, where neither Redwald nor Ethelfrid would be able to find him. Edwin thanked him for his warning, but refused to be the first to break covenant with his host by showing a doubt of his protection, and wearily exclaimed: "If I must die let me die here, rather than begin again that life of a fugitive which I have already led for so many years in every province of Britain." His friend left him and he remained alone with his sad thoughts in the darkening night.

Suddenly a man whose face and garb were alike unknown to him, stood before him and asked him why he sat there so mournfully on his seat of stone, while all within the palace were wrapped in sleep. "What is it to thee," said the weary exile, "where I choose to spend the night?" "But I know," answered the stranger, "both why thou art here, and why thou art so sad and what thou fearest. Now what wouldst thou give to any one who should free thee from thy anxieties and persuade Redwald not to deliver thee into the hands of thy enemies?" "All that I possess," said Edwin. "And what if he assured thee that thou shouldst overcome thine enemies and become a king greater than any English king before thee?" "I would give the gratitude which he deserved to any one who could confer on me such benefits." "And how, if he could point out to thee a new way of life and salvation better than any that thy fathers have known? Wouldst thou hearken to his voice and obey his counsels?" "Assuredly I would," said Edwin. The stranger put his hand upon his head and said: "When next thou shalt receive this sign, remember what thou hast promised and fulfil it." With that the stranger, whether he were living man or spirit, zealous missionary or martyred apostle, vanished into the darkness. A little cheered by the vision but still melancholy and anxious, Edwin was sitting yet before the palace when lo! his friend the courtier returned to him with joy in his countenance and said: "Arise, dismiss thy cares, go to thy couch and slumber with a quiet mind. The danger is past. The queen, to whom in secret Redwald disclosed his purpose, persuaded him not for any of Ethelfrid's gold to sell his far more precious kingly honour, or sacrifice the friend who had sought his protection in extremity." When day dawned it was seen that Edwin's friend had spoken truly. The king dismissed Ethelfrid's messengers with a final refusal, and knowing now that he would have to face that king's anger, resolved to anticipate the blow and to restore the fugitive to his kingdom. Hastily collecting his army he came upon the surprised and imperfectly prepared Ethelfrid on the banks of the Idle, a little river of Nottinghamshire, and there won a decisive victory. It was true that Redwald's own son, Regenheri, perished in the fight, but Ethelfrid himself was also slain, and the power of Bernicia for a season annihilated. It was a memorable day for the dwellers in the fens by the Humber, and six centuries later the historian, Henry of Huntingdon, still heard the proverb: "As when the Idle river grew foul with Anglian blood."

This great battle which for the time overthrew the Bernician dynasty and gave the dominion of all Northumbria to Edwin of Deira was fought probably in the year 617. Edwin, who was born in 585, and whose life since he was a child of three years old had been passed in exile, was therefore a man thirty-two years of age when he thus recovered his father's kingdom. The sons of Ethelfrid fled to the Celts of Scotland, and at least one of them sought the friendly shelter of Iona. Edwin no doubt fixed his capital at York, that great and important city which under its Anglian name of Eoforwac carried on the traditions of Roman Eburacum. The fact that the Roman name subsisted still with so little change in the language of the conquerors makes it probable that there was here no such utter destruction and desolation as at Anderida and Chester, but that there was a continuous civic life from the departure of the last Roman soldier to the enthronement of the first Anglian king. How gladly would we exchange much of the scanty knowledge of the invasion that we do possess for the details of the capture of the Roman capital of the north;* but over this conquest, as well as over that of the sister city of Londinium, there hangs a pall of impenetrable darkness. The lines of the Roman city may still be traced with considerable precision; the noble ruin of the multangular tower clearly marks its western corner, but we have not yet recovered, possibly shall never recover, the site of the once stately edifice where the Roman Dux Britanniarum dwelt aforetime, and where in all probability the Anglian kings of Deira held their court. There, however, we may safely imagine Edwin enthroned; from thence his armies marched forth along one or other of the great network of Roman roads which centred at Eburacum. One of his earliest conquests was probably that of the British kingdom of Elmet or Loidis

* This remark was made by Professor Freeman.

which still lingered on in the dales of the West Riding, but seems to have come to an end about this time. Having consolidated his power over Northumbria, Edwin became the mightiest of all the English kings. The title of Bretwalda was recognised as rightfully belonging to him, and all the other kings of Britain, Anglian, Saxon, Celtic, for a time at least acknowledged him as in a certain sense their superior. Even the islands of Man and Anglesey were added by him to his dominions, the latter island probably deriving from this conquest by the Angles the name which it still bears. Only Jutish Kent still maintained its independence, and with its king Edwin before long formed a close tie of alliance. An unexplained phenomenon in these first ten years of Edwin's reign, during which, still heathen, he seems to have been pursuing a career of unbroken success, is the disappearance of East Anglia from the scene. It was the might of Redwald the East Anglian which broke the power of Ethelfrid on the great day of the battle at the river Idle, and yet we hear of Edwin, still apparently in the lifetime of his benefactor, establishing his supremacy over all the kings of the Angles and Britons, including therefore among his subject allies even Redwald himself.

It was probably about the year 624 when Edwin was in full middle life, and his sons, by his first Mercian wife, were growing up towards manhood, that he made proposals of marriage to the Kentish princess, Ethelburga. She, like himself, must have been middle-aged. Her father, Ethelbert, had been for some years dead, and her brother, Eadbald, had the disposal of her hand. Mindful of the stripes and the warnings of Laurentius, Eadbald was now loyal in his adherence to Christianity, and replied to Edwin's messengers "that it was not lawful to give a Christian maiden in marriage to a pagan, lest the faith and sacrament of the heavenly King should be profaned by intercourse with an earthly king who was ignorant of the worship of the true God." To this objection (a remarkable one as coming from the offspring of the union between the Christian Bertha and the pagan Ethelbert) Edwin replied that he would do nothing contrary to the Christian faith of the princess if she became his bride; that she might bring with her as many ministers of that faith as she pleased, whether male or female, and should have full liberty of worship along with them; and, moreover, he held out hopes that he himself might become a convert to Christianity if on examination by the wise men of his kingdom it should be found more holy and worthier of the Most High than the religion which it offered to supersede. After this reassuring statement, Eadbald's objections were withdrawn. Ethelburga was sent northwards to meet her bridegroom, and in her train came Paulinus, who was now consecrated on July 21, 625, by Archbishop Justus, bishop of York, which was virtually equivalent to bishop of Northumbria.

Paulinus, who is certainly the noblest figure in the Roman mission to England, was constant in preaching the Christian faith in season and out of season to the men of Northumbria. He met at first with but little success, but a year after his arrival, in April 20, 626, a foully attempted crime brought him in a strange way nearer to his goal. The history of Wessex for some generations after the dethronement of Ceawlin in 592 is obscure and inglorious. Her once powerful kings seem to have accepted without a murmur the supremacy first of Kent and then of East Anglia, and if now they resented the rapidly extended dominion of Northumbria they sought to overthrow it not in fair fight but by the dastardly hand of the conspirator. The kings of the West Saxons at this time were Cynegils and Cwichelm, the latter of whom, perhaps in concert with his colleague, sent an assassin named Eomer, armed with a poisoned dagger, to the court of Edwin. The king was then dwelling in a royal villa near the Yorkshire Derwent (one of the many English rivers bearing that name), and there Eomer presented himself with a pretended message from his master. While Edwin listened intently to his words he drew the deadly weapon from its sheath and made a sudden onslaught upon the king. A faithful thegn named Lilia, who dearly loved his lord, having no shield ready to hand, rushed in between and broke the force of the blow, but not even the sacrifice of his life saved the monarch from a wound; and before Eomer was hewn down by the swords of the surrounding soldiers he had succeeded in stabbing one of them named Fordheri with his fatal weapon. That very night—it was the night of Easter Sunday, 626—Edwin's queen was delivered of a daughter, to whom was given the name of Eanfled. Touched by the mingled congratulations and exhortations of Paulinus, Edwin gladly consented that his infant daughter, along with eleven members of his household, should receive baptism on the eve of the following Whitsunday. For himself, though he was inclined to listen to the advice of Paulinus, all other matters had to be postponed to the great campaign of vengeance which, as soon as he had recovered from his wound, he undertook against the vile West Saxon murderers. In this campaign he was completely successful. Having slain five kings and much people, and returned victorious from the war, he at once abandoned the worship of idols and began seriously to consider the question of making a formal profession of Christianity.

It was apparently during this religious interregnum that the King and Queen of Northumbria received each a letter from Pope Boniface V. The letters, verbose and unpersuasive in style, can hardly have had much influence on the fresh and vigorous intellect of the Northumbrian king, but no doubt the fact that they should have been written at all by the father of western Christendom was felt as a compliment to Edwin's greatness. Still, however, the king hesitated before making a final breach with the traditions of his fathers and accepting Christ instead of his ancestral Woden. Unable to dismiss the subject from his thoughts he sat much apart in solitary places and there mused upon the parting of the ways. While he thus sat one day, Paulinus came unbidden into his presence, laid his hand upon his head and said: "Rememberest thou this sign?" With that the scene outside the East Anglian palace came back vividly into Edwin's memory. He was about to fall at the feet of Paulinus, but the bishop lifting him up said in a gentle voice: "Behold thou hast escaped by the Divine favour the snares of thine enemies: thou hast received the kingdom which was promised thee: delay not to stretch out thy hand and grasp the third blessing, even eternal life."*

Thus admonished Edwin determined to delay no longer his profession of Christianity, but wisely resolved to associate as many as possible of his counsellors with him, and to make the great change the act of the nation rather than of the king alone. Then followed the memorable and well-known scene in the Witenagemot, or meeting of the wise men, perhaps at York, perhaps at the royal villa by the Derwent. When the subject of the proposed change of faith was mooted in the assembly of the elders, its first and most strenuous advocate was found to be the chief priest Coifi, who complained that his past years spent in zealous service of the gods had brought him no proportionate share of the royal favour. To this sordid calculator of the worldly advantages to be derived from this or that form of faith, succeeded an unnamed ealdorman who, in words as well fitted to

* In telling this story Bede hints that Paulinus received by supernatural means the particulars of an earlier supernatural appearance; but he does not put forward this theory very confidently, and we may, perhaps, sufficiently account for the incident if we suppose that Paulinus himself, unknown at that time to Edwin, was the chief actor in the first scene, the memory of which he revived at an opportune time to strengthen the wavering faith of the king.

the twentieth century as to the seventh, painted the short, perplexing and precarious life of man "like a sparrow flitting through your hall, O king! when we are seated round the fire at supper-time, while the winds are howling and the snow is drifting without. It passes swiftly in at one door and out at another, feeling for the moment the warmth and shelter of your palace, but it flies from winter to winter and swiftly escapes from our sight. Even such is our life here, and if any one can tell us certainly what lies beyond it, we shall do wisely to follow his teaching." Moved by these and similar arguments the elders and counsellors of the king, unanimously as it would seem, voted for the proposed religious revolution.

After Paulinus had expounded to the assembly the doctrines of Christianity, Coifi exclaimed: "Long ago had I suspected that the things which we were worshipping were naught, for the more earnestly I sought for truth in that worship the less did I find it. Now I openly profess that in this new preaching alone is the way of eternal life to be found. O king! let us at once give over to the flames the temples and altars which we have consecrated so vainly." The king gladly consented, but asked who should deal the death-blow. "I," said Coifi. "Who more fitting than I to destroy, in the new wisdom which is given me, the idols which I worshipped in my folly?" He besought the king to give him arms and a war-horse, and though the multitude, who knew that it was forbidden to one of their priests to bear arms or to ride on anything but a mare, deemed him to be insane, he mounted the charger, rode to a great temple in the neighbourhood, hurled his lance into its sacred precincts and called upon his companions to give to the flames the shrine itself and all the enclosures by which it was surrounded from the gaze of the multitude. A hundred years afterwards men still showed at Goodmanham on the Derwent, east of York, the ruins of this great iconoclasm.

The overthrow of the old faith was followed by the visible triumph of the new. On Easter eve, 627, just a year after his escape from the dagger of the man of Wessex, Edwin was baptised by Paulinus in the new wooden church of St. Peter at York, a church which he was shortly to replace by a more elaborate edifice in stone. His sons by the Mercian princess before long followed his example: his young children, the offspring of Ethelburga, and even a little grandson Yffi, son of Osfrid, together with a great number of the nobles of the court, were all solemnly received into the Christian Church. The preaching of Paulinus, so long resultless, now seemed to be bearing abundant fruit. Up in remote Bernicia, where the royal villa of Yeavering nestled under a hill, an outlying sentinel of the Cheviots which still bears the name of Yeavering Bell, Paulinus was engaged for twenty-six consecutive days catechising and baptising in the river Glen the multitudes who flocked to him. Returning to Deira, to the Roman station of Cataractonium, he there baptised many converts in the river Swale, no church or oratory having yet been erected for Christian worship. In his zeal he overpassed the strict limits of Northumbria: he crossed the Humber, preached the Gospel in Lindsey, converted the "prefect" of the city of Lincoln, and baptised a multitude of people at noon-day in the river Trent, King Edwin himself honouring the ceremony by his presence. One of the many converts who went down on that day into the river with Paulinus described the scene to a youth who when an abbot, in his reverend old age, passed the tradition on to Bede, telling him that the great missionary was a man of tall stature, slightly stooping, with black hair, thin face, aquiline but slender nose, in his general aspect at once venerable and awe-inspiring. His constant attendant was a certain deacon James, a courageous and energetic man, who also lived to be a contemporary of the historian.

In after years of turbulence and discord men looked back on the reign of Edwin as a sort of golden age. They said that then a woman with her new-born babe might cross Britain from sea to sea unharmed by any man. In many a place where he saw a clear fountain bubbling up beside the public way he would order stakes to be erected, upon which brazen pots were hung, and none dared to touch them save the thirsty travellers for whose use they were designed. His state was indeed kingly. Not only in war was his standard displayed; but in peace also, as he was journeying from villa to villa and from province to province, attended by a long and brilliant train of servants, a banner with a tuft of feathers, called by the Romans tufa and by the English thuuf and hinting perhaps at something like imperial dignity, was borne before the mighty king of Northumbria.

But this splendour of regal power was early overshadowed. It was not, after all, from Eburacum that the word of power was to go forth which was to bind the various Teutonic races of England into one nation. The Anglian power was not thoroughly established over Wales, and already the destined rival of Northumbria, the Mercian kingdom, was rising into baleful pre-eminence. Singularly enough, it was from these two powers which are said to have sheltered Edwin in the time of his evil fortunes that his ruin came. Cadwallon, King of Gwynedd, descended from that

Maelgwn whom Gildas vituperated under the name of "The Great Dragon of the Island," was son of Cadvan, at whose court, it is said, Edwin had passed his boyhood. Doubtless Cadwallon keenly resented the position of inferiority to which his nation had been reduced by Ethelfrid's great victory of Chester, which shut them off from Strathclyde, as Ceawlin's victory of Deorham had shut them off from Devon and Cornwall. When Edwin, once Cadvan's humble guest, had become the mightiest prince in Britain, Cadwallon, unwilling to accept his yoke, had taken refuge—so say the Welsh annals—in Ireland. He had now returned and was determined to strike one more blow for independence and for liberty of passage to Strathclyde. With this intent he formed an alliance with the ruler of Mercia, Penda, who became king in 626, a year before Edwin's baptism; who was still pagan; and who in his dull ferocity was as typical a specimen of the old faith as Edwin of the new. The alliance of the Welsh Christian and the English pagan for the overthrow of the newly born Christianity of Northumbria was scarcely felt to be unnatural, so intense was the bitterness engendered by the Paschal controversy and the varying fashions of ecclesiastical tonsure.

The armies met at Heathfield, which is identified with Hatfield Chase on the north-east of Doncaster, on October 12, 633. We have no details of the encounter: we only know that Edwin was defeated, that he and his eldest son Osfrid were slain, and that Cadwallon and his ally roamed in savage wrath over the plains of Yorkshire and Northumberland. The Christian, even more ferocious than the pagan, spared neither sex nor age, recognised no claim to mercy drawn from the profession of one common faith, and vowed (this surely when out of hearing of his ally) that he would root out the whole brood of Angles from the land of Britain.*

Edwin's second son fled for refuge to the court of the Mercian king, and was afterwards slain by him, in violation of his sworn promise of protection. The widowed Ethelburga fled to the court of her brother, the King of Kent, under the escort of Paulinus. The royal infants—such was the terror of the times—were separated from their mother, and it was left for a brave soldier named Bass, one of Edwin's thegns, to bring to the Kentish court the girl Eanfled, her brother Wuscfrea, and their little nephew Yffi, the orphaned son of Osfrid. The widowed queen afterwards sent the

* It must be remembered that this is the Anglian version of the story, possibly unjust to Cadwallon, and that the Britons had the wrongs of two centuries to avenge.

boys to the court of her cousin, Frankish Dagobert, that they might be safe from the new rulers of Bernicia, but both died in infancy in that foreign land. As for Paulinus he seems to have bowed his head to the storm of the recrudescent paganism of Northumbria. He vacated his Yorkish see, and was appointed Bishop of Rochester, in succession to Romanus, who had been drowned in the Mediterranean when sent on a mission to Rome. He died in 644. The ill-starred union of Mercian paganism and British fanaticism seemed to have accomplished its purpose. Northumberland was a wilderness and Northumbrian Christianity a vanished dream.

IX.

OSWALD OF BERNICIA

When the cause of Christianity and, as connected with it, the hope of eventually building in the new England a civilised and well-ordered state seemed at its darkest, light arose from an island in the Hebrides; it spread to a rough storm-beaten rock on the Northumbrian coast; it illumined one of the noblest and loveliest pages in the history of our nation, the reign of Oswald of Bernicia.

The conversion of the southern Picts to Christianity is believed to have taken place more than two centuries before the date that we have now reached. Near the close of the fourth century when the Roman empire had already begun to crumble into ruin, St. Ninian, a Briton educated at Rome, filled with veneration for the soldier-saint, Martin of Tours, came to the region between the Roman Wall and the Grampians, preached Christianity with much success to the Picts who dwelt in that country, and built a monastic church dedicated to St. Martin, on one of the promontories of Galloway which project south into the Irish sea. This church, built of stone, and thereby differing from the humbler wooden churches of the period, was called Candida Casa (a name represented in its modern successor Whithern), and it is said to have been still in course of erection when Ninian heard of the death of the holy man in whose name he dedicated his beautiful "white house." Nearly two centuries passed away. There was much intercourse of various kinds between the dwellers in the Hebrides and their neighbours the Scots of Ireland. The Dalriadic kingdom, Scottish (that is Erse) by race and Christian by religious profession, was set up in Argyll and the adjacent islands; but the Picts north of the Grampians whose relations to Dalriada were generally hostile, remained obstinately heathen. All this was changed by an event which took place about the year 563—the arrival of St. Columba from Ireland. Whatever accretions of superstitious legend may have grown up around the name of this saint, the historic importance of the great apostle of the Picts cannot be denied, and can hardly be over-stated.

Born in Donegal, in the year 521, a scion of the princely clan of the Hy Neill, descended from Irish kings both on his father's and his mother's side, the young Irishman in his boyish days showed such zeal in his attendance at church that his baptismal name of Colum was changed to Colum-cille or Columba of the church. He was ordained priest, but the bent of his religious temper like that of most of his Irish contemporaries was all towards the monastic profession. During his early middle life he was busily engaged in founding monasteries, the first in point of date being that of Derry, and the most famous that of Durrow in the diocese of Meath. But in his fortieth year, 561, he became entangled in one of the ever-recurring civil wars of his distressful country. A great battle was fought at Cuildremhne, in Connaught, near the boundary between that province and Ulster. Columba's kinsfolk, the northern Hy Neill, prevailed and the King of Ireland, commanding the clans of the southern Hy Neill, was defeated. Though his friends' cause triumphed, the battle appears in some unexplained manner to have injured Columba's religious position in his native country. He seems to have been excommunicated by some of his brethren, possibly on account of his alleged responsibility for the strife. At any rate he now resolved to quit his country and, perhaps as a penance for his sins, to take up his abode in some place from which he could not even see the shores of his beloved Ireland. Such a place, after some wandering, he found in the then little known island of Hy, famous to after ages under the name of Iona; where, as tradition tells, he ascended a hill which still bears the name of Cul-ri-Erin (back turned to Erin), and when he found that no line of the Irish coast, however dimly seen, could thence be discerned on the horizon, amid all the cluster of surrounding islands, he determined to make that little spot his dwelling-place. Iona is separated from the much larger island of Mull by a channel about one mile broad. It is only three miles long, and from a mile to a mile and a half in breadth; yet in this little space there is considerable variety of scenery; hills, the highest of which attains to an elevation of 320 feet, "retired dells, long reaches of sand on shores indented with quiet bays, little coves between bare and striking rocks, and on the west wild barren cliffs and high rocky islets opposed to the sweep of the Atlantic."* As Bede says: "it is not large but computed as containing five families according

* Skene, Celtic Scotland, ii., 89.

to English reckoning." (The word "families" is rendered "hides" in the English Chronicle, and this is an important passage as showing what were the average dimensions of a "hide of land" in early Saxon times.) The ruins now visible on the island are those of a Benedictine abbey of the thirteenth century. No traces remain of the buildings, probably wooden, raised by St. Columba, but there are many interesting natural features which may be recognised in the nearly contemporary life of the saint written by the ninth abbot of Iona, Adamnan.

The objects which Columba set before himself after his migration to Iona were political as well as religious. His kinsmen, the Scots of Dalriada, were harassed and oppressed by the pagan Picts in the east of the island, whose king, Brude, had in the year 560 inflicted a crushing defeat on the Scottish king, Gabhran. Columba would fain convert the Pictish conqueror to Christianity, and at the same time obtain more generous treatment for his beaten countrymen; and by the magic of his personality he achieved a striking success in both directions. King Brude in 565 embraced Christianity, and relations of peace and friendship were established between him and the man whom, in 574, Columba succeeded in placing on the throne of Dalriada, Aidan, Prince of Strathclyde. The thirty-four years of Columba's life, after his great migration, were spent in establishing monasteries in the land of the northern Picts, in the Hebrides and in his native Ireland, to which he paid several visits, and where the once excommunicated partisan was now an honoured, almost worshipped guest. These Columban monasteries, "the family of Iona" as they were called, were of a distinctly different type from that of the monasteries of the Benedictine rule. Like all the Irish monastic establishments they partook largely of the tribal character. The tribe gave the land, contributed to the support of the monks, had a right to receive, apparently without special charge, their religious ministrations, and in certain circumstances had also a right to nominate one of its members as abbot, though the first claim upon this coveted office resided in the family of the founder. It was thus that the first nine abbots of Iona were all descended from the same family, the northern Hy Neill, from which St. Columba himself had sprung. This tribal character of the monasteries suited the genius of the Celtic populations, and was one reason of the success of the missionaries in converting them to Christianity. It has been truly said* that "these large monasteries, as in their external aspect they

* By Skene, u.s., ii., 63.

appeared to be, were in reality Christian colonies into which converts, after being tonsured, were brought under the name of monks."

The large part thus played by the monasteries in the work of conversion impressed in its turn a peculiar character on the churches of Ireland and Hebridean Scotland, rendering them more exclusively monastic and less purely episcopal than the churches of Italy and Gaul. This divergence resulted in part from the nature of things, and was due to the differences of place and time in which the conversion of the several countries was respectively effected. The Bishops of Lyons and Vienne, of Toledo and Seville began their work while the Roman Empire was still standing, were to some extent moulded by its form, shared the prosperity and the influence of its great towns and were essentially magnates of cities. Columba, his comrades and his pupils, came into a much ruder and more primitive state of society. The rough tribal rulers whom they converted had scarcely any cities worthy of the name. The new missionaries planted their monasteries in such rural places as promised them the supply of their simple wants, or even only safety from the attacks of a midnight foe—often on an island in a lake or surrounded by the ocean—and there, not so much by eloquent preaching as by mere rightness and simplicity of living, succeeded in converting whole populations to the religion of Christ. The conversions thus obtained seem to have been for the most part more genuine and more durable than those which were first effected in the large cities of the old Roman world and from thence radiated outwards into the country.

It has seemed necessary to emphasise this distinction between the two types of ecclesiastical organisation (the fourth century Gaulish and the sixth century Irish Churches) because the difference reappears in our own history. The Roman mission under Augustine and his successors, and especially under Paulinus in Northumbria, seems to have gone on the old urban and episcopal lines, while the far more successful mission from Iona, with which we have now to deal, was monastic, many-centred and rural. In the year 597, the very year of Augustine's arrival in England, St. Columba died. He is one of the most vividly seen personalities of the early Middle Ages: a man of somewhat hot temper in youth, softened and controlled in later life, with a stately beauty of feature which seemed to correspond with his princely descent, and with a kind of magnetic power of attracting to himself the devotion of his followers, a lover of animals and beloved by them. One of his natural gifts was an extraordinarily strong and resonant voice which, when he sang the psalms of the church, could be heard distinctly for more than a mile. A great open-air preacher, an organiser and a poet—he eagerly championed the cause of his brother bards before an Irish synod—he might, perhaps, not unfittingly, be called the John Wesley of the sixth century.

In 615, about eighteen years after the death of Columba, when his fellow-tribesman Fergna was ruling, fourth in the series of abbots, at Iona, a party of refugees from the south crossed the little channel and landed on the shore of the island, craving shelter and sanctuary. They were some of the attendants of Ethelfrid, the late King of Bernicia, who had been slain "when the river Idle ran foul with Anglian blood," and they brought, besides other noble youths, Oswald, that king's second son, and implored the brethren to protect him from the avenging might of Edwin. There was no shadow of a claim for this young Anglian, son of an obstinate pagan, on the hospitality of the Irish monks, but the request was willingly granted. Oswald and the young nobles his companions were kindly received, were soon baptised, and instructed in the doctrines of Christianity, and growing up to manhood on the sequestered Hebridean isle, probably looked forward to no other sort of life than that which was led by the simple-hearted monks their entertainers.

All this was changed, in 633, by the great and unlooked-for catastrophe of Heathfield. The two Northumbrian kingdoms, united under the strong rule of Ethelfrid and Edwin, fell once more apart. Osric, cousin of Edwin, son of his uncle Elfric, ruled in Deira, and Eanfrid, eldest son of Ethelfrid, in Bernicia. These two young princes, each of whom had made profession of the Christian faith, both apostatised and returned to paganism. Possibly the sordid calculations by which Coifi had justified his renunciation of the faith of his fathers weighed with them now in the opposite scale, and they felt themselves justified in deserting the Christians' God, who had abandoned their land to the tender mercies of Penda and Cadwallon. But the triumph of paganism was short. Osric, who with inadequate forces besieged Cadwallon while holding the "municipium" of York, was killed and his whole army cut to pieces by a sudden sally of the Welsh king. This happened in the summer of the year which followed the battle of Heathfield, and, apparently in the following autumn, Bernician Eanfrid, coming with twelve chosen warriors to treat of peace with Cadwallon, was treacherously slain by his orders. So full of gloomy memories was this year, 634, that the monkish chroniclers, who afterwards drew up a scheme of Anglian chronology, decided that it should not come into the number of the years, and silently included it in the glorious reign of him who succeeded the apostates.

This successor was Oswald, who came from Iona evidently determined to play the part of a Christian hero-king, and who endured to his life's end steadfast in that decision. By one bold stroke he delivered his nation, Bernicia, from the Cambrian ravagers. "When he arrived after the death of his brother Eanfrid with a small army, and fortified by the faith of Christ, the wicked general of the Britons with the immense forces which, as he boasted, nothing could resist, was slain by him at the place which is called in the English tongue Denisesburn,' that is, the stream of Denis." So runs the first simple statement of Bede as to this important encounter which for ever settled the question whether the Celt or the Teuton was to be supreme in Northern Britain. From Bede himself, as a kind of afterthought, and from Adamnan, the biographer of St. Columba, we get some additional particulars which enable us to see more clearly if not the strategic features of the battle at least what was passing in the minds of the combatants. It seems that the battle itself was fought not at "Denisesburn" but at Heavenfield, a little on the north of the Roman wall, which probably was an important element in the problem that the Anglian king, with his great inferiority of forces, had to solve.* The great Roman work, striding across the country in its uncompromising way, here traverses a high moorland which separates the main stream of the Tyne from its northern affluent, and in this portion of its career it is from 700 to 800 feet above the level of the sea. Though none of its stones are here remaining, we can yet trace the high mounds and deep fosses of its companion, the line of fortification on the south, which is known by the name of the vallum. Between these two lines, that of stone and that of earth, ran the Roman road, still probably in Edwin's day capable of being traversed, notwithstanding 230 years of neglect. Along this road Cadwallon may have marched, and by it he may have encamped for the night, while somewhere, behind either wall or vallum, Oswald may have placed in ambush his father's veterans. He himself was in a mood of religious and patriotic exaltation. On the day before the battle he had in his sleep a vision of the blessed Columba, whom he had never seen

* Nennius (Hist. Brit., § 64) says "in bello Catscaul". Cat is an old English word for battle; caul is probably corrupted from guaul, the word elsewhere used by Nennius for the Roman wall (cf. §§ 23 and 38).

with the eyes of the flesh. The saint's beautiful face shone with angelic brightness: his figure rose majestic till it seemed to touch the clouds: he spread his mantle over the Anglian camp. Addressing Oswald in the words which Moses spake to Joshua he told him to be strong and of a good courage, for the Lord would be with him. Let him march out on the following night to battle: his foes should be all scattered in flight, and the Welsh king should be delivered into his hands.

Awaking, Oswald assembled his council, told them his dream and received the unanimous promise of the army that if they won the victory they would make profession of the Christian faith. He then caused a large wooden cross to be prepared and a hole to be dug, in which it was firmly planted, he himself holding it erect with both hands while his soldiers filled in the soil. When this was done he cried to the host with a loud voice: "Let us all bend our knees and together call upon God Almighty, the Living and the True, that He in His pity will defend us from our proud and cruel foe: for He knoweth that this is a just war that we have undertaken for the deliverance of our people." All obeyed his command and prayed to the God of the Christians. That night, just before dawn, they moved out of camp, attacked the probably unsuspecting Britons, and inflicted upon them a crushing defeat. Many of the enemy must have perished on the wide moorland; some who probably fled southwards with Cadwallon, their king, were whelmed in the deep waters of the Tyne. Cadwallon himself met his death (how we know not) on the banks of the little Rowley Burn, some five miles south of the Tyne and ten miles from the field of battle. Such was the event which ruined the British hopes of a reconquest of the island, which confirmed the endangered work of Ethelfrid, ratified the victory of Chester, cut off the Britons of the south from their kinsmen in Strathclyde, and confined the former to that mountainous rectangle of territory which we know as Wales. The son of the slain king, "Cadwallader the Blessed," perhaps strove for a time to maintain the high, almost imperial pretensions of his father, but his long reign seems to have been on the whole disastrous, and when he died a pilgrim at Rome in the year 681, the Welsh chronicler himself admits that "thenceforth the Britons lost the crown of the kingdom and the Saxons gained it."* The two centuries which followed the battle of Heavenfield are the darkest and dreariest in the history of Wales.

Returning in triumph, as Columba in vision had promised him, Oswald

* Brut y Tywysogion, s.a., 681.

proceeded to his father's wooden palace at Bamburgh, and from thence, apparently with little difficulty, extended his rule over all Northumbria. In Bernicia he would, of course, as the son of Ethelfrid, find many loyal hearts ready to greet him; and even Deira, now that Edwin and his progeny were off the stage, had possibly a welcome for the man who was not only the deliverer from British oppression, but also on his mother's side descended from the old line. For it will be remembered that Acha, wife of Ethelfrid, was daughter of Aelle of Deira.

Thus, then, did Bamburgh, which is now a lonely village by the German Ocean, become "the royal city," the most strongly fortified abode of the most powerful king in Britain,* the centre of a realm which stretched from the Humber to the Firth of Forth, and apparently, through the rest of the seventh century, the destined capital of England, if England should ever attain to unity. The traveller who now visits this dethroned queen of Northumbria will see much that, however noble and picturesque, must be eliminated by an effort of the imagination if he would picture to himself the Bamburgh of King Oswald. The massive keep that "stands four-square to every wind that blows," dates from the reign of Henry II.; the great hall of the castle now ingeniously restored by a modern architect, was originally of the time of Edward I.; some of the still existing buildings were reared by a benevolent ecclesiastic in the reign of George III.; but the natural features of the place are unchangeable and unchanged, and in looking upon them we know that we behold the same scenes that met the eye of the conqueror of Cadwallon. Such is the rock itself, an upheaved mass of basalt upon whose black sides the tooth of time seems to gnaw in vain; such are the long sandy dunes which gather round its base; such the Inner and Outer Farne Islands, fragments of basalt rising out of the ocean at distances ranging from three to six miles from the castle; such the far-off peninsula, which when the tide flows, becomes Holy Island; such the long range of Cheviot on the western horizon, snow-covered for many months of the year. Such, we might almost say, is the fierce wind which, from one quarter or another, seems for ever attacking the lonely fortress, and which assuredly battered the "timbered" palace of Oswald as it now batters the time-worn fortress of the Plantagenet.

Scarcely had Oswald seated himself on the Northumbrian throne when he began to labour for the conversion of his new subjects to Christianity,

* "Urbs regia" (Bede, iii., 6); "urbs munitissima" (Simeon of Durham, Historia Regum, § 48).

a Christianity, however, not altogether after the fashion which Paulinus had taught to Edwin of Deira, but rather according to that which he himself had learned of his friends, the monks of Iona. The abbot Seghine paid him a visit, probably soon after his accession, and heard from his own lips the marvellous story of his vision of Columba and the victory of Heavenfield; and one of his monastic family was despatched to teach the Northumbrians the religion of Christ. This missionary was a man of narrow intellect and austere temper, who soon returned to Iona with the unwelcome tidings that it was but lost labour to try to teach a nation so barbarous and untamable. At the council whereat this report was rendered sat a man, probably in early middle life, the monk Aidan. "It seems to me, my brother," said he, "that thou hast been somewhat too hard on these poor unlearned folk, and hast scarcely remembered the apostolic precept to give milk to babes till such time as they may be able to understand and to keep the more sublime commands of God." The eyes of all in the council were turned upon the speaker who had so opportunely spoken words of wisdom. "Aidan shall be bishop," "Aidan shall be ordained to preach to the Northumbrians," was the unanimous decision of the assembly. He accordingly went southward, and for the next sixteen years (635–51) was the great missionary bishop of Northumbria.

It must have seemed to Aidan when he visited the palace of the king, his patron, as if it was a special act of Providence that had fixed that palace where he found it. For here on the storm-beaten Northumbrian coast, within six miles from the royal dwelling, lay an island whereupon he could establish his monastery, and wherein he could be out of the world yet within reach of the world like his prototype Columba in Iona. This island which was given him by the king for his possession, bore then and has borne intermittently ever since the name of Lindisfarne; but even at this day for once that its legal designation of Lindisfarne is mentioned, you shall hear it a thousand times called by the endearing appellation of Holy Island, given to it probably twelve centuries ago when it first received the imprint of Aidan's sandals. The island is but a small one, only about 1,000 acres in extent, with three fair-sized farms, and a population of about 800 persons, chiefly engaged in fishing, and in winter often hard pressed for subsistence. The beautiful ruins of the Benedictine abbey, the parish church, the castle, built in the Commonwealth period, all belong to ages long posterior to the time when it first became "Holy Island"; but here, as at Bamburgh, the natural features of the landscape are so unchanged that it requires but little effort of the imagination to enable the beholder to travel backward through the centuries to see Cuthbert praying among the sea-gulls, or Aidan slowly pacing the long spit of sand which lay between him and the palace of the king. It will be seen that it is spoken of as an island, and such for all practical purposes it has ever been; for though on the north it stretches out a long sandy arm to the mainland, and at dead low water travellers may reach it from thence all-but dry shod, still their path, traversing three miles of wet sand and leading them through the waste of waters on either hand, seems to sever them from the mainland rather than to unite them thereto, and the inhabitants are at this day islanders in heart and feeling.

Here then dwelt the Celtic apostle of Northumbria, and from hence did he diffuse that influence which accomplished the lasting conversion of the northern Angles to Christianity. In this work he was powerfully aided by King Oswald. In all the history of Christian Church and state during eighteen centuries there are few fairer chapters than that which deals with the intercourse between Oswald and Aidan. There was evidently something in the character of the Celtic bishop which won for him more than the veneration, the love, of the Anglian king. Aidan was a man of absolute simplicity of character, intent on one purpose alone, that of spreading the Christian faith in the kingdom of Northumbria, utterly indifferent to wealth, and fame, and power, and yet without that harshness and austerity which the men of one idea so often display, and which made many of the noblest of medieval saints unloveable. Herein, and in his genuine, not feigned, contempt of riches we trace a certain resemblance between the saint of Lindisfarne and the saint of Assisi. Bede describes the character of Aidan with an enthusiasm all the more trustworthy, because he regretfully observes that "his zeal for God was not according to knowledge, since he kept the day of the Lord's Pascha according to the manner of his race, that is from the fourteenth day to the twentieth." He says of him, however, that "herein did he chiefly commend his doctrine to others in that he taught none otherwise than as he lived among his friends"; words which remind us of Chaucer's often quoted description of the "Poure Persoun of a Toun":—

But Criste's loore and his Apostles twelve
He taughte, but first he folwed it hymselve.

It was a strange, but, as Bede says, a most beautiful sight, when the missionary who as yet had not fully mastered our English tongue would preach to the people; when Oswald, whose boyhood passed at Iona had made him master of the difficult Gaelic tongue, stood forth as interpreter, and translated to his own grim warriors and to the servants of his palace "the words of the heavenly life" as they fell from the lips of Aidan. Occasionally, but not too often, for he dreaded the fascinations of a court, Aidan would accept the royal invitation and appear with one or two of his clergy in the great hall at Bamburgh. Even then after a short and hurried repast he would go forth speedily with his friends to read the Scriptures, to chant the Psalter, or to pray. But the scene enacted at one such courtly festival lingered for generations in the memory of men. It was Easter day (the heterodox Easter, as it may be feared), and the king and the bishop had just sat down to the mid-day meal. The bishop was on the point of stretching forth his hand to bless the royal dainties which were served in a splendid silver dish, when the king's almoner abruptly entered and told his master that a multitude of poor persons gathered from all quarters had arrived, and were sitting in the streets and in the courtyard of the palace, plaintively demanding alms from the king. Thereupon Oswald at once ordered the victuals to be distributed among the beggars, and the dish itself to be broken up into fragments, one of which should be given to each of them. Aidan, who was himself a most generous benefactor of the poor, was so delighted with the deed that he clasped the king's right hand and exclaimed, "May this hand never see corruption!"

Devoted as Oswald was to the Christianisation of his people he was no pious roi fainéant, but a strong and successful monarch who made his power felt at least from the Firth of Forth to the Bristol Channel. Bede tells us, perhaps with some unconscious exaggeration of the glory of his native Northumbria, that "he received under his sway all the nations and provinces of Britain, which are divided into four languages, those of the Britons, the Picts, the Scots, and the Angles." As he evidently here uses "Angles" as equivalent to Angles and Saxons, this sentence represents Oswald as accomplishing more than Egbert was to achieve two centuries later, and as practically the lord of our whole island. Consistently herewith he represents him as the sixth of the Bretwaldas; and Adamnan, who at first calls him merely "regnator Saxonicus," says that after the victory of Heavenfield he was "ordained by God emperor of the whole of Britain." But all these statements must be taken with considerable reservation. Oswald wielded evidently during the seven years of his reign the predominant power in the island, but we are not to think of him as interfering with any of the details of administration in Wessex or East Anglia, still less in Wales or among the Scots of Dalriada. With Wessex, indeed, we are expressly told that he formed ties both of relationship and of religion. When Cynegils, King of the West Saxons, who had been converted to Christianity by the preaching of Birinus, was baptised, his godfather, the man who, according to ecclesiastical phrase, "received him emerging from the sacred laver," was Oswald of Bernicia, who also became his son-in-law, accepting from the old West Saxon king the hand of his daughter in marriage.

From the character of our one chief authority, Bede's Ecclesiastical History, it naturally but unfortunately follows that we are left in almost total ignorance of the political events in Oswald's reign. Gladly would we know, for instance, whether the fierce Mercian, Penda, bowed his head even for a time under the yoke of Northumbrian supremacy, but on this point we are left without information. There are hints of earlier wars and fightings between the two states, but all that we can certainly say is that on August 5, 642, Oswald and Penda met in battle at a place called Maserfield,* and that though Penda's brother fell in the fight the Mercian king "was victorious by diabolic art," and Oswald lay dead on the battlefield. He died praying: when he saw himself girt round by the Mercian host and knew that his death was inevitable, he cried aloud: "Lord, have mercy on the souls of my army," and the remembrance of this prayer passed into a proverb: "'Lord, pity their souls,' as Oswald said when he was falling to the ground."

Oswald was in his thirty-eighth year when he died, the second Northumbrian prince in the prime and vigour of his days, who had fallen before the elderly barbarian, Penda. The brutal heathen had his head and hands severed from the body and fixed on stakes; but before long, at a turn of the wheel of fortune, these relics, now deemed to be endowed with miraculous power, were carried to distant sites where they met with more honourable treatment. The head was deposited in the monastery at Holy Island, and in after years shared the migrations of the relics of St. Cuthbert: the hand, "the uncorrupted hand" which Aidan had blessed, was enshrined at Bamburgh: the body, by the order of Oswald's niece, Osthryd, now Queen of the Mercians, was reverently laid in the monastery of Bardney in the centre of Lincolnshire. In his lifetime Oswald had, with some display of force, extended his dominion over this

* Generally identified with Oswestry (Oswald's tree) in Shropshire.

South-Humbrian land, mindful of which fact the patriotic monks were loth to receive the body of their conqueror, but a pillar of fire hovering at night over the coffin showed them that the corpse to which they were refusing admittance would be a precious and wonder-working relic, and turned their aversion into eagerness for its possession. Numerous in fact were the miracles alleged to be wrought by the dissevered fragments of the kingly body, and even by the dust of the battlefield on which he had fallen. The day of his martyrdom, August 5, was appropriated to the cult of Saint Oswald, and the fame of the new saint and his wonder-working relics spread rapidly not only in England but in Ireland and on the Continent.

X.

OSWY AND PENDA

The Mercian victory of the Maserfield was doubtless followed by a ravaging expedition into Northumbria. When the waters of the flood subside we find that country again split into the two kingdoms of Bernicia and Deira. In the former reigned Oswy (or Oswiu), brother of the martyred Oswald; in the latter, Oswin, son of that Osric, Edwin's cousin, whose one year's reign preceded the accession of Oswald. For seven years (644–651) these two kings reigned side by side in the northern land, but before their further career is described it is necessary to turn back and consider more closely the history of that midland kingdom which was running so even a race with Northumbria for the supremacy in Britain.

The causes and the stages of the development of the Mercian power, and even the origin of the Mercian state, are alike hidden from us. All that can be said is that in the early part of the seventh century we find the Mercians, an Anglian tribe, manifesting themselves in force in Staffordshire and Shropshire along the Welsh March from which they perhaps derived their name. As the century proceeds, they conquer or ally with themselves the Middle Anglians, who seem to have inhabited Leicestershire and some of the country adjacent thereto; as well as the South Angles in Buckinghamshire, Bedfordshire, and Hertfordshire, who sooner or later became incorporated in the new state. The agent in these great changes was probably Penda himself, the strong-willed pagan who, in 626, at the age of fifty, ascended the Mercian throne, which he occupied for nearly thirty years. Of his alliance with Cadwallon of Wales, and his successful wars with the Northumbrian kings, Edwin and Oswald, enough has already been said in previous chapters; but his dealings with Wessex and East Anglia require some further notice.

In the year 628, as we learn from the Chronicle, Cynegils and Cwichelm fought with Penda at Cirencester and made a treaty there. These are the two Kings of Wessex, apparently reigning together as father and son, who sent the assassin to deal that murderous blow at the life of Edwin which was foiled only by the self-devotion of the loyal thegn, Lilla. That event and the retaliatory campaign of Edwin against Wessex no doubt preceded by some years this war of 628 between Wessex and Mercia. Of the details of the treaty by which the war was ended we know nothing, but it has been conjectured with some probability* that it included a cession of the north-western conquests of Ceawlin to Mercia, and the acceptance by Wessex of the line of the Thames as her northern boundary.†

Penda's next intervention in the affairs of his southern neighbours took place in 645, three years after his overthrow of Oswald. Wessex had in the meantime become Christian, chiefly through the preaching of a certain Birinus, who had received his commission from Pope Honorius on his assurance "that he would scatter the seeds of the holy faith in the innermost parts of England whither no teacher had preceded him." The orthodoxy of Pope Honorius has been sorely attacked on account of his unfortunate vacillations on the subject of the Monothelete heresy, but his evident interest in the conversion of our remote island should be allowed to plead on his behalf as at least one who was zealous for the Christian faith. Birinus discharged the commission entrusted to him with energy and success. We have but little authentic information as to his life, but it seems clear that in respect of the conversion of the kingdoms he held the same relation towards Wessex that Augustine had held to Kent, Paulinus to Deira, and Aidan to Bernicia. The influence of Northumbrian Christianity aided the zealous missionary, and, as we have seen, Oswald of Bernicia stood sponsor for his future father-in-law when in the year 635 Cynegils, the aged King of Wessex, received the sign of baptism. Cwichelm, son of Cynegils and partner of his throne, the chief actor apparently in the murderous attempt upon Edwin of Deira, followed his father's example in the following year, but died soon after, and when old Cynegils died (641) five years later, he was succeeded by another son, named Cenwalh, who still persisted in heathenism. Soon, however, as Bede remarks, he who refused the offer of the heavenly kingdom, lost his earthly crown. Growing tired of his wife, who was a daughter of Penda, he divorced her, and this repudiation naturally brought upon him the wrath of the Mercian king. Expelled from his kingdom (645) by the victorious arms of Penda,

* By Freeman: Norman Conquest, i., 36 (3rd ed.).

† Except parts of Oxfordshire and Buckinghamshire surrounding Dorchester.

Cenwalh took refuge in East Anglia, at that time the most enthusiastically Christian of all the English kingdoms, with the possible exception of Kent. The persuasions of the East Anglian king, Anna, induced him to make profession of Christianity, and when, after three years' exile (648), he succeeded in recovering his ancestral kingdom, Cenwalh continued faithful to his new creed, and for the remaining twenty-eight years of his reign he ruled as a Christian king. Thus Wessex, before the seventh century was half way through, accepted the faith of Christ.

The place which witnessed the baptisms of these West Saxon kings, and in which Birinus fixed his episcopal seat, deserves a passing notice. The Dorchester of Oxfordshire (which must on no account be confounded with the county-town of Dorset) is now a pleasant but obscure village on the left bank of the Thames about twelve miles south-east of Oxford. It is in a country full of archæological interest. High on a hill to the west rises what has been truly called "the mighty camp of Sinodun," a relic apparently of pre-Roman times; and nearer may be traced the so-called "dykes" of the Thames, the work probably of Roman engineers. In the village itself is a fine old abbey church with architecture of various ages, a church which might yet serve on occasion as a cathedral. There is also a great charm in the antique appearance of the place with its picturesque houses, some of them dating from the seventeenth century. Brought thus in contact with the spirit of the past, and freed from the importunate clamours of the industrial present, the traveller finds it not hard to re-create the scenes of the yet more distant past, to imagine Birinus preaching in his little wooden church, or Cynegils and his thegns riding through the swollen river. But for all this, it is hard to bring home to oneself the truth that this village was an ecclesiastical, and almost a literary centre, while Oxford, if it existed at all, was an obscure cluster of cottages; that she was the ecclesiastical metropolis, first of Wessex and then of Mercia, and that royal Winchester and stately Lincoln are both in a certain sense the daughters of Dorchester.

The shelter which King Anna gave to the fugitive Cenwalh was an act of generous courage in the ruler of a country which had already suffered much and was to suffer more at the hands of the terrible Penda. It will be remembered that Redwald, King of East Anglia, who had shown hospitality to Edwin, died a heathen, though more than tolerant of Christianity; but his successor, Earpwald (617–28), yielding to the persuasions of the Northumbrian king, allowed himself to be baptised.

After a short reign Earpwald was assassinated by a worshipper of the old gods.* Heathenism and anarchy then prevailed in East Anglia for three years, at the end of which time Sigebert the Learned, brother or half-brother of Earpwald, returned from Gaul, in which country he had spent some years, having incurred for some reason the hatred of Redwald. In Gaul he had become a Christian and had pursued those studies which had procured for him his surname "the Learned." When raised to the East Anglian throne, he successfully attempted the reconversion of the country to Christianity, from which it never afterwards relapsed. He also—a noteworthy fact—"established a school in which boys might be instructed in letters," following herein the example set him by the King of Kent, and bringing his school teachers from Canterbury. In all his works, scholastic and religious, he was zealously aided by Felix, a missionary-bishop from Burgundy, who had fixed the seat of his episcopate at Dunwich, a city on the coast of Suffolk, long since swallowed up by the ocean. While the trained ecclesiastic, Felix, supplied the organising and educating influences needed by the infant Church of East Anglia, an enthusiastic energy was imparted to it by an Irish monk named Fursa, a man of vivid imagination, full of his marvellous revelations of the world of spirits, one whom, when we read the story of his visions as it is told us by Bede, we are almost persuaded to call the unlettered Dante of the seventh century. As men in Florence said when they saw the poet pass, "That man has been in hell," so the awe-struck Angles of Norfolk and Suffolk noted on the cheek and shoulder of Fursa the scars of the burning inflicted upon him for a slight offence by the foul fiends whom he had seen in one of his visions; and they remembered how in the depths of winter, and though he was thinly clad, the sweat streamed down his face while he rehearsed the terrible story.

Thus then, in the fourth decade of the seventh century, East Anglia became Christian: and already in her history was manifested that extraordinary desire of men in high places to save their own souls at the cost of leaving their duties to their fellows unfulfilled, which was, it may be said, the glory and the shame of Anglo-Saxon Christianity. After two or three years of reigning, Sigebert abdicated in 634, received the tonsure, and retired to a monastery. He was succeeded by his cousin Egric, but ere the new king had been long on the throne, the terrible Penda (probably crossing the fens which separated the two kingdoms) invaded

* "A viro gentili nomine Ricberto" (Bede, Hist. Ecc., ii., 15).

East Anglia (637?). Some remembrance of Sigebert's capacity and valour in war seems to have dwelt in the minds of his late subjects, who saw themselves out-numbered by the Mercian hosts. They surrounded the monastery, and when their clamorous cries for Sigebert failed to draw him from his retirement, they pulled him out by main force and compelled him to place himself at their head. But he, mindful of his vow, refused to arm himself with any other weapon than a rod, and remained passive through all the tumult of the battle. He was slain and Egric with him; the East Anglian army was cut to pieces, and Penda, as usual, triumphed.

It will be observed, however, that in these inter-Anglian contests annexation scarcely ever follows victory. The conquered people choose another king, over whom the conqueror no doubt asserts some sort of supremacy, and all goes on as before. So was it now. Anna, the son of Eni, of the royal East Anglian stock, but how nearly related to Sigebert we are not informed, succeeded his kinsman and reigned for some seventeen or eighteen years (637–654). During this time, as we have seen, he gave shelter to the fugitive King of Wessex, Cenwalh, and converted him to Christianity. He is chiefly noted for his "saintly progeny" of daughters and granddaughters, some of whom married into the royal houses of Kent and Mercia, carrying thither their enthusiastic zeal for the propagation of the Christian faith, and nearly all of whom became eventually abbesses in Britain or Gaul. The reign of this excellent king came to an end about 654. It is scarcely necessary to state the cause of his death. He was slain, probably slain in battle, by the nearly octogenarian Penda. Thus had three kings of East Anglia as well as two kings of Northumbria fallen before the all-conquering Mercian. But the tale of his victories was well-nigh told. Let us turn back to consider what had been happening in Northumbria during the twelve years that had elapsed since the death of Oswald.

Two kings, as has been said, with perplexingly similar names, had been, perhaps by some tumultuary vote of their countrymen, raised to the two now separate Northumbrian thrones: Oswy, son of Ethelfrid, to reign in his great grandfather Ida's palace at Bamburgh, as king of Bernicia; Oswin, collateral descendant of Aelle and Edwin, to reign at York over Deira. Soon after his accession Oswy, who though only about thirty years of age, was a widower with at least two nearly grown-up children, sent a priest named Utta, "a man of much gravity and truth, and for that reason held in high honour even by princes," to solicit from the king of Kent the hand of his niece Eanfled, the exiled daughter of

Edwin of Deira. It was arranged that Utta should travel to Kent by land, but—perhaps from fear of robbers—he was to return with the maiden by sea. Before his departure the priest sought Aidan's blessing and prayers for his safe journey. The saint foretold that he would meet with contrary winds, rising to a tempest, but gave him a bottle of holy oil to cast upon the raging waters. All happened as Aidan had foretold. The ship in which Utta and his precious charge were embarked was assailed by a tremendous storm: no anchors would hold; the sailors, finding the ship beginning to fill with water from the waves that swept over her, gave themselves up for lost. Then the priest, remembering Aidan's gift, poured oil from his flask upon the waters and the sea ceased from its raging. Probably the violence of the storm has been somewhat exaggerated by the narrators; but it is interesting to note that modern seamanship does not disdain to use an expedient which in the seventh century was deemed miraculous. One object in Oswy's matrimonial alliance was doubtless that of strengthening his claim on the men of Deira by his union with Edwin's daughter. Another result which he perhaps did not foresee was the revival in an acuter form of the strife between the Roman and Celtic Churches for the possession of Northumbria, since Eanfled represented the Roman Christianity of Augustine and Paulinus, while Oswy, like Oswald, had learned in his youth the Christianity of the Hebrides which was represented by his friend the saintly Aidan.

It was probably more or less the aim of every Northumbrian king to reunite the two kingdoms over which Edwin and Oswald had ruled as one realm. Thus Oswy may from the beginning have seen with impatience the rival power of Oswin of Deira. The latter was a man dear alike to martial thane and to devout Churchman: "fair of face, tall of stature, pleasant of speech, courteous in manner, and open-handed both to the noble and to the base-born. This truly royal dignity of his, displayed both in his looks and in his actions, won for him the love of all, so that from nearly all the [other] provinces [of the land] men of noblest birth flocked to do him service."

To this kingly soul was conjoined the virtue, rare in kings, of humility, to illustrate which Bede tells a well-known story. It appears that Aidan, from his island home in Lindisfarne, now often extended his missionary journeys far and wide through Deira, and, though he made a point of travelling on foot, had accepted from Oswin the present of a horse to enable him to cross the manifold rivers of Yorkshire. Meeting one day a poor man who asked of him an alms, and having apparently no money in his scrip, he gave to the astonished beggar the horse with all its royal trappings, "for he was very pitiful, a nourisher of the poor and, so to speak, a father of the miserable." When the king heard this he very naturally asked the bishop the reason of his strange procedure. "I had specially chosen that horse for your use, and if it was a question of giving horses to beggars at all, I had others, much cheaper ones, in my stable which would have served your purpose as well." Hardly with justice Aidan answered: "What art thou saying, O King? Is my steed, the offspring of a mare, dearer to thee than that poor man, a son of God?" And thereupon they went into the palace to dine. The bishop sat apart in his own place; the king who had just come in from hunting stood at the fire with his courtiers warming himself. Suddenly the reproving words of the bishop darted into his soul. He ungirded himself of his sword, which he handed to a courtier, and hastening to the bishop fell at his feet and asked forgiveness, "for never henceforward will I cavil at any act of thine in giving from my treasures what thou wilt to the children of God." The bishop assured him of his forgiveness and bade him sit down joyfully to the feast. Oswin obeyed, and his merry laugh soon resounded through the hall, but the mantle of his late sadness fell upon Aidan who began to weep. "Why these tears, my father?" said a priestly companion in the Celtic speech which the men of Deira could not understand. "I know," answered the bishop, "that this king will not live long. I never saw so humble a prince, and this people is not worthy to have such a ruler."

Too soon were Aidan's forebodings justified. In the seventh year of Oswin's reign the disputes between the two Northumbrian kingdoms reached a head, and their armies met in the field near Catterick, in Yorkshire. Finding himself hopelessly out-numbered, Oswin dismissed his soldiers to their homes and fled to the house of one of his followers named Hunwald whom he believed to be a loyal friend. Unfortunately Hunwald betrayed him to Oswy, whose officer Ethelwin was admitted into the house by the treacherous host and slew Oswin, together with his faithful henchman, Tondheri, who had shared his flight. This deed, which was evidently considered no fair act of war, but a foul and detestable murder, took place at Gilling (near Richmond in Yorkshire), on August 20, 651. At the request of Queen Eanfled, Oswin's near kinswoman, a monastery was erected on the spot by Oswy as a sort of expiation of his crime. Prayers in that monastery were daily offered for the souls of the two kings, the murderer and the murdered, but the blot on Oswy's memory remained. Twelve days after the death of his royal friend and disciple (Aug. 31, 651), Aidan also died after having for seventeen years held the see of Lindisfarne. The shortness of the interval after Oswin's death, and the close connexion with that event in which it is mentioned by Bede, seem to authorise the conjecture that grief at this treacherous murder of a Christian prince by his professed brother in the faith may have hastened the death of the toil-worn prelate. He died, not at Lindisfarne, but at a certain villa regia "not far from the city," says Bede, "of which I have already spoken." It is generally assumed, perhaps too hastily, that this royal villa was on the site of the modern village of Bamburgh, close to the foot of the rock on the top of which stood undoubtedly both the palace and the town of Bebbanburh. A tent was spread for the dying saint contiguous to the church on its western side. He died leaning against a buttress of the church, and the lovers of miracles noticed that when the village and the church were wrapped in flames in the course of one of Penda's ravaging expeditions, this buttress against which the dying saint had leaned his head was the only part of the fabric which survived the conflagration.

The Northumbrian ravages of Penda may possibly have been of frequent occurrence. Besides that just mentioned there was at least one more in the lifetime of the saint, possibly soon after the death of Oswald. In this expedition also he sought by the aid of fire to achieve the conquest of the fortress which, in fact, remained impregnable till the invention of gunpowder. Destroying all the hamlets in the immediate neighbourhood of the royal city, he collected their ruins together, an immense mass of wooden beams, brushwood, straw-thatch and other inflammable materials, and piling them up against the lowest end of the cliff, waited for a favourable breeze to kindle his fire. It happened that at this time Aidan had retired from monastic Lindisfarne to the yet more solitary Farne Islands, where, but for the myriads of sea-fowl which resort thither in the breeding season, he could be alone with his Creator. Looking across the two miles of sea which separated him from Bamburgh, the saint saw clouds of smoke arising and balls of fire flying high over the castle walls. With hands and eyes uplifted towards heaven he cried: "See, O Lord, what ills Penda worketh." Thereat, says the legend, the wind changed, the flames beaten back from the fortress were driven upon the besiegers, who, with some of their number badly burned and all utterly affrighted, at once desisted from the siege of the city.

But there must have been peaceful intervals in the long duel between Mercia and Northumbria. In one of these intervals, Alchfrid, Oswy's son, sought and obtained the hand of Penda's daughter, Cyneburga, in marriage. This led to a similar request from Penda's son, Peada, King of the Middle Angles, for the hand of Alchfleda, daughter of Oswy. He was told that the only terms on which his suit could be successful were that he and all his people should receive the Christian faith. His brother-in-law, Alchfrid, strongly urged him to the same conclusion, and he consented to listen to the teaching of the Christian priests. When he heard of the promise of a heavenly kingdom, the hope of a resurrection and of future immortality, he declared that he would gladly accept such a religion as that, even though no virgin-bride was to be the prize of his conversion. He came in 653 with a long train of thegns, soldiers and servants, and was baptised by Finan, Aidan's successor, at a royal villa called Ad Murum, close to the Roman wall, and twelve miles from the sea. The conversion of Peada was followed by the mission of four priests to the Middle Angles, that is the inhabitants of Leicestershire. The preaching of these men, seconded by the royal influence, was most successful, and practically the whole of that tribe came over to the new faith. Mercia, properly so called, on the west of the country of the Middle Angles, was still heathen, but even there Penda did not prohibit the preaching of Christianity. He does not seem to have had any deep-rooted objection to the doctrine of the Nazarene, though it was not for him, the descendant of Woden, to worship a deity so unlike the gods of his fathers. He did not, however, conceal his hatred and contempt of those men who, professing the faith of Christ, did not bring forth works according thereto, saying that they were poor and despicable wretches who did not obey the God in whom they professed to believe.

At last when the old king was close upon his eightieth year, the ever-smouldering quarrel with Northumbria broke out again into flame. Oswy felt that the repeated raids of Penda must by some means be brought to an end. He offered quantities of costly royal ornaments as the price of peace, but in vain. Penda would give no promise to cease from ravaging. "Then," said he, "if the barbarian will not be mollified by our gifts, let us offer them to the Lord God as the price of victory." His daughter dedicated to sacred virginity; twelve estates given for the foundation of as many monasteries; these were his vows to the Most High, and having made these promises he moved forward with confidence to the war, though his army was much smaller than that of the enemy; though his young son, Egfrid, was a hostage in Penda's hands; though his nephew, Ethelwald, Oswald's son, who had been elected King of Deira, was apparently on the side of the enemy; and though Ethelhere, brother of the martyred Anna, now marched to battle in the host of the terrible pagan who had bound East Anglia to his chariot-wheels.* Alchfrid, son of Oswy, fought by his father's side, notwithstanding his affinity with Penda. If we may trust the fitful light of Nennius's history, Penda was again in this attack on Northumbria allied with the Britons, and Catgabail, King of Gwyneth, went with him to the war, but by a stealthy night march evaded the necessity of fighting.

The armies met on the banks of the Winwaed, possibly the Went, a stream in the West Riding of Yorkshire. The exaggerated traditions of a later day assigned to the Mercian king thirty regiments, each as large as the little army of Oswy, under the command of as many noble generals. Evidently, however, there was no little treachery in Penda's camp. The Welsh king, as we have seen, deserted on the night before the action. Ethelwald, in the hour of conflict, drew off his troops, and from a safe distance watched the event of the battle. Possibly there were others in the Mercian army who at heart sympathised with the Christian king. At any rate, Oswy won a signal victory (November 15, 655). Nearly all the thirty Mercian generals, including the East Anglian Ethelhere, were killed. Multitudes of fugitives were drowned in the waters of the Winwaed, swollen with autumnal rain. Most important of all, the octogenarian Penda, the slayer of five kings, perished in the fight, and with him fell the last hopes of English heathendom.

....

* In some way which is not explained, Ethelhere was himself "the author of the war". Possibly as suggested by Mr. Bates (Archæologia Aeliana, xix., 182–91), his marriage with a great niece of Edwin gave him some claim to the throne of Deira.

XI.

TERRITORIAL CHANGES—
THE CONFERENCE AT WHITBY—
THE GREAT PLAGUE

The victory by the Winwaed left Oswy undoubtedly the mightiest king in Britain. It may be convenient to enumerate here the chief territorial changes during the latter half of the seventh century which can be discerned between the succession of bishops and the miracles of saints that form naturally the chief subject of Bede's Ecclesiastical History.

1. Northumbria, at any rate after Oswy's victory, may have stretched along the eastern coast from Aberdeen or the Cromarty Firth nearly to the Wash. We are distinctly told that "he subdued the nation of the Picts or at least the largest part of them to the Anglian kingdom," and it is generally agreed that this must refer to the Picts north of the Firth of Forth, which was at this time the ordinary Anglian boundary. Southward, the dominions of which Oswy was overlord probably now included the whole of Yorkshire. It seems, however, to have been an accepted principle that when the overlord was king in Bernicia there must be an under-king in Deira. For seven years, as we have seen, the comely and gracious Oswin, either as equal colleague or as such under-king, reigned in Deira (644–51). After his murder and the consequent extinction of the direct male line of the descendants of Aelle, Oswald's son, Ethelwald, ruled over the southern kingdom. Did his dubious conduct on the battle-plain of the Winwaed fail to secure for him the favour of his victorious uncle? We cannot say, but it is an ominous circumstance that soon after that event he vanishes from the scene and is replaced by Alchfrid, son of Oswy by his first marriage. We have heard of this prince as assisting in the conversion of his brother-in-law, Peada, to Christianity; we have seen him fighting by his father's side against his father-in-law, Penda; we shall find him taking a leading part in the discussions about the date

of Easter and generally befriending the Roman party; but besides these facts we hear also of some action on his part, possibly in the way of overt rebellion, whereby he added to the "labours" of his father. Whatever the date of this rebellion, if such it were, after 664 we hear no more of Alchfrid.

The mystery, however, that hangs over the life and death of Alchfrid almost heightens the interest which is attached to a monument raised to his memory, the celebrated Bewcastle Cross. There in the midst of a wide and desolate moor, as desolate, perhaps, now as it was twelve hundred years ago, rises an obelisk fourteen and a half feet high, once surmounted by a cross which has now disappeared, bearing in Runic letters the sacred name "Gessus Christus" (so must our Anglian ancestors have spoken of the Saviour), and an inscription which, though not yet deciphered beyond dispute, certainly says that the stone was raised as a memorial of "Alchfrith, son of Oswy, and aforetime King." Other runes give us the names of Alchfrid's wife, Cyneburga, of her sister (?) Cyneswitha, and of her brother Wulfhere, King of Mercia. An inscription seems to record that it was reared in the first year of his brother Egfrid, that is in 670. This date gives additional interest to the quaint but not ungraceful specimens of Anglian art with which the obelisk is enriched, to the flowing tracery of vine-leaves and grape-clusters, the birds and dogs, the figures of John the Baptist and our Lord, and (in the lowest compartment of all) the standing figure of a man with a bird on his wrist, perhaps King Alchfrid himself with his falcon. Even should the reading of one line of the inscription, "Pray for his soul's great sin," prove too fanciful to be accepted by future students, we have in the other utterances of this monument enough to invest with a peculiar interest the name of Oswy's son and Penda's son-in-law.

After the death of this prince, two younger sons of Oswy are spoken of on somewhat doubtful authority as successively holding the position of Deiran under-kings. It seems clear that there was in the two provinces, Bernicia and Deira, a certain reluctance to coalesce, an unwillingness of each to submit to the king chosen by the other, which it is not difficult to understand. Whatever may have been its cause, this tendency to estrangement between its two great provinces had doubtless something to do with the early downfall of Northumbria.

The southern boundary of Oswy's kingdom was at this time a somewhat uncertain one. In the first place, what is now the county of Lincoln, or, as it was then called, Lindissi, was for generations the regular prize of war between Northumbria and Mercia. It was added to his dominions by the victorious Edwin, and if lost through his defeat by Penda, it was recovered by Oswald, but, as we have seen, so little was his yoke beloved that the monks of Bardney in Lincolnshire at first refused to give shelter to his bones. Under Penda it was doubtless again annexed to Mercia, and probably shared the fortunes of that middle kingdom until, between 671 and 675, it was recovered from Wulfhere, son of Penda, by Oswy's son and successor, Egfrid. It was once more regained for Mercia by Ethelred, probably about the year 679, and apparently never after owned the sway of a Northumbrian king.

2. After the victory of the Winwaed, Oswy seems to have been virtually master of Mercia. He continued his son-in-law, Peada, as under-king of Southern Mercia, that is the part of the kingdom south of the river Trent, but he apparently kept Northern Mercia in his own hands. In the spring of the following year, however, at the very time when the newly converted nation was celebrating the Easter festival, Peada was murdered, and dark suspicions prevailed that his young Christian wife was an accomplice in the crime. It is not hinted that Oswy himself had instigated the deed, but doubtless the horror of it added to the dislike with which the people of Mercia viewed the Northumbrian rule. Three years after old Penda's death, three of his veteran generals successfully conspired against the Northerner, brought out of his hiding-place a young son of their late master, named Wulfhere, whom they had till then successfully concealed, expelled Oswy's thanes, and restored the independence of the Mercian kingdom, apparently with its old boundaries. The new king Wulfhere was a zealous Christian—as indeed, strange to say, were all the children of Penda—and reigned for seventeen years well and gloriously (659–675). We hear of no attempt by Oswy to recover his supremacy over Mercia, although, as we have seen, his son did recover that shuttle-cock of battle, Lindsey. Wulfhere's chief wars seem to have been with the Kings of Wessex, over whom he won several victories. The extent of his power is most clearly shown by the fact that having formed a friendship with Ethelwalh, King of the South Saxons, and persuaded him to be baptised, he handed over to him the Isle of Wight and the district occupied by the Meonwaras in the east of Hampshire, which he had wrested from the King of Wessex. The son of Penda officiated as godfather to the new convert, whose example in accepting the Christian faith was followed by

many of his thanes and soldiers, but not as yet by the bulk of the South Saxon people.

3. Of political events in the kingdom of the East Angles in the period now under review, we find scarcely a trace. Shut off from the rest of England by the great fen-lands, which covered almost the whole of the modern counties of Cambridge and Huntingdon, East Anglia seems to have generally kept the even tenour of her own solitary way, which was at this time the way of holiness. If we may judge of the people from their rulers, we should be inclined to conjecture that, under the influence of the preaching of Felix and Fursa, this isolated district of England was passing through a phase of religious fervour like that which made its counties the stronghold of Lollardy in the fourteenth, and of Puritanism in the seventeenth centuries, sending at the latter period so many stern enthusiasts to fight in the new-modelled army of Cromwell. Of course, in the seventh century religious zeal took a direction which would have brought it into fierce collision with the Ironsides of Naseby and Marston Moor. All the fairest fruits of Christianity at this time were ripened in the cloister, and a monastic life seems to have had irresistible attractions for the ladies of the royal East Anglian race. King Anna, who, as we have seen, fell in battle against Penda in the year 654, left three daughters, two of whom were the wives of kings, but all of whom ended their lives as abbesses in a convent, and in the next generation two daughters of one of these saintly ladies (one of them also a queen consort) followed their mother's example.

4. Very different at one time was the religious history of the kingdom of the East Saxons, represented by the two modern counties of Essex and Middlesex. When we last heard of the affairs of this little kingdom Mellitus had been contemptuously driven forth from his episcopal seat in London because he refused to administer the white bread of the communion to the heathen sons of King Saberct (617?). Since that time a generation had passed away, and Essex was still heathen. The king now reigning in London—one of the many Sigeberts who about this time perplex the student of Anglo-Saxon pedigrees—was, we are told, a friend and a frequent visitor to Oswy of Northumbria. In the halls of Bamburgh and Ad Murum the conversation often turned on religious subjects; and "How," said the Northumbrian king, "can you think that these things are gods, which are made by the hands of men? You take a piece of wood or stone, and what is not needed for the purpose of idol-making you either

burn in the fire or shape into some common household utensil which, when it is done with, is pitched out of doors and trodden under foot of men. How can these things be divine? We must think of the true God as incomprehensible, unseen, omnipotent, eternal, the righteous ruler of the world, who does not dwell in perishable substances but has His eternal seat on high. We can understand, too, that the beings whom He has created, if they will learn His will and do it, shall receive from Him eternal rewards." Many dialogues of this kind at last produced an effect. The East Saxon king was baptised by Finan of Lindisfarne, Aidan's successor, at the same royal villa of Ad Murum which had witnessed the baptism of Peada, the Mercian. Returning to his own kingdom he sought to bring his subjects over to his new faith and sent to Oswy for a missionary (653). Hereupon Cedd, one of a family of zealous Northumbrian converts who had been preaching Christianity in Mercia, was recalled from his work in the Midlands and sent to Essex, where he carried on a most successful mission, was consecrated as bishop, and, apparently for the first time, founded the church of London on a secure basis. Sigebert, however, was slain after a reign of some years by two noblemen of his kindred who were offended by his meek submission to the counsels of the bishop, and after one intervening reign,* two kings named Sighere and Sebbi reigned over the East Saxons jointly, but always in subjection to the overlordship of Wulfhere, King of Mercia, whose "sphere of influence" evidently included all the south of England with the doubtful exception of Wessex.

The accession of these two kings probably took place soon after 660, but dates as well as accurate pedigrees are grievously wanting for all this portion of history. In 664 a terrible pestilence, which ravaged Essex as well as all the rest of England, shook the newly-born faith of the people and divided their rulers. Sighere and all his subjects openly apostatised from the faith of Christ, sought out the old half-ruined heathen fanes, and began once more to worship the idols replaced therein. Sebbi, on the other hand, and the men under his sway remained steadfast in their profession of Christianity. Nor does the relapse into heathenism of the other half of the kingdom seem to have been of long continuance. The zeal of the overlord Wulfhere soon remedied that error. He sent his Mercian bishop, Jaruman, on a mission to the East Saxons, the third which had been despatched to that wavering people, and Jaruman, backed by the authority of his sovereign, without much difficulty overturned once more the idol-altars

* That of Swithelm.

and brought back the recalcitrant East Saxons within the embraces of the Church. From this time onwards London, its bishops and its commerce become of ever-increasing importance in the pages of the historians.

5. The political history of Kent during this period offers little of interest. The king whose name figures most largely in the pages of Bede is Erconbert (640–64). He married Sexburh, daughter of Anna, one of the devout East Anglian family, and, partly perhaps owing to her influence, Church and State were more closely welded together in this than in any of the other kingdoms. "He was the first of all the English kings who by his princely authority ordered the idols throughout his kingdom to be abandoned and destroyed, and the fast of the forty days [of Lent] to be observed. And in order that these commands might be despised by none, he proclaimed fit and proper punishments against the transgressors." Thus in Kent we have reached the second stage in the establishment of Christianity, which is now no longer merely tolerated or approved by the sovereign but dominant and in a certain sense persecuting.

6. The obscure history of the South Saxon kingdom has been already touched upon in connexion with that of Mercia. Suffice it to remind the reader that under the protecting hand of the great Midland king, who evidently wished to make of this kingdom a counterpoise to the power of Wessex, it included not only the modern county of Sussex but also the Isle of Wight and a good deal of the east of Hampshire; and that though its royal family were Christian the bulk of the people remained idolators. This religious isolation of the South Saxon people is generally attributed to the fact already alluded to, that they were separated from the rest of England by the mighty forest of the Andredeswald, that "dark impenetrable wood" which yielded in later ages to the axes of the charcoal-burners of Sussex and Kent, so that the country which we call the Weald is now left comparatively bare and treeless. It is hard for us who now know the chief town of the coast of Sussex as virtually a suburb of London, to imagine the time when Sussex, isolated in its heathen barbarism, remained virtually another world to the inhabitants of Essex and Middlesex.

7. The history of the West Saxon kingdom, for which such a brilliant future was reserved in the coming generations, is for the seventh century obscure and uninteresting. Partly, of course, this may be accounted for by the fact that our one transcendent authority for this period, Bede, is himself a most patriotic Northumbrian, and cares little for distant Wessex. But even after

making allowance for this weighting of one of the scales, it is impossible not to recognise the fact that in the West Saxon line during the greater part of the seventh century we meet with no such powerful personalities as Edwin, Oswald, and Oswy, nor do we find there any symptoms which would have warranted a beholder in looking for the eventual appearance of the splendid figures of Alfred, Edward, and Athelstan.

As we have seen, the fortunes of Wessex in her conflict with Mercia were at this time generally unprosperous. In 628 there was the disastrous war with Mercia. Then came the preaching of Birinus, the baptism and death of Cynegils and his son, the accession of the still heathen Cenwalh and his expulsion by his enraged brother-in-law of Mercia. He returned, perhaps, on the invitation of his kinsman Cuthred, to whom he made an enormous grant of property (3,000 "lands" or hides) at Ashdown in Berkshire. Having embraced Christianity in his exile, he completed the conversion of Wessex to the new faith. Unsuccessful as he seems generally to have been in his wars with Mercia, he met with better fortune in his campaigns against the southern Britons. In 652 we are told that he fought—assuredly with the "Walas," though this is not expressly stated—at Bradford-upon-Avon. He thus apparently completed the conquest of Wiltshire, and it may well have been within a generation after Cenwalh's victory that Aldhelm, Abbot of Malmesbury, built that quaint little church, dedicated to St. Lawrence, which still stands overlooking the south-country Bradford, and which is nearly the best surviving monument of true Saxon architecture. Six years later (658) Cenwalh again fought with the Welsh at Peonnum (or the Pens, generally identified with Pensel Wood on the south-eastern border of Somerset), and this time we are distinctly told that he drove them as far as the river Parret. The larger half of the county of Somerset thus became definitively West Saxon, and the far-famed sanctuary of Glastonbury and the poetic valley of Avalon now owned the sway of a king who, though a Saxon, was also a Christian.

An important acquisition certainly: yet the very fact that it had still to be made, illustrates the extremely gradual character of the Saxon conquest of Britain. Two hundred years have now elapsed since the accepted date of the landing of Hengest, one hundred and seventy since Cerdic, one of the latest of the invaders, set foot on the shore of Southampton Water, and yet the West Saxons have only just crossed the Mendip Hills; nearly half of Somerset and the whole of Devonshire and Cornwall have yet to be won. The other records of the reign of Cenwalh relate to his battles, generally unsuccessful, with the Mercian kings. His fellow-Christian, young Wulfhere, ravaged what was left of West Saxon territory north of the Thames, as far as Ashdown. While the territory of Wessex had been in some degree growing towards the west, it was, as we have already seen, curtailed towards the east by the loss of the district of the Meonwaras and the Isle of Wight which were handed over by Wulfhere to Sussex. Altogether there was little in the fortunes of the West Saxon dynasty under Cenwalh, or under the obscure rulers who followed him, to betoken that the hegemony would one day be theirs. When towards the end of the century Caedwalla and Ine appear upon the scene, the prospect somewhat brightens, but the victories of the first and the laws of the second must be dealt with in a later chapter.

From this brief review of the relations of the various English kingdoms to one another towards the close of the seventh century, it will be abundantly evident how far we yet were from anything like national unity. There does not even seem to be any dawning feeling of fellowship of race. Angle wages with Angle and Saxon with Saxon a long and embittered warfare; and more than once a Mercian or West Saxon king avails himself of British help to win the victory over his kinsfolk. If Anglo-Saxon unity was at length obtained, and we know that it was not till far on in the tenth century that it was even approximately realised, this result was due undoubtedly to two great causes: the influence of the national Christian Church and the necessity of self-defence against the Scandinavian invaders. With the first of these causes alone we have here to deal. It cannot be doubted that zeal for their new-born Christian faith was already in some measure drawing the English kings together. When Oswald of Bernicia stood sponsor for West Saxon Cynegils, when his brother Oswy persuaded East Saxon Sigebert to forsake the follies of idolatry, a moral bond of union was formed, which might be developed into a political relationship. The consciousness of common interest in the Civitas Dei might well become, and eventually did become, a consciousness of fellow-citizenship in one great country.

In order however that the Church might exert this unifying influence on English politics it was essential that she should be of one mind herself; but at this time the unfortunate division between the Roman and the Celtic Churches on the utterly unimportant questions of the shape of the tonsure and the right calculation of Easter did much to prevent so desirable a consummation. Utterly unimportant they seem to us, and probably few ecclesiastics of any school of thought would now deny their triviality; but there is a well-known law of theological dynamics that the bitterness of feeling between rival Churches is in inverse proportion to the magnitude of the issues between them; and so it proved at this crisis. Owing to the different quarters from which the different English kingdoms had received their Christianity, the religious map of England was divided in the following manner. Kent and East Anglia were firm in their following of Rome. Wessex also, which had been won for Christianity by Birinus, was steadily, though perhaps not enthusiastically, Roman. Bernicia, till late in the reign of Oswy, clung firmly to the teachings of Iona. Deira seems to have been generally on the same side, though the remembrance of the teaching of Paulinus, kept alive, as it was, by the teaching of his follower James the Deacon, had probably modified the strength of its Celticism; and Alchfrid the king, influenced by the persuasions of his friend Cenwalh, King of Wessex, had embraced with fervour the party of Rome. Mercia and Essex, both of which had been evangelised by Northumbrian missionaries, seem to have been somewhat half-hearted in their adherence to the Celtic traditions.

Such being the condition of things, Oswy, in conjunction with his son and colleague, Alchfrid, convoked in the year 664 a synod at Streanæshalch to discuss the thorny question of the difference between the Churches. The place was well fitted to be the scene of a memorable meeting. Its Saxon name, which, according to Bede, signified lighthouse-bay, well indicates that conspicuous cliff on the Yorkshire coast which we now know so well by the more common-place name of Whitby, given to it some three centuries later by its Danish destroyers and rebuilders. Hither, to this wind-beaten rock, had the holy Hilda, great-niece of Edwin of Deira, removed her convent from the more northern Hartlepool; and here she dwelt, ruling her double monastery of monks and nuns in all gentleness and purity, while the little Elfleda, Oswy's youngest daughter, whom he had vowed to God on the eve of his great battle with Penda, was growing up under her tuition into all the virtues of a perfect nun, and preparing to take her place one day as abbess of the convent. To the student of English literature Whitby monastery is for ever memorable as the home of the first English poet, Caedmon, who there, while sitting in the cow-byre, received the command from a heavenly visitor to sing "the beginning of things, the going forth out of Egypt, the suffering and the resurrection of the Lord."

At this place, then, all that was eminent for holiness in the infant Church of Northumbria came together to discuss the then all-important question of the true date for the keeping of Easter. However uninteresting from a religious point of view this question may now appear, the practical inconvenience of its unsettled condition was clearly seen in the household of King Oswy. Here was he, following the Celtic usage, celebrating his Easter feast on the fourteenth day of the lunar month which included the vernal equinox, while his wife, Eanfled, daughter of Edwin and granddaughter of Ethelbert of Kent, refused to recognise as a possible Easter any Sunday earlier than the fifteenth of the same month. Hence it might possibly happen, nay, in the very next year after the council it actually would have happened, that in the very same palace the king would be celebrating Easter Sunday with all the feasting and the gladness which were considered the suitable accompaniments of the day of the Lord's resurrection, while the queen and all the holy men and women of her party would be sitting in the sadness of Lent preparing to follow in imagination the Dolorous Way by which on the successive days of Passion week the Saviour would be led up to the crowning grief of Calvary. The difference, as the fair-minded Bede is careful to explain, was not the same as that which separated the so-called Quarto-decimans from the Western Church, and which was finally condemned at the Council of Nicæa. That party, adhering strictly to the Jewish usage, celebrated Easter at the same time as the old Passover on "the fourteenth day of the first month," on whatever day of the week that day might happen to fall. Not so, however, with the sons of Iona. Columba, Aidan and all the saints of the old Celtic Church remembered the Crucifixion on a Friday and the Resurrection on a Sunday, whether those days fell on the fourteenth or sixteenth of the lunar month or not. Thus the correct date for the Christian seasons for both parties had to be arrived at by a compromise between the week reckoning and the month reckoning; the only question at issue being the form of that compromise and the limits of permitted deviation. The Celt contended that the pendulum must swing between the fourteenth and the twentieth days of the moon's age; while the Roman ecclesiastic allowed it to swing only between the fifteenth and the twenty-first. A small difference truly to cause such long and heated arguments, yet, as we have seen, where a house was divided against itself on this question, it might occasion no little practical inconvenience.

There was much that was illogical and unscientific in the arguments on both sides of the controversy. The fathers from Iona were fond of appealing to the authority of the beloved Apostle John, which, so far as it proved anything, proved not their contention but that of the old, universally condemned Quarto-decimans. The supporters of the Roman usage loudly asserted the necessity of following St. Peter, who certainly cannot be proved, nor can with much probability be even conjectured, to have ever expressed an opinion on the point at issue between the Churches. Much stress did they also lay on the unchanging custom of the Roman Church, whereas that Church had in fact shown its good sense by modifying its calendar in some important particulars in deference to the calculations of the more scientific fathers of Alexandria. Doubtless the real arguments, appealing to the heart rather than to the head, were on the one side the remembrance of saintly Christian lives, such as those of Columba and Aidan, producing a natural reluctance to admit that such men had lived and died in grievous error; and on the other side a feeling of impatience that the inhabitants of a few rocky islands in the wild Atlantic should set their judgment against the richly endowed and stately Churches of Paris, Arles and Vienne, of Milan and of Rome.

On the Celtic side of the controversy were ranged the saintly Hilda herself, and Colman, Bishop of Lindisfarne, who, after the short intervening episcopate of Finan, had succeeded to the dignity held by the universally venerated Aidan. It was probably hoped, too, that King Oswy would be a stout defender of the usages which he and his brothers had learned in their long boyish banishment at Iona. On the other side, eager for union with Canterbury and Rome, stood Eanfled, the queen, and her step-son, Alchfrid of Deira. There, too, was James the Deacon, the follower of Paulinus, who for thirty-one years had maintained the cause of Roman Christianity in Deira. Highest in ecclesiastical rank on this side was Agilbert the Frank, Bishop of Dorchester, a learned man who had studied for some years in Ireland—then a great centre of theological study—but had apparently not cared to add the knowledge of Anglo-Saxon to his other accomplishments, for we are told that Cenwalh, King of Wessex, once his friend and admirer, growing weary at length of his "barbarous" way of talking, planted down at Winchester a rival bishop who could talk with him in Saxon. This gave Agilbert such offence that he resigned his diminished see of Dorchester, and returned to Gaul, where he was appointed Bishop of Paris. That migration was, however, yet in the future, and it was still as Bishop of the West Saxons, though possibly of the divided see, that Agilbert appeared to support his sovereign's friend, Alchfrid, in the great controversy. The hint about Agilbert's "barbarous" Frankish language is especially interesting to the philologer as showing how widely the language of the Franks, probably from its admixture with degenerate Latin, was beginning to diverge from the kindred Anglo-Saxon. Two generations previously at the court of Ethelbert, the Kentish courtiers seem to have conversed without difficulty with the companions of their Frankish queen.

When all were seated, King Oswy arose and made a speech on the need for unity of practice between men who were all seeking the same heavenly kingdom. Let them inquire which was the true rule for the calculation of Easter, and all follow that. He then called on his own bishop, Colman, to set forth the reason for his rule. Colman replied with the usual reference to the holiness of his predecessors and to the authority of the beloved Apostle John. Bishop Agilbert being called upon to reply, acutely conscious of his inability to speak in the English tongue, prayed that the task of replying might be assigned to one of his disciples, named Wilfrid the presbyter, who fully shared all his opinions and could clearly set them forth in the king's own language without the intervention of an interpreter.

Herewith there stepped on to the stage of English history an actor who was never to be long absent thence through more than forty troublous years. Wilfrid, who was now about thirty years of age, was the son of a Northumbrian thegn, a youth brought up in the rude luxury of a rich Anglian's hall, with horses, armour and goodly raiment at his disposal; but at the age of fourteen a harsh step-mother in his home, and some instinct of aspiration after a holier life, sent him to Lindisfarne, where he learned much, but gradually became dissatisfied with the Celtic position of isolation from Rome. Queen Eanfled, encouraging his disaffection, assisted him to visit the court of her cousin, Erconbert of Kent, from whence in his twentieth year he set out for Rome. On his way through Gaul the bright and handsome Northumbrian had offers of worldly preferment and a rich marriage from the Archbishop of Lyons, but refusing all such worldly advantages, he pressed on to "the tombs of the apostles." Though to the reader of the pontifical annals, Rome in the middle of the seventh century, with its Monotheletic controversy and its Lombard wars, may not seem a very inspiring theme, it is clear that the great world-city, with its stately ruins and statelier church-organisation, exerted a powerful fascination over the mind of the young Northumbrian, and during all the rest of his life we find him, like another Loyola, staunch in his resolve to live or die for the defence of the Holy See. He learned from a certain Archdeacon Boniface "the daily lessons from the four gospels, the reasonable mode of calculating Easter, and many other things relating to the discipline of the Church of which he had been ignorant in his own country," and then returning through Gaul he again visited his friend, the Archbishop of Lyons, and received from him the monastic tonsure. The archbishop was still minded to make him his heir, and apparently with some such expectation Wilfrid remained for three years in attendance upon him. By one of those reverses of fortune to which the courtier-prelates of Merovingian Gaul were frequently subject, Wilfrid's patron lost both office and life, and Wilfrid himself narrowly, and only on account of his foreign origin, escaped sharing his doom.* Returning at last (in 658), after long wanderings, to his native Deira, he there found Alchfrid reigning, a man like-minded with himself in his preference of Rome to Iona. He settled eventually in a monastery at Ripon, from which Eata, friend and pupil of Aidan, had been expelled on account of his adherence to the Celtic usages by the hotly partisan king. Here Wilfrid, a year before the convocation of the synod, had been ordained as priest by Bishop Agilbert and installed as abbot of the monastery, which seems to have been to the end of his days the most dearly loved of his homes.

Such was the man, already well versed in the Paschal controversy, and deeply tinged with the Roman and Gaulish contempt for the religion of the Hebrides, to whom the grateful task was assigned of demolishing the arguments of Colman. "The Easter which we observe," said he, "is that which I myself have seen celebrated at Rome, home and burial-place of the two great apostles. Wheresoever I journeyed, intent on learning and on prayer, throughout Italy and Gaul I found this feast celebrated. This feast, Africa, Asia, Egypt, Greece, nay, and the whole Christian world through all its various nations and languages do observe, save only these two obstinate nations, the Picts and the Britons (inhabitants of the two furthest isles in the ocean and of only a part even of them), who do with stupid energy strive against the opinion of the whole world." So spoke the haughty, foreign-fashioned ecclesiastic; and when we have heard this first tactless utterance of his, we are the better able to understand why

* The whole of this story about the so-called Dalfinus, Archbishop of Lyons, as related by Wilfrid's biographer is encompassed with historical difficulties. See Bright's Early English Church History, pp. 218 ff. (3rd ed.).

all the forty years of his episcopate were more or less passed in strife. Colman plaintively asked if Wilfrid would call the blessed apostle John stupid. Wilfrid replied that St. John like St. Paul might do many things to conciliate Jewish prejudice, and that after all, his usage being that of the earlier Quarto-decimans, did not coincide with the Celtic Easter which must always fall on a Sunday. "No," he ended, "you who shut out the 21st day of the moon from your calculation, agree neither with John nor with Peter, neither with the Law nor with the Gospel."

The debate then drifted off into a discussion of "the cycle of Anatolius,"* and an appeal by Colman to the virtues of Columba and his successors who had kept the Celtic Easter. "Surely," he pleaded, "the miracles which they had wrought showed that their teaching was acceptable in the sight of God." "I do not deny," answered Wilfrid, "that these men of whom you thus speak were God's servants. I think that if any Catholic calculator had come to them and taught them the better way, they would have obeyed his monitions. And however holy your, or I would rather say our, Columba may have been, however mighty in signs and wonders, can you prefer his authority to that of the blessed Prince of the Apostles, to whom the Lord said, 'Thou art Peter, and on this rock I will build My Church, and the gates of hell shall not prevail against it, and I will give thee the keys of the kingdom of heaven'?" As Wilfrid made this closing quotation the king turned to Colman and said: "Is it true that these words were spoken by the Lord to Peter?" "It is true, O king!" was the answer. "Can you produce any instance of a similar power conferred on your Columba?" "We have none," answered Colman. Said the king: "Do both parties agree without controversy on this point, that these words were spoken pre-eminently to Peter and that to him the keys of heaven were granted by the Lord?" Both answered: "We do." Thereupon the king thus announced his conclusion: "Then I say to you that this is the door-keeper whom I am loth to contradict, and whose ordinances I desire to obey to the utmost of my power, lest haply when I arrive at the doors of the kingdom there shall be none to open them unto me if I have lost the favour of him who keeps the keys thereof."

The Bernician king evidently conceived of heaven as of a Northumbrian palace hall: and not unnaturally he, who knew his hands to be stained with the blood of his gracious kinsman Oswin, desired to enlist the sympathies of the most powerful patron possible on his side against the

* An attempt to arrange the recurrences of Easter in a cycle of 19 years.

day when he should have to plead for entrance therein. Oswy's decision was, of course, final. All over Northumberland the Roman customs as to Easter and the tonsure now prevailed. Bishop Colman, who could not reconcile himself to the new ways, abdicated his see and returned to Iona, accompanied by all the Irish monks from Lindisfarne and by thirty Anglian brethren who shared their opinions. From Iona he afterwards went to Ireland and founded a monastery on an island off the coast of Mayo, which had not a very successful career. Cedd, bishop of the East Saxons, who had acted as interpreter and to some extent as mediator between the two parties, accepted the decision of the synod, and returned to enforce it in London and the rest of his diocese. Everywhere now throughout Teutonic Britain unity with Rome was established, and little more than a century elapsed before all the Celtic communities in Iona, in Ireland, even in sturdy recalcitrant Wales, had adopted the Roman Easter and the coronal tonsure.*

The change was one which probably ought upon the whole to be considered beneficial. Unity was the thing now most needed, both politically and ecclesiastically, and unity had to be achieved by the State through the Church. It was, therefore, well that this pebble, which broke the full flow of the stream towards unity, should be removed out of the way by the synod of Whitby. It was well, also, that there should be no hindrance to free and full intercourse between the ecclesiastics of England and those of the continent. True, the civilisation of Italy and Gaul in the seventh century was nothing to boast of. To Cicero or to Marcus Aurelius it would have seemed like barbarism: but it was superior to the barbarism of the Saxon, perhaps in some respects superior even to the undoubtedly high civilisation, at this time, of Celtic Tara and Armagh. Still it was not all gain that resulted from the decision of the synod of Whitby and the rupture of the spiritual bond that had bound Lindisfarne to Iona. Even Bede, with all his loyalty to Rome and abhorrence of the Celtic Easter, seems to feel this fact; else why does he introduce just at this point an eloquent panegyric on the simple life of Colman and his predecessors, their genuine poverty and the faithfulness with which they at once handed to the poor any money which they received from the rich? "At that time the religious habit was held in great veneration, so that wheresoever cleric or monk appeared, he was joyfully welcomed by all as the servant of God;

* The southern Irish conformed in 634; the northern Irish in 692; the northern Picts, 710; the monks of Iona, 716; the Britons in Wales, 768.

those who met him on the road with bent necks rejoiced to receive the blessing of his lips or of his extended hand: they listened eagerly to his words of exhortation. The priests and clerics of that day had no care for anything else but preaching, baptising, visiting the sick—in a word, for the salvation of souls. So utterly were they delivered from the poison of avarice, that no one of them would receive land or presents even for the building of monasteries, unless absolutely compelled to do so by secular rulers." In these and similar sentences Bede hints at the degeneracy of his own times and seems to mourn that more of the spirit of Iona had not lingered in the Anglian Church. In Columba, Aidan, Colman and their disciples, as has been already said, we seem to see something of that absolute indifference to wealth, that kinship with Nature and her children, that almost passionate love for Poverty and the Poor which, six centuries later, was to shed a halo round the head of Francis of Assisi. These men were zealous missionaries, "humble and holy men of heart": the men who were about to replace them in the organised and regularly affiliated Church, though by no means devoid of missionary zeal, nor of the spirit of self-denial, were before all, great ecclesiastics and lordly rulers of the Church.

The year 664 which witnessed the assembling of the synod at Whitby was, for other reasons, a sadly memorable one to the English nation. In that year, on May 1, there was a total eclipse of the sun, and this, to the unscientific minds of our ancestors, seemed to be in some mysterious way connected with a terrible visitation of pestilence which, apparently in the summer and autumn, swept over our island, beginning at the southern shore and from thence passing northward till it reached Northumbria, and crossed over into Ireland; everywhere carrying off multitudes of people. On July 14, Erconbert, King of Kent, and Deusdedit, archbishop, both died within a few hours of each other, apparently smitten by the pestilence. Later on, probably in the same year, Tuda, the new Bishop of Lindisfarne, and Cedd, the interpreter-bishop of the Whitby synod, fell victims to the same wide-wasting enemy. We have already had occasion to notice the effect which this terrible calamity had in causing many of the East Saxons to relapse for a time into idolatry. The stories concerning the plague with which Bede crowds his pages are generally of the edifying death-bed sayings uttered by its victims and the visions of supernal bliss vouchsafed to them before their departure. Intent on these spiritual aspects of the visitation, and not sparing his readers one of the miracles which he had heard of as marking its course, Bede has not recorded any of its physical symptoms as Thucydides has done in his memorable description of the Plague of Athens. We learn, however, from other sources* that it was intensely infectious, that one of the symptoms was inflamed swellings, and that the faces of the patients were tinged with a ghastly yellow colour. Probably, therefore, it belonged to the same type of disease as the yellow fever which is now so suddenly fatal in tropical countries. We perceive from Bede's narrative that its force was not expended by the visitation of 664, but that it returned at intervals during the next twenty years, and that there was one outbreak of especial violence in the year 686 from which Bede's own monastery of Jarrow suffered severely. The coadjutor-abbot Eosterwine of the sister convent of Wearmouth died of the plague in his thirty-seventh year; and at Jarrow the pestilence carried off all the monks who could read or preach or sing the antiphons, save only the abbot Ceolfrid and one little boy whom he had trained. The old man and the child kept up an abridged form of the daily service without the antiphons for one week. Then, as the tears of Ceolfrid had almost prevented him from taking part in this mutilated service, they summoned up courage to sing the whole psalter through, antiphons and all, till at last a full choir had been trained to help them to bear the burden. It is generally believed, though it cannot be proved, that the little boy who thus officiated with Ceolfrid was Bede.

In reading Bede's Ecclesiastical History it is impossible not to be struck with the especial severity wherewith the plague raged in the monasteries both of men and women. At Lindisfarne, at Ely, at Wearmouth and Jarrow, at Carlisle, at Barking and at Lastingham in the East Riding of Yorkshire, the plague committed great ravages, often carrying off nearly all the inmates. The manager of a modern school or hospital will not be surprised at this, when he remembers that the monastic rule enjoined the use of woollen garments and prohibited linen; that the more ascetically disposed monks or nuns washed themselves only three or four times in the year; and that the monks lay down to rest in the same woollen garments and with the same unloosed shoes which they had worn and in which they had worked throughout the day. This self-denial, especially in the sons and daughters of princely houses, sprang from a noble motive: it had been perhaps originally ordained as a protest against the luxurious life of the young Roman nobility for whom

* Chiefly Celtic. See Bright's Early English Church History, p. 237, n. 2.

The Bath and Wine and Women made up life.

But it was none the less a calamity for Europe that an unnatural and unneeded divorce should have been made between Christianity and cleanliness. Sanitary science, during the long medieval centuries and even for some time after they had ended, had little chance of making its way in the world. Exactly one thousand years after the pestilence of 664 were felt the first foreboding symptoms of the Great Plague of London.

*****

There is little else to record as to the reign of Oswy of Bernicia after the departure of the ecclesiastics from Whitby. In consequence of the death of Archbishop Deusdedit, the two Kings of Northumbria and Kent took counsel "concerning the state of the English Church" (this joint action of North and South in an ecclesiastical matter was itself an important event), and decided to send one of the late archbishop's clergy named Wighard to Rome that he might there be consecrated as his successor. This step was taken probably in the year 667, and though at the time unsuccessful, for Wighard and nearly all his companions died of pestilence soon after their arrival in Rome, it led to important results.

Towards the end of his reign Oswy suffered from declining health. Like so many other kings and ecclesiastics of Anglo-Saxon stock, he desired to go to Rome and, if it might be, end his days there, and he would fain have had Wilfrid, now a consecrated bishop, as guide of his journey. With this view he offered large moneys to the young ecclesiastic—the very offer seems to show the difference between Wilfrid's character and Aidan's—but apparently the disease made too rapid progress for the fulfilment of his design. The journey to Rome had to be abandoned; Oswy died on February 15, 671,* and Egfrid his son, son of Eanfled and grandson of Edwin of Deira, reigned in his stead.

* For the reasons for dating Oswy's death in 671 rather than a year earlier according to the text of Bede, see Plummer's note on H. E., iv., 5.

XII.

KING EGFRID AND THREE GREAT CHURCHMEN: WILFRID THEODORE, CUTHBERT

The purely political events of the reign of Egfrid, as far as we know them, are soon told. Coming to the throne, as we have seen, in the year 671, he reigned for fourteen years. At the very beginning of his reign he gained (says Wilfrid's biographer) a great victory over "the bestial hordes of the Picts who, chafing at their subjection to the Saxons and hoping to throw off the yoke of servitude," mustered "like a swarm of ants under the leadership of an audacious chieftain named Bernhaeth, but were attacked by Egfrid at the head of his cavalry and utterly routed. So great was the slaughter that two rivers were filled with the corpses of the slain, and the victorious Northumbrians passed dry-shod over them in pursuit of the foe." About four years later, apparently, Egfrid fought Wulfhere, King of the Mercians, defeated him and put him to flight, and thus won back that debatable land, the province of Lindsey. In 679 he fought a great battle on the banks of the Trent with Ethelred, Wulfhere's brother and successor, who had married his sister Osthryd. The victory in this battle perhaps remained doubtful, but it brought sore distress in its train, for in it fell Egfrid's brother Alfwin, under-king of Deira, a youth eighteen years of age, who was, we are told, "much beloved by both provinces." It seemed as though this calamity would cause the flame of war to burn more fiercely than ever between the Northumbrian and the Mercian kings, but the Archbishop Theodore interposed his peaceful counsels. The amount of wergeld to be paid as compensation for the death of Alfwin was arranged by him. Lindsey was probably handed back to Mercia, and a treaty of peace, which remained unbroken for many years, was concluded between the two kingdoms.

In the year 684, against the advice of St. Cuthbert and all his best counsellors, King Egfrid, for reasons which we can only conjecture, sent an army to Ireland and "miserably wasted that harmless nation which hath ever been most friendly to the nation of the English; so that not even churches and monasteries were spared by the hostile band." The Irish defended themselves to the best of their ability, but had at last to take refuge in curses and prayers to heaven for vengeance, the answer to which, in the opinion of the English historian, was not long in coming. For in the next year Egfrid, again refusing to listen to Cuthbert's counsels, rashly ventured on an expedition against the Picts dwelling north of the Firth of Forth. The enemy, feigning flight, drew him into the recesses of the mountainous country, then turned and fell upon him, cutting the greater part of his army to pieces and slaying the king himself. The scene of this battle, which was fought on May 20th, 685, is not mentioned by Bede, but is given by other authorities as Nechtansmere or Nechtan's Fort (Dûin Nechtan), and is identified with Dunnichen, about five miles east of Forfar.

By the battle of Nechtansmere Northumbria's fair prospects of permanently holding the hegemony of the English states were for ever destroyed. "From that time," says Bede, "the hopes and the manhood of the Anglian [Northumbrian] kingdom began to dissolve and to fall into ruin. For the Picts recovered the lands once possessed by them, which the Angles had held; also the Scots [men of Dalriada] who were in Britain, and a considerable part of the Britons recovered their freedom. Many of the English nation were slain with the sword, or bound to slavery or else escaped by flight from the land of the Picts." Among the latter was Trumwine, the Northumbrian Bishop of Abercorn on the Forth, who fled from his see and had to beg for an asylum for himself and his followers from the monks of Whitby. Apparently the result of this battle was the loss by Northumbria of all the territory north of the Cheviots and the Solway as well as of the southern part of the kingdom of Strathclyde. The Northumbrian kingdom survived indeed for some centuries and even recovered for a short time some part of its lost territories, but it survived for the most part in a maimed and enfeebled condition like the Athenian state after the battle of Aegospotami. The prestige of the kingdom was gone; no more did any great Bretwalda issue his commands to subject princes from his rock-built palace at Bamburgh; and soon anarchy and intestine feuds completed the ruin which had been begun on the fatal day of Nechtansmere.

Such, as has been here indicated, is the short and disastrous political history of Egfrid's reign; but to understand its true significance we must devote some attention to the biography of three great churchmen whose lives were closely intertwined with that of the Northumbrian king. They are:—

Wilfrid, who lived from 634 to 709; Theodore, who lived from 602 to 690; and Cuthbert, who lived from 630 to 687.

After Bishop Colman, disheartened by the defeat of his party in the synod of Whitby, had left Northumbria and returned to Iona, an Irishman named Tuda, an advocate for the Roman Easter, was consecrated as his successor, but, as has been said, died almost immediately afterwards, a victim to the plague which was ravaging England. On his death there was a discussion between the Northumbrian kings and the Wise Men of the kingdoms who should be elected to the vacant see. The choice naturally fell on Wilfrid, the champion of the Roman cause, young, noble and victorious. At the same time it seems to have been generally agreed that the seat of the episcopate should be removed from sea-girdled Lindisfarne, too full perhaps of the memories of Iona, to York, the capital of Deira, the city whose walls and palaces, even in their ruin, testified to the greatness of that Rome with whom Northumbria was now entering into such full and perfect fellowship. Objecting, however, that it was difficult to find in Britain bishops to perform the act of consecration, who were not more or less tainted with what he called the heresy of the Quarto-decimans, Wilfrid begged that he might be sent to Gaul to receive consecration there from bishops in undoubted communion with the Roman see. The kings consented: a ship, a retinue of attendants and a large store of money were placed at Wilfrid's disposal that so the new bishop (whose preference through life was always strongly marked for the gorgeous and the stately) "might arrive in very honourable style in the region of Gaul." The journey was successfully performed: a great assembly of twelve bishops was convened at Compiègne (664); among them Agilbert, late bishop of Dorchester, now of Paris, Wilfrid's ally at the Whitby synod, doubtless now rejoicing at finding himself once more among men to whom his speech was not strange. These men received Wilfrid in the presence of all the people with demonstrations of high honour: they made him sit on a golden chair which was then, according to their usual custom, lifted on high and borne by the hands of bishops alone into the oratory, while hymns and canticles sounded through the choir.

Were the stately ceremonies and the well-furnished episcopal dwellings of Merovingian Gaul too attractive to the æsthetic soul of Wilfrid, and was he loth to return to the rude wooden churches and the rough untrained psalmody of his fatherland? This can only be conjectured, but it seems certain that he committed one of the great errors of his life by lingering too long, certainly for more than a year, in Gaul, instead of returning at once to Northumbria and there beginning his episcopal career. At last, in the year 666, he set sail for England, accompanied, says his biographer, by 120 armed retainers besides his clerical followers. The clergy sang loud their psalms, to cheer the arms of the rowers, but in the midst of their psalmody a mighty tempest arose and drove them on the coast of Sussex. The inhabitants, still heathen and barbarous, flocked to the stranded vessel and began to strip it of its treasures and to divide its passengers among them as their slaves. Wilfrid offered them money and spoke words of peace and conciliation, but the natives proudly answered, "All is ours that the sea throws up on the shore." Meanwhile, a priest of the Saxon idolatry, standing on a high mound near the shore, ceased not to curse the Christian strangers and sought by his magic arts to render vain their efforts for deliverance. At last one of Wilfrid's companions flung a stone—"a stone," says his biographer, "blessed by all the people of God"—which hit the high priest on the head and wounded him to the death. His fall discouraged the South Saxons; the 120 soldiers fought bravely with the much larger forces of their foes; Wilfrid and his clergy prayed like Moses, Aaron and Hur upon the mountain; the Saxons were thrice repulsed, and at length victory, cheaply earned by the loss of five of Wilfrid's followers, crowned the exertions and the prayers of the Northumbrians. A miraculously early tide floated the vessel off the shore and she reached Sandwich without further misadventure.

But when at last Wilfrid reached his diocese, he found unpleasant tidings awaiting him there. Weary of his long delay, King Oswy had appointed Bishop Ceadda (famous in English hagiology as St. Chad) to the bishopric of York. The act was certainly irregular, and Wilfrid had good cause to complain, but with more meekness than might have been looked for, he accepted the rebuff and retired to his dearly loved monastery of Ripon, a place which more than all others, except perhaps Hexham, was enriched by his labours and preserves his memory. Moreover, at the request of Wulfhere of Mercia and Egbert of Kent he undertook some volunteer episcopal work in those two kingdoms, travelling about with his band of singers, masons, and teachers of every kind of art, and everywhere founding monasteries or reforming them according to the strict rule of St. Benedict which he had minutely studied at Canterbury.

After three years this parenthesis in Wilfrid's life came to an end, owing to the intervention of the new archbishop, Theodore, to whose history we now turn. We have seen that the Kings of Northumbria and Kent, taking counsel together after the death of Archbishop Deusdedit, sent Wighard to Rome as the bearer of their request that he might be consecrated archbishop, and that after their arrival in Rome Wighard and nearly all of his companions fell victims to the pestilence then raging in the Eternal City. Thereupon the Pope, Vitalian, whose courage and skill had already been displayed on the occasion of the unwelcome visit of the Emperor Constans to Rome, deliberated anxiously with his council on the question whom he should send as archbishop to Canterbury in place of the dead Englishman. After some hesitation and two refusals of the dignity, his choice fell upon Theodore, a learned Greek monk, who was at that time living in Rome and who had possibly come over to Italy in the train of the Emperor Constans. Theodore, who was, like the apostle Paul, a native of Tarsus in Cilicia, was now sixty-six years of age, and dreaded not so much the duties of the office as the hardships of the long journey to a remote and chilly island. However, the abbot, Hadrian, an African, who had himself refused the offered dignity and had recommended Theodore to the Pope, volunteered to accompany his friend, having already twice made the journey through Gaul; and Vitalian, who seems to have entertained some groundless fear as to the perfect orthodoxy of this Greek monk on the great question of the Monothelete controversy, gladly consented to this arrangement. But however free Theodore might be from Greek errors of doctrine, the fashion of his tonsure, which professed to be after the example of St. Paul, and which consisted in the shaving of the whole head, declared but too plainly to the world his Greek origin. He had therefore, after being ordained sub-deacon, to wait four months till his hair had grown sufficiently to enable him to receive the Roman tonsure, which made a crown of baldness on the top of the head. He was then consecrated archbishop by Vitalian, and set forth on May 27, 668, with his friend Hadrian for his distant diocese. His journey through Gaul seems to have been performed in a very leisurely manner, and we are expressly told that he tarried for a long time with Agilbert, by whom he was cordially received, and with whom he doubtless had much conversation concerning affairs on the other side of the channel. Meanwhile Egbert, King of Kent, being informed of the events which had happened at Rome, sent his "prefect" Radfrid to escort

Theodore into his kingdom. But notwithstanding this special embassy, we are told—and the information throws a curious light on the European politics of the time—that Ebroin, the all-powerful mayor of the palace, would not permit Hadrian to accompany his friend, because he suspected that he was the bearer of some message from the Emperor to the kings of Britain, which might be adverse to the interests of the Frankish kingdom. It is with some surprise that we learn that a statesman of the seventh century contemplated the possibility of a combination of England and Constantinople against France. After a time Ebroin, having satisfied himself that no secret embassy such as he feared had ever formed part of Hadrian's instructions, permitted him to follow Theodore, by whom he was made abbot of the great monastery of St. Peter and St. Paul at Canterbury, the Westminster Abbey of the Kentish kingdom.

Theodore of Tarsus arrived at Canterbury and was enthroned there on May 27, 669, thus commencing a memorable career, which lasted for more than twenty-one years. "Soon," says Bede, "having traversed the whole island wherever the tribes of the English abode, and being heartily welcomed and listened to by all, he spread abroad the right way of living and the canonical rule for the celebration of Easter; Hadrian everywhere appearing as his companion and helper. For he was the first of the archbishops to whom the whole Church of the English agreed to give the hand of fellowship." We see at once how great a step towards national unity, at least as far as the English people was concerned, was taken under the guidance of this Oriental stranger, who came from under the shadow of Mount Taurus. Unfortunately there is no evidence that he did anything to break down the middle wall of partition which the arrogance of Augustine had raised between the English and the Welsh Churches; while, to the yet unreconciled Celts of Ireland and the Hebrides his very appointment was in the nature of a challenge.

Bede proceeds to describe to us how Theodore's copious stores of learning, both sacred and secular, were made available for the people. He tells us of the multitude of disciples who flocked to his daily lectures and those of his friend Hadrian; of the knowledge "of the metrical art, of astronomy and of ecclesiastical arithmetic," which, along with the sacred Scriptures, they imparted to their hearers. "A proof hereof is," says he, "that to this day there survive some of their disciples, who know the Latin and Greek tongues as well as that wherein they were born. Nor in fact were there ever happier times since the days when the English first landed in Britain, since now, under the leadership of most valiant and Christian kings, they were a terror to all the barbarous nations; the desires of men were strongly directed towards the new-found joys of the heavenly kingdom; and all who desired to be instructed in the sacred Scriptures had teachers near at hand, who could impart to them that knowledge." There can be no doubt that Theodore possessed a genius for organisation such as had not been displayed by Augustine or any of the subsequent prelates, and that to him more than to any other single person is due the structure of the Anglo-Saxon Church, such as it remained till the Norman conquest. One change which he perceived to be necessary for the good of the Church, but which also inevitably tended towards the augmentation of his own power, was an increase in the number of bishoprics. Hitherto the tendency had been to have one bishopric only for each of the English kingdoms, an arrangement quite unlike that which had generally prevailed throughout the Roman empire, in some parts of which almost every town that was above the rank of a village had its own episcopal ruler. Such great unwieldy bishoprics as Northumbria, Mercia or Wessex, were not likely to be administered efficiently by a single bishop, while, on the other hand, their very magnitude suggested dangerous thoughts of rivalry with a primate whose immediate sway extended only over a part of Kent. Thus Theodore was impelled by every motive, public and private, to strive to break up the existing bishoprics into smaller portions. In that process the wise but masterful old man certainly did not show himself to any undue extent a respecter of persons.

One of the first cases in which Theodore had to exert his archiepiscopal authority was that of the bishopric of York. However aggrieved both king and people might have been by Wilfrid's long-delayed return, there was no doubt that the intrusion of another bishop into a see already filled was entirely contrary to the canons; and, moreover, from the strict Roman point of view Ceadda's consecration to the episcopate was not safe from attack, inasmuch as two "Quarto-deciman" bishops had taken part therein. When all these various objections were stated by Theodore to Ceadda, the simple-minded and unambitious old man at once declared his willingness at Theodore's call to resign a dignity of which he had never deemed himself worthy. "No: not the episcopate," was Theodore's answer. "To that I will reordain you with all due formalities; but stand aside for the present from this see, which of right belongs to Wilfrid." Thus Wilfrid, after three years of suspension, was once again bishop of the great diocese of York, extending from the Humber to the Firth of Forth, or even beyond. For Ceadda meanwhile a place was quickly found, the scarcely less important bishopric of Mercia; and Theodore's regard for the saintly old man was shown by ordering him no longer to perform his long episcopal journeys on foot, but to ride through his diocese. When Ceadda hesitated, mindful of his beloved Aidan's example, Theodore insisted, possibly himself provided him with a steed, at any rate with his own archiepiscopal hands lifted him into the saddle. Ceadda's tenure of the Mercian episcopate was short, as he fell a victim to the plague in 672. He died, however, not only in the odour of sanctity, but, what is better, surrounded by the unfeigned love of his monastic brethren, and able to speak even of the Angel of the Pestilence as "that lovable guest who hath been wont of late to visit our brotherhood."

All the ecclesiastical events which have been described in this chapter, save the last, took place in the reign of Oswy. In the year 671, as we have seen, a new monarch, Egfrid, ascended the Northumbrian throne. He had already been for some years the nominal husband of one of the saintly members of the East Anglian family, Etheldreda, a daughter of King Anna, but she, though Egfrid was her second husband, was at heart a devoted nun and insisted through life on keeping her virginity unstained. Here was already cause for trouble in the Northumbrian palace, trouble which was aggravated by the interference of Wilfrid, who, in defiance of apostolic precept and the Church's law, made himself the champion of the cause of the disobedient wife, and at last (probably in the first or second year of Egfrid's reign) with the hardly won consent of her husband arrayed her in the veil of a "sanctimonialis femina." She retired first to the monastery of Coldingham, then ruled by Ebba, the aunt of Egfrid. After a year's residence therein she became abbess of the great convent which she had herself founded in the Isle of Ely on lands devised to her by her first husband. There, after bearing rule for seven years, she died. The signal triumph of religious zeal over worldly ambition and luxury which her life displayed was celebrated in enthusiastic and acrostic verse by her admirer Bede. She was undoubtedly one of the most popular saints of the Anglo-Saxon epoch, and her name in the abbreviated form of Audrey still possesses a certain attraction for Englishmen.

The place which Etheldreda had vacated by the side of Egfrid was at once filled by a second wife named Ermenburga, who was persistently hostile to Wilfrid, and is accordingly likened to Jezebel by his enthusiastic biographer. There was, however, much in Wilfrid's position at this, the most glorious period of his career, which might well rouse the jealousy of the secular rulers of the nation. Between 671 and 678 he was probably the foremost man in all Northumbria. He built great basilicas, the marvels of the age, at Hexham* and at Ripon.† At the dedication of the basilica at Ripon, Wilfrid stood before the altar, which was draped in purple and marvellously enriched with gold and silver, and there rehearsed, in the presence of the Northumbrian kings, the great gifts of landed property which the royal house had bestowed upon the Church, and also enumerated the places which had belonged in old time to the British Church and to which, though then desolate, it was evident that the English Church meant to assert her claim. When his sermon was ended a great feast was spread, to which the kings and all their followers were invited, and which lasted amid great rejoicings for three days and nights.

Of Wilfrid's wonderful churches no trace now remains above ground. We are told that the church of Hexham was "supported by various columns" (perhaps taken from Roman temples) "and many porches, adorned with walls of wondrous length and height, and with variously winding passages, leading now up, now down, by stately staircases." Both at Ripon and Hexham the crypt "carried deep down into the earth with marvellously smoothed stones" still remains; and at Hexham inscriptions, bas-reliefs and the shape of the stones employed show us all too plainly that the Roman camps along the line of the wall were the quarry from whence Wilfrid's marvellously smoothed stones were obtained. But the great bishop was not giving all his time to his architectural labours. He rode from end to end of his diocese, ordaining priests and deacons in great numbers, and attracting to himself the love and devotion of the powerful abbots and abbesses, who very generally, either by present transfer or by testamentary disposition, arranged that he should become lord of the lands of their monasteries. Many Anglian nobles also sent their sons to be brought up in the bishop's house, in order that they might either by his introduction enter the life of religion, or if they preferred the profession of arms, might by him be recommended to the king. In everything that Wilfrid touched the same note of sumptuous magnificence might be discerned. Thus, on the day of the dedication of the church at Ripon, he presented to it "the four illuminated Gospels traced in purest

---

* Hagustald.

† In Hrypum.

gold on purple parchment, which he had caused to be transcribed for the welfare of his soul, also a bookcase for these books, all made of the purest gold and adorned with the most precious jewels." But all this pomp and splendour (though coupled with personal abstinence and the practice of monastic austerities) was rearing up for Wilfrid a host of lifelong enemies; at their head Queen Ermenburga, who ceased not to remind her husband of "all the worldly pomp of Bishop Wilfrid, his riches, the multitude of his abbeys, the grandeur of his buildings, and the numberless host of his followers adorned with royal raiment and equipped with arms."

The jealousy which the royal pair felt at the greatness of the Bishop of York was powerfully aided by their alliance with Archbishop Theodore. For the formation of this alliance it is quite unnecessary to accept the biographer's story of bribes out of ecclesiastical property offered by the king and accepted by the archbishop. On the contrary, it might almost have been foretold by any one who was acquainted with the two men, Wilfrid and Theodore, that they must necessarily sooner or later come into collision. They were both men of great intellectual stature, both devoted to the Roman obedience and intent on bringing the English Church fully into that obedience, but they would do it in different ways. Theodore, as Metropolitan of the whole land, would enforce Church order, subdivide the unwieldy dioceses, and make his strong hand felt by every bishop and abbot in every corner of the English kingdoms. Wilfrid had no thought of resigning any part of his power over his vast diocese, in which he was virtually independent. Nay more, faint as are the traces of such a scheme in history, it is difficult not to suppose that Wilfrid was cognisant of Gregory's original plan for the establishment of two independent archbishoprics in Britain, one at London and the other at York, and hoped to convert—as was actually done half a century later—his bishopric into an archbishopric. Such an arrangement would be far more in accordance with ecclesiastical precedent throughout the Roman empire than that which actually prevailed, since the general usage had been to place the Metropolitan in the chief city of the province. All the venerable associations which now cluster round the name of Canterbury should not cause us to forget the fact that it is merely owing to a series of accidents (foremost among them the relapse of the East Saxons into idolatry) that the chief pastor of the English Church now bears the title of Archbishop of Canterbury. Either Londinium or Eburacum, pre-eminently the latter, had better right to give an archbishop to England than the little insignificant city of Durovernis.

Intent on his schemes of Church reform and full of the paramount authority symbolised by his archiepiscopal pallium, Theodore visited Northumbria and found there in the royal palace a ready acquiescence in his grand project for the division of the diocese. He at once, in Wilfrid's absence, ordained three new bishops who were to divide among themselves a large part of his diocese, leaving him probably the city of York and a certain part of Deira as his portion.* It was a strong measure to adopt, certainly, not courteous nor perhaps canonically correct in the absence of the bishop whose diocese was thus invaded; and it is no wonder that Wilfrid sought an interview with the king and archbishop, and demanded by what right they, without any cause of offence alleged against him, thus defrauded him in robber-fashion of property given him by the king for God's service. They answered, says his biographer, in the presence of all the people with the memorable words: "No accusation is made against thee of having done injury to any man, but the decision which we have come to in thy case we will not change." Hereat Wilfrid signified his intention of appealing to Rome (678) against this unjust act of spoliation. The flatterers who surrounded the king laughed aloud at his words, but he turned round and rebuked them sternly, saying: "You laugh now, evidently rejoicing at my condemnation, but on the anniversary of this day bitterly shall ye weep to your own confusion." And in fact men noted with awe that it was on the exact anniversary of Wilfrid's interview with the king that the body of the beloved under-king, Alfwin, was brought back to York from the battlefield on the banks of the Trent, and was received by all the people with tears and rent garments and passionate lamentations.

And now began that long duel between prelate and king, with visits to Rome, confiscations, imprisonments, reconciliations, repentances, which lasted with some intermissions and some changes in the person of the royal disputant, for nearly thirty years, and which in some of its vicissitudes reminds us of the contention between Henry Plantagenet and Thomas Becket. It is a history with much intrinsic interest, and rendered additionally interesting to us by the fact that the Life of Wilfrid by Eddius, in which it is recorded, was written some years before the Ecclesiastical History of Bede, and is probably the earliest extant piece

* This is Eddius' account of the transaction. According to Bede a dispute arose between Egfrid and Wilfrid. The latter was deposed and then his diocese was divided.

of Latin writing that has proceeded from an Anglo-Saxon pen. Skilfully escaping from the toils of his enemies (whose emissaries by a laughable mistake attacked and plundered a harmless bishop named Winfrid instead of him), Wilfrid landed in Friesland, made friends with the king of the Frisians, and began that career of missionary enterprise in Germany which was continued by his disciple, Willibrord, and in later years by the West Saxon, Boniface, with vast results on European history. He then travelled through Gaul, visiting King Dagobert II., whom, when an exile in Ireland, he had sped on his way to France, and thus had helped to recover his father's throne. Dagobert's gratitude now showed itself by assisting Wilfrid on his journey to Rome. In Italy he was befriended in a similar way by the Lombard King Perctarit, who had himself once led the life of a hunted fugitive, and refused to surrender him to his foes. Arriving at Rome, where he spent the winter of 679–80, he laid his complaint before the recently consecrated Pope, Agatho the Sicilian, and claimed his protection. A council was held in the Lateran basilica, where Theodore's representative, a monk named Coenred, stated the case for Canterbury. Wilfrid's petition was read, setting forth that he did not refuse to consent to the division of his bishopric, but claiming that he should be consulted as to the persons intruded upon him as colleagues; and the synod having listened to the representations of "the most holy Archbishop Theodore" and "the God-beloved Bishop Wilfrid" decided in favour of the latter.

Armed with this papal decree, and not doubting of the triumph which it would procure for him, Wilfrid presented himself at the Northumbrian court, but was at once accused of having obtained the decree by bribery, thrown into prison and despoiled of his personal possessions. One of the most precious of these, a reliquary, was appropriated by Ermenburga to her own use, and always carried about by her, whether she abode in her bedchamber or rode abroad in her chariot. Wilfrid's first place of imprisonment was the royal city of Bromnis.* On the refusal of the governor, whose wife had fallen dangerously ill, to act any longer as jailer of so holy a man, Egfrid sent him to another of his cities named Dynbaer (Dunbar), another proof, if any were needed, how far northward at this time stretched the kingdom of Northumbria. At last after he had undergone a rigorous imprisonment for nine months, the dangerous illness of Ermenburga (which seemed to take the form of demoniac possession), and

* Site not known.

the entreaties and warnings of the saintly Ebba, brought about Wilfrid's liberation from the dungeon, but not his restoration to his bishopric. He went forth as an exile into Mercia, where he was favourably entertained by a nephew of King Ethelred and received land for the foundation of a monastery. But as Ethelred was Egfrid's brother-in-law, he soon ordered Wilfrid to quit his kingdom. He turned his steps to Wessex and there for a little space had rest, but soon was expelled thence also, King Centwine having married Ermenburga's sister. It is easy to see how hard the lot of a fugitive from one of the English courts might be made by the matrimonial alliances that were so frequent between them.

Thus expelled from Christian England the hunted fugitive turned his thoughts to the land of the South Saxons: "a heathen province of our race" (says the biographer) "which for the multitude of its rocks and the density of its woods remained impregnable by all the other provinces." Here Ethelwalh, himself a Christian, as we have seen, was reigning over a still heathen people, and to him Wilfrid confided the whole story of his wrongs. The king made with him a covenant of peace so strong that, as he declared, no terror of the sword of any hostile warrior and no gifts however costly should avail to move him from the troth then plighted. In this inaccessible corner of the land which we now name Sussex, Wilfrid remained for five years, preaching the story of the creation of the world, its redemption, the day of judgment, the rewards and punishments to come, with such eloquence and fervour that he achieved the conversion of the entire people, thus ending in the year 686 the long spiritual campaign for the conversion of England which was begun in 597 by the arrival of Augustine. King Ethelwalh gave him his own villa of Selsey for his episcopal seat, adding to it a gift of land amounting to eighty-seven hides.

During Wilfrid's sojourn in Sussex his unreconciled enemy King Egfrid died. The story of his death brings us into close relation with our third great churchman, Cuthbert, to whose life we now turn. Born somewhere about 630 in the region of the Lammermoor Hills, the young Cuthbert, when he was tending sheep by the River Leader, saw one night in a vision angels carrying a holy soul into heaven. He found afterwards that it was on the same night, August 31, 651, that the venerable saint, Aidan, had died. He waited not, however, for this confirmation of his faith, but at once transferred the sheep to their owners and descended into the valley of the Tweed to seek admission into the recently founded monastery of Melrose. After some years' residence there, he went in the train of the

Abbot Eata to Ripon; but on the arrival of Wilfrid at that place fresh from Rome, and with a grant from King Alchfrid in his hand, the whole party of Celtic-trained monks, Cuthbert among them, were forced to leave the pleasant valley of the Nidd and return to Melrose on the Tweed. There, however, ended his antagonism to the new teaching. Whether actually present or not at the synod of Whitby, he certainly accepted its decisions, and after some years was sent by his friend, Eata, to govern as prior the monastery at Lindisfarne. It was not altogether an easy task to rule the monks on Holy Island after the revolution which the decrees of the synod had caused, but more by gentleness than by sternness Cuthbert succeeded in enforcing discipline, all the more readily perhaps as in food, in vigils, in dress, he set an example of rigorous austerity. But after all, neither as prior nor afterwards as bishop did he ever care for the possession of power. In character he much more closely resembled Aidan than either Theodore or Wilfrid. He loved to be alone with Nature and with God, and was ever moving about among the country folk and "stirring them up" by his conversation rather than by set sermons "to seek after the heavenly crown." There is still shown in a cleft of the basaltic range of low hills on the mainland overlooking the winding shore of Holy Island a cave, affording bare shelter from the rain and none from the wind, where the saint is said to have passed some months of his life. "Cuddy's Hole" is to this day the name given to it by the neighbouring farmers.

Often, too, he seems to have retired to the little island which still bears his name and which lies at a short distance from the ruined abbey on Holy Island, being like Lindisfarne itself island or peninsula according to the state of the tide. There, while apparently still holding the office of prior, he "began to learn the rudiments of a solitary life," and when his education was completed and his spirit braced for the great renunciation, he gave up his office of prior (676) and withdrew to the more utter seclusion which was afforded by one of the little group of Farne Islands, about five miles from Holy Island and two or three miles from the rock of Bamburgh. These rocky islets, some thirty or forty in number, are now furnished with two lighthouses; and the memory of Grace Darling, the courageous daughter of an old lighthouse keeper, rivals but does not eclipse the fame of St. Cuthbert. Countless flocks of sea-birds make these rocks their breeding place; and there are seen the eider ducks, bold in their gentleness, which calmly hatch their young within a few feet of the intruding wayfarer, and whose tameness, attributed to the miraculous working of the saint, has procured for them the name of "Saint Cuthbert's Chickens." Was it the loneliness of these weather-beaten rocks or the sad cry of the sea-birds that procured for them the evil reputation of being "unfit for human habitation by reason of the number of malign spirits by whom they were haunted"? Howsoever that may be, it is admitted that at the approach of the man of God the evil spirits departed and the place at his prayer became completely habitable. Here then Cuthbert built for himself a little round cell made of large unwrought stones and turf, and so constructed that he could see from it nothing of earth or sea, but was forced to keep his eyes ever fixed on the heaven above him. Here, after dismissing the few brethren who had helped him in his labours, Cuthbert lived absolutely alone for eight years, enjoying the heavenly visions, but also wrestling with the awful spiritual terrors, which have ever been the portion of the anchorite.

At length in 684, Tunberct, Bishop of Hexham, one of Theodore's intruding prelates, having been for some reason deposed from his see, a synod was held at "Twyford" on the Alne (probably the modern Alnmouth) to consider the question of the appointment of his successor. In this synod, at which Theodore himself presided, the name of Cuthbert was suggested and received with unanimous approval. It was, however, no easy matter to induce the anchorite thus to return to the common abodes of men. At last a deputation of nobles and ecclesiastics, headed by King Egfrid himself and by Trumwine, Bishop of Pictland, accomplished the difficult task, and on March 26, 685, Cuthbert received at York the episcopal charge at the hands of Theodore and six other bishops. He still, however, remained so far faithful to the wind-swept shores of the North Sea that he chose Holy Island for his episcopal seat, persuading his old friend Eata to migrate from thence to the busier diocese of Hexham.

It must have been during the long negotiations which preceded the consecration of St. Cuthbert that he pressed upon the unwilling king his vain dissuasions against the barbarous Irish expedition. Equally vain, as we have seen, was his attempt to dissuade Egfrid from that disastrous expedition against the Picts, which was undertaken in the very first months of Cuthbert's episcopate. At the time of Egfrid's invasion of Scotland Cuthbert was abiding at the Roman city of Luguvallium (Carlisle), which had been bestowed upon him by the king at his consecration. There also was dwelling the queen, Ermenburga, Wilfrid's enemy, who had gone for shelter during this warlike time to a convent ruled by her sister. While

Cuthbert was going round the walls of the city on the afternoon of Saturday, May 20, escorted by the king's reeve, Paga, and by a multitude of the citizens, he suddenly stood still, leaning on his staff. With downcast face he gazed upon the ground, then looked up at the darkening sky and said with a deep groan: "Perhaps even now the conflict is decided." He would not more plainly impart his fears, even to his own clerical companions, but hastening to the convent warned the queen to be ready to depart on the Monday for York "lest haply the king should have fallen." On Sunday he preached a sermon which hinted at some coming trouble. On Monday came the tidings of the fatal field of Nechtansmere, fought on the very day and hour when Cuthbert had his telepathic warning of the disaster.

Egfrid's widow, Ermenburga, according to her enemy Eddius, "after the slaughter of the king, from a she-wolf became one of God's lambs and was changed into a perfect abbess and a most excellent mother of her [monastic] family." Apparently there was no issue of her marriage with Egfrid, who was succeeded by his half-brother or nephew Aldfrid, either a son or grandson of King Oswy. He had been for some years an exile in Ireland and the Hebrides, and had acquired a considerable store of learning in the Celtic monasteries, so that he was generally known as Aldfrid the Learned. The twenty years' reign of Aldfrid (685–705) was marked by few striking events. Northumbria, as we have seen, was now shorn of her greatness and was no longer the leading power in Britain. It was probably as much as Aldfrid could do to preserve his weakened and diminished kingdom from conquest by its Pictish and Mercian neighbours. It will suffice briefly to indicate the further fortunes of the three great Churchmen whose lives had been of late so closely intertwined with that of Egfrid.

The newly consecrated bishop Cuthbert did not long sustain the weight of the uncongenial mitre. In 686 he made another journey to Carlisle, on which occasion he gave the nun's veil to the widowed Ermenburga. Here also he received a visit from an old friend of his named Herbert, who like him led the life of an island-hermit but amid far different scenes from the stormy Farnes. Herbert dwelt on an island of "that very large lake from which the young waters of the Derwent issue forth"—in other words, on St. Herbert's Isle in Derwent-water—and had been accustomed to pay a yearly visit to Cuthbert and to hear from him counsels concerning the life eternal. He now besought his friend, whose whole soul was filled with thoughts of his coming end, to pray that they might both die at the same time, a longing which was in fact fulfilled. Soon after Christmas Cuthbert returned to his lonely dwelling on the Farnes: at the end of February he was seized by his last illness. The monks of Holy Island prayed to be allowed to minister to him in his extreme weakness, but it was not till near the very end that he suffered them to enter his cell. In the morning of March 20, 687, after many faintly uttered words of advice and farewell, the great anchorite passed away. There was no English saint, till Thomas Becket was slain before the altar in Canterbury, who filled half as large a space in the memories of the English people, at any rate in the North of England, as Cuthbert of Lindisfarne. The strange migrations of his corpse in later centuries, the magnificence of its final resting-place, the wide domains and princely revenues of the Bishops of Durham, whose chief claim to lordship was derived from the fact that they were the guardians of his tomb—all these things fixed deep in the mind of the medieval Englishman the greatness and the glory of the shepherd of the Lammermoors. Eight centuries after his death we find the soldiers of "the bishopric" rejoicing over the fall of James IV. on the field of Flodden, and tracing therein the manifest workings of the anger of the saint, whom he had offended by the demolition of his castles at Ford and Norham.

We pass from the hermit to the archbishop. Of Theodore of Tarsus there is little more which need be related here save that soon after Egfrid's death he became reconciled to Wilfrid; asked him to come to London to meet him, and (according to Eddius) made him a full apology for all the injustices which he had committed towards him, even expressing a desire that Wilfrid might succeed him in his archbishopric. He died on September 19, 690, in the eighty-eighth year of his age after an archiepiscopate of twenty-two years, and was laid to rest in the abbey of St. Peter and St. Paul, along with many other primates and princes of Kent.

The long exiled Bishop Wilfrid was at last, soon after the death of Egfrid, permitted to return home and restored to some portion of his lost grandeur (686–87). The death of the hostile king, interpreted by Wilfrid's partisans as the judgment of heaven on his despoiler, had probably something to do with this change of policy, to which also his reconciliation with the archbishop largely contributed. His restoration was not, however, by any means to all his old dignities, though he was once again in possession of his favourite abbeys of Hexham and Ripon. And even this restoration was only for a time. After five years of peace the eternal dispute broke out again on Wilfrid's refusal to acknowledge the lawfulness of some of the acts of Theodore. He was banished from Northumbria and took refuge in Mercia, where he dwelt for ten years (692–702). Then came one more journey to Rome, undertaken by the brave old man in the sixty-ninth year of his age. His appeal succeeded, but, as before, the decree in his favour failed to change the purpose of the Northumbrian king. Aldfrid was still immutably fixed in his determination to modify nothing in that decision "which formerly the kings, my predecessors, and the archbishop with their councillors did form, and which afterwards we, with the archbishop sent us from the apostolic see and with almost all the [spiritual] rulers of our race in Britain, confirmed. That decision," said he to Wilfrid's messengers, "so long as I live I will never change for the writings which, as you say, you have received from the apostolic see." Scarcely had this answer been returned when the Northumbrian king was stricken with mortal sickness, an event in which the partisans of Wilfrid not unnaturally thought that they could trace the vengeance of Heaven for his audacious contempt of the papal mandate. It was believed that on his death-bed he repented of his behaviour towards Wilfrid and expressed his intention of being reconciled with him in the event of his recovery, but he died in 705 after lying speechless for many days, and was unable to give effect to his intentions if such intentions ever existed.

On the death of Aldfrid a certain Eadulf, of whose relationship to the royal family nothing is known, usurped the throne. Aldfrid's son Osred was a boy of eight years old, but the faithful friends of his father, headed by Berthfrid, who is described as "a noble next in dignity to the king," gathered round him in the fortress-city of Bamburgh. To quote Berthfrid's words, as related to us by Wilfrid's biographer who, of course, views all events in relation to the fortunes of his hero: "When we were besieged in the city which is called Bebbanburg and everywhere girt round by the forces of the enemy, having only that narrow rock on which to dwell, we came to the conclusion amongst ourselves that if God would grant to our royal boy the kingdom of his father, we would promise God to fulfil those things which the apostolic authority had ordained concerning Bishop Wilfrid. No sooner had we made this vow than the hearts of our enemies were changed: with quickened steps they turned towards us swearing to be our friends; the doors were opened; we were freed from that narrow dwelling; our enemies fled and we recovered the kingdom."

This is all the information that we possess concerning a domestic revolution which, probably on account of its extremely short duration, is unnoticed by Bede. It seems to be clear that during the two months of his usurped reign Eadulf absolutely refused to redress the grievances of Wilfrid, but that in the early months of Osred's reign a great synod was held near the river Nidd in Yorkshire to settle finally the wearisome business. The boy-king presided: Bertwald of Canterbury was there with all the bishops and abbots in his obedience. There, too, was Elfleda, the daughter long ago vowed by Oswy to the service of God, now and for many years past sitting in the seat of the venerated Hilda as abbess of Whitby: "a most wise virgin," says the biographer, "ever the best consoler and counsellor of the whole province." She was a great friend of Cuthbert, and had probably at one time shared the general Northumbrian or, at least, Bernician dislike to the all-grasping Bishop of York; but the letter which the aged Theodore had written, almost from his death-bed, beseeching her to become reconciled to Wilfrid had perhaps changed her mind towards him, and she now strongly pressed his claims and vouched for the fact that her step-brother Aldfrid on his death-bed declared his intention of complying with all the demands made on his behalf by the apostolic see. The result of the deliberation which followed was that the king, his nobles and all the bishops swore to maintain peace and concord with Wilfrid, and on that same day gave him the kiss of peace and broke the bread of communion with him. At the same time the abbeys of Ripon and Hexham, with all their revenues, were restored to him, and the thirty years' war was at an end. This result was after all a compromise, and, as has been well pointed out by Dr. Bright, a compromise less favourable to Wilfrid than that which had been made before. He had lost the bishopric of York and had to be content with the less important bishopric of Hexham, but he recovered possession of all his domains and monasteries in Northumbria and Mercia.

Wilfrid had now four years of peace at the end of his stormy life. Not long before his death he "invited two abbots and certain very faithful brethren, to the number of eight in all, to meet him at Ripon, and commanded the key-bearer to open his treasury, and to set forth in their sight all the gold and silver with the precious stones, and then ordered them to be divided into four parts according to his judgment." He explained that it had been his intention to make yet another journey to Rome and offer one of these four portions at the shrines of the Virgin and the saints. Should death prevent him from carrying this design into effect, he charged them to send messengers to offer the gifts in his stead. Of the remaining portions one was to be given to the poor for the redemption of his soul; another was to be divided between the rulers of his two beloved abbeys Hexham and Ripon, "that they may be able by their gifts to win the friendship of kings and bishops"; the last was to be distributed among the friends and companions of his exile to whom he had not yet given landed possessions. From the minute account which the biographer gives of the whole scene, it seems probable that he was one of the six faithful brethren permitted to gaze on the opened treasury, and one of the companions of the exile who received a share in the bequest.

After some further arrangements about the future government of the abbey of Ripon, Wilfrid journeyed into Mercia, on an invitation from King Ceolred, reached the monastery of Oundle in Northamptonshire, and there, in 709, after a short sickness, ended his days, in the seventy-sixth year of his age. In the forty-six years of his episcopate he had dedicated churches and ordained bishops, priests and deacons past counting. His body was taken to Ripon and there interred with great solemnity. The abbots of his two chief monasteries believed that they had secured in the departed saint a heavenly intercessor of equal power with their apostolic patrons St. Peter and St. Andrew, and their faith was confirmed when, at a great meeting on the anniversary of his death, they beheld at night a white circle in the heavens reaching all round the sky and seeming to encompass the monastery of St. Peter at Ripon with its protecting glory.

The life of Wilfrid with all its strange vicissitudes of triumph and disgrace is confessedly one of the most difficult problems in early Anglo-Saxon history. The enthusiastic panegyric of Eddius, the conventional praise and strange reticence of Bede, leave us still greatly in the dark as to the real cause of the hostility of the leading men of Northumbria, both in Church and State, towards one who seemed made to be a victorious leader of men. The vast blanks in the history can now be supplied only by conjecture, and any such conjectural emendation would probably be unjust to one or other of the disputants, to Wilfrid, to Theodore or to Egfrid. Only this much may with confidence be asserted, that the dispute, bitter as it was, turned on no question of doctrine or of morals; hardly in the end on any question of Church government. It is the possession of the great monastic properties, both in Northumbria and Mercia, which seems to be the real bone of contention between Wilfrid and his foes, and when we read of the large possessions wherewith these were endowed, ten "families" to one monastery and thirty to another (domains probably equivalent to at least 1,200 and 3,400 acres), and when we see the well-filled treasury blazing with gold and jewels, which after all his reverses gladdens the aged eyes of Wilfrid at the close of his career, we are, perhaps, enabled to understand a little more clearly what was the unexpressed grievance in the mind of the Northumbrian kings and bishops against their greatest ecclesiastic. With justice he exclaimed again and again, "What are the crimes of which you accuse me?" They had, it would seem, no crimes to allege against him, but the king felt that the vast wealth which he had accumulated made him a dangerous subject, and the bishops thought that he had abused the great position which he had achieved by his victory at Whitby, to secure for himself an unfair share of the new riches of the Church. Whatever view may be taken of the struggle, the very fact of its existence and of the somewhat sordid interests at stake shows us how far we have already travelled in less than two generations from the days of Oswald and Aidan. The victory of the Roman Easter was not all pure gain to the churches of northern Britain.

XIII.

THE LEGISLATION OF KING INE

We have now nearly reached the end of the seventh century of our era, and we may well take note of the fact that it was, not for England only, a century of great religious change. The world-famous Hegira of Mohammed happened in 622, when Edwin was reigning in Deira. Throughout the reigns of the great kings at Bamburgh the invincible armies of Islam were sweeping over Syria and Egypt, overthrowing the ancient kingdom of Persia and for seven long years laying siege, all-but successful siege, to Constantinople. It may be well for us children of the Saxon to be reminded that our profession of Christianity is not older than the Mussulman's allegiance to the faith of the Prophet. Our ancestors were idolators at the same time as the ancestors of our Mohammedan fellow-subjects in the east; the same century saw both our own forefathers and theirs converted from polytheism to monotheism, from chaotic Nature-worships to "the religion of a book."

A very noticeable figure in the south of England at the close of this century was Cadwalla, King of the West Saxons. The kingdom of Wessex had fallen after the death of Cenwalh in 672 into dire confusion and disorder. Cadwalla, who was descended in the fourth generation from the great fighter Ceawlin, was one of the many claimants for the throne. His first victories, however, were not won over any rival competitors for the West Saxon crown, but over his South Saxon neighbours. Between Wessex and Sussex there seems to have existed in these early centuries an enduring blood-feud. The enmity was not likely to be lessened by remembrance of the fact, already mentioned, that in 661 Wulfhere, King of Mercia, had wrested the Isle of Wight and part of Hampshire from the West Saxons and handed them over to his convert and godson, Ethelwalh of Sussex. Against Sussex, therefore, Cadwalla, "that most strenuous young man of the royal race of the Gewissas," while still an exile, about

685, directed the arms of the followers whom he had gathered round him in the forests of Chiltern. He was at first successful, slaying King Ethelwalh and laying waste the land of Sussex with cruel and depopulating slaughter, but was repulsed by two ealdormen who acted as regents after the death of the king. Just at this time, however, Cadwalla seems to have made good his claim to the crown of Wessex, and with the forces of the whole West Saxon kingdom now at his back, he set himself to recover the lost provinces of Wight and the Meonwaras, and at the same time to extirpate the idolatry which still lingered in that conservative Jutish population. Herein he seems to have been abetted by the zealous Wilfrid, who notwithstanding his friendship for Ethelwalh was willing to work for the good of the Church with Ethelwalh's destroyer, and who received from him as the reward of his co-operation one fourth of the 1,200 hides into which the Isle of Wight was divided.

King Cadwalla, though an apostle of Christianity, reflected, of course, some of the barbarism of his age. There were two lads of royal blood (brothers of the last king of Wight) who had escaped to the mainland, but whose hiding-place was unfortunately discovered. Cadwalla, who had been wounded in the wars and was resting for a time at a house not far distant, ordered that the youths should be slain; but a certain Cyniberct, abbot of the monastery of Redbridge, came to Cadwalla's bedside and made earnest intercession, not for the lives of the hapless lads, but that before their execution "they might be imbued with the sacraments of the Christian faith." The request was granted. The two young princes were converted and baptised, and when the executioner made his appearance "they joyfully submitted to the temporal death by which they doubted not that they should pass over into the everlasting life of the soul."

The war of Wessex with Sussex continued and soon brought in Kent also, which came to the help of its southern neighbour. After two years' ravaging of Kent, the king's brother Mul, by some sudden turn of fortune, fell into the hands of the men of that land (687), and they in their rage and exasperation burned him and twelve of his followers alive, a savage deed, which was like to have made a truceless war between the West Saxons and the men of Kent. Strange to say, however, this work of revenge was not long engaged in by the brother of the victim. In the year 688, after little more than two years of bloody reign, Cadwalla, stricken with satiety or remorse, went on pilgrimage to Rome. He had two great desires: "to be baptised at the threshold of the apostles and to be speedily freed from the flesh that he might pass into eternal joy." Both desires were granted. The devout Syrian Pope, Sergius I., baptised him by the name of Peter on April 10, 689, and on the 20th, while yet wearing the white robes of a catechumen, he died of Roman fever. He was buried in the great church of St. Peter, and a Latin epitaph in twelve elegiacs was carved over his tomb. The meteoric career of "the most strenuous Cadwalla" who reigns and ravages for two years and a half, and at thirty dies "in Christ's garments" at Rome, and is buried at St. Peter's, forms one of the strangest pages in Anglo-Saxon history.

Cadwalla's successor, a remote kinsman named Ine, descended from Cerdic, but not from Ceawlin, reigned for thirty-seven years (688–726) over the West Saxons. In the sixth year of his kingship the blood-feud with Kent was ended by a treaty under which the men of Kent bound themselves to pay 30,000 coins of some kind (the denomination is not clearly stated) for the murder of Mul. The West Saxon king seems to have had but little difficulty in holding down Sussex, which before the end of the eighth century altogether disappears from the list of the kingdoms. He probably established some sort of protectorate over Essex, since (apparently about 693) he calls Erconwald, Bishop of London, "my bishop." In 715 he fought with Ceolred, King of Mercia, at Wodensburh.* As the result of the battle is not stated we may, perhaps, infer that the victory was doubtful. The chief operations of the West Saxon king seem, however, to have been on his Western borders which were notably extended by him. In 710 he and his kinsman Nun, king of the South Saxons, fought against Geraint, king of the West Welshmen, and it was probably to mark and to secure the increase of territory thus won that Ine built the fortress of Taunton in the valley of the Tone.

On the other hand there were, as so often happened in the disorganised West Saxon house, troubles with the king's own kinsfolk. In 721 it is said "Ine slew Cynewulf the Etheling." In the next year, Ine's own queen, Ethelburga, appears as the demolisher of the newly raised fortress of Taunton. Apparently, however, she was warring for, not against her husband, and we may, perhaps, safely connect this entry with those which immediately follow it: "Ealdbert went into banishment into Surrey and Sussex, and Ine fought with the South Saxons," and (725) "Ine fought with the South Saxons and there slew Ealdbert the Etheling whom he had

* The identification of this place with Wanborough, near Swindon, is disproved by Stevenson (Eng. Hist. Rev., xvii., 638).

before expelled from his kingdom." If we are not erroneously combining these scanty notices, Ealdbert an Etheling of the royal house rebelled against his kinsman, seized the new fort of Taunton, was besieged therein by the martial consort of Ine, and on the storming of that stronghold fled into Sussex, where, three years after, he was defeated and slain by the West Saxon king.

In 726, sated apparently with rule and strife and victory, the elderly Ine followed the example of his predecessor, resigned the crown to a kinsman—apparently a remote kinsman—named Ethelheard, and performed the great pilgrimage to Rome, "desiring in this life to wander round the neighbourhood of the holy places, that he might win a kinder reception from the holy ones in heaven." According to William of Malmesbury* the king's wavering and procrastinating temper was definitely turned towards the Roman pilgrimage by the exhortations of his wife Ethelburga who acted the following parable in order to give weight to her words. It happened upon a day that the king and his court left a certain tun in which they had been dwelling with a profusion of regal luxury. By Ethelburga's orders the steward filled the rooms of the royal abode with rubbish, allowed cattle to wander through it, defiling its floors, and placed a sow which had just littered, in the royal couch. Persuading the king, on some pretext or other, to go back to the tun, she turned his natural surprise at the hideous change into an argument for relinquishing the world. "Where, lord husband, are now the pomps and delights of yesterday? Like a river hastening to the sea is all the glory of man. As hath been the delight of our life here so shall be our torments hereafter." With these words and with the sight of the squalid habitation, she persuaded him at once to perform the great renunciation for which she had so long vainly laboured. The death of Ine was apparently not so sudden or so dramatic as that of his predecessor, but there can be no doubt that he died in Rome and never returned to his native land.

The especial interest, for us, of the reign of Ine lies in the fact that he was the first King of Wessex who published written laws for the guidance of his subjects. Till his time such legislative activity as existed among our ancestors had been confined to the kingdom of Kent, where it had evidently been called into being by the organising and civilising influence of the Roman ecclesiastics. "These are the dooms which Ethelbert the king gave forth in Augustine's days": so runs the title of the document which now stands first in the collection of Anglo-Saxon

* Gesta Regum Anglorum, i., 35 (first recension).

laws. This document is little more than a schedule of the fines to be paid for various offences committed. Though later legislators are a little less dry and curt in their utterances, the general character of their work is not greatly different. As with most of the barbarian codes the repression of crime and the redress of injuries is their first care. They say little about rights, much about wrongs. The rules which guided the devolution of property, and the various customs which made up "folkright" were, no doubt, deeply engraved on the minds and hearts of the people, and it is not from any formal enactment of a royal legislator, only from casual allusions to them, that we have to learn their nature and their history.

After the death of Ethelbert, law-making activity seems to have slumbered for two generations. Then about the year 680, Hlothere and Eadric, who were apparently joint kings of Kent, put forth a small collection of "dooms" adding some items to Ethelbert's list of offences and penalties. Eadric's son, Wihtred, in the year 696, issued another set of laws, dealing more with offences against morality and religion—with adultery, Sabbath-breaking, the worship of devils, the eating of flesh in Lent, and so forth. The strong ecclesiastical influence under which Wihtred's laws were framed is evidenced by the preface which is to this effect: "When Wihtred the most gracious king of Kent was ruling, in the fifth year of his reign (696), ... the 6th day of October, in the place which is called Berkhamstead, there was gathered together for counsel an assembly of great men. There was Berwald, archbishop of the Britons, also Gybmund, bishop of Rochester: and every rank of the churches of the land spake in concord with the obedient people. Then did the great men with the consent of all men 'find' these dooms and added them to the law-customs of Kent, as is hereafter said and spoken."

The expressions used in this and many similar prefaces in the collection of Anglo-Saxon laws indicate that which is probably incapable of definition, the sort of share which the leading men of Church and State had in the royal legislation. Laws are passed in the name and by the authority of the king, but he is no uncontrolled autocrat, and for any important change in the "law-customs" of the people, the great men of the realm must share the responsibility.

We may now turn from the rather obscure and elliptical "dooms" of the Kentish kings to the much fuller and more interesting laws of Ine of Wessex which seem to have been promulgated about 693, a year or two before those of Wihtred. Like the latter they were framed "with the counsel and consent of my two bishops, Hedde of Winchester and Erconwald of London, and of all mine ealdormen and the oldest witan of my people and also of a great assembly of the servants of God." "My father Cenred" is also named among the royal advisers, thereby raising a difficult question as to Ine's accession to the throne while his father was still living. The preface ends, "And let no ealdorman nor any of our subjects after this seek to turn aside any of these our dooms."

As it is impossible to give here anything like a complete digest of the Anglo-Saxon laws, we may leave unnoticed the ordinances for the repression of crime—especially the crime of theft—which constitute the larger part of the document before us, and may confine our attention to those paragraphs which deal with the tenure of land and with the ranks and orders in the West Saxon state.

In all the earlier stages of a nation's life, before the people have begun to flock into great cities, there is no subject of more vital importance than the relation of the Folk to the Land. In the seventh century in England this was doubtless governed chiefly by old unwritten customs which needed not to be formally enunciated because they were universally understood. Two precious sentences, however, in Ine's laws give us a glimpse of the agricultural life of that day, and, combined with information drawn from other sources, enable us in some measure to reconstruct the rural community as it then existed. "A ceorl's homestead[*] should be fenced in, winter and summer. If he be unfenced and his neighbour's beast rush in by the opening which he has left, he shall receive nothing on account of [the damage done by] that beast, but must drive it out and bear the loss" (§ 40). "If ceorls have a common meadow[†] or other divided land[‡] to fence, and some have fenced their portion, others not, and [stray beasts[§]] eat their common arable or pasture, then those who are responsible for the opening shall pay the others who have fenced their portion for the injury that is done and take such compensation as is due from the [owners of the intruding] cattle" (§ 42).

This law shows clearly that we are here in presence of an institution, the existence of which is proved by sentences of Tacitus, by charters of Anglo-Saxon kings, by manor-rolls of many succeeding generations down to the

* Weorthige.

† Gaers-tun.

‡ Gedal-land. Mr. Seebohm translates "land divided into strips".

§ There is evidently an omission of some such words.

very last century, the so-called Open Field System. This system was not socialistic nor what we understand by the word communistic, and yet it may truly be described in terms drawn from the life of to-day as a system which formed "a community of shareholders."* Such a community was settled, by what means, peaceful or warlike, we need not inquire, on some land cleared, perhaps, from the forest where they founded what we should call a village, but what they called a tun or a ham,† to which they gave the name of their own little tribe or kinship. The memory of the Yslings may have quite died out from suburban Islington, and Birmingham is no longer the little Mercian ham where once the Beormings clustered, but there seems no sufficient reason to doubt that from some such settlements as these sprang the numerous tons and hams which dot the map of England and have given their names to a stalwart progeny in America and at the Antipodes.‡

In the village settlements thus formed, of course, the main business of the inhabitants was agriculture, and this appears to have been conducted mainly on the Three Field System in which the land that was not reserved for pasture was put one year under wheat sown in the winter, the next year under oats or barley sown in the spring, and the third year lay fallow. Now the peculiarity of the Open Field System is this, that instead of each owner having his own bit of land separate from the rest, in which he could practise this rotation of crops by himself, the community as a whole had three large districts undergoing that rotation, and in each of these districts the ceorl (as the Anglo-Saxon village shareholder was called) had a number of separate strips of land, as a rule not adjacent to one another, assigned to him, and in the cultivation of these strips he was probably for ever helping or being helped by the owners of the strips adjoining. The system appears to us inconceivably complicated and absurd: it can hardly be even understood without reference to a map§

* Vinogradoff, The Growth of the Manor, p. 150.

† The nature of the difference between the tun and the ham has perhaps yet to be discovered. For brevity's sake the former word only will be used in the following discussion. Neither "town" nor "township" is a quite satisfactory translation.

‡ The theory that place-names containing the element ing necessarily points to a settlement by a community, though generally accepted, is contested by Prof. Earle and Mr. Stevenson, who consider that ing is sometimes merely the equivalent of the genitive singular (Eng. Hist. Rev., iv., 356).

§ Such as those in Seebohm's Village Community.

in which we see the strips of varying width, but generally a furlong in length, lying side by side for a while, and then in another group starting off at right angles to their former direction, but always preserving this strip-like formation. Looking on such a map we can better understand what King Ine meant when he talked of the gedal-land or divided land which it was the duty of the ceorl owner to fence; since, obviously, if the end of his strip abutted on the forest or on the pasture in which the cows of the community were feeding, his carelessness in leaving it unfenced would work annoyance and loss to many others besides himself.

The causes and the origin of this remarkable system are lost in prehistoric darkness. It has been well said* that "it is the more remarkable, because with all its inconveniences of communication, all its backwardness in regard to improvements, all its trammels on individual enterprise and thrift, all its awkward dependence of the individual on the behaviour of his neighbours, it repeats itself over and over again for centuries, not only over the whole of England but over a great part of Europe." One thinks that some idea of future repartitions, some desire to prevent any one individual or family from getting too strong a grip of the land, must have been at work here as with the Germans in the first Christian century, of whom Tacitus wrote: "They change their fields year by year, and there is still land left over."† To continue the previous quotation: "the system was particularly adapted to the requirements of a community of shareholders who were closely joined together in the performance of their work, the assertion of their rights, the fulfilment of their duties and the payment of their dues."

If we now inquire what was the extent of the land thus strangely divided which was generally owned in the seventh century by the Anglo-Saxon ceorl, we shall find that the determining factor is his ability to grapple with the necessary cultivation of the soil; or, in other words, the size of his estate is expressed in terms of his ploughing power. The normal English plough-team consisted of eight oxen yoked two and two together; and the land which it was possible to plough by such an ox-team was called in English a hide, in the Latin of the later lawyers a carucate.‡ The extent

* By Vinogradoff, l.c., 176; compare also Maitland, Domesday Book and Beyond, p. 337.

† Germania, xxvi.

‡ From caruca, a plough. There is a general correspondence between the two terms hide and carucate, but it would not be safe to treat them as always precisely equivalent to one another.

of a hide was not always precisely the same even in the earliest times,* and in later times there are puzzling differences in its dimensions, but as a rule it seems safe to estimate it at 120 acres.

If a husbandman had only two oxen (in which case he would generally have to rely on co-operation with his neighbours to get his land tilled) he could only hope to cultivate the fourth part of a hide. This was called a yard-land in Old English, or a virgate† in legal Latin. An even smaller division was the ox-gang or bovate (the eighth of a hide), which belonged to the husbandman who had but one ox to contribute to the common ploughing.‡

The question now arises, "What was the ordinary holding of the Anglo-Saxon ceorl during the first ages after his settlement in the land, and what was his social position?" The answer, of course, must be mainly conjectural, but especially when we consider the language of Bede, and his Anglo-Saxon translators, who use "family" as the equivalent of "hide," it seems probable that the hide, whatever its dimensions may have been, was the normal holding of the ceorl in his day, and all the indications derived from the history of the seventh century seem to point to the conclusion that the ceorl was a free man, proprietor of the land which he cultivated, liable to service in the fyrd or national army, and to certain ecclesiastical payments, but in every other relation independent. Metaphors are dangerous things, but we may probably with safety characterise the numerous and sturdy class of ceorls as the backbone of the Anglo-Saxon community.

On the other hand, whatever the normal property of the ceorl might be, it is certain that in the course of time holdings would be split up and the size of proprietorships would vary. While some ceorls—as we shall

* The size of a hide might partly depend on the nature of the soil. Obviously in some soils a team of six oxen would accomplish a much larger day's work than in others. Kemble, The Saxons in England, i., 101, argues for a hide of about 33 acres.

† From virga = a yard.

‡ For convenience of reference the following table is appended, but it must be remembered that these are rather average results than scientifically exact formulæ. See Vinogradoff, Villainage in England, p. 239, for varying sizes of Hides, Virgates and Bovates.

1 Bovate or Ox-gang = 15 acres.

2 Bovates = 1 Virgate or Yard-land = 30 acres.

8 Bovates or 4 Virgates = 1 Carucate or Hide = 120 acres.

see later on—might become owners of as many as five hides and thus "attain unto thegn-right," many more would see their holdings dwindle into virgates and bovates; perhaps even* the virgate or yard-land would become the typical holding of the descendant of the original ceorl-settlers. The owner of 15 acres or even of 30 acres in those days when "intensive" cultivation was unknown, would not be able to do much more than provide food for himself and his family, and in a rough, undemocratic age would be deemed a person of little account in comparison with the great thegn or the abbot of a wealthy monastery who sat in the king's council and affixed his cross to the king's charters. Thus we can easily understand how the status of some, by no means of all the ceorls might already towards the close of the seventh century be slowly changing from absolute independence into ill-defined subjection or payment of rent to some great neighbouring land-owner whom he was learning to call his hlaford, or lord.†

Owing to the peculiar mode of its division the arable land of the tun has attracted the largest share of our attention. It is not to be forgotten, however, that surrounding the three great open fields which at one time or another came under the plough, there was also a large meadow in which there was "common of pasture" for the cattle belonging to the members of the tun. Surrounding this, again, and disparting one tun or ham from its neighbour, there would generally be found a belt of forest-land, as to which we have some interesting utterances from the mouth of the West Saxon legislator. The great economic use of the forest, in addition to the provision of fuel, was its supply of "mast" for the swine, whose flesh was an important part of the food of the people. In the forty-fourth of Ine's laws it is ordained that if any one cut down a tree under which thirty swine could take shelter he shall pay a fine of thirty shillings. In the twentieth law we are introduced to "a foreigner or other stranger"—probably in most cases a Welshman—pushing towards us through a trackless forest. "Comest thou peaceably?" is evidently the question that rises to the lips of the Saxon ceorl as he sees the figure in outlandish garb dimly moving through the trees. If the stranger would dispel suspicion he must either wind his horn or shout at frequent intervals; otherwise the West Saxon may assume that he is a thief and either slay him or capture

* As alleged by Mr. Seebohm.

† The laws of Ine which speak of the subjection of a free man to a lord are 3, 21, 27, 39, 67 and 74.

and hold him to ransom. In the former alternative, however, he must at once make the matter known and swear that he took the dead man for a thief; otherwise he will be liable to judicial process at the hands of the dead man's kinsmen. Again,* if a man burns a single tree in a forest, and is afterwards convicted, he shall pay the full fine of sixty shillings, for "Fire," says the law-giver, "is a thief," a secret, furtive creature that may do much mischief. But if a man goes boldly into the forest and cuts down trees for his own use, he shall be fined thirty shillings for the first tree so felled and so on up to ninety shillings, but no more, however extensive may have been his depredations, for "The axe is a tell-tale." He could not have wielded it so long in the forest without a ringing sound which should have arrested the attention of the forester.

Of course there was an exception to the general law of the mutability of holdings in the case of the house of the ceorl with the little bit of land surrounding it. This, which we should call a homestead, was called in Anglo-Saxon a weorthig, and the fortieth law (already quoted) warned the ceorl that this must be kept always well fenced winter and summer, and that if any gaps were left in the hedge surrounding it he would have no claim against a neighbour for any damage that might be done by that neighbour's beast rushing in through the opening.

The whole of the labour on the land of a ceorl who had the normal holding of a hide would certainly not be performed by himself and his family. We have frequent references in the laws to a servile class, generally known as theows, but sometimes—chiefly in the laws of the Kentish kings—as esnes. We may conjecture that this class was originally formed for the most part out of vanquished Britons spared by their conquerors; probably also from among the descendants of yet earlier strata of population, enslaved by the Britons themselves. It was certainly recruited by the so-called wite-theows, men probably originally of the class of ceorls, who having committed some crime and being unable to pay the pecuniary penalty for their offence were condemned to penal servitude, and in such a case generally forfeited the freedom of their descendants as well as their own. Probably the larger number of theows were in bondage to land-owners of higher rank than the ceorl, but one of the laws of Ethelbert of Kent† shows that at any rate the possession of a slave by a ceorl was not a thing altogether unknown. Our information as

* Law 43.

† Law 16. Ceorles birele evidently means a ceorl's female slave.

to this servile class is, however, very imperfect, and relates chiefly to the floggings to which they may be subjected for various offences.*

Though the position of the great body of the ceorls, if it has been rightly stated here, was that of partners in a free and independent agricultural community, it must be admitted, as previously said, that we have already in the laws of Ine traces of another, probably an increasing class of gafol gelders or rent-payers. Land in these cases was held by free men under a lord, to whom payments had to be made in kind whenever the lord visited the tenant. In Saxon Britain, as in Frankish Gaul, the king and his chief nobles lived on the produce of their estates, not by drawing half-yearly rents and converting them into money, to be spent in their own distant palaces, but by moving about from tun to tun, from vill to vill, and calling upon their tenants for supplies of food which were consumed upon the spot by themselves and their retainers, doubtless with much wassail and jollity. From an estate of ten hides the lord was entitled to claim ten vessels of honey, three hundred loaves, twelve ambers of Welsh ale, thirty ambers of clear ale, two full-grown oxen or ten rams, ten geese, twenty hens, ten cheeses, a full amber of butter, five salmon, twenty pounds weight of fodder, and a hundred eels.†

From the consideration of the middle and lower classes of Anglo-Saxon society we ascend to consider the rather difficult questions connected with the higher ranks of that society, the thegns, the eorls, the ealdormen, about whom the Laws and the Chronicles inform us. In this examination we should be left in almost hopeless darkness were it not for two institutions both well known in all the collections of primitive Teutonic law, and both very repugnant to our modern ideas of justice, wergild and (so-called) compurgation.

The essential principle of the wergild was compensation in money to the kindred of a murdered man, in order to induce them to abstain from righting or avenging themselves by force. Far back in the dimmest ages

* Vinogradoff (Growth of the Manor, 202) minimises the element of personal slavery in the early Anglo-Saxon community: "Even in the earliest stage of English life it could not be said that English society was a slave-holding one.... Slavery turns out not to be a fit economic and social basis for a primitive, half-agricultural, half-pastural society: the slaves are difficult to keep and awkward to deal with.... They are mostly provided with small households of their own and used as coloni."

† Ine, 70. The amber is said to have contained four bushels, but Maitland (Domesday Book, etc., p. 440, n. 6) doubts its having been so large.

of the Teutonic foreworld the historical student discerns a period when all wrongs were avenged by the stroke of the broad-sword. The right, and more than the right, the sacred duty, of vengeance was handed on from father to son, and the circle widened from kinsman to kinsman, till the terrible blood-feud was like to destroy a tribe or even a nation. Then at some period far back in the ages, the idea was conceived of exorcising the spirit of revenge by the wand of pecuniary compensation. Let the relatives of a murdered man receive a wer, a payment in money, proportioned to his rank and position in the tribe, and, the family honour being thus satisfied, let them forego the right to revenge. If the injury were something less than death—if it were maiming, mutilation, the abduction of a wife, unprovoked words of insult—a proportionate payment in the nature of wer was made to the sufferer himself. The wer was purposely fixed high according to the value of money in those days, and if the offender were unable to pay it, he and sometimes his family with him became the bondslaves of the injured party. There was thus an element of prevention as well as of compensation in the punishment inflicted. But in all this we do not find any thought of punishment inflicted by the state to avenge the injured majesty of the law; nothing of that feeling which now makes the murder of the most degraded outcast a matter which must be inquired into with the utmost diligence by the police and punished by the hands of the executioner. This thought was indeed in some degree expressed by the wite or fine for murder, breach of the peace and so on, which was paid to the king or to one of his officers, but this fine was generally less in amount and always less in importance than the venerable wergild payable to the kindred.

The amount of wergild was elaborately proportioned to the station in society of the injured party—twice as high for the nobleman as for the squire, three times as high for the squire as for the yeoman (if one may be permitted to use as a very rough approximation the terms current in modern society); but it is important to remember that obligation in this system of law went hand in hand with privilege. If the wer for an injured thegn was high, it was on the level of that wer that he would have to atone to the king for offences committed by him against the law of the land.* The wergild tariff, however, though frequently referred to, is not regularly set forth in the laws either of Ethelbert or of Ine, an omission common to it with many of the other Teutonic codes, especially that of

* Ine, 11, 12.

the Lombards. Probably the amount of wer payable in each case was so well known through long usage that the legislator deemed it needless to set it forth anew, but it is possible also that there was a variable element left, in some cases, to be the subject of bargaining between the two kins of the injurer and the injured. Some broad lines of demarcation, however, may be clearly traced. We know that the ceorl was called a twy-hynd man, because the ordinary compensation for his violent death was 200 shillings. A Welshman, however, who owned that single hide of land which seems to have been the normal property of the well-to-do ceorl, was entitled to a wergild of only 120 shillings, but if he so prospered as to become the owner of five hides of English soil then his wergild rose to the proportionate amount of 600 shillings.

The class next above the ceorl, the class corresponding with the gentry of modern times, the large land-holders who do not happen to hold any official position at the king's court, were in the ninth century spoken of as thegns; and that word may, for convenience, be used here, though it is perhaps doubtful whether it was yet used as the simple designation of a class. In the word thegn the thought of soldiership and of service to the king seem almost inseparably blended. In the poem of Beowulf thegns seems to be equivalent to warriors.; while in the charters of Anglo-Saxon kings the Latin equivalent of thegn is almost invariably minister. In the laws of Ine these men seem to be generally spoken of as gesithcund, men who by birth were entitled to be comrades and attendants of the king; and it is almost certain that they are identical with the twelf-hyndemen, their wergild being fixed at 1,200 shillings. Higher than this these laws do not enable us to go, but the tenor of later legislation supports the conjecture that the wergild for an ealdorman or for a bishop was 4,800 shillings, for an archbishop or etheling (member of the royal house), 9,000 shillings, and for the king himself, 18,000 shillings.*

It will be seen that the Ealdorman is here put on a level with the Bishop. At the point of West Saxon history which we have now reached, there seems to have been one ealdorman to every shire. He commanded the fyrd of his shire in battle, he presided along with the bishop and the reeve in the shire-gemot, of which later laws than Ine's inform us: and altogether his position may perhaps be best imagined by comparing it with that of a modern lord-lieutenant of a county.

....

* There seems to have been a tendency as legislation advanced to increase the distance in respect of wergilds between the king and his subjects.

*****

Some further light on the ranks and orders in the Anglo-Saxon kingdoms is shown by the rather copious ordinances on the subject of that judicial process which is generally called compurgation. This name is not technically correct, as it is of ecclesiastical origin and belongs to later times than those with which we are now dealing; but we have not yet naturalised "oath-helping" as the Germans have naturalised eid-hilfe, and the word ath-fultum, occasionally used in the Anglo-Saxon laws, has not yet attained the same degree of currency as wergild. With the word "compurgation," therefore, we must for the present rest satisfied.

We first meet with this custom in the fourteenth law of King Ine, who says, "If any one be accused of brigandage he shall clear himself by 120 hides or pay accordingly." We naturally inquire what is meant by "clearing oneself by 14,400 acres," and we receive further light on the question when we come to law 19 which tells us that "a king's retainer (geneat) if his wer is 1,200 shillings may swear for 60 hides if he be a communicant," on which the later Latin translator adds the gloss, "for 60 hides, that is for six men."

We now see more plainly the meaning of "swearing by 120 hides." A man accused of such a grave crime against society as brigandage must, in order to prove his innocence, procure the attestation of at least two king's tenants (each presumably holding sixty hides of land) or twelve land-owners (each owner of ten hides), and they must swear that they believe him innocent. This is "oath-helping" or "compurgation." This swearing process is, as has been often pointed out, not in the least like our modern examination of sworn witnesses to fact, nor does it contain the promise of our modern trial by jury. It is much more akin to the privilege allowed to the defendant of "calling witnesses to character," a privilege which, where the evidence is only circumstantial, often has an important influence on the verdict. It must be admitted that even with us the force of such evidence frequently depends in some measure on the social status of the witness-bearers, but we should shrink from making the bald statement that a man accused of murder must produce two persons paying income-tax on £10,000 a year, or twenty persons at £1,000 a year, to declare their belief in his innocence.

The amount of "swearing power," if it may be so called, belonging to each class of men is not very clearly stated. From the passage quoted above, with its Latin gloss, one is inclined to suppose that the ordinary ceorl swore for ten hides. It has been recently argued* that he swore only for five or perhaps six hides. There is, however, evidently something factitious in the ownership of land thus theoretically assigned to him. We may say, certainly, that the ordinary ceorl did not possess five, much less ten hides of land; nor were all thegns, who had probably the same swearing power as the king's geneat, possessed of sixty hides, say 7,200 acres. We may therefore rather look upon the number of hides for which ceorl, thegn and king's thegn were entitled to swear as a conventional mode of stating for the guidance of the judge, the weight that was to be attached to their testimony when they gave it on behalf of a man accused of crime. Perhaps also there was in this curious tariff of credibility an attempt to ascertain the extent to which the belief of the vicinage could be relied on in the prisoner's behalf. The ordinary ceorl, cultivating perhaps only one hide, but mingling with a certain number of his fellow ceorls in the exercise of his daily toil, might vouch for the opinion of the owners of ten hides; while the king's retainer, from his wider field of observation, could vouch for the belief of a district six times as large.

From a consideration of the laws of Ine and other nearly contemporary sources, we may, perhaps, safely arrive at the following general conclusions as to the nature of the social edifice in the eighth century. At the summit of that edifice we find, of course, the king. He is king as yet of only a few English shires, a monarch of far less importance than the Frankish kings before they sank into inefficiency, yet a much greater man than many who had borne the same title in preceding centuries. In the early history and charters of the Anglo-Saxons we are struck with the large number of persons who bear the title of cyning or rex. Edwin slays five kings when fighting against the Saxons. Four kings were reigning at the same time in Sussex, three in Essex. There were kings of the Hwiccas (Worcestershire and Warwickshire) and a separate kingdom of the Middle Angles and of Lindsey, all of which vanished leaving no trace in the so-called "Heptarchy" of later historians.†

All this, though partly accounted for by the tendency to treat the kingdom as a family estate and to divide it up at the king's death among his

* Chadwick, Anglo-Saxon Institutions, pp. 144–48.

† See Chadwick, chapter viii., for references on this point.

surviving sons, shows also that there must have been a strong movement in the opposite direction, a tendency towards unity and consolidation to produce the three comparatively large and powerful kingdoms of Mercia, Wessex and Northumbria, which are practically all that are of historic importance in the eighth century.

It may have been partly on account of the increasing majesty of the royal name that the nobility (if we may thus speak of the classes reaching from the throne down to the lowest stratum of thegn-hood) became, what perhaps they had not been originally, a class of ministri and milites, servants to the king in peace and in war. Writers on the early constitution of the Germanic states are accustomed to dwell on the distinction between the primeval "nobility by birth" and its successor, "nobility by service." Without denying the probability that nobles of the first kind existed among the invaders of England, we must admit that in the Anglo-Saxon kingdoms as we know them it is the second species, "nobility by service," in the king's court with which we find ourselves chiefly brought in contact. When the king takes counsel with his witan it is with the archbishop and bishops, with the ealdormen, the king's thegns and the "exalted councillors" (gethungenan witan) in their various degrees that he deliberates, with their concurrence that he makes laws for the welfare of the realm, and by their cross-made signatures that his charters granting land are attested. We do not appear to have any accurate information as to the time of meeting of the witan (witenagemot). Nor was the place of meeting by any means always the same even for each Saxon kingdom, though Winchester, Kingston, and in later times London, were frequent homes of the West Saxon witenagemot.

The functions of this great council of the wise men of the realm, the degree to which they shared or controlled the royal power in matters of legislation, of finance, of the defence of the country, are better learned by watching the course of national history than from any attempt to frame a definition of that which was essentially vague, fluctuating and incoherent. The relation between the witenagemot and the medieval parliaments of the Plantagenets must be felt to be only one of rather faint analogy. In some respects the contemporary ecclesiastical councils of Visigothic Spain, at any rate in their later phases, present a much closer correspondence of type. It certainly seems, from the language of the Chronicle, that the English witan, like those councils, had a powerful voice in the election of the king, though, unlike the Spanish councillors, the Wise Men of Wessex were, in their choice, for the greater part of the time confined to one royal line, the men "whose descent goeth unto Cerdic."*

NOTE ON ANGLO-SAXON MONEY

To understand properly the information about wergilds supplied to us by the Anglo-Saxon laws, we must devote a little attention to the Anglo-Saxon currency. Our ancestors a thousand years ago used for the most part the same pecuniary language that we use to-day. They generally spoke of pounds, shillings and pence; and the clerkly ecclesiastics who had to translate these words into Latin employed the Libra, Solidus and Denarius, which have given us the well-known symbols £ s. d. This translation, however, into the terms of Roman currency has done nothing but confuse our own monetary history. Libra as the translation of pound is unobjectionable, but solidus—the only coin of that name that obtained wide currency, the solidus aureus of Constantinople—was a gold coin of which 72 went to the pound of gold, and was in intrinsic value equal to about thirteen shillings of our present money. No scilling that any Anglo-Saxon legislator ever dealt with had any such intrinsic value as this. Similarly the denarius, the true denarius of the republic and of the early empire, was a silver coin intrinsically worth about eightpence of our present currency. No penny in any Anglo-Saxon coinage ever approached this value; and the translation of denarius by penny has introduced confusion even into some well-known passages of the English Bible. Let us, therefore, for the sake of clearness, wholly disregard the pretended Roman equivalents, and confine our attention to the true, long-enduring Saxon denominations, the pund, the scilling and the penig.

1. The pund meant a pound's weight of silver. It was purely a "money of account," as no coin representing this value was ever struck by any Anglo-Saxon king. According to the present value of metals, it would be worth intrinsically somewhat less than £2 sterling.

2. The scilling was also only a money of account, represented by no actual coin. Its derivation (from scylan, to divide) seems to point to the fact that it was originally a portion of a silver ornament, probably a torque or an armlet broken off and cast into the scale, for payment by weight of the trader's demand. Even so, as we may remember, St. Oswald ordered his beautiful silver dish to be broken up and distributed

* Chadwick (Excursus, iv.) takes a different view and practically denies the elective power of the witan.

to the starving crowd, who would take these scyllingas into the market and exchange them there for the needed food. At a later time the scilling acquired a definite value, which, however, varied much in the different English kingdoms. The Kentish scilling was one-twelfth of a pound; the Wessex scilling, one-forty-eighth; and the Mercian, one-sixtieth.

3. But however much the scilling might vary, the penny (pending, pening or penig) seems in all the English kingdoms to have ever borne the same proportion to the pound which it bears at present, namely, as 1 to 240. This enables us to state the varying values of the scilling in the following manner:—

The scilling of	Kent =	20	peningas.
Do.	Wessex =	5*	"
Do.	Mercia =	4	"

Here at last, in this lowest and humblest denomination, we get something which is not a mere "money of account." The silver pennies of the Anglo-Saxon kings, which reach from the middle of the eighth century right down to the Norman conquest, and whose successors formed practically the only money of the country until the reign of Edward III., are the glory of the numismatic collector, but suggest strange thoughts as to the stage of civilisation reached by a country whose only coin was a little bit of silver, one-twentieth of an ounce in weight.

A few words must be said (1) as to the intrinsic value, and (2) as to the purchasing power of these moneys.

(1) As to the first question we are met by the practical difficulty of deciding what is the present value of silver. Not thirty years ago silver was worth fully 4s. 6d. an ounce, or £2 14s. a pound; now it fetches about half that price. But if we take, for convenience, the larger quotation, representing the old-fashioned ratio between gold and silver of 15½ to 1, we get roughly the following results:—

The pund = £2 14s. in intrinsic value.

Scilling of	Kent = 1/12 of a pound	= 4s. 6d.	in intrinsic value.
Do.	Wessex = 1/48 "	= 1s. 1½d.	"
Do.	Mercia = 1/60 "	= 10⅘ pence	"

The penig = about two pence and three farthings "

(2) The "purchasing power" of money in those days is of course a different and a far more difficult question. As every one knows, since the

* There are some indications that in early times the shilling of Wessex may have contained only 4 peningas.

discovery of America and the opening up of enormous fresh sources of supply of the precious metals, prices have been altogether revolutionised, and the "purchasing power" of an ounce of gold or silver has been enormously lessened.

The following are a few indications given us by the laws of Ine and some of his successors as to the prices prevalent in his time:—

1. An ewe with one lamb, 1 scilling (= 1s. 1½d.).

Present value, £2 10s. Ratio 1 to 44.

2. Maintenance of a peasant's child, 6 scillings (6s. 9d.) per annum plus a cow in summer and an ox in winter.

Equivalent to our time to about £6. Ratio 1 to 17.

3. A peasant's blouse was worth 6 peningas (1s. 4d.).

This was probably a rather elaborate affair, and if hand-worked might be worth at the present time £1 10s. Ratio 1 to 22.

4. A sheep's fleece, 2 peningas (5½d.).

Present price, 7s. Ratio 1 to 15.

From the laws of Athelstan:—

5. A good horse, 24 scillings (£1 7s.).

Present price, £40. Ratio 1 to 30 nearly.

6. A sheep, 1 scilling (1s. 1½d.).

Present price, £2. Ratio 1 to 35.

From the law concerning the Dunsaete (Welsh mountaineers) (tenth century):—

7. A mare, 20 scillings (£1 2s. 6d.).

Present price, £25. Ratio 1 to 22.

8. A "swine," 1⅗ scilling (1s. 10d.).

Present price, £1 10s. Ratio 1 to 16.

9. A sheep, 1 scilling (1s. 1½d.).

Present price, £2. Ratio 1 to 35.

10. A goat, ⅖ of a scilling (5½d.).

Present price, 15s. Ratio 1 to 33.

It will be seen from the above rough calculations how impossible it is to get any fixed proportion between the purchasing power of money in Anglo-Saxon times and in our own. As to one very important element, the price of grain, we have no satisfactory information; but from the records of later centuries (from the thirteenth onwards) it seems probable that, with frequent and violent fluctuations, it generally ruled relatively higher than the price of cattle.

On the whole, for historical purposes, if the reader mentally translates the scilling of Wessex into the pound sterling of our own day he will probably not go far wrong.

It may be well to add a few other monetary terms belonging chiefly to the later centuries of Anglo-Saxon history.

1. The Mancus was one-eighth of a pund: or 30 penings. The name is said to be derived from the Arabic. The Mancus in the time of Athelstan was the standard price of an ox.

2. The Thrymsa of Mercia was originally a gold coin (derived from the Roman tremissis), but afterwards the word was used to denote a unit of value, the equivalent of 3 penings.

3. The Sceatt was very nearly equivalent to the pening; but 250 not 240 went to the pund.

4. The Mark, a Danish word, denotes the equivalent of half a pound.

5. The Ora was the eighth part of a mark. It was held to be equivalent to 2½ scillings of Wessex, but there is some difficulty in the equation of these Danish and Saxon currencies. According to Domesday Book the Ore contained 20 pence, and accordingly the Mark would be equal not to 120 but to 160 pence. On the other hand, Ethelred's laws, iv., 9, say that the pound contained 15 ores. This would make the Mark if it was half a pound equivalent to 7½ ores.

(See Chadwick, l.c., chapter i., for a discussion of this perplexing question.)

XIV.

THE EIGHTH CENTURY

The eighth century was in many ways a memorable one for Europe and Asia. In the east it was the period of the greatest splendour of the Caliphs of Baghdad; at Constantinople it saw the rule of the strong, stern iconoclastic emperors who set the spiritual authority of the popes at defiance; in Italy it beheld the downfall of Lombard rule, in Spain the subjection of nine-tenths of the country to the domination of the Moors.

Even more important than any of these events were the changes which were going forward in the wide regions subject to the dominion of the Franks. Here the star of the great Austrasian house, which was represented by Charles Martel, Pippin and Charlemagne, was steadily rising. In this century they shouldered aside the last feeble representative of the Merovingian race, and seated themselves visibly on that Frankish throne behind which they and their sires had stood so long as mayors of the palace; and in the end, aspiring yet higher, at the very end of the century the greatest of the race received the imperial crown and was hailed as Carolus Augustus by the people of Rome in the city of the Cæsars.

In this last series of events, as it happened, Englishmen self-exiled from their country took a prominent part. Willibrord, the apostle of the Frisians, baptised Pippin and foretold the exaltation of his house. Wynfrith, otherwise known as Boniface, following in his footsteps, persuaded or compelled Frisians, Thuringians and Hessians to embrace that religion which his own forefathers had accepted only three generations before, and with the religion induced them to accept also the ecclesiastical discipline of Rome. In his later missionary operations, gentle or forcible, he was strongly supported by the Austrasian Pippin, whom he repaid for that support by crowning him King of the Franks just half-way through the century. Moreover, it was another Englishman, the Northumbrian Alcuin, head of the great school for ecclesiastics attached to the church of York, who towards the close of the century accepted Charlemagne's invitation to take up his abode at the Frankish court; became, so to speak, his literary prime minister, and being full himself of the memories of classical Rome, had no inconsiderable share in persuading his patron to revive the glories of the great world-empire, to pass from the condition of a mere King of the Franks into that of Roman Emperor.

Thus, in this eighth century the Anglo-Saxon race was in various ways making its mark on Europe; and in our own island its literary history during this period is not without interest; but politically the century is one of the most sterile in all our annals. It was an age of little men, of decaying faith, of slumberous inaction, or else of sanguinary and chaotic strife. Northumbria especially, during this period, was falling fast and far from her former high estate. Mercia and Wessex were engaged in perpetual objectless war, not ennobled by any great names or chivalrous deeds. Yet possibly even this dreary time was looked back upon in the next century as a golden age, for it was, almost till its close, unmarked by foreign invasion. In the year 793 a new and more disastrous chapter was opened by the appearance on the horizon of the ships of the Vikings.

The unsatisfactory character of this portion of English history is no doubt partly due to the fact that at an early stage we lose the guidance of that great writer to whom we are indebted for almost all that gives freshness and life to the preceding narratives. Bede, the father of English history, finished his great work in 731, and died four years later, in 735. Hitherto he has been speaking to us about the lives of other men; it is now time to listen to what his disciples have told us concerning his own. Born about the year 672, soon after the death of Oswy, Bede was taken as a child of seven years old to the newly founded monastery of Monkwearmouth, and there or in the sister monastery of Jarrow he passed the rest of his life. He was thus not only the child of the convent but in a pre-eminent degree the spiritual heir of Benedict Biscop, the nobly born and cultured Northumbrian, who had founded these two monasteries, had built in their precincts two stately stone churches "after the manner of the Romans which he always loved" (far superior doubtless to the uncouth wooden churches which satisfied most of the Anglo-Saxon builders), had enriched their libraries with precious manuscripts and pictures—the trophies of five journeys to Rome—and had imported artisans from Gaul to teach the Anglo-Saxon the hitherto unknown mystery of the manufacture of glass. It is an interesting fact that of both these two foundations of Benedict Biscop some vestiges still remain, almost unique specimens of early Anglo-Saxon art. In the porch of the parish church of Monkwearmouth are some cylindrical "baluster-shafts," and some slabs covered with beautiful Anglo-Saxon knot-work. In the parish church of Jarrow, surrounded as it now is by smoking furnaces and clanging steam-hammers, there are portions of a wall undoubtedly anterior to the Norman conquest, and possibly belonging to the very fabric which, as an inscription tells us, was dedicated in the fifteenth year of king Egfrid and the fourth year of abbot Ceolfrid (probably 685). Under this abbot, who ruled Wearmouth as well as Jarrow, Bede spent more than thirty years of his life, the years of boyhood, youth and early middle age. With him, according to the pathetic story already related, he probably sustained as a boy of fourteen the whole burden of chanting the antiphones, when all the rest of the choir were laid low by the terrible pestilence. By him doubtless his studies were directed in later life, when as a studious youth he entered the convent library and began to pore over the manuscripts, sacred and profane, the splendid copies of the Vulgate, the treatises of the Fathers, the poems of Lucretius, Horace, Ovid and Virgil, wherewith the literary enthusiasm of Benedict had enriched his monastery.

In 716 the abbot Ceolfrid, in the seventy-fifth year of his age, resigned his office and started on a pilgrimage to Rome. He travelled slowly, and had only reached the city of Langres in Champagne, when the weakness of age conquered him, and he lay down and died. His attempted pilgrimage has, however, a special interest for us, since it has recently been discovered that one of the manuscripts which he took with him on his journey as an offering to the Holy Father was none other than the celebrated Codex Amiatinus, now preserved in the Laurentian Library, at Florence and, by the admission of all scholars, the chief authority for the text of Jerome's great translation of the Scriptures.

Bede survived his old preceptor nearly twenty years, following up with patient industry the literary career upon which Ceolfrid had started him. In 731 he completed the great work on The Ecclesiastical History of the English Nation, which has made his name immortal; but besides this he wrote a vast number of treatises: on The Interpretation of Scripture, on The Nature of Things, on Grammar and on Astronomy, and two chronological works entitled De Temporibus and De Temporum Ratione. His books show an especial interest in the computation of time, the natural result of his study of the great Easter controversy, the echoes of which must have been still resounding in the days of his childhood. He was unquestionably the most learned man of his age, perhaps one might safely say the most learned man of the early Middle Ages. He was—what even the great Pope Gregory was not—a Greek scholar; and his Latin style, formed doubtless on a careful study of the classical authors in the library of the convent, is eminently pure, and free from turgidity and affectation. His history, in fact, comes as a delightful surprise to the student who has had to struggle with the barbarous Latinity of papal epistles, or the astounding grammatical blunders of Bede's Frankish counterpart, Gregory of Tours. All this intellectual attainment on the part of the monk of Jarrow is the more surprising when we remember how short was the interval which separated him from actual barbarism. Bede's father possibly, his grandfather almost certainly, were rude illiterate pagans; yet we find their near descendant writing Latin which might almost have passed muster at the court of Augustus, and by his saintly life and happy death illustrating the noblest qualities of the Christian character.

Bede's life ended on May 9, 735. Though the story of his death is one of the best known in English history, it may hardly be omitted here. For some months before the end he had suffered much from difficulty of breathing. The long and weary night watches were gladdened with psalmody; sometimes with the repetition of his own Anglo-Saxon verses, one of which may be thus translated:—

Let not man take thought too deeply
Ere his last and lonely journey.
Ponder as he may, he knows not
What of good and what of evil
Shall befall his parting spirit.

He wept with his weeping disciples; then he changed to rejoicing and gave thanks to God for all, even for his chastisements. "As Ambrose said, so can I say, too, 'I have not so lived that I need be ashamed to abide longer with you; yet neither do I fear to die, for we have a good Lord'." In the intervals of sacred song he continued his literary labours, dictating to a youth by his bedside a translation of the early chapters of John's gospel, together with some extracts from a treatise by Isidore of Seville. This latter was probably one of the Spanish bishop's scientific works, for Bede said: "I do not want my lads to read that which is false, nor that after my death they should spend fruitless labour on this thing." The amanuensis said, "There is yet one chapter of the book which thou art dictating, but

I think it too hard work for thee"; but Bede answered, "No, it is easy; take thy pen and write speedily." When the dictation was all-but ended, he distributed his little treasures, spices, napkins and incense, among his friends in the monastery. Then said the scribe, "There is yet one more sentence not written down." This was dictated. The scribe said, "It is done." "Thou hast said truly," answered Bede. "It is finished. Help me to sit in yonder place where I have been wont to pray, that sitting there I may call upon the name of the Father." And thus, seated on the pavement of his cell and chanting with laboured breath the Gloria Patri, the father of English history passed away.

In connexion with the name of Bede, allusion must be made to one or two of his contemporaries who made this period illustrious in the history of English literature. The herdsman-poet Caedmon has already been mentioned in connexion with the conference at Whitby. The date of his death is not recorded, but it probably occurred before the close of the seventh century. Though recent criticism has thrown some doubt on his authorship of the poems which were formerly attributed to him, there can be no doubt that his was a great name in the young literature of the Anglo-Saxon race, and if Bede, though writing in Latin, may be considered as standing by the fountain-head of English prose, Caedmon must be allowed to hold the same place in relation to English poetry.

Aldhelm, abbot of Malmesbury and first bishop of Sherborne, was probably considered by his contemporaries the greatest scholar of his age. Like so many of the great ecclesiastics of this period, Aldhelm was of noble birth, a kinsman, said some, of King Ine himself. Trained in the monastic school of Hadrian at Canterbury he imbibed from his Italian instructors a large amount of classical learning, but not that purity of taste which caused his younger contemporary Bede to use his learning with discretion. Whatever may have been his literary failings, there was a fascination about his personal presence and an earnestness in his religious character which won for him a large number of loyal disciples, enabled him to develop the little community gathered by an Irish saint into the famous monastery of Malmesbury, and made him the literary apostle of Wessex. According to his great panegyrist, William of Malmesbury, he combined in his style the excellencies of various nations. Some fastidious readers in the twelfth century found his works heavy reading. "Unreasonable judges are they," said William, "who do not know that every nation has its own different style of writing. For the Greeks write in an involved style, the Latins in a guarded one, the Gauls write with splendour, the English with pomp.... But if you will carefully read Aldhelm's writings you will think him a Greek by the acuteness of his intellect, a Roman by his brilliancy, and an Englishman by his pomp." The "pomposity," or in other words, the turgidity of his style has been found quite intolerable by later scholars, but was probably considered an enviable gift by his countrymen, only just emerged from barbarism. At any rate even to the pompous and somewhat pedantic churchman much may be pardoned in consideration of the charming anecdote, related on the authority of King Alfred, that Aldhelm in his younger days seeing the "semi-barbarous" people accustomed, as soon as Mass was finished, to stream away to their houses without listening to the words of the preacher, took his station on the bridge by which they needs must pass and there sang merry ballads of his own composition, till he had gained the ear of the hurrying crowd, after which he changed his tune, gradually interwove with his song the words of Scripture, began to speak to them of serious things, and, in short, won back to sanity and devotion the citizens whom he might vainly have endeavoured to coerce by the terrors of excommunication. Aldhelm was chosen Bishop of Sherborne in 705 and died in 709.

The names just mentioned are those of men of a somewhat earlier generation than Bede, and belong, in fact, rather to the seventh century than to the eighth. Not so with the last upon our list, Cynewulf, who was born not many years before the death of Bede and whose literary activity was displayed in the latter half of the eighth century. We have in this poet a remarkable instance of a man whose very existence had been forgotten by his countrymen, and whose name, till a few years ago, was absent from the most carefully written histories of our literature. In the year 1857, however, a German professor* discovered Cynewulf's name in a charade prefixed to a collection of Anglo-Saxon riddles. The clue thus followed led to other discoveries, and now by the general consent of scholars many poems formerly attributed to Caedmon are reclaimed for his fellow-Northumbrian Cynewulf. The Riddles which are sometimes attributed to this poet are considered by those who have studied them to show, amid much misplaced ingenuity, considerable sensitiveness to the beauties of Nature, and some power of description of the battle and the banquet. It is interesting to observe how rapidly in these early Middle Ages a literary fashion spread from country to country over the whole

* Heinrich Leo.

west of Europe. Almost at the same time when the Northumbrian poet was composing his curious poetical riddles, Paul the Lombard and Peter of Pisa were discharging at one another acrostic riddles and enigmatic charades at the court of Charlemagne.

The most important of all the poems which have been conjecturally assigned to this author is the beautiful "Vision of the Holy Rood," some lines of which are carved upon the Ruthwell Cross still existing in Dumfriesshire. In this poem the author describes the appearance to him in a dream of the holy wood which had once been a tree in the forest, and was then cut down and fashioned into a cross for the punishment of criminals, but received with awe upon its arms the sacred body of the Lord of mankind. The Rood speaks:—

Then the young hero, who was mightiest God,
Strong and with steadfast mind,
Up to the cross with steps unfaltering trod
There to redeem mankind.
I trembled, but I durst not fail,
I on my shoulders bare the glorious King.
They pierce my sides with many a darksome nail,
And on us both their cruel curses fling.

The death, the burial and the resurrection of the Lord are related in a similar strain of reverent compassion for the Almighty Sufferer, and the Rood finally charges the poet to reveal the vision to all men, inasmuch as the day is coming when Christ will ask who there is that for His name will taste of bitter death as He did on the cross.

There is something which must needs move our sympathy when we see the passion of pitying love with which these simple-hearted sons of warriors received the story of the suffering Saviour. But, as has been already said, the tide of religious emotion which had flowed so freely in the seventh was already beginning to ebb in the eighth century. This decay of religious life in England, or at any rate in Northumbria, is vouched for in the memorable letter which Bede wrote shortly before his death to his friend Egbert, who had just been consecrated bishop and was shortly to become Archbishop of York. The letter itself is a model of wise exhortation, boldly but respectfully tendered by an aged saint to a man, his junior in years but his superior in ecclesiastical rank. Bede is evidently sure of the goodness of his pupil's intentions, but anxious lest he should not have sufficient force of character to make head against the corruption of the times. Ever since the death of King Aldfrid, which happened thirty years before (705), the decline in morals had gone on at a rapid pace. He holds the bishops largely responsible for this degeneracy. They have insisted on retaining dioceses larger than any one man could possibly administer. They have, for filthy lucre, given their consent to all sorts of grants which should never have been made. They and their clergy have clutched eagerly at the shepherd's hire, leaving the flock unfed. "There are, as we hear, many farms and villages on lonely mountains or in brambly wildernesses, in which for many years the face of a priest has never been seen, and neither baptisms nor confirmations are ever performed, and yet not one of the dwellers in such places is ever allowed to escape from the payment of church-dues."

But the greatest scandal of all in Bede's day seems to have been the foundation of pseudo-monasteries by noble and wealthy laymen, who intended anything rather than the leading of a life of religious austerity. Intent apparently on securing the creature-comforts which a well-endowed monastery afforded; intent also on escaping under the pretence of a religious life the duties of military service for their king and country, these pseudo-abbots would obtain a large grant of land from the king, and would there rear their unholy convents, in which, freed from all laws, human or divine, they would live their lives of licentious ease, waited on by troops of menial monks, who had generally been themselves expelled from genuine monasteries, by reason of their irregular lives. Nay, sometimes these impostors would go even further, and persuade a foolish king to grant them a piece of land adjoining the first donation, and would there erect a nunnery in which their wives might, without taking any regular vows, pretend to be the guides and rulers of maidens vowed to Christ.

These abuses had gone so far that the service of the state was seriously impaired thereby. The lavish grants of land, both to the genuine and the sham monasteries, had so impoverished the king that he had no reserve land, from which to reward the sons of his thegns or poor soldiers who had served him well in war. Hence these young men either sped across the seas to countries which held out the hope of a better career, or, being unable to marry, abandoned themselves to illicit love and sank down into the lowest depths of sloth and immorality. Bede's recommendation was that as there were so many of these places which were profitable neither to God nor man, with no true service to God performed in them, and quite useless for the defence of the realm, they, or at any rate one of them, should be seized and converted into the seat of a new and much-needed bishopric. Such a deed, far from being blamable as sacrilege, would deserve the praise due to a most virtuous action. Subjection of all monasteries to some external supervision and control; the suppression of as many as possible of those nests of hypocrisy and vice, the sham monasteries; and the formation of many new bishoprics—these were the remedial measures which lay nearest to the heart of Bede. Whether Archbishop Egbert, a noble and pure-minded man, friend of one king (Ceolwulf) and brother of another (Eadbert), was able to carry into effect any of Bede's reforms it is impossible to say; but the subsequent course of Anglo-Saxon history seems to point to a negative conclusion. It was, perhaps, partly in these paradises of sin, in the pseudo-monasteries of England, that the virility of the nation was sapped and the way prepared for so many a miserable surrender to the Danish invaders.

In the general decline of morals during the eighth century NORTHUMBRIA was especially conspicuous, if we may draw any conclusion from its political history. In the course of that century fifteen kings swayed the sceptre, and of these, five were deposed, five murdered, two voluntarily abdicated the throne. It is no wonder that Northumbria, once so glorious, now became the basest of the kingdoms; that Charlemagne, on hearing of one of these murders, called the Northumbrian Angles "a perfidious and perverse nation, worse than the pagans, murderers of their lords"; or that the northern kingdom was found utterly unable to cope with the storm of Danish invasion when it beat upon its shores. It would serve no good purpose to give the names and dates of accession of all these kings, most of whom are to us mere names in an arid chronicle, but we may single out for special notice two who reigned in the first half of the century, Ceolwulf and Eadbert.

Ceolwulf, a descendant of Ida but not of Oswald's line, in the words of William of Malmesbury "mounted the trembling summit of the kingdom" in the year 729. He is memorable for us as the friend of Bede and the sovereign to whom he showed and dedicated his Ecclesiastical History; and for his liberality to the Church he was looked upon with much favour by ecclesiastics. But the throne did not cease to tremble when he ascended it. In 731 he was taken prisoner, no doubt, by some of his rebellious subjects, was forcibly tonsured and consigned to a monastery. He was, however, soon restored to his kingdom and reigned, it would seem, with comparative tranquillity for six years, during which time he must have received and may have read the Ecclesiastical History. In 737 "thinking it contrary to the gravity of the Christian character to be immersed in worldly affairs," he abdicated the kingdom and became a monk at Lindisfarne. The abdication and the monastic profession were this time probably voluntary. The rare sanctity which he displayed in the convent procured for him the honour of burial near the tomb of St. Cuthbert and miracles were believed to be wrought at his grave.

The chosen successor of Ceolwulf was his cousin Eadbert (737–58), a strong and strenuous ruler who once more pushed the Northumbrian border far into Scotland, adding a part of Ayrshire to his dominions, and so impressing the surrounding states with the terror of his name that the Angles of Mercia, the Picts, the Scots and the Britons of Strathclyde, all remained at peace with him during the greater part of his reign and delighted to do him honour. By a combination of circumstances, probably unique in English history, the brother of this powerful king was Egbert, archbishop of York (734–66), the prelate to whom Bede addressed the letter of counsel just quoted. Egbert's tenure of the see was in itself memorable. He was the first occupant of that see after Paulinus to hold the rank of archbishop and to receive his pallium from the pope. He did for the church library at York what Benedict had done for Jarrow and Wearmouth, obtaining for it large stores of precious manuscripts and laying the foundation of that great ecclesiastical school the glory of which culminated in Alcuin. As for his brother, King Eadbert, his fame spread far and wide, and in him the glory of Oswald and of Oswy seemed about to be revived. But towards the close of his reign his fortune changed. In the year 756, when he had been nineteen years on the throne, he, in alliance with the King of the Picts, led an army against the strong city of Alclyde, the modern Dumbarton, which was the capital of the kingdom of Strathclyde. The allied operations were at first successful. Alcuith surrendered on August 1, but only nine days later almost the whole of Eadbert's army perished in its march through Perthshire. We have no hint of the cause of the disaster, but we may, if we like, imagine a well-planned ambuscade in some Perthshire glen, an anticipation by nearly a thousand years of the battle of Killiecrankie.

Was it depression of spirits at this lamentable change in his fortunes, or was it merely that weariness of reigning which overcame so many Anglian kings, that drove Eadbert into the monastery? In the twenty-first year of his reign, notwithstanding the earnest dissuasion of his neighbour-kings, some of whom, we are told, offered to add part of their realms to his if he would continue to reign, Eadbert, "for the love of God, and desiring to take the heavenly country by storm, received on his head St. Peter's tonsure," and handed over his kingdom to his son Oswulf. He continued in his religious seclusion for ten years till his death in 768, and was buried at York in the same porticus of the church which held his brother, the archbishop, who had died two years before him. There is some reason to suppose that after the unfortunate issue of Eadbert's campaign in 756, the border of Bernicia being withdrawn a long way to the south, the capital of that kingdom was transferred from Bamburgh to Corbridge in the valley of the Tyne, some seventy miles south-west of Bamburgh. Corbridge was the Corstopitum of the Romans, a station on the northern Watling Street, and still shows some interesting relics of Roman occupation. About the same time we find indications that Cataractonium, now Catterick, the most northerly Roman station within the limits of Yorkshire, became a royal residence, perhaps as a supplemental palace to that at Eburacum. Thus we see that even four centuries after the departure of the legions the charm of Roman civilisation still lingered round the places where they had dwelt, though these are represented in our own day by villages whose very names are obscure except to antiquaries.

In the latter half of the century the lawful line of Northumbrian kings, the sons of Ida, was frequently broken by usurpers of unknown lineage, chief among whom were a certain Ethelwald Moll and his son Ethelred. The latter, an impiissimus rex, in the language of the chronicler, reigned from 774 to 779, was expelled in the latter year, and returned in 790 to wreak vengeance on the princes of the lawful line. The two sons of his predecessor, when apparently little more than children, were lured from their sanctuary in the cathedral at York by promises of safety and protection, and were drowned in Windermere by order of the usurper. Their cousin Osred, who had for a short time worn the crown, was similarly enticed from the Isle of Man, captured and slain. Ethelred sought to strengthen himself by an alliance with Offa, the powerful King of Mercia, whose daughter Elfleda he married at Catterick in 792, the year of Osred's murder. But for all his precautions he could not escape the usual fate of Northumbrian kings. In 796 he was slain "by his own people" at Corbridge.

The man who sat upon "the trembling throne" at the end of the century was a certain ealdorman named Eardulf, who six years before his accession had had a narrow and, as some men thought, miraculous escape from death. The tyrant Ethelred, whose anger he had somehow incurred, ordered him to be executed outside the gates of the monastery of Ripon. The monks with solemn chants bore his body to the church for burial and left it for the night at the lych-gate. There soon after midnight some faithful follower found him still alive and helped him to escape. His resurrection seems to have been concealed from Ethelred, and, as has been said, the year 800 found him reigning as king over Northumbria.

*****

From Northumbria we turn to the central kingdom of MERCIA. The eighth century was the time of the greatest glory of that kingdom, and for many years it seemed as if from that quarter rather than from Wessex would come the needed consolidation of England; as if Lichfield, rather than Winchester or even London, might be the destined capital of the country. It was chiefly under two kings, Ethelbald and Offa, whose united reigns occupied eighty years (from 716 to 796), that Mercia attained this high position. Penda's grandson, Ceolred, King of Mercia, died insane in 716, being thus punished, according to St. Boniface, for the sins which he had committed in defrauding the Church of her possessions and making the vowed virgins of her convents minister to his lusts. He was succeeded by a remote relation, Ethelbald, who was not a lineal descendant of Penda, and whom, jealous of his great qualities, Ceolred had driven forth from his court. In his fugitive wanderings Ethelbald had visited more than once the far-famed sanctuary of Crowland,* where amidst the vast fens of Lincoln and Cambridgeshire, dotted over with desolate forest-islands, the holy man Guthlac, the Cuthbert of Mercia, had made for himself a hermit's retreat, and, with only two servants for his companions in that infinite loneliness, had practised austerities surpassing those of the hermits of the Thebaid. Guthlac had the usual experiences of the fever-stricken solitary, being assailed at night by demons with great heads, hideous faces, long horse-like teeth and horrible harsh voices, which croaked forth temptation, in the language not of the Angle but of the Briton. This sorely buffeted but eminently holy man, who died in 714 at the age of forty-one, and whose life in the wilderness lasted only fifteen

* This name, or rather Cruland, was afterwards corrupted into Croyland.

years, had during that term acquired great renown as a saint. His fame spread far and wide through Mercia, and people of all ranks flocked to him for healing or for counsel. Among these was the outcast Ethelbald, to whom Guthlac predicted that he should soon without strife possess the Mercian throne, a prophecy which was shortly fulfilled when his cousin and enemy was stricken with madness, while sitting at the banquet with his gesiths all round him.

Ethelbald swayed the sceptre of Mercia for forty-one years (716–57). He was evidently a strong and strenuous, if somewhat unscrupulous ruler. In the early part of his reign he had so completely cowed Wessex and conquered the other four southern kingdoms, that Bede, writing the concluding paragraphs of his history in 731, could say: "All the southern provinces up to the boundary of the Humber, with their respective kings, are subject to Ethelbald, King of the Mercians." In 733 we find him capturing Somerton, the chief town of the Sumorsaetas; in 740 he turns his arms northwards and takes advantage of Eadbert's absence on his Pictish campaign to ravage Northumbria. But in his last years fortune frowned upon him. In 750 Cuthred II., King of Wessex, apparently an active and valiant man, rose in rebellion, and in 752 won a great victory over Ethelbald at Burford on the slopes of the Cotswolds, putting him to ignominious flight. Never apparently did Mercia recover the supremacy over Wessex which she lost on that battlefield, and in 757 Ethelbald, who must have been an unpopular master of his household, perished by a night attack of his own guards. Notwithstanding his early friendship for St. Guthlac, Ethelbald was not a pious nor even a moral king. There is preserved a remarkable letter addressed to him by St. Boniface,* in which the apostle of Germany, while praising the vigour and justice of his government, rebukes him for his outrageous profligacy, and expresses his fear that some great national judgment, like the Moorish conquest of Spain, will fall upon the kings and peoples of England for their luxury and immorality—a remarkable prophecy, as it must have seemed to later generations, of the Danish ravages.

After a short interval of unrest the Mercian throne was filled by Offa, a distant relation of Ethelbald, who reigned for nearly forty years (757–96), and who in some ways seems to deserve the title of the greatest of Mercian kings. The everlasting contest with Wessex was renewed, and Offa's victory at Bensington in Oxfordshire (779) did something towards

* Ep. 73 (Mon. Hist. Germ., Epist. iii., 340).

obliterating the disgrace of Burford and probably gave what is now the county of Oxford to the middle kingdom. From various causes Offa had now acquired so great a predominance that he was able to carry into effect a change in the ecclesiastical geography of England which was little less than a revolution. This was the creation of a new archbishopric for the Midlands. We may imagine that he reasoned in this wise: "Northumbria has now its archbishopric at York. The archbishop of Canterbury is too much overshadowed by the greatness of my rival of Wessex. Why should not I, the most powerful king in Britain, have an archbishop of my own here in Mercia?" This reasoning prevailed. In 787 a synod, ever after known as "the contentious synod," was held at Chelsea, and thereat, we are told, seven out of the twelve dioceses of the southern province were placed under the archbishop of Lichfield, being rent away from their dependence on Canterbury. The meaning of this change is obvious. There were now three great English kingdoms: Northumbria, Wessex and Mercia, and three corresponding archbishoprics, York, Lichfield and Canterbury. The Thames was the boundary between the central and southern provinces, except that Essex with Middlesex was included in the latter. East Anglia was evidently, in ecclesiastical matters as well as in things political, subject to Mercia, a fact which accounts for the abrupt entry in the Chronicle for 792* (794): "Offa, King of the Mercians, ordered the head of Ethelbert, King [of the East Angles], to be struck off." The new ecclesiastical arrangement lasted for only sixteen years. In 803 Offa's successor Cenwulf voluntarily restored all the metropolitan rights of the see of Canterbury.

There is one still existing memorial by which the name of Offa yet survives in the mouths of men. This is Offa's Dyke (called by the Welsh Clawdd Offa), a great earthen rampart flanked by a ditch, which ran from the mouth of the Dee to the mouth of the Wye, a distance of some 130 miles, and divided the territories of the Mercians from those of the Welsh. For a considerable portion of its course this rampart is still visible, in some places only as a low bank but in others showing a height of 30 feet to the summit of the mound from the bottom of the ditch on its western side. It nearly corresponds with the present boundary between England and Wales, except that it cuts off from England a portion of Hereford and the whole of Monmouth. In part of its course it is duplicated by another

* It is now recognised that the dates in the Chronicle from 754 to 851 are two, or in some cases three years behind the true dates.

embankment called Wat's Dyke, about three miles to the east of it, and this work also, in the belief of some antiquaries, belongs to the age of Offa. Though we are distinctly told, on good authority, that the object of this huge work was military defence, it is probable that, like the Vallum in Northumberland and the Pfahlgraben in Germany, it was also a geographical boundary, and served a useful purpose in time of peace, as marking the limit of two rival jurisdictions and clearly indicating to which of them pertained the duty of punishing robbery or murder committed on either side of the border. This dyke probably commemorates the result of the "Devastation of the southern Britons wrought by Offa" which is noted by the Cambrian Annals under the years 778 and 784; and the effect of these campaigns seems to have been to push back the Welsh frontier from the Severn to the Wye—no unimportant augmentation of the Mercian kingdom.

The diplomatic correspondence of the period shows us how large loomed the figure of Offa in the eyes of his contemporaries. Pope Hadrian I. in writing to Charlemagne calls him absolutely "rex Anglorum," and at the same time earnestly expresses his disbelief in a rumour which had reached his ears that the two kings of the Franks and the Angles were plotting his own deposition from the papacy, and the appointment of a Frankish ecclesiastic in his place. This, however, was probably an idle rumour, set afloat by some of Hadrian's enemies in order to work upon the fears of the elderly pontiff. Offa, himself, seems to have received the legates of the Holy See with reverence and to have availed himself of their help in regulating the affairs of his new archbishopric. Moreover, he ordained, probably as a thank-offering for the papal assistance in this matter, that his kingdom should send a yearly offering of 365 mancuses (about £130), one for each day in the year, to the holy see.

There were, however, some difficulties connected with the frequent English pilgrimages to Rome; too frequent according to Alcuin for the good repute of the Anglo-Saxon dames who engaged in them; and too frequent, as the tax collectors of Charles the Great considered, by reason of the number of merchants who, under the guise of holiness, transacted a profitable business in the transport of specie and merchandise. These difficulties were, however, set right by a friendly letter from Charles to the effect that true pilgrims should receive all due protection from him, but that merchants masquerading as pilgrims must pay the regular customs dues. This letter, written in 796, was accompanied by the present of a belt, a Hunnish sword and two silken vestments, part of the huge spoil taken in the previous year from the robber hold of the Avars. It seems to have healed an old estrangement between the two kings dating from 789, the result of the failure of matrimonial negotiations between them. Charles had solicited the hand of Offa's daughter for his son and namesake, and Offa had been willing to consent, on condition that Charles's daughter, Bertha, should become the bride of his son, Ecgferth. On this point, however, the negotiations broke down, owing to Charles's well-known reluctance to part with any of his daughters. For a short time the relations between the two kingdoms were sorely strained, and decrees forbidding the entrance of merchants were issued by either angry sovereign, but gradually the dispute died down, perhaps partly owing to the mediation of Alcuin, who was English by birth and loyal to his English friends, but Frank by adoption and a true subject to Charles. At last, as we have seen, all wounds were healed by the application of an Avar baldric, a sword and two mantles.

Offa died in 796, and his son and successor Ecgferth followed him to the grave in four months. This untimely death of a young and hopeful prince was, according to monastic writers, a punishment for the many crimes of his father, especially for the execution of the East Anglian Ethelbert. Cenwulf, who succeeded to the Mercian throne, was not of Offa's line, though like him a collateral descendant of Penda. Of his reign, which lasted well on into the ninth century (796–821), nothing need here be said, save that in its third year he invaded Kent, which had revolted from his rule and set up a rival king named Edbert Pren, possibly a descendant of the old Kentish line. Edbert was defeated and taken prisoner by the soldiers of Offa, who, after cutting out his tongue and chopping off his hands, sent him as a prisoner into Mercia. With all its vaunted prosperity, the central kingdom does not seem to have made great progress in civilisation since the days of Penda.

*****

Save for some conflicts with Wales, in which the Cymri appear generally to have been worsted, the history of the WEST SAXON kingdom in the eighth century consisted chiefly of that protracted struggle with Mercia which has been briefly sketched in the foregoing pages. But the story of the death of Cynewulf in 786 is told in the Chronicle with such vividness and in such detail that an attempt must be made to reproduce it here. Cynewulf, a kinsman of the victorious Cuthred, had expelled that king's successor, Sigebert, and driven him into exile. After thirty years of reigning, Cynewulf had to meet the face of the avenger, Sigebert's brother, Cyneheard, who is called in the Chronicle "the Etheling." Learning that the king, slenderly guarded, was visiting a woman at Merton, Cyneheard with a band of his gesiths surrounded the house and rode through the gate of the great courtyard to the door of the lady's bower. Surprised and unable to summon his guards, the king rushed to the door, and in the narrow entrance defended himself bravely and with success till he caught sight of the Etheling. Then with a sudden burst of rage he dashed forward, sorely wounded his enemy, but was himself surrounded and slain by Cyneheard's men. Meantime the lady's cries aroused the king's thegns who were in the great hall, ignorant of what had happened, and they hastened to the scene of tumult, each running as fast as he could. The Etheling, who had no quarrel with them, offered them quarter and money in return for peace, but they refused his terms and continued fighting, outnumbered as they were, till they were all slain but one man, "and he," says the chronicler apologetically, "was [only] a Welshman, a hostage and already sorely wounded."

Next morning, when the main body of the king's thegns, whom he had left behind when he rode to Merton, heard what had happened, they galloped to the house, headed by the Ealdorman Osric, but found the Etheling in possession and the gate of the courtyard closed against them. A parley was called, and Cyneheard offered the new-comers their own terms in money and land if they would join his party and win for him the kingdom, adding with uncomprehended irony: "There are kinsmen of yours now with me in the house, and they, I know, will never leave me." "No kinsman," answered the thegns, "can be dearer to us than our lord, and we will never follow his murderer." The offer of quarter which they in turn made to the Etheling's gesiths was rejected with equal scorn. "We care no more for your offer," said they, "than did your comrades for ours, and they"—now at last the truth came out—"were all slain with the king." Then followed fierce fighting round the gates, till at last the king's thegns, who were the stronger party, forced their way in and slew the Etheling and all the men with him, save one who had already received many wounds and was godson to Ealdorman Osric by whom his life was preserved. Once again we note the unshakable fidelity of the "comrades" to their lord.

On the death of Cynewulf, Beorhtric (786–802), a distant kinsman, succeeded to the West Saxon throne. Royal genealogies were by this time in much confusion, and all that the chronicler could say concerning his descent was that "his right father's kin goeth unto Cerdic." Beorhtric's reign, in itself unimportant, is chiefly interesting to us by reason of a certain competitor, for the time an unsuccessful competitor, for the crown. This was none other than a young man named Egbert, who, it was said, could trace his line back through a brother of King Ine to Ceawlin and so to Cerdic. His father, Ealhmund, had been under-king of Kent, whether under Mercia or Wessex it would be difficult to say; indeed the whole of Egbert's early career is veiled in obscurity. All that seems to be certain is that he had pretensions of some kind to the kingship of Wessex, which made him obnoxious to Beorhtric and forced him to seek shelter at the Mercian court. Thence, however, he was driven in 789 when Beorhtric obtained in marriage the hand of Offa's daughter, Eadburh. Ethelred of Northumbria having soon after married another daughter of the same house, there was evidently no safe resting-place in England for the fugitive prince, who betook himself to the court of Charles the Great and there abode for thirteen years till the death of his rival. In 802, Beorhtric died, and Egbert, returning to England, seems to have been without opposition raised to the West Saxon throne.

According to Asser, the biographer of Alfred the Great, the death of Beorhtric was due to his wife. That daughter of Offa, if Asser may be trusted, as soon as she had established her influence in the West Saxon palace, "began in her father's manner to act tyrannically." She undermined to the utmost of her power the king's best counsellors by slandering them to her husband, and those whom she could not thus displace she removed by poison. A draught of poison which she had thus prepared for a young man greatly beloved by Beorhtric was inadvertently tasted by the king and caused his death, which of course involved Eadburh's downfall. Carrying with her great hoards of treasure, she sought the Frankish court where her husband's rival, Egbert, had so lately been sheltered. As she stood in the hall of audience and offered rich presents to the emperor, Charles said to her, perhaps in jest: "Choose, Eadburh, which you will have, me or my son who stands here with me under the dais." She thoughtlessly answered: "If I may really have my choice, I choose your son, inasmuch as he is the younger of the two." Whereupon Charles answered with a smile: "If you had chosen me, you should have had my son, but now since you have chosen him you shall have neither." An improbable story truly, but one which shows the sort of legend which already ere the end of the ninth century was springing up around the name of Charlemagne. Eadburh, however, received from the emperor the gift of a great abbey which she ruled for some time. Then, being convicted of unchastity, she was expelled from the convent, wandered over Europe, begging her daily bread, and died at last in misery at Pavia. Such was the end of the daughter of the mighty Offa. So detestable, says Asser, was the memory of Eadburh's crimes that for generations the West Saxons would not allow the wife of one of their kings to be called queen, but would only allow her the title of consort.

XV.

EARLY DANISH INVASIONS—EGBERT AND ETHELWULF

Two entries which strictly belong to the eighth century have been reserved for this place, because they are rather foreshadowings of what was to befal in the years after 800, than characteristic of what was happening in the years preceding it. At some unnamed date in the reign of Beorhtric, King of Wessex, but probably about the year 790, the Chronicle tells us that "first came three ships of Northmen.* And then the reeve rode thereto and would fain drive them to the king's vill, for he knew not what [manner of men] they were and there they slew him. These were the first ships of Danish men that sought the land of the English race." This short but ominous entry is a tocsin ringing in 300 years of strife. The words of the Chronicle and of its copyist Ethelweard seem to suggest that the ships' crews came with peaceful intent; that the king's reeve—a man whose office was something like that of steward or bailiff—tried to exact some payment from them, and for that purpose to force them to enter some royal settlement, but found to his cost that these were no sheep that would stand quiet for his shearing, but fierce war-wolves, capable of turning upon him with hungry teeth and rending him in pieces.

This first affray with the Danes evidently took place in Wessex; and, if we may believe the historian Ethelweard, the royal vill where the reeve resided was Dorchester. But the Scandinavians having seen, as the Saxons did before them, "the nothingness of the natives," of course came again, and this time (793) to Northumbria. Dire presentiments had already cowed the hearts of the people; hurricanes blew and lightnings flashed,

* The words from Haerethaland which follow in the text are thought by Steenstrup (Normannerne, ii., 15–20) to be an interpolation. In the following chapters the example of the Chronicle will generally be followed, in calling the Scandinavian invaders Danes, without entering on the debated question which of them came from Denmark proper and which from Norway.

and (if we like to trust the chronicler) fiery flying serpents hurtled through the air. Then came a great famine, and then (June 8) "the heathen men" [Danes] "miserably destroyed God's church at Lindisfarne with rapine and slaughter." The desecration of so holy a place shed horror through western Christendom. "It is now," wrote Alcuin to the Northumbrian King Ethelred, "about 350 years that we and our fathers have dwelt in this most beautiful country, and never before has such a terrible thing befallen Britain as that which we have now suffered from the pagans. Nor was it, in fact, thought possible that a voyage of that kind could ever have been made"—a strange illustration of the lost seamanship of the Anglo-Saxons. "Lo now the church of St. Cuthbert is stained with the blood of the priests of God. It is despoiled of all its ornaments. The most venerable place in Britain has been given to pagan nations for a prey."

The ninth century, upon which we now enter, too truly verified the forebodings of the prophets of evil. It began indeed in glory, with Charles the Frank acclaimed at Rome as Augustus, and meditating the revival of the old Roman empire in all its splendour, the protection of the widow and the fatherless, the humbling of all lawless power, the foundation of St. Augustine's City of God. But the new empire had scarcely been founded when it began to crumble; all through the middle years of the century it sank lower and lower into the morass. With the deposition of Charles the Fat in 887 and his death in 888 the last Carolingian emperor vanished from the scene. Saracen pirates ravaged the shores of the Mediterranean, besieged Rome (846), rifled the tombs of the apostles and hurled their lances at the mosaic picture of Christ in the apse of St. Peter's. Ere the century was ended, Hungarian Arpad was renewing in Central Europe the ravages of Attila. Everywhere there was "distress of nations with perplexity"—perplexity made all the more terrible by the fact that the popes themselves, the men to whom Europe looked for counsel and for cheer, were throughout this century for the most part men of poor and feeble character. It was the age which saw the posthumous condemnation of Pope Formosus, the age in which the malevolent credulity of a later generation placed the fable of Pope Joan.

But greater than all the other calamities which befel Europe during this period was unquestionably the misery caused by the raids of Scandinavian free-booters. A well-known story describes how Charles the Great saw the ships of the Northmen approaching the city in Provence where he then dwelt. As soon as the pirates perceived that they would have to deal with the great emperor himself, they sheered off in well-advised caution, but Charles stood at the eastern window of his palace gazing at their departing sails, and as he gazed he wept. None of his courtiers durst ask him the reason of his tears, but he himself deigned thus to explain them: "I weep for sorrow that they should have dared in my lifetime to approach this coast, and because I foresee how much misery they will cause to those who come after me." Whatever may be the truth of this story, there is no doubt that Charles's alleged prophecy was fatally verified. Engrossed as we generally are by the story of Danish ravages in England, we are apt to forget that, at least in the ninth century, France and Germany suffered nearly as much from the same calamity. All round the coast from Denmark to Spain, wherever a broad estuary invited their presence, there the Danish pirates entered and ravaged. The Elbe, the Rhine, the Seine, the Loire and the Garonne were all furrowed by their keels. Hamburg, Paris, Rouen, Bordeaux, Marseilles and countless other cities were sacked by them; some, especially Paris, more than once.

A student of Scandinavian history may well inquire, not why the raids of the Northmen were terrible in the ninth and two following centuries, but why they had not begun long before. Here was a poor and hardy population, inhabiting a country so deeply indented by the sea that it was impossible for its sons to be mere landsmen; in fact a population which for more than a thousand years has been more enthusiastically seafaring than any other in the world. Within a few days' sail of their homes were the shores of Britain and of Gaul, countries peopled by races which had lost their old love of the sea, and were for the most part sunk in swinish pleasures; rich countries, too, according to the estimate of that day, everywhere studded with convents in which pious women or unwarlike men were hoarding up gold and silver and jewels for the glory of the White Christ. There was yet no settled order in any of the Northmen's own lands. The history of Denmark, Sweden and Norway in the seventh and eighth centuries is mere chaos. The title of king was easily earned and easily lost. In the sagas of the Heimskringla piracy is treated as the normal occupation of every young Northman of noble birth. "Eric's sons warred much in the eastern lands, but sometimes they harried in Norway." "There harried Olaf and slew many men, and burned some out of house and home, and took much wealth." Entries such as these (though of a rather later date than we have yet reached) occur on almost every other page of the great Icelandic epic, and give us the impression that the young Scandinavian gathered ships together and "harried" the Baltic lands or the shores of the German or Atlantic Ocean, in the same way in which the young Englishman went the grand tour in the eighteenth century, or in the nineteenth became owner of a ranch.

The ships of the vikings, if we may judge from the few specimens preserved in the museums of Denmark and Norway, though well built of their kind, were not much better than large open boats, undecked, averaging about seventy feet long, and drawing not more than four feet of water. They had only one mast with a square sail, and they trusted rather to rowing than to sailing for their progress. Except on the largest ships, about fifteen or sixteen men at a time, with a like number relieving them, and sixty or seventy fighting men, or a hundred in all, may have been the complement of a viking ship. There was no difference between prow and stern, and the vessel could be worked in either direction, the steering being managed by an oar at the side. The high-pointed prow at either end was often fashioned into the likeness of some animal, generally a dragon or a serpent. It is evident that such a craft as these, however well adapted for navigation in the long sheltered fiords of Norway, would not be very safe in an Atlantic storm.* It is probable, therefore, that the Northmen would be careful observers of the weather, and would generally choose a season of calm weather for slipping across the German Ocean. Once arrived at the English or Irish coast, they would choose some island near to the mainland and make it their lair, from whence they might issue forth to plunder and destroy. Especially convenient for their purpose, as for that of their Saxon predecessors, were such islands as Sheppey and Thanet, separated from fertile Kent only by narrow channels in which the dragon-ships could lie sheltered from winds and waves. Dear also to the heart of the Northman buccaneer were the estuaries of great rivers, Humber, Severn, Thames, Seine and Loire. Here they could collect their ships, scattered perchance in the course of their passage over the ocean, could watch the movements of the militia gathering for the defence of the country, and then at the right moment could row rapidly up the broad stream, capture and sack some unsuspecting city, and gather great store of gold and jewels from some rich cathedral. This, the collection of treasures from the more civilised lands of the south, was, after all, the chief incentive to the early vikings in their wild sea-rovings. Herein they were like the first generation of Elizabethan adventurers in the Spanish main, to whom the plunder of the

* See Keary, The Vikings in Western Christendom, pp. 139–42.

Plate-fleet seemed the supreme object of desire, though with the viking, as with the buccaneer, thoughts of settlement and of conquest came later, and they who had come to ravage remained to rule.

The Here,* the great Danish armament which appears and reappears so often in the pages of the Chronicle—one imagines the studious monk in his scriptorium trembling as he writes the very word—seems to have been generally composed of foot soldiers hewing with swords or wielding their great two-handed battle-axes, armed with strong round shields and with byrnies or coats-of-mail, and beginning the fight by sending a cloud of javelins at their foes. Gradually, however, they learned the advantage of possessing a force of cavalry; and one of their first exploits on landing was to scour the country for horses, by means of which they could ravage the land far and wide where their ships could not carry them. They were, however, in strictness mounted infantry rather than cavalry. Their horses bore them swiftly to the battle-field. When they had reached it they dismounted and fought on foot.

Not even the Icelandic Sagas with all their poetic fire can win us to unmixed admiration of the lives of these freebooters. They had some noble qualities, but notwithstanding these they were still barbarians. They were ancestors of the most chivalrous nations of Europe, and they possessed some of the qualities inherent in chivalry, such as courage, endurance, loyalty, honour to the women of their tribe. But on the other hand—if any reliance is to be placed on the statements of the Chronicle—they would often swear most solemnly to a treaty and then ride away and break it. They often tortured their captives; their hands were heavy on the weak, on little children and on women. This is the less to be wondered at, since owing to the poverty of their country they often left their own new-born children to perish. Their blows fell with especial ferocity on the churches and monasteries of Britain: a fact which may probably be accounted for by the fact that these were the chief treasure-houses of the invaded lands.

The assaults of the Danes upon the Saxons, like those of the Saxons upon the Romanised Britons, fall naturally into three periods,† the first

* 'Here' is simply the Anglo-Saxon equivalent for army; but in the Chronicle it almost invariably means the Danish army, while fyrd is the word used for the English troops, which were in the nature of a mi

† This fact has been especially emphasised by Freeman, Norman Conquest, i., 43–45.

of robbery, the second of settlement, and the third of conquest. The chronological limits of these three periods may be approximately fixed as follows: pillage, from 790 to 851; settlement, from 851 to 897; conquest (after a pause of nearly a century), from 980 to 1016.

Terrible as were the ravages of the Scandinavian invaders, it is generally admitted that on the whole the benefit which resulted therefrom was greater than the suffering. That benefit was the consolidation of Anglo-Saxon England into one kingdom. In the thirty-seven years of the reign of Egbert of Wessex he attained, by steps which we are about to trace, to a supremacy which was probably wider than that of any of the Bretwaldas who had preceded him, and which in some degree justifies the popular conception of his position as founder of the English monarchy, though the unity of England was not in truth realised till a century later. But other Bretwaldas had been nearly as powerful as Egbert, and their overlordship in the hands of feeble descendants had melted away, while the "particularism" of the several lesser kingdoms had again successfully asserted itself. It may be doubted whether Egbert's supremacy would not have gone the way of all the previous supremacies, but for that terrible series of Scandinavian invasions which seemed at the time to threaten not merely the prosperity but the very life of Anglo-Saxon peoples. For a century the terrible struggle continued and then ended for a time, to be renewed indeed with almost equal fury after an interval of rest; but the effect of that first fierce discipline was greatly to weaken if not altogether to destroy the spirit of particularism in the Anglo-Saxon states. After Athelstan's death in 940 there was scarcely any serious thought of reestablishing Mercia or Northumbria as a separate kingdom from Wessex. Hard and cruel were the blows stricken by the hammer of Thor, but they had the effect of welding Angles, Saxons and Jutes into one people.

The upward career of EGBERT of Wessex (802–839) must now be briefly described. As has been said, he returned from exile on the death of his foe, Beorhtric, and apparently without a contest was raised to the West Saxon throne. On the very day of his accession there was a great fight between the Mercians, commanded by the Ealdorman of the Hwiccas and the West Saxons under the generalship of the Ealdorman of Wilts. Both Ealdormen were slain, but victory is said to have rested with the men of Wiltshire. With this exception, the first thirteen years of Egbert's reign passed in peace. Cenwulf of Mercia, whose dominions, including, as they did, Kent, Sussex, Surrey and Essex, wrapped Wessex all round to the east, was too powerful to be lightly assailed. When Egbert's old patron, Charlemagne, died in 814, there was nothing to betoken that the exile whom he had befriended would achieve anything more than a petty and precarious West Saxon royalty. In the following year, however, the long-interrupted movement westward was once more resumed. Egbert "harried West Wales from east to west"; in other words, he overran Cornwall from the Tamar to the Land's End. Though the process of subjugation was not yet complete, this was the beginning of the end of Cornish independence.

In 821 Cenwulf, the powerful King of Mercia, died, and there were troubles in the palace at Lichfield. After the murder of his son, a child of seven years old, and the deposition of his brother, an usurper named Beornwulf obtained the crown. The discords thus caused gave Egbert the opportunity for which he had probably long waited. He declared war on Beornwulf, met him in battle at Ellandune, probably in the north of Wiltshire, and after a most bloody fight completely defeated him. Intent on gathering at once the most important fruits of victory, Egbert sent his son Ethelwulf to the region of Kent, where his own father had once held sway. Baldred, King of Kent, the vassal of Mercia, was expelled; the three south-eastern counties and Essex, which included the city of London, gladly accepted the rule of Egbert, who was represented by his son Ethelwulf as under-king, and the long struggle between Mercia and Wessex for the possession of that corner of England was at an end. East Anglia, with her bitter memories of Mercian perfidy, to which her King Ethelbert had fallen a victim thirty years before, now rose in rebellion, relying on the protection of Egbert, and succeeded in defeating and slaying the Mercian king (826?). After Beornwulf's death Mercia could no longer offer any effectual resistance. Egbert was soon acknowledged as overlord, and thus by about the year 829 he had brought under his supremacy, though not under his personal rule, the whole of England south of the Humber, and acquired the mysterious title of Bretwalda, which (if the Saxon Chronicle may be trusted) had been borne by no other sovereign since the death of Oswy, a century and a half before.

The conqueror next moved against Northumbria, whose king Eanred did not dare to accept the offer of battle. At Dore, among the hills of North Derbyshire, not far from Sheffield, "the Northumbrians met him and offered him obedience and peace, and with that they separated the one from the other." This transaction undoubtedly meant the acceptance of Egbert as overlord, and his supremacy was thus at last assured over the whole English portion of the island. Nor did he rest content herewith, for in the next year "he led an army against the men of North Wales and reduced them to humble" (though not permanent) "obedience."

The last four years of Egbert's life were disturbed by the raids of the Danish invaders. For forty-one years after the raids in which the Northumbrian sanctuaries were pillaged, the Northmen seem to have left England unmolested, but during this time they had been sailing round the north of Scotland, occupying the Hebrides and grievously harrying, all but conquering, Ireland. Now in 835 Egbert, already a man advanced in years, heard the grievous tidings that "heathen men were ravaging the Isle of Sheppey." Thus the Danes, like the Jutes four centuries earlier, began their hostile operations with one of those curious semi-islands which clustered round the coast of Kent. Sheppey, however, was higher up the estuary of the Thames than Hengest's Isle of Thanet. Next year the Danes appeared on the coast of West Dorset. The crews of thirty-five ships appeared off Charmouth, not far from Lyme Regis. Egbert himself led his men to battle; there was a terrible slaughter, in which two bishops and two ealdormen fell, and—ominous confession of the West Saxon chronicler—"the Danes held the place of slaughter." Still, however, we have no hint of permanent occupation.

Two years later, in 838, there was a perilous combination of Northman and Celt. "A mighty fleet" [evidently Danish] "came to West Wales and they" [Danes and Cornishmen] "made an alliance to fight against Egbert. When he heard that, he went forth and fought with them at Hengestdune, and there he put to flight both Welshmen [Cornishmen] and Danes." At Hingston Down, a high moorland overlooking the Tamar, about four miles north of the place where the great Saltash bridge now spans the creek, this important victory was won. It was the last piece of work that the old warrior accomplished. In 839 he "fared forth," surely not without some dark forebodings of the hard struggle that lay before his descendants; and ETHELWULF his son reigned in his stead. The new king seems to have ruled in person only over the ancestral Wessex, forming the recently acquired kingdoms in the south-east of the island into a dependency, of which his brother Athelstan was made under-king.

The teacher to whom the education of Ethelwulf when a boy had been entrusted by his father, and who retained considerable influence over him in manhood, was an ecclesiastic of noble birth named Swithun, who is chiefly now remembered on account of the meteorological phenomena connected with the day devoted to him in the calendar (July 15, 971).* The gentle and devout character of Ethelwulf seems to have retained through life the impress of the teaching of the unworldly St. Swithun, but he had also another counsellor by whom he was often braced to the performance of the difficult work of reigning. This was Ealhstan, a stirring warrior-prelate, who in 848 won a great and bloody victory over the Danes, at the mouth of the Parret, in Bridgwater Bay, fighting side by side with the ealdormen of Somerset and Dorset. Ealhstan was bishop of the great diocese of Sherborne (including the counties of Somerset and Devon), while Swithun in 852, towards the end of Ethelwulf's reign, was enthroned in the more dignified see of Winchester.

The influence, in some respects the diverging influence, of these two counsellors of the king is probably described with truth by the twelfth century historian, William of Malmesbury. "These two eminent bishops, seeing the king to be of somewhat dull and lethargic temperament, stirred him up by frequent admonitions to the performance of his kingly duties. Swithun, who looked on worldly things with disgust, moulded the mind of his lord to the love of things heavenly. Ealhstan, who thought that secular matters also should not be neglected, animated him to the war against the Danes, himself often furnishing money to the royal treasury, himself setting the battle in array. Any one who reads our annals will find that many such affairs were resolutely begun and gloriously ended by him." The historian, however, remarks that he cannot give Ealhstan the unmingled praise which he would willingly offer, because of his unjust encroachments on the rights of the monastery of Malmesbury.

Almost every year of Ethelwulf's reign has its annal in the Chronicle, telling of Danish ravages. The storm beat most persistently on Wessex. Southampton (840), Portland (840), Charmouth (843), the mouth of the Parret (848), Wembury (?) (854), were all scenes of battle with the Danes, generally, but not always, disastrous for the English. The other parts of the country did not escape unharmed. In 841 Lindsey, East Anglia and Kent saw widespread slaughter. In 844 Redwulf, King of Northumbria, met his death at the hands of the invaders. In 851, three hundred and fifty

* This date, as will be seen, is not that of his original burial, which probably took place near the beginning of July, 862, but the date of the "translation" of his remains to the cathedral, which was accomplished more than a century later.

ships came to the mouth of the Thames; their crews took Canterbury and London by storm, and put to flight the king of the Mercians who had advanced to meet them. There, however, their success ended. Crossing the Thames into Surrey, they were met by Ethelwulf and his eldest son Ethelbald leading the West Saxon fyrd. Battle was joined at Ockley, on the edge of the chalk downs which look into the adjoining county of Sussex, and there the West Saxon king in the words of the Chronicle, "made the greatest slaughter among the heathen army that we have heard of till this present day, and there gained the victory."

However complete the victory of Ockley might be, its importance is much diminished by the entry which precedes it in the Chronicle: "And the heathen men for the first time took up their quarters over winter in Thanet." We thus enter on the second of the above-mentioned periods—the stage of settlement, that in which the Danes came to England, not merely to plunder and then depart, but to fix their abode permanently in the country. This choice of Thanet as their winter quarters must, to the men of Kent who knew anything of the history of their ancestors, have seemed an ominous recurrence to the strategy of Hengest and Horsa four centuries previously. There was trouble also from an older enemy. The men of Wales were now governed by one of the greatest of their early kings, Rhodri Mawr (Roderick the Great, 844–77); and it seems that the distress of the Saxons under the Danish attacks gave the Welsh courage to rise against the traditional enemies of their race. In 853 Burhred, King of Mercia, acting by the advice of his witan, made formal application to Ethelwulf for help against "the men of North Wales." The very fact that such an application was needed, and that it came from the king and council of the Mercian realm, shows how far England was from having yet attained to that complete unity which has been incorrectly associated with the name of Egbert. However, the expedition which Ethelwulf now undertook against the Cymri, in alliance with Mercia, seems to have been successful, and the marriage of Burhred to Ethelwulf's daughter, celebrated at Easter-tide, doubtless cemented the alliance and may have been a step towards federation.

Again in this year 853 there was fighting both by land and sea against the heathen in Thanet. Many men on both sides were slain and drowned. The two ealdormen who led the forces of Kent and Surrey were at first victorious, but—as often happened—let victory slip from their unskilful hands, and both fell on the field of battle. This and many similar entries bring vividly before us the typical Saxon ealdorman, leading the fyrd or militia of his shire to battle, displaying plenty of courage and risking his life freely in the service of his country, but showing little skill in organising a campaign or even in grasping its fruits when they fell into his lap. On the other side we see the men of the Scandinavian islands and long fiords, children of the sea, equally ready to fight on it or on the land—artful, ruthless, courageous, and with a splendid ignorance of defeat. Such were the ravens who were now fixing their talons deep in our exhausted England. Our next entry is: "In this year" [855] "heathen men first remained over winter in Sheppey."

It might have been supposed that the West Saxon king would need all his energies to put his kingdom in an adequate state of defence and to organise all round the coast an efficient system of resistance to the all-penetrating Northmen. Instead of this we find him, with some surprise, in this very year 855, "going to Rome with much pomp," remaining there for a twelve-month, visiting the Frankish court on his way back, and returning, elderly widower that he was, with a bride thirteen years old. This strange episode of the pilgrimage was the fulfilment of a long-cherished design, and may have been partly due to the pious counsels of St. Swithun, but certainly does not raise our opinion of the king's wisdom, while the marriage adventure looks like mere fatuity. Before Ethelwulf's departure he made that celebrated donation to the Church which used to be considered as the introduction of the tithe-system into England, but which was really "the devotion of a tenth part of his private property to ecclesiastical purposes."* He took with him his youngest and favourite son Alfred, who though still but a little child had already, two years before, made the same pilgrimage. Travelling through France he was received with royal honours by Charles the Bald, king of that country, and escorted by him to the boundary of his kingdom. He perhaps arrived in Rome in time to see the pontiff Leo IV., who on Alfred's previous visit had laid his hands in benediction on the head of the child. On July 17, however (855), the old pope died, and Ethelwulf and his boy must have witnessed the tumultuous proceedings which followed, and the state of practical civil war between the Lateran and St. Peter's which filled the streets of Rome with clamour, till at last about the end of September the iconoclast anti-pope Anastasius was finally overthrown and Benedict III. took his seat on the chair of St. Peter. It is a curious

* Stubbs, Const. Hist., i., 249, and 258.

fact, but probably a mere coincidence, that precisely at this point of papal history the romancing chroniclers of the Middle Ages have inserted the fable of "Pope Joan," the learned and eloquent Englishwoman who, as they averred, came to Rome in male attire, habited as an ecclesiastic, was unanimously chosen pope and wore the tiara for some months or even years, till her sex was unfortunately disclosed in the midst of a public procession. If any further proof were needed of the absurdity of this story (which is no Protestant invention but passed current through many medieval centuries), it might be furnished by the absolute silence of the English chroniclers, some of whom may well have conversed with members of the retinue of the West Saxon king.

Ethelwulf's devout liberality is recorded by the contemporary papal biographer, though his Italian ear has failed to catch or to retain his barbarous name: "At this time a king of the Saxons named ... leaving his goods and his own kingdom, came for prayer with a multitude of followers to the thresholds of the Apostles Peter and Paul in Rome. And he gave to St. Peter a crown of pure gold weighing four pounds; vessels of pure gold weighing two pounds; a sword bound with pure gold; two smaller images of pure gold; a paten of silver gilt, Saxon work, four pounds; a vestment of purple with a golden border; a white surplice all of silk, embroidered and gold bordered; two large curtains of gold tapestry.* Then the Saxon king, on Pope Benedict's request that he would employ the gold and silver [which he had brought with him] in giving largesse to the people in St. Peter's church, dispensed gold to the bishops, presbyters, deacons and all the rest of the clergy and chief men of Rome, but he gave small silver coins to the common people."†

A more obviously useful exercise of Ethelwulf's liberality was connected with the Schola Saxonum, which is said to have been founded by his predecessor, Ine, or by the Mercian Offa. In this schola (something probably between a convent and an academic hostel) young Anglo-Saxons destined for the ecclesiastical profession probably dwelt for months or years, learning the Latin of the missal and the tones of Gregorian plain-song. Its memory even yet lingers in Rome, for the Church of the Holy Spirit in "the Leonine city" having been placed near the school of the Saxons still bears the name of "San Spirito in Sassia." The schola had, however, been unfortunately destroyed by fire in the year before

* The translation of some of the terms used is conjectural.

† Liber Pontificalis, ii., 148 (ed. Duchesne).

Ethelwulf's visit, and patriotism as well as piety prompted him to spend on its restoration some part of the treasure which he had brought from England.*

After a year's residence in Rome, Ethelwulf returned to England, visiting on the way the court of his much younger contemporary, Charles the Bald,† whose daughter Judith, a young girl of thirteen, he brought home with him as his wife, much to the astonishment, doubtless, of his subjects and to the annoyance of his sons by his first marriage. Though it is nowhere distinctly so stated, it seems probable that this extraordinary second marriage of Ethelwulf had some connexion with an event which clouded the last years of his life, the rebellion of his eldest son Ethelbald. This young man had probably exercised some of the functions of a regent during his father's absence, and now stood arrayed in arms to repel him from his kingdom. The fact that he was abetted by the energetic Bishop Ealhstan and by the ealdorman of Somerset, who had helped Ealhstan to win his great victory over the Danes in Bridgwater Bay, suggests the possibility that this rebellion may not have been due merely to the ambition of an undutiful son, but may have been prompted by a patriotic desire to wrest the helm of the state from the hands of an inefficient pilot. Happily, though Ethelwulf had many partisans, shocked by what they deemed the unnatural conduct of Ethelbald, civil war was avoided. The gentle old man agreed without much difficulty to an arrangement whereby the western portion of the kingdom, the richer and fairer part, was handed over to his son, he himself retaining the eastern portion. The young Queen Judith, who had been crowned before her departure from France, now took her place on the royal throne side by side with her husband, notwithstanding the "infamous custom" of Wessex which, as has been said, on account of the evil example of the daughter of Offa, forbade the consorts of West Saxon kings to sit on the throne or to bear the name of queen.

....

* This restoration of the Schola Saxonum rests only on the authority of William of Malmesbury, and is doubted, but hardly disproved, by Mr. Stevenson in his edition of Asser, pp. 245–46. Notwithstanding the high authority of Monseigneur Duchesne, quoted by Mr. Stevenson, it does not seem to me probable that the scholæ peregrinorum were essentially military establishments, though they may have assumed somewhat of that character under the stress of the Saracen invasions in the ninth century.

† Charles the Bald was at this time thirty-two years of age. Ethelwulf cannot have been less than fifty and may have been considerably older.

Less than two years after his return from Rome, on January 13, 858, Ethelwulf died. His will was much talked of and was considered by his biographers a model for all future generations. After directing how his kingdom and his property should be divided between his sons, he ordained that throughout his dominions one man in ten, whether a native or a foreigner, should be supplied with meat, drink and clothing by his successors until the Day of Judgment, always supposing "that there should still be men and cattle in the land and that thc country should not have become quite desolate," a striking evidence of the anxieties caused by the Danish invasions. True to the last to his affection for Rome, he left a hundred mancuses (twelve and a half pounds of silver) to buy oil for the lights of St. Peter's, the same sum for the lights of St. Paul's (outside the city), and another hundred for the apostolic pontiff's own private use. It does not seem possible to accept the theories of some recent writers who would fain represent Ethelwulf as a wise and capable statesman, the deviser of large continental alliances for defence against the Northmen. On the contrary, he was probably a man of slender intellect and feeble will, but devout, unworldly and affectionate, by no means the least lovable of Anglo-Saxon sovereigns.

XVI.

ETHELWULF'S SONS—
DANISH INVASIONS TO THE BAPTISM OF GUTHRUM

During the twenty years which followed the death of Ethelwulf four of his sons successively filled the West Saxon throne, namely, Ethelbald, Ethelbert, Ethelred, and Alfred. As the last named is to us incomparably the most interesting figure, it will be well to insert here some particulars relating to his childhood which were purposely omitted from the preceding chapter. For these particulars, as for almost all that makes the great king a living reality to us, we are indebted to the little book De Rebus Gestis Aelfredi, written by the Welsh ecclesiastic, Asser.*

The question of the date of Alfred's birth is beset with some difficulty, but on the whole it seems safest to assign it to the year 848. The place of his birth was undoubtedly Wantage in Berkshire, about twenty-five miles from Reading. Throughout his life his chief exploits had reference to the valley of the middle Thames, and if any one county more than another may claim an interest in his glory, it is that county which, as Asser says, "has its name from the wood of Berroc, where the boxtree grows most plentifully." The mother of Alfred was Osburga, whom Asser describes as "a very religious woman, noble of intellect and noble by birth, daughter of Oslac, the renowned butler of King Ethelwulf, and descended from the old Jutish kings of the Isle of Wight."

In 853, when Alfred was only four or five years old, he was sent by his father to Rome "with an honourable train of nobles and others." The Chronicle says that Pope Leo "anointed him as king and adopted him as his godson." The pope himself, in a still extant letter to Ethelwulf,

* The reader is referred to the Appendix for an account of the controversies which have arisen respecting this book. It is enough to say here that we seem to be justified in accepting it as a contemporary, and in the main a truthful account of the life of the great king. It ends, however, with the year 887.

tells the king that he has "invested his son with the girdle, insignia and robes of the consulate after the manner of Roman consuls." It is difficult to suppose that Ethelwulf, who had four strong sons older than Alfred, can have wished the little five-year-old child, much as he loved him, to be anointed as king. It has been suggested as a possible explanation of the ceremony that some of the West Saxon retinue, who saw the child invested in the splendid trabea of the consul, and were told that these were the robes once worn by the men who wielded kingly power in Rome, attached to the ceremony a political importance greater than was its due. Two years later the boy again went to Rome, accompanying his father on the visit already described. He returned with him through France, and doubtless witnessed the marriage ceremony which gave him a step-mother six years older than himself.

It is probably to the interval between his first and second visits to Rome that we must refer the episode of the ballad-book prize, the best-known story of Alfred's childhood. That story must be told in Asser's own words:—

"His father and mother loved him greatly, more than all his brethren; and so, too, did all men in his father's court, in which he was ever nourished. As infancy grew into boyhood, he appeared more comely than all his brethren and pleasanter in countenance, in speech and in manners. From his very cradle, notwithstanding the practical bent of his disposition, his intellect, noble as his birth, inspired him with an earnest desire for wisdom, but, sad to say, through the shameful neglect of his parents and guardians, he remained unlettered till the twelfth year of his age or even later. He was, however, both by night and day an earnest and frequent listener to the recitation of Saxon poems, and being an apt pupil he easily retained them in his memory....

"Now one day his mother showed to him and his brothers a certain Saxon book of poetry which she had in her hand, and said: 'Whoever shall soonest learn this codex to him will I give it,' at which word he, being urged by some Divine inspiration, and also attracted by the beauty of an initial letter in the book, anticipating his brothers (older than he in years but not in grace) answered his mother thus: 'Will you really give that book to him who shall soonest understand and repeat it to you?' 'Yes, I will,' said she with a happy smile. Hereupon he at once took the book from her hand, went to a master and read it,* and having read it he

* Tunc ille statim tollens librum de manu sua magistrum adiit et legit. Quo lecto matri retulit et recitavit.—Asser, De Rebus Gestis Aelfredi, § 23.

took it back to his mother and recited it to her." It is probable that Asser here intended only to describe the quickness of the child's apprehension and the strength of his memory. The story has nothing really to do with Alfred's learning to read, which, as we are told, did not take place till his twelfth year or even later. He took the book to his master, learned the contents from him and repeated them accurately to his mother. The words "and read it," which are the sole stumbling-block to those who would thus understand the narrative, are possibly due to some slip of the copyist* or to the confused way in which Asser tells his tale.

From the story of Alfred's childhood we return to the main stream of Anglo-Saxon history. As has been said, Ethelwulf died in the beginning of 858. His second son, Ethelbert, probably succeeded him in the eastern half of his kingdom, while ETHELBALD, the eldest, and possibly the over-lord, reigned in the west. The only notable fact, and that a disgraceful one, in Ethelbald's reign was his marriage to his father's young widow, Judith of France. Though the first marriage was perhaps one only in name, the unlawful union excited the disapprobation of all Western Europe, and the premature death of Ethelbald in 860 was probably regarded as a Divine judgment on the sinner. Soon after her second husband's death Judith returned to France, and having after two years eloped with her father's handsome forester, Baldwin, obtained with difficulty the paternal forgiveness, and permission to contract lawful wedlock with her lover. Baldwin, who received a grant of the borderland of Flanders with the title of count or marquis, was the ancestor by Judith of a long line of Baldwins, who gave to their dominions the name of Baldwinsland, and one of whom in 1204 donned the imperial buskins and was crowned by his fellow-crusaders at Constantinople Emperor of Rome. From the same romantic union of Baldwin and Judith sprang also in the seventh generation Matilda, the wife of William the Conqueror.

ETHELBERT, the second son of Ethelwulf, who succeeded to the throne and reigned for six years (860–66), probably added the western half of the kingdom to the eastern, and thus ruled over the whole country south of the Thames. He held it, says the chronicler, "in good agreement and much peacefulness," but already upon his reign was cast the shadow of coming calamity. "In his days," says the Chronicle, "there came a great fleet to land and broke down Winchester." It is true that the invaders were

....

* As Mr. Stevenson suggests, if et be a copyist's mistake for qui (both represented by contractions), the difficulty would vanish.

afterwards defeated and put to flight by the ealdormen of Hampshire and Berkshire, but it is alarming to see the facility with which they gained possession of the capital of Wessex. No doubt this was owing to the fact that the English had made no systematic attempt to keep up the great fortresses which they had inherited from the Romans and which they themselves in their earlier invasion had laid in ruins.* All this was to be altered ere the end of the century by the fortifying hand of Alfred.

On the death of Ethelbert the third brother, ETHELRED, mounted the menaced throne and reigned for five troublous years (866–71). He was assisted in the labour of governing and fighting by his brother Alfred, who bore the title, unique in Anglo-Saxon history, of Secundarius. Apparently he and Alfred were fonder of one another than any others of the royal brethren, and had it not been for his early death he had perhaps achieved renown as enduring as that of his successor. The West Saxon was indeed a menaced throne. Already a year before the death of Ethelbert the fiercest of all the Scandinavian storm-winds had begun to blow. The Danes were now bent upon settlement, not merely on pillage. In 865 "the heathen army encamped in Thanet and made peace with the men of Kent, who promised them money therefor, and under cover of the peace and the promised money, the army stole away by night up country and harried all Kent eastwards." Thus was set the fatal precedent of the payment of ransom. We hear with no surprise that next year there came a mighty heathen army to England and took up their winter quarters in East Anglia. There the sailors supplied themselves with horses and made peace—such peace as it was—with the inhabitants.

Next year (867) the heathen host moved northwards, crossed the Humber and made for York. The affairs of Northumbria were in their usual confusion. Osbert, the lawful king, had been driven out, and another king of non-royal blood named Ella had grasped the reins of power. This is that Ella to whom, in sagas, is assigned the possession of the pit full of serpents into which was thrown the viking Ragnar Lodbrog. Late in the year the two rivals agreed to join their powers and march against "the army." Having mustered a large force, they marched to York, already occupied by the Danes, and took the city by storm. Some of the Northumbrians, too confident of victory, entered the city. The walls which were still standing severed their army in twain. A terrible slaughter was made of them, "some within and some without." Both the rival kings

* This is pointed out by Mr. Oman in "Collected Essays" in Alfred the Great.

were slain and the miserable Northumbrian remnant made peace with "the army." In the next year, 868, the Danes, who had now no thought of returning home, invaded Mercia and took up their winter quarters at Nottingham. Burhred, King of Mercia, by the advice of his witan called on his West Saxon brothers-in-law for help. They marched with the fyrd of Wessex to Nottingham, but finding the Danes strongly entrenched durst not attack them. "There was no serious fighting there"; the men of Mercia had to make their own peace, and the West Saxon fyrd returned inglorious to their homes.

In 869 "the army" remained quartered in York, doubtless strengthening their hold on Deira, which was rapidly becoming a mere Danish province. But next year (870) witnessed an event, one of the most memorable in the whole story of Scandinavian invasion, an event which led to the canonisation of an English prince, and called into existence the stateliest but one of English monasteries. The king of East Anglia at this time was a young man named Edmund, of pure and noble character. The legends of later centuries have been busy with the story of his boyhood, representing him as a native of Nuremberg, chosen as his heir by an East Anglian king as he went on pilgrimage to Jerusalem, sent to England, and after many romantic adventures, obtaining the kingdom of his patron. Though this traditional history be set aside as altogether untrustworthy, it is difficult to resist the conclusion that there was some strain of foreign blood in King Edmund's ancestry, regal though it seems to have been.* However this may be, all the authorities agree in fixing his accession to the throne at a very early period of his life, and it is probable that, though he had already reigned for about sixteen years, he was not much past the thirtieth year of his age when in 870 the Danes, under the command of two brothers named Inguar and Ubba, leaving Mercia, invaded East Anglia and took up their winter quarters at Thetford. Battle was joined on November 20, and the invaders won a decisive victory, of which they made use to spread themselves over the country and destroy all the monasteries which abounded in that pious land.

Both the Chronicle and Asser seem to imply that King Edmund,

* Florence of Worcester's words (borrowed from St. Edmund's earliest biographer Abbo), "Ex antiquorum Saxonum prosapia oriundus," seem, according to the usage of the time, to refer to the Old Saxons of the continent. If he had meant merely to say "from an old Saxon family," he would probably have said "antiqua" rather than "antiquorum".

"fighting fiercely," was slain on the field of battle; but it is hardly possible altogether to reject another widely credited version of the story, according to which the young king was taken prisoner on the battle-field; was offered his life by Inguar on condition of renouncing his faith and accepting the heathens as his over-lords; steadfastly refused in any way to compromise his profession of Christianity; was tied to a tree and made a target for the Northmen's arrows; till at last the Danish leaders took pity on his sufferings and ordered the executioner to strike off his head. This story, which is said to have been often told by Dunstan, who had it from Edmund's armour-bearer, was universally believed two generations after his death, and procured for the East Anglian king the title of saint and the crown of martyrdom.

The battle in which St. Edmund was defeated was fought at Hoxne, about twenty miles east of Thetford. The martyr's body, according to the legend, was found miraculously guarded by a wolf, and after an interval of thirty-three years was transferred to the town of Beadoricesworth, about ten miles south of Thetford, where, in the course of time, the magnificent abbey of Bury St. Edmund's rose above the relics of the saint. Strange to say, the Danish King Canute was the most enthusiastic of the earlier benefactors of this monastery and ever professed an especial reverence for the memory of the martyred king. St. Edmund soon became one of the most popular of English saints, a popularity sufficiently attested by the ancient churches, between fifty and sixty in number, distributed throughout more than half the counties of England from Durham to Devonshire, which are still dedicated to his memory.*

In the course of the same campaign, Inguar and Ubba came to Peterborough, then called Medeshamstede; and, as a monk of that abbey pathetically relates, "they burned and brake, slew abbot and monks, and so dealt with what they found there, which was erewhile full rich that they brought it to nothing." And thus ended the year 870.

The year 871, a famous date in English history, "the year of battles," the date of Alfred's accession, now dawned upon the distracted land.† Berkshire was the great battle-ground which was invaded in January

* Studies in Church Dedications (ii., 327), by Miss Arnold-Forster.

† In describing the events of this year the writer follows the guidance of the late Mr. W. H. Simcox, who personally identified most of the battle-sites, and the results of whose investigations are contained in an excellent paper in the English Historical Review, i., 218–34.

by a Danish host fresh from the slaughter of St. Edmund and his East Anglians. They came to "the royal town which is called Reading," situated on the southern bank of the Thames, took it and entrenched a camp on its southward side between Thames and Kennet. A party of plunderers headed by two jarls* rode westwards as far as the little village of Englefield, about six miles from Reading, where they were stopped by Ethelwulf, ealdorman of Berkshire, who had taken up a position on a hill overlooking the valley of the Pang. In the encounter which followed, the Danes were defeated, one of the jarls named Sidroc was slain, and the scanty remnant of his troops crept back to the Danish camp at Reading. Four days after this engagement, the royal brothers Ethelred and Alfred, having mustered the troops of Wessex, came to Reading, cut off many of the straggling plunderers, and tried to storm the Danish camp. But the heathen made a fierce sally; the Christians were repulsed; the brave ealdorman Ethelwulf was slain, and the enemy held the field of slaughter.

Emboldened by this victory the Danes again sped westward, possibly intending to harry Somerset and Wiltshire, and occupied Aescesdune, which Asser translates "the hill of the ash,"† and which has been generally identified with what are now known as the Downs or as Ashdown Hills. These are a chalk ridge some 600 or 700 feet in height, which runs for about ten miles east and west through the northern part of Berkshire and divides the valley of the Thames from that of the Kennet. The Saxons marched after the enemy in haste and both nations arrayed themselves for battle. The Danes held the higher ground: the centre of their army being commanded by their two kings, Halfdene, brother of Inguar, and Bagseg; while the wings were under the command of the numerous jarls who followed their standard. On the Saxon side it was arranged that Ethelred should encounter the kings and Alfred the jarls. But when the heathens began to march down the hill, and the Saxons should have received the word to spring forward to meet them, that signal was not given from the royal tent. There knelt Ethelred, listening to Mass, and refusing to stir

* The title of the Danish battle leaders, next in rank to the king.

† On philological grounds Mr. Stevenson disputes the propriety of this translation and asserts that Aesc must be the name of a person. The present appearance of Ashdown Hills seems, however, to correspond admirably with Asser's description. It is better not to complicate the discussion by an argument derived from the strange figure of a White Horse (so-called) cut upon their northern side, as that figure, with all its picturesque interest, is not a safe guide to a historical identification.

till the rite was ended. "He would not," he said, "abandon the service of God for that of men." On Alfred, therefore, rested the responsibility of assuming the chief command and leading the whole army to battle. It is probable, though not distinctly so stated by Asser, that Ethelred, against whose personal courage no imputation is made, soon emerged from his tent and hastened after his fighting "fyrd" men. A single stunted thorn-tree, still standing apparently when Asser wrote, marked the spot where the clash of the opposing armies was deadliest and where the battle-shouts were heard the loudest. Long and desperate was the encounter, but at last, near night-fall, the Saxons prevailed and the heathens fled in utter confusion, leaving dead on the field Bagseg, the king, five jarls and many thousands of the rank and file, whose bodies covered the whole broad ridge of Ashdown.

It was a great victory, certainly, but like so many other battles in this strange campaign it was utterly indecisive. The Danes who had succeeded in reaching their stronghold, now marched southward, apparently threatening Winchester: Ethelred and Alfred followed them, and after another tough fight were defeated at Basing, near to the site of that far-famed "Loyalty House" which eight centuries later was held so gallantly and so long by the Marquis of Winchester for Charles I. against the army of the Parliament. The Danish victory at Basing, however, was, as we are expressly told, "a victory without spoils." The invaders seem to have renounced their intended attack on Winchester and turned back to their entrenched camp at Reading. Two months pass, during which some of the nameless battles that bring the tale of this year's conflicts up to nine, may have been fought. When the veil again lifts we find the Danes apparently attempting to turn the English left, marching the whole length of Berkshire to Hungerford, and seeking to penetrate into Wiltshire. The next battle was fought on the edge of Savernake Forest; Ethelred and Alfred each put their enemies to flight, "and far into the day they had the victory," but after many had fallen on either side, the Danes held the field of slaughter. The chronicler's entry is extremely enigmatical, and we are perhaps allowed to conjecture that in the moment of victory Ethelred received a mortal wound which changed the fortunes of the day, for our next entry is as follows: "And the Easter after King Ethelred died, having reigned five years, and his body lieth at Wimborne." As we are told at the same time that "a mickle summer army came to Reading," we may consider that two events stand out clearly in these April days of

871, the arrival from over-seas of a great fresh body of troops, who had not wintered in England, to reinforce their countrymen at Reading; and the death of King Ethelred, whose body was not taken to be buried in his own city of Winchester, but, probably owing to the disturbed state of the country, had to be interred in the nearer minster of Wimborne in Dorsetshire. There his epitaph (not contemporary) records that he died "by the hands of the pagans."

The accession of ALFRED to the throne, in 871, on his brother's death, seems to have passed almost unnoticed in the deadly earnestness of the great encounter. There were battles at Reading and at Wilton, in which, as usual, the Saxons seemed to be on the point of winning when the Danes, turning at the right moment on their disorderly pursuers, changed defeat into victory, and kept possession of the battle-field. They were, however, by this time as much wearied and wasted by the events of this awful year as the Saxons themselves, with whom they now made peace, a peace which, as the historian remarks with surprise, they kept for four years unbroken.

During these years, however, from 872 to 875, they were greatly strengthening their hold on the northern kingdoms. After besieging London and putting it to a heavy ransom, they marched through Mercia, occupied successively Torksey on the Trent and Repton in Derbyshire, dethroned Alfred's brother-in-law, Burhred (874), and set up in his stead "a foolish thegn named Ceolwulf," who bound himself by oaths and hostages to hand Mercia back to his new lords whenever they should demand it. Burhred, heart-weary of the strife and the toil of his twenty-two years of reigning, went to the paradise of Anglo-Saxons, Rome, died there and was buried in the new church of St. Mary which Pope Leo IV. had built in the precincts of the Saxon school.

In the next year, 875, while part of the Danish force went to Cambridge and took up their quarters there, a vigorous detachment, headed by the fierce Halfdene, crossed the Tyne and invaded Bernicia, whose inhabitants had driven out a puppet-king named Egbert, reigning there as vassal of the Danes. This spasmodic stroke for liberty was cruelly avenged by the ravage of the till then unharried province. It was probably at this time that the Christian civilisation of Northumbria, such as we find it in the pages of Bede, received its death-stroke. Under the leadership of Halfdene, as Symeon of Durham informs us, the Danish army indulged in a wild revel of cruelty, first mocking and then slaying the servants and handmaidens of God, and in short spreading murder and conflagration from the eastern to the western sea. The devastation was not confined to the Anglian kingdom; the Picts on the north and the Britons of Strathclyde on the north-west shared in the general ruin.

This invasion of Halfdene's set in motion a pilgrimage which was full of significance for the ecclesiastical history of Northumbria, the memorable migration of the body of Saint Cuthbert. Now, at last, under the terror of the pagan hosts, the little isle of Lindisfarne, which for 240 years had been the spiritual capital of Bernicia, relapsed into its pristine loneliness. Seeing the widespread ravage wrought by the heathen men, bishop Eardulf resolved on flight, but could not bear to leave behind the uncorrupted body of the patron saint. He called into council Edred, abbot of St. Cuthbert's monastery at Carlisle, who reminded him of the saint's own words: "Dig ye up my bones and find a home elsewhere as God may direct you, rather than consent to the iniquity of the schismatics." St. Cuthbert's forebodings perhaps pointed to a recrudescence of the Easter controversy, but the churchmen rightly held that they were applicable to the far more terrible invasion of the Danes. Accordingly they took up the body of the saint (still incorrupt, according to the legend): they took also its companion relics, the head of St. Oswald, some bones of St. Aidan and of the three bishops who followed him; and provided with these precious talismans they set forth on their first great pilgrimage. For eight years they wandered: at first like sheep over the moors of Northumbria; then they came down to the western coast at Workington, and were on the point of setting sail for Ireland when a wind which sprang up, as if by miracle, drove them back upon the shore. In the hurry of the abortive embarkation they dropped into the sea the precious and beautifully illuminated Lindisfarne Gospels, but miraculously recovered the treasure after many days. This manuscript is still preserved in the British Museum, showing stains as if of sea-water on its pages.

At last, in 883, five years after the peace which will mark the conclusion of this chapter, the uncorrupted body and its weary guardians found rest at the old Roman station of Chester-le-Street, eight miles south of Newcastle, under the shelter of the rule of a converted Dane, Guthred, son of Harthacnut. "He gave them," says the chronicler, "all the land between Wear and Tyne for a perpetual possession, and ordained that the church which they were about to build should be constituted a sanctuary, that whosoever for any cause should flee to the saint's body should have respite for thirty-seven days from his pursuers." Such were the magnificent possessions and privileges bestowed on the minster which now rose at Chester-le-Street by the old Roman highway, and which, after a little more than a century, were to be transferred in 995 to the more famous sanctuary at Durham.

The year 876 marked the end of the truce and the renewal of the Danish attacks on Wessex. Three Danish kings, one of whom was the famous Guthrum, after wintering in Cambridge, stole past the West Saxon fyrd, and apparently by a series of night marches succeeded in reaching Wareham. Here, surrounded by the rivers Piddle and Frome, they could feel themselves as secure as in the islands of Thanet or Sheppey. Worsted, however, by blockade rather than by battle, the Danish kings came to terms with Alfred. They gave hostages once more of their most honourable men and swore upon a certain sacred armlet—an oath, says the chronicler, which they had never given to any other people—that they would truly depart out of the kingdom. Not all of "the army," however, kept this solemn compact. Hostages and oath notwithstanding, the mounted men rode off to Exeter and entrenched themselves there. King Alfred's pursuit with the infantry of the fyrd was vain. Fortunately, however, the fleet which should have co-operated with the Danes was overtaken by a fierce storm, and 120 ships filled with warriors were dashed to pieces on the rocks of Purbeck. Disheartened by this calamity, the Northmen at Exeter once more swore great oaths, gave hostages and marched forth from Wessex to their own now vassal kingdom of Mercia.

This happened in the autumn of 877. Soon after Twelfth night, at the beginning of 878, another gang of plunderers came suddenly to the "royal villa" of Chippenham, probably hoping to capture the king himself. With a small band of followers Alfred escaped to the woods and morasses of Athelney in Somerset; but though they thus missed their chief prize, this invasion of Wessex, for some reason unknown to us, came nearer to success than any which had preceded it. From Chippenham as a centre the Danes harried the country far and wide; they drove many of the inhabitants across the sea; those who remained had to accept them as their lords; it seemed as if Wessex would have to follow the example of Mercia and Northumbria, and bow its neck to the Danish yoke. Meanwhile Alfred, in the little island of Athelney—an island then, because surrounded on all sides by marshes, but an island now no longer—was gathering his faithful followers round him and quietly preparing for the recovery of his throne.* The little band of his followers wrought at the construction of a rude fortress, which was finished by Easter, and which proved impregnable by the heathen assailants. Behind this earthwork the West Saxon king "greatly stood at bay," and from hence he and the men of the Somerset fyrd, who gathered round him under their ealdorman Ethelnoth, made several successful sallies against the enemy.

Ere long there came to cheer them the tidings of a great victory gained by the men of Devon, near Bideford Bay, over a Danish army which seems to have been commanded by Ubba, the murderer of St. Edmund. After wintering in South Wales, Ubba had crossed the Bristol Channel, landed in Devonshire and besieged the soldiers of the fyrd in a poorly fortified stronghold which they had constructed and which was called Cynuit.† The fort had no spring of water near it, and the victory of the invaders seemed assured, but despair gave courage to the besieged, who sallied forth at dawn, took the besiegers by surprise, and slew of them eight hundred. Only a scanty remnant escaped to their ships; the great raven standard, the flapping of whose wings betokened victory, was taken, and Ubba himself was among the slain. The death of the royal martyr of East Anglia was thus at length avenged.

At last, close upon Whitsuntide, Alfred emerged from the forest of Selwood, which seems to have hitherto served him as cover, collected round him at "Egbert's Stone" the men of three counties, Somerset, Wilts and Hants (who, as the chronicler beautifully says, "were fain of their recovered king"), and by two days' marches came up with the Danish army at Ethandune.‡ Here he won a crushing victory. The Danes fled to their fortified camp, probably at Chippenham; Alfred pursued them, shut them up in their stronghold and besieged it for a fortnight. Then came offers of submission, and a promise to withdraw from Wessex. Hostages and oaths were again offered to the conqueror, and—what was

* At this point the Chronicle of St. Neots, a late and untrustworthy authority written perhaps early in the twelfth century, inserts the well-known story of the burning of the cakes, which does not form part of the genuine text of Asser's Life.

† The site of this fortress has been much discussed but is not yet satisfactorily settled. See Stevenson's Asser, p. 262.

‡ Edington in Wiltshire, a little east of Westbury. Near this place is another White Horse, at Bratton Castle, but we have not sufficient evidence to connect this with Alfred's victory.

more significant—"the army promised that their king, Guthrum, should receive the rite of baptism."

Alfred returned to the neighbourhood of Athelney, and there waited for the pagan chief's fulfilment of his promise. He was not disappointed; Guthrum came with thirty of his chiefs to Aller, near Athelney, was baptised and received in rising from the font the Saxon name of Athelstan. It is probable, though not expressly stated, that his thirty warriors were baptised with him. The two kings then went together to Wedmore, a royal vill under the Mendips, where Alfred for twelve nights gave the new convert hospitable entertainment. Guthrum-Athelstan laid aside the white robes of the catechumen at the end of a week, and departed laden with gifts by his spiritual father. "The army" cleared out of Wessex and marched to Cirencester. The most dangerous of Alfred's wars with the Danes was ended, and the land had rest for fourteen years.

XVII.

ALFRED AT PEACE

The fourteen years which followed the Peace of Wedmore (878 to 892) were, as has been said, in the main years of peace, and may be considered to justify the heading of this chapter; yet that peace was not all unbroken, nor was Alfred's Danish godson always a placid and peaceful Christian. There were still some slight heavings of the barbarian sea, which must be shortly described before we turn to the much more interesting subject of Alfred's peaceful labours. The main condition of the Peace of Wedmore was that the Danes should evacuate Wessex. The agreement that the Watling Street should be the boundary between the two nations cannot be stated to have been one of the conditions of the peace now concluded. We have, in fact, no accurate information as to the territorial arrangements of 878. The extremely interesting document called Aelfredes and Guthrumes Frith (the peace of Alfred and Guthrum) must belong to some later year than the meeting at Wedmore, and the course of the history seems to justify us in assigning it to the year 885 or thereabouts.*

After Guthrum and his men had lingered for some time in the neighbourhood of Cirencester, they marched across England to East Anglia (879), and made a permanent settlement there, "occupying and dividing the land." This probably means that they exchanged the destructive excitement of the life of the viking for the peaceful existence of the husbandman. But when, five years later, in 884, a division of "the army" which had been ravaging Gaul came to Kent and besieged Rochester, the sight of their fellow-countrymen, harrying on the other side of the Thames estuary, seems to have been too much for Danish self-control. Guthrum "broke peace with King Alfred," and probably sent some of his men to help in the siege. Alfred, however, set to work to besiege the besiegers, who had "wrought another

* This was pointed out half a century ago by Dr. Reinhold Schmid, the accurate German editor of the Anglo-Saxon laws.

fastness round themselves," and in the end forced them to abandon their enterprise, leave their horses as the prize of victory, and depart over seas. He then proceeded to chastise the East Anglian Danes for their breach of faith, sending a fleet against them from Kent which won a signal victory. Notwithstanding a subsequent defeat, his operations must have been on the whole successful, for he rescued London from the Danish yoke and concluded, probably in 885, that treaty with Guthrum which as before said is still extant, bearing the title of Alfred's and Guthrum's frith.

If the provisions of Wedmore had made the Watling Street the boundary between the two nationalities, which is doubtful, the treaty now concluded was certainly more favourable to the English. It went from the Thames northwards "up the Lea to its source, then straight on to Bedford, and then up along the Ouse to the Watling Street," which throughout a large part of its further course became practically the boundary of the two nations. This line gave to the English king London, previously abandoned to the Danes, and with London the region round it north of the Thames and west of the Lea, which had previously formed part of the kingdom of Essex, but which now, perhaps, received a special organisation of its own, and the name that it has since borne for ten centuries, Middlesex. It also gave to Alfred the larger and fairer half of Mercia, being in fact all that portion of the midland counties which lies south and west of the London and North Western Railway,* together with half of Hertfordshire and two-thirds of Bedfordshire. But then, on the other hand, it is true that the rest of Mercia, East Anglia, Essex (mutilated) and Northumbria were practically handed over to the Danes, either as personal rulers or as over-lords. This surrender has often been treated as a wise and politic act of self-sacrifice on Alfred's part, a view which was the natural result of the historical teaching which spoke of Egbert and his descendants as unquestioned monarchs of all Anglo-Saxon Britain. Now, however, that we see what a precarious and shadowy thing was the supremacy of the ninth century Kings of Wessex over northern and midland England, a supremacy which under a feeble king like Ethelwulf perhaps almost

....

* It is interesting to note that the Watling Street is still the chief boundary between the counties of Warwick and Leicester. Through a large part of its course the London and North Western Railway so nearly coincides with this old Roman road that the traveller faring northwards may consider himself to be looking forth from the right-hand window over the "Danelaw" and from the left over "Saxony".

vanished into nothingness, we can see that the settlement which generally (though incorrectly) goes by the name of the Peace of Wedmore was not so great a sacrifice on Alfred's part as we used to imagine. Bitter doubtless it was to Alfred as to every patriotic heart among the "Angel-cyn" to see the Dane so firmly rooted in the north and east of England, but that was the actual position of affairs, and he, as a statesman, was bound to recognise it. On the other hand, the larger half of Mercia now came under Alfred's personal rule and was irrevocably joined to his realm, and this great new kingdom was now preparing to enter the lists against the Scandinavian invaders with a fairer prospect of success than could ever have been entertained by the disunited, mutually suspicious states of the "Heptarchy." As has been already pointed out, the Dane was the real though involuntary creator of a united England.

It is worth our while to notice the language of the great frith which thus settled the boundary of the two races. It professes to be concluded "between Alfred, king, and Guthrum, king, and all the witan of the English kinship, and all the folk that is in East Anglia, for themselves and for their offspring." "If any man be slain, as we hold all equally dear, both Englishmen and Danes, the penalty shall be eight half-marks of pure gold,* but if he be a ceorl or freed-man on gafol [rented] land, the penalty shall be 200 scillings." "And we all agreed on this day when men swore their [mutual] oaths that neither bond nor free shall fare unto the [Danish] army without leave, nor shall any one of them come to us. Should it happen that one of them wishes to have business with us, or one of us with them, in respect of land or cattle, that is to be permitted only on condition of his giving hostages for the observance of the peace and as a testimony that he has a clean back," in other words, that his past record is that of a peaceable neighbour.

Evidently the continuance of friendly relations between the two races, parted only by two small streams and the old Roman road, was felt to be precarious, and both rulers agreed that the less they mingled with one another the better.

* The value of the mark of pure gold is not yet clearly ascertained. Mr. Chadwick (Studies in Anglo-Saxon Institutions, p. 50) argues from this passage that a single mark of gold = 300 scillings, and that the fine hereby imposed was 1,200 scillings, equal to the wergild of a West Saxon noble. But in that case one would have expected to have some more distinct indication of rank than is contained in the words "gif man ofslagen weorthe".

*****

It is pleasant to turn from the monotonous story of the conflict with the Danes to the subject of Alfred's family life. In 868, three years before "the year of battles" and his own accession to the throne, he married a noble Mercian lady named Ealhswith, daughter of Ethelred, ealdorman of the Gaini(?), and descended on her mother's side from the royal family of Mercia. By this lady (who survived him three years) Alfred had five children who grew up. The eldest, Ethelfled, when little more than a child, was given in marriage to Ethelred, ealdorman of the Mercians, and became, after her father's death, a personage of great importance, ruling her mother's country with spirit and success under the proud title of "Lady of the Mercians." The next child, Edward, who was eventually his father's successor, had for his especial companion his sister Elfrida. "When he was not hunting or engaged in other manly exercises, he was with her learning the psalter or books of Saxon poetry, showing affability and gentleness towards all, both natives and foreigners, and ever in complete subjection to his father." In after life the two playmates were widely separated. The boy became Edward the Elder, one of the greatest of English kings; the girl was sent across the seas to become the wife of Baldwin II. of Flanders, son of Judith of France, and her husband the handsome forester. After more than two centuries the brother and sister playmates were once more to meet in the persons of their progeny, when Elfrida's descendant Henry Beauclerk, son of Matilda of Flanders, married Matilda of Scotland, descended in the seventh degree from Edward the Elder. Of the two other children of Alfred, we know only that Ethelgiva was early dedicated to the monastic life, becoming Abbess of Shaftesbury; and that Ethelweard, the youngest of the family, was a pupil in a court school founded by his father, probably in imitation of the similar institutions founded by Charlemagne, in which the sons of the nobility and some others were taught to read books both Latin and Anglo-Saxon, and also learned to write. Ethelweard (who must not be confounded with his kinsman of the same name, author of a chronicle) seems to have specially profited by this training, and was probably the most learned member of his family.

An obscure statement of Asser's with reference to Alfred's marriage reveals to us the fact that the great king's life was in some mysterious way one long battle with disease. From early boyhood he suffered from some malady which caused him grievous pain. In his twentieth year, just about the time of his marriage, this malady left him, but was succeeded by another which caused him at intervals yet sharper pain, and always kept him in terror of its recurrence. This affliction endured from his twentieth till his forty-fifth year, if not longer.* These hints, obscure as they are, heighten our admiration of the heroic spirit with which Alfred, often suffering from acute bodily pain, with the ever-present fear of attacks either by disease or by the Danes, set himself to fulfil his duties towards his subjects in the wide and comprehensive sense in which he understood them. Of his wisely planned and efficient schemes for the defence of his realm from hostile invasion something will be said in the next chapter. We are now concerned with his earnest endeavours to dispel the intellectual darkness which brooded over his country, yet of which only the king himself and a few chosen friends were fully conscious.

It is clear that in the course of the century which elapsed between the death of Bede and the birth of Alfred, the intellect of England had suffered a terrible relapse into ignorance and barbarism. It was not the inroads of the Northmen alone which had brought about this result, though, of course, the ruin of so many Northumbrian monasteries and the destruction of so many manuscripts were influences unfavourable to the cause of learning. But independently of Scandinavian ravages, England herself was becoming barbarised. In Northumbria the beacon light of Christianity and culture, which had once shone so brightly, was quenched in the blood of her kings, murdered and murderers. In Mercia there was a little more interest in literary pursuits, but apparently there only; East Anglia and Wessex were intellectually dead. As Alfred himself says, in the preface to his translation of Pope Gregory's Regula Pastoralis: "Even before all this burning and ravaging [by the Danes in the reigns of Ethelwulf and his sons], when the churches were still filled with books and sacred vessels, and God's servants abounded, yet they knew very little of the contents of their books, because they were not written in their own idiom." "Formerly men came from beyond our borders, seeking wisdom in our own land; now, if we are to have it at all, we must look for it abroad. So great was the decay of learning among Englishmen that there were very few on this side Humber, and I ween not many north of it,

* For some valuable suggestions on the mysterious subject of Alfred's diseases see Plummer's Life and Times of Alfred the Great, pp. 28, 214.

who could understand the ritual [of Mass] or translate a letter from Latin into English. No, I cannot remember one such, south of the Thames, when I came to the throne."

To help him in the arduous task of once more bringing the English race under the influence of literary culture, nay, rather to teach him who yearned to be the teacher of his people, Alfred sought the aid of learned ecclesiastics beyond his own borders. With much earnestness he invited the Welshman Asser, his future biographer, to repair to his court. From Mercia he imported Plegmund, who became in 890 archbishop of Canterbury, and Werferth, who eventually returned to the midlands as bishop of Worcester. From St. Omer came Grimbald, who was consecrated abbot of the new minster founded by Alfred at Winchester; and from the lands near the mouth of the Elbe came John the Old Saxon, whose ancestors had probably fought hard for heathenism against Charlemagne, but who was himself a learned ecclesiastic. He helped Alfred much in his literary work, and was made by him abbot of his monastery at Athelney; an uneasy post, for two of his monks contrived a villainous plot against his life and his reputation, but were foiled by the vigorous resistance made by the stalwart Old Saxon, who had been a warrior in his youth, when the would-be murderers set upon him by night in the lonely convent church.

These were the chief of Alfred's literary assistants, and with their help he enriched his people with translations of some of the most highly prized works which the dying Roman world had bequeathed to Teutonic Europe.

1. The passage quoted above concerning the decay of learning in England comes from the king's translation of Pope Gregory's Regula Pastoralis, or as Alfred calls it his Herd-book. In this book the great pope to whom England was so largely indebted for her Christianity, gave many excellent hints as to the character, duties and special temptations of the Christian pastor. In his preface, King Alfred explained the reasons which had moved him to undertake the work of a translator. He marvelled that none of the good and wise men who had been in England before him had anticipated him in the work, but concluded that this was because they expected that learning would flourish yet more instead of decaying, and that another generation would be so familiar with Latin as to need no translations. Then on the other hand he remembered how the Old Testament itself had been translated from the Hebrew, first into Greek and then into Latin, and from thence, at any rate in part, into the languages of

the other Christian nations of Europe; and on this precedent he resolved to act. "For it seems to me desirable," he said, "that we should turn some of the books which all men ought to know into that language which we can all understand, and so bring it to pass (as we certainly may do if we only have rest from our enemies) that all the free youth of England, sons of men of substance, shall devote themselves to learning in their early years before they are fit for other occupations; that they shall first learn to read English writing, and then if they are still willing to continue as pupils and desire to rise to the higher ranks of the state, that they shall be taught the Latin language."

The king then proceeds to describe his mode of translation: "sometimes word for word and sometimes meaning for meaning; as I learned the sense from Plegmund, mine archbishop, and Asser, my bishop, and Grimbald and John my mass-priests." He describes the measures which he has taken to supply every see in his kingdom with a copy of the book, enriched with an aestel (clasp or book-marker?) worth 300 scillings, and commands in God's name that no man shall take the aestel from the book or the book from the minster. "Thank God! we have now abundance of learned bishops, but we know not how long this may continue; and I therefore ordain that each book be always kept in the place to which now I send it, unless the bishop himself desire to borrow it, or give a written order for its loan to another."

2. In order that his subjects might have some knowledge of the history of that great and splendid Roman past which lay in ruins behind them, Alfred, always with the help of his ecclesiastic friends, translated the seven books of the History of Paulus Orosius against the Pagans. The selection was in many respects an excellent one, for Orosius, a Spanish ecclesiastic of the fifth century and a friend of St. Augustine, has here set forth, in a concise manner and fairly interesting style, all that his contemporaries knew of the history of the world from the building of Babylon to Alaric's capture of Rome. He was credulous and inaccurate, and his work, except for the events of his own age, has no scientific value, but as a manual of ancient history for the young Anglo-Saxon nobleman it could hardly have been surpassed. Both Alfred, however, and his readers must have been somewhat unnecessarily depressed by its perusal; for as the book had a polemical bearing, adversus Paganos, and was intended to show that the calamities which were befalling the Roman empire in the fifth century were not due to its adoption of the Christian faith, its author was naturally led to exaggerate the misery

of the world in preceding ages. While enumerating, therefore, all the murders, pestilences and earthquakes of which he could find mention in the 5,617 years that had elapsed since the creation of the world, he omits to notice the long interspaces of quiet happiness which there had been in some ages and some countries of the world, and he has no praise for the progress which Humanity had made in some departments of life from Sardanapalus to Constantine.

King Alfred and his teachers were evidently sometimes at a loss to understand the meaning of their author, and it is amusing to see the ingenious arts by which in such cases they evaded the difficulty. They decided, no doubt wisely, that the unabridged history would be too long for their Saxon students, and therefore practised severe compression. Unfortunately for us this compression applies much more to the later portions of the history, where Orosius's testimony is valuable, and where his translators might have added something of importance, than to the earlier books where neither he nor they have anything to say that we care to hear. The long account of Cæsar's campaign in Gaul is reduced within the limits of a single sentence, and even the story of his British campaigns is shortened, though here we derive from the translation the fact that in Alfred's opinion the site of Cæsar's third battle was "near the river that is called Thames, near the ford that is called Wallingford."

Incomparably the most interesting, however, of Alfred's interpolations is made at the very beginning of the history, in the long geographical description which Orosius thought it his duty to prefix to his work. In translating this chapter the king has allowed himself very great freedom and sometimes has not improved upon his author; as when he volunteers a statement, borrowed doubtless from some classical geographer, that Scotland (by which, of course, he means Ireland) lies over against the Wendel Sea (or Mediterranean) at its western end. But when he comes to speak of the Teutonic and Scandinavian lands, he breaks quite away from Orosius and gives us a detailed ethnological description of Northern Europe, which, though in some of its details not easy of interpretation, is far more valuable than the meagre Orosian sentences for which it is exchanged. And then, suddenly, without any pretence of following his author's guidance, he introduces the weather-beaten forms of two Norwegian pilots, Ohthere and Wulfstan, and imparts to his subjects and to posterity the information which they had given him as to their voyages in the North Sea and the Baltic.

Of these two men Ohthere, "who dwelt northmost of all the Northmen," was the most adventurous. He told how he had sailed northward as far as any of the whale-hunters go, keeping the waste land on his right and the wide sea on his left hand. Then, leaving even the whalers behind, he had sailed northward for three days more, at the end of which time he found the coast turning suddenly to the east and then to the south. After this he had anchored his ship at the mouth of a great river. In other words, this bold seaman had doubled the North Cape, entered the White Sea, and probably cast anchor at the mouth of the river Dwina, somewhere near the site of the modern Archangel. The conversation of this old salt concerning the whales and walruses of the Polar Sea, the Fins and their reindeer, their accumulated skins of martens and bears, and feathers of sea-birds, which constituted the sole wealth of those desolate regions, evidently made a deep impression on the mind of "his lord King Alfred." Though we may be inclined to smile at the naïve literary device which introduced all these details into the history of a Spanish presbyter who lived some five centuries earlier, we must be grateful to the king who preserved for us this record of the exploits of the Franklins and the Nansens of that long-vanished age.

3. It was not, however, only the history of the Biblical and classical ages which Alfred desired to render accessible to his people. He knew that the deeds of their own forefathers since they had entered the land of Britain, were worthy of their remembrance, and he rightly judged that the great struggle with the Danes, in which he was himself engaged, would soon be History, as memorable as anything that was recorded in the pages of Orosius. With this view, as Geoffrey Gaimar, a historian of the twelfth century, says, "He caused to be written an English book of adventures and of laws of the land and of the kings who made war." In other words, Alfred's orders brought into being the Saxon Chronicle. As its latest editor* says: "The popular answer is in this case the right one. The Chronicle is the work of Alfred the Great. The idea of a national chronicle, as opposed to merely local annals, was his, and that this idea was realised under his direction and supervision, I most firmly believe. And we may, I think, safely place in the forefront of the Chronicle the inscription which encircles Alfred's jewel [found at Athelney in 1693 and now in the Ashmolean Museum at Oxford], AELFRED MEC HEHT GEWYRCAN, 'Alfred ordered me to be made'."

* Plummer, Two Saxon Chronicles, ii., civ.

4. In further pursuance of the same plan a translation of Bede's Ecclesiastical History from Latin into Anglo-Saxon was made, as we have reason to believe, either by Alfred's own hand or under his immediate supervision. As this book had become a kind of classic among churchmen, Alfred allowed himself here less liberty than in some of his other translations. Some letters, epitaphs and similar documents are omitted, and there is an almost complete erasure of the chapters relating to the wearisome Paschal controversy. In other respects the king's translation seems to be a fairly accurate reproduction of the original work.

5. Last, and in some ways most interesting of all the literary labours of Alfred, comes his translation of the Consolation of Philosophy by Boethius. This is a book which, after enjoying during the early Middle Ages a popularity perhaps somewhat greater than its merits, has fallen since the revival of learning into much less deserved oblivion. In it Boethius, a Roman nobleman who was cast into prison and eventually executed by order of the Gothic king Theodoric, sets forth the comfort which came to him in his wearisome imprisonment by meditations on Divine Philosophy. The problem which perplexed him and which Philosophy, the spiritual companion of his solitude, sought to solve, was the world-old one, "Why do the wicked flourish and why are the righteous afflicted?" Strange to say, though Boethius was a Christian, and was even in a certain sense a martyr for the Catholic faith, the Christian solution of the problem is kept almost entirely out of sight, and the answers suggested are such as might have been given by Socrates or Epictetus. Boethius believes in a Divine Ruler of the universe, and the general tendency of the book is towards the strengthening of belief, but it is belief rather of a theistic than of a definitely Christian type. However with all its defects and all its strange silences, the book was one which had a great attraction for many of the noblest minds of a bewildered Europe, and not least for the great West Saxon king, who, struggling against the depressing influences of disease, and ever dreading a fresh outburst of the Danish volcano, felt that he, too, like the author, had much need of "the Consolation of Philosophy." In his other translations he had been working for his people; in this, which was probably executed towards the close of his reign, he was, perhaps, working rather for himself, for the solace and fortification of his own troubled spirit.

We have seen that Alfred did not take a slavish view of the duties of a translator; and in his Boethius he is more lordly than ever, omitting, adding, altering with a sublime contempt for mere verbal accuracy. It is, however, these very changes which make the book so precious to a student of Alfred's own character. We see therein what were the thoughts which were most akin to his nature; we learn something of the secret springs of his actions; we can almost listen to the conversations which he held with his bishops and thegns in the great wooden palace at Winchester.

In the first place, he gives to the whole inquiry a more religious turn than he found in the original. For "Nature" he substitutes "God"; he sometimes introduces the name of Christ; he speaks of the Judgment-day, and his language has throughout that distinctly religious tone which is so strangely absent from the meditations of Boethius. He takes us into his royal council and tells us the principles upon which he has sought to administer the state, using for his instruments three sorts of ministers, men of prayer, men of war, and men of work, for all of whom suitable maintenance must be found out of the land. He expands a slight sentence of Boethius in praise of friendship into a noble passage, in which he declares that true friendship is not an earthly but a heavenly blessing; that all other objects of desire in this world are sought after in obedience to some selfish motive, but a true friend we love for love's own sake and because of our trust in his truth, hoping for no other return. "Nature joins friends together and unites them with an inseparable love, whereas by our worldly goods and the wealth of this life we more often make foes than friends."*

Boethius puts into the mouth of Philosophy some words deprecatory of too great regard for noble birth; but Alfred says boldly on his own account that "true high birth is that of the mind not of the flesh," a memorable utterance in the mouth of the man whose lineage "went unto Cerdic" and who according to the songs of Saxon bards was descended from Woden. There are also in this most interesting translation many passages which show Alfred's keen perception of the beauties of Nature, his unfailing interest in geography, and his knowledge of Saxon folk-lore (as illustrated by his allusion to the bones of Weland the Smith), besides some which reveal his naïve ignorance of well-known facts of ancient history, as when he describes the sella curulis as a kind of carriage, or when he tells us that Cassius was another name for Brutus. One sees

* Quotations are given from Mr. Sedgefield's translation, which has the great merit of distinguishing Alfred's interpolations by a different type from the original text.

with pleasure that the wise king had a certain gift of humour, and that he could at times be even sarcastic. He alone, not his author, is responsible for the following remark attributed to Philosophy: "Two things honour and power can do, if they fall into the hands of a fool: they can cause him to be respected and even revered by other fools." Whosoever would get at the heart of this great man, the true founder of the English kingdom, and discover his inmost thoughts, should carefully study Alfred's translation of Boethius, and observe where he neglects and where he reinforces from his own experience the maxims and arguments of the Roman statesman.

To the interval of comparative peace with which we are now dealing we may probably assign the reorganisation of the royal household. Apparently service in the palace was conducted on parallel lines with service in the army, being performed in both cases by men who had houses of their own to govern and lands of their own to cultivate. The king, therefore, ordained that the household should be divided into three portions, each of which should take palace-duty ("night and day," says the biographer) for one month, and then, being relieved by another detachment, return home for two months' furlough. The same principle of threefold division prevailed partially in the simple budget of Alfred's exchequer. He divided, says Asser, all the revenue which was yearly collected by his officers into two parts, one of which was devoted to secular and the other to religious uses. Of the secular portion one-third was paid to the household, according to their respective dignities and special services; one-third to the workmen of various nationalities whom he had gathered about him for his great works of building and restoration; and one-third to the foreigners—probably for the most part scholars or professors of some liberal art—who flocked in great numbers to his court. Of the religious half of his revenue, one-quarter went to the poor, one-quarter to the two new monasteries founded by him at Winchester and Athelney, one-quarter to the court school, and the remainder promiscuously to the various monasteries in Wessex and Mercia, and the needy churches in Britain and even in Gaul and Ireland.

One of the most extraordinary of the king's benefactions, one which we might well have doubted had it not been vouched for by the contemporary evidence of the Chronicle, is thus described therein: "And that same year [883 for 882] Sighelm and Athelstan carried to Rome the alms which he had vowed to send thither when he was fighting the [Danish] army at London: and also to India to St. Thomas and St. Bartholomew." Of the campaign before London in the course of which this vow was made we have no more definite information. The sending of alms to Rome is easily understood, but the mission of West Saxon almoners to "St. Thomas's Christians" in India is indeed a marvellous fact if true. Unfortunately the tendency of modern criticism is somewhat unfavourable to the genuineness of the entry.*

*****

Though we know not the exact year when Alfred's Dooms were compiled, this will be the best place for a brief statement of the legislative work of the great king.

"These are the dooms which Alfred the king chose, in order that no man should deem them otherwise than according to his will." Such is the opening sentence of the laws. Then follows an elaborate table of contents including Ine's laws as well as his own; and then, strangely enough, we have almost the whole of four chapters of the book of Exodus (xx.-xxiii.), containing the Ten Commandments and the Mosaic code of civil law in all its archaic simplicity and with all its Draconian sternness: the principle of "an eye for an eye and a tooth for a tooth"; "whosoever doeth this or that he shall surely die," the keynote of the whole. Then, however, comes a reference to the mission of "the Lord's Son, our God, who is Jesus Christ, who came into the world, not to destroy the law but to fulfil it, and to increase it with all good things. With mild-heartedness and humility did He teach."

Thereupon follows a description of the Council of Jerusalem as given in the fifteenth chapter of the Acts of the Apostles, and a rehearsal of its decrees about "abstaining from fornication, from things offered in sacrifice to idols, from things strangled and from blood." The acts of this council end with the Golden Rule (omitted from the manuscripts on which the Received Text of the New Testament is founded, but inserted in Codex Bezae and several early authorities), "And that which ye will that other men should not do to you, do not ye to other men." "On this one doom," says the king, "let each man meditate that he may judge each one rightly; nor needs he any other law-book. Let him seek for no other

* Against the genuineness of the passage are its omission from Ã, the earliest and best MS. of the Chronicle, from Asser, and from the original text of Florence of Worcester. See Stevenson, Asser, pp. 287–90.

doom upon his neighbour than he would be willing to have pronounced upon himself."

But, as Alfred proceeds to show, since the conversion of many nations to Christianity, synods have been held at which bishops and other distinguished witan have been present, and these assemblies, for the sake of the "mild-heartedness" which Christ taught, have commuted the death-penalty for the offences named in the Mosaic law to money payments on the scale set forth by them; and such payments may, therefore, without sin be taken by the secular lords to whom they are made payable. Only, there is one crime for which no money payment must be suffered to atone; and that is treason against a man's rightful lord, because Almighty God ordained no remission of punishment to those who despised Himself, nor could His Son give any such remission to the traitor who delivered Him to death; and He ordered that a man should love his lord even as himself.

These passages give us an interesting glimpse of the mental process which governed the compilation of Alfred's law-book. In the same spirit in which he translated Orosius and Gregory for his subjects' benefit, he sets before them what he considers the source of all legislation, the divine ordinances given amidst the thunders of Sinai. He then shows how that law was modified by the teaching of Christ; he rehearses the several points of the decree of the Council of Jerusalem, and thence glides by an easy transition to that tariff of compensations and fines (payment of wergild and wite) by which, in his day, atonement might be made for all offences, with the one exception here so emphatically insisted on, the crime of treason against a man's natural lord. Of course, modern historical science cannot concede to Church synods the credit of this great change, which we believe to have been wrought possibly through long ages in the forests of Germany—namely, the change by which the blood feud slowly gave place to the exacted wer: but doubtless Christian ecclesiastics accepted the principle, perhaps in many instances regulated its application; and King Alfred was so far right in claiming the authority of the Church for the practice of money compensation instead of the relentless severity of some of the ordinances of Exodus. The conclusion of Alfred's Prologue is important as indicating what was the legislative competence of the king and how he shared it with the witan.

"I then, King Alfred, gathered these laws together and caused them to be written down, selecting many which pleased me from among those ordained by my predecessors. And many of those which I liked not I abrogated by the counsel of my Witan, ordaining some different way for the future. For I did not dare to set down in writing many of my own suggestions, not knowing how they would be liked by those who should come after. But whenever I found in the laws passed in the days of my kinsman Ine, or of Offa, King of Mercia, or of Ethelbert, the first English convert to Christianity, anything that seemed to me to be most justly decided, such laws I gathered in and the others I left out."

Generally speaking, Alfred's laws differ from those of Ine, and still more from those of Kentish Ethelbert, in the direction of greater leniency, the amount of fine payable for injuries to the person being almost always considerably reduced. This tendency, when we compare Alfred's and Ethelbert's laws, is at first sight obscured by the fact that the fines imposed by the latter are expressed in terms of the Kentish scilling, which was worth four times as much as that of Wessex, but when we have made the necessary correction for this difference, it comes out very clearly. Thus the fine for cutting off the thumb was in Ethelbert's code the equivalent of 80 shillings of Wessex, while under Alfred it was only 30. For the like injury to the middle finger it was respectively 32 and 15 shillings; for the "gold" or ring finger, 24 and 17.

This remarkable diminution in the scale of pecuniary punishments was probably due, not simply to "mild-heartedness" on the part of the king and his witan, but also to the economic effect of the Danish ravages. So much of the portable wealth of the country had been carried off from hall and monastery to the homesteads of Scandinavia, that the value of gold and silver remaining in the land was sensibly increased, and a fine which was reasonable at the beginning of the eighth century became exorbitant at the close of the ninth. This abatement of pecuniary penalty is modified in a singular way in the case of forest trespass. It may be remembered that by the laws of Ine, a man going into a forest and felling timber for his own use was liable to a fine of 30 scillings for each tree so felled, up to three, but that 90 scillings was the maximum penalty. Now, by the laws of Alfred the penalty for each tree so felled was only 5 scillings, but there was no maximum. A forest-thief, therefore, who cut down twenty trees would fare worse under the new law than under the old. One would like to know what were the developments in English forestry which led to this singular modification of the law.

Our attention begins to be directed to the public assemblies for the transaction of business, the local moots which, as we know from other sources, had judicial as well as administrative duties to discharge, arranging the levy of men for the fyrd and raising money for the equipment of ships, as well as settling important questions of inheritance and disputes about property. It was important that such meetings should not be disturbed by the brawls of unruly partisans of the litigants, and accordingly we find it enacted that "if any man fight before the king's ealdorman in the gemot (meeting), he shall pay his wer and wite as the law ordains for any assault that he may have committed, and in addition shall pay a fine (wite) of 120 scillings to the ealdorman."

Law 42 in Alfred's code illustrates in an interesting manner that gradual transition from the blood-feud to the law-suit which was perhaps the most important conquest of Teutonic civilisation. By the various sections of this law it is provided that no man who has a grievance against another shall fight his foe until he has first demanded justice of him. That done, however, and justice denied, he may, if he have a sufficiently strong body of friends to back him, besiege the defendant for seven days. Should that blockade bring about a surrender and a disarmament, he must keep his adversary in custody for thirty days, sending word to his kinship that they may come and pay the mulct for which the prisoner is liable. What is to happen if the surrender does not take place at the end of the seven days, or the payment at the end of the thirty, we are not informed, but it seems to be implied that the claimant may then fight and even slay his enemy without guilt. If the plaintiff have not sufficient power to besiege his foe, he must ride to the ealdorman and demand his aid. Failing that, he must seek redress of the king, before he takes it upon himself to fight his foe. Moreover, a man might always fight for his lord or his kinsman without incurring the penalties of blood-guiltiness, and so too he could wage "lawful war" with the seducer of his wife, his sister, or his mother. We see that the ideas of the old blood-feud and of the so-called "Fist-right" still lingered in the mind even of so wise and religious a legislator as Alfred. Redress of wrongs by the action of courts of law might be the ideal, but in the actual Saxon world private warfare must still be allowed, and all that the king could hope to accomplish was to confine it within narrow bounds and regulate its procedure.

On the condition of the servile class, the theows and esnes, in the time of Alfred, not much light is thrown by Alfred's Doom-book. We learn, however, that there was already a large class of free-men working for wages, for whose holidays, amounting in all to about thirty-six days in the year, the forty-third of Alfred's laws made provision. From this enactment the theows and esnes are expressly excluded, but it is provided that all men in servile condition shall have the four Wednesdays in the Ember-weeks, on which days they are graciously permitted to make a present of their labour to any one who may have helped them in God's name, or even to work for themselves. There is also a curious provision (law 20) exempting from liability the lord of a monk who has received money on deposit which he has failed to restore. This passage coincides with some others which seem to indicate that owing to the ruin of the monasteries wrought by the Danes, many of the monks, in order to keep body and soul together, accepted a servile position on the estate or in the house of some great landowner.

There are other indications that during the two centuries which had elapsed since the legislation of Ine, the tendency which was even then observable, towards the formation of large landed estates and the lessening of the number of free and independent ceorls, had been going forward. One cause which probably contributed to this result was the conversion of Folkland into Bookland: two terms which, after puzzling a whole generation of English historians, have at last, it may be hoped, yielded up their secret to the patient research of a foreign student of our institutions.[*] Folkland, it seems now safe to say, was "family land held by common right and without written evidence."[†] Bookland was, as it is called by a Latin interpreter,[‡] terra testamentalis, land over which the owner had full power of disposition by will, and his right to which rested on some "book" or written document, not on folk-right and immemorial custom. A striking illustration of the difference between the two kinds of property is afforded by the will of a certain ealdorman Alfred who was a contemporary of his great namesake the king.[§] This nobleman leaves the bulk of his large property, which is expressly stated to be bookland, to his widow and "our common bairn" Aldryth: but there is also a son,

....

* Professor Vinogradoff in his essay on Folkland contributed to the English Historical Review, vol. viii.; further illustrated by his Growth of the Manor.

† "Terra popularis, communi jure et sine scripto possessa." This was Spelman's definition (1626), and Vinogradoff shows good ground for reverting to it with a slight modification, instead of adopting Allen's theory that the folkland was land owned by the nation like the ager publicus of Rome.

‡ See Cnut's laws, ii., 13.

§ Kemble, Codex Diplomaticus, No. 317; Birch, Cartularium Saxonicum, No. 558.

probably not born in wedlock, for whom he wishes to make provision. After leaving him a certain small "bookland" property, he adds: "If the king will let him have the folkland in addition to this bookland, then let him have and enjoy it"; if not, the widow is to convey to him certain other bookland estates. It is argued with much force that here we have the case of a nobleman owning large properties which have been conveyed to him by perhaps recent "books," written instruments of purchase and sale, royal donations and the like. But he has inherited also another, probably smaller, property which has been in his family from time immemorial, is his by folk-right, and is called folkland. But this property is held subject to certain customary laws of inheritance, and is perhaps liable to reversion to other members of the kinship in default of male heirs. The ealdorman hopes for the king's intervention on behalf of his son should any difficulty be made about his succession to the folkland, and, failing that, desires that the loss shall be made up to him out of the bookland estate, over which his disposing power is incontestable.

If, as there is reason to believe, the cases of conversion of folkland into bookland were frequent throughout the later Saxon centuries, if the slumbering rights of succession of distant members of the kinship were being barred by "books" granting the land to members of the royal household, to convents and churches, or simply confirming ordinary commercial transactions of sale and exchange, it is easy to see that the class of "twy-hind" ceorls would be sensibly diminished and the possessions of the "twelf-hynd" man, the thegn or the king's retainer visibly increased. All these causes would augment the number of poor and struggling freemen who, especially in times of war and invasion during "the clash of mighty opposites," were glad to sacrifice some part of their precarious independence by "commending" themselves to the protection of some powerful landowner.

XVIII.

ALFRED'S LAST DAYS

From the peaceful labours which had occupied him for the last seven years, Alfred was recalled to the weary work of war by tidings of the return of the dreaded here to the English coast. During those seven years the chronicler had been nervously noting the deeds of "the army" beyond seas. They had been fighting chiefly in the north of Gaul, pressing up the rivers Somme, Seine and Marne, and even laying close siege for ten months (November, 885, to September, 886) to the city of Paris itself, a siege which the Emperor Charles the Fat had raised, not by arms but by the ignominious payment of tribute. It is easy to trace a connexion between these vehement attacks on Frankish territory and the resistance which, in our own country, from Athelney onwards, had been so valiantly offered by Alfred. But now the process was reversed, and the Northmen, severely handled by a Frankish king, were thrown back upon England. In the year 887 Charles the Fat, who had disgusted his subjects by his ignominious treaty with the Danes, was deposed from his imperial dignity, and Arnulf, his nephew, was chosen king by the Franks east of the Rhine, by whose aid he won for himself, nine years after, the grander title of emperor. In 891 he won a great victory over the Danes near the modern city of Louvain. Hereupon the Scandinavians, recognising that "Francia" was for the present closed against them by the might of this new German king, decided to try their fortune once more on the other side of the channel.

The operations of the five years that followed (892–896*) are described by the Chronicle in great detail and with unusual vividness and vigour. A recent editor† calls the six or seven pages devoted to these campaigns "the most remarkable piece of writing in the whole series of chronicles."

* Not 893–97 as Chronicle.

† Earle, Two Saxon Chronicles (1865), p. xvi.

It is allowable to conjecture that such a narrative, if not from Alfred's own pen, comes from some person in the immediate neighbourhood of the king. Fresh and vivid, however, as the narrative is, it is not easy to discover therefrom the precise sequence of events. Different bands of Danes are seen to be operating in different parts of the kingdom, and the difficulty which they probably felt in combining their efforts meets also the historian who seeks to combine their narratives. Here it will be sufficient to indicate some of the principal stages of the contest.

The invasion of 892 seems to have been made by two bodies of Danes, acting to some extent independently of each other. "The great army" which had been defeated by Arnulf at Louvain, went westwards from Flanders to Boulogne, embarked from the latter port "with horses and all" in a fleet of 250 ships, and sailed across to the Kentish coast. According to their usual custom they made use of a river channel to penetrate into the interior; but the river up which they fared and which probably entered the sea at Lymne, has long since disappeared in that region of silted-up streams. Up the river they towed their ships for four miles, and there they found a "work" half finished and defended by a few rustics. Their capture of this work well illustrates a remark of Asser's that "of the many forts which Alfred ordered to be built, some were never begun and others, begun too late, were not finished when the enemy broke in upon them by land and sea," causing tardy repentance and shame on the part of the disobedient builders. The Danish army then constructed for themselves a "work" at Appledore, some twenty miles west of Hythe. The nature of these "works," of which we hear so much at this point of the history, is explained to us by the Frankish chronicler who describes the Emperor Arnulf's victory in 891, and who tells us that the Northmen "had according to their usual manner fortified themselves with wood and heaped-up earth."* The description points to a mound crowned with a palisading, such as the Romans had used to protect their encampments.

Meanwhile another horde, not so large as the first, and fleeing, not so much from the conquering sword of Arnulf, as from the famine which waited upon their own destructive footsteps, having crossed the channel with eighty ships, had entered the Thames and made a "work" in Kent near the Isle of Sheppey. The leader of this band was the far-famed Haesten or Hasting, a pirate who had sailed up the Loire to ravage Central Gaul in the year 866, and in the twenty-six years which followed had not often rested

* Reginonis Chronicon, a. 891.

from the work of devastation. Between these two invading armies Alfred took up a position (893) in the great Andredesweald which stretched along the whole length of Kent and Sussex dividing the two counties, and from thence or from the burhs or fortresses which he had erected, forays were constantly made with some success on the unwelcome visitors. So things seem to have remained through the winter. At Easter the larger host, having broken up from Appledore, wandered through Hants and Berks, ravaging as they went. The young "Etheling" Edward, son of Alfred, being informed of their movements, and having collected his troops, pursued the spoil-laden plunderers and came up with them at Farnham. He fought them and gained a complete victory; the booty was all recovered and the robbers in their desperation swam the Thames without waiting to find a ford, and made their way up the little stream of the Hertfordshire Colne to the river island of Thorney. There apparently Edward was forced to leave them, for the fyrd was divided into two parts, each bound to serve for six months only. The time for relieving guard had now arrived, and while one half was marching "thitherward" (to the front) and the other half homeward, the favourable moment passed away for pursuing the Danes, whose king had been wounded in the late encounter. Some of the enemy penetrated to the coast, collected a hundred ships and sailed westward to make a raid on Devonshire, whither Alfred was forced to follow them.

Leaving "the great army" for a time, we turn to follow the fortunes of Hasting. It seems that he had pretended to imitate the example of Guthrum (who had died three years before, at peace with Alfred), and had expressed his willingness to become a Christian. He gave hostages, swore oaths of peace and friendship, and was probably baptised along with his two sons, the godfathers being Alfred and his son-in-law Ethelred of Mercia, his stout ally in all these campaigns. But some turn in the fortunes of war, perhaps the disloyal attitude of the Danes of Northumbria and Mercia, who were hungering for war, sent Hasting again into armed opposition. He made a "work" at Benfleet in the south-east corner of Essex, and as soon as it was finished he began, as the chronicler says with indignation, to harry that realm of Mercia which Ethelred, his godfather, was bound to defend. Alfred, who had been summoned to Exeter by the tidings of another Danish raid, now returned rapidly to London where a strong burh had been built, a stout-hearted body of citizens having been sworn to defend it. Marching forth with these and with his own troops, he assailed the "work" at Benfleet and carried it by storm. Great spoil was found there as well as many women and children—a sure token that the Northmen had come to settle in the land. All the treasure was gathered within the safe shelter of London-burh, but Alfred, recognising the obligations of spiritual kindred, though Hasting had so soon forgotten them, restored to the old pirate his wife and her two sons. After this the two Danish armies seem to have united and to have made a great "work" at Shoebury in Essex, not far from the abandoned Benfleet. Hasting henceforward fades out of the narrative, possibly unwilling to continue to fight against his generous foe.*

The avowed union of all the men of the "Danelaw" (as the district settled by the Danes was now called), both in East Anglia and Northumbria, gave a new character to the war. It was no longer a mere descent of sea-rovers on Kent or Devonshire; it was a terrible internal struggle, and all along the Watling Street, the boundary between the two kingdoms, the shuttle of war flew swiftly. Leaving their camp at Shoebury, the Danes marched up the valley of the Thames and across the country to the Severn. But now the whole forces of the kingdom were collected for the contest. Not only Ethelred of Mercia but "the Ealdormen of Wilts and Somerset and such of the king's thegns as were then at home at the works, gathered together from every town east of the Parret, from both sides of Selwood, from the north of the Thames and the west of the Severn, and with them came also"—a memorable addition—"some part of the North Welsh race." Evidently the Welshmen had learned by experience that there were worse enemies than the Saxons, and probably also the righteous rule of Alfred had won their confidence. The army thus collected marched after the Danes and came up with them at a place called Buttington on the Severn. For many weeks the two armies sat watching each other, the river flowing between them. At last, after the Danes had eaten most of their horses, they sallied forth and crossed the river to fight. The battle which followed was a bloody one, many of the king's thegns falling; but the slaughter on the Danish side was greater, and victory remained with the English. Back into Essex fled the beaten remnant of the army, but having ere winter gathered to them many helpers from the Danelaw, and having entrusted ships and wives and property to the care of the East Angles, they once more followed the Watling Street into Cheshire, which

* In Eng. Hist. Rev. (1898), xiii., 444, Mr. W. C. Abbott argues that Hasting is possibly identical with Hásteinn, one of the first settlers of Iceland.

for some reason or other (possibly connected with the Danish conquest of Ireland) they persistently made the objective of their campaign. Day and night they marched, till they came to the estuary of the Dee. Here, still surrounded by its grass-grown walls, lay the silent and ruined city which had for near four centuries resounded to the shouts of the twentieth legion, "Valerian and Victorious." In its desolation it yet bore the name of "the camp of the legions" (lega-ceaster), but it was "a waste Chester." A Chester it is still, by its picturesque medieval architecture pre-eminent above all others of its kind, but happily no longer waste. The fyrd hastened with all speed after the here, but failed to overtake them ere they had taken refuge in the ghostly city. They had, therefore, to be satisfied with destroying all the cattle and corn in the neighbourhood, slaying some straggling Danes and leaving nought but a hungry wilderness round the survivors. The blockade of Chester (894) was not a strict one; before long the Danes, urged by famine, broke out of the city, and escaping into the friendly Danelaw marched across the country to the island of Mersea at the mouth of the Blackwater, not far from their old winter quarters in Essex. At the same time the invaders who had been troubling Devonshire sailed homeward, but on their way harried the west of Sussex, until the burg-ware (townsfolk) of Chichester issued forth to battle, routed them, slew many hundreds, and captured some of their ships. Throughout this second Danish war, the martial ardour of the inhabitants of the burhs built or refortified by the king is very conspicuous.

It was now apparently 895, the fourth year since the great scip-here had appeared off the coast of Kent. The Danes who had wintered in Mersea, still hankering doubtless after the spoil of London, sailed round to the estuary of the Thames and towed their ships up the sluggish waters of the Lea, which now forms the boundary between Essex and Middlesex. Here, about twenty miles above London—that is, probably in the neighbourhood of Bishop Stortford—they wrought a "work," and remained encamped for six months. When summer came a multitude of the burg-ware of London marched forth to storm the Danish work. This time, unfortunately, civic valour did not triumph. The burg-ware were put to flight, and four of the king's thegns, who had been acting as their leaders, were slain.

Autumn was now approaching and it was important that the men of Essex should not be attacked while they were gathering in their harvest. Accordingly Alfred encamped in the neighbourhood of London. One day he rode up the Lea to reconnoitre the Danish position, and something in the course of the river suggested to his mind, fertile in expedients and enriched by the study of ancient historians, that it might be possible so to obstruct it as to hinder the escape of the Danes. The scheme ripened; he set two bodies of troops to erect works above and below the station of the ships. Ere the works were finished the Danes saw that their position was being made untenable; they abandoned the ships—probably by night—and marched off, still no doubt through the friendly Danelaw, till they came to Bridgnorth on the Severn, where they again wrought a work and fixed their winter quarters. While the fyrd rode after them towards the north, the men of London-burh came out and captured the ships, some of which they broke up and others, the more serviceable, they towed down stream to London. Such was the strange campaign of the Lea. Any one who knows the Lea in its present conditions, who has seen the sleepy bargemen gliding along from lock to lock, the anglers sitting all day on the banks which Izaak Walton has made classic ground, all the indescribable restfulness and tranquillity of the scene, will feel the contrast between this peaceful Present and the days when Alfred's men were toiling at their noisy labours and when the heathens howled forth their execrations on finding their passage barred by the Saxons.

In the following summer (896) "the here went some to East Anglia, some to Northumbria, and those who were moneyless got them ships and fared over sea to the Seine. Thus had the army," says the chronicler, "not utterly broken all the English race. But they were more fearfully broken during those three years by pestilence both of cattle and of men, especially because the most eminent of the king's thegns died in those three years." The chronicler then gives the name and rank of the chief victims of the plague: the bishops of Rochester and Dorchester, the ealdormen of Kent, Essex and Hants, a king's thegn of Sussex, the town-reeve of Winchester, a grand constable (king's horse-thegn) and many others.

Though the great land invasion was thus defeated, the king had still to deal with a harassing swarm of sea-pirates, whose long ships named "ashes," built of the wood of the ill-omened ash tree, were constantly appearing off the southern coast, often manned by insurgent Danes from East Anglia and Northumbria. In order to grapple with these pestilent enemies Alfred turned shipbuilder. He may have already taken some steps towards this end, but the following entry in the Chronicle for the year 897 (= 896) is the earliest definite information that we receive as to the beginnings of England's navy: "Then King Alfred bade build long ships against the ashes; they were full nigh twice as long as the others. Some had sixty oars, some more. They were both swifter and steadier and eke higher than the others. They were not built on Frisian nor yet on Danish lines, but as he himself thought that they might be most serviceable."

An engagement of no great importance, which is, however, described in great detail by the chronicler, took place between the pirates and nine of the new ships which had been despatched by Alfred to stop their depredations, and had sealed them up in some estuary or land-locked bay (such as Brading harbour) in the Isle of Wight. While the tide was high the crews of the big English ships captured and slew to their hearts' content, but when the tide ebbed they were left aground, as the chronicler says, "very inconveniently" half on one side of the estuary and half on the other, with the Danish ashes, also aground, between them. At dead low water the shore was firm enough for the Danish pirates to climb down out of their ship, paddle across the sands and challenge a fight with the crews of the three English ships nearest to them. For such small contending forces the battle seems to have been a bloody one. One hundred and twenty Danes fell and sixty-two English, but among these latter were many men of high rank, a king's reeve and a king's companion (geneat), and also many of the Frisian captains and sailors whom Alfred, knowing their nautical skill, had attracted to his service. When the battle was ended, in came the flowing tide, on which the Danish ships could float out to sea while the larger ships of the new navy were still lying "very inconveniently aground." So the three pirate ships escaped for the time, but they were sorely strained and damaged, so that they could not all sail round the coast of Sussex. Two were wrecked on that coast, and their crews being brought to Winchester and led into the king's presence, were ordered by him to be hanged. This order was not like the usual clemency of the king, but he probably felt that it was necessary to repress with a strong hand movements which were now no longer warfare but mere brigandage. The third ship escaped both the winds and the English pursuers, and landed her crew, a troop of sore-wounded and weary men, on the East Anglian coast.

Not more than four years of rest seem to have been granted to Alfred after the repulse of this last invasion before death ended his labours. There can be little doubt that some part at least of that plentiful literary harves which was described in the preceding chapter belongs to these closin years. Especially interesting is it to note that, according to the judgment of the most careful modern inquirers, the king's metrical translation of Boethius should be referred to this period. The proem to that translation alludes to "the manifold worldly cares that oft troubled him both in mind and body" when he was turning it from Latin into English prose, and then again to the cares, apparently the yet heavier cares, "that in his days came upon the kingdom to which he had succeeded," but which did not prevent him—so high was his value for the great Consolatio—from "working it up once more into verse" as the reader may now behold it. All these cares were now at an end, and ended, too, all his noble toil for the defence, the enlightenment and the guidance of his people. He died on October 26, 900,* in the fifty-third year of his age, and was buried in St. Swithun's monastery at Winchester. In 903, however (according to the legend told by William of Malmesbury), as "the delirious fancies of the canons" declared that the king's ghost, resuming possession of his corpse, wandered at night through their cells, the royal remains were transferred to the New Minster, founded by his son in fulfilment of a plan which Alfred himself had formed and had confided to his friend and spiritual adviser, Grimbald the Frank. In the reign of Henry I. the monks of New Minster migrated from their narrow domain within the city to a large nd convenient site called Hyde Mead, on its northern side, and in their ıigration they took with them the body of the king. At the suppression the monasteries Hyde Abbey fell into decay, and near the close of eighteenth century the Hampshire magistrates purchased the site for purpose of erecting thereon a county jail. The tombs were ruthlessly ıed, the stone coffins were turned into horse troughs, the lead which red a coffin, presumably Alfred's, was sold for two guineas, and ently the dust of the great king himself was scattered to the winds. der of the Danish army could have shown greater zest in the work cration. This New Minster at Winchester was consecrated by one d's friends, Archbishop Plegmund, and numbered another of his Grimbald, as first on its list of abbots. Its records, known as the ınasterii de Hyda, furnish us with some valuable information g the reigns of Alfred and his sons.

he great king himself, several of the chroniclers, especially his Ethelweard, and Florence of Worcester, have celebrated his

y; but the Chronicle gives the date 901, and Mr. Stevenson, Eng. Hist. 8), xiii., 71, argues strongly for 899.

praises in fitting terms, but his best epitaph is contained in three simple words of an unknown scribe of the twelfth century, "Alfred, England's Darling." His fame and the glory of his noble character have grown brighter as the centuries have rolled by, and at this day he is really nearer to the hearts of Englishmen than all, save one, of his successors.

NOTE ON THE EXTENT OF THE DANELAW

The political boundaries of the Danish state recognised after the Peace of Wedmore have been sufficiently indicated by historians, and it may be said that for all practical purposes they nearly coincide with the old Roman road called the Watling Street, the sphere of Danish influence lying to the north and east, that of Saxon influence and rule to the south and west of that line, which, as previously remarked, coincides very nearly with the line of the London and North Western Railway. There is, however, another question both interesting and important: "To what extent did the Danish population fill up the district thus assigned to them?" In other words, "How far did the ethnological coincide with the political boundary?" This is a question which we have not as yet sufficient materials to answer fully or accurately. Much study and much patient research on the part of our local antiquaries, study of dialects and research in sepulchral tumuli, will probably be needed before we can say with certainty: "Here the old Anglian population remained preponderant, and here the Danish or Norwegian immigrants so filled the land as to make it practically a Scandinavian district." But in the meantime some help is gained from a consideration of the place-names in the several districts of England; only we must beware of looking at the conclusions thus arrived at as final and irreversible.

Broadly, however, we may say with some confidence that place-names ending in ton, ham, yard and worth are Saxon or Anglian; those ending in by, thorpe and toft are Danish; in thwaite, garth, beck, haugh, and fell, Norwegian; in borough, probably Anglian; in wick or wich, if inland, Saxon, if near the sea-coast, Danish. Applying these tests we find evidence of considerable Danish settlements, but no Danish preponderance, in Norfolk and Suffolk. The great fen district round Peterborough seems to have been an impassable barrier, and we find no Danish names to the west of it; on the other hand, the Humber and the Wash must have been constantly visited by the ships of the vikings, for their shores swarm with Danish names. As has been said by Mr. Isaac Taylor,* "A district in Lincolnshire, about nine miles by twelve, between Tattersall, New Bolingbroke, Horncastle and Spilsby, would appear to have been more exclusively Danish than any other in the kingdom. In this small space there are some forty unmistakably Danish village names, such as Kirby, Moorby, Enderby, etc., all denoting the fixed residence of a Danish population." "The Danish local names radiate from the Wash.† In Leicestershire, Rutland, Northamptonshire and Yorkshire the Danish names preponderate over those of the Anglo-Saxon type; while Cambridgeshire, Huntingdonshire, Bedfordshire and the adjacent counties, protected by the fens, present scarcely a single Danish name." There can be no more striking proof of the absolute preponderance of the Danish element in the north-east corner of Yorkshire (where probably the influence of the invaders radiated from the estuary of the Tees) than the fact that Streanæshalc itself, the Anglian sanctuary, home of St. Hilda and meeting-place of the great Paschal Synod, meekly bowed its head to the alien yoke and accepted the Danish name of Whitby.

In the midland counties the most striking proof of the numerical superiority of the Danes was exhibited by the powerful confederation of the five boroughs, Leicester, Lincoln, Nottingham, Stamford and Derby. It is true that only one of these bore an unmistakably Danish name, but the part which they played politically, their strong offensive and defensive alliance, seems to confirm the generally accepted conclusion that the five boroughs were essentially a Danish confederation. Going further north we find very slight indications of Danish settlement in Durham and Northumberland. This part of Northumbria the invaders seem to have visited only for ravage, not for settlement, being satisfied to leave it under the rule of some subservient earl, who might or might not be of their own race. Further north still, across the Scottish border, Danish names die out altogether; but when we go far enough we find abundant traces of the other great stream of Scandinavian invasion, the Norwegian, and about this a few words must be said in reference, not to Scotland (Shetland, Orkney, Hebrides, etc.), but to the western coast of England.

The place-names of Cumberland and Westmorland must always have arrested the attention of careful philologists. While the names of mountains and rivers, such as Helvellyn, Blencathra, Glaramara,

* Words and Places, pp. 175–76.

† Might it not be added "and from the Humber?"

Derwent, are for the most part of Celtic origin, we find a great number of names of villages and some also of hills and streams which evidently are Scandinavian rather than Celtic. Such are all the multitudinous thwaites and ghylls, the garths and haughs, and the frequently recurring beck for a stream, and fell for a high hill. Mr. Robert Ferguson called attention to the fact that this multitude of non-Celtic terminations—so remarkable in a country which actually bears the name of the Cymri—pointed to a large immigration of Scandinavians, not, however, of the Danish but of the Norwegian type. Of such immigration we have scarcely a hint in the chroniclers, but the philological evidence adduced by Mr. Ferguson* is so strong that his conclusion has been generally accepted by ethnologists. As to the date of this migration, his theory is that after the Saxon king Edmund in 945 had overrun the district of Cumbria and had left it wasted and bare of people, the Norwegians from their stronghold in the Isle of Man, discerning their advantage, covered the Solway with their ships, and pouring into that land of mountains and lakes and long stream-watered valleys—a land so like their fatherland—settled there and made it their own. This migration he would therefore place in the latter part of the tenth century, between the just mentioned Cumbrian campaign of Edmund (945) and the similar campaign of Ethelred (1000) which was undertaken, Henry of Huntingdon says, against "the Danes" yet involved the ravaging of Cumberland.

However this question of the date may hereafter be settled, there can be little doubt that the race which peoples these two most picturesque counties of England is pre-eminently of Norwegian origin. There seems to have been two other settlements of Scandinavians which deserve remark. One was in that curious peninsula of Cheshire, called the Wirral, between the estuaries of Dee and Mersey, a region which teems with Norse names; and the other, an exceptional instance of a Norse settlement south of the Watling Street, was in the promontory of Pembrokeshire, where a number of towns and villages, of which the best known is the watering-place of Tenby, attest by their names their Danish origin.

* The Northmen in Cumberland and Westmorland (1856).

XIX.

EDWARD AND HIS SONS

With the death of Alfred and the accession of his son EDWARD (called in later times "the Elder," to distinguish him from his descendants, "the Martyr" and "the Confessor") we enter upon a new century. Like its predecessor, the tenth century was for Europe generally a time of gloom, dismay and depression. The break-up of the empire of Charlemagne went on with increasing rapidity, the imperial title itself becoming the prize of obscure Italian princes until, about the middle of the century, the great Otto I. of Saxony (962–73) did something to restore its lustre and to bring back the Italian peninsula within the sphere of the imperial unity. In some measure, too, he succeeded in rehabilitating the office of the papacy, cruelly discredited by the intrigues of two profligate women, Theodora and Marozia, who had placed their lovers, their husbands and their young and licentious sons on the most venerated throne in Christendom. In France the Carolingian line was yielding to the same process of decay which had destroyed its Merovingian predecessor; and thirteen years before the end of the century Hugh Capet followed the example of Pippin and, thrusting the descendants of Charlemagne into the background, became the acknowledged king of the diminished territory of France; a position in which he was somewhat overshadowed by the greatness of his nominal vassals, the Norman dukes descended from Rollo. For France and Germany it is true that the invasions of the Northmen had practically ceased, but the ravages of the Hungarians during the first half of the century were a terror to Europe. In England, however, this age was not nearly so dark a time as many of its predecessors. In fact the tenth century saw the Anglo-Saxon monarchy attain its highest point of power and prosperity, though it also before its close saw it sink to the lowest depths of misery and degradation.

The first five years of Edward's reign* were disturbed by the rebellion of his cousin Ethelwald, son of Ethelred. According to the theories of strict hereditary succession which have since prevailed, Ethelwald's title as representative of an elder son was incontestable, and in fact Alfred himself according to these theories was but a usurper, yet it need hardly be said that these theories had no place in the Anglo-Saxon polity. The son, if a minor, or for any other reason unsuitable, had no indefeasible right to wear his dead father's crown. Among the Saxons, as with most of the other Teutonic nations, the two principles of inheritance and election were closely, we are inclined to say illogically, blended. The new king must be of the royal race; in the case of Wessex his line must "go unto Cerdic"; but he must also be "chosen and raised to be king" by the witan, the wise men or senators of the kingdom. This ceremony had been duly complied with at Edward's accession, and therefore he was rightful king though sprung from a younger branch of the royal house. Moreover it was a matter of reproach against Ethelwald that he had "without the king's leave and against the bishop's ordinance married or cohabited with a woman who had before been hallowed as a nun." Yet for all this he did not lack adherents, some of whom probably held that he was wrongfully excluded from the throne.

Ethelwald's rebellion was announced to the world by his occupation of a royal vill at Badbury in Dorsetshire, near his father's sepulchre at Wimborne. Thither rode the new king with a portion of the local fyrd, but found all the approaches to the place blocked by order of the insurgent Etheling. It was rumoured that Ethelwald had said to his followers, "Here will I die or here will I lie": nevertheless his heart failed him when it came to the pinch, and he stole away by night to Northumbria, vainly pursued by the men of King Edward. The Danish army in the northern realm accepted him for their king; the men of East Anglia joined them, and after three years all marched through Mercia, ravaging as they went, as far as Cricklade in Wiltshire. At the approach of Edward with his fyrd, the insurgents moved rapidly northwards with the spoil which they had gathered. Edward pursued, and ravaged all their land between the Cambridgeshire dykes and the river Ouse, as far northward as the fens. He then sounded a retreat, but the men of Kent, eager for the fight, though

* Edward's reign probably lasted from 900 to 924, but owing to discrepancies between the MSS. of the Chronicles no date in the reign can be stated with certainty, the differences varying from one to three years.

seven times ordered to withdraw, continued to face the enemy. The battle which ensued was evidently a defeat of the Saxons, and cost the lives of two ealdormen and many distinguished nobles of Kent. Practically however it was as good as a victory, since Ethelwald, "who enticed the Danes to that breach of the peace," lay dead upon the field. Peace seems naturally to have followed upon his death, and thus was ended in 905 what might have been a dangerous civil war.

The chief work of Edward's reign was the conquest of the new Danish kingdoms of East Anglia, Essex and the remainder of Mercia. The settlement which followed the Peace of Wedmore, a wise and statesmanlike compromise at the time, had ceased to be applicable to the existing state of affairs. At every serious crisis of the West Saxon state the Danes beyond Watling Street at once broke the frith, and their dreaded "army" crossed the Saxon border. It was time that this intolerable state of things should be brought to an end, and to its termination Edward, himself "a man of war from his youth," and with an army of Saxon veterans at his back, now successfully devoted himself. We hear of him in 910 beating the Danes at Tettenhall in Staffordshire; in 911, at some place unnamed, winning a great victory over the Northumbrian Danes—a victory in which two kings, many jarls and holds (earls and chief captains) and thousands of soldiers of meaner rank were slain. Then, in 912, he "took possession of London and Oxford, and all the lands thereto belonging." This however was apparently no fresh conquest, but only a peaceful resumption of territories previously appertaining to Mercia. In 913 he fortified Hertford, encamped at Maldon in Essex, and received the submission of the greater part of that kingdom. In 914 and 915 the chief victories seem to have been won not by the king in person, but by the warlike energies of the local militia. In the former year they defeated a plundering host of Northamptonshire and Leicestershire Danes at Leighton Buzzard, and stripped them of their accumulated spoil. In the latter, operations after a long interval were begun anew by marauders from beyond sea. A scip-here, or naval armament, from the coast of Brittany, made its unwelcome appearance at the mouth of the Severn and captured a Welsh bishop whom Edward ransomed for forty pounds (of silver); and then the men of Hereford, of Gloucester and of all the nearest burhs came out against them, slew one of the two jarls who commanded them and the brother of his colleague, and drove them into a "park" or enclosed space, which the men of the fyrd beset so closely that the Danes were forced to give hostages for their peaceable departure from the country. Apparently, however, they broke their promises, stole away by night and made two hostile descents on the coast of Somerset, one at Watchet and one at Porlock, both of which were successfully repulsed. After betaking themselves to the two islands of Flatholme and Steepholme, in the middle of the Bristol Channel, and seeing many of their number die of sheer starvation on those desolate islands, the remnant departed, first to South Wales and then to Ireland, and were heard of no more.

The largest share of the credit for the conquest of Danish Mercia must be given to Edward's manlike sister, Ethelfled, "lady of the Mercians." Daughter herself of a Mercian princess and married to a husband (Ethelred) who was probably related to the royal line of Offa, she seems after her husband's death in 911 to have still commanded, to an extraordinary degree, the love and loyalty of the Mercian people, and to have wielded the warlike resources of the Midland kingdom with wonderful energy and success. Each year she struck a heavy blow either at the men of the Danelaw, on her right, or at the Welsh of Gwynedd—now no longer friendly to the Saxon—on her left. With her, as with her brother, the plan of campaign, generally centred round some burh which the English ruler built in the hostile territory and defended against all comers. After Chester had been repaired, probably by Ethelred, the chief fortresses built and defended by his widow were Bromesberrow, near Ledbury in Herefordshire, Shrewsbury, Bridgnorth, Stafford, Eddisbury in the forest of Delamere, Warwick, Chirk in Denbighshire, Warburton and Runcorn in the south of Lancashire. While some of these forts were within, most of them were decidedly beyond the Watling Street line, and their erection betokened the recovery for the English of an important portion of the Danelaw. The Denbighshire fort is evidence of the determination of the high-hearted "lady of the Mercians" to reduce her Welsh neighbours to obedience; a determination which was shown still more plainly when in June 19, 916, she sent the Mercian fyrd into South Wales, took Brecon by storm and captured the wife of the Welsh king with thirty-four other persons, probably nobles of his court.

By this time, however, the conquering career of Ethelfled was drawing to a close. Towards the end of July, 917, she "with the aid of God obtained the burh which is called Derby, with all pertaining thereto." The victory, however, was not bloodless. "There were slain within the gates four of her thegns, of those who were dearest unto her." The next year by the same Divine aid "she gained peaceable possession of the burh of Leicester and subdued to herself the largest part of the here that owned allegiance thereto. Also the men of York promised obedience, and some gave bail, while others confirmed with oaths their covenant to be under her rule." Apparently the Lady of Mercia was destined to become also Lady of Northumbria. Not so, however. "Very swiftly after this covenant was made, twelve nights before midsummer (918) she died at Tamworth, in the eighth year that she had held power with right lordship over the Mercians. And her body lieth at Gloucester in the east porch of St. Peter's Church." From this entry it appears probable that Tamworth was the favourite residence of the Lady of the Mercians as it had been of her royal predecessors.* What was the precise nature of the political relation between Ethelfled and her royal brother, it is perhaps impossible to discover. Clearly the status of Ethelred and his wife was not kingly. He is correctly spoken of as ealdorman and as hlaford (lord), while she is described as hlæfdige (lady); yet in all her actions, in her military movements, her sieges and her treaties, she seems to act as independently as Penda or Offa. Probably the term which is sometimes used in the Chronicle, mund-bora (protector), most fittingly expresses the relation which during Ethelfled's lifetime Edward held toward his sister. She is not absolutely independent, yet she governs her subjects, marches her armies about, and promotes her well-beloved thegns to honour, as seems meet to her. She is a subject-ally, most faithful and most valiant of all allies, and he, should she ever need to call upon him for help, will not fail as her "protector."

Whatever may have been the precise nature of the peculiar relation between Wessex and Mercia, it came to an end soon after the death of Ethelfled. She left, indeed, a daughter named Elfwyn, who seems for about eighteen months to have wielded her mother's authority, but in 919, "three weeks before mid-winter," she was deprived of all power over the Mercians and led away into Wessex. There are some slight indications in the Chronicle that this obliteration of Mercia as a semi-independent state was not altogether acceptable to the people of the middle kingdom. However this may have been, Edward, now sending forth into the field the united armies of Wessex and Mercia, carried forward with irresistible might the process of the unification of the kingdom. The burhs which he erected between 913 and 924 rounded off the work of Ethelfled.

* Offa calls it his palatium regale in one of his charters (Birch, Cart. Sax., 240).

These were Hertford, Bedford, Huntingdon and Towcester in the East Midlands, Maldon and Colchester in Essex, Stamford in Lincolnshire, Nottingham and Bakewell in the country of the Peak, Thelwall in Cheshire, and Manchester, the last being expressly stated to have been "in Northumbria." The work of subduing and over-aweing the Welsh was not forgotten. In 921 Edward built a burh at Wigmore in Herefordshire, in sight of the long range of Radnor Forest, and another at the mouth of the Cleddau in Pembrokeshire, a proof that his arms had penetrated as far as to Milford Haven.

Round all these newly built burhs the tide of battle fiercely ebbed and flowed ere the people whom they were meant to hold down patiently submitted to their domination. Thus we hear of an unsuccessful assault by "the army" of East Anglia and Mercia on the burh at Wigmore; of "the army" breaking the frith and marching against Towcester. "And they fought against it all day and thought to carry it by storm, but the folk that were therein defended it till help came, whereupon they departed ravaging as they went." In consequence of this attack, unsuccessful as it was, Edward surrounded Towcester with a stone wall which it had not previously possessed. The enemy vainly endeavoured to imitate Edward's castle-building policy. The Danes of Huntingdon and East Anglia built a great fort at Tempsford on the river Ouse (a little south of St. Neots), "and thought that they should therefrom with battle and un-peace win back to themselves more of this land." But they were disappointed, for the people from the nearest burhs having gathered themselves together, fought against Tempsford and overthrew it, slaying the Danish king and two of his jarls, and all who were found fighting therein.

The year which is marked in the chief manuscript of the Chronicle as 921 but which probably was in truth 918, saw the full tide of English successes, and in consequence we now hear of the complete submission of East Anglia and Essex to the rule of Edward. "To him submitted much folk both of the East Angles and the East Saxons, who had been erewhile under the Danish power, and all the 'army' in East Anglia swore to oneness with him, that they would all will that which he willed, and be at peace with those with whom he was at peace, whether by sea or land. And the here that belonged to Cambridge chose him specially for lord and protector (mund-bora) and confirmed this by oaths as he commanded them." In 919, the year after the death of Ethelfled, three kings of North Wales and all the North Welsh kin sought Edward to be their lord. His conquest of Nottingham followed, and here we observe with interest that he garrisoned the newly captured fort with Danes as well as with Englishmen; also that all the folk that were in Mercia submitted to his rule, whether they were Danes or Englishmen.

Thus then we now have Edward not wielding the shadowy power of a Bretwalda, but actual king, personally ruling over all the lands south of the Humber, acknowledged as over-lord by North Wales, probably also by Northumbria. Did his overlordship extend yet farther north? Did Scotland recognise him as supreme king? That question seems to be answered decisively in the affirmative by the celebrated entry in the Chronicle for the year 924 which probably should be corrected to 921. After describing Edward's operations in the midlands, his building a bridge over the Trent between the two burhs of Nottingham, his going from thence into the Peak country and ordering a burh to be built as near as possible to Bakewell, the chronicler thus proceeds: "Him chose as father and lord the Scottish king and all the Scottish people; and Raegnald, Eadulf's son [king of Northumbria], and all the dwellers in Northumbria whether they were Englishmen or Danes or Northmen or any others, and eke the king of the Welsh of Strathclyde and all his people [did the like]." The facts here related, as far as they concern the men of Strathclyde and Northumbria, are not seriously disputed, though one may note in passing the distinction now first met with between "Danes" and "Northmen" or Norwegians. But how as to Edward's over-lordship of Scotland, which seems to be vouched for by the beginning of the sentence, and which was made, four centuries later by his namesake, Edward Plantagenet, the basis of a claim to exercise the rights of lord paramount? The answer to that question has involved historians on both sides of the Border in fierce debate. It is, of course, impossible here to do more than sketch the bare outline of the controversy, but so much as this must be attempted.

The champions of the English claim to supremacy over Scotland* maintain that "in 921 Edward received—what no West Saxon king had ever before received—the submission of the Scots and the Strathclyde Welsh.... In the Latin phrase they commended themselves to him; they promised him fidelity and put themselves under his protection." "There was nothing strange or degrading in this relation; it was the relation in

* Especially Freeman, whose words are quoted in the rest of this paragraph. But see also for a later vindication of the correctness of the chronicler's statement, Plummer, Saxon Chronicles, ii., 131.

which in theory all other princes stood to the Emperor."* "From this time to the fourteenth century the vassalage of Scotland was an essential part of the public law of the isle of Britain. No doubt many attempts were made to cast off the dependent relation which had been voluntarily incurred; but when a king of the English had once been chosen 'to father and to lord,' his successors never willingly gave up the position which had thus been bestowed upon them."† On the other side, Scottish historians‡ naturally point to the fact that it is a Saxon chronicler who makes the statement from which such mighty consequences are deduced. The law does not allow a suitor to make evidence for himself; but here is an alleged "commendation" of which we have no hint in the records of the king and the nation by whom it is alleged to have been made; only in the chronicles of the pretended receiver. They further throw doubt on the genuineness of the passage and suggest that it may be a late interpolation. One argument against its genuineness is that it seems to represent the "commendation" as taking place in the heart of Derbyshire, whereas such a transaction would naturally have been performed on the boundary of the two kingdoms. Another and more serious objection is that Raegnald of Northumbria is here named as taking part in the "commendation" in the year 924, whereas "in the Irish annals, at this period most accurate and trustworthy authorities for all that relates to the family of Raegnald,"§ the death of this chieftain is assigned to a date three years earlier, 921.

The question at issue, now merely academic but once of vital importance to the two countries, has been much complicated by subsequent transactions, alleged cessions of Lothian and Strathclyde on terms of feudal dependence, homage rendered by Scottish kings for possessions in England and so forth. The allegation of fact made by the English chronicler seems entirely worthy of credit. Doubtless for polemical purposes such a statement if made by a Scottish authority would have been more valuable; but the writer of the Chronicle was a contemporary; his work though not very luminous and often careless of strict chronological accuracy, certainly impresses one's mind with a general feeling of its honesty and good faith; there is no trace of interpolation in the manuscripts (which are all long antecedent to the reign of Edward

* Historical Essays, i., 60, 62.

† Norman Conquest, i., 59.

‡ Robertson, Skene and Lang.

§ Robertson, Scotland under her Early Kings, ii., 397.

I.); nor is there any very obvious reason why a monastic scribe writing at Winchester or Canterbury should have invented the transactions here detailed if they never happened. When the entry is carefully examined and compared with similar passages in the same Chronicle, it is seen that the writer is not committed to the statement that the interview took place at Bakewell. Nor will the objection drawn from the date of Raegnald's death appear formidable to any one who knows how loose is the chronology of the Chronicle everywhere, but especially in this part of it, in which, for reasons quite unconnected with this controversy, its latest editor considers that all the events are post-dated by three years.

If then we accept as probably true the statement that "the Scottish king [Constantine II.] and all the Scottish people chose Edward as father and as lord," what does that statement imply? It is perhaps a mistake to introduce the word "commendation," though that word may pretty nearly describe the nature of the transaction. But the word itself, though known to the Franks and occurring in the Bavarian law-book, does not seem to have been ever used by our Anglo-Saxon ancestors. The Teutonic word mund-byrd (protection), which most nearly corresponds to it, is not used of the transactions of 921, though it is used shortly before concerning the men of Huntingdon who "bowed to King Edward and sought his frith (peace) and his mund-byrd." In such a difficult and obscure discussion, it is surely better to keep quite close to the original words of the historian, avoiding all mention of "commendation" and far more of "vassalage," which last term, as all agree, does not correctly represent any relation established in Britain early in the tenth century. Let us repeat simply that the King of Scots "chose Edward as father and as lord."

What then was the meaning of that choice? Did it make "the vassalage of Scotland an essential part of the public law of the isle of Britain"? The word "vassalage" no one would insist upon; but may we not also demur to the expression "the public law of the isle of Britain" at this period of its history? Where is there a trace in that age of such a refined juristic conception? Is not everything in the relation between the races and kingdoms of Britain vague, ill-defined, anarchic? The Danes make a frith and break it; the West Saxons establish some kind of supremacy over the Mercians; Edward's personal rule is advanced as far as the Humber; he becomes thereby undoubtedly the most powerful man in Britain; Scots, Northumbrians and Britons of Strathclyde take note of the fact and desire to become allies—we may safely say subject-allies—of so mighty a prince, whom they accordingly take "as father and as lord." That is all that has yet happened. There was something here which on the one hand, as the current of the age swept on towards feudalism, might have been developed into lordship and vassalage, or, on the other, might have utterly disappeared. In the next reign the very districts which have thus acknowledged the superiority of Edward are found fighting against his son. Under such a weak king as Ethelred the germ involved in the transaction of 921 must have disappeared altogether. No one can suppose that the Redeless King, who could not defend his own throne against the attacks of the Danes, was in any sense "father and lord" of Scotland. Thus the question, which is academic to us now, was or should have been equally academic in the thirteenth century. Whatever other grounds Edward I. might have for claiming high-lordship over Scotland, the dead and buried rights or duties or courtesies of 921 ought not to have been imported into the controversy.

Shortly after the events last described, at the end of 924 or the beginning of 925, King Edward died at Farndon* in Mercia. Only sixteen days after his death his son Elfweard died also, and father and son were both buried in the New Minster at Winchester. Edward, though one of the noblest of his race, was a man much less richly endowed with intellectual gifts than his father. We cease to hear of works undertaken for the instruction of his subjects, and the great Chronicle begins to languish in his reign. His character also seems to lack some of the beauty of his father's; one can hardly imagine Alfred dealing with Ethelwald or with Elfwyn exactly in the same manner as his son. But he was essentially a soldier, probably a strict disciplinarian, and he, with the help of that Amazon, his sister, carried strongly and steadily forward the great work which their father had begun, the recovery of England for the English.

*****

ATHELSTAN, who now succeeded to the throne, and who reigned, probably, from 924 to 940, was much the eldest of the remaining sons of Edward. The others were but children, while he was thirty years of age at his father's death. Although he cannot have been more than six years old when Alfred died, we are told that his comely face and winning

* It was pointed out in the Athenæum for Nov. 4, 1905, that this place rather than Farringdon, in Berkshire, corresponds with the Farndune of the Chronicle.

ways so endeared him to his grandfather that the latter made him "a premature soldier," robing him in a scarlet mantle and girding him with a little sword, golden-scabbarded, and hung round his neck by a jewelled baldric. Moreover, Alfred is said to have prayed that the royal child might one day have a prosperous reign. It is not very easy to reconcile these stories with the fact, alleged by William of Malmesbury, that the stain of illegitimacy rested on his birth. The same authority tells us that he was the son of Egwinna, a noble lady, and then in another place describes her as the daughter of a shepherd, marked out by a dream for high destiny, and introduced to Edward by his old nurse, at whose cottage he was visiting. It is difficult entirely to reject the statement that there was something irregular about Athelstan's birth which caused difficulties about his accession even in that age, not fastidious about the strict principles of legitimacy. There is also something slightly suspicious about the emphasis which the chroniclers lay on the premature death of his half-brother, Elfweard, as if, had that event not occurred, he would have been at least a partner in the throne, if not its sole occupant. We need not, perhaps, greatly concern ourselves with William of Malmesbury's story of a certain Alfred, the rival of Athelstan, who opposed his elevation to the throne on the ground of his illegitimacy, went to Rome to state his case before the Pope and died in the act of taking an oath, presumably a false oath, in its support. All this, though it raises a suspicion that for some reason or other the accession of Athelstan was not wholly unopposed, is too doubtful and legendary to be made the ground-work of serious history. We can only say that Athelstan's day was a glorious one, if there were some clouds which hung round its sunrise. It should, perhaps, also be mentioned that Athelstan when a boy had been entrusted by his grandfather to the care of Ethelred and Ethelfled, and seems before his accession to the West Saxon throne to have been specially connected with Mercia.

The coronation of Athelstan took place at Kingston-on-Thames, which for the rest of this century was the chief crowning place of English kings. In the new king, whatever may have been the clouds overhanging his birth, or the difficulties attending his accession, we have a more splendid type of English royalty than has yet been displayed even by the great kings of Northumbria. By his family alliances, by the renown which he inherited from his father, and by that which he achieved for himself as the successful champion of his people, he obtained a commanding position among the rulers of western Europe, and he early assumed and not doubtfully vindicated for himself the proud title of "lord of the whole of Britain."

By the marriages of his half-sisters, the daughters of Edward, Athelstan was brought into close connexion with the most powerful rulers of France and Germany. Not powerful it is true, though highly placed, was his brother-in-law, the unfortunate Charles the Simple, King of France (893–929), who married Edgiva, was dethroned and died in a dungeon; but his son, Louis IV. ("d'outre mer"), after having been smuggled out of Laon in a truss of straw, was brought to England by his devoted mother; was reared at the court of Athelstan; recalled to his native country and played the part of the king of France not altogether unsuccessfully for eighteen years (936–54). A too powerful subject of these Carolingian kings, one whose greatness overshadowed their throne and whose son eventually succeeded in winning it for himself, was Hugh the Great, Duke of France. This nobleman sought another of Athelstan's sisters in marriage, even the Lady Eadhilda, in whom as a chronicler says "all the elements of beauty which other women have in part, naturally flowed together in one." The messenger who came to urge this suit, and who was himself Athelstan's first cousin,* brought with him gorgeous gifts, precious relics, consecrated swords, lances and banners. Among the presents may be specially noted an onyx vase (surely of antique workmanship) so skilfully carved that on it you seemed to see the corn waving, the vines putting forth their shoots, the figures of men moving, and swift horses prancing in their golden trappings. The pleadings of the ambassador or the splendour of the gifts prevailed. The lovely Eadhilda became the wife of Hugh the Great, though not for her but for a successor was reserved the honour of being the mother of the new line of kings of France. When German Otto, the future Roman emperor, wished to wed one of the same royal sisterhood, he seems not to have proffered so humble a request, but in lordly fashion to have signified his pleasure that a princess should be sent unto him. Thereupon, Athelstan sent two of his sisters, Edgitha and Elfgiva, that Otto might choose between them. He chose Edgitha, whose marriage seems to have been a happy one, and who was much loved by the German people. Elfgiva, who remained on the continent, had to be satisfied with the humbler position of wife of a sub-Alpine prince.

A striking feature of Athelstan's policy was his friendship for the Scandinavian powers. He probably saw that notwithstanding all that

* Adolf, son of Baldwin of Flanders.

England had suffered at the hands of the Danes, the Northmen were tending towards the condition of an organised state, and that it would be wise for "the lord of all Britain" to cultivate their friendship. His reign coincided with the last years of the long reign of Harold the Fair-haired, the first king of Norway, and the legend of the dealings of the two kings with one another, though probably untrue in the letter, may well illustrate the relations between the two kings as remembered by the people.

"One day a messenger of Athelstan appeared at the court of Haarfager (the Fair-haired one) bearing a sword whose hilt was enwrought with gold and silver and set with most precious gems. The messenger said: 'Here is a sword which King Athelstan sendeth thee, bidding thee take it withal'. Harold grasped the sword, and the envoy completed his message thus: 'Now hast thou taken the sword according to our king's bidding. Henceforth thou must needs be his thegn.' Harold dissembled his vexation and next year sent a ship to England under the command of his favourite champion, Hawk High-breech, into whose keeping he gave the little Hakon, the son of his old age by his bondwoman, Thora. Norseman Hawk was hospitably entertained by the king and bidden to a right worthy feast in the city of London. After due greetings interchanged, the old captain took the boy and set him on Athelstan's knee. 'Why dost thou do that?' said the king. 'Because King Harold thus ordereth thee to foster the child of his bondwoman,' was the reply. The king was angry and began to feel for his sword, but the messenger said: 'Thou hast set him on thy knee, and now thou mayest murder him if thou wilt, but not so wilt thou make an end of the sons of King Harold'."* These sons were in truth an almost countless throng, and the wars and tumults of them, their sons and grandsons, kept Norway in an uproar for a century. The little lad, however, who sat on Athelstan's knee at the great London banquet was actually reared at the English court and grew up to be King of Norway, being known as Hakon the Good, and endeavouring with no great success to convert his people to Christianity.

The determination of Athelstan to be "lord of all Britain" naturally urged him northwards, since all the region south of the Humber was, or seemed to be, securely resting under the dominion of Wessex. Into the extremely difficult and obscure history of the Kings of Northumbria after the death of Guthred, the friend of the monks of St. Cuthbert, it is not necessary here to enter. A variety of Sihtrics, Anlafs and Godfreys

* Heinskringla, Story of Haarfager, 41 and 42.

flit across the scene, and the confusion is increased by the fact that there are generally two contemporaneous princes bearing the same name. It may be remarked in passing, however, that this is the period of Danish pre-eminence in Ireland (whose capital, Dublin, is a memorial of Danish rule), and that the fortunes of the two sets of invaders in Northumbria and in Ireland were almost inextricably intertwined. Also that we have traces of an Anglian dynasty still existing at Bamburgh, though probably owning the overlordship of Danish kings.

Almost immediately after his father's death, Athelstan had an interview at the Mercian capital, Tamworth, with Sihtric the Dane, King of the Northumbrians. Sihtric received Athelstan's sister (his only sister of the full blood) in marriage, and probably agreed, as part of the compact, to embrace Christianity. Next year, however, he died, after having, according to some of the chroniclers, repudiated both his new wife and his new religion. Hereupon Athelstan marched northward (probably in 926), expelled Sihtric's successor, Guthfred, and his son, Anlaf, from the country, and "assumed the kingdom of the Northumbrians," thus for a time—it was only a short time—governing directly and not as overlord the whole of what is now England except Strathclyde.* The Chronicle adds that he subjugated all the kings who were in this island—Howel, King of the West Welsh (Cornishmen); Constantine, King of Scots; Owen, King of Gwent (North Wales); and Ealdred, son of Eardulf of Bamburgh. One of the conditions of the peace which was ratified (probably at Emmet in Holderness) on July 12, 926, was that all idolatry should be strictly forbidden. Possibly we have here a combination of the Christian powers in Britain; Saxon, Anglian and Celtic against the heathen Danes.

If such a combination were formed, it did not long endure, for eight years later, in 934, we find Athelstan again moving northward to fight against the kings of Scotland and Strathclyde. The monk of Durham who records this fact takes care to mention that on his journey Athelstan presented the church of St. Cuthbert at Chester-le-Street with many costly ornaments and no fewer than twelve vills, and that he charged his brother, Edmund, in the event of his falling in battle, to bring his body

* It was probably at this time that Athelstan, as we learn from William of Malmesbury, rased to the ground the fortress which the Danes had aforetime built in York, "that there might be no place in which these perfidious ones could take refuge," and generously divided among his men the vast booty which he found there.

back to St. Cuthbert's minster and bury it there. "Having defeated the two kings both by sea and land, he subdued Scotland to himself," says the same chronicler. This was certainly a most precarious subjugation if it ever took place, for after the lapse of three years, in 937, Athelstan had to face the mightiest combination of his foes that any English king had yet had to encounter; and the very soul and centre of that combination was the hoary Scottish king, Constantine, who had chosen Edward "to father and to lord," and whom in this entry he is represented as having utterly subdued.

The chief factors in this combination were besides Constantine, his son-in-law, Anlaf (son of the Northumbrian Sihtric), king of the Danes settled in Ireland; another Anlaf, cousin of the former, and also king of the Irish Danes; and Eugenius, king of Strathclyde. Such a formidable combination between two pagan and two Christian kings is in itself a proof of the fear inspired by the growing power of Athelstan. King Anlaf is said* to have owned 615 ships with which he sailed to join his allies of Scotland and Cumberland.†

The great battle of Brunanburh, in which Athelstan defeated the confederate army, has been celebrated in a war-song which is in some respects the most interesting relic that has been preserved of Anglo-Saxon literature. Unfortunately a tantalising obscurity rests upon the site of the battle. Numerous identifications have been suggested, but without discussing or criticising these it may be allowable here to mention one, of which it may at least be said that it has not been proved to be impossible. On the coast of Dumfriesshire in Scotland rises a range of mountains which look across the sandy Solway to the mountains in Cumberland, and according to popular tradition have strange weather-sympathy with their Cumbrian brethren. Here is the high hill of Criffel, which whenever Skiddaw is wrapped in cloud, wears his cloud-cap likewise, and here is the long, flat-topped, altar-shaped hill of Burnswark which overlooks

* By Symeon of Durham, not by the Chronicle, which here is singularly barren of information except such as is contained in the "Lay of Brunanburh".

† The twelfth century chronicler, Florence of Worcester, says that with these ships he entered the Humber; and this statement has been frequently copied by later historians. It is not, however, to be found in any contemporary or nearly contemporary record, and it is now generally regarded with suspicion, for the obvious reason that an invader, coming from Ireland with the intention of co-operating with the Kings of Cumberland and Scotland, would be more likely to land on the western than on the eastern coast of Britain.

Annandale and once dominated the old Roman road, the northern continuation of the Watling Street. This road led in the second century from the wall of Hadrian to the wall of Antoninus, from Carlisle to the neighbourhood of Glasgow. The multitude of Roman camps which skirt this hill or are to be found in its near vicinity, show that it was once a most important military position, and such in some measure it may well have continued to be far on into Anglo-Saxon times; the Roman roads still, after the lapse of so many centuries, being the best, often the only, roads available for the march of armies.

One of these Roman camps bears, and apparently has always borne since the Anglian occupation, the name of Birrens, which is evidently connected with the name Birrenswork or Burnswark given to the altar-shaped hill above it. Now the scene of the great battle was evidently close to some great hill-fortress. This is testified by the varying forms of the name, which is called by Ethelweard Brunandune, by Florence of Worcester Brunanburgh, by Symeon of Durham Weondune or Etbrunnanwerc or Brunanbyrig, and by Geoffrey Gaimar (a twelfth century writer, but one who often gives us curious little scraps of valuable information) Bruneswerce or Burneweste. It is evident that in these last forms the name approaches very near to the local form, Burnswark, which has finally prevailed. It seems probable that Athelstan, marching rapidly northward to meet the confederate hostile armies, met them in the great north-western road in Annandale, near the point where Anlaf Sihtricson had just landed his troops; that the battle raged, as the ballad tells us, ymbe Brunnanburh, all round the camp-scarred hill of Burnswark, and that when Anlaf fled "over the yellow sea" (on fealene flod) it was the sand-laden waters of the shallow Solway Firth that witnessed his ignominious flight.

The ballad which is here inserted in the Chronicle, lightening up its dull pages with a gleam of Homeric brilliance, is familiar to every English student,* and it will therefore not be necessary to do more than to gather up the information—not very copious or minute—which is vouchsafed to us by the minstrel in his rushing career of song. The two chief English heroes were King Athelstan himself, "liberal bestower of bracelets," and his half-brother Edmund Atheling, a youth about seventeen years old. Under their guidance the men of Wessex and Mercia broke down the

* Especially since it was turned into spirited yet closely literal English verse by Tennyson, from whose poem a few passages are here quoted.

stubborn shield-wall of the confederate army. The battle began at sunrise and lasted as long as the daylight.

Five young kings put asleep by the sword-stroke,
Seven strong earls of the army of Anlaf
Fell on the war-field, numberless numbers
Shipmen and Scotsmen.

The Danish leader was hard pressed by the victorious army; with few followers he escaped to his warship and saved his life by a scurrying voyage "over the fallow flood." Especially does the minstrel triumph over the humiliation of the old Scottish king, Constantine, the same who thirteen years before had chosen Athelstan's sire "to father and to lord."

Also the crafty one, Constantinus,
Crept to his North again, hoar-headed hero.
Slender reason had he to be glad of
The clash of the war-glaive—
Traitor and trickster and spurner of treaties,—
He nor had Anlaf
With armies so broken a reason for bragging
That they had the better in perils of battle
On places of slaughter,—
The struggle of standards, the rush of the javelins,
The crash of the chargers, the wielding of weapons,
The play that they played with the children of Edward.

*****

Never had huger slaughter of heroes
Slain by the sword-edge, such as old writers
Have writ of in histories,
Happed in this isle, since up from the East hither
Saxon and Angle from over the broad billow
Broke into Britain with haughty war-workers who
Harried the Welshman, when Earls that were lured by the
Hunger of glory gat hold of the land.

The Anglo-Saxon Tyrtaeus in this shrill song of triumph naturally makes no mention of the losses on his own side, but we learn from another source* that two of Athelstan's cousins, Elwin and Ethelwin, fell "in

* William of Malmesbury, Gesta Regum, ii., 135.

the war against Anlaf," which probably means at Brunanburh. However, one-sided as all our information is about the great battle, it cannot be doubted that it was a real and important victory for the English.

The campaigns in Northumbria were apparently the most memorable events in the reign of Athelstan, but we hear also of his forcing the king of Wales to pay him tribute, of his visiting Cornwall, probably in hostile guise, of his expelling the "West Welsh" from Exeter and turning it into a purely Saxon city. He thus fixed the Tamar as the limit against the old British population in the south of England, as the Wye had been fixed further north.* It is clear that he came somewhat nearer than any of his predecessors to the position which would have been described in feudal times as lord paramount over the whole island. It is not only that he is generally described in the charters, which he granted with lavish hand to the monasteries, as rex totius Britanniæ, sometimes substituting for Britannia the half-mythical word Albion, which he must have learned from his ecclesiastical friends. Nor is it only that he first uses of himself the Greek word Basileus, which was regarded with awe throughout Western Europe as expressing the mysterious majesty of the Cæsars at Constantinople. These titles might be regarded as only the ornaments of style affected by the clerks of this period, or as the pompous assumptions of regal vanity; but when we find the meetings of the witan attended, and Athelstan's charters signed, by Welsh kings (Howel, Juthwal and Morcant) who are styled sub-reguli; when we find, even at a meeting of the witan held as far south as Buckingham (in 934), the attesting signature of "Ego Constantinus subregulus," and when we know that this is Constantine II., King of Scots (900–43), we feel that there was something real in Athelstan's claim to be lord of all Britain; and the story of Constantine's commendation of himself to Edward the Elder becomes decidedly more probable, even though "that old deceiver" did afterwards break his frith and stand in arms against his patron on the field of Brunanburh.

Athelstan does not seem to have ever married, and we may perhaps conjecture that he purposely abstained from leaving issue who might contest the claims of the legitimate descendants of his father. With one doubtful exception his relations with all his half-brothers and sisters seem to have been not only friendly but affectionate. That exception relates to his half-brother Edwin, as to whom the Chronicle for the year 933 simply asserts: "Now the Etheling Edwin was drowned in the sea." Symeon

* Ibid., 134.

of Durham, however, or rather the Cuthbertine annalist from whom he quotes,* has this ugly entry under the same date: "King Athelstan ordered his brother Edwin to be drowned in the sea." This annal grew by the time of William of Malmesbury into a long and fanciful narrative, which William himself only half believed, and which connected the death of Edwin with some opposition to Athelstan at the time of his accession to the throne, on the ground of his illegitimacy. This evidently legendary story need not weigh greatly with us, and is at least balanced by the statement of Henry of Huntingdon, that Athelstan "was moved to tears by the news of the drowning of his brother, a youth of great vigour and of fine disposition."†

The person and character of Athelstan are painted in bright colours by later historians; his manly stature, his yellow hair interwoven with threads of gold, his free and easy manner of joking with laymen, while meek and reverent towards ecclesiastics, his majestic deportment towards the nobles of his realm, and his condescension to the poor; qualities all of which so endeared him to his subjects that we should probably not err in calling him the most popular of all the West Saxon kings. He was a most generous giver to the Church, and his martial piety, as displayed in the curious document‡ called the Prayer of Athelstan, breathes a spirit not unworthy of a David or a Joshua. He died in the prime and vigour of his life, in the forty-seventh year of his age, October 27, 940, three years after the battle of Brunanburh, and he was succeeded by his half-brother Edmund. He was buried in the abbey of Malmesbury, where, by his order, the bodies of his two young cousins who fell at Brunanburh had already been laid.

Athelstan was succeeded by EDMUND, who reigned from 940 to 946, and he by Edred, who reigned from 946 to 955. The reigns of these two young kings, sons of Edward the Elder, will be best considered together, as they make but one act in the drama, the struggle with Danish revolts in the northern kingdoms. The personal history of the two brothers, as far as we know it, is soon told. Edmund, "the dear deed-doer" of Anglo-Saxon minstrelsy, who had already fought well at Brunanburh, was eighteen years old when he came to the throne. He was twice married:

....

* Probably of the tenth century, therefore nearly contemporary.

† See Plummer, Saxon Chronicles, ii., 137, and Freeman, Hist. Essays, i., 10–15, for a full discussion of the question.

‡ See Birch, Cartularium Saxonicum, 656.

his first wife, Elgiva, who after her death was recognised as a saint, bore him two sons, Edwy and Edgar, both of whom reigned after him. His second marriage was childless. Edmund was evidently a man of much force of character, and if his policy in some respects differed from that of his predecessor—the Heimskringla, contrasting him with Athelstan, says that "he could not away with Northmen"—still, had his reign been prolonged for the thirty or forty years which might reasonably have been expected, he might have rivalled the glories of Edward or of Athelstan. In fact, however, it was prematurely cut short by a felon stroke, the story of which gives us a strange picture of life in the West Saxon court. It was the feast of St. Augustine, May 26, 946; the king and his thegns were banqueting at the royal vill at Pucklechurch in Gloucestershire. A robber named Liofa, who six years before had been banished for his crimes, entered the hall, and striding up to an ealdorman to whom the king had just sent a dish from the royal table, sat himself down beside him. The guests, deeply drinking, did not notice the intrusion, but the king's dish-thegn bade him begone and was at once assaulted by the robber. Enraged at the man's insolence the king leaped up from his seat, grasped Liofa by the hair and hurled him to the ground. Hereupon the robber unsheathed a dagger and drove it with all his force into the king's heart. The royal servants rushed upon him, and after receiving many wounds, succeeded in tearing him limb from limb. But the robber had dealt a mortal stroke. The valiant deed-doer, Edmund, in the twenty-fifth year of his age, was laid in the tomb at Glastonbury, near the flowering thorn of St. Joseph of Arimathea, and Edred, his brother, reigned in his stead.

EDRED, who was probably about twenty-three when he was solemnly crowned at Kingston-on-Thames, suffered from chronic dyspepsia and died when but little over thirty. Thus his reign, like that of his great ancestor, Alfred, was one long battle with disease, but he seems to have followed that ancestor's example and not to have neglected his kingly duties for all his sufferings. He came much under the influence of the rising churchman Dunstan, and was also in some measure guided by the counsels of his mother, the widowed Edgiva. Faint as are the colours of Edred's portrait, he seems to have been not the least deserving of the princes of his line. The attitude of these two brothers towards the other rulers of Britain is somewhat less lordly than that of Athelstan. The proud claim to be "King of all Britain" disappears almost entirely from their charters, and is generally replaced by the more modest title "King of the

English," to which, however, is often added "governor and ruler of the other nations round about." Thus the claim to predominance in Britain is not wholly dropped, but it is put in a somewhat less offensive form than by the victor of Brunanburh. The Greek word "Basileus," doubtless attractive by reason of its very strangeness, still sometimes makes its appearance; but Edmund's favourite epithet for himself is "Industrious," probably a translation of the Saxon "daed-fruma" (deed-doer), by which the minstrels of the people sang his praises. In a world which had seen, not long before, the degenerate race of the fainéant kings of France, deed-doer was an epithet full of meaning.

Let us pass to the history of Danish revolts and their suppression. From the short and often obscure statements of the chroniclers, it is hard to discover what amount of permanent success resulted from the victories of even the most prosperous kings. It certainly seemed as if Athelstan had made himself undisputed King of Mercia and overlord of Northumbria, yet, if we may trust Symeon of Durham, Edmund at the very outset of his reign had once more to accept the Watling Street as the boundary between himself and a Danish ruler, that ruler being apparently Anlaf Sihtricson who had been defeated at Brunanburh, but who now reappeared in Northumbria and fixed his capital at York. In the next year (942) a fragment of ballad assigns to "the dear deed-doer" the deliverance of the Five Boroughs (Leicester, Lincoln, Nottingham, Stamford and Derby) from Danish thraldom. But these very five boroughs, though undoubtedly containing a large Danish population, were expressly or by implication included in the conquests of Edward and Ethelfled. Evidently much is left unwritten of this portion of English history. It seems probable that at the coming of Anlaf there had been a general rising of the Danelaw, and that the suppression of this revolt, being more complete than the earlier conquest, took a stronger hold on the popular imagination. Hence it was that the poet chronicler of Edmund's reign attributes to him, not to his predecessors, the deliverance of the native population:—

Under the Northmen need-constrained
In heathen bondage long time chained.

The result of Edmund's Mercian campaign seems to have been a treaty of peace, negotiated by the two archbishops Oda and Wulfstan on the lines of the peace between Alfred and Guthrum. Anlaf and his brother-king Raegnald were baptised, Edmund acting as their sponsor; and the Watling Street was again made the boundary between Englishman and

Dane. The peace thus concluded lasted but a year. In 943 Anlaf and his Danes were again in Mercia, and—ominous conjunction—Wulfstan, Archbishop of York, was abetting the invaders. They stormed Tamworth, they took much spoil and great was the slaughter, but on Edmund's approach they retired to Leicester where they were besieged by the king. Notwithstanding the escape of Anlaf and the rebel archbishop, Edmund was victorious, and next year (944) he invaded Northumbria and drove out his two rebellious god-sons, who appear no more upon the scene.

In the following year, 945, Edmund ravaged all "Cumbraland," a region which probably included all that was left of the old kingdom of Strathclyde south of the Solway, the northern portion having been gradually appropriated by the Scottish kings. We now come to another of the great academic battlefields between English and Scottish historians. We are told by the chronicler that having ravaged Cumberland, "he let it all to Malcolm, King of Scotland, on condition that he should be his fellow-worker both on sea and land." What was the relation thus established between Edmund and Malcolm I. who had succeeded "the hoary old deceiver" Constantine? Of course a feudal lawyer of the twelfth century pondering these words would discover in them a regular case of the relation of lord and vassal. But they do not in themselves seem to imply more than friendship and alliance, and it is admitted that the fully developed feudal theory was not yet known in England. As with the "commendation" of 921, we may probably conclude that the transaction would mean anything or nothing according to the after course of events, and the shifting of the centre of gravity between the two contracting parties. In itself this "cession of Cumberland" was probably a politic measure, as it enlisted the sympathies of the Scottish "fellow-worker" on the English side and interposed a barrier between the vikings of Dublin and their Northumbrian fellow-countrymen.

On the assassination of Edmund in 946, Edred seems to have taken up the endless task and laboured at it successfully. "He took to the kingdom and soon subdued all Northumbria to his power, and the Scots swore to him oaths that they would do all his will." Wulfstan, the turbulent or patriotic archbishop of York, plays a prominent and singular part in Northumbrian politics during the reign of Edred; and princes of the royal houses of Norway and Denmark also bear a hand in the perplexing game. One such was Eric Blood-axe, son of fair-haired Harold of Norway, who when driven forth from his kingdom by Hakon the Good, Athelstan's foster-son, sailed for the Orkneys, ravaged Scotland and the northern parts of England, but on receiving a message from Athelstan, who reminded him of the old friendship between himself and his father, made peace, consented to be baptised along with his wife and children, and became for a time the peaceful under-king of Northumbria. This settlement had endured during the life of Athelstan, but on Edmund's accession, Eric, knowing that he was not beloved of the new king, and hearing a rumour that he would set another king over Northumberland, renounced his allegiance to Winchester, resumed his viking life, gathered together a new "scip-here," chiefly from among the Irish Danes, harried Wales and all the southern coasts of England, but ere long fell in battle against the English.

Another Eric, the son of another Harold, then appeared upon the scene. This was the son of Harold Blue-Tooth, King of Denmark. In 948 the witan of Northumbria, headed by Archbishop Wulfstan, chose this Danish prince for their king, though but a year before they had solemnly plighted faith to Edred. Enraged hereat the Saxon king marched northwards and "harried over all Northumberland." So ruthless or so careless was the work of destruction that even Wilfrid's famous minster at Ripon perished in the flames. During Edred's homeward march the Danish garrison of York sallied forth, and overtaking the rear of his army at Chesterford* inflicted upon it grievous slaughter. Exasperated by the defeat, Edred, whose weak health perhaps made him exceptionally irritable, meditated a second ravage of Northumbria, but consented to forego his revenge when the witan of the northern kingdom expelled Eric and paid compensation for the injury which had been inflicted by their countrymen. We need not follow minutely the fortunes of King Eric. Expelled and restored twice, if not thrice, in the anarchy of Northumbria, he is said to have perished in 954, "deceitfully slain" (according to Roger of Wendover) "with his son and his brother in a lonely place which is called Stainmoor, by the treasonable contrivance of Earl Oswulf." This event is memorable as finally closing the book of Northumbrian royalty. Oswulf of Bamburgh succeeds to the chief place in the northern province with the title of earl, and henceforth we hear no more of kings in Northumbria.

The strange career of the rebel archbishop, Wulfstan, came speedily to an end. In 952 Edred ordered him to be imprisoned in a fortress "because he had been often accused to the king," or according to William of Malmesbury, "because he meditated desertion to his countrymen." Prob-

* Possibly Chesterfield.

ably the phrase "his countrymen" means merely the men of Northumbria. It is, however, possible that Wulfstan may have been of Danish descent. We have clearer information as to the Danish descent of his contemporary Oda, Archbishop of Canterbury. It certainly throws a strange light on the relation of the two races, as well as on the ecclesiastical history of the period, that the first and possibly the second of the highest places in the English Church should have been filled by scions of that still barely Christianised stock. In 954, the year of the extinction of the Northumbrian kingdom, Edred thought himself safe in giving to Wulfstan the Mercian bishopric of Dorchester, where, three years after, he died. The only other noteworthy event in the reign of Edred was "a great slaughter" which in his usual passionate way he ordered to be made among the inhabitants, probably the Danish inhabitants, of Thetford in East Anglia in revenge for their murder of the abbot Eadhelm (952). Three years after this, on Nov. 23, 955, Edred died at Frome in Somerset and was buried in the old monastery at Winchester. No nightly appearances in his case, as in that of his great ancestor, seem to have troubled the repose of the dwellers in the convent.

XX.

EDGAR AND DUNSTAN

"On the death of Edred, EADWIG [or EDWY] succeeded to the kingdom. Two years afterwards, his younger brother Edgar succeeded to the kingdom of the Mercians."

"In 958, Oda, Archbishop of Canterbury, separated King Edwy from his wife Elfgyfu, because they were too near akin."

"In 959, King Edwy died on the 1st of October, and Edgar his brother succeeded to the kingdom as well of the West Saxons as of the Northumbrians and Mercians, being then about sixteen years old."

Such is the only information (with one important exception) vouchsafed us in the Chronicle concerning the short reign of the unfortunate Edwy, who when about fifteen years of age succeeded his father Edmund. These sentences suggest much—internal discord, fraternal rivalry, a matrimonial union condemned by the Church, the early death of a broken-hearted husband—but they tell us nothing as to the causes of these events. Later historians have believed that they found the clue to the mystery in the one sentence which has not yet been quoted. "And in the same year [957] Abbot Dunstan was driven away over sea." However this may be, the story of Edwy's reign is so inextricably intertwined with the life of this man, the most famous English saint between Cuthbert and Becket, that for a little space history must give place to biography.

Dunstan was born about the year 925, near the commencement of the reign of Athelstan. His birthplace was in the immediate neighbourhood of the great Abbey of Glastonbury; his parents must have belonged to the higher ranks of Anglo-Saxon society, since he numbered two bishops and certain members of the royal household among his near kinsmen and was in some way related to a niece of Athelstan's. Glastonbury was probably the only great sanctuary in which the religious life of the Celt had flowed on without interruption into a Teutonic channel; and it may have been on account of its old British traditions that it became the resort of "certain Irish pilgrims who looked on that place with great affection, especially on account of their reverence for the younger Patrick, who is said to be there resting in the Lord."* Taught by these men, the boy early acquired great familiarity with Scripture; he received the tonsure and performed some of an acolyte's duties in the church of the Virgin, but was not as yet definitely vowed to a religious life. He seems to have been admitted as a lad to some place about the court of King Athelstan, who probably often visited the royal estate of his own great ancestor at Wedmore, a few miles from Glastonbury. But the future archbishop's experience of court life was not a pleasant one. He was evidently a lad of quick intelligence with a nervous and sensitive frame, a soul much exercised by the joys and the terrors of the world of spirits. He had already seen some visions, and in the delirium of fever had climbed to the roof of the church at Glastonbury, his safe descent wherefrom was accounted a miracle. His young kinsmen, the pages of the court, with their rough and fleshly natures, could not tolerate this pale and pious playfellow, and they treated him as bullying schoolboys in later generations have often treated an unpopular comrade. At last, by an accusation of extracting from Latin books a knowledge of unholy arts, they obtained an order for his expulsion from court, which they emphasised in their own brutal way by throwing him into a marshy pool, and then trampling him down into the stinking mud. The poor victim escaped to the neighbouring house of one of his friends, but on arriving there was set upon by the dogs, who in his besmirched figure scarcely recognised a human being, much less one of their master's friends. When they heard his voice, however, they at once gave him a warm canine greeting, whereupon the young saint wept at the contrast between the friendliness of the dog and the cruel animosity of man.

At this point Dunstan had come to the parting of the ways. "The ancient enemy of mankind," says his biographer, "sorely tempted him with suggestions of the delightfulness of family life, and the love of woman," but, on the other hand, his kinsman, Elphege, Bishop of Winchester, strongly urged him to become a monk, and to this advice he yielded after a sharp attack of some sickness, in the nature of bubonic plague, from which he was like to have died. It was no doubt the great monastery of Glastonbury in which he made his profession. Near to that monastery was

* Life of Dunstan, by B. (a Saxon monk, nearly contemporary).

the dwelling of an elderly lady named Ethelfled, a relative and patroness of Dunstan. The saint in his old age sometimes told the story of the barrel of mead which in answer to Ethelfled's prayers was miraculously replenished, when a sudden visit from her uncle Athelstan found her without sufficient provision of liquor for all his thirsty courtiers. He told too of the white dove which he saw alighting on the roof of the blessed matron's house when she lay a-dying, and of the converse which on his entering her room he found her holding with an invisible heavenly visitor.

In Dunstan's monastic life, both now and later on when he had attained to high office in the Church, there was always room left for other occupations besides prayer and psalmody. We are told that "in the intervals of his study of sacred literature, he diligently cultivated his talent for playing on the harp, as well as for painting, and that he became a skilful judge of all articles used in the household." At the request of a devout lady who was his friend, he sketched out for her a design for a stole with various kinds of patterns, which she could afterwards embroider with gold and gems. A bell was long preserved at Canterbury fashioned by the saint's own fingers; and late in life he presented to Malmesbury Abbey an organ, bells and stoup for holy water, all of his own manufacture.

After the accession of Edmund, Dunstan, who was still but a youth, was recalled to court, and probably on account of his literary qualifications "was numbered among the royal chiefs and princes of the palace." What precise official rank these words betoken it would be difficult to say; but whatever it may have been, he soon lost it through the machinations of his enemies, who probably again whispered in Edmund's ear the old accusation, "Dunstan traffics with the powers of darkness." Bowing his head to the storm, Dunstan prepared to quit the realm, and taking advantage of the presence at court of certain messengers from "the eastern kingdom," he begged them to procure him an asylum in that land. What is the meaning of these words "the eastern kingdom" is by no means clear. Germany has been suggested, but on the whole it is perhaps slightly more probable that the biographer—not a very accurate writer—means by these words to describe East Anglia. That region, though not strictly a kingdom, was still bound by a somewhat loose tie to Wessex, and was at this time ruled by a great noble named Athelstan, who, though properly speaking he was only an ealdorman, was known in the common speech of men as "the half-king."

Whatever may have been the exact name of Dunstan's intended place of refuge, it was not, in fact, necessary for him to betake himself thither. The court was at this time staying at Cheddar, that well-known and beautiful village at the foot of the Mendips, where steep cliffs and stalactite caves attest the wonder-working presence of the limestone formation. One day Edmund, while hunting, became separated from his companions, and found himself following the hounds and the stag alone. In its desperation the hunted animal made for the cliffs, leaped from the top and was dashed to pieces. The hounds followed, and the king followed also, pulling in vain at the bridle of a hard-mouthed horse, and seeing a terrible death immediately before him. In that moment Edmund reviewed his past life, and thought with satisfaction: "I do not remember to have ever wittingly injured any man." But then Dunstan's name came into his mind. "Too true! I have injured Dunstan. O God, if Thou wilt preserve my life, I will be reconciled to Thy servant." The horse stopped, on the very edge of the precipice, and the king's life was saved.

Meanwhile, however, the first act of the delivered king was to send for Dunstan, provide him with a horse and ride with him to Glastonbury. After offering prayer, the king took the monk's right hand, gave him the kiss of peace, led him up to the abbot's chair and seated him thereon, saying: "Be thou occupant of this seat and a faithful abbot of this church. Whatever may be lacking for the performance of divine service and the due observance of your holy rule, I will supply it from my royal bounty." Thus was Dunstan, still in very early manhood, installed as abbot in the great historic house of Glastonbury. The Benedictine rule, if it had been adopted in this monastery, had become much relaxed, but Dunstan at once set to work to restore the discipline of the brotherhood. He enlarged the buildings, and collected round him a crowd of young followers, whom he instructed in Holy Scripture, so that from this monastery, as from a school of the prophets, many deans, abbots, bishops, even some archbishops went forth to guide and govern the English Church. At this point of the story we hear much of Dunstan's conflicts with the Powers of Darkness, conflicts which were believed to endure throughout his monastic life. Now the Evil One appeared to him in the form of a bear, now as a dog, now as a fox, shaking his tail in terror and shrinking from the keen glance of the holy man. All these appearances and others like them, which later ages delighted to record and to magnify, belong to the intellectual pathology of the cloister and are not to be specially attributed to the spiritual discernment or the cerebral excitability of this particular recluse, though we may be permitted to observe that they occupy a more prominent place and are of a more grotesque character in the authentic Lives of Dunstan than in the pages of Bede. Unfortunately they have, by their frequent repetition, somewhat obscured the real greatness of the alleged devil-fighter, both as ecclesiastic and as statesman.*

After the death of Edmund (of which the saint is said to have had supernatural warnings) his successor Edred took Dunstan into high favour and committed to him the charge of his treasure and of many of the deeds relating to his various estates, besides the precious things accumulated by the old kings his predecessors. All these were deposited at Glastonbury. Moreover, Edred desired to make his friend bishop of Crediton, but Dunstan refused, nor could even the entreaties of the king's mother, Edgiva, though she had great influence with him, prevail upon him to consent to take the nominal charge of so distant a diocese. When Edred's long struggle with disease was nearing its end, he ordered Dunstan to bring to him the treasures committed to his charge that he might make a death-bed division of them among his kinsfolk. The saint complied with the order, visited Glastonbury and had gone several stages on the return journey, when he heard a voice from heaven saying: "Behold! now King Edred has departed in peace." A yet greater marvel! his horse, hearing the same voice and "being unable to bear the presence of the angelic sublimity," fell down and died on the road. When Dunstan reached the palace he found that his patron's death had taken place at the very same hour at which he had received the heavenly communication.

We have now reached the same point in Dunstan's life at which we had already arrived in the history of the kingdom. Edred dead, and the boy-king Edwy seated on the throne (955), we come to the well-known scene at the coronation banquet. Dunstan's biographer tells us that after the great ceremony had been performed, when according to the unanimous choice of all the English nobles, Edwy had been anointed and hallowed as king, he suddenly leaped up and left the merry banquet and the company of his own nobles, whom he forsook for the companionship of two high-born dames, Ethelgiva and her daughter Elfgiva. These ladies were of royal descent, Edwy's near relations; and it is a plausible conjecture, though

* The celebrated story of the Devil and the hot tongs is not told by any contemporary of Dunstan's, but by the much-romancing Osbern about 130 years after his death. The identical pair of tongs with which the saint is said to have seized the Devil's nose is still shown at the priory of Mayfield in Sussex.

only a conjecture, that the elder lady may have acted as foster-mother to the king, who had lost his own mother in childhood. It was natural, if not politic, for the boy-king (still scarcely fifteen years of age) to leave the company of the grim warriors and hoary churchmen who composed his witan, and to refresh himself with the livelier talk of his child-sweetheart and her mother. But the nobles of the witan felt themselves insulted by the king's departure, and Oda, the Archbishop of Canterbury, who had Danish blood in his veins, in a loud and angry voice gave utterance to the general discontent. "Let some one," he said, "be chosen who shall bring back the king to take his place, as is fitting, at our merry banquet." All others refused, not liking to face the women's wrath, but at last Abbot Dunstan and his relative Kinsige, Bishop of Lichfield, were chosen for the disagreeable task. When they entered the royal apartment they found the crown cast carelessly on the ground and the king seated on a couch between the two ladies. "We are sent," said they, "by the nobles to beg you to return at once to your fitting place at the board and not to disdain to mingle in the joyous feast of your thegns." The boy at first refused and the women scolded, but Dunstan raised the king from the couch, put his crown becomingly on his head and led him back, an obviously reluctant banqueter, to the company of his nobles. Such was the scene, natural and intelligible enough and worth studying for the sake of the light thrown by it on the habits of our forefathers in the tenth century, but by no means justifying either the praise or the blame which have been bestowed on the chief actors therein, especially the foul imputations which the monkish biographer has cast upon the characters of "the two she-wolves," as he terms them, the ladies Ethelgiva and Elfgiva.*

Dunstan's intervention at such a time was not likely to recommend him to royal favour, and it is with no surprise that we read the Chronicle's entry for the year 957: "In this year abbot Dunstan was driven away over sea." Even his own friends were partially alienated from him, for his biographer lays the blame of his banishment and the confiscation of his goods not only on "the impudent virago, that Jezebel," Ethelgiva, but also on "the secret machinations of his own disciples, whom he himself had nurtured in their tender years with the nectareous sweetness of his teaching." This is one of several indications that the struggle, a very obscure one and difficult to understand, which took place during Edwy's

* An excellent summing up of the whole case will be found in E. W. Robertson's Historical Essays, p. 192.

short reign, was not, as was formerly supposed, a struggle between the boy-king on the one hand and an arrogant and united Church-party on the other. There were ecclesiastics on both sides, and Edwy, at any rate, was no declared enemy of the Anglo-Saxon Church. There are in the Saxon Cartulary copies of grants made by him to Glastonbury, to Bath, to Worcester, to Abingdon and many other monasteries. But there are also grants made by him in surprising numbers to the thegns of his court, and this lavish generosity looks like a sign of weakness and may have had something to do with the revolt against his authority.*

Notwithstanding the uproar at Edwy's coronation, the lady Elfgiva, who was one of the persons blamed for his absence from the feast, became soon afterwards his wife. To one document which is assigned to the year 956 the names of Elfgiva, "king's wife," and Ethelgiva, "king's wife's mother," are attached as witnesses. It was not till two years after this time that, according to the Chronicle, "Oda, Archbishop of Canterbury, separated King Edwy from his wife Elfgiva because they were too near akin" (958). At this point Edwy's wife and her mother disappear from authentic history. Writers of little judgment, the earliest of whom lived a century and a half after the event, tell us distressing stories of the branding of Elfgiva's face with a hot iron, of her or her mother's flight into Ireland, return and miserable death under the cruel operation of ham-stringing. The authority for these tales is poor, their style legendary, the confusion which they make between Ethelgiva and Elfgiva an additional reason for distrust. On the whole, though a painful suspicion may rest on our minds that there was some basis of fact underlying these ghastly traditions, we are not bound to accept them as history. In any case no one has a right to impute these cruelties, if ever committed, to Dunstan, who was almost certainly still in exile at the alleged date of their infliction.

The cartularies further show us that under the reign of Edwy his venerable grandmother Edgiva, widow of Edward the Elder, was deprived of some portion of her property, which she recovered after the accession of Edgar. It is evident, from this and other indications, that many personal and political questions were involved in the revolution which has next to be described; and it is probable that the great ecclesiastical controversy which sounded so loud through the next twenty years had no connexion therewith. Of that revolution itself we have most scanty details. The chiefs of the realm, we are told, dissatisfied with Edwy's government,

* The short reign of Edwy furnishes 150 pages to the Cartularium Saxonicum.

proclaimed as king his brother EDGAR, a boy of some thirteen years old. We hear of no battles. A compromise was soon arranged, by the terms of which Edgar reigned in the lands north of the Thames, and Edwy south of that boundary. We may probably trace here some remains of the old jealousy between the kingdoms. Edwy retained the allegiance of loyal Wessex, while Mercia, glad of any pretext for recovering her lost independence, rallied round the standard of his brother and was joined by East Anglia, under whose "half-king" Athelstan and his wife Elfwen, Edgar had been reared from infancy. This compromise was arranged in 957, and in the following year, or in 959, Edwy died and Edgar reigned alone over the whole kingdom. There is no suggestion of foul play, but it is natural to conjecture that Edwy's early death was caused by worry and disappointment at the unfortunate turn which his affairs had taken both in his household and in his kingdom.

The accession of Edgar to the Mercian throne was speedily followed by the recall of Dunstan from exile.* When the young abbot was sent away "over-sea" by the offended Edwy, he sought shelter in Flanders, then ruled by a grandson of Alfred the Great, Count Arnulf the Old. His temporary home was the great monastery of St. Peter's at Ghent, and his observation of the strict discipline there maintained by the abbot doubtless stirred his emulation to begin similar reforms in the monasteries of England. On his return from banishment he was promoted to the office of bishop of the Mercian see of Worcester. To Worcester in 959 the see of London was added, a strange instance of plurality but probably a temporary expedient resulting from the determination of the old queen Edgiva and the other advisers of Edgar that the highest place in the English Church should eventually be filled by the great reformer. The old Danish archbishop Oda died, probably in 958. His immediate successor, Elfsige, of whom it was related that he spake vaunting and contemptuous words of the late archbishop, striking with a staff insultingly on his grave, was soon punished for his irreverence. On his way to Rome to receive the pallium, he caught so severe a chill in the snows of St. Bernard that he died in the land of the stranger. A second successor, Beorhthelm, was appointed in 959, immediately before Edwy's death, but was unceremoniously deposed by Edgar in the following year to make room for Dunstan. This

* The Chronicle and the biographers agree in postponing Dunstan's return till after Edgar's accession to the undivided realm, but his signatures to charters seem to require an earlier date.

great saint, who had now reached the zenith of his orbit, ruled the Church of England with eminent wisdom and success for twenty-eight years, from 960 to 988, but evidently his sphere of action was not confined to the Church. It is probable that much of the success of the undoubtedly successful reign of Edgar was due to the advice of Dunstan, and if the saint's biographers would but have retrenched one half of the miracles which they have recorded in his honour, and would have described some of the affairs of state which he guided to a right issue, they would have conferred a great benefit on history, and they would probably have placed their favourite's name high beyond the reach of doubt among the Christian statesmen of England. At present that reputation, great as it is and much as it has grown of recent years, is rather a matter of highly probable inference than of actual proof.

Politically the reign of Edgar the Peaceful, as we know it, is somewhat barren of events and seems to have been characterised by almost unbroken tranquillity. Save for the facts that in 966 "Thored son of Gunner harried Westmorland," and that three years later "King Edgar commanded the land of Thanet to be ravaged," no military operations are recorded in the Chronicle; and so great is the obscurity that we do not even know whether the first operation was undertaken in obedience to, or in defiance of, the orders of the king. Nor can we tell whether the ravage of the Isle of Thanet was a penalty for some movement of revolt or a precaution against its occupation by the Danes. On the whole, the latter hypothesis is perhaps somewhat the more probable.

But by far the most memorable event in Edgar's reign, and the event with which his name and Dunstan's are chiefly connected, was of an ecclesiastical kind, the famous monastic reform. This movement was not, as it used sometimes to be considered, primarily a struggle like Hildebrand's on behalf of the celibacy of the clergy: it was essentially a struggle for the reform of the relaxed discipline of the convents, and the restoration to monks, strictly so called, of houses and lands which had been gradually filched from them by the hybrid order of canonici. These men may be considered as occupying a half-way position between the parish priest and the professed monk. Following the canon, the rule framed by Chrodegang, Bishop of Metz, in the latter part of the eighth century, these canonici, priests leading a collegiate life, were bound to chastity and obedience but not to the renunciation of all private property. Thus their standard was in some respects lower than that of the regular monks, and if their rivals are to be trusted—which is perhaps doubtful—they fell far below even that lowered standard. The staid and decorous William of Malmesbury laments that his beloved monastery had been turned into "a stable of clerics." Florence of Worcester says that Edgar "cast out from the convents the impostures of clerics," and many similar passages might be quoted, in which the monks speak with the utmost bitterness of their canonical rivals.

The great reform, however, with which the names of Edgar and Dunstan are associated, consisted not merely in the casting forth of the canons and the restoration of Benedictine regulars to their homes. It was also part of a great general movement for the purification of conventual life and the uplifting of the standard of morals in the whole Christian community; a movement which began in Eastern France, spread thence over Flanders, Germany and Italy, and will be for ever associated with the venerable name of the monastery of Cluny, founded in 910 by William, Duke of Aquitaine. In the monastery of Cluny and the religious houses which followed its example, the rule of St. Benedict was restored in more than its old strictness. The chanting of the whole Psalter every twenty-four hours; silence so nearly total that the monks almost lost the habit of speech; the entire prohibition of the flesh of four-footed animals for food; coarse clothing of a dun colour; absolute obedience to the ecclesiastical superior, and the entire prohibition of private property; these were the chief points of the restored monastic discipline which Dunstan brought back with him from the Continent.

Three other ecclesiastics besides Dunstan threw their weight into the reforming scale. The first was the venerable archbishop, Oda the Dane, who, however, died in 958 or 959 while the movement was still in its infancy. His nephew Oswald, who was consecrated bishop of Worcester in 961, and who eleven years later received in addition to that dignity the archiepiscopal mitre of York, was after Dunstan the most eminent churchman of the age, and zealously seconded the efforts of his brother of Canterbury. The most active, however, as well as the harshest and most unpitying of the reformers, was Ethelwold, Bishop of Winchester, who was, like his teacher Dunstan, of noble birth and had served as a lad in Athelstan's palace. He was also like Dunstan skilful with his hands, and left behind him bells and other implements of religious service, the products of his own cunning handicraft. After ruling the monastery of Abingdon he was, in 963, consecrated to the see of Winchester, where he carried out the work of reform with a high hand. Both the Old and New Minsters at Winchester had been filled with canonici many of whom were married. To all Ethelwold offered but one choice: "Assume the monastic habit or depart hence." All but three departed, and Chertsey and Milton Abbas in Dorsetshire were then similarly purged. The last monastery was situated without the bounds of Ethelwold's diocese, but he seems to have held from the king a kind of roving commission to rebuild and reform monasteries wherever he would. In pursuance of this commission Ethelwold next visited the great monasteries of the fen country, Ely and Medeshamstede (now known as Peterborough). In their most flourishing time these monasteries must have worn a somewhat desolate appearance, standing as they did in the midst of the waste of waters which then covered half Cambridgeshire. Of Peterborough the chronicler expressly tells us that owing to its having been "fore-done by heathen folk, Ethelwold found nothing but old walls and wild woods." Here then no extrusion was necessary; all that the reformer had to do was to rebuild the fabrics and once more to instal in the restored abbeys the industrious monks, who would again make these oases in the fen lands to blossom as the rose.

The Abingdon chronicler tells us of these good deeds of Ethelwold, naturally magnifying the glory of his convent's most famous abbot. Strangely enough we do not hear of any actual foundation of a new monastery at Canterbury, or expulsion of canonici from the precincts of the old one, by Dunstan himself, though we know that he was heart and soul with the new movement. In fact, Dunstan's tolerance of the canons, even at Canterbury, and his abstention from deeds of violence in furtherance of the reform, are singularly at variance with the character for persecuting harshness which he has somehow acquired in English history. So, too, his fellow archbishop, Oswald, far gentler than Ethelwold, if a little more energetic than Dunstan, seems always to have preferred persuasion to force. At Worcester, instead of expelling the canons from the cathedral church of SS. Mary and Peter, he founded a new monastery which he attached to a new cathedral, and these younger institutions gradually supplanted the old in popular favour.

*****

Next to ecclesiastical affairs the pageants of the peaceful king's reign seem most to have attracted the attention of his contemporaries. When he had been already reigning as sole king for more than thirteen years and had attained the thirtieth year of his age, he was solemnly "hallowed" as king on Whitsunday in the old Roman city of Bath (973). The reason for this long delay in the king's coronation is not obvious, but possibly, as the words of the coronation service seem to have expressly hailed him as "King of the Saxons, Mercians and Northumbrians,"* the ceremony may have been postponed till some unrecorded transactions, peaceful or warlike, with the chiefs of the Danelaw secured their presence at the pageant and showed that the words of the coronation service were not an idle vaunt. "And straightway after the hallowing," says the Chronicle, "the king led all his naval force to Laegeceaster [Chester], and there came unto him six kings to meet him, and all plighted faith with him that they would be his fellow-workers on sea and on land." This is that celebrated meeting of Edgar with his British under-kings of which later chroniclers are so proud. Both Florence of Worcester and William of Malmesbury, writing in the early part of the twelfth century, record that eight kings were constrained by Edgar to come to his Witenagemot, to bind themselves to him by an oath of perpetual fidelity, and then to row him in solemn pomp upon the river Dee, while he sat in the barge's prow in regal magnificence. "He is reported to have said that now at last his successors might boast that they were truly kings of the English since they would inherit the honourable precedence which was thus accorded him." The two historians give us the names of these eight kings: Kenneth of Scotland, Malcolm of Cumberland, Maccus, "the archpirate" (that is, the Viking), "king of many islands" (possibly Man and the Hebrides), and five Welsh kings whose names need not here be recorded, especially as one at least of them is incorrectly reported. It is interesting, however, to find this act of vassalage admitted by a Welsh annalist, though the scene of it is transferred, with much probability, from Chester to Caerleon-upon-Usk—much nearer than the former city to the scene of Edgar's coronation. "And five kings from Cymry," says the Brut-y-Tywysogion, "Edgar compelled to come to his court, and in Kaerllion-ar-Wyse he commanded them to row him in a bark while he himself sat at its prow." Upon the whole, this celebrated water procession seems to be attested upon sufficient and trustworthy authority.†

....

* See Robertson's, Historical Essays, p. 211.

† As pointed out by Mr. W. H. Stevenson in the English Historical Review (1898), xiii., 506, an important attestation to the meeting of the kings (though

In this connexion a romantic legend may be related which meets us in the pages of William of Malmesbury. He tells us that Edgar, though strong and wiry, was of small stature, and that this caused Kenneth of Scotland to remark that he marvelled why such great territories should be willing to be subject to such a pigmy of a king. The saying was carried by tale-bearers to Edgar, who sent for Kenneth as if he were about to consult him on some most important secret of state. He drew him apart into a lonely wood, offered him his choice of two swords which he had brought with him, and called upon him to prove his strength in a hand-to-hand encounter. "For it is a base thing for a king to babble at a banquet and not be willing to prove his words in fight." Hereupon Kenneth fell at Edgar's feet and implored his forgiveness for words which, as he protested, had only been spoken in jest.

From the same source—one, it must be admitted, of secondary authority—we derive the well-known story of the yearly tribute of 300 wolves' heads which he imposed on the Welsh king, Juthwal, a tribute which is said to have been paid for three years and then of necessity discontinued because the breed of wolves was exterminated. Magnifying in similar fashion the resources and the renown of the peaceful king, Florence of Worcester tells us that he collected a fleet of 3,600 strong ships, one-third of which, when Easter was past, were ordered to muster in the north of the island and sail to the Straits of Dover, one-third on the east for a voyage to the Land's End, and one-third on the west which sailed to Cape Wrath. Thus was the whole island circumnavigated and safeguarded against invasion by a foreign foe. There is probably some historic fact at the bottom of this story, but no one need accept the enormous numbers vouched for by Florence.

The chief characteristic of Edgar's reign was the peace which he maintained in the land and which contrasted so painfully with the troubled reign of his son. Hence, doubtless, was derived the surname of the Peaceful, which is that by which he is known in the pages of Florence of Worcester There was something brilliant and attractive in

not to the water procession) is furnished by the ecclesiastical author Elfric, himself a contemporary of Edgar and a pupil and friend of bishop Ethelwold. In his poetical Life of St. Swithin, written about 996, he contrasts the happy days of Edgar with the disastrous reign of his son, and says: "All the kings of this island of Cymri and of Scots, eight kings, came to Edgar once upon a time on one day and they all bowed to Edgar's government".

his personality, and the staunch support which he gave to the victorious party in the Church was sufficient guarantee that his good deeds would not be forgotten. Yet even the monastic chronicler, as an honest man, could not dissemble the fact that the bright and comely little king was no saint. He quotes from a poem which after praising the piety of Edgar and magnifying his power "before whom mighty kings and earls gladly bowed" concludes thus:—

But one misdeed he did, aye all too oft,
The evil customs of strange folk he loved,
And heathen manners into this our land
Too fast he brought,
And hither introduced outlandish men
And hurtful people drew unto the realm.
But God's grace grant him that his well-done deeds
Weigh heavier in the balance than his sins,
And guard his soul upon the longsome road.

It will be seen that the poet speaks of introducing foreign vices and hurtful heathenish customs, but does not distinctly charge Edgar with personal immorality. Later historians, more out-spoken, tell a story, which seems to have some foundation in fact, about his seduction of a novice named Wulfthryth, whom he is said to have carried off from the abbey of Wilton, and by whom he had a daughter named Edith, who took the vows of a nun and died an abbess. The long delay of Edgar's coronation (which happened, as we have seen, in the fourteenth year of his reign) has been connected by later writers with this intrigue, and with an alleged penance inflicted on the king by Dunstan, who is said to have forbidden him to wear his crown for seven years. Chronological arguments, however, prove the untruth of this theory.* Edgar's first wedded wife was apparently Ethelfled the Fair, who was known also by the epithet of "the Duck." She was the daughter of a certain Ordmaer whom Edgar seems to have ennobled by bestowing upon him forty hides of land at Hatfield, thus giving him the appanage of an earl, though his birth would appear to have been insufficient to qualify him for exalted office.† By this lady Edgar was the father of a son known in English history as Edward the Martyr. The married life of the beautiful Ethelfled, however terminated, whether by her death or divorce, must have been a short

* Robertson's Historical Essays, p. 203.

† Ibid., p. 169.

one, for in 964 Edgar married another woman celebrated for her beauty, Elfthryth or Elfrida, daughter of the Earl Ordgar, who became ealdorman of Devon and possibly of the two adjoining counties of Somerset and Dorset.* Elfrida, however, had been previously married, her first husband being Ethelwold, ealdorman of East Anglia and son of "the half-king" Athelstan. Elfrida exercised undoubtedly a baneful influence on English history throughout the closing years of the tenth century; and arguing perhaps from these known tendencies of her character and from Edgar's evil record for sexual immorality, later writers, especially the poetical historian, Geoffrey Gaimar, have constructed a long and unsavoury romance, according to which Ethelwold, having first deceived his master as to Elfrida's beauty and thus secured her for himself, was afterwards murdered like Uriah the Hittite in order to make way for his royal rival. This story, also, though long accepted by historians, vanishes at the touch of criticism which clearly shows that Elfrida's first husband died at least two years before her marriage with Edgar.† But however innocent may have been the story of the peaceful king's courtship of his second wife, there can be no doubt that when she was once seated in the palace her influence on the lives of its inmates was disastrous.

Edgar survived his coronation but two years. He died in the thirty-third year of his age, July 8, 975, and was buried in the Abbey of Glastonbury, which he and his father had so highly favoured.

* As stated by Robertson, ibid., p. 168.

† See Freeman's Historical Essays, first series, 15–25, for a refutation of the legend of Elfrida's marriage.

XXI.

EDWARD THE MARTYR—
OLD AGE OF DUNSTAN—
NORMANS AND NORTHMEN

Of the two sons left by Edgar, one, EDWARD, son of "Ethelfled the Duck," was about thirteen years old, and the other, Elfrida's son, Ethelred, was but seven at the death of their father. This being so, it is surprising that there should have been any debate as to which son should succeed to the vacant throne. Possibly the kinsfolk of Elfrida, a powerful clan, may have raised doubts as to the regularity of Edgar's marriage to Ethelfled, or they may have insisted on the superior position of the child Ethelred as the son of a queen, for Elfrida, first of all royal consorts since Judith, wife of Ethelwulf, had been permitted to bear that envied name.* The debate was, however, decided, apparently by the united influence of the two archbishops, Dunstan and Oswald, in favour of Edward, upon whose head the crown of England was placed by the kindly hands of the Archbishop of Canterbury.

The politics of the short reign of Edward, which lasted barely four years, are as obscure and difficult to trace as the cause of its premature close. It is clear, however, that immediately on the death of Edgar there was a certain reaction against that king's monastic policy. It was in Mercia that this reaction was most powerful, and the leader in the movement was the ealdorman Elfhere, "enemy of the monks," as the Chronicle calls him; "most wicked of consuls," as he is styled by the classically minded Henry of Huntingdon. There was a certain Oslac, earl of Northumbria, who was driven into banishment by Elfhere, and from the way in which his name is mentioned we are led to conjecture that he was a partisan of the monks.

* See Robertson's Historical Essays, pp. 166–71. There is no evidence that Elfrida shared her husband's coronation, but she is the first king's wife after Judith to sign charters as Regina.

Then was in Mercia's land, as I have heard,
Widely and everywhere the Maker's praise
Laid low on earth; then many were out-driven,
God's learned ministers. Then much must mourn
The man who in his breast bore burning love
To God who made him. Then the Glorious King,
The Lord of Victories, Who the heavens doth rule,
Was too much scorned, and shattered were His rights,
Then forth was driven the hero bold of mood,
Oslac, the hoary-headed veteran,
The wise, the eloquent. He forth must fare,
Forth from the land, over the billow's roll,
Over the gannet's bath, the whale's domain.
Yea, o'er the water's throng, bereft of home.
Then too was seen, high in the firmament,
That star appearing, which brave men of old,
Men wise of soul and skilled interpreters,
Widely denoted by the comet's name;
Thus through the nations was the Ruler's wrath
Broadly proclaimed and Famine marked its path.

Thus sings the monk of Winchester. He of Peterborough, after also deviating into verse, adds in quiet prose: "In this year (975) there were great disturbances throughout England; and Elfhere the ealdorman ordered the demolition of many monasteries which king Edgar had erewhile ordered the holy bishop Ethelwold to establish. And at the same time the great earl Oslac was banished from England."

There are hints, especially in the life of St. Oswald of York, that Elfhere's anti-monastic policy was connected with a certain amount of spoliation of the abbey lands, which were probably in some measure distributed among his followers. On the other hand, we hear that Ethelwin, Ealdorman of East Anglia, son of "half-king" Athelstan and brother-in-law of Elfrida, zealously opposed Elfhere's policy and championed the cause of the monks. A yet more strenuous defender of the order was his brother, Alfwold, who slew a certain man accused by him of fraudulently obtaining some of the abbey lands of Peterborough. Desiring to obtain absolution for the deed he went to Winchester to beg it of bishop Ethelwold. In his penitence and remorse, Alfwold in his hostel unloosed his shoes and went, humble and barefooted, to meet the great bishop. But

Ethelwold, knowing in whose cause he had stricken the blow, would have none of such needless humiliation. He went forth clad in full vestments, with holy water, cross and thurible to meet "the general and defender of the Church." Prayers were offered, the acolytes replaced the shoes on the feet of the Church's champion, and the rest of the day was spent in rejoicings. "Thus did the pious chieftain of the East Angles defend all the possessions of the monasteries with great honour, wherefore he was called the Friend of God."

Concerning the actual cause of the struggle we are very imperfectly informed. The East Anglian chiefs were joined by Brihtnoth, ealdorman of Essex, brother-in-law of "the half-king," and for some time it seemed as if the dispute would have to be settled by force of arms. Happily this was averted, and in three meetings of the witan, held probably in three successive years, 977, 978 and 979 (the last after the death of Edward), it was perhaps arranged that the two parties should compromise on the basis of uti possidetis, the monasteries in East Anglia and Essex not being disturbed, but those in Mercia not being restored to the monks, at any rate during the lifetime of Elfhere.

At the first of these Witenagemots, which was held at Kirtlington, in Oxfordshire, Sideman, the aged Bishop of Crediton, who had been the young King Edward's teacher and guide, suddenly expired. At the second, which was held in an upper chamber at Calne, in Wiltshire, the floor suddenly gave way and "all the chief witan of the English race" were precipitated into the room below. Some were killed and many suffered grievous bodily harm. Apparently almost the only one who escaped quite unhurt was the Archbishop Dunstan, "who stood up upon a beam." Naturally, so remarkable an escape brightened the halo which shone round the archbishop's name. In later legends the accident was magnified into a kind of heavenly judgment between the monks and their opponents; while some modern historians, remembering Dunstan's great mechanical skill, have seen in it a cunning device for ridding himself of his enemies. Happily we are not constrained to adopt either hypothesis, and the last suggestion is certainly inadmissible. It would probably tax the ingenuity of the ablest engineer of modern times to contrive such an apparent accident so as to kill part of the assembly. Miracle and fraud may therefore both disappear from the discussion. The event, which undoubtedly happened, is only one of several indications of the unsoundness of Anglo-Saxon building. There seems reason to suspect that in the tenth century the political and the domestic architecture of England were both equally insecure, and that the apparent glory of the reign of Edgar the Peaceful rested on many rotten timbers which made easy the collapse of the kingdom under Ethelred the Unready. Perhaps, also, we may conjecture that the deaths of so many of England's chief men and wisest counsellors left the field open for meaner, weaker, more treacherous statesmen.

In the same year (978) Edward's short reign came to a bloody end. The circumstances of his death are somewhat obscure, though there can be no doubt that he was foully murdered on March 18 at Corfe in Dorsetshire. We have no contemporary evidence directly connecting his step-mother with the crime, but this silence, as all chroniclers for the next thirty years would be somewhat in fear of Elfrida and her son, cannot be counted strong evidence in her favour. On the other hand, there is some evidence that Corfe, the scene of the murder, was the place where Elfrida was at the time dwelling with her boy, and all the later historians speak unhesitatingly as to the quarter from which the blow came, though, unfortunately (as we so often find to be the case), the further removed they are from the date of the event, the more they profess to know about its details. Thus the biographer of St. Oswald, who wrote about thirty years after the murder, tells us that a conspiracy was formed against the king by Ethelred's thegns, and carried into effect when the young king, "desiring the consolation of fraternal love," paid an evening visit to the house where his brother was residing with the queen. The partisans of Ethelred gathered round Edward, who was alone and unguarded. The butler came forward "ready to serve in his lowly office"; one of the thegns seized the king's right hand as if to kiss it; another grasped his left hand and inflicted on him a mortal wound. The king called out in a loud voice: "What are you doing, breaking my hand," and then fell dead from his horse, which was also mortally wounded by the conspirators. "No chant was raised; no proper rites of burial performed; the renowned king of the whole country lay covered with a cheap garment, awaiting the resurrection day. After the lapse of a twelvemonth, the glorious duke Elfhere [of Mercia] came to Wareham, found the body lying there naked but incorrupt, and transferred it to Shaftesbury, where it received honourable burial." This account looks a little more like a political conspiracy and less like a mere private assassination than the story told in the twelfth century by William of Malmesbury, according to which the kingly boy returning from the chase, tired and thirsty, called at his step-mother's abode, asked for wine, and while drinking the stirrup-cup was treacherously stabbed by one of Elfrida's henchmen; fell from his horse, and with one foot in the stirrup was dragged along by the frightened steed, a long track through the forest being marked by the blood of the dying king. This, which is in some respects the more romantic version of the story, is that which has found its way into the received text of English history. The feelings of the people concerning this tragedy may be gathered from the ballad which was embodied in the Chronicle.

Never was worse deed done by Englishmen
Than this, since first they sought the British land.
Men murdered him, but God him magnified.
In life Eadward was an earthly king;
Now after death he is a saint in heaven.
His earthly kinsmen durst not him avenge,
But grievous vengeance wrought his Heavenly Sire.
On earth his foes his memory would efface,
But the Supreme Avenger spread abroad
In earth and heaven remembrance of that crime.
They who in life refused him reverence,
Now bow on bended knee before his bones.
Thus may we see how wisdom of mankind,
Their clever counsels, their persuasive words,
Are but as nothing 'gainst the thought of God.

Here we can perceive, deep in the heart of the writer, a smouldering fire of indignation against some persons highly placed and beyond the reach of man's revenge, by whom the deed of wickedness was wrought. The misery which fell upon the nation in the long and dreary reign of Elfrida's son is heaven's answer to the cry of the innocent blood. Without the Church's sanction, without any strict warrant for the epithet, the instinct of the people gave to the victim of Corfe the name which he has ever since borne in history, "Edward the Martyr."

The new king, ETHELRED, a boy of ten years old, was crowned at Kingston-on-Thames a fortnight after Easter, the two archbishops and ten bishops taking part in the ceremony. Dunstan addressed to him, as he had done to his father before him, a sermon on the duties of his kingship, and is said, but on somewhat doubtful authority, to have uttered at the same time foreboding words as to the calamities coming upon the kingdom, in punishment for the crime which had given Ethelred the crown. It seems clear that he withdrew more and more from a share in the civil, perhaps even in the ecclesiastical, government of the realm, and spent the ten years of life which yet remained to him chiefly in religious retirement; in preaching to the crowd of unlearned persons, lay and clerical, male and female, who gathered round him "to be fortified day and night with the heavenly salt"; in practising those mechanical arts which he had loved from boyhood; and in sitting on a bench in the scriptorium correcting some of the manuscripts which formed part of the treasure of Canterbury.

In the year 986, however, Dunstan was roused from his meditations by the extraordinary conduct of young Ethelred, who "on account of certain dissensions besieged Rochester, and being unable to take it, invaded and laid waste the patrimony of St. Andrew." Some light is thrown on this remarkable entry by a document* issued twelve years later, in which Ethelred laments that his youthful simplicity was imposed upon by a certain Ethelsin, an enemy of God and man, and that by his advice he violently abstracted from the church of Rochester a rural property at Bromley, which he now restores. Dunstan, we are told, warned the king of the punishment which waited on such crimes, and eventually induced him by a ransom of 100 pounds of silver to raise the siege of Rochester. Hereupon he prophesied that "such a king who preferred money to God, silver to the apostle, the gratification of his avarice to the earnestly expressed desire of his spiritual father, would draw down on himself and on his kingdom such calamities as the English nation had never yet experienced. But he himself, as he had been told by the mouth of the Lord, should not live to see this righteous retribution." And so it proved. Two years later, on May 19, 988, Dunstan expired, probably in the sixty-fourth year of his age.

That Dunstan was a great saint and a great statesman cannot be doubted. No small man could have produced the impression which he produced on his own and on later generations. But what were his own actual achievements in Church and State it is not easy to discover through the veil of turgid obscurity woven by his biographers, who are more intent on recording childish miracles than on painting for us a truthful and vivid portraiture of the great archbishop. Doubtless the alleged miracles of the saint were not all the accumulation of later ages. Partly on account of his

* Kemble's Codex Diplomaticus, 700.

mechanical skill and partly from the peculiarities of his own temperament, a certain thaumaturgic atmosphere seems to have surrounded Dunstan even in his lifetime. With this we can now dispense; but while we closely study his life, some of the old misconceptions as to his character fall away. He was evidently not the grim and crafty ecclesiastic whom in our childish days we used to fancy him. On the contrary, with all his enthusiasm for monkhood, his influence was in fact a moderating one on the party of monastic reform. Far from being of a cruel nature, he seems, from such indications as are furnished us, to have been a man of genial and lovable disposition. He is now generally regarded as a great administrator, and a man of wide and statesmanlike views; though, as was before remarked, strict proof of this has hardly yet been adduced. But he seems also to have been through life a man of nervous, perhaps even of hysterical, temperament, renowned and envied for his power of shedding copious floods of tears; a man who saw visions and dreamed dreams; and, above all, a man who believed himself to be engaged in a perpetual personal encounter with the Prince of Darkness, who was to him as real and familiar a presence as the ealdorman of Mercia or the canonici of Glastonbury.

*****

Before entering on that dreary period of Danish desolation which now lies before us it will be well to say something as to certain events which had been happening in France, Denmark and Norway, and which were about to exercise an enormous influence on the next stages of development of the English nation. The dukes of Normandy, the French kings of the race of Capet, the Angevin ancestors of our Plantagenet monarchs, all date their origin, or at least their greatness, from the tenth century, from the period between the death of Alfred and the accession of Ethelred. It is necessary also to take note of the immediate ancestors of the Danish kings who were about to make themselves actual sovereigns of England.

The Scandinavian invasions, which tended indirectly towards the consolidation of England, wrought powerfully towards the disintegration of the Frankish empire. The ignominious treaty which the last emperor of the direct line of Charlemagne, his great grandson Charles the Fat, made with the Danes to induce them to desist from the siege of Paris, and which had to be paid for by a large ransom, was one of the causes which led to his deposition from the imperial throne (887). A younger branch of the Carolingian house continued for just a century longer to wear the title of Kings of Francia, but their personal domain became gradually restricted to a little tract of territory surrounding the city of Laon, and they were ever more overshadowed by the greatness of the family of Robert, rightly called the Strong, who, though himself a Saxon alien of somewhat obscure origin, had shown conspicuous valour in the Danish wars, and whose two sons, Odo and Robert, both crowned as Kings of France, were the heroes of the mighty siege of Paris. For thirty-three years (923–56) Hugh the Great, son of this second Robert and grandson of the first, was far the most powerful man in France: Duke of Francia, Burgundy and Aquitaine, Count of Paris and Orleans, Lay Abbot of St. Martin of Tours. But though a kingmaker, son and nephew of kings, he always refused to be king himself. His son, Hugh Capet, more ambitious or less scrupulous, in 987 pushed aside the last powerless descendant of Charlemagne, and ascended that glorious throne which was uninterruptedly occupied by his descendants, Valois, Plantagenet, Bourbon, till the awful day of August, 1792, when the Swiss Guards fell fighting in front of the Tuilleries.

The Norman dukes, who also in this tenth century climbed up into all but regal state, bore an important part in this revolution. The hitherto received story of the settlement of the Northmen under their leader Rolf or Rollo in the fair province to which they gave their name has been subjected of late to much adverse criticism,* and has been so seriously shaken that hardly anything but the bare fact survives indubitable, that there was such a settlement in the early part of the tenth century; that either in 911 or, as is rather more probable, in 921, Rolf "commended" himself to the French king Charles the Simple; and that he became his "man" in return for the cession of a large district on the Lower Seine. This transaction resembled in some respects the arrangement made a generation before, between Alfred and Guthrum. It was the surrender of part of the kingdom to ensure the safety of the remainder, the change of a pertinacious enemy into a fairly faithful friend. The cession of Normandy to Rolf was, however, in some ways a more signal success than Alfred's cession of East Anglia to Guthrum. Though the Frankish historians persisted for generations in calling Rolf's people pirates, the

* Especially by Sir H. Howorth, Archæologia, xlv., 235–50.

new-comers soon assimilated all and more than all the civilisation of their Frankish neighbours; and Norman literature, Norman chivalry, Norman architecture became the envy of Europe.

On Rolf's death or abdication in 927 his son, William Longsword, became duke and reigned for fifteen years. He was a man of keen and polished intellect, with many noble, even with some holy, aspirations, but with a strange duality in his nature, perhaps the result of the mingled strain of Viking and Romanised Frank that was in his blood, for his mother is said to have been a Frankish lady of noble birth. A conflict had begun between two sections of his subjects, between the men of Rouen and its neighbourhood, who were fast becoming Frenchmen, and the men of the district round Bayeux, who remained obstinate Danes; and in this conflict William veered first to one side, then to the other. Moreover in the confused welter of French politics he played an eminently inconsistent and unwise part, showing that amidst the intriguing, grasping but adroit counts of Northern Gaul he never felt himself completely at home, but was uneasily conscious that he was still looked upon by them as dux piratarum. He would fain have been faithful to the royal line, to which his father owed his legalised position in the country; and in 936 he heartily co-operated with Hugh the Great in bringing back Athelstan's nephew, Louis IV. d'Outremer, from his English exile and crowning him king; but, changeable as a weather-cock, he was almost as often found among the enemies of Louis IV. as in the ranks of his friends. Unfaithfulness begat unfaithfulness; the man who had been on each side in every quarrel made himself enemies all round, and in 942, having been treacherously invited to a conference on an island in the Somme, he was there foully murdered by a band of noble conspirators, among whom we regret to find Arnulf of Flanders, grandson of our own Alfred, first and foremost.

On the death of William Longsword, his little son Richard, though not born in lawful wedlock—this was almost the rule in the Norman line—was unanimously accepted as his successor. The boy, only ten years old, was soon plunged into a whirlpool of troubles, from which even his father's old and faithful counsellors could hardly have extricated him, had he not himself shown that cool, patient, self-sustained courage which earned for him his historical surname, "the Fearless." Though the Norman historians may have somewhat embroidered the romantic history of his captivity and escape, there can be little doubt that two dangerous neighbours, King Louis IV. and Count Hugh the Great, coveted the orphan boy's inheritance; nor that, but for the loyalty of the Norman warriors to the son of their dead chieftain, and the astute management of two or three of his father's old friends, they would have succeeded in making it their own. Soon after the death of William Longsword King Louis came to Rouen, ostensibly as the friend and protector of the little duke. He seems, however, to have practically taken the government of the country into his own hands, while the boy Richard, who was transferred to the court of Laon "that he might be there educated as beseemed a Christian prince," found the school of knighthood every day becoming more like a prison. However, Richard's faithful guardian, Osmund, succeeded in smuggling him out of the castle, according to the legend, "in a truss of hay." The Normans, tired of the financial exactions of the ministers of Louis, rose in open revolt and gathered round their just recovered prince; the invasion of Louis with a formidable army was neutralised by that of Harold, a chieftain from Scandinavia, who, in 945, on the urgent appeal of Richard came to the help of his brother-Northmen. A battle followed, the battle of the Dive, in which Louis was utterly defeated, and he was soon after taken prisoner. Thus were the tables now turned, Louis who was of late the jailer being now the captive; nor did he regain his liberty till he had surrendered the rock fortress of Laon, almost his last remaining possession, to the omnivorous Count Hugh the Great, and had—so say the Norman writers—formally released Duke Richard from all ties of feudal dependence. Whether this be literally true or not, there is no doubt that Richard "commended" himself to the count of Paris. Thus even before Hugh Capet became King of France, the duke of Normandy was already his most powerful vassal. This fact, coupled with the steady and effectual help which Richard gave to the younger Hugh in his patient upward progress to the throne, deserves to be remembered when in later ages we have to deal with the relations, more often hostile than friendly, between the Norman-English vassal and the French lord paramount.

At the period which we have reached in English history, the date of the death of Dunstan (988), Richard the Fearless was a middle-aged man of fifty-five years. He had been reigning for forty-five years, and was the father of a numerous progeny—not born in wedlock—by a Danish woman named Gunnor, whom he married after the death of his lawful wife Emma, sister of Hugh Capet. His marriage with Emma was childless. In the year 996 he died and was succeeded by his son Richard the Good.

*****

The origin of the house, which in after ages bore the name of Plantagenet and which held in the tenth century the countship of Anjou, is hidden in clouds of legend; but the legend itself does not dare to say that their forebears were always noble, nor to assign to them, as to so many of their princely contemporaries, a descent from the great Emperor Charles. The legendary ancestor of the Counts of Anjou is a certain Tortulf or Tertullus, a Breton forester to whom a doubtful Carolingian king, probably Charles the Bald, is said to have assigned a woodland district known as the Blackbird's Nest (Nid de Merle), on condition of repelling the Danish attacks on the valley of the Loire. The special interest attaching to the history of the Angevin counts, in addition to the fact that they were the ancestors of so many of our English sovereigns, lies in the tenacity of purpose with which they pursued their policy of aggrandisement, gradually converting their little marchland on the east of Brittany, a small and precarious possession, into an extensive and powerful state in one of the fairest regions of France. With their Breton neighbours on the west, with Maine and Normandy on the north, they were frequently at war, but their most bitter and enduring conflicts were with the Counts of Blois on the east, and it was at their expense that the most important of the Angevin conquests was effected. This is a fact which it will be well to bear in mind when we find Henry of Anjou and Stephen of Blois, heirs of a feud which had already lasted in France for two centuries, contending on English soil for the crown of England.

*****

The history of Denmark during the first century and a half of the Viking raids is involved in great obscurity; but about the time when Edward the Elder was reigning in England we emerge into clearer light, and find a king named Gorm the Old reigning over a united Denmark, with, however, some obligations of vassalage towards the German king, Henry the Saxon. On his death or abdication towards the middle of the tenth century began the long and prosperous reign of Harold Blaatand (Blue-

Tooth), which lasted for about fifty years and was the great period of consolidation for the Danish kingdom. In 977 Harold, in conjunction with two Norwegian allies, made an expedition to Norway by which he obtained possession of a considerable part of that country and acquired a sort of feudal supremacy over the whole. In his relations with the German emperors Harold was less fortunate. He was apparently compelled to submit to Otto I., and as one of the conditions of peace, he and his son Sweyn were forced to receive Christian baptism. The conversion of the son at any rate was not sincere, and dissensions broke out between him and his father. The old king was defeated and fled the country. He was restored for a short time, again attacked by Sweyn, and died of his wounds received in battle.

Thus, in the fourteenth year of Ethelred's reign, the throne of Denmark was occupied by the stern pagan Swegen or Sweyn. No tenderness will he show to Christian churches or monasteries in any land that he may invade; and any king or people that shall do him wrong may expect to receive terrible retribution.

The early, doubtless in large measure legendary, history of Norway, as told in the Heimskringla Saga, is full of romantic interest, but is beside our present purpose. The great unifier of the Norwegian kingdom was Harold Fair-hair, whose long reign ended before the middle of the tenth century. In the eleventh year of his age he found himself lord of a small kingdom between Lake Wener and the Dovrefield Mountains. When he came to manhood he wooed the fair Gytha for his wife, but the damsel declared that she would marry no man who did not rule the whole of Norway, as Gorm ruled all Denmark and Eric the whole of Sweden. Hereupon Harold, having vowed not to cut his hair till he had accomplished the prescribed task, began a series of expeditions northwards, which did in the course of years make him master of the whole of what we now call Norway. He married Gytha, but she was only one of many wives and concubines by whom he begat countless children, whose wars and alliances, whose rivalries and reconciliations, fill Norwegian history in the tenth century as English history in the fifteenth is filled by the broils of the Plantagenets. This is that Harold who sent the infant Hakon to be educated at the court of Athelstan; and Hakon, as has been said, having been educated by his great foster-father in the Christian religion and trained in all arts that became a Saxon Etheling, went back to his fatherland, reigned there after his father's death as Hakon the Good, and vainly endeavoured to

Christianise his people. Another Harold and another Hakon followed in quick succession, sometimes owning, sometimes rejecting, the overlordship of Denmark. At the period which we have now reached, the rising star is that of Olaf Tryggvason, great-grandson of Fair-hair, not yet king of Norway but a great and popular Viking, whose name will be heard with terror in Essex and in Kent, in Sussex and in Hampshire.

XXII.

ETHELRED THE REDELESS

The story of the long reign of Ethelred consists of little else than the details of Danish invasions, large payments of ransom to the raiders, and the king's dealings with the Dukes of Normandy, at whose court he was at last obliged to take refuge.

Though many historical verdicts have been reversed in our day, Ethelred the Redeless, the man devoid of counsel—this rather than "the Unready" is the best translation of his distinguishing epithet—still remains unchampioned under the stigma of incompetence as great as was ever displayed by any occupant of the English throne. When we read the record of his disastrous reign, when we see how systematically he left undone the things which he ought to have done, and did, with fitful and foolish energy, the things which he ought not to have done, we are inclined to ask, "Was this man bereft of reason?" If he had been absolutely insane we should probably have had a distinct statement to that effect in the Chronicle, but it may, perhaps, be suggested that there was some hereditary weakness in his family which in his case affected the fibre of his brain. Royal families not renewed by any admixture of plebeian blood have sometimes shown a tendency to become worn out. We must remember that the descendants of Cerdic had now been reigning for five hundred years. As compared with the young and parvenus dynasties which were coming up into power from the ranks of sailors and huntsmen and tillers of the soil; as compared with the Norman dukes, the Capetians and the Angevins, the Kings of Wessex were an old and apparently a weakening stock. There was certainly brain-power enough in an Alfred, an Edward and an Athelstan, but perhaps even with them physical hardly kept pace with mental energy. Alfred the Great was a life-long sufferer from disease. If he and his son completed each his half century of life, that was more than was attained by most of their immediate descendants. Athelstan lived but to the age of forty-six; Edred, a chronic invalid, died at thirty; Edwy probably under twenty; even Edgar, whose reign seemed a long one, at thirty-two. Edmund and Edward the Martyr died violent deaths, and therefore they do not come into this calculation. Ethelred himself, though he lived long enough to inflict untold misfortunes on his country, died at the age of forty-eight. All this looks like a decay of physical power in the house of Cerdic, which may in some degree account for the fatal "redelessness" of Ethelred. It is true that there was a revival of the old heroic energy in his son Edmund Ironside, but even that is coupled with a very short life (we cannot be sure that his death was due to foul play); and in his half-brother, Edward the Confessor, though he lived to the age of sixty-two, there is a sort of anæmic saintliness which marks him out as the fitting son, intellectually though not morally, of his "redeless" father.

The story of the reign of Ethelred is given us in the Chronicle with a minuteness of detail such as we have not found there since the days of Alfred. It is evidently the work of a contemporary, of one who saw and groaned over the calamities of his people, and who was moved to passionate indignation by the mingled folly and wickedness of the rulers of the land. This part of the Chronicle is then a document of the highest value for the historian, and yet it is one which requires to be used with some caution on account of the motive by which it is unconsciously inspired. That motive is the strong tendency which always leads a beaten army or a beaten nation to argue that the enemy did not fight fairly, or that "the pass was sold" to them by some traitor in the camp. It is quite possible that all the accusations brought by the chronicler are true, especially that the inexplicable treasons of Elfric and Edric were as monstrous as he describes them; but it is also possible that they may have been magnified by a patriotic scribe, looking round for some scapegoat to bear his people's sins; and in any event what we have to remember is that we are here reading what are virtually the articles of an opposition journalist. It is just possible, therefore, though hardly probable, that in some cases Ethelred's ministers and generals, or even Ethelred himself, if they could be heard in their own defence, might somewhat mitigate the severity of the sentence passed upon them. A few of these criticisms are here inserted, but even these will hardly give a sufficient idea of the tone of condemnation which pervades the whole long reign of Ethelred in the pages of the Chronicle.*

....

* The following passages are almost all taken from the Peterborough version of the Chronicle which was based for this part of the narrative on a Canterbury Chronicle. Hence, doubtless, the fulness of the entries relating to Kent.

998. "The Danes came to the mouth of the Frome and ravaged Dorset at their will. The fyrd was often gathered together against them, but as soon as they should have all got together, then ever for some cause was flight determined on, and so the Danes in the end always got the victory. So they quartered themselves for the second time in the Isle of Wight, drawing their provisions from Hampshire and Sussex."

999. "The army again came round into the Thames and moved thence up the Medway to Rochester. Then came the Kentish fyrd against them and there were they firmly locked in fight. But, alas! the Kentish men too quickly gave way and fled, because they were not supported as they ought to have been. Thus the Danes held the place of slaughter, and took horse and rode far and wide as they chose, and ravaged well-nigh the whole of West Kent. Then the king took counsel with his witan, and decided that they must go against the enemy with ship-fyrd and also with land-fyrd. But when the ships were ready, then some one delayed from day to day and harassed the poor folk who were on board the ships, and ever, when things should have been forwarder they were later, from one time to another, and so they let the army of their enemies grow, and they were always retiring from the sea and the Danes were ever following hard after them. Thus at the end the great ship-fyrd accomplished nothing but oppression of the people and waste of money and the emboldening of their foes."

1006. "The Danish fleet came to Sandwich, and the crews did as they had ever done, harrying, burning, murdering wheresoever they went. Then the king called out all the people of Wessex and Mercia, and they lay out all the autumn, arrayed against the enemy, but all availed nothing as so often before; for in spite of all this the Danish army marched just where they pleased, and the fyrd itself did the country folk every harm, while neither the home army (inn-here) nor the foreign army (ut-here) did them any good. As soon as the weather grew wintry, the fyrd went home, and the Danish army after Martinmas, November 11, came to their resting-place in the Isle of Wight and helped themselves to all that they wanted from every quarter. Then in mid-winter they sallied forth through Hants and Berks to their comfortable quarters at Reading, and there did as they pleased, kindling their beacons [blazing villages] wherever they went. Thus fared they to Wallingford which they burned down, and they then went along Ashdown to Cwichelms-law,* and there abode, out of pure

* Now corrupted into Skutchamfly Barrow, eight and a half miles from the White Horse in Berkshire.

bravado, because it had been often said that if once they got to Cwichelms-law they would never get back to the sea. They then went home by another way. The fyrd was assembled at Cynete (?), and they there joined battle, but soon was that [English] army put to flight, and afterwards they carried their booty down to the sea. Then might the people of Winchester see the invading army, insolent and fearless, marching past their gates to the sea; and they spread over fifty miles from the sea, gathering food and treasure."

It would be tedious to follow the chronicler's example and relate in detail all the events of these successive raids, which recur with melancholy monotony through thirty years. The reader is therefore referred to the accompanying table for the list of the districts successively ravaged by the invaders.

Year.

982 Portland, by three ships' crews landing in Dorsetshire. (London burnt; possibly an accidental fire.)

988 Watchet in Somerset. Goda, a Devonshire thegn slain.

991 Ipswich ravaged. Battle of Maldon. Brihtnoth slain. First payment of gafol (tribute) to the Danes.

993 Bamburgh stormed. Great booty taken. Both banks of the Humber ravaged.

994 Brave defence of London, attacked by Olaf and Sweyn. Essex, Kent, Sussex, Hampshire. Second payment of gafol.

997 Cornwall, Devon, Wales, Watchet, Lydford, Tavistock.

998 Mouth of the Frome, Dorset, Isle of Wight. Sussex and Hants forced to supply provisions.

999 Rochester: Kent.

1001 Battle at Alton in Hampshire. Devonshire. Taunton burnt. Exmouth defended. Penhoe and Clist (in Devon). Bishops Waltham in Hampshire burnt.

1002 Marriage of Ethelred with Emma of Normandy. Massacre of St. Brice's Day. Third payment of gafol.

1003 Exeter stormed and looted. Wilton, Sarum.

1004 Norwich, Thetford. Brave defence of Norfolk by Ulfkytel.

1005 Great famine throughout England.

1006 Sandwich, Isle of Wight, Reading, Wallingford, Cwichelms-law.

1007 Fourth payment of gafol.

1008 Ships ordered to be built all over England.

1009 Failure of the new navy. Canterbury, Isle of Wight, Sussex, Hants,

Berks, both banks of the Thames, Oxford. London vainly attacked. Local payment of gafol by East Kent.

1010 Ipswich, Thetford, Cambridge, Oxfordshire, Bucks, Bedford, Tempsford (in Bedfordshire), Northampton, Canning Marsh (in Somerset).

1011 Canterbury.

1012 Martyrdom of Archbishop Alphege. Fifth payment of gafol.

1013 Mouth of the Humber, Gainsborough. King Sweyn at Sandwich. Northumbria and all the country north of Watling Street submit to him. Oxford, Winchester, Wallingford, Bath, Devon and London submit to Sweyn. Flight of Ethelred and his family to Normandy.

1014 Death of Sweyn (Feb. 3), Ethelred recalled. Canute, son of Sweyn, King of the Danes, occupies Lindsey. Mutilation of Northumbrian hostages by Canute. Sixth payment of gafol.

1015 Dorset, Wilts, Somerset ravaged.

1016 Warwickshire, Buckinghamshire, Bedfordshire, Huntingdonshire; along the fens to Stamford. Lincolnshire, Nottinghamshire, York, submission of Northumbria, London repeatedly attacked. Death of Ethelred (April 23). Edmund Ironside king. Battle of Assandune. The kingdom divided between Canute and Edmund. Death of Edmund Ironside (Nov. 30). Canute sole king.

Dreary and depressing as is the general course of the narrative of these successive invasions, we have in the early years of the war, not from the chronicler but from an unknown contemporary poet, a graphic account of a battle in which the Northmen were valiantly met and all but defeated. The hero of the battle was Brihtnoth, ealdorman of Essex, brother-in-law of the half-king Athelstan, and champion of the monks against Elfhere of Mercia. The scene was laid at Maldon in Essex, where the dark stream of the Blackwater begins to discharge itself into its broad tidal estuary. The date was 991, the thirteenth year of Ethelred. The poet brings before us the ealdorman Brihtnoth arraying his men-at-arms on the shore of the Blackwater. He rides up and down their ranks, bidding them hold their shields with firm grasp and fear naught. He alights from his horse and stands beside "his friends, his own hearth-warriors," of whose staunch service he has often made proof. While he is standing on the bank a Viking herald shouts forth his threatful message: "The bold sailors have sent me to thee to say that thou must forthwith send to them a ransom of golden rings. It will be for your profit by this payment to forego the flight of spears; and you shall then have peace with the men of the sea."

At this Earl Brihtnoth gripped tight his shield and shook his slender ashen spear and poured forth his words of wrath: "The tribute we will give you is naught but flying spears, the edge of deadly iron, the old and trusted sword. Go back and tell the folk who sent thee, that here stands an earl with his warriors who will defend this country, the land of noble Ethelred, to the uttermost. Now that you have visited our land you shall not depart all softly to your homes bearing no marks of battle on your bodies. Rather shall point and edge settle our differences: grim will be the sword-play ere we pay you tribute."

After this interchange of defiances, the troops on either side were drawn up in battle array, but it was some hours before they could close in conflict. The estuary of the Blackwater was still filled by the flowing tide, and one bridge over the narrower part of the stream, by which the enemy might have crossed, was valiantly defended by three Saxons. "Finding these bridge warders all too bitter," the Northmen moved up stream to find a ford. The earl, in the pride of his soul, allowed many of the hateful people to come to land, shouting aloud: "Listen, warriors! Free space is now granted you to come quickly to us. Come as warriors to the war. God only knows who shall hold the field of slaughter." "The wolves of rapine" tramped through the water, holding high their shields over their heads, and found, when they reached the shore, Earl Brihtnoth waiting to receive them. He had bidden his men "to weave the war-hedge with their shields" (that is to make the shield-wall) and hold it firmly against the foe. Then rose high the war of battle, the ravens gathered together at the sound, and with them came the eagle, greedy for his prey.

With true Homeric fervour the poet describes the incidents of the battle that followed. Brihtnoth was wounded early in the fight by the spear of a Viking, but succeeded in giving his antagonist a death-wound by his javelin.

Blithe was then the chieftain,
Laughed the moody man: "I thank Thee, Lord of heaven,
For this glorious day's work Thou to me hast given."

Soon, however, he received another more deadly wound from a Norse arrow, and though for a little space he still fought on, ere long "to earth fell the golden-hilted sword, nor might he longer hold the hard knife or wield the well-loved weapon." But still the hoary warrior bade the youths fight on and show a bold front to the foe, and as he lay he looked toward heaven and said:—

Thankful I remember, Lord of Nations,
All the joys I in this world have tasted.
Now this one thing do I crave in dying
From Thy hands, O merciful Creator!—
That Thy grace be on my parting spirit,
That my soul in peace to Thee may journey,
To Thy presence, O Thou Lord of Angels,
And that of the Hell-crew none may harm her.

Uttering these words he died, and his corpse was barbarously hacked by the bands of the heathen. Soon were his two squires, Elfnoth and Wulfmaer, lying dead beside him, having freely given their lives for their lord. And now was seen the difference between the brave men and the infamous (nithings). Now fled from the battle those who loved it not. First in flight was Godric, to whom his good lord had in past days given many a noble steed, but who now leapt on his master's horse and fled fast from the battle, spreading panic among the soldiers, who thought when they saw the well-known steed that it was Brihtnoth himself who was thus fleeing from the encounter. Offa, a thegn of Brihtnoth, upon whom the command of the remnant of the army seems now to have devolved, had said only the day before when they were holding gemot (whereat Godric had probably been speaking loud and boastful words):—

Many speak valiant words in council hall,
Who in the time of need from honour fall.

And now Godric's cowardice made vain his words. Then did a young warrior named Elfwine, grandson of an ealdorman of Mercia, speak heart-cheering words to his fellows, reminding them of all the brave old times that they had shared together in Brihtnoth's banquet-hall, drinking mead and talking of hard-won victories.

Now shall not the brave thegns, my countrymen, upbraid me,
That I from this day's fighting have shamefully departed,
And sought my home unwounded, when there my chieftain lieth,
Hacked by the hostile broadswords. That were my worst disaster.
Alas! that there my kinsman, my dead lord, lies before me.
Then many of the sailor host Offa laid low in battle,
But all too soon the chieftain brave himself received his death-blow,
Redeeming thus the promise he to his lord had given,
"Either we twain to castle triumphant ride together
Safe to our homes, or elsewise we both in battle perish,

Sore wounded, life out-bleeding upon the field of slaughter."
So lay the noble Offa all thegn-like by his master.

The poem both begins and ends abruptly, and is evidently a fragment, but we know from the Chronicle that the valour of Brihtnoth's henchmen was vain to restore the battle, and that Maldon was a Northmen's victory. The chief interest of the poem lies in the fact that it so vividly brings before us the devotion of the thegns to their "dear lord" (wine drihten), reminding us forcibly of the words of Tacitus concerning the ancestors of these men nine centuries before. "The man is disgraced for the rest of his life who leaves the battle-field having survived his chief. The chiefs fight for victory, the 'companions' for their chief." Also, unfortunately, the poet reveals to us the existence of treachery and cowardice in the Saxon host. We shall soon come upon notorious instances of men who imitated the panic-breeding flight of the base Godric rather than the noble stand of Brihtnoth and his henchmen.

We may gather from the lay of Brihtnoth some notions of the manner of fighting in use among the Saxons. The battle was evidently fought on foot, horses being merely used to convey some of the warriors to the field of battle. The chief weapon seems to be the spear (gar or franca), and next to it the dart (dareth), though of course the sword (sweord) and dagger or knife (mece) are also used. The use of the bow and arrow (boga and flan) seems still to be rather exceptional, at any rate on the Saxon side. The chief arms of defence are the byrne or ringed coat of mail and the bord or shield made of linden wood. To "weave the war-hedge" (wyrcan thone wighagan) with closely interlocked shields is the first duty of an army on the defensive; to break the shield-wall (brecan thone bordweall) is the highest act of assailant valour.

*****

At the outset of the battle of Maldon we heard the messenger of "the sea men" suggesting the terms on which they were ready to sell an ignominious immunity from ravage. It was in 991, the very year of that battle, that the first payment of what is generally called Danegeld was made.* "And in that year," says the chronicler, "it was first decided

* The term Danegeld seems to be properly applicable to the tax imposed on the king's subjects in order to provide for the payment to the Danes. The payment itself is generally called gafol in the Chronicle.

that men should pay gafol to the Danish men on account of the many terrible things which they wrought on the sea coast. That was at first 10,000 pounds. This was the counsel of Archbishop Siric" (Sigeric of Canterbury, 990–94).* Of course this easy and ignominious remedy for the miseries inflicted by the invaders was only a palliative, not a cure, and the short breathing-time purchased by the payment not having been utilised as it was by Alfred to put the country in a better state of defence, when the importunate beggars came again, they had to be bought off at a higher figure. The following table shows the dates and amounts of the successive payments of gafol:—

991	First Payment	10,000 pounds of silver
994	Second Payment	16,000
1002	Third Payment	24,000
1007	Fourth Payment	36,000
1009	Local Payment, East Kent	3,000
1012	Fifth Payment	48,000
1014	Sixth Payment	21,000
		158,000 pounds of silver

This sum, if we take the pound weight of silver at fifty-four shillings, would be equivalent in intrinsic value to £426,600 sterling, or if we take the "purchasing power" of money in the tenth century at twenty times its present amount, it would be equivalent to a drain of £8,532,000 from a thinly peopled and exhausted country. Probably, as the drain went on, the purchasing power of the silver that remained would be enormously increased and the above estimate may therefore be too small. The chronicler in most cases simply records the fact that the king and his witan promised gafol to the army (sometimes gafol and food) on condition that they should cease from evil; but under the year 1011, after enumerating the districts of England, equivalent to sixteen of our present counties, all of which they had ravaged in that one year, he adds:

* It is stated in Ethelred's Treaty with Olaf (Liebermann, i., 220–228) that the sum promised to the invaders was "22,000 pounds of gold and silver". The document is, on other grounds, an interesting one, as it seems to show a serious effort to secure permanent peace between the two nations.

"All these misfortunes befel us through evil counsel (un-raed) because people did not choose either to pay them gafol in time or else to fight with them; but when they had done about as much evil as they could possibly do, then people made truce and peace with them.... And nevertheless for all this truce and peace and payment of gafol, they went everywhere in bands and harried the country and captured and slew our poor people."

In order to meet these terrible demands upon the treasury, Ethelred imposed the tax called Danegeld, which was possibly the first tax paid in money and not in kind. The amount of this tax in Saxon times does not seem to be clearly stated. Abolished by Edward the Confessor in 1052, it was revived and made much more oppressive by the Conqueror long after all fear of Danish invasion had ceased, and though its discontinuance was frequently talked of, it does not finally disappear from the treasury rolls till the year 1163.* So persistent is the clutch of the tax-gatherer when he has once fastened his claws upon his victim.

*****

In 992 we have the first of the long series of "inexplicable treasons"† of Elfric, ealdorman of Hampshire and Berkshire. The king and all his witan had decided that all the ships that were of any value should be collected in London. The command of this naval armament was entrusted to Ealdorman Elfric, with three colleagues, two of whom were bishops, and they were ordered to intercept the invading host while still upon the high seas. But Elfric gave private warning to the Danish leaders, and on the evening before the day on which the battle was to have been fought, he stole away by himself from the fyrd, to his great disgrace. The result was that the Danish fleet escaped, all save one ship, the crew of which was slain; and the Danes in their turn caught the ships of East Anglia and London at a disadvantage, and wrought a mighty slaughter among them, capturing the very ship, all armed and equipped, in which Elfric had been. As a punishment apparently either for this or for yet another treason, his son Elfgar was next year blinded by order of the king. And yet ten years later (1003), when a great fyrd had been collected out of Wiltshire and Hampshire, Ealdorman Elfric was again placed in command of it. "But," says the chronicler, "he was again at his old tricks. As soon as the two armies were so near together

* Stubbs' Constitutional History, i., 118, 623.

† Freeman, Hist. of Norm. Conq., i., 279.

that they could look into one another's faces, he feigned himself sick and began retching and spewing, and called out that he was suddenly taken ill. Thus did he betray the folk that he should have led to battle. For when the general is cowardly, then is all the army terribly hindered." This is the last time that Elfric is mentioned as in command of an army; but we hear of him (or another ealdorman of the same name) thirteen years later (1016) falling at the battle of Assandune. We may, perhaps, doubt whether he was really a deep-dyed traitor or only a man of weakly and nervous constitution, unable to face "the flight of spears" and quite unfit to be put in command of the smallest detachment of soldiers.

In 994 a united effort for the conquest of England was made by a Norwegian and a Danish chieftain. The Norwegian was Olaf Tryggvason, great grandson of Harold Fair-hair, hero of a hundred romantic stories, "fairest and strongest of all men and in prowess surpassing all men talked of by the Northmen." He had already visited England as a foe and had borne a chief part in the battle of Maldon. The Dane was Sweyn, son of Harold Blue-tooth, whose early career has been already described. In the autumn of 994 the two comrades with ninety-four ships sailed up the Thames and fiercely attacked the city of London on September 8, the Feast of the Nativity of the Virgin Mary, thinking to set it on fire. "But there," says the Chronicle, "God be thanked, they experienced more harm and mischief than they ever thought that any citizens should do unto them. For the holy mother of God showed her mild-heartedness unto those burghers and delivered them from their enemies." The marauding bands then departed and "wrought the most ill that any man could do in burnings and harryings and man-slayings by the sea coast of Essex, in Kent, in Sussex and in Hampshire," and after "they had worked indescribable evil," the king and his witan decided to make the second great gafol payment of £16,000, and "the army" after once mustering at Southampton, was billeted through the whole land of Wessex while the silver was being collected. The terms of peace being thus settled, Ethelred sent a solemn embassage to Olaf, consisting of Elfheah and Ethelweard. Both these were in their different ways men worthy of note. Elfheah or Alphege, who was at this time bishop of Winchester, became twelve years later archbishop of Canterbury, and as we shall see suffered cruel martyrdom at the hands of the Danes. Ethelweard, an ealdorman of Wessex, seems to be clearly identified with the chronicler generally known as Ethelweard, who was of royal blood (being descended from

Alfred's elder brother, Ethelred I.), and whose turgid and obscure narrative occasionally sheds a glimmer of light on the dark places of Anglo-Saxon history. The English ambassadors conducted Olaf to Andover; and there he was led "with much worship" into the presence of Ethelred, who bestowed upon him kingly gifts and received him from the bishop's hands, when the baptismal rite had been performed. Under the spell of these new religious influences, Olaf promised that "he would never again come against the English race in unfriendly guise," a promise which, as the chronicler says, he well fulfilled. Next year (995) he made himself master of the Norwegian kingdom, and succeeded in inducing all the Norwegian chiefs, north and south, to become converts to Christianity. After a reign of five years full of romantic adventures,* the Norwegian hero fell in a great sea-fight against the combined forces of his former ally, Sweyn of Denmark, and his namesake, Olaf of Sweden. For fourteen years (1000–14) Norway lay under the yoke of the confederate kings. The increase of power thus obtained by Denmark may have had something to do with the success of Sweyn's schemes for the conquest of England.

*****

Powerless as Ethelred was to defend our island from her foes, he could at least imitate their ravages in that portion of it which was not under his immediate rule. "In the year 1000 he marched into Cumberland and harried very nearly the whole of it." Even here, however, his unrivalled genius for failure showed itself. His ships—the remnant probably of those collected in the previous year—were to have met him at Chester and co-operated in his campaign. This they failed to do, but "they sailed to the Isle of Man and ravaged there." These last words throw a little light on what is otherwise not only an obscure but an utterly purposeless proceeding. We know from other sources that Man was an island stronghold of the Norse pirates, and there are, as we have seen, indications that from thence a stream of Scandinavian settlers passed into Cumberland towards the close of the tenth century. It is true that Norse rather than Danish seems to have been the character of the settlement in the Isle of Man, but as the Scandinavian sea-rovers were still acting generally in concert against the English, this fact need not prevent us from seeing in this Cumbrian raid an act of energy on Ethelred's part against the Danish invaders.

* Freeman, Hist. of Norm. Conq., i., 279.

*****

Two strangely contrasted events, a marriage and a massacre, fill up the record for 1002. There had been apparently some desultory warfare between Ethelred and Richard the Good, son of Richard the Fearless, duke of Normandy. An expedition against the Cotentin, the western horn of Normandy, had proved, like many of Ethelred's undertakings, unsuccessful, and now the English king, his first wife being dead, in order to strengthen himself by a foreign alliance, sued for and obtained the hand of Richard's sister Emma in marriage. The bride was brought over to England with much pomp in the spring of 1002 by the magnates of the realm who had been sent to escort her. An attempt was made to change her name to the Saxon Aelfgyfu (Elgiva), but the Norman "Emma" is that by which she has ever been known in history. She bore to Ethelred two sons, Alfred and Edward (the Confessor). Queen Emma, who was known as the "gemma Normannorum," was probably beautiful after the fair type of her Scandinavian ancestors, but her character is not an attractive one, and indirectly her connexion with the royal family of Wessex wrought much harm to England. Henry of Huntingdon (writing of course after the Norman conquest) makes the extraordinary statement that "from this union of an English king with the daughter of a Norman duke, the Normans justly, according to the law of nations, challenged and obtained possession of the English land." He goes on to say, however, that a certain man of God had prophesied that because of the enormous crimes of the English people, their addiction to murder, treason, drunkenness, and neglect of the house of the Lord, "an unlooked-for dominion should come upon them from France, and even the nation of the Scots, whom they held most vile, should also rule over them to their deserved confusion."

After narrating the payment of the third gafol to the Danes (24,000 pounds), the chronicler proceeds: "In that year the king ordered all the Danish men who were in England to be slain on St. Bricius' Day, November 13, because the king was informed that they wished to plot against his life and afterwards against the lives of all his witan, and so to have the kingdom easily for themselves." A most extraordinary statement is this, describing an event even more unintelligible than the other events in this inexplicable reign. The alleged murder of all Danish men reminds us of the Sicilian Vespers, but the historical parallel may be deceptive.

The Chronicle speaks only of the murder of "Danish men"; the statements of later Chronicles extending the massacre to women and children are probably oratorical amplifications. Henry of Huntingdon gives us an interesting personal touch when he says: "In our boyhood we heard from some very ancient men that the aforesaid king sent letters to each city, according to which the English on the same day and hour, either hewed down the unsuspecting Danes with their swords or, having suddenly arrested them, burned them with fire." Notwithstanding statements like this, it may be safely asserted that all the thousands of Danish men who were scattered over England, in the Danelaw and elsewhere, did not perish on St. Brice's Day. Nor is this probably the Chronicle's meaning. We learn from another version of the Chronicle that in the previous year (1001) Pallig, whom we know to have been a Danish jarl and brother-in-law of King Sweyn, "fell off from Ethelred, contrary to all the assurances that he had given him, although the king had well gifted him with villages and gold and silver"; and that he had joined the Danes who were invading Devonshire. On the somewhat doubtful authority of William of Malmesbury we are assured that this Pallig, his wife and child were killed in the massacre. This may suggest to us that the real character of the event of St. Brice's Day was a kind of coup d'état; the summary and treacherous execution of all the Danes who of recent years had flocked into Wessex and taken service in the court and camp of Ethelred. Even so, the deed was sufficiently atrocious, but not impossible, as the murder of all the Danes on English soil would certainly have been.

*****

Passing over some important events, among them the brave defence of East Anglia by its ealdorman Ulfcytel ("No worse hand-play did the Danes ever meet with from Englishmen than that which Ulfcytel gave them"), we come to the year 1008, for which the Chronicle gives us the following important but perplexing entry: "Now the king bade that through all England men should regularly build ships, that is for 300 hides ... and for 10 hides a skiff, and for 8 hides a helmet and coat of mail."

There is evidently something omitted in this sentence, and it is generally agreed that the "Worcester" version of the Chronicle which fills up the lacuna with the words "one great ship" has much to recommend it, though the scribe himself may not have understood correctly the meaning of the passage. We may perhaps draw from it this conclusion, that in each county every unit of three hundred hides was called upon to furnish one large warship; the owner of ten hides (1,200 acres?) a light skiff not much bigger than a boat, the owner of eight hides (960 acres?) a helmet and a coat of mail. Whatever difficulty there may be in this obscure passage, it is interesting to note that we have here the origin of "ship-money." The great case of Rex v. Hampden in the Exchequer Chamber was connected by a distinct chain of causation with the Danish sea-rovers' movements in the early years of the eleventh century. As usual, these large preparations came to nothing, although (says the chronicler) "as the books tell us, never in no king's day were so many ships seen in England as were now gathered together at Sandwich." But domestic dissension and one man's treachery ruined all (1009).

The new traitor who now emerges from obscurity, and for the next ten years exercises a malign influence on England's fortunes, is Edric Streona, who was in 1007 set over Mercia as ealdorman. Florence of Worcester ascribes to him the murder of Elfhelm, ealdorman of Northumbria, in a forest near Shrewsbury, and thus draws his general character: "The aforesaid Edric, son of Ethelric, was a man of low origin, whose tongue had procured for him riches and rank, clever in wit, pleasant in speech, but one who surpassed all the men of his time in envy, faithlessness and cruelty." We have here a more dangerous type of man than his predecessor Elfric; a man who will not be afraid to lead armies to battle, though it may be to their deliberately planned ruin; a man who will have the courage to plot and execute crimes which would have been too much for the delicate digestion of Elfric. Edric had a large band of brothers, who no doubt shared the profits and the enmities which attended his sudden elevation. One of these named Brihtric accused a nobleman named Child Wulfnoth to the king, evidently hoping to profit by the forfeiture of his estates. Thus driven into rebellion, Wulfnoth took to piracy, persuaded twenty ships' crews out of the king's fleet to join him, and ravaged the southern coast like a Dane. Brihtric with eighty ships went forth against him, boasting that he would bring back Wulfnoth, alive or dead, but he was overtaken by a terrible storm which battered and thrashed the ships and drove many of them on shore. These Brihtric burned; the others were with difficulty conveyed up the Thames to London. Thus, through the intrigues of one man, Edric's brother, did the great naval force waste its energies on an inglorious civil war, "and we had not," says the chronicler, "the happiness nor the honour that we hoped to derive from an efficient navy any more than in previous years." Of course now, when "the immense hostile army came to Sandwich, there were no ships to meet it." The Danes landed in Kent, besieged Canterbury, were bought off by a special local gafol of 3,000 pounds, and marched on into Berkshire, harrying and burning. For once Ethelred showed some energy, made a levy en masse of his people, outmarched the Danes and was on the point of cutting off their retreat to their ships. The English peasant soldiers of the fyrd were keen to attack them and avenge the burning of their homesteads and the slaughter of their brethren, "but it was all hindered, now as ever, by Edric the ealdorman." In November the invaders took up their winter quarters in Kent, drawing their supplies from the counties on both sides of the Thames, "and many a time they attacked the town of London. But God be thanked, she yet stands sound and well, and they have ever fared ill before her walls."

*****

The years 1011 and 1012 were made sadly memorable by the successful siege of Canterbury and the murder of its archbishop. The siege lasted from September 8 to 29, and it is hinted that it would not so soon have ended but for the treason of Elfmaer, Abbot of St. Augustine's, whose life had once been saved by the archbishop whom he now betrayed. This archbishop was Elfheah or Alphege, whom we met with seventeen years before when he was sent, as bishop of Winchester, to negotiate with Olaf Tryggvason. He had been for six years archbishop of Canterbury, when he had to witness the capture of the hitherto inviolate city of St. Augustine by the pagans. Besides the archbishop, other great persons, a king's reeve, a bishop and an abbess were taken prisoners, but these latter seem to have been allowed to ransom themselves. "Abbot Elfmaer"—significant entry—"was suffered to depart." The Danes searched the city through and through; and the spoil collected and the ransoms paid doubtless made this raid one of the most profitable of their speculations. The archbishop, however, was a perplexing prize. His captors had formed extravagant ideas of what an archbishop's ransom ought to be, and when they named their price, the archbishop would not hear of his flock being subjected for his sake to such a terrible exaction; and not only would do nothing himself, but positively forbade all the faithful to take any steps towards procuring his ransom.

Seven months was the venerable captive kept in the Danish camp, while the fruitless negotiations went on. At last on April 19, 1012, when the Danes were all excited by the arrival of the largest gafol that Ethelred had yet paid them, a gafol amounting to 48,000 pounds weight of silver; and when their hearts were also merry with wine brought from the shores of the Mediterranean, the archbishop was brought forth from his prison. The rude tribunal before which he was brought bore a name long afterwards well known in England: it was called "the hustings." The time was Saturday evening, the eve of the first Sunday after Easter; the scene strangely dissonant with the many peaceful vespers of the archbishop's past. The drunken barbarians, singing perchance some of their fathers' rude war-songs, began to pelt the aged prisoner with the bones left over from their banquet, with the skulls of the oxen which they had slaughtered. Even so in Valhalla, according to the Viking mythology, had the gods amused themselves by pelting the invulnerable Balder with stones and other missiles, until the blind Hoder, inspired by mischief-working Loki, hurled the fatal mistletoe, which alone had power to deprive him of life. The brutal game went on and the air was filled with the drunken laughter of the barbarians at the old man's misery. At last one of their number named Thrum, who had been confirmed by the archbishop only the day before, with kind cruelty clave his head with a battle-axe. "He fell down dead with the blow and his holy blood was spilled upon the earth, but his saintly soul went forth into God's kingdom." The martyrdom, for such in truth it was, took place at Greenwich. Next day the barbarians suffered the saint's body to be removed to London, where it was received with all reverence by the bishop and burghers of the city, as well as by the bishop of Dorchester, and by them deposited in St. Paul's cathedral. "And there," says the Chronicle, "does God now show forth the wonder-working power of the holy martyr." The translation of the remains to Canterbury will be described in a future chapter. Under the altered form of Saint Alphege, the name of the murdered archbishop still appears in the calendar of the English Church, which commemorates the day of his martyrdom, April the 19th.

*****

Up to this point the Danish invasions of this period have been mere plundering and blackmailing raids, apparently with no thought of permanent conquest. Had that been the aim of the sea-rovers, all this cruel burning and slaughtering would have been beside the mark: for why should a conqueror utterly ruin a land which he meant to rule? In 1013, however, a change came over the character of the invasions. They became part of a regular scheme of conquest; and the old Danish king who brought with him Canute,* his son, determined to make the country his own. Sweyn landed in the estuary of the Humber: Northumbria, Lindsey and the Five Boroughs submitted to him and gave him hostages, whom he sent to the ships to be kept under his son's guardianship. He ordered the inhabitants to feed and mount his soldiers; he restored the full Danish dominion over all the country beyond the Watling Street as it existed in the darkest years of the ninth century. He then crossed the Watling Street, harrying the midland counties. Oxford submitted, so did Winchester. He marched against London, losing many of his foolhardy soldiers in crossing the Thames. London as usual made a brave defence. Ethelred was there, and with Ethelred a strange ally, none other than Thurkill the Dane who had commanded the invading army in 1009. It was Thurkill's men who had captured Canterbury and murderously pelted the holy Elfheah; but according to one contemporary authority Thurkill himself had tried to save him, offering the murderers all his treasures, "except only his ship," if they would but be merciful. Possibly the remembrance of that scene, or some lessons in Christianity which he may have learned from the captive archbishop, induced him now to lower the Raven-banner and take service under Ethelred. Possibly, too, it was this notable defection which caused Sweyn to come over in person and pluck the ripe fruit, lest it should fall into the hands of one of his subjects.

The Danish king next moved westward to Bath, and received the submission of that ancient city and of all the western thegns, each one of whom had to give hostages, who were sent like the others to the Humber to be kept under Canute's guardianship. Even the brave citizens of London saw that it was useless further to prolong the contest.

* The name of this well-known historical personage was undoubtedly Knut or Cnut. It is so written both in the Scandinavian Sagas and in the English Chronicle. But the Latinised form Canutus preserves the remembrance of a helping vowel which may have been often used, even by contemporaries, at least in England. At this day the Danish name Knothe is always pronounced Kinnoté in Northumberland. The important point is to remember that the accent is on the last syllable: Canúte, not Cánute.

They submitted, gave hostages and joined with the rest of England in acknowledging Sweyn as "full king." There are indications that this great revolution was prompted not merely by the desire to end in any manner the dreadful period of Danish ravagings, but also by utter disgust at the character of Ethelred, who seems to have been not merely incapable but also lustful and cruel. In the years which we have been traversing, there are some strange entries in the Chronicle recording executions, blindings, confiscations, no doubt inflicted at the command of Ethelred; and William of Malmesbury, in quoting a letter from Thurkill to Sweyn, makes him thus describe the condition of England and her king. "The land is a fair land and a rich, but the king snores. Devoted to women and wine, he thinks of everything rather than war, and this makes him hateful to his subjects and ridiculous to foreigners. The generals are all jealous of one another: the country-folk are weak, and fly from the field at the first crash of battle." This letter is probably not authentic, but its words show what was the traditional character of "the redeless king."

Recognising that his sceptre was broken, Ethelred sent the Lady Emma and her two sons across the sea to her brother in Normandy. He himself lingered for a while, first on shipboard in the Thames; then in the Isle of Wight, where he seems to have spent his Christmas; and then he too escaped to "Richard's Land," as the chroniclers call the duchy of Normandy. Thus then had Sweyn, the heathen and the parricide, king of Denmark by inheritance and of England by conquest, reached the summit of his earthly ambition: and having reached it, he was speedily removed by death. According to the legend related by Symeon of Durham, his death was a punishment for his contemptuous behaviour towards St. Edmund of East Anglia. Often had he spoken in a disrespectful manner of this martyred king, declaring that his saintship was an idle tale; and, what was more serious, he had announced to the monks of St. Edmundsbury that unless by a certain day a heavy tax which he had laid upon their monastery was paid, he would march thither with his men, give the sanctuary to the flames and put its inmates to death with a variety of torments. On the very day before his threatened expedition he was sitting on his horse at Gainsborough surrounded by the armed assembly of his warriors. Suddenly he cried out, "Help me, comrades! help! yonder is Saint Edmund who is coming to slay me." While he was thus speaking, an unseen hand transfixed him with a spear: he fell from his war-horse and died at nightfall in great agony. Such is the legend. The Chronicle records only the simple fact that "at Candlemas on February 3, 1014, Sweyn ended his days, and all the fleet chose Cnut for their king." The dead monarch seems to have reigned as "full king" over England for barely a month after the flight of Ethelred. His death led to a sudden shifting of the scene.

*****

"Then all the witan, lay and clerical, resolved that they would send for King Ethelred, and they said that no lord should be dearer to them than their natural born lord, if only he would govern more righteously than he had done aforetime. Then the king sent hither his son Edward with his messengers, and bade greeting to all his people, and said that he would be to them a gracious lord and would amend all the things of which they complained, and that everything which they had done or said against him should be forgiven, on condition that they would all firmly and loyally adhere to him. Thus was full friendship made fast between them with word and pledge on either side; and they pronounced every Danish king outlawed from England for ever. Then came King Ethelred in spring-tide home to his own people, and gladly was he received by all of them."

It was an easy matter for the witan to declare every Danish king an outlaw; to expel the young and vigorous Canute from the kingdom was a very different affair. At this time the Dane's strongest position was in Lincolnshire, his naval base of operations being still doubtless the estuary of the Humber. The men of Lindsey had resorted to him at Gainsborough, and had undertaken to supply him with horses and to go forth together with him and harry. But now when Ethelred with "a full fyrd" appeared in Lincolnshire, Canute who was not ready for fight, stole away to his ships and sailed forth from the Humber, leaving "the poor folk whom he had deceived" to their king's vengeance. Ethelred then "harried and burned and slew every man who could be got at." Evidently the long years of war had thoroughly brutalised both the combatants. Canute, enraged probably by the proceedings of the witan, sailed round to Sandwich, and there landed the luckless hostages who had been delivered to his father by the northern shires in 1013. He chopped off their hands and noses and then, apparently, let them return to their homes. This savage mutilation is the greatest piece of barbarity that stands recorded against him. Meanwhile the portion of the fleet which Thurkill commanded lay at Greenwich, and from thence, though professing to support the cause of Ethelred, ravaged the country as much as they pleased. Thus for the unhappy peasants there was little to choose between Thurkill and Canute.

In the following year, 1015, there was a great meeting of the witan at Oxford, and here Edric, of whose treasons we have lately heard but little, distinguished himself by a characteristic piece of villainy. There were two thegns, probably brothers, named Sigeferth and Morcar, men with large estates and holding highest rank in the Five, or as they were now called, the Seven Boroughs (York and Chester were perhaps the two new additions to the old group). These men Edric, when he met them at the witenagemot, invited into his chamber and there he treacherously slew them. According to the somewhat doubtful story of William of Malmesbury, he had first made their henchmen drunk, and then when they, too late, sought to avenge their lords, Edric's followers overpowered them, chased them into the church of St. Frideswide and slew them there. The king was evidently consenting to the death of these men, and purposed to bestow their broad lands on their murderer. But now came a strange overturn. Sigeferth's widow had been by royal order conveyed to Malmesbury, probably with the intention of immuring her in the convent. Thither also, after a short interval, went the king's son, the Etheling Edmund Ironside, whom we now hear of for the first time, but who was to be the protagonist in the next two years' combat. He wooed the widow of Sigeferth; he perhaps promised to take vengeance on her husband's murderers; he married her, contrary to the king's command, and then early in September he marched to the Seven Boroughs, presented himself as the avenger of the murdered thegns and the heir of one of them, made himself master of all their domains and received the submission of their people.

The king was now lying at Cosham,* stricken with mortal sickness, and could exercise little influence on the course of events. The hopes of the nation must have all rested on Edmund, who certainly showed in these two years courage and activity, though he may have inherited some of his father's incapacity for reading the characters of men. Thus, notwithstanding the breach between them, which he should have known to be deadly, he accepted the offered help of Edric Streona who repaired to his standard in the north, only to exercise his usual paralysing influence on the army, and then deserted to Canute, inducing the crews of the forty ships at Greenwich to follow his example.

England was now, in 1016, divided in a fashion not seen before. All

* In Hampshire, near Portsmouth.

Wessex was submissive to Canute and gave him horses and hostages, while the district of the Seven Boroughs and probably the whole of Northumbria went with Edmund, heir by marriage of the influence of Sigeferth. He summoned the Mercian fyrd to his standard, but the men replied, curiously enough, that "it did not please them to go forth, unless the king were with them, and they had the support of the burgesses of London." Apparently the Etheling Edmund was more than half suspected of being a rebel against his father, and in the strange confusion of the strife the approval of the brave citizens of London was the only irrefragable sign and seal of rightful lordship. With some difficulty the sick king was brought from London, where he then abode, to the northern fyrd, but being alarmed by rumours of a conspiracy against his life, he quitted the camp and returned to London. "Thus the summoning of the fyrd availed nothing more than it had ever done before."

The junction of Edmund's forces with those of Uhtred, earl of Northumbria, might seem to promise more effectual resistance to the foreigner. Practically, however, it resulted in nothing more than a series of harryings in Shropshire, Staffordshire and Cheshire, from which Uhtred was suddenly recalled by the tidings that Canute had marched northwards and was already nearing York. Uhtred abandoned his harrying and hastened to meet the enemy, but in presence of Canute's superior force was obliged to submit, acknowledge the Dane as his king, and give hostages. The submission availed him naught. After this surrender he and another powerful Northumbrian named Thurcytel were put to death by Canute. This crime also was attributed to the malign influence of Edric Streona. The struggle now centred round London. There was the sick king; thither his son Edmund went to meet him. Thither was Canute sailing with his ships, but ere he arrived, an enemy stronger than he had found entrance. On April 23, 1016, King Ethelred died, and this dreariest of all English reigns came to an end. Old as Ethelred seems to us by reason of the evils which he had so long inflicted on his country, he was still only in the forty-ninth year of his age.

*****

"After the death of Ethelred, all the witan that were in London and the citizens chose EDMUND for king, and he boldly defended his kingdom while his time was," which was only for seven months. Canute, who was obstinately set on the conquest of London, made a canal on the south side of the Thames and passed his ships through it, so as to bring them into the main stream above the strongly defended bridge. After two battles in Somerset and Wilts the English king came to the help of the citizens and defeated the Danes at Brentford. His army, however, was somewhat lacking in discipline, for "many English folk were drowned in the river through their own carelessness, pushing on beyond the main body of the fyrd in the hope of taking booty." In the battles which followed on the Orwell, in Mercia, in the island of Sheppey, Edmund was generally victorious; but all such success was counterbalanced by the disastrous return of Edric to the English army and by Edmund's acceptance of his help. "Never was worse counsel adopted than that." The last and greatest of the long series of battles was fought at Assandune, in the flats of Essex between the Thames and the estuary of the Crouch. Here, after a long and fierce encounter, victory fell to the Danes, it is said through the treachery of Edric, who was the first to take flight and who spread panic through the English ranks by displaying a severed head, which, he shouted, was the head of Edmund Ironside. In this battle fell the old traitor Elfric and a very different man, the brave East Anglian Ulfcytel, besides many other thegns. There, in fact, fell the flower of the English manhood.

It seemed clear that neither of the opposing forces could utterly crush the other. By the mediation of Edric a meeting was arranged between the two kings at Olney, an island in the Severn not far from Gloucester. A payment, we are not told of what amount, was made to the Danish army, and the kingdom was divided between the combatants, Wessex to Edmund, Mercia and Northumbria to Canute. London, faithfully following the house of Cerdic, was included in the peace, and the now reconciled Danish mariners were allowed to take up their winter quarters in the city by the Thames. A peculiar relation, somewhat embellished by the fancy of later historians, seems to have been established between the two young partners in the kingdom. Brotherhood in arms was perhaps sworn to between them; it is alleged that the survivor of the twain was assured of the inheritance of his partner. Whatever may have been the precise nature of the tie, it was soon dissolved. On November 30, 1016, Edmund Ironside "fared forth," and was buried by the side of his grandfather, Edgar, at Glastonbury. He was only about twenty-three years of age. A death so opportune for the purposes of Canute and his followers naturally arouses suspicion. Later historians had no hesitation in making

Edric the murderer. There is also something in the after-life of Canute which looks like remorse for some great crime committed against his brother-king. On the other hand it is but justice to say that there is no hint of foul play in any contemporary authority; and the death of the young king may perhaps be accounted for by the fearful labours and anxieties of his last two years of warring and reigning.

The period which we have lately traversed is one of those dreary times which a patriotic historian would gladly blot out from the annals of England, and one is half inclined to resent the exceptional fulness of detail with which it is treated in the Saxon Chronicle. Yet it is a time which the student of our social history cannot afford to overlook. If the thirty years' war in the seventeenth century left deep scars on the face of Germany, which were still visible after the lapse of two hundred years, we must surely believe that the wounds inflicted by the incessant ravages and harryings of the Danes for more than thirty years were also deep and long lasting. The utter demoralisation of king and people, the apparent rottenness of the body politic, as manifested in the course of the struggle, abate much of our first feeling of patriotic regret for the Norman conquest, suggesting as they do the reflection that these Saxons, if left to themselves, would never have made a strong and stable nation. Much as we condemn the conduct of Ethelred, we may be inclined to conjecture that all the mischief was not wrought in his reign. We should perhaps do wisely in mistrusting a good deal that is told us about the glory and the greatness of the reign of Edgar. After all, it was in that king's days that traitors such as Elfric and Edric were growing up into maturity. Had Edgar left the country a really strong, well-organised state, it could hardly have gone down so speedily before the assaults of the sea-rovers. Probably the new and nobler life breathed into the Saxon people by the great Alfred lasted during the reigns of Edward and Athelstan and not much longer.

XXIII.

CANUTE AND HIS SONS

When in 1016 Edmund Ironside died, there could be little question that CANUTE must be sole King of England. It was true that Edmund had left two sons, Edmund and Edward, but they were mere babes and it was no time for a protracted regency. In the older generation, of the numerous progeny of the redeless Ethelred (nine sons and six daughters), there were still left only three whose claims could deserve consideration. These were Edwy, the son of his first marriage, and two boys, Alfred and Edward, sons of Emma. These latter, however, besides the disadvantage of their youth—they cannot have been more than twelve years of age—were still absent from England, at the court of their uncle Richard, Duke of Normandy. They seem therefore to have been left altogether out of the reckoning at this juncture, though one of them a generation later was to ascend the throne of England, and to be known under the name of Edward the Confessor. There remained, therefore, as claimant, of the immediate family of Ethelred, only his elder son, Edwy, who was probably in his twentieth year, or thereabouts, but who seems to have borne a high character for wisdom and prudence. But there was another shadowy competitor for the crown who also bore the name of Edwy, with the strange epithet, "King of the Churls." In our complete ignorance of this man's previous history we can only guess from whence he emerged. One such guess is that he claimed to be descended from his namesake, the brother of Edgar, and that, having put himself forward as champion of the free tillers of the soil (a class doubtless sorely suffering from thirty years of anarchy), he was called in derision "King of the Ceorls." However this may be, neither Edwy could stand for a moment against the might of the young Dane, already the acknowledged sovereign of all England north of the Thames, and with the terrible "army" at his back, ready at the giving of a signal to break loose from their winter quarters and resume their terrible harryings of the land. Canute had apparently no difficulty in decreeing that both the Edwys should be banished the realm, nor shortly after in putting the son of Ethelred to death.

The two infant sons of Edmund Ironside were sent by Canute to the King of Sweden, it is said with a request that they might be quietly put out of the way. The Swedish king, however, declined to make himself the Dane's executioner, and passed the children on to the King of Hungary. Forty years after our present date, one of them having returned to England became, not indeed himself a king, but father of a Scottish queen, and ancestor, through her, of many generations of English sovereigns. As to the manner in which Canute acquired the power of dealing thus summarily with the descendants of Cerdic, there is some uncertainty. One version of the Chronicle says that he was "chosen to be King of all England," and so far confirms the elaborate account of Florence of Worcester. This author says that there was a great meeting of the witan in London, and that Canute interrogated them as to the nature of the agreement made between him and Edmund Ironside at Olney, whereof they had all been witnesses. "Was anything then said about the right of brothers or sons to succeed Edmund in Wessex, if he should die in Canute's lifetime?" Thus interrogated, they said that they knew for certain that Edmund destined no portion of his kingdom for his brothers, either in his lifetime or after his death, but that he looked to Canute as the future helper and protector of his sons till they should reach the age of kingship. "But herein they called God to witness of a lie," hoping to win the king's favour thereby. According to this story, Canute's election to the throne by the witan of London was the result of hard swearing; but the Scandinavian authorities assert, and some modern historians believe, that the exclusion of Edmund's brothers from the succession was really part of the compact of Olney. The question must probably be left unsettled. What is not doubtful is the full and undisputed power which the young Danish conqueror ever thereafter wielded in England, and the peace and comparative prosperity which for near twenty years she enjoyed under his sway. Wisely distrustful of his own ability to direct personally the details of government throughout the whole kingdom, Canute at once divided it into five districts, four of which he placed under rulers with delegated power. East Anglia he placed under the government of Thurkill the Dane, once the ally of Ethelred, but now his own henchman. What was once Deira was assigned to Yric or Eric, also a Dane, who seems, as before, to have made York his capital. In old Bernicia English lords of the family of Uhtred still held sway. Mercia was handed over to the notorious Edric Streona, while Wessex, the heart and centre of Anglo-Saxon monarchy, was reserved for Canute's own especial rule. Here, and not in any of the Scandinavian lands across the sea, he resolved to make his home for the remainder of his life. All these great lords-lieutenant (as we should call them) were probably called earls, a title copied from the Danish jarl which was now gradually supplanting the old English ealdorman.

Two of these newly appointed earls did not long enjoy their dignities. In 1017 the old traitor Edric Streona was put to death by Canute: "most justly," says the latest recension of the Chronicles. Florence of Worcester asserts that "Canute ordered him to be killed within the palace, because he feared that he might one day be circumvented by his plots, as had often been the fate of his former lords, Ethelred and Edmund." He may have been, as he is depicted in the Chronicle, one of the vilest of men, or he may have been merely a great opportunist, the Talleyrand or the Sunderland of a shifting and difficult period; but even so, it is hard for a man of that stamp to convince his new employer that he has really changed front for the last time. Thurkill of East Anglia fell into disgrace in 1021 and was banished. After two years he was restored to favour, yet not brought back to England, but entrusted with the regency of Denmark. There is some evidence that he, like Edric, had married a daughter of Ethelred; and there is reason to suppose that not only the sons, but even the sons-in-law, of the late king were viewed with suspicion by Canute.*

In the first year of his reign, on July 31, 1017, the young Danish king, now about twenty-two years of age, took to wife Emma of Normandy, widow of Ethelred, and probably thirteen years his senior. As to the motives for this somewhat surprising marriage we have no sufficient information. It may have been due to a politic desire to secure the friendship of Normandy; it may have been Canute's wish to present to his English subjects an appearance of continuity in the domestic life of the palace of Winchester; or there may have been—who knows?—a romantic passion engendered when the future bride and bridegroom met during the negotiations after the siege of London.† The new queen certainly seems to have faithfully complied with the spirit of the Scriptural precept about

* This is Freeman's suggestion, Norman Conquest, i., 415.

† This also is Freeman's suggestion (u.s., i., 411).

the bride's forgetting of former ties, but need she also have forgotten the children of her former marriage? The son whom she bore to Canute, and who was named Harthacnut, was the object of her fondest affection. Canute evidently ousted the memory of the inglorious Ethelred, whose sons Alfred and Edward lingered on at their uncle's court, apparently forgotten by their mother, and with no effort on her part to bring about their return from exile.

It was perhaps only a coincidence, though an unfortunate one, that the second marriage of Emma, like her first, was accompanied, if not by a massacre, by a considerable sacrifice of human life. In 1017 Canute ordered the execution not only of Edwy, of the seed royal, and of Edric the traitor, but of "Northman, son of Leofwine the ealdorman, and Ethelweard, son of Ethelmaer the Fat, and Brihtric, son of Elfheah in Devonshire." The last name is for us meaningless: Ethelweard is interesting as denoting the grandson of Ethelweard the Chronicler, the "Patrician," as he calls himself; the man of royal descent and of pompous diction. The name of Northman, son of Leofwine, deserves further notice as being our first introduction to a family which was to play an important part in the next half-century of English history. For five generations, since the very beginning of the eighth century, the family of Leofwine had borne a high place in the kingdom of Mercia. This Leofwine himself in 997 signed charters as dux, that is ealdorman, of the province of the Hwiccas. It was his son Northman who now, we know not on what pretext or under what cloud of suspicion, was put to death by Canute. The king's wrath seems not to have extended to the other members of Northman's family; for his father Leofwine at once received the earldom of Mercia, vacated by the death of Edric, and there are some indications that his son Leofric received a minor earldom, possibly that of Chester, which may have been previously held by the slain Northman.*

About the same time as the family of Leofwine, a rival family, one which was to engrave its name yet more deeply on the pages of English history, begins to make its appearance, not yet indeed in the Chronicles, but in those invaluable charters which show us by the names of the attesting witnesses who at any given period were the most prominent personages in the English court. Godwine, son of Wulfnoth, is a man over whose ancestry there hangs a cloud of mystery, the result partly of the poverty of Anglo-Saxon nomenclature, which makes it often difficult to identify

* See Freeman, u.s., i., 737–40.

the particular Wulfnoth or Edric or Ethelweard of whom we are in quest. There are stories about him of a romantic kind, according to which he, as a cowherd's son, had the good fortune to meet a king or an earl who had lost his way after one of the battles between Canute and Edmund; gave him a night's shelter, and was rewarded by patronage which enabled the future Earl Godwine to get his foot planted on the first rung of the official ladder. For these stories, which we find chiefly in chroniclers of a much later age, there appears to be no sufficient foundation. On the whole it seems probable that he was the offspring neither of a thegn nor of a theow, but sprang from some middle stratum of Anglo-Saxon society. Whatever his origin may have been, he was evidently a man of energy and capacity, and he rose rapidly in the favour of Canute, who was perhaps glad to obtain the services of new men, neither suspected of too strong an attachment to their former master, Ethelred, nor branded with the shame of his betrayal. Already, in 1018, he had the rank of earl, of what district we are not informed. He is said to have accompanied Canute in 1019 on a visit which he paid to Denmark; and to have distinguished himself in a war against the Wends, probably in Pomerania, and on his return to England he was raised to the high and novel position of Earl of the West Saxons. Up to this time the kings of Cerdic's line, while ruling other parts of England by ealdormen or earls, had kept Wessex, the cradle of their dynasty, under their own personal control: and their example was followed by Canute himself at the beginning of his reign. He had now, however, by the death of his obscure and contemptible brother Harold (1016), become the wearer of the Danish crown; and possibly cherishing visions of other and more widely reaching Scandinavian conquests, he determined to keep his hands free from the mere routine of government even in royal Wessex, and therefore handed that province over to the administration of his young and loyal henchman, Godwine. About the same time he further secured the new earl's attachment to the Danish dynasty by marrying him to Gytha, daughter of his cousin, Thurgils Sprakalegg, and sister of his own brother-in-law, Ulf the Jarl. Such a connexion brought the new man, Godwine, very close to Danish royalty. It is possible* that, during all the earlier part of his career, Earl Godwine seemed to the English people almost more of a Dane than a Saxon.

The country was now so tranquilly settling down under Canute's rule that he felt himself able to dispense with the presence of "the army."

* As suggested by J. R. Green, Conquest of England, 479.

To him, as the chosen and anointed ruler of England, the marches and counter-marches, the harryings and the burnings of these fierce "sea-people" would be as little agreeable as to Alfred or Ethelred. One last and fearfully heavy gafol, no less than 72,000 pounds of silver, the equivalent probably of £1,500,000 sterling in our day, had to be raised and paid them, besides a further sum of 10,500 pounds, paid by the citizens of London alone. The army then, in 1018, returned to Denmark, only forty ships and their crews remaining with their peacefully triumphant king. Everything showed Canute's desire to banish the memories of rapine and bloodshed which for so many years had been gathering round his father's name and his own. He is said by one writer to have erected churches on all his battle-fields: he certainly did so (in 1020) on the bloodiest of them all, on Assandune. Earl Thurkill (not yet fallen into disgrace) with the archbishop of York, and many bishops, abbots and monks, joined in hallowing the minster there erected, a ceremony in which some have seen not only a commemoration of Canute's "crowning mercy" but also an act of reparation for some share, direct or indirect, in the death of his Iron-sided rival. Another object of his devotion was East Anglian Edmund, who had been so barbarously done to death by Ingwar and Hubba. To this saint, it may be remembered, old Sweyn was said to have had a particular aversion, and from his ghostly apparition he was believed to have received his death-stroke. To appease the spirit of this royal martyr was now one of Canute's most cherished desires. He reverenced his memory with a devotion as especial as his father's hatred, and he, apparently, first gave to the great monastery of St. Edmundsbury that character of magnificence which distinguished it for so many centuries and gave it a place in the foremost rank of English sanctuaries.

In the seventh year of the new reign, 1023, Canute made the greatest of all reparations, that to the memory of the good archbishop whom drunken Danish seamen had brutally slain. The body of St. Alphege had been for some eleven years resting in St. Paul's Church at London. It was more fitting that it should be laid in his own metropolitan church of Canterbury, and thither accordingly it was translated by the king's orders. The delight with which Englishmen saw this tardy reparation to their dead countryman's memory, rendered by a Danish king, shines forth in the enthusiastic pages of the Chronicle. The writer describes how "by full leave" of the king, archbishop Ethelnoth and Bryhtwine, bishop of Sherborne, took up the body from the tomb; how "the glorious king and the archbishop and suffragan bishops and earls and a great multitude, clerical and lay, carried on a ship St. Alphege's holy body over the Thames to Southwark, and committed the holy martyr to the care of Ethelnoth and his companions, who then with a goodly band and with winsome joy bare him to Rochester. Then on the third day came the Lady Emma with her kingly bairn Harthacnut [aged five], and they all with great pomp and gladness and singing of psalms bare the holy archbishop into Canterbury." The whole proceedings occupied seven days, and on June 15, 1023, the martyr's body was finally deposited on the north side of the altar in Christ Church.

In like manner as Canute had honoured the memory of St. Edmund of East Anglia and St. Alphege of Canterbury, is he said to have dealt with the sepulchre of Edmund Ironside at Glastonbury. Towards the end of his reign he determined (says William of Malmesbury in his classical style) "to visit the Manes of him whom he was wont to call his brother Edmund. Having offered up his prayers, he placed upon the tomb a pallium inwoven with divers colours, representing figures of peacocks, which may still be seen there." By his side stood Ethelnoth, archbishop of Canterbury, the seventh monk who had gone forth from Glastonbury to preside over the English Church. Before leaving the venerable minster in which rested the bones of so many of his predecessors, Canute gave a charter confirming to the church of the Virgin Mary in Glastonbury all its previous privileges. This charter was said to be given "by the advice of Ethelnoth, the bishops and my nobles, for love of the heavenly kingdom, for the pardon of my crimes and the forgiveness of the sins of my brother King Edmund."

With the description of these expiatory rites our information as to the internal history of England under Canute comes to an end. This part of the Chronicle is extremely meagre, but probably its very sterility is partly an illustration of the proverb, "Happy is the nation that has no annals." After all the agonies of the Danish invasions, now that a wise and masterful Dane sat upon the English throne, the land had rest for twenty years. In external affairs Canute played an important part, which we shall have to consider in relation to (1) Scotland, (2) the Empire and the Papacy, and (3) Norway.

(1) Events of great and lasting significance took place on the Scottish border in the reign of Canute, but to understand them we must go back into the reign of his predecessor, and take up for the last time the story of the wanderings of the incorruptible body of St. Cuthbert. For 112 years

that precious relic had reposed at Chester-le-Street, but in 995 Bishop Aldhun, who had for five years presided over the diocese which still bore the name of deserted Lindisfarne, filled with fear of Danish invasions and "forewarned by a heavenly oracle," carried the body farther inland, to the abbey of Ripon. After four months it was considered safe to re-transport it to its former home; but when the bearers reached a certain place on the banks of the Wear, called Wrdelau, the holy body became immovable as a mountain and refused to be carried an inch farther. It was revealed to a monk named Eadmer that the neighbouring hill of Dunhelm, splendidly and strongly placed in the midst of a fruitful land, and overlooking the windings of a beautiful river, was meant to be the saint's next and final resting-place. Thither accordingly, with joy and gladness, the holy body was carried. The little wattled church which was erected over it was the predecessor of a noble cathedral, the grandest specimen of Norman architecture that our country can boast: and Bishop Aldhun, who lived for twenty-four years after the translation, was the first of the long line of bishops of Durham.

Almost at once we find the prelates of this see important factors in Northumbrian politics. Aldhun gave his daughter, Ecgfrida (born no doubt before he became an ecclesiastic), in marriage to "a youth of great energy and skilled in military affairs," named Uhtred, who was practically taking the management of affairs out of the hands of his father, Earl Waltheof, as that aged man, self-immured in Bamburgh, was doing naught for the defence of his country. Thus, when in 1006 Malcolm II., King of Scots, taking advantage, doubtless, of the distracted state of England during the Danish invasions, collected the whole army of Scotland, entered Northumbria, laid it waste with fire and sword, and then besieged the new city of Durham, it was Uhtred who gathered troops together and went to the help of the bishop, his father-in-law. As old Waltheof still continued inactive he, on his own responsibility, summoned the fyrd of Northumberland, joined it to that of the citizens of York, and with the large army thus collected fell on the Scottish besiegers of Durham and won a complete victory. King Malcolm only escaped with difficulty, and a multitude of his followers were slain. The anonymous chronicler* who relates these events, tells us that "the daintier heads of the slain, with their hair inwoven according to the then prevalent fashion, were by Uhtred's

* Author of the tract, De Obsessione Dunelmi, added to the history of Symeon of Durham.

orders carried to Durham, fixed on stakes, and placed at intervals round the circuit of the walls, having first been washed by four women, to each of whom he gave a cow as the reward of her labours." That little detail concerning the women's payment for their ghastly toil looks like a bit of genuine tradition.

Such was the great English victory of 1006. Now for its fatal reversal twelve years later. The victorious Uhtred, who had become in the meantime Earl of Northumbria and son-in-law of Ethelred, was, as we have seen,* put to death by order of Canute, or rather perhaps assassinated at his instigation by a private enemy, just as the struggle between the Danish and English kings was coming to a crisis. The Danish earl, Eric, whom Canute had set over Deira, and the Englishman, Eadwulf Cutel, who had succeeded to some portion of his brother Uhtred's power over Bernicia, were probably known by Malcolm to be inefficient men, not likely to combine for the common defence. In 1018, having made his preparations and formed an alliance with Eugenius the Bald, King of the Cymri of Strathclyde, Malcolm crossed the Firth of Forth and marched through Bernicia as far as the Tweed. The men of Northumbria were already disheartened by the appearance of a comet which for thirty nights had been hanging, ominous, in the midnight sky; and too truly were their forebodings justified. At Carham, a place on the southern bank of the Tweed, a little above Coldstream, almost within sight of the future battlefield of Flodden, the two armies met in fight. "Then were the whole people" (says Symeon of Durham) "from Tees to Tweed on one side, and there was an infinite multitude of Scots on the other." Malcolm's victory on this occasion was far more decisive than his defeat had been twelve years earlier. "Almost the whole English force with its leaders perished." To Aldhun, the aged Bishop of Durham, the tidings of this defeat—all the more bitter because sustained at a place which for three centuries had formed part of the patrimony of St. Cuthbert—came as an actual death-stroke. "Me miserable!" said he, "that I should have lived so long, to behold this lamentable slaughter of St. Cuthbert's men. Now, O Confessor! beloved of the Lord, if I have ever done aught pleasing in thy sight, repay me, I pray thee, by not suffering me any longer to survive thy people." His prayer was granted. After a few days he died: the first but not the last Bishop of Durham to have his life made burdensome by the incursions of the Scots.

* See supra, p. 396.

This battle of Carham, fought in the second year of Canute's reign, deserves more attention than it has generally received from English historians. It was more important than Brunanburh, we might perhaps say only a little less important than Hastings, for by it the Border between England and Scotland, which had fluctuated through many centuries, was finally fixed at its present limitary streams and mountains. Edinburgh, it is true, seems to have been lost to the Scots some sixty years before the time that we have now reached,* but the rich and beautiful country of the Lothians was only now finally abandoned by the English, "surrendered" (says the anonymous chronicler) "by the very base and cowardly Eadwulf, who feared lest the Scots should revenge upon him the death of all the men of their nation who had fallen in battle against his brother. Thus was Lothian added to the kingdom of the Scots." It was for us English a loss disastrous and irretrievable. Our only compensation is to be found in the fact that the large Anglian population thus transferred to the northern kingdom so leavened its speech, its institutions, its national character, that the Scotland of the Middle Ages was Anglian rather than Gaelic in its dominating tendencies.†

Towards the end of his reign—in 1031 according to the authority, here somewhat doubtful, of the Saxon Chronicle—"Canute went to Scotland, and the Scots' king Malcolm submitted to him and became his man, but that held only a little while. Also two other kings, Maelbaethe and Jehmarc." Of the last of these two kings we know nothing. Maelbaethe seems to be the same person as the Macbeth of Shakespeare's tragedy.‡ He was not yet a king, but obtained the Scottish crown in the year 1040 by slaying the young king Duncan, grandson and successor of Malcolm II. It will be seen that the chronicler says nothing about fighting on Canute's part. Malcolm II. seems to have bowed to the inevitable and quietly acknowledged the claim of Canute as English king to the homage of his Scottish neighbour, a claim which might mean anything or nothing according to the characters of him who demanded that homage and him who rendered it. It is interesting to observe that the author of the Heimskringla, in his account of the negotiations between Canute and St.

* In the reign of Indulph (954–962) according to a Pictish chronicle quoted by Skene, Celtic Scotland, i., 365.

† It does not appear necessary to discuss the previous question of the alleged "cession of Lothian" by Edgar, the evidence for which is very slender.

‡ As to this identification, see Skene, Celtic Scotland, i., 397, 405–6.

Olaf, King of Norway, puts into the mouth of the latter these words: "And now it has come to this, that Cnut rules over Denmark and over England, and moreover has broken a mickle deal of Scotland under his sway." The parleyings here described are supposed to have taken place five or six years before 1031, the actual date of Canute's Scottish expedition, but from traditional history such as this is, minute accuracy as to dates is not to be looked for.

(2) Towards the end of the year 1026* Canute made his memorable pilgrimage to Rome, a journey which certainly was an important event in itself, and is almost unique in the history of English royalty. It is true that Ceadwalla, Ine and Ethelwulf had made the same pilgrimage, but after Canute the next crowned English king to visit Rome was His now reigning Majesty, Edward VII. We have, unfortunately, no details of Canute's journey, but we know from foreign sources that he was present at a ceremony of high political importance, the crowning of the "Roman" Emperor Conrad II. and his Empress Gisela on Easter day, 1027.

The line of Saxon emperors, made memorable by the great deeds of the three Ottos, came to an end in 1024 on the death of the ascetic emperor, St. Henry II. The dukes, counts and bishops of the empire, assembled under the open sky on the meadows of Kamba, after some debate chose as his successor Conrad the Salic, a nobleman of Franconia, that beautiful land watered by the Main which now forms the northern half of the kingdom of Bavaria. The dynasty inaugurated by his election lasted for another century (1024–1125), and then gave place to the nearly allied Hohenstauffens of Swabia. This Franconian dynasty it was which, under three emperors bearing the name of Henry, fought with the Papacy the stubborn fight of the Investitures, which "went to Canossa" and warred with Hildebrand. Conrad, the new emperor, was a strong, masterful, knightly man. The pope who crowned him and before whom Canute kneeled in reverence, was John XIX., one of the series of cadets of the house of Tusculum whom the counts of that little hill-fortress intruded for half a century on the chair of St. Peter. But though this pope's elevation was sudden and irregular—the same day saw him a layman, prefect of the city, and pope—he seems to have borne a respectable character, quite unlike that of his nephew and successor, the dissolute lad who

* Certainly not 1031, as stated in the Chronicle. Canute's presence at Conrad's coronation makes this date impossible. So considerable an error throws doubt on the chronological accuracy of, at any rate, this part of the Chronicle.

took the name of Benedict IX. (1033–1046). No doubt the aristocratic count-pope bore himself with becoming dignity in the solemn ceremony of the emperor's coronation, which was graced by the presence of two sovereign princes, our own Canute (the splendour of whose retinue and the liberality of whose almsgiving excited general admiration) and Rudolf III., descendant of Charlemagne and last king of Burgundy. There were, however, troubles and disorders in the somewhat anarchic capital of Christendom. The archbishops of Milan and Ravenna had a dispute about precedence, which ended in a street-brawl between their followers and in the flight of him of Ravenna. Worse still, the German soldiers of the emperor had a fight with the people of Rome, in which many lives were lost, and by which Conrad's wrath was so fiercely kindled that it could only be appeased by the appearance of the Roman citizens barefooted and disarmed before the German Augustus, abjectly entreating his forgiveness. All this Canute must have witnessed, but nothing seems to have weakened the impression of awe and reverence for the apostolic city, made by his residence in Rome.

In a letter to his people, written from Rome and preserved for us by two of the twelfth century historians, William and Florence, Canute sends greeting to the two archbishops, the bishops and nobles, and all the English people, gentle and simple. He informs them that his long-cherished desire to visit Rome, there to pray for the forgiveness of his sins and the welfare of his people, has at length been gratified. He has visited the sepulchres of Peter and Paul and every other sanctuary within or without the city. At the great Easter festival he has met not only Pope John and the Emperor Conrad, but all "the princes of the nations," from Mount Garganus (in Apulia) to the Tyrrhene Sea, and has received gifts from all, especially from the emperor; vessels of silver and gold, mantles and robes exceeding precious. Further, from the emperor and from King Rudolf, he has obtained an assurance that none of his subjects, whether English or Dane, shall any longer be harassed with the heavy payments at the mountain passes or the exorbitant customs-duties with which they have been hitherto afflicted. Nor shall future archbishops, visiting Rome in quest of the pallium, pay the immense sums which have heretofore been demanded of them. Finally, the king assures his loving subjects of his desire to administer equal justice to all. Let no shire-reeve or bailiff think to curry favour with him by the oppression of his subjects. "I have no need that money be accumulated for me by unjust exactions." "But let all the debts which according to ancient custom are due from you [to the Church] be regularly paid; the penny for every carucate ploughed; the tithe of the increase of your flocks and your herds; the penny for St. Peter at Rome; the tithe of corn in the middle of August, and the Church-scot at the feast of St. Martin. If all these dues are not regularly paid, I shall on my return to England execute unpitying justice on the defaulter."

The new emperor was evidently struck by the statesmanlike character of the Anglo-Danish king, and thought it good policy to draw closer the relations between them. Canute's daughter, Gunhild, was betrothed to Conrad's eldest son, and in 1036, when she had attained a suitable age, the marriage was consummated. She died, however, after two years of wedlock, leaving an infant daughter who afterwards became Abbess of Quedlinburg. A year after her death her husband ascended the imperial throne under the title of Henry III. Conrad the Salic also ceded to Canute such rights—perhaps even then vague and ill-defined—as the empire claimed to possess over the frontier province of Sleswick, thus making the river Eider the acknowledged boundary between Germany and Denmark. Hence, and from the later union between the provinces of Sleswick and Holstein, sprang in the course of ages that bitter controversy which was cruelly solved in our own day (1864) by the cannonade of Düppel.

(3) The pilgrimage to Rome came midway between two expeditions to Norway, one, a failure, in 1025–1026, the other, in 1028, triumphantly successful.

The most renowned King of Norway in Canute's time, and the great champion of her newly recovered independence, was that strangely compounded man who was known by his contemporaries as Olaf the Thick, but whom after ages have reverenced as Saint Olaf (1015–1031). "In stature scarce of the middle height, but very thick-set and strong of limb: with light-red hair, broad-faced, bright and ruddy of countenance, fair-eyed and swift-eyed, so that it was terrible to look him in the face when he was angry," this energetic descendant of Harold Fair-hair, after many reverses, succeeded in establishing himself on the throne of Norway, and at once set to work to destroy the lingering remains of heathenism in the north of his kingdom, smashing idols, making diligent inquiry into the secret "blood-offerings" of horses and oxen, slaying, banishing, fining all who still persisted in idolatrous practices. To strengthen himself against the inevitable revival of the Danish claim of sovereignty, Olaf wooed the elder, and married the younger daughter of his namesake the King of

Sweden, and formed a fairly stable alliance with that neighbour state. In the early years of his reign, according to the story of the Heimskringla (in which much fiction is, doubtless, blended with fact), Canute the Rich sent an embassy to Olaf, calling upon him peacefully to submit to his claims, to become his man, and thus save him the necessity of coming with war-shield to assert his right. To this demand Olaf sent an indignant negative. "Gorm the Old thought himself a mighty king, ruling over Denmark alone. Why cannot his descendant be satisfied with Denmark, England and a mickle deal of Scotland? Is he minded to rule alone over all the Northlands, or does he mean, he alone, to eat all the kale in England?"

For the time Canute had to be satisfied with this bold reply; but in 1025 he set forth with a great naval armament from England. A great battle followed, at the mouth of the Holy River, at the extreme south of what is now Sweden.* Here, by a clever manœuvre of the allied Kings of Norway and Sweden, Canute's great ship, The Dragon, was caught in mid-stream and well-nigh sunk by an avalanche of suddenly unloosed floating timbers. He was delivered by the timely appearance of Jarl Ulf with his squadron of ships, but the battle was lost. "There fell many men," says the Chronicle, "on the side of King Canute, both Danes and Englishmen. And the Danes held the place of slaughter."

Soon after this unsuccessful expedition came the event which has left perhaps the deepest of all the stains on the memory of Canute, the murder of his brother-in-law and deliverer, Jarl Ulf, "the mightiest man in Denmark after the king." At a noble banquet which Ulf had prepared for his kinsman, the king sat scowling gloomily. To lighten his mood Ulf suggested a game of chess, in the course of which one of the king's knights was placed in jeopardy. "Take back your move," said Canute, "and play something else." Indignant at this style of playing, Ulf knocked over the chess-board and rose to leave the room. "Ha!" said the king, "runnest thou away now, Ulf the Craven?" He turned round in the doorway and said: "Craven thou didst not call me when I came to thy help at the Holy River, when the Swedes were barking round thee like hounds." Night fell: both slept: but next morning Canute said to his page: "Go to Jarl Ulf and slay him." The page went, but returned with bloodless sword, saying that the Jarl had taken refuge in the church of St. Lucius. Another man, less scrupulous, slew him in the church-choir and came back to boast of the deed. After this desecration the monks would fain have closed their

* In Scania, which then belonged to Denmark.

church, but Canute insisted on their singing the Hours of divine service there, as if nothing had happened. As usual, his penitence took the form of liberality. So great were the estates with which he endowed the church, that far and wide over the country-side spread the fame of St. Lucius.

When Canute recommenced operations in 1028 after his pilgrimage to Rome, not war but internal revolution gave him the victory. He seems to have had a superiority in naval forces over both the allied kings. The Swedes, being home-sick, scattered back to their own dwellings. Olaf fled to Russia, and a Thing, summoned by Canute at Trondhjem, proclaimed him king over all the land of Norway. It is evident that Olaf's forceful, sometimes even tyrannical, proceedings had alienated many of his subjects; but moreover Canute the Rich had, we are told, for years been lavishing gifts on the Norwegian nobles. "For it was indeed the truth to say of King Cnut that whenever he met with a man who seemed likely to do him useful service, such a man received from him handfuls of gold, and therefore was he greatly beloved. His bounty was greatest to foreigners, and especially to those who came from furthest off." This description, given us in the Heimskringla, of Canute's practisings with the subjects of St. Olaf, suggests the question whether similar arguments had not been used with Edric Streona, and whether the decision of the Saxon Witenagemot in Canute's favour may not have been bought in the same manner as that of the Norwegian Thing.

We must not further follow in detail the fortunes of the dethroned King of Norway. Two years after Olaf's expulsion from the kingdom he returned (1030), but fell in battle with his own hostile countrymen. When the inevitable reaction in favour of his memory set in, his body was carried to Trondhjem and buried under the high altar of the cathedral church. Miracles soon began to be wrought by his relics: there was a tide of pity and remorse for their fallen hero in the hearts of his people, who found themselves harshly dealt with by their Danish rulers. Before long Norway recovered her independence, and then Olaf was universally recognised as not only patriot but saint. The Church gave her sanction to the popular verdict, and St. Olaf, or St. Olave, as he was generally called in England, was accepted as one of the legitimate saints in her calendar, July 29 being set apart for his honour. Though not to be compared for holiness of character with our own St. Oswald, or even with Edwin of Deira, he soon became an exceedingly popular saint, especially with his old Danish antagonists. More than a dozen churches were dedicated in his name in England, chiefly in the district where Danes predominated. The most celebrated of these was St. Olave's in Southwark, which gave its name, corrupted and transformed, to the "Tooley Street" of inglorious memory.

Of the closing years of the reign of Canute little is recorded. There are stories, uncertain and mutually contradictory, of hostilities between England and Normandy, arising out of Duke Robert's championship of the claims of the English Ethelings, sons of his aunt Emma. Whatever truth there may be in these narratives, they must be referred to the latter part of Canute's reign, as Duke Robert did not come into possession of the duchy till 1028. We may, if we please, assign to the same period the well-known story of his vain command to the sea to retire, a story which is told us for the first time by Henry of Huntingdon, about 120 years after the death of Canute. As Henry tells it, the courtiers, the blasphemous flatterers of the monarch, disappear from the scene, and it almost seems as if Canute himself, in one of those attacks of megalomania to which successful monarchs are liable, really thought that he could command Nature as if she were one of his own thegns. Learning better doctrine from the voice of the sea, he thenceforth abjured the vain ensigns of royalty and hung his crown on the cross of the Redeemer. To the same peaceful years we may assign the equally well-known incident of Canute being rowed in his barge over the fens in the cold days of early February, and hearing the song of the monks of Ely as they celebrated the Purification of the Virgin Mary:—

Cheerly sang the monks of Ely
As Cnut the king was passing by.
"Row to the shore, knights!" said the king,
"And let us hear these churchmen sing,"

—an interesting ditty for us, as showing that the word "knights" still kept that meaning of "servants" or "retainers" which it had when the New Testament was translated into Anglo-Saxon. In the Gospels the disciples of Christ are always called His "leorning-cnichtas."

King Canute died at Shaftesbury on November 12, 1035, and was buried at Winchester in the Old Minster where rested so many of the descendants of Cerdic. Owing to his early appearance on the scene and the various parts which he had played, we unconsciously attribute to him a greater age than he actually attained. He was probably little, if at all, over forty years of age when he died. The transformation of character which he underwent, from the hard, unscrupulous robber chieftain to the wise, just and statesmanlike king, is one of the most marvellous things in history. Perhaps the nearest approach to it is to be found in the change wrought in the character of Octavian. Both Canute and Augustus were among the rare examples of men improved by success.

He left four children, Sweyn and Harold Harefoot by a wife or concubine named Elgiva of Northampton; Harthacnut and Gunhild by Emma of Normandy. The gossip of the day alleged that Sweyn and Harold were not really Elgiva's children, but the sons of ignoble parents foisted by her on her credulous husband. This tale, however, though echoed by the Chronicle, may have been an invention of the partisans of their rivals. What is certain is that both Elgiva and Emma survived Canute. Either, therefore, the former was no legally married wife, or else she was divorced to make room for the Norman "Lady." But the marriages of these Scandinavian princes, Norse and Norman, were regular only in their irregularity.

Whatever may have been the testamentary intentions of the dying Canute, the practical result of his death was to divide his great empire in the following manner: Norway to Sweyn (who died a few months after his father), Denmark to Harthacnut, and England to HAROLD HAREFOOT. Of the latter, the Peterborough text of the Chronicle says: "Some men said that Harold was son of King Canute and Elgiva, daughter of Ealdorman Elfhelm; but this seemed very incredible to many men." Of the two surviving sons of Canute who now for a few years fill the chief place in English history, it must be said that they represent only the first and worst phase of their father's character, displaying none of the nobler, statesmanlike qualities of his later years. We sometimes see in modern life a man who has struggled upwards from the lowest ranks of society, acquiring a refinement and a culture which he fails to transmit to a wealthy but coarse-fibred son. So was it with the sons of Canute, two dissolute young barbarians who degraded by their vices the ancient throne which they were permitted to occupy.

The events which immediately followed the death of Canute, obscure in themselves, are variously stated by our different authorities; but it seems clear that the old division between Mercia and Wessex again made itself manifest and was connected with another division, that between the two great houses of Godwine and of Leofwine. An assembly of the witan was held at Oxford, at which "Earl Leofric (son of Leofwine) and nearly all the thegns north of the Thames and the sailors in London, chose Harold as king over all England," leaving to Harthacnut the rule over Denmark, in which country he was then living and reigning. There was apparently no talk of a reversion to the old line, to the sons of Ethelred or Edmund. The dynasty of Canute represented peace with the Danes, a respite from the terrible ravages of the previous generation; and it was probably valued and clung to for this reason, even as, 500 years later, English parliaments clung to the house of Tudor, notwithstanding all the flaws in their title, as a security against the revival of the Wars of the Roses.

This conclusion, however, was not unanimous. The witan at Oxford had to reckon with the opposition of Wessex, under its powerful earl Godwine, with that of "the Lady" Emma, surrounded by a strong body of her dead husband's house-carls or body guards (an organisation of which the Chronicle now first makes mention); and with such force as the lad Harthacnut from distant Denmark might be able to bring to bear for the vindication of his claims. A compromise was arranged, which amounted in substance, though perhaps not in form, to a division of the kingdom. "It was decided that Emma, Harthacnut's mother, should sit at Winchester with the house-carls of the king, her son, and hold all Wessex under his authority, and Earl Godwine was her most devoted servant."

This arrangement had in it no element of permanence and might at any moment be upset by the arrival of Harthacnut. He was, however, but a lad of eighteen, much involved apparently in the cares of his Danish kingdom. To Harold Harefoot, the Norman exiles, sons of Ethelred and Emma, full-grown men, with a hope of possible support from their cousin, the great Duke of Normandy, might well seem the most dangerous competitors for his crown. In order to entice these rivals into his power, Harold is said to have caused a letter to be forged, purporting to come from "Queen Emma, a queen only in name," and complaining of the daily growing strength of the usurper, "who is incessantly touring about among the cities and villages, and by threats and prayers making for himself friends among the nobles." "But they would much rather," said the letter, "that one of you reigned over them, than he to whom they yield enforced obedience. Wherefore I pray that one of you will come to me swiftly and secretly to receive wholesome counsel from me, and to learn in what way the thing upon which I have set my heart can be accomplished."* On the receipt

* This story of the forged letter is taken from the author of the Encomium Emmæ, who, as a contemporary, and as one who actually conversed with

of this message Alfred, the younger of the two brothers, betook himself to the friendly coast of Flanders and thence to England, accompanied by a small band of followers, recruited from among the inhabitants of Boulogne, instead of the large body of troops which Baldwin of Flanders offered him. Finding one part of the coast occupied by a hostile force, he sailed to another, probably nearer to Winchester; and set forth to meet his mother, thinking that he had now escaped from all danger. He had not reckoned, however, with the astute Earl Godwine, who was now no longer the zealous adherent of the queen-dowager, but was prepared to make his peace with Harold by the sacrifice of her son.* He met the young Etheling, swore to become his "man," guided him to Guildford, billeted his followers about in various inns, caused them to be supplied with meat and drink—especially the latter—in great abundance, and so left them, promising to return on the morrow.

That night, while they were all sleeping the deep sleep of well-plied banqueters, the men of Harold came upon them, stealthily removed their arms, and soon had them all fast in handcuffs and fetters. The cruel vengeance which followed, taken upon disarmed and helpless prisoners, excited the deep indignation of Englishmen, and found vent in a ballad, some lines of which have made their way into that manuscript of the Chronicle which is attributed to Abingdon:—

Some they blinded; some they maimed;
Some they scalped, some bound with chain;
Some were sold to grievous thraldom;
Many were with tortures slain,
Never was a bloodier deed done
Since to England came the Dane.

There is a persistently repeated story that a cruel parody of the Roman decimation was inflicted on these unfortunates. By that old custom lots were cast, and every tenth man so selected was handed over to the executioner. Now nine out of ten were slain and only the tenth survived, nor was even he certain of life; for after the massacre it seemed to the tyrant's agents that too many still survived and the sword devoured anew.

Queen Emma, seems to be entitled to credence, notwithstanding some strange misstatements, due, perhaps, rather to insincerity than to ignorance.

* Mr. Plummer (Saxon Chronicles, ii., 210–15) argues that Godwine's hostile action towards the Etheling was taken in the interest not of Harold but of Harthacnut.

As for the unhappy Etheling himself, he was taken round by sea to the Isle of Ely and there imprisoned. An order having been received for his blinding, he was held down by four men while the cruel deed was done. He seems to have survived for some weeks or months, and moved about, a saddening figure, among the once cheery monks of Ely; but ere long he died, either from the shock of the operation, or, as one author hints, from insufficiency of food. It seems clear that these cruelties were not perpetrated by Godwine himself, who judiciously disappeared as soon as he had left the slenderly guarded prince at his supper table at Guildford; but neither the judgment of his contemporaries nor that of posterity, with one eminent exception,* has acquitted the great Earl of Wessex of complicity in the crime.

The abortive expedition of Alfred, and the defection of Earl Godwine, left the dowager-queen in a precarious position. Moreover, the hearts of Englishmen had begun to turn away from Harthacnut who, as they thought, tarried too long in Denmark, and towards Harold, who was, after all, the son of a Saxon mother (whether gentle or base born), and who, notwithstanding the cruelty and craft which he had shown in the affair of the Etheling Alfred, had qualities of physical strength and fleetness which gained for him a sort of rude popularity with his subjects. Thus it came to pass that in 1037 "Queen Emma was driven out of the country," as the chronicler laments, "without any tenderness of heart, against the raging winter." She went to the court of the hospitable Baldwin, her nephew by marriage, who assigned to her a dwelling in the city of Bruges and a princely maintenance. Of this, however, she took only a small part, sufficient for her absolute needs, and gratefully refused the rest, saying that she could do without it. So says the Flemish priest, who doubtlessly met her about this time, and who, in gratitude for favours received, composed the Encomium Emmæ, on which, in the absence of better sources, we have to rely for many details of her history.

The election of Harold as king of the whole of England, which now took place, did not pass without some opposition, especially from the archbishop of Canterbury, Ethelnoth. When ordered to perform the ceremony of consecration, he flatly refused, declaring that at Canute's command he had vowed to recognise only Emma's son as his lawful successor. He would not presume to keep, in defiance of the king, the crown and sceptre, which had been committed to his charge, but,

* Freeman, Norman Conquest, i., 489–501 and 779–87.

laying them on the altar he left them to Harold to deal with as he would, only declaring that none of his suffragan bishops should presume, on pain of excommunication, to crown this king or to grant him episcopal benediction. How the dispute ended Emma's partisan does not inform us. Probably Harold, like Napoleon, crowned himself; but we are told that the refusal of the episcopal benediction so rankled in the young king's breast that he relapsed into something like paganism. When others in Christian fashion were silently gliding into church for Divine worship, he (the swift-footed hunter) would be surrounding the woods with his dogs and cheering them on to the chase, or sometimes indulging in less innocent occupations. Clearly, here was a monarch who had little love for the Church, and whose character may therefore have been painted a little too darkly by ecclesiastical chroniclers.

After making an ineffectual appeal for help to Edward, her surviving son by Ethelred, Emma at last succeeded in inducing Harthacnut to leave his beloved Denmark and attempt the invasion of England. He arrived at Bruges, probably towards the end of 1039, with sixty-two ships, and having no doubt made other large preparations for a hostile expedition, but none of these were needed. Harold Harefoot died on March 17, 1040, and was buried at Westminster. On his death a deputation was sent to Bruges to invite HARTHACNUT to assume the crown, "and men deemed that they did well in doing so." Sore, says the encomiast, was the lamentation of the widows and orphans of Bruges, who deemed that by the departure of the Lady Emma they were losing their best friend; but she of course accompanied her son.

Too soon the men of both nations found that they had not done so well as they supposed, in inviting the lad from Denmark to reign over them. The crews of his ships were clamouring for money, and to appease them the new king laid upon his subjects a heavier Danegeld than had been exacted all through the reigns of Canute and Harold. Then the Danegeld had been for sixteen ships, at the rate of eight marks for each rower; now Harthacnut claimed the same rate of pay for his whole fleet of sixty-two ships. It was indeed "a stern geld," and the attempt to levy it caused violent popular commotions. A terrible hurricane had blown the previous year, probably injuring the harvest, and the high price of corn resulting therefrom caused the gafol to be felt the more bitterly. "Thus all men that had before yearned after Harthacnut became unfriendly to him. He devised no kingly deed during all his reign, and he caused the dead body of Harold to be taken up and shot into the marsh." Worse than this, he took a cruel revenge on the whole of Worcestershire for the murder of two of his house-carls whom he had sent to exact the "stern geld" from the citizens of Worcester. An insurrection had broken out; the house-carls had taken refuge in a turret of the minster, but had been discovered, dragged forth and slain. Hereupon, the enraged king ordered Godwine, Leofric and all the great earls, to assemble their forces; and sent them, six months after the murder, with orders to harry both city and shire. The inhabitants, forewarned, took refuge on an island in the Severn, and made so vigorous a defence that their lives were of necessity spared; but the minster was burnt, the country was laid waste and the house-carls of the king, with the followers of the earls, returned laden with booty to their homes.

Now at last, during the short reign of Harthacnut, a brighter day dawned for the banished son of Ethelred. Edward was invited over from Normandy and was "sworn in as king"; that is, probably, associated in some way with Harthacnut as ruler of the land, and recognised as his destined successor in the event of his early death, which seems to have been considered not improbable. The only other event recorded of the reign of Harthacnut, "the king who devised nothing kingly," is his complicity in the murder of Eadwulf,* earl of Bernicia, who had possibly made himself conspicuous as one of Harold's partisans. He seems to have been invited to court that he might be formally reconciled to the new king, but on his way he was murdered by his nephew, Siward the Strong, who was already earl of Deira, and now, receiving as the reward of his crime his victim's earldom of Bernicia, ruled once again as the kings of Northumbria had ruled aforetime, over the whole wide region from Humber to Tweed.

Harthacnut's end was worthy of his life. On a day of June, 1042, a great feast was given by a Danish nobleman, Osgod Clapa, in honour of the marriage of his daughter. To this banquet the king was, of course, invited, and "as he stood at his drink he suddenly fell to the ground and was seized with dreadful convulsions. Those who were near took him up, but he never after spake a word. He died on the 8th of June, and all the people accepted Edward as their king, as was his right." Harthacnut died in the twenty-fifth year of his age, having not quite completed the second year of his reign. Like the old Saxon kings, and like Canute his father, he was buried in the Old Minster at Winchester.

* Son of Uhtred and nephew of Eadwulf Cutel.

XXIV.

LEGISLATION OF THE LATER KINGS

In the period which followed the Norman Conquest "the laws of good King Edward" was a phrase often on the lips of Englishmen; yet it was but a phrase, for Edward the Confessor, on the threshold of whose reign we are now standing, added, as far as can be ascertained, no laws to the Anglo-Saxon collection. Danish Canute, on the other hand, holds an honourable place in our legal history; for his Dooms, which fill one hundred pages in Liebermann's volume, show somewhat of the instinct of a codifier as well as a genuine desire to deal equal justice to the Danish and the English inhabitants of the land.

From the death of Alfred—the last king whose laws have been specially dealt with—till the death of Canute, an interval elapsed of more than 130 years or about four generations, and in almost every reign some fresh Dooms received the sanction of the reigning king and his witan. It will be well for us briefly to survey the course of this legislation and to see what light it throws on the social condition of the country, and what changes it reveals in political institutions. When we consider the laws of this period from a social and economic point of view, one fact stands out at once in strong relief. The immense majority of these laws relate to one crime, theft, and to one form of that crime, the theft of cattle. We have before us a population of herdsmen and sheep-masters whose chief concern it is to guard their live stock from the sly, roving cattle-lifter, and to recover them when thus purloined. Herein these tenth-century laws bear a striking resemblance to the border laws, the code according to which, in the fourteenth, fifteenth, and sixteenth centuries, rough justice was administered between cattle owners and cattle raiders on both sides of the Scottish border.* Sometimes,

* It is perhaps not a mere coincidence that some even of the special terms of the Leges Marchiarum are also to be found in the laws of Edgar and Ethelred. Such are foul or ful for "guilty," and trod for the track of a stolen beast.

too, the grievances which we hear of in these laws and the rough redress of those grievances which they contemplate, seem to carry us into the same world of which we have read in stories of the Wild West of America only one generation ago. It seems probable that the immense importance thus assigned to the possession and the theft of cattle is partly due to the fact that, owing to the settlement of Danes on the north-east of the Watling Street, a large part of England had now become like Northumberland and Roxburgh, a "border country," and was subject to all the insecurity of that position.

In order to give greater assistance to the owner of cattle, Edward the Elder ordained that every landowner should have men in readiness on his land to guide those who were seeking to recover their lost property; and these men were straitly warned not for any bribe to divert the owner from his quest, nor give shelter to any convicted thief. Athelstan directed that if any one claimed a beast as his rightful property, he should get one out of five persons nominated by the judge to swear "that it is by folk-right his"; and the defendant must get two out of ten persons similarly nominated, to swear the contrary. But, perhaps, the most interesting of all this class of ordinances is that contained in the Judicia Civitatis Lundoniæ, framed by the chief officers of Church and State, the bishops and reeves (or representatives of the king), not without the consent of all the citizens. We have in these ordinances, under the sanction of Anglo-Saxon royalty, some wonderfully modern devices for the interposition of the community, to lessen the loss inflicted by robbery on the individual.

The document begins: "This is the decision which the bishops and the reeves who belong to London, have made and secured with pledges in our peace-guild, whether of nobles or of commonalty" (eorlisce or ceorlisce), "to supplement the enactments made at various meetings of the witan." The first chapter ordains that the punishment of death shall be inexorably inflicted on any thief over twelve years of age stealing goods to the value of more than twelve pennies, and that any one endeavouring by force of arms to rescue a thief shall pay a fine of 120 shillings to the king.

The second chapter introduces us to a curious arrangement between the citizens, in the nature partly of a Trade Protection Society and partly of a Society for Mutual Insurance against Theft. "Each one of us shall pay four pennies to a common stock within twelve months, in order to indemnify the owner for any animal which may have been stolen after that time, and we will all join in the quest after the stolen animal. Every one who has a beast worth thirty pennies shall pay his shilling, except poor widows who have no patron or land." It may be said, Why is the prescribed payment four pennies at the beginning of the law and a shilling at the end? The answer no doubt is that London still adhered to the currency of Mercia, in which only fourpence went to the shilling. The contributors were to be arranged in ten groups of ten each, the oldest of whom was to serve notices and keep the accounts; and these ten seniors with "an eleventh man" whom they were to choose, were to form a sort of governing board, keeping the money and deciding as to contributions into, and payments out of, the common fund. Every man who heard the summons must join in the quest after the stolen animal so long as the trace remained. The quest was to be continued either on the northern or southern march till every member of the guild who had a horse was riding it. He who had no horse of his own must go and work for a lord who should ride in the quest instead of him. Then comes the question at what rate were the stolen beasts to be valued. The ordinary tariff of compensation is as follows:—

For a horse 10 shillings.

For an ox 30 pennies or 7½ shillings.

For a sheep 5 pennies or 1¼ shillings.

For a stolen slave (theow), half a pound = 30 shillings.

Apparently if the thief was captured and compelled by a court of law to refund a higher price than any of the above, if, for instance, he was made to pay for a valuable ox ten shillings instead of seven shillings and a half, the surplus was divided among the members of the guild, the owner receiving only the sum to which he was entitled under the tariff.

The ordinance continues: "Whosoever takes up that which is the common cause of all of us shall be our friend. We will all be one, in friendship and in enmity. The first man to strike down a thief shall receive twelve pennies from the common purse for having made so good a beginning. The owner of a stolen animal is not to relax his diligence" (because of the insurance), "but must pursue it to the end, and he shall be reimbursed for the expenses of his journey out of the common fund.... We will meet once a month if we have leisure ... with filling of casks and everything else that is suitable, and we must then see which of our decisions have been complied with, and the twelve men shall have their food together, and eat as much as seems good to themselves and dispose of the food that is left [to the poor] according to the will of God."

The state of society here presented to us is one of peculiar interest.

We seem to see these cattle-owning citizens of London, whose flocks and herds were grazing outside the walls of the city in Smithfield or Moorfields. They follow the track of their stolen beasts across the wilds of Middlesex or Surrey ("the Northern and the Southern March"). When the cattle are caught, fierce vengeance is taken on the depredator. If the pursuit fails, the luckless owner can, after all, console himself with the tariff price which he receives from the guild treasury. And then once a month they meet to settle the affairs of their guild, "with filling of casks and everything else that is suitable," and so a vista is opened, at the end of which after the lapse of centuries, we behold the stately banquets of the Guild-hall of London.

It is possible that to this need of grappling with agrarian crime we owe the institution of the Hundred which was a prominent feature in the organisation of medieval England, after as well as before the Conquest, and exists, though now little more than a survival, even in our own day. It is at least worthy of notice that the first clear mention of the Hundred-court, which is in the reign of Edgar, occurs in close connexion with the theft of cattle, and we might almost be justified in saying that this is the main business which in those beginnings of its existence was thought likely to come before it.

There has been much discussion as to the kind of unit, five-score of which made up the Anglo-Saxon Hundred, but on the whole the prevailing opinion seems to be that it was composed, in theory at least if not invariably in practice, of a hundred hides or households.* The charter, if we may so call it, of the Hundred-court is furnished us by a document which is believed to date from the reign of Edgar and which begins: "This is the arrangement, how men shall hold the Hundred. First, that they always gather themselves together once in four weeks: and that each man shall do right to the rest. Second, that they set forth to ride after thieves. If occasion arise, let a man [whose beast has been stolen] give notice to the Hundreds-man, and he then to the Tithing-men, and let them all fare forth as God shall point the way, that they may arrive there [at the place where the beast is hidden]. Let them do justice on the thief as was before ordained by [King] Edmund, and hand over the price to him who

* Compare Vinogradoff, The Growth of the Manor, p. 144; Chadwick, Anglo-Saxon Institutions, 239–48, and the remarkable article by Mr. W. J. Corbett in vol. xiv. of Transactions of the Royal Historical Society, N.S., on the "Tribal Hidage".

owns the animal and divide the rest [of the fine] half to the Hundred and half to the lord."

We observe that we have here a regular local court, armed with very summary powers and able to inflict fines, probably heavy fines, after it has restored the value of the stolen property to the rightful owner. Of these fines, however, the Hundred-court may retain for itself only half, the other half going to "the lord." The assumption that there will be in every case a lord, who will thus share in the profits of the criminal jurisdiction exercised by his neighbours of the Hundred, seems to mark a step towards the manorial jurisdiction of later centuries and strikes a somewhat different note from that sounded in the laws of Ine. It would seem that there was a tendency among powerful and lawless men to treat the Hundred-court with contempt and ignore its jurisdiction. "If any one shall put difficulties in the way and refuse to obey the decision of the Hundred and this is afterwards proved against him, he shall pay 30 pennies to the Hundred: and for a second offence 60 pennies, half to the Hundred and half to the lord. If he do it the third time he shall pay half a pound (120 pennies), and for the fourth offence he shall forfeit all that he has and be outlawed, unless the king allow him to remain in the land." By the time that Canute took the matter in hand* sharper remedies had been found to be necessary. He who refused the judgment of the Hundred was fined—apparently for the first offence—30 shillings, not pennies. For a similar contempt of the Earl's court he had to pay a fine of 60 shillings, and twice that amount for despising the judgment of the king.

Before passing from the subject of the Hundred, it should be observed that the corresponding institution in most of the Danish counties of England was called the wapentake, a name which is said to be derived from that clashing together of their weapons whereby the Scandinavians, like their Teutonic predecessors in the days of Tacitus, were wont to signify their assent to the propositions laid before them by the masters of their assemblies. The counties in which the Wapentake generally took the place of the Hundred were York, Lincoln, Nottingham, Derby, Leicester and Rutland.†

"And let men seek the Hundred-gemôt in such manner as was arranged aforetime, and three times in the year let them hold the Burh-gemôt and

* Cnut, ii., 15 (in Liebermann, i., 320).

† Rutland was not, however, formed into a separate county till after the Norman Conquest.

twice the Shire-gemôt, and there let the bishop of the shire and the ealdorman be present, and there let both of them expound God's law and the world's law." By these words of King Edgar* we are brought into contact not only with the Hundred, but also with two other organisations still very prominent in the political life of England, the Borough and the Shire.

The Burh or Burg, in the sense of a fortified town, first comes into notice about the beginning of the tenth century and is evidently the offspring of the Danish invasions. Not that the word was not before that time in familiar use among the Anglo-Saxons,† but that it seems rather to have denoted the walled enclosure round the dwelling of a great landowner, than the close-packed streets of a medieval borough. The breaking of such a burh (burh-bryce), the forcible entry into the precincts of a dwelling, was punished by the laws of Ine and Alfred with fines carefully graduated according to the rank of the owner. "A king's burh-bryce is 120 shillings; an archbishop's, 90; another bishop's or an ealdorman's, 60; a twelf-hynd man's, 30; a six-hynd man's, 15 shillings. The breaking down of a ceorl's hedge (edor-bryce) is 5 shillings."‡ The meaning of the law evidently is, that "the man whose wer is 600 shillings will probably have some stockade, some rude rampart round his house; he will have a burh, whereas the ceorl whose wer is 200 shillings will not have a burh, but will only have a hedge round his house."§

It was into a country full of unwalled tuns or villages, and scattered country houses calling themselves burhs, but poorly protected by moat and stockade, that the Danes came pouring in the reigns of Egbert, Ethelwulf and Alfred. Winchester itself, as we have seen, was "broken down" by them. York and London were taken, and apparently in this, the first stage of their invasion, no town which they seriously attacked was able to resist their onslaught. But then the invaders gave their victims a lesson in self-defence. As soon as they had taken up a position in town or country they fortified themselves by erecting a strong "work" (the word is of constant occurrence in these pages of the Chronicle), and

* Edgar, iii., 5 (ibid., 202).

† Burg is, of course, one of the best-known words of the common Teutonic stock. It is enshrined in Luther's hymn "Ein' feste Burg ist unser Gott," and in hunting for the traces of Roman encampments in Hesse and Nassau, I have found that the name by which they are best known in the countryside is "Die alte Burg".

‡ Ine, 45 (Liebermann, i., 108); Alfred, 40 (ibid., 72).

§ Maitland, Domesday Book, etc., p. 184.

the hardest part of Alfred's task was often the capturing of these hastily reared Danish fortifications. In the years of peace between the invasions of Guthrum and of Hasting, Alfred, imitating his opponents, reared many burhs which he filled with armed men. The establishment of these forts which stood up as islands out of the hostile sea, had evidently much to do with the deliverance of the land from the flood of Danish invasion in the terrible years between 892 and 896. The entry of the Chronicle for the year 894 tells us how a portion of the invading army was attacked "by bands of Englishmen, almost every day and night, both from the fyrd and also from the burhs; for the king had divided his fyrd into two parts so that they were always half at home and half out, except the men whose duty it was to hold the burhs." And a little farther on we hear of the valorous deeds of the burh-ware of Chester and of London, which had an important influence on the successful issue of the war.

We have seen, in a previous chapter, how the stalwart brother and sister, Edward and Ethelfled, reconquered central England for the English, and how they secured their conquests by the great line of forts which they planted everywhere along and sometimes far within the frontier which had divided the two nations. Chester, Shrewsbury, Bridgnorth, Stafford, Warwick, Bedford, Huntingdon, Manchester and many more, were burhs which owed their foundation or renewal to the stout-hearted Lady of the Mercians and her brother. It must not be forgotten, however, that the bulk of the population around, and even in some of these burhs, must have remained Danish. Leicester, Stamford and Nottingham are included in the list of forts founded by Edward and his sister, yet they with Lincoln and Derby made up that Danish confederation of the Five Boroughs with which Edmund had to fight in 942 and which went over so readily to Sweyn in 1013.

In the main, however, we may no doubt consider these new, strongly fortified burhs or, as we may now venture to call them, "boroughs" as the homes of loyal Englishmen, keen for resistance to an invading foe, but also keen for commercial enterprise. Very early the kings perceived the importance of insisting on internal peace and orderly life within the limits of the borough. Thus Edmund claims for it the same right of inviolate sanctuary as for the church itself. "If any man seek refuge in a church or in my burh and any one thereafter assault him or treat him ill, he who does this shall be liable to the same punishment as is aforesaid." Where security was thus provided for, against external enemies by thick walls and deep ditches, against internal strife and anarchy by the proclamation of the king's peace, wealth was sure to accumulate. Markets were fixed in boroughs, and in order to guard against the ever-dreaded theft of cattle it was ordained with increasing stringency that purchases and sales should take place within their limits. By a law of Edgar* it was directed that in every [large] borough thirty-three men should be chosen as "witnesses"; in the smaller boroughs and the hundreds twelve would suffice; and from these we must suppose a smaller number were chosen to attest the validity of every sale by which cattle changed hands. Judging from the example of Londonburh, the greatest of all the boroughs, we may conclude that in these trading, fighting, debating communities much of the most vigorous life of England was to be found in the tenth and eleventh centuries.

We have to note in passing that the obligation to assist in the maintenance and repair of these national defences was one of those which pressed upon all free Englishmen. Fyrd-fare, burh-bote and bridge-bote, the duty of serving in the national army, the duty of building or repairing fortresses, and the like duty in respect of bridges, constituted the triple obligation, the often-mentioned trinoda necessitas, from which no estate of thegn or of ceorl, with whatever other immunities it might be favoured, was ever, except in very rare cases, allowed to be exempt.

*****

Returning to the consideration of King Edgar's law about local government we observe that it ordains that the shire-gemôt shall be held twice a year under the presidency of the bishop of the shire and the ealdorman. The question of the origin of the existing forty counties into which England is divided is an extremely interesting one, but it can hardly yet be said to have received its final solution. We can see at a glance that some of our counties such as Kent, Essex, Middlesex, Sussex, Surrey, represent old kingdoms or sub-kingdoms of the early "Heptarchic" period. Norfolk and Suffolk are but the two divisions of East Anglia. Yorkshire and Northumberland may stand fairly well for Deira and Bernicia, the generous endowment of St. Cuthbert's tomb being interposed between them in the shape of the county of Durham. The formation of the three counties of Cumberland, Westmorland and Lancashire out of Celtic Strathclyde and its adjoining territory is a late and somewhat obscure piece of history; while on the other hand the

* IV., 2, 4 and 5 (Liebermann, i., 210).

emergence of Cornwall, Devon, and perhaps we may add Somerset, out of the former kingdom of West Wales, is pretty easily understood by what the Chronicle tells us of the successive victories of West Saxon kings. Wessex itself, as we see from the Chronicle, must have been at an early period, at any rate in the course of the eighth century, divided into its four often-mentioned shires, Hampshire, Berkshire, Wiltshire and Dorset. When, however, all these older counties have been dealt with, there yet remains before us an interesting question as to the formation of the counties which are still known colloquially as "the shires," the score of counties which lie between the Thames and the Humber, between Wales and East Anglia, and which evidently represent pretty fairly the old kingdom of Mercia. These, as a rule, cluster each one round some borough which has given its name to the county. One half of these are called after strong places which, as we are distinctly told, owed their foundation or their renewal to Edward and Ethelfled; these ten being Cheshire, Shropshire,* Staffordshire, Nottinghamshire, Leicestershire, Huntingdonshire, Bedfordshire, Hertfordshire, Warwickshire and Herefordshire, and we may reasonably conjecture that the remaining shires were carved out nearly at the same time and on a similar plan. There is a great and obvious distinction between all these midland shires named after one central burh, and counties which recall the name of a tribe such as the Sumorsaetan or the South Saxons. The reason for that distinction is evidently that the Mercian shires were made as part of a definite political organisation, after the repulse of the Danish invaders by whom many of the old landmarks had been overthrown.† It is probable that many territorial divisions which would have become counties, had Mercia kept the peaceful tenor of her way through the ninth and tenth centuries, districts such as those of the Pecsaetan in the county of the Peak and the Gyrwas in the county of the Fens, may have disappeared from the map of central England owing to the ravages of the Danes. That map is in fact, as remarked by Maitland, a palimpsest, under whose broad black county-names many erased characters lie hidden.‡

....

* If Ethelfled's fortress of Scergeat may be identified with Shrewsbury.

† As Freeman puts it: "I believe the cause of this distinction [between Somerset and Northamptonshire] to be that West Saxon England was made only once, while Mercian England had to be made twice" ("The Shire and the Gâ" in English Towns and Districts, p. 124).

‡ Some of these names are probably contained in that curious document, the Tribal Hidage, on which Mr. Corbett has commented in Transactions of the Royal Historical Society, vol. xiv., N.S.

We have seen that a law of King Edgar's ordains that the ealdorman shall sit by the side of the bishop at the meeting of the shire, and shall expound worldly law while the bishop gives utterance to the divine. In the early period of the West Saxon monarchy, when there was an ealdorman to every shire, this enactment causes no difficulty; but it is clear that during the course of the ninth century there was a constant tendency to lessen the number of ealdormen and increase the size of their dominions, and we can then no longer say that every shire had its own ealdorman. Some men like Ethelred, brother-in-law of Edward the Elder, ealdorman of Mercia; like Athelstan the half-king of East Anglia; and like all the later Northumbrian earls, ruled over territories as large as the old Anglo-Saxon kingdoms. In the reign of Canute we have seen that three earls—as the ealdormen were now called—ruled over three-fourths of England. If the law of Edgar still continued in force, we must imagine these great officials travelling from shire to shire, and holding the gemôt in each. It is a probable suggestion, however, that when the power of the ealdorman was thus widely extended, new officers, the shire-reeves, from whom our modern sheriffs derive their title, were called into being, in order to administer the counties under the ealdorman. This suggestion can hardly, however, be yet spoken of as more than a conjecture.*

The ealdorman, as was just now remarked, changed his title in the eleventh century for that of earl. There can be no doubt that this change was due to Danish influence and was an imitation of the word jarl, by which the chiefs of the Danish host were often designated. Eorl was, however, also a word known to the Anglo-Saxons, and by its use in the laws of Ine and elsewhere it seems to have been very nearly equivalent to thegn. In the laws of Ethelred of Kent, of Alfred and of Athelstan, it is frequently used as the antithesis to ceorl, "no man whether eorl or ceorl" being used in the same way that "gentle or simple" was used in the middle ages. Between this generic use of the word, however, and the title of powerful rulers like Leofric and Godwine there was a wide and important difference; and to avoid confusion it seems better to use the word earl only in its later signification, in which it replaces the term ealdorman and is equivalent to the Danish jarl and the Latin comes. One important point to notice is that never before the Norman Conquest does the title of earl become absolutely hereditary, though there are certain great families which seem to have had practically an overwhelming

* See Chadwick, Anglo-Saxon Institutions, 262.

claim to share the earldoms among them. No earl, however, even in the latest days of the Anglo-Saxon kingdom, seems to have had a recognised right of transmitting his earldom to his son.*

We have several incidental evidences of the social changes wrought by the two unquiet centuries between Egbert and Canute. The tendency of all those marches and counter-marches, those harryings and hardly held "places of slaughter," to depress the peaceful cultivator and raise the mere fighting man, is shown by a curious document called "The Northern People's Laws" (North-leoda laga) and supposed to date from the tenth century. In this document we have the most complete table of wergilds that is anywhere to be found in Anglo-Saxon law.† In the following table they are, for convenience of comparison, converted into West Saxon shillings of five penings each:—

The Wergild for the king is 18,000 shillings.

Archbishop and Etheling 9,000 shillings.

Bishop and ealdorman 4,800 shillings.

Hold and king's high-reeve 2,400 shillings.

Mass-thegn (priest) and secular thegn 1,200 shillings.

Ceorl 160 shillings.

Here we see that the ceorl, the free agriculturist, has sunk in the social scale. He was a two hundred, he is now only a hundred and sixty man. The wergilds in the upper ranks of society are, perhaps, unaltered, but, as before remarked, we have very imperfect information about these till we come to this very document. The important thing to observe is the position of the hold. This is a Danish word and signifies properly a fighting man. Here, however, this simple Danish warrior, possibly without any large landed possessions, has only by his sword carved his way up into a position in which he boasts a wergild fifteen times as great as that of the honest Saxon ceorl. He is half as big a man as a bishop or ealdorman, and twice as big as an ordinary thegn.‡

....

* If any exception is to be made to this statement it will be with reference to the half-independent earls of Bamburgh.

† The wers are calculated in the Scandinavian or, perhaps, Northumbrian money, the thrymsas, each equivalent to three penings.

‡ See Vinogradoff (The Growth of the Manor, p. 131) on this illustration of "the arrogant superiority of the Danish conquerors". He remarks on the growth of the pretensions of the invaders since the treaty between Alfred and Guthrum which put the Northmen warriors only on the same level as the twelf-hyndmen, or ordinary thegns.

*****

Another interesting document which dates probably from the reign of Canute is that which is called the Rectitudines singularum personarum,* and is a compendium of the whole duty of man, or at least of the services which he is bound to render to those above him in the social order. The thegn has his obligations—in the language of a much later age, "property has its duties as well as its rights"—he must be "worthy of his book-right," that is, observe the conditions of his charter and do three things on account of his land, serving with the fyrd, burh-building and bridge-work. Also on many estates other obligations accrue at the king's behest: such as making the fence for the game on the king's demesne; the equipment of a war-ship; keeping watch on the coast, at the royal headquarters or in the fyrd; alms-giving; Church-scot, and many other payments of various kinds.

The Geneat seems to have belonged to a class dependent on a lord, but in a certain sense superior. He had "to pay rent (land-gafol) in money or in kind, to ride and guide, lead loads, reap and mow, cut the deer-hedge and keep it in repair, build and fence round the fortress, make new roads to the tun, keep ward and go errands far and near just as one may order him about." It is evidently supposed, however, that he has a horse, probably several horses of his own, although he has to be thus submissive to the bidding of a lord. We may, perhaps, see in these geneats the descendants of ceorls who, under the pressure of the times, have lost their absolutely independent position and have been fain to "commend" themselves to the protection of some great thegn or religious house.†

The cottager (cotsetla) is personally free and does not pay rent, but he has to render a certain amount of service to his lord in return for his holding, the normal size of which is five acres. The amount of service varies according to the custom of different estates; but a very usual arrangement is that he shall work every Monday throughout the year for his lord and three days every week in harvest time.

"The Gebur's duties," says the document, "are various; in some places they are heavy, in others they are quite moderate." He seems, however, to have somewhat less of personal freedom than the men belonging to either of the two previous classes. His minimum of work is for two days in the

....

* Schmid, p. 371; Liebermann, p. 444.

† This is Professor Vinogradoff's view, Growth of the Manor, p. 233.

week; he has to put in three days, not only in harvest time, but from the beginning of February to Easter; and all the time from Martinmas (Nov. 11) till Easter he may be called upon, in rotation with his fellows, to lie out at night beside his lord's fold keeping watch over the sheep. On some lands the gebur pays gafol of honey, on some of meat and on some of ale. The lord provides him with implements for his work and utensils for his house, but then, per contra, when his time has come to take the journey (of death) his lord takes all that he leaves behind. Evidently the gebur is, if not yet actually a serf, in a condition much nearer serfdom than either the geneat or the cotsetla.

After this follow descriptions of the duties of the bee-keeper, the pork-butcher, the swine-herd, the sower, the shepherd, the wood-ward and many other agricultural labourers; the whole forming a most interesting picture of a large and well-managed English estate in the eleventh century.

*****

In studying the laws of Alfred's successors throughout the tenth century, we are struck by the evident desire of the royal legislators to draw tighter the reins of government and to combat the tendencies towards disintegration and anarchy which they found in the body politic. Under Edward the Elder the great pact between Alfred and Guthrum was the corner-stone of the social fabric and to deal out equal justice between Englishman and Dane was the chief aim of a righteous ruler, but, unfortunately, the king found that he had much cause to complain of timid, corrupt and inefficient servants. The offence of oferhyrnesse, contempt of the royal word and commandment, is one which is now first mentioned, and of which we often hear afterwards from Edward and his descendants. Of this offence, punishable by a fine of 120 shillings, any gerefa ("reeve" or magistrate) was guilty who failed to administer justice according to the testimony of the sworn witnesses, or to hold his gemot once in every four weeks for the administration of justice. Oferhyrnesse was also the offence of any person who presumed "to cheapen except in a port," that is, to conduct any process of bargain and sale except within the limits of a market town and in the presence of a port reeve, to whose testimony he could afterwards appeal to prove that he was not dealing in stolen goods.

Strong and vigorous ruler as Athelstan was, he needed to put forth all his powers in order to repress the growing tendency to anarchy and injustice.

"If any of my gerefan," says he, "disobey this edict or be more slack concerning this matter than I have ordained, he shall pay the penalty of his oferhyrnesse, and I will find some one else who will attend to what I say.... I have learned that our peace is worse held than I like, and my witan say that I have borne it too long. I have therefore ordered that all such peace-breakers shall get out of my kingdom with wives and children, and all that they have, and shall go whither I direct. If they return to this realm they shall be treated like thieves caught in the act." King Athelstan's influence, however, was not always exerted on the side of increased severity. The citizens of London record that he conveyed to the archbishop his opinion, that it was a lamentable thing that so young a man as one between the ages of twelve and fifteen should be put to death for any offence, or any man for stealing a chattel of less value than twelve pennies, and that he altered the law accordingly, raising the limit of age and of value in both cases.

In order to make the punishment of crime, especially of the one most common crime, cattle-stealing, more certain, it was ordered by Edward the Elder[*] that every man should have his geteama, a person doubtless of known character and position, who would act as his advocate or guarantor in any transactions of purchase and sale. It was probably a development of the same idea when Edgar ordained as follows: "This then is what I will, that every man shall be under a borh whether he be within boroughs or without them and that witnesses be appointed in every borough and in every hundred."[†] The law was repeated and strengthened by Canute who thus announced his decision: "And we will that every free man if he be over the age of twelve years shall be included in a hundred and a tithing, that he may have right to clear himself from accusation and right to receive wer if any one assail him. Otherwise he shall have none of the rights of a free man be he householder (heorth-faeste) or follower. Let every one then be brought into the hundred and have a borh, and let the borh hold him and bring him at all times to judgment. Many a powerful man wishes by hook or crook to protect his man and thinks that he can easily do it, whether he be free or theow. But we will not tolerate this injustice."[‡]

....

* Edward, i., 1 (Liebermann, i., 138).

† Edgar, iv., 3 (Liebermann, i., 210). This law is important as it helps us clearly to distinguish between burh, a borough, and borh, an association for mutual defence and for the enforcement of mutual responsibility.

‡ Cnut, ii., 20 (ibid., i., 322).

Of this institution of the tithing, whereby the poorer class of free men were grouped together in clusters of ten, we heard among the citizens of London in the reign of Athelstan. That grouping was for purposes of mutual protection; this seems rather to be in order to enforce mutual responsibility. It is not to be wondered that organisms, so low down in the social system, have not made much mark in the Anglo-Saxon law-book; but it seems to be generally agreed that from them was derived that institution of frank-pledge which, under the Norman kings, was so efficient a machine for the repression of disorder.

*****

In the laws of the later Anglo-Saxon kings we seem to hear less about oath-helping and much more about ordeals than we heard in the laws of their predecessors. Does this change betoken the growth of superstition or a decay of honesty and public spirit and a diminished confidence in the veracity of the oath-helpers? The chief modes of ordeal among the Anglo-Saxons were three, and an accused person seems to have had his right of choosing between them. In all there was a direct appeal to the Almighty to show by the ordeal the innocence or guilt of the accused; and the Church by solemn services, prayers and fastings gave her sanction to the appeal. (1) If the ordeal was by cold water, the accused person was hurled into a vessel of water, after a prayer had been uttered that "the creature, water" might reject this person if he were guilty or receive him if innocent, according to the course of nature, into her bosom. In this ordeal to float was fatal, to sink was salvation. (2) In the ordeal of fire the accused must carry a mass of red-hot iron weighing one pound a distance of nine feet, or must plunge his hand up to the wrist into a vessel of boiling water to pick out of it a stone. After either of these trials the hand was bandaged and sealed up. If, after the lapse of three days, when the bandages were removed, there was raw flesh visible, the man was guilty, if the hand showed clean skin he was innocent. If the crime laid to his charge were that of conspiring against the king's life, then the ordeal must be of threefold severity; the mass of hot iron must weigh three pounds, or the arm of the accused must be plunged in up to the elbow. (3) The ordeal of the test-morsel (corsnaed) was chiefly practised upon ecclesiastics and consisted in the obligation to swallow a piece of bread or cheese upon which a solemn anathema had been pronounced for any but an innocent partaker. As Ethelred said in one of his laws:[*] "If an accusation is laid against a servant of the altar who has no friends and who cannot call upon any oath-helper, let him go to the corsnaed and there fare as God shall will."

*****

The judicial processes even in the ordinary courts of the realm certainly seem to us sufficiently blundering and barbarous; but at the end of the period which we are now considering, other courts of private jurisdiction were coming into being, and whether they administered better or worse justice who shall say? In the reign of Canute we first find a clear case of a grant of sake and soke to the Archbishop of Canterbury, a kind of grant which was given with lavish hand by the king whose reign lies next before us, Edward the Confessor.[†] Without entering upon the question whether the Danish king was really the first to bestow this special privilege upon his courtiers, lay or ecclesiastical, we may safely assert that, at any rate in the eleventh century, our kings were freely attaching judicial functions to the ownership of lands. For this is, undoubtedly, what is meant by these words sake and soke, or sac and soc. The first probably means a "matter" or "cause";[‡] the second, "a seeking out" or "inquiry." The meaning in any case is clear. The abbot or wealthy thegn who "had sake and soke" had, merely in right of the king's grant, and generally as appurtenant to the land which the king had given him, the right to try causes of dispute arising in his district. Apparently that right included both what we should call civil and criminal causes; and, of course, the right must have carried with it power to enforce his decisions, and also—no unimportant matter—the right to receive the fines and other profits arising from the administration of justice.

What may have been the limits of this jurisdiction—for there must surely have been some causes too grave for any mere holder of sake and soke to meddle with—and how it may have impinged upon the sphere in which shire-mot and burh-mot exercised their powers, are questions the

* Ethelred, viii., 22 (Liebermann, i., 266).

† See Maitland, Domesday Book, etc., p. 260. He thinks it probable that many grants of similar privileges of an earlier date have perished.

‡ The German sache, preserved in our expression "for God's sake," and the like (Maitland, Domesday Book, etc., p. 84).

answer to which is not yet before us. It is evident, however, that we have here judicial tribunals which might very easily grow into the manorial courts which flourished under the Norman and Plantagenet kings and the survivals of which exist among us to this day. And altogether the whole effect produced on our minds by a comparison of the laws of these later kings with the laws of the heptarchic kings is, that during the three centuries which elapsed from Ine to Canute the distinction between classes had been growing broader, that the eorl was mightier and the ceorl much weaker than in that older stratum of society; that, though certainly feudalism was not yet materialised in England, the spirit which prompted it was in the air; and that, possibly, even without any Norman Conquest, something like the Feudal System might have come, by spontaneous generation, in our land.

XXV.

EDWARD THE CONFESSOR (1042–1066.)

EDWARD, son of Ethelred, last visible scion of the old royal West Saxon stock, seems to have succeeded, on Harthacnut's death, without opposition, to the throne of his forefathers. If the most powerful man in the kingdom, Earl Godwine, had any reason to fear the accession of the brother of the murdered Alfred, he determined to run all risks, and by actively co-operating in the new king's election to establish a claim on his gratitude which might outweigh the remembrance of the deeds done by the zealous adherent of Harold Harefoot. The large influence of Godwine in the king's counsels did not imply, as it would have done some years before, the continuance in power of the king's mother. On the contrary, in the very next year after Edward's accession, and seven months after his coronation at Winchester, the king, with his three most powerful subjects, Godwine, Leofric and Siward, rode from Gloucester to Winchester (November 16, 1043), and coming suddenly upon "the Lady" Emma, deprived her of all the vast treasures that she had accumulated, "her lands, her gold, her silver and her precious things untellable," and ordained that she should live thereafter, unimprisoned indeed, but deprived of all her ancient state, in the royal city of Winchester. Thus she lived on for eight years longer, till her death on March 14, 1052; but in all the stirring scenes which preceded that event the busy, managing "Old Lady"* seems to have taken no part. Her party, if she had one, struck down by that hasty ride of the king and his three nobles, never after raised its head. The reason assigned by the chronicler for this harsh procedure toward the widow and mother of two kings, seems to bear the stamp of truth. "This was done," he says, "because she was, before, very hard on

* Sco ealde Hlaefdige is the term used in the Chronicle to describe the queen-dowager. It will be remembered that there was in Wessex a peculiar distaste to the title "Queen".

the king her son, and she did less for him than he would, both before he was king and afterward," meaning no doubt both before and after his association with Harthacnut. In other words, the queen-dowager, who evidently disliked her first husband and gave all her pent-up love to her second, had become so complete a Dane at heart that she would not lift a finger to help the surviving son of Ethelred, and for this unfriendliness she was sorely punished when he had power to avenge his wrongs.

Soon after Emma's downfall, the place of "Lady" in the palace of Winchester was again filled, by the marriage of Edward to Edith, daughter of Earl Godwine (January 23, 1045). It was a marriage only in name; for the king, to the admiration of his monastic biographers, retained through life the virgin purity of his saintliness; but the daughter of Godwine undoubtedly exercised some influence on the counsels of her royal spouse, though in what direction that influence was exerted is one of the not fully solved riddles of this difficult reign. The reign is difficult, chiefly because of the singular nullity of the sovereign's character. Religious and kindly natured, Edward (who received after his death the half canonisation conveyed in the title of "Confessor") seems to have had scarcely a will or mind of his own. He is always under the dominion of some stronger nature, Saxon earl, or Norman bishop, or wedded queen: and it is rarely possible to discover what were his own true sympathies and antipathies. We have constantly to guess to which of his councillors we must attribute the praise or the blame of the actions which were nominally his own.

To avoid confusion, it will be well to describe the events of this reign under four heads: foreign relations; internal troubles; wars with the Scots; and wars with the Welsh.

To us, who judge after the event, the dissolution of the splendid Anglo-Scandinavian Empire of Canute seems a natural and inevitable consequence of the death of its founder; but in all likelihood it was not so regarded by contemporary observers. Both Magnus of Norway and Sweyn of Denmark may well have aspired to rule England as heirs or quasi-heirs of Canute the Rich, and in order to guard against their attacks, the new King of England was compelled to keep a large fleet in readiness, which was generally assembled at Sandwich.

Magnus of Norway was a bastard son of St. Olaf's, whose very name bore witness to the irritable temper of his father. His mother, Alfhild, when in travail, was brought nigh unto death, and when the child was born the by-standers were for long in doubt whether it were alive. But the king was asleep, had given strict orders that he should never be roused from his slumbers, and none, not even his favourite minstrel Sigvat, dared to disobey. Fearing lest the child, dying unbaptised, should become "the devil's man," a priest hastily baptised it, the minstrel standing godfather, and giving it the name Magnus in honour of Carolus Magnus, "the king whom he knew to be the best man in all the world." (And this was full two centuries after the death of Charlemagne.) The anger of the awakened king, when he learned what had happened during his slumbers, was charmed away by the smooth-tongued Sigvat. Thus did the name Magnus enter not only into the dynastic lists, but into the common family nomenclature of Norway and Iceland.

The child Magnus, grown to man's estate and succeeding to his father's kingdom, vindicated the unconscious prophecy of his name, and was for a time the greatest monarch of the North. Whereas in the previous generation, Denmark had conquered Norway, it now seemed probable that Norway would conquer Denmark, so hard was the king of the latter country pressed by Magnus. This Danish king was Sweyn, not, of course, the son of Canute, who had died some years before, but Sweyn Estrithson, son of the murdered Ulf (of the overthrown chess-board) and of Canute's sister, Estrith. As Ulf's sister was Gytha, wife of Earl Godwine, Godwine's many sons and daughters were of course first cousins to the King of Denmark.

In the year 1047 Sweyn Estrithson, vigorously attacked by Magnus, sent an earnest petition to England that fifty ships might be despatched to his succour. "But this seemed an ill counsel to all people, because Magnus had great sea-power, nor was it adopted." Unhelped, Sweyn was expelled from his kingdom. The Danes had to pay money to their conquerors—a new and bitter experience for them—and to own Magnus for their king. There, however, the career of Norwegian conquest stopped. In that very year, Magnus, when riding through the forest, was thrown violently by his shying steed against the trunk of a tree and received an injury from which he died. His uncle, Harold Hardrada, who succeeded him, and who will be heard of again in the history of England, could not prevent Denmark from reverting to its former ruler, Sweyn Estrithson, who founded there a dynasty which endured for 300 years.

Though schemes of conquest, such as are attributed to Magnus, died with him, there was some renewal of the old piratical raids. In 1048 two Norse buccaneers came with twenty-five ships to Sandwich, were repelled from Thanet, but successfully raided Essex, and sailing thence to "Baldwin's land" (Flanders), found there a ready market for the fruits of their cruel industry. The shelter given by Flanders to these and other depredators, induced Edward to acquiesce the more willingly in a proposal made to him by his kinsman, the Emperor Henry III., that he should help to guard the narrow seas against Baldwin, who had broken out into rebellion against the empire, had demolished the palace reared by Charlemagne at Nimeguen, and had done many other ill turns to his sovereign lord. To punish these despites Henry had gathered a large army, and Edward helped him by keeping guard with a fleet at Sandwich. No naval engagement followed, but the pressure thus effected by land and sea was effectual, and before long "the emperor had of Baldwin all that he would."

The Emperor Henry III., who thus drew Edward into the circle of European politics, was chiefly memorable for the beneficial influence which he exerted on the papal court, procuring the election of bishops of high character, generally Germans, instead of the dissolute lads who had been too often of late intruded into the papacy. One of the best of Henry's German popes was Bruno of Toul, who ruled as Leo IX. from 1048 to 1054. To him in the year 1049 Edward, by the advice of his witan, sent as ambassadors the Bishops of Sherborne and Worcester, to pray for absolution from a vow of pilgrimage to the Holy Land, which he had made in his years of poverty and apparently hopeless exile. The Witenagemot represented to him with good reason that the fulfilment of such a vow would now be inconsistent with his higher duties to his country and his subjects; and the aid of the pope was sought to cut the casuistic knot. In the following year the two bishops returned, bringing the papal absolution from the vow of pilgrimage, coupled, it is said, with an injunction to build or restore a monastery in honour of St. Peter, and fill it with monks who should spend their days in prayer and psalmody. The condition was one in itself delightful to the heart of the pious king. From the unfulfilled vow of pilgrimage, from the journey of the two bishops to Rome, and from the reply of the venerable Leo, sprang that noble sanctuary, the name of which will endure as long as men speak the English language, the great Abbey of Westminster.

*****

The internal history of England during the twenty-two years of Edward's reign is chiefly a record of the struggles of two or three great nobles for supremacy in his councils. It is true that some measures were taken for lightening the burdens of the people. "In the year 1049," says the Abingdon chronicler, "King Edward paid off nine ships and they went away with their ships and all: and five ships remained, and the king promised them twelve months' pay. In the next year he paid off all the shipmen." The result is told us by his brother chronicler: "In 1052 [1051] King Edward took off the army tax (here-gyld) which King Ethelred formerly instituted. It was thirty-nine years since he began it: and this gyld oppressed the English people during all that time. This tax ever claimed priority over all the other gylds by which the people were in various ways oppressed." As has been pointed out,* the tax here spoken of is not the Danegeld, a levy of money to be paid as blackmail to foreign invaders, but it is here-gyld, "army tax," or rather, in strictness, "navy tax," a levy of money to be paid to the naval defenders of the country, an imposition therefore which may be fittingly compared to the ship money of the Middle Ages. But the previously quoted entry concerning the exactions in the reign of Harthacnut shows how easily the here-gyld might be increased till it became an intolerable burden, and we can thus the better understand the joy of the nation at its removal.

The position of Edward appears during the whole of his reign to have been not unlike that of the later kings of the two first Frankish dynasties. If he were not a mere roi fainéant, a puppet in the hands of an all-powerful Mayor of the Palace, he was at any rate like a Carolingian Louis or Lothair, with large theoretical claims, with little real power, and quite overshadowed by a few great earls, who had not indeed yet made their offices hereditary; who were still in theory removable officers of the crown; but who ruled wide provinces, raised considerable armies among their own house-carls, and above all, possessed wealth probably much exceeding any that could be found in the treasure-house of the king. One of these great French nobles, Hugh the Great, had so played his cards as to prepare the way for the elevation of his own son to the actual seat of royalty, when the time should come for its relinquishment by the descendants of Charlemagne. It seems not improbable that the example of Hugh the Great was much before the eyes of Godwine, and that through life he kept steadily in view the possibility that sons issuing from his loins might one day sit upon the English throne, now after five centuries about to be left vacant by the dying dynasty of Cerdic.

* By Freeman, Norman Conquest, ii., 124–25 and 615.

Godwine, Leofric and Siward: these were the three greatest names in the English Witan when Edward came to the throne, and all three should be still memorable to Englishmen; Godwine, by reason of his great place in history, and the other two by reason of their renown in English poetry; Leofric being commemorated in the Godiva of Tennyson, and Siward in the Macbeth of Shakespeare.

The kingdom of England, imperfectly welded together by Egbert and Alfred, and since then modified by the large infusion of Scandinavian blood into its northern and eastern districts, showed throughout this period a strong tendency to split up again into its three old divisions, Northumbria, Mercia and Wessex. Northumbria, as we have seen, was reconstituted as one earldom by the bloody deed of Siward the Strong, who slew his uncle Eadwulf, and so joined Bernicia to Deira. A strong, stern, unscrupulous Dane, whose martial character is attested by the well-known story of his death (hereafter to be related), he nevertheless seems to have ruled well his great province and was apparently a loyal subject of King Edward.*

Leofric, son of Leofwine, was sprung, as has been said, from a family which for more than two centuries had been eminent in Mercia, and it is probable that he and his offspring bore with unconcealed dislike the overshadowing competition of the great upstart house of Godwine. He is often spoken of as Earl of Mercia, and perhaps had some sort of pre-eminence over other earls in that district, but his immediate jurisdiction seems to have been confined to the three counties of Cheshire, Shropshire and Staffordshire. Godwine's nephew by marriage, Beorn, son of Ulf and Estrith, was quartered on his eastern flank in Derby, Nottingham, Leicester and Lincoln. Sweyn, Godwine's eldest son, ruled the Mercian counties of Hereford, Gloucester and Oxford, besides a part of Wessex. Well might the proud Mercian noble feel that his title was but a mockery, while such large slices of Mercia were given to his rivals. Both Leofric and his wife Godiva were munificent benefactors to the Church. Whatever may be the foundation for the beautiful legend of Godiva's absolute surrender of herself for the lightening of her people's burdens, we certainly should not, from his record in history, have inferred that her husband Leofric was an avaricious or close-fisted lord.

We turn to the earldoms which throughout the greater part of Edward's

* For some years the county of Huntingdon was strangely added to Northumbria as a portion of his earldom. For the complicated question of the limits of the earldoms under Edward, see Freeman, Norman Conquest, vol. ii., note G.

reign were subject to the family of Godwine. He himself held, of course, that great and enriching office, the earldom of Wessex, which had been long ago conferred upon him by Canute, and which practically included all the lands south of the Thames; excepting that Somerset and Berkshire appear to have been carved out of them, to form what in later times would have been called an appanage for his eldest son, Sweyn, in addition to the three Mercian counties which, as we have already seen, were included in his earldom. His second son, Harold, called Earl of the East Angles, ruled not only the two strictly East Anglian shires, but also Huntingdon, Cambridge and Essex, which probably included Middlesex.* The three sons who came next in order, Tostig, Gyrth and Leofwine, were but boys at the time of Edward's accession and were as yet unprovided with earldoms; but even so, it is evident if we look at the map, that more than half, and that the fairest half, of England was subject to Earl Godwine and his family.

Of the character of this man, certainly the most powerful and probably the ablest Englishman of his time, very varying judgments were formed, even in his lifetime; and after his death the antipathy of the Norman and the regretful sympathy of the Saxon writers, naturally led to very divergent estimates concerning it. Nor is the controversy even yet ended; for the enthusiastic championship of the great historian of the Norman Conquest has not unnaturally provoked an equally vigorous storm of censure. To the present writer he does not appear a high-minded patriot, nor yet, considering the age in which he lived, a detestable villain. Hard, grasping, capable, remorseless, intent on the aggrandisement of his family, and by no means successful in forming their characters, he nevertheless may be credited with a certain amount of love for his country, and for the Anglo-Danish race which now peopled it. Himself English by birth and Danish by marriage and by all his early official training, he was determined that, if he could help it, no third element should be imported by the Norman sympathies of the king, to oppress the common people and to snatch away the prizes of government from the nobles. It is when he risks life and dearly loved treasure in maintaining this contention, that he seems to us almost a patriot.

The first shock to the stately edifice of Godwine's power was given by the disordered passions of his eldest son. In 1046, after a successful campaign in Wales, "when Sweyn was on his homeward journey, he

* Freeman, u.s.

ordered that the Abbess of Leominster [named Edgiva] should be fetched unto him, and he had her as long as he pleased and afterwards let her go home." Such is the short dry record by the chronicler, of a deed which shocked the not too sensitive conscience of the eleventh century, and which appears to have led to the dissolution of the nunnery of Leominster, the outlawry of Sweyn and the allotment of his earldom to others. It seems, however, from later allusions to the matter, that it was not the forcible abduction but the lascivious seduction of a consecrated virgin of which the son of Godwine was guilty. Sweyn betook himself in 1047 to that refuge of all English outlaws, "Baldwin's land," and from thence after a time went to Denmark, where by some crime or immorality of the nature of which we are not informed, he "ruined himself with the Danes." In 1049 he returned to England, and began to hover about the coasts of Kent and Sussex, off which the king was lying with a fleet, operating against Baldwin of Flanders and watching the proceedings of another outlaw, Osgod Clapa. This man, who had once been in high favour at the English court, had held the office of Staller or Chamberlain, and had been honoured by the presence, the ill-omened presence, of Harthacnut, at his daughter's marriage feast, but had now fallen into disgrace, and led for some years the life of a buccaneer, imitating the ravages of the old Vikings and requiring the manœuvres of a royal fleet to keep him at bay. The Chronicle has much to tell us about Osgod Clapa's and his wife's movements, but he possesses for us no political significance, and we have only to note his death which happened "suddenly in his bed," as the chronicler tells us, in the year 1054.

Returning to the tempestuous career of the outlawed Sweyn, we find that his petition for forgiveness was at first rejected by the king, influenced as it was supposed by the criminal's brother and cousin, Harold and Beorn, who were averse to surrendering his forfeited earldom. Then some change seems to have come over the more generous Beorn, who, on Sweyn's entreaty that he would intercede for him to the king, consented to do so, and set off with him to march along the Sussex shore, making for the king's station at Sandwich (1049). Many were the oaths which Sweyn had sworn to him, and "he thought that for his kinship's sake he would not deceive him." Thus beguiled he fared forward, putting himself ever more completely in the outlaw's power; and even when his cousin proposed that instead of journeying eastwards to Sandwich, they should go westwards to the little town of Bosham, a favourite haunt of the

Godwine tribe, off which his ships were lying at anchor, the unsuspecting earl consented. "For my sailors," said Sweyn, "will desert me, unless I show myself speedily among them." But when they had reached the place and Sweyn proposed that they should go together on board of his ship, Beorn, whose suspicions were by this time aroused, stoutly refused to do so. Resistance was now too late. Sweyn's sailors forcibly laid hold of Beorn, threw him into the boat, and tightly bound him. They then rowed him to the ship, spread sail, and ran before the wind to Exmouth, where the prisoner was slain and buried in a deep grave, from which his friends afterwards lifted his body, that they might carry him to Winchester and bury him beside his uncle, King Canute. After such an atrocious and dastardly crime, one would have expected that Sweyn, if he could not be laid hold of and brought to justice, would at least have been banished from the society of all honourable men. And for the moment, though he escaped as usual to Baldwin's land and dwelt at Bruges, he was solemnly proclaimed a nithing or vile person (the most ignominious term in the Teutonic vocabulary) by the whole host, with the king, his brother-in-law, at their head. Yet with that fatuous facility in wrong-doing which seems to mark the conduct of all leading Englishmen in this bewildering century, by the mediation of Ealdred, Bishop of Worcester (afterwards Archbishop of York, and by no means the worst of the ecclesiastics of the period), Sweyn was brought back from his exile in 1050, his outlawry reversed, and his old earldom, which involved the rule over five counties, restored once more to his own keeping. The only thing that can be said in his favour is that he does seem to have felt some remorse for his many crimes. When next year he shared the general downfall of his house and was once more driven into banishment, instead of scheming for his return and restoration to power, he went on pilgrimage to Jerusalem, visited the sacred shrines, and died on his homeward journey at Constantinople (Michaelmas, 1052).

The history of the Godwine family is now modified by events at King Edward's court, which gave them the opportunity of assuming the character of national champions against the dominion of foreigners. We hear a good deal about the Norman favourites who flocked to Edward's court, but it is not easy to ascertain how numerous these were, or how far a king, all whose nearest relations were Normans, and who had spent the best years of his life in a foreign land, exceeded the limits of moderation and good policy in bestowing lands and offices on his friends of foreign birth. Among these were the kinsfolk of his own sister, Godiva, whom it would be hard to blame him for having invited to his court, though one of them, her second husband, Eustace, Count of Boulogne, when he came sorely offended the Saxons by his insolent demeanour. Another, Ralph, sometimes called Ralph the Timid, Godiva's son by her first husband, was entrusted by his uncle with the earldom of the Magasaetas, corresponding to the modern county of Hereford. A feebly arrogant man, he too probably added not a little to Edward's unpopularity, and he appears to have gathered round him a number of his countrymen, whom the Chronicle calls sometimes Frenchmen (Frencysce) and sometimes Welshmen.* These men seem to have been already anticipating the baronial oppressions of a later century, and building their strongholds to overawe the common folk. Of one such fortress the patriotic chronicler writes that the foreigners had erected a castle in Herefordshire in the district of Earl Sweyn, and there wrought all the harm and disgrace that they could do to the king's men.

The ecclesiastically minded Edward, however, seems to have chosen his chief friends from among the Franco-Norman churchmen whom he had known in his youth. Chief among these was Robert Champart, formerly Abbot of Jumièges on the Lower Seine, whom Edward made Bishop of London near the beginning of his reign, and who, according to an often-quoted story, obtained such an ascendency over the feeble mind of his patron that "if he said that a black crow was white, the king would rather trust his mouth than his own eyes." Owing to the feeble health of the Archbishop of Canterbury, Robert of London probably had from the first a controlling voice in the affairs of the southern province, and when at last, in October, 1050, the aged Eadsige was gathered to his fathers, Edward desired to make his favourite ecclesiastic archbishop. There was, however, an undercurrent of opposition; the chapter met in haste without the royal mandate and elected one of their number, Aelfric, archbishop. The monastic candidate was a relation of Earl Godwine's, who put forth all his influence to procure the confirmation of his election, but in vain. The Norman's power over the king was too great; at the Witenagemot held in London at Midlent, 1051, Robert Champart was appointed Archbishop of Canterbury. He went speedily to Rome and returned with

* Welisce menn.—Of course the word Wealas and its derivations meant simply non-Teutonic and had no necessary connexion with the British population of what we now call Wales.

the indispensable pallium. This rebuff to Earl Godwine was perhaps the first indication of the precarious tenure of his power. At any rate from this time onward, if not before, the influence of the king's clerical master was thrown heavily into the scale against him.

Such apparently was the state of affairs at the English court, and such the smouldering fires of jealousy and distrust, when in the summer of 1051 Eustace of Boulogne came on a visit to his brother-in-law. The visit paid, he and his retinue took the homeward road through Kent, and after baiting at Canterbury, made for Dover as their resting-place for the night. When the little troop were still some miles short of Dover, he and his men dismounted, put on their coats of mail and thus rode on, martial and menacing. When they reached Dover they showed at once their intention to take up their quarters wherever it pleased them. They were probably not without some legal justification for what seems to us a somewhat high-handed procedure, for Count Eustace was son-in-law and brother-in-law of English kings, and royal personages in the west of Europe seem to have possessed in the eleventh century some rights of compulsory hospitality similar to those of which we hear so much in later centuries under the name of "purveyance." It was therefore probably not so much the claim itself as the insolent manner in which it was urged by armed foreigners, which exasperated the citizens of Dover. A quarrel arose between one of the Frenchmen and the householder upon whom he was quartered. The householder received a wound which he repaid by a mortal blow. Thereupon the count and his men mounted their horses, and attacked the householder, whom they slew on his own hearthstone. A general mêlée followed, the result of which was that twenty of the citizens were slain, and nineteen of the strangers, many of whom were also wounded. Count Eustace, with the survivors of his train, made his way back to the king, and in angry tones, concealing his own followers' misconduct, called for vengeance on the men of Dover. Hereupon Earl Godwine was summoned to the royal presence and ordered to execute the king's wrath against the citizens. This command he absolutely refused to obey. The men of Dover belonged to the county which he had longest ruled and with which he was most closely connected,* and he would have nothing to do with that which he considered to be their unjust chastisement. It was then decided (apparently under the Norman archbishop's influence) that a Witenagemot should be held at Gloucester,

* Some doubt has been thrown on the early connexion of Godwine with Kent.

at which the old charge of complicity in the death of the Etheling Alfred was to be brought against Godwine. The great earl, moreover, had at this time on foot an expedition against the "Wealas" (that is Frenchmen), who were distressing the inhabitants of Herefordshire, from the castle which they had there erected. That matter, and the counter-accusations brought by the "Wealas" against Godwine, were apparently to be also discussed at the Gloucester meeting of the witan.

Things seemed to be gathering up towards a civil war, in which Godwine and his sons would have had against them, not only the king and his French favourites, men like Robert of Jumièges and Ralph the Timid, but also Siward of Northumberland and Leofric of Mercia, who were hastening with their armies to the help of the king. This last fact seems to show that the tyrannical conduct of Edward's Norman kinsmen was not the sole question at issue in this summer of 1051. Jealousy and dread of the overmastering power of the house of Godwine also had their share in the great debate, nor perhaps were the old rivalries between the one southern and the two northern kingdoms altogether absent. It seemed as though a collision between the fyrds of Northumbria and Mercia, and those of Wessex and East Anglia was inevitable; but even at the eleventh hour wiser counsels prevailed. To some of the leaders on the king's side the thought occurred, that the impending battle would be a grievous mistake, "inasmuch as almost all that England had of noblest was in the two armies, and a battle between them would but bring one common ruin and leave the land open to invasion by the enemies of both." On Godwine's side also there was great unwillingness "to be compelled to stand against their royal lord." Thus a peace—as it proved only a precarious peace—was patched up, and all subjects in dispute were referred to a great national meeting of the witan, which was to be held in London at Michaelmas.

By consenting to this delay, and by changing the venue from Gloucester to London, the Godwine party seem to have thrown away their chances. The earl and his sons came to his dwelling at Southwark with a great multitude of West Saxons, "but his army ever waned, and all the more the longer he stayed." The magic of the king's name was still too mighty to be resisted. The thegns who were in subjection to Harold were told to transfer their allegiance to the king himself; Sweyn the seducer was once more outlawed; the negotiations soon became a mere desperate appeal from the Godwine party for hostages and safe conduct, and at last they received the royal ultimatum: "Five days in which to clear out of the country, or judgment against you," probably on the old charge of complicity in the murder of Alfred, combined with new charges of treachery against the king. Hereupon the whole family took their departure. Godwine with his wife and three of his sons, Sweyn, Tostig and Gyrth, went to the patrimonial Bosham, "shoved out their ships, betook them beyond sea, and sought the protection of Baldwin, with whom they abode the whole winter." There was especial fitness in those exiles seeking shelter in "Baldwin's land," for immediately before the downfall of the Godwine family Tostig had become the bridegroom of Judith, sister of Baldwin V., the reigning Count of Flanders. The other two sons, Harold and Leofwine, rode hard to Bristol, vainly pursued by Ealdred, Bishop of Worcester, whom the king had ordered to capture them. Much buffeted by storms, they beat out from Avonmouth, and at last arrived on the coast of Ireland, where they spent the winter as guests of Diarmid, King of Leinster. To complete the ruin of the family, Godwine's daughter Edith, "who had been hallowed to Edward as queen, was forsaken by him; all her property in land, in gold, in silver and in all things was taken from her," and she was committed to the care of her husband's half-sister, the Abbess of Wherwell in Hampshire. Well may the chronicler who records these events say: "It must have seemed a wonderful thing to any man that was in England, if any man had said beforehand that so it should happen, inasmuch as he was so high uplifted that he ruled the king and all England, and his sons were earls and the king's darlings, and his daughter [now sent to a nunnery] was wedded and married to the king."

Soon after the expulsion of Godwine and his sons a memorable event occurred: the landing in England of William the Norman, who came on a visit to the king in 1051. In 1035, the year of the death of Canute, Robert Duke of Normandy, King Edward's first cousin, had died at Nicæa in Bithynia on his way home from the Holy Land. Before starting on this pilgrimage he had presented to the nobles of Normandy his illegitimate son, William, child of Herleva, the daughter of a tanner of Falaise, and called upon them to recognise him as his successor. The child was only about seven years old, but as his father said, "He is little but he will grow, and if God please he will mend." Moreover, his lord paramount, the King of France, had promised to maintain him in his duchy. The nobles were loath to accept as their future ruler one whose illegitimacy for various reasons was considered more disgraceful than that which tarnished the shield of many of his ancestors, but being in some degree constrained, perhaps surprised, by the sudden action of their masterful duke, they consented and acknowledged themselves the "men" of the little bastard. When the tidings of Duke Robert's death in the distant Orient arrived, no rival candidate was set up, and the plighted faith of the Norman nobles was not formally violated, but there seems to have been a general relapse into anarchy. Private wars between noble and noble were waged continually. Three guardians of the boy-duke were slain, one after another, and two attempts were made to kidnap, perhaps to murder him. But out of this welter of warring ambitions and treasons sometimes fomented by the liege-lord in Paris who had sworn to protect him, the young duke gradually grew up a bold, athletic, soldierly man; chaste and clean-living, though himself the child of illicit love; devout, though when occasion arose he could defy the thunders of the Church; beyond everything self-centred and capable of holding on through long years to an ambitious project once formed with infinite patience, and of carrying it into bloody effect without a shadow of remorse. Four years before his visit to England, in 1047, William, with the help of his liege-lord, Henry of France, had defeated the rebellious nobles of his duchy in the great battle of Val-es-dunes, a few miles east of Caen. In 1048 he took the two strong castles of Domfront and Alençon on the frontier between Normandy and Maine, thus preparing the way for the conquest of the latter country which followed six years later (1054), and which made him without question the most powerful of all the vassals of the French king.

Even as it was, however, he was already a mighty prince when he came, probably in the autumn of 1051, to visit his elderly cousin, a man in all respects as utterly unlike himself as it is possible to imagine. A fateful visit indeed was that, though its details are passed over in provoking silence by all the chroniclers and biographers both of host and guest. When we remember that the man who thus came as a visitor to our land was he from whose loins have sprung all the sovereigns who have ruled over us for eight centuries, how gladly would we have heard some circumstances of this peaceful invasion: of his first sight of the white cliffs of Dover; his voyage up the Thames; his intercourse haply with some of the merchants of the rising city of London; his talks with his temporarily widowed cousin in his palace in the west of London, near the island of Thorney; but for all this we have only imagination to draw upon. The strangest thing is that though during this visit some promise was almost certainly made, or some expectation held out by Edward, that William should be the heir of his kingdom, even this though constantly alluded to by the Norman writers is never by them definitely connected with this visit. Of one thing we may be tolerably sure that the visit indicates the high-water mark of Norman influence at Edward's court. Robert of Jumièges, the all-powerful archbishop of Canterbury; William, the king's chaplain, bishop of London; Ulf, another chaplain, and a scandal to his profession, bishop of the vast diocese of Dorchester—all these were Normans, while Godwine, the Englishman, and his progeny of earls were all absent from the kingdom. Are we wrong in conjecturing that but for that absence the visit had never been paid? However, after a stay probably of a few weeks, William returned to his own land, and shortly after another member of his house, that one to whom all his claims to interfere in English politics were indirectly due, set forth on a longer journey. "On March 14, 1052, died, the Old Lady, mother of King Edward and Harthacnut, named Imme [Emma], and her body lies in the Old Minster [Winchester] with King Canute."

There can be no doubt that dislike of the arrogance of Edward's Norman favourites was one cause, though possibly not the sole cause, of the remarkable revolution which took place in the year 1052. All through the winter of 1051–52 Godwine in "Baldwin's land" and Harold in Ireland were preparing their forces, in order to compel a reversal of the decree of exile against them. Edward's counsellors were also on the alert, and prepared at Sandwich a fleet of such strength that when Godwine with his ships issued forth at midsummer from the neighbourhood of Ostend he found the royal armament too strong for him and declined battle. Then followed three months of indecisive action, in which, curiously enough, the chief events recorded are the raiding expeditions against certain districts of England, made by the men who professed to come as her deliverers. "Earl Godwine hoisted sail with all his fleet and went westwards right on to Wight and harried the country there so long until the people paid them as much as they ordered them to pay." This sounds more like Vikings extorting gafol than like the patriot statesman coming to deliver his country from foreign oppression. "Then did Harold return from Ireland with nine ships and landed at Porlock, and much folk was there gathered against him, but he did not shrink from procuring him food. He landed and slew a good lot of people* and helped himself to cattle and

* "Mycelne ende thes folces," says the Peterborough chronicler; "thirty good thegns," say the Abingdon and Worcester chroniclers, "besides other folk."

men and property as it came handy," and then sailing round the Land's End, joined his father at the Isle of Wight, and so they sailed together to Pevensey. Meantime the royal fleet was weakened by continual desertion. The old Kentish loyalty to Earl Godwine revived in full force, and "all the butse-carlas (common sailors) of Hastings and all along by that coast, all the east end of Sussex and Surrey and much else thereabouts came over to Godwine's side and declared that they would live and die with him."

Thus Godwine's fleet rounded Kent, reached the northern mouth of the Stour and sailed up towards London; some of the ships, however, improving the occasion by sailing inside the Isle of Sheppey and burning the town of King's Milton. On September 14 Godwine was at his old home at Southwark, his troops drawn up in array on the Surrey bank of the Thames, his ships waiting for a favourable tide to pass through the bridge and encompass the king's dwindling fleet. Battle, however, between Englishmen and Englishmen, now as in the previous year, was felt to be a terrible thing. The men of London were decidedly favourable to the cause of the banished earls, and when their humble petition to the king for the renewal of his favour to them met with stern refusal, it was all that Godwine could do to prevent the popular discontent from breaking out into some sudden act of mutiny. This state of tension did not last long. The foreign favourites saw that their cause was lost; they scattered, some to the west, some to the north; Robert of Canterbury and Ulf of Dorchester rode out of the eastern gate of the city, and after slaying and otherwise maltreating many young men (who probably sought to stay their flight) reached the Naze in Essex and there got on board a crazy ship, which crazy as it was, seems to have borne them in safety over to Normandy. "Thus," says the chronicler, "did he, according to the will of God, leave his pallium here in this land, and that archiepiscopal dignity which not according to God's will he had here obtained."

The Frenchmen gone, peace was easily negotiated between the cipher-king and his powerful ministers. To Earl Godwine, his wife, his sons and his daughter, full restitution was made of all the offices and all the property of which they had been deprived. "The Lady" was fetched back from her convent and again installed in the palace. "Friendship was made fast between Godwine's family and the king; and to all men good laws were promised, and outlawed were all the Frenchmen who before perverted law and justice,* and counselled ill-will against this land, save

* Literally "had raised up un-law and deemed un-dooms".

those (few) persons whom the king liked to keep about him, because they were loyal to him and to his people." At a great meeting of the witan, held outside of London, Earl Godwine appeared and made his defence, clearing himself, we are told, before his lord King Edward and before all the people of the land, of all the things that were laid to his charge and to that of his sons.

The chief agent in these negotiations was Stigand, Bishop of Winchester, a very noticeable figure in the ecclesiastical history of the times, a busy, diplomatising person who had been a keen partisan of the Lady Emma's; had shared her downfall and had afterwards been appointed to the bishopric of Winchester, which he now exchanged for the archiepiscopal see of Canterbury, practically, though not canonically, vacant by the flight of Robert of Jumièges. His position, which was already in the eyes of strict churchmen a doubtful one so long as his predecessor lived, was not improved by his tardy journey to Rome in the year 1058 in quest of his pallium, for he had the misfortune to receive it from the hands of a Pope, Benedict X., who, though apparently chosen in a regular manner, did not second Hildebrand's reforms, and being deposed in favour of Nicholas II., bishop of Florence, figures in ecclesiastical history as an anti-pope. A pallium conferred by such hands was held to bring with it no blessing; on the contrary, by committing the English metropolitan to the losing party, which opposed the famous Gregory VII., it had a very important influence on subsequent events, and gave to the buccaneering expedition of William the Bastard something of the character of a religious crusade.

To the great earl himself the revolution of 1052 brought no long enjoyment of power. Godwine fell sick soon after his landing in England, and though he recovered for a time, his health was evidently much shaken. In the following year, when King Edward was keeping Easter at Winchester with Godwine, Harold and Tostig for his guests, as they sat at meat, the earl "suddenly sank down by the king's footstool, bereft of speech and strength. They carried him into the king's bower, hoping that the attack would pass off, but it was not so. He continued so, speechless and powerless, from Easter Monday till the following Thursday [April 15, 1053], when he died. He lieth there within the Old Minster; and his son Harold took to his earldom (Wessex), resigning that which he had hitherto held (East Anglia), which was given to Elfgar," son of Leofric and Godiva. In the face of this perfectly straightforward and circumstantial account given by the Saxon chronicler, of the death of an elderly statesman, after a hard and laborious life, from a stroke of apoplexy or paralysis, it is unnecessary to reproduce the idle legends of Norman historians two generations later, who represented that death as the fulfilment of a blasphemous imprecation of the divine vengeance on himself if he had had part or lot in the murder of the Etheling Alfred.

Earl Harold succeeded not only to the earldom but also to the political predominance of his father, and for the remaining thirteen years of Edward's reign we may safely consider him as the real ruler of the kingdom. Only it must be observed that though Harold was the king's efficient man of business, the chosen companion of his sports and of his leisure was another brother, Tostig, who in the year 1055 received the earldom of Northumbria. This peculiar position of favour in the palace and absenteeism from his province led to complications which will be related hereafter. For the present our notice of the internal affairs of the kingdom may close with the fact that in the year 1057 the Etheling Edward, son of Edmund Ironside, came to England accompanied by his wife, Agatha, a kinswoman of the Emperor Henry III., and by what a Saxon ballad-maker quaintly calls "a goodly team of bairns." Probably it was the intention of the older Edward that his namesake should succeed him on the throne, though he may have at times vacillated between the more remote but known kinsman in Normandy and the nearer stranger from Hungary. But whatever the king's intentions may have been, they were foiled by sickness or some less innocent agency. "We know not," says the chronicler, "for what cause that was done that he might not see his kinsman, King Edward. Woe was that wretched mishap, and harmful to all this people that he ended his life so soon after he came to England, for the unhappiness of this poor folk." There is a mystery in all this which it is vain now to try to penetrate. Only one cannot help again remarking the lack of virility in these latest scions of the house of Cerdic. Assuredly neither William the Bastard nor Harold Godwineson, would have been content to linger out forty years of life in exile, nor when returned to their native land would have been so easily snuffed out of existence as was this prince, the descendant of fifteen generations of West Saxon kings.

*****

We pass from the internal affairs of England to the notices, scanty, but possessing for us a peculiar interest, concerning wars with Scotland in the reign of Edward. We have seen that in 1018 the Scottish king, Malcolm II., by his victory at Carham wrested from Northumbria all its territory north of the Tweed. This king died in 1034, the year before the death of Canute. His own death seems to have been a violent one, but he had certainly murdered the man who, according to the complicated law of succession then prevailing, had the best right to succeed him on the throne, and had thus secured the succession for his grandson, a lad named Duncan. The short reign of this young man—it lasted only six years—was marked by some exciting events. In the year 1035 he led "an immense army" across the Border and laid siege to the new city of Durham. The siege lasted a long time, but in a successful sally of the besiegers the greater part of the Scottish cavalry was destroyed, and in the disordered flight of the army the infantry were also cut to pieces, and their heads being collected and brought within the walls were stuck upon stakes to adorn the market place of the city of St. Cuthbert. Then followed war, on the whole unsuccessful war, between Duncan and his cousin Thorfinn, the Scandinavian earl of Orkney and Caithness. Duncan was driven southward, and in August, 1040, he was murdered by the general who had hitherto been fighting his battles, Macbeth, Mormaer or Earl of Moray. There was nothing in this event to take it out of the ordinary category of royal murders in Scotland at this time. It took place not under Macbeth's own roof but on neutral ground, at a place called Bothgowanan or the Smith's bothie; the victim was not the venerable greybeard whom Tragedy brings before us, but a young man still "of immature age," whose grandfather had not many years before killed the brother of Macbeth's wife and ousted her family from the royal succession. In fact, we may almost say, looking to the vicissitudes of the two families who at this time alternately ruled Scotland, that it was Duncan's turn to be murdered. Macbeth, who reigned from 1040 to 1058, seems to have been on the whole a good king, though reigning by a more than doubtful title. It is possible that he imitated his contemporary Canute by going on pilgrimage, as a chronicler tells us that in the year 1050 Macbeth, king of Scotland, scattered silver broadcast among the poor of Rome.

Such was the man against whom, in 1054, Siward the Strong, earl of Northumbria, moved with a large army accompanied by a fleet. Siward being himself brother-in-law of the murdered Duncan was uncle of the young Malcolm Canmore, who was now seeking to recover his father's throne. We have also a hint from a later historian that there were Normans in the Scottish army. It is suggested, on rather slender evidence, that these were some of Edward's favourites, displaced by the revolution of 1052, who had taken refuge at the court of Macbeth; and it is possible that their presence there may have had something to do with Siward's expedition. However this may be, it is clear that a battle was fought on July 27, in which the Northumbrian earl was victorious, but at a heavy cost. His own son, Osbeorn, was slain ("with all his wounds in front," as his father rejoiced to hear), and his sister's son, Siward, as well as many of his own and the king's house-carls. Some of these house-carls, we are expressly told, were Danes as well as Englishmen. There was a great and unprecedented capture of booty, but Macbeth himself escaped. He reigned, though probably with broken power, for four years longer, till 1058, in which year he was finally defeated and slain by Malcolm III. This prince, who is generally known by his epithet of Canmore (the Large-headed), is he who by his marriage with Margaret, daughter of the Etheling Edward, brought the blood of the old Saxon kings into the veins of the royal family of Scotland and indirectly into that of England also. Matilda, wife of Henry Beauclerk, daughter of Malcolm Canmore and Margaret, is the link which connects the Saxon with the Norman dynasty, Alfred with Victoria.

The year after his invasion of Scotland (1055) old Siward the Strong died of dysentery. Of him is told the well-known story that when he found his death drawing nigh, he said: "What a shame it is that I, who could not find my death in so many battles, should now be reserved for an inglorious death like that of a cow. At least arm me with coat of mail, sword and helmet: place my shield on my left arm, my gilded battle-axe in my right hand, that I, who was strongest among soldiers, may die a soldier's death." His command was obeyed, and thus honourably clad in armour he breathed out his soul. The great earldom of Northumbria, made vacant by the death of Siward, was bestowed on the king's favourite brother-in-law, Tostig, who, however, held it not for long. Siward's son, Waltheof, seems to have been little more than a child at his father's death, but, though now passed over in the distribution of earldoms, he received, ten years after, the earldom of two southern counties, Northampton and Huntingdon, which had once formed an outlying portion of his father's dominions, and he had a great share in the events which followed the Norman Conquest.

*****

The affairs of Wales, during the reign of Edward the Confessor, centred chiefly round the person of Griffith ap Llewelyn, "the head and shield and defender of the Britons," as he is called by a Welsh chronicler; a terrible thorn in the side of England, as he must have appeared to his Saxon contemporaries. This man, whose father, Llewelyn, died in 1021, soon after achieving the supremacy in Wales, had been for sixteen years throneless and probably an exile. In 1039 Griffith slew the King of Gwynedd (North Wales), and being himself of a North Welsh house became practically supreme over all the Britons. And not over the Britons only did he win victories. "During his whole reign," says the Chronicle of the Princes, "he pursued the Saxons and the pagan nations and killed and destroyed them and overcame them in a multitude of battles." The life of a Welsh king at this time was necessarily one of continual turmoil. There was the ever-present rivalry between Gwynedd and Dyved (North and South Wales), barely held in check from time to time by the strong hand of such an one as Griffith. There were "the pagans," the Danes of Dublin and Wexford, always ready to cross the narrow seas and harry the Welsh coast. Apparently the Christian Irish must sometimes have shared in these raids, for "the Scots" (which doubtless still means the Irish) are frequently alluded to as enemies of Griffith. In addition to this there was the long feud with Mercia, which had lasted for so many centuries, but which was now occasionally interrupted when it served the purpose of both Wales and Mercia to combine against Wessex.

In 1039, in the first year of Griffith's reign, he won a great victory over the Mercians at "the Ford of the Cross" by the river Severn, slaying Leofric's brother, Edwin, "and many good men besides," as the Saxon chronicler admits. Then there was a check to Griffith's career of victory. In 1042 he was taken prisoner by the pagans of Dublin, but two years later we find him at the head of his forces, defeating the Danish invaders with great slaughter. A namesake and rival, Griffith, son of Rhyddarch, whose father had reigned in South Wales, stirred up rebellion against him in 1046, but he was defeated by a joint expedition of Griffith, son of Llewelyn, and Earl Sweyn, son of Godwine. This co-operation of Wales and Mercia is memorable for more reasons than one, since it was on his return from this expedition that Sweyn Godwineson sinned that great sin with the Abbess of Leominster which ruined his career and, for a time at least, blighted the fortunes of his father.

There were some smaller skirmishes between Welshmen and Englishmen, but, omitting these, we pass on to the year 1055, when a war broke out which was partly caused by the discords and rivalries of English nobles. Godwine was now dead, and Harold was all-powerful. Leofric of Mercia, Godiva's husband, still lived, but must have been an old man, since we find his grandsons, only ten years later, men in the vigour of manhood. For some reason or other—it is difficult not to see the hand of the great rival family in the affair—a charge of treason was brought against Leofric's son, Elfgar, who had, we may remember, received the earldom of East Anglia when it was resigned by Harold on succeeding to Wessex. A general Witenagemot was now summoned to London, before which "Earl Elfgar was charged with being a traitor to the king and to all the people of the land, and he confessed this before all who were gathered there, though the words shot forth from him against his will." So says the Peterborough chronicler, a strong partisan of the Godwine family. The Abingdon chronicler, who disliked them, says that "The Witenagemot in London outlawed Earl Elfgar without any guilt on his part." The Worcester chronicler vacillates and says, "almost without guilt of his." It is hopeless now, after the lapse of eight centuries and a half, to retry a cause which excited such differences of opinion among contemporaries. What is undoubted is that Elfgar's earldom was given to Tostig Godwineson, who had just received the great earldom of Northumberland, and that the outlawed Elfgar betook himself to Ireland, raised there a fleet of eighteen ships and sailed across to Wales, where he threw himself on the hospitality and help of Griffith ap Llewelyn. With a great force of Irishmen and Welshmen Griffith marched against Ralph, the timid Earl of Hereford. This man, the king's nephew, had collected a large number of the militia, but, in order probably that he might follow the French fashion of fighting, had mounted them on horses, the consequence of which was that "ere a single spear had been thrown, the English people fled, forasmuch as they had horses, and a good lot of them were slain, about four or five hundred, and not one on the other side." Thus was Hereford laid at the mercy of the invaders, among whom there were probably some of the "pagans." They carried the city by storm, burned both it and the minster, thereby breaking the heart of the good Bishop Athelstan, its builder; slew the priests in the minster and many others besides, and carried off all the treasures.

A proclamation went throughout almost the whole of England for the gathering of a fyrd at Gloucester, and Harold took the command. But then "people began to speak about peace": a conference was held at Billingsley in Shropshire; and, as the Worcester chronicler sarcastically remarks, "when the enemy had done all the harm that was possible, then people took counsel that Earl Elfgar should be inlawed again and receive once more his earldom." But though peace and friendship were supposed to have been "fastened" at Billingsley, war with Wales broke out again next year (1056), apparently in part owing to the martial ardour of Harold's mass-priest, Leofgar, who succeeded the good old Athelstan as Bishop of Hereford. This extraordinary person, to the amazement of the chronicler, had worn his moustaches all through his priesthood until he was bishop;* and now "he abandoned his chrism and his rood, his ghostly weapons, and took to his spear and his sword after he had become bishop and so joined the army against the Welsh king, and was there slain and his priests with him; Elfnoth the sheriff also and many other good men; and the others fled away" (June 13, 1056). A dreary campaign followed, with much waste of horses and men, but at last old Leofric, with Harold and the universal pacificator, Bishop Ealdred, succeeded in making a peace, one of the conditions of which was Griffith's oath that he would be King Edward's loving and loyal under-king. Two years after, however, Elfgar, now Earl of Mercia and the head of his family (old Leofric having died the year before), was again expelled and again restored by the help of his Welsh friend, co-operating apparently with a certain Magnus, who brought ships from Norway, but about whom our information is very unsatisfactory.

It was probably about this time that the union between Wales and Mercia was made yet closer by the marriage of Griffith to Aldgyth, the beautiful daughter of Elfgar. His career, however, was drawing to a close. Successful as his expeditions had generally been, his people seem to have grown tired of the constant fever of strife with their neighbours. In 1063 war again broke out, and this time Harold was determined to deal a crushing blow. A sudden march to Griffith's castle at Rhuddlan, on the north coast of Wales, failed to accomplish the arrest of the king, but was marked by the burning of the town and all the ships in the harbour with their tackle. In May, Harold sailed from Bristol all round Wales, receiving hostages

* This is Mr. Plummer's excellent suggestion for the interpretation of a passage in the Chronicle which had previously baffled the commentators.

and promises of obedience from the people; and Tostig meanwhile operated with a land force in the interior of the country. On August 5 Griffith was slain by some of his own followers, "because of the war which he waged against Earl Harold," and his head, with the prow of his ship and the ornament thereon, was brought as a trophy to the conqueror. Thus, as a Welsh chronicler says, "The man who had been hitherto invincible was now left in the glens of desolation, after taking immense spoils and after innumerable victories and taking countless treasures of gold and silver and jewels and purple vestures."

The kingdom was handed over to two brothers of Griffith on the usual conditions of oaths of fealty, hostages and tribute: but how little such promises availed in the disordered condition of the country, was seen two years after when a hunting lodge, which Harold, hoping to have the king there as his guest, began to build at Portskewet in Monmouthshire, was destroyed (August 24, 1065) by Caradoc, son of another Griffith, who was ruling in South Wales. Nearly all the men who were engaged on the work were slain, and the ample stores there collected were carried away. "We do not know who first counselled this piece of folly" (the building of a hunting-lodge in an enemy's country) is the dry remark of the Worcester Chronicle.

*****

From these border wars we must now return to watch the course of events at Edward's court during the closing years of his reign. The year 1064, which is an absolute blank in the Saxon Chronicles, is generally chosen for an event, undated, perplexing and mysterious, namely, Harold's visit to the court of William the Norman, and his oath of fealty to that prince. About this oath, his subsequent breach of which figured so largely in the indictment preferred against him on the battlefield of Hastings, Norman writers have much to say, Saxon writers nothing, nor does the witness even of the Normans always agree together. It is impossible to doubt the truth of the main outlines of the story, but unfortunately it is equally impossible to fill in the details. Did Harold go to Normandy with express purpose to assure William of his nomination by Edward as the successor to his throne? Did he go thither in order to obtain the liberation of two of his kinsmen, hostages once given to the English king and transferred to the keeping of the Norman duke? Or was his visit to Rouen involuntary and accidental, the result of shipwreck and felonious detention by a lawless count? All of these versions of the story have been given, and though the last is the one which is generally received and on the whole the most probable, to speak with any certainty on the question seems impossible. All that will be attempted here will be to describe some of the chief scenes of the fatal journey as they are depicted in that all-but contemporary record, the Tapestry of Bayeux.

We see Harold taking leave of the aged king who, white-bearded, and adorned with crown and sceptre, is seated on his throne. With hawk on hand, preceded by his dogs and followed by his squire, Harold rides to the family property at Bosham and enters the church at that place to worship. He embarks, and crosses the channel with a favouring breeze filling his sails. There is no suggestion in the pictures of storm or shipwreck, though these seem to be almost required by the course of events. Whatever the cause may have been, Harold, when he lands in the territory of Guy, Count of Ponthieu, is arrested by the count's orders, and is conducted, still with the hawk on his hand, but with dejected countenance and with spurless heels, to Beaurain, where he is imprisoned. Parleys (no doubt as to the amount of ransom demanded) follow with his captor: but at this point William of Normandy's messengers arrive, who vigorously plead the cause of Harold and press for his liberation. The result of the negotiations and of the payment by the Norman duke of a heavy ransom (as to this the Tapestry is silent) is that Guy conducts his prisoner to William, who receives him in his palace as an honoured guest. William and Harold undertake together a campaign in Brittany under the shadow of Mont St. Michel. The soldiers are seen crossing the river Couesnon (the boundary between Normandy and Brittany), and holding high their shields above their heads as they wade the water breast-high. Some of the men are in danger of being swallowed up by the quicksands, from which they are drawn by the strong arm of the tall-statured Harold. At the close of this campaign Harold is knighted by Duke William, who with one hand places the helmet on his head, and with the other fastens the straps of his coat of mail.

Then follows at Bayeux the fateful scene of the oath-taking. The duke, attended by his courtiers (a full assembled parliament according to the poet Wace), sits on his throne, and Harold stands before him between two great coffers, which (as we know from other sources) were filled with the bones of some of the greatest saints in Normandy. He puts a hand on each coffer-lid and swears; but what is the purport of the oath? The Tapestry itself simply says that he makes his oath to Duke William. Of the Norman writers some represent him as swearing that he will marry William's daughter, Adela (a little damsel not half his age); others, as becoming in the fullest sense of the word William's vassal; others as undertaking to hand over to him the Castle of Dover; but almost all give us the impression that in some way or other Harold was cognisant of William's determination to assert his claim as heir to his cousin of England, and promised to aid him therein when the occasion should arise. What burden an oath thus exacted under duress should have laid upon the conscience of the swearer, and how the contract was affected by the undoubted fact that the consent of the witan was necessary for any disposal of the crown either by Edward or by Harold, are questions of casuistry on which much has been said, but which need not be discussed here. We note, however, that the Tapestry gives no support to the often-repeated story that Harold was beguiled into taking the oath on relics of greater and more awful sanctity than he was aware of. Whether the whole episode were mere misadventure or the failure of some cunningly devised scheme on Harold's part, one cannot but marvel at the lightness of heart with which he threw himself into the power of the most dangerous of all his rivals, at a time when he needed all his vigilance and all his ability in order to secure the splendid prize for which he had so long been labouring.*

The year following that usually assigned to Harold's visit to Normandy (1065) witnessed another revolution in the fortunes of one member of the Godwine family. Tostig, Earl of Northumbria, was, as has been said, an especial favourite at court, and seems to have been the best beloved brother of the royal "Lady," Edith. He was, not, however, by any means equally popular with the men of his own Northumbrian earldom, who seem to have complained both of his frequent absences and of the stern, almost bloodthirsty, character of his government when he did appear among them. There was a general rising of all the thegns in Yorkshire and Northumberland; they decreed in some tumultuous assembly the outlawry of their earl, then hunting in Wiltshire with the king; they massacred all the men of his household, whether English or Danes, upon whom they could lay their hands, and seized his weapons stored up in the arsenal at

* It must always be remembered that we have nothing but bare conjecture to go upon for the date of Harold's visit to Normandy. There are some reasons for placing it much earlier than 1064.

York, his gold, his silver and all his money about which they could obtain information. These massacres and robberies seem to have taken place both at York and Lincoln; and the insurgent thegns then proceeded to elect a new earl to reign over them. This was the young Morkere, grandson of Leofric. Elfgar, the twice-banished Earl of Mercia, was now dead; his eldest son, Edwin, had succeeded him in Mercia, and to Edwin's younger brother, Morkere, was given the splendid but difficult office which had been wrested from Tostig. In support of their rebellious acts—for they were nothing less—the northern thegns marched to Northampton, where Morkere was joined by his brother, Edwin, at the head of the Mercian fyrd and—ominous conjunction—-of many Welsh auxiliaries. Once more civil war seemed inevitable, but the good offices of Harold were sought for as mediator between the insurgents and the king. He failed, however, to reconcile the Northerners and his brother; and after two gemots held at Northampton and at Oxford the negotiations ended in an entire surrender to all the demands of the rebels (October 28, 1065). The outlawed Tostig went over sea with his wife and followers to his brother-in-law, Count Baldwin; the grant of his earldom was confirmed to Morkere, and the insurgent army at last returned northward, not, however, till they had so wasted Northamptonshire with fire and sword and carried off such quantities of cattle that it was years before that county recovered from their ravages.

What was the precise part taken by Harold in this revolution, which implied in some degree the depression of the house of Godwine and the elevation of the rival house of Leofric, it is very difficult now to discover. Everything that he did may be fully accounted for and justified by a patriotic abhorrence of civil war, a recognition of the fact that his brother's government had been arbitrary and unpopular, and a noble willingness to place the welfare of England before the private advantage of his own family. On the other hand, there are curious traditions as to an enmity subsisting from boyhood between the two brothers, Harold and Tostig, and some even of their contemporaries averred that the whole revolution was planned by Harold for the overthrow of his brother. This suggestion seems most improbable, but it is evident that, whether as a cause or consequence of the disgrace of Tostig, Harold does from this time forward unite himself more closely to the house of Leofric, whose granddaughter, Aldgyth, widow of the Welsh king, Griffith, and sister of Edwin and Morkere, he seems to have married about this time. This marriage, which rendered it impossible for him to fulfil one at least of the articles of his covenant with William of Normandy, may have been the first intimation to his great rival that Harold regarded the promise made to him as of none effect.

Whatever may have been Harold's feelings as to his brother's disgrace, there can be no doubt that it cut King Edward to the heart, and probably, as one of his biographers hints, hastened his end. He was now apparently a little over sixty years of age, a man of moderate stature, with milk-white hair and beard, with broad and rosy face, white and slender hands and a certain royalty of aspect. Already perhaps that belief in the healing efficacy of his touch had begun to spread among the multitude, which engendered the mass of miracles wherewith his memory was afterwards loaded. These miracles being strangely supposed to be in some way specially connected with the royal office, led to the practice of "touching for the King's evil," which was continued till the reign of the last Stuart.

Through all these later years of his reign he had been intently watching the progress of his great church in the Island of Thorney by the Thames. Its foundations of large square blocks of greystone, its apsidal end, its central tower and two towers at the west end with their beautiful bells, and the long rows of its columns with their richly adorned bases and capitals, are enthusiastically described by his biographer. He came to Westminster on December 21, 1065, "and caused the minster to be hallowed which he had himself built to the glory of God and St. Peter and all God's saints, and the hallowing of this church was on Childmass day" (December 28), but he was not himself present at the hallowing, and his death took place on Twelfth night (January 5, 1066).

The death-bed sayings of the old king, as reported by his biographer, are perhaps best known in Tennyson's poetical version of them, but have, even unparaphrased, a poetical beauty of their own. After describing the vengeance of God which was coming upon England for her sins, and his pitiful prayer to the Most High that this punishment might not endure for ever, he repeats the words which he has heard from the saints whom he has seen in vision: "The green tree which springs from the trunk, when it has been severed thence and removed to a distance of three acres, shall return to its original trunk and shall join itself to its root whence first it sprang. Then shall the head again be green and bear fruit after its flower; and then may you certainly hope for better times." Most of the bystanders listened with awe and wonder to the dying king's prophecy, but Archbishop Stigand, with his hard worldly wisdom, said: “The old man is in his dotage.”

But Edward not only uttered this perplexing prophecy; he also, there can be little doubt, uttered some words which amounted to a bequest of his crown, as far as he had power to bequeath it, not to William but to Harold. There seems no reason why we should reject the story told in the quaint verses of the Chronicle—

Nathless, that wisest man, Dying made fast the realm
To a high-risen man, Even to Harold’s self,
Who was a noble earl: He did at every tide
Follow with loyal love All of his lord’s behests,
Both in his words and deeds: Naught did he e’er neglect
Whate’er of right belonged Unto the people’s king.

“And now was Harold hallowed as king, but little stillness did he there enjoy, the while that he wielded the kingdom.”

XXVI.

STAMFORD BRIDGE AND HASTINGS

Upon the death of Edward the Confessor the election and coronation of HAROLD, son of Godwine, followed with the briefest possible interval. No serious notice seems to have been taken, at the time, of any claim to the crown which might be made on behalf of Edgar the Etheling, grandson of Edmund Ironside, the undoubted heir, on what we call legitimist principles, of the house of Cerdic. Though the year of Edgar's birth is doubtful, he was certainly little more than a boy at his great-uncle's death, and it is probable that the ascertained weakness of his character made the Wise Men of the kingdom unwilling to entrust even the nominal government of England at such a critical time to his nerveless hands.

The election of Harold was undoubtedly contrary to all the traditions of West Saxon royalty, but there are some considerations which may have made it seem a less revolutionary proceeding, and the new king somewhat less of an upstart, than they have appeared to later ages. Let the cloud which rests over Godwine's birth and parentage be admitted, but it must be remembered that Harold was on his mother's side a near kinsman of Canute, that in his veins flowed the blood of Gorm the Old and Harold Bluetooth, kings of Denmark in the preceding century, and that the then reigning King of Denmark was his own first cousin. As has been already said, Godwine and his tribe must have always appeared half-Danish to the Saxon people, and though the claims of the house of Cerdic were disregarded by his election they had been equally disregarded by the elections of Canute, Harold and Harthacnut of whom Harold Godwineson may have seemed in some sort the natural successor.

But that this view of the case would not be accepted in Normandy, all men knew full well, and none better than the new king himself. The Bayeux Tapestry, almost immediately after its picture of Harold enthroned, represents "an English ship coming to the land of Duke William." Whatever this may mean, whether the flight of some Norman favourite to his native land, or a desperate attempt at self-exculpation and reconciliation on the part of Harold, it is followed with ominous rapidity by the picture, "Here William orders ships to be built," in which the axes of the woodmen are felling the trees of the forest; that again by a picture, "Here they drag the ships to the sea," and that by a lively scene, "These men carry arms to the ships and here they drag a cart with wine and arms." After this in a scene which is not pictorially represented and at a date of which we are not accurately informed, William assembled his barons at Lillebonne and endeavoured to obtain from them a vote in favour of an expedition for the assertion of his rights to the throne of England. The expedition, however, appeared to the Norman nobles too dangerous, the naval power of England too great to give a hope of success, and notwithstanding the eloquent pleadings of William's trusty henchman, William Fitz Osbern (son of one of the murdered guardians of his childhood), the assembly broke up in confusion without giving the desired promise of support. The assent, however, which he had been unable to obtain from the united baronage of the duchy, he succeeded in winning by entreaties and promises from the barons singly in private conference. The contingents of men, the numbers of ships which each baron undertook to furnish, were all set down in a book, in which were found the names not only of William's own subjects but of volunteers from the neighbouring provinces of Brittany, Maine and Anjou. It was, so to speak, the memorandum of a great Joint Stock Company of conquest, which was entered in that "Domesday Book of the Conquerors,"* and though the precise rate of dividend was not there set down, it is evident that the lordships and estates in the doomed land, which William promised to his shareholders, bore some definite relation to the size of their contributions.

It remained only, according to medieval ideas, to get the blessing of heaven's representative on the great spoliation. William had himself in his earlier days all-but brought an interdict on his realm by his marriage with Matilda of Flanders who, for some reason not very clearly explained, was held to be canonically unfitted to be his wife. But that breach with the Holy See had been healed through the mediation of the great churchman Lanfranc, Prior of the Abbey of Bec; and Lanfranc's influence may probably now have been employed to obtain from Pope Alexander II. a formal approval of the invasion of England. The oath of Harold, so

* Freeman, Norman Conquest, iii., 300.

solemnly taken and so flagrantly broken, and his marriage to Aldgyth, after having promised to marry William's daughter Adela, may possibly have been pressed against him at the court of Rome and may have helped towards the composition of the bull which was now issued denouncing Harold as a usurper and proclaiming William as Edward's rightful heir. It is probable, however, that in the mind of Hildebrand, the master-spirit of the papal court, though not yet actually Pope, the independent attitude which the English Church had sometimes assumed, and notably the unfortunate fact that Archbishop Stigand had, during the lifetime of his own predecessor, received his pallium from the anti-pope Benedict X., were the chief reasons for the Church's enthusiastic partisanship on the Norman side. The word Crusade was not yet heard in the Christian world, nor was it to be heard till near thirty years later, when Peter the Hermit at the Council of Clermont was to utter his fiery declamation against the misbelievers; but a virtual crusade was preached against Harold and his adherents, and all Europe knew that whenever William's shipbuilding should be ended and he should be ready to sail, his troops would march to battle under the protection of a banner consecrated by the successor of St. Peter.

The Norman preparations, begun in the early months of 1066, lasted on through the summer and almost up to the autumnal equinox. Meanwhile, a portent in the heavens and the attacks of another foe were depressing the spirits of Englishmen. Soon after Easter "the comet star which some men call the hairy star," which had for some time been creeping nearer to the sun, unnoticed in the early morning hours, began to blaze forth in the north-west in the evening sky. From April 24 till May 1 was the period of its greatest brilliancy, and it probably disappeared early in June. In the Tapestry we see six men pointing fearful fingers towards a star which trails a rudely drawn streamer of light behind it, and we are informed that "These men are marvelling at the star." The comet here depicted is now known to be one which regularly returns to our firmament at intervals of some seventy-five or seventy-six years. Its return in 1758 verified the prediction of the astronomer Halley, then no longer living, and it is expected that once more in the year 1910 Englishmen will be gazing upwards, and with less fearful hearts than of old, will "wonder at the star."

The less shadowy terror of the spring of that year came from the king's banished brother Tostig, who now by right or wrong was determined to win back his lost earldom. He had gathered a considerable force of ships and men, no doubt chiefly in "Baldwin's land," among the subjects of his brother-in-law; and he had probably already made overtures of alliance to the Duke of Normandy and the King of Norway. He came, however, unaccompanied by allies "from beyond sea into Wight with as large a fleet as he could procure and there people paid him both money and provisions; and he went thence and did all the harm that he could along the sea-coast until he came to Sandwich." The naval armament which Harold had collected in anticipation of the Norman attack availed to keep the southern coasts clear from further ravages by Tostig, who took on board a large number of butse-carlas, some willingly and some unwillingly, and steering northwards entered the Humber, and began to ravage Lincolnshire. The two northern earls, Edwin and Morkere, however, having summoned the fyrd succeeded in driving him out of the country. Most of his butse-carlas took the opportunity to desert, and with a dwindled force of twelve smacks he sailed for the Forth. The Scottish King, Malcolm Canmore, took him under his protection and helped him with provisions, and there he abode all summer.

The delay of these summer months, during which invasion was impending from two quarters at once, was disastrous for England. When Harold had collected his fleet and army, "such a land force both by land and sea as no king of the land had ever gathered before," he went to the Isle of Wight and there lay at anchor all the summer, keeping the land force always close beside him on the coast. Had William made his invasion then, it may fairly be conjectured that he would never have sat on the throne of England. But when the day of the Nativity of St. Mary (September 8) was come, the men's provisions were exhausted, and it was impossible to keep them longer under the standards. They were accordingly allowed to go home, and the king rode up to London, while his fleet sailed round to the Thames, and meeting unfortunately with bad weather, many of the ships perished ere they reached their haven.

If Harold thought that peril from either of his foes was over for that year he was terribly mistaken. Even while the fleet and army were scattering from the Isle of Wight, the whole aspect of affairs in the north was being changed by the sudden and unexpected arrival off the northern coast of Harold, King of Norway, with an immense fleet of more than three hundred ships. This Harold, surnamed Hardrada (the man of hard counsel), was, even if we may not believe all that the saga-men told concerning him, one of the most romantic figures of the time. A half-brother of the sainted Olaf, by whose side he fought when but fifteen years old at the fatal battle of Stiklestadt, he appears, after some four or five years of a fugitive existence, as one of the chiefs of the Varangian soldiery at the court of Constantinople. The tall statured Scandinavian—his height is said to have been nearly seven feet—rose rapidly in the Byzantine service, and it was hinted that the inflammable Empress Zoe would have gladly welcomed him as one of her numerous husbands or lovers. The life of a soldier was, however, more to his taste than the dissipations of a luxurious court. He wrought great deeds in the eastern waters and shared with the veteran Byzantine general, George Maniaces, the glory of a temporary re-conquest of Sicily. Even then, however, that element of keen egotism in his character which won for him his title of Hardrada made itself visible; and his country's skalds delighted to tell of the clever but dishonourable stratagem by which he out-witted his brother general when they were casting lots for choice of quarters. Strange to say, one of the most interesting memorials of this Norwegian chief is still to be seen amid the lagunes of Venice. There, in front of the noble gateway of the arsenal, sit two great marble lions, brought by the Venetian general Morosini from the Piraeus, trophies of that fatally memorable expedition in which he converted the Parthenon into a ruin. On the flanks of one of these lions is a nearly effaced Runic inscription, recording the conquest of the port of Piraeus by three chieftains with Scandinavian names. "These men," says the inscription, "and Harold the Tall, laid considerable fines on the citizens because of the insurrection of the Greek people." With difficulty Harold escaped from the prison in which he was confined by the jealous caprice of Zoe, and after charging over the great chain which was stretched across the Bosphorus, sailed out into the Euxine and thence up one of the great rivers into the heart of Russia. The king of Novgorod gave him his daughter Elizabeth to wife, and in the year 1045 Harold reappeared laden with treasure in his native Norway. He was sometimes the ally, sometimes the foe of his nephew Magnus the Good, on whose premature death in 1047 he succeeded peaceably to his throne. For fifteen years he waged almost incessant, generally successful, war with the King of Denmark, but in 1062 he concluded a treaty with that prince, which left him free to attempt the larger and more daring enterprise to which he was tempted by the example of Canute and the overtures of Tostig, even the conquest of England.

Harold made first for the Orkneys, then under the rule of the sons of the Norseman, Earl Thorfinn. From thence he sailed along the coast of Scotland, till, either in the Forth or the Tyne, he met his promised ally, Tostig, who "bowed to him and became his man." They went both together, landed in Cleveland, which they harried; set fire to Scarborough; and at last reaching the mouth of the Humber, sailed with all their enormous fleet up that river and the Ouse, and landed near York. The Earls Edwin and Morkere came forth to meet them with as large a force as they could muster, but were utterly defeated in a great battle fought at Fulford, two miles from York, on September 20, 1066. The two earls escaped alive from the field, but were unable to make any further opposition to the invaders, who entered York in triumph and received the submission of the city. "Then after the fight came Harold and Tostig into York with as many people as to them seemed good, and they took hostages from the city and also received provisions, and so went thence to their ships, having agreed to full peace, that they [the people of York] might all go south with them and conquer this land." It was to be an expedition of Northumbrians, Scots and men of Orkney, as well as Norsemen, under the command of Harold Hardrada, against Harold Godwineson and the men of Mercia and Wessex.

The invaders had in this instance reckoned without their host. They thought they had only the young and somewhat inefficient sons of Elfgar to deal with, whereas the namesake of Hardrada, "Harold our king" (as one of the chroniclers calls him), had heard the unwelcome news of their presence in his kingdom, and with almost Napoleonic swiftness of decision, was bearing down upon them. It was only on September 8 that he had dismissed his fleet and army in Hampshire. His journey to London may have occupied a day or two, and we know not how soon the tidings of the invasion reached him; but already on September 24, with all the fyrd that he could assemble in the south, he was at Tadcaster, and on the following day he marched through York. Hardrada and Tostig, whom he had perhaps hoped to surprise cooped up within the city, had marched eastwards some seven or eight miles to Stamford Bridge, on the river Derwent, where they expected to receive the hostages whom Yorkshire was to offer for her fidelity. Against them marched the English Harold, so suddenly, and with such successful precautions against their obtaining information of his movements, that at first when Hardrada saw afar off the steam of the horses and thereunder fair shields and white byrnies (coats of mail), he asked Tostig what host that might be. Tostig answered that they might be some of his kinsmen coming in to seek the king's friendship, but that he feared it meant "unpeace," and so it proved. The host drew nearer and nearer, and like the flashing of the sunlight reflected from a glacier was the gleam of their weapons.*

There was a short parley ere the armies closed. English Harold sent to offer his brother a third of his kingdom, that there might be peace between them. "'Tis pity," said Tostig, "that this offer was not made last winter. Many a good man had then been living who now is dead, and better had it been for the whole realm of England; but if I accept these terms, what shall Harold of Norway have in return for his labour?" Then came the celebrated answer (and it is worthy of note that the Norse story-teller has preserved it): "Seven foot's room, or so much more as he may need, seeing that he is taller than other men." Tostig honourably refused to make any peace by the sacrifice of his ally; and the battle was joined, a terrible battle which lasted all day long and wrought great slaughter. The English at last succeeded in breaking the invaders' shield-wall, and, surrounding them on all sides, poured their missiles upon them with deadly effect. Mad at this breach in his ranks, Hardrada leapt in front of his men and made a clear space round him, hewing with both his hands, but he was at last wounded in the throat by an arrow and fell dead upon the field. There was a little lull in the conflict, and Harold Godwineson offered peace to Tostig and the surviving Northmen, but they all whooped out with one voice that they would rather fall each one across the other than take peace of the Englishmen. Tostig seems to have fallen in this second battle. Then another pause, and a host of men, well-armed but breathless, came rushing up from the Norwegian ships in the river. They wrought great havoc in the English ranks, and had well-nigh turned the fortune of the day; but it was not to be. The new-comers were so spent with their march, that at last they threw away their "byrnies" and so fell an easier prey to the English axes.

So ran the story of the fight of Stamford Bridge as told by the descendants of the Norsemen. The English chronicler, with much less detail, describes Harold Godwineson's unlooked-for attack upon the Scandinavians. According to him, the bridge itself was the key of the position and victory was impossible for the English until it was crossed. In its

* The following description of this battle is taken for the most part from the Saga of Harold Hardrada in the Heimskringla, and has no doubt a good deal of the character of fiction.

narrow entrance one Norwegian long held the English host at bay: an arrow availed not to dislodge him, but at length one of Harold's men crept under the bridge and pierced him through the corselet. Then the king of the Englishmen came over the bridge and the victory was won. Great slaughter was made both of the Norsemen and Flemings, but Olaf, the son of Harold Hardrada, was left alive. With him, with a certain bishop who accompanied him, and with the Earl of Orkney, the English Harold made terms. "They all went up to our king," says the chronicler, "and swore oaths that they would ever keep peace and friendship with this land; and the king let them depart with twenty-four ships. These two folk-fights [Fulford and Stamford Bridge] were both fought within five days" (September 20 to 25, 1066).

Short time had Harold for rest at the great northern capital, York. It was probably in the earliest days of October that news was brought to him that on September 28 William of Normandy had landed at Pevensey. Let us hear the story of what happened from that day to the fatal October 14 in the few simple words which are all that the only Saxon chronicler (he of Worcester) can bring himself to devote to the subject. "Then came William, Earl of Normandy, into Pevensey, on the eve of St. Michael (Sept. 28), and as soon as his men were fit [a possible allusion to sea-sickness which they had endured], they wrought a castle at Hastings-port. Tidings of this were brought to King Harold, and he gathered then the great host and came towards him at the Hoar Apple Tree, and William came against him at unawares ere his people were mustered. But the king nevertheless withstood him very bravely with the men who would follow him, and there was a mighty slaughter wrought on both sides. There was slain King Harold and his brothers, the Earls Leofwine and Gyrth, and many good men, and the Frenchmen held the place of slaughter."

"He dies and makes no sign." This is all that the Saxon chroniclers, whose guidance we have followed through six centuries, or any native English historians have to tell us of the death of the Saxon monarchy. One is half disposed to leave the matter there, and not to repeat the stories, many of them, as we may suspect, falsely coloured or absolutely untrue, and often quite inconsistent with one another, with which the Norman chroniclers and poets have enriched their jubilations over England's downfall. But as this can hardly be, an attempt will be made to present only the broad outlines of the story, omitting all reference to recitals obviously fictitious, and for brevity's sake declining to enter into any of the controversies which have been fiercely waged round certain parts of the narrative.

By about the middle of August William's preparations were completed, and his fleet, collected near Caen at the mouth of the river Dive, was ready to sail. For a whole month the wind was contrary to them—a fateful month during which, as we know, but as William possibly did not know, Harold's crews were being paid off and his army disbanded. A slight westward veering of the wind enabled the ships to creep a hundred miles up the Norman coast to St. Valery, at the mouth of the Somme. Some vessels seem to have been lost by storm, but at last, after a fortnight's further detention at St. Valery, a favourable breeze blew—men said as the result of the exhibition of the relics of the saint and prayers for his intercession—and on the night of September 27 the fleet set forth on the great expedition. Though one chronicler puts the number of ships as high as 3,000, we are informed on what seems to be good authority* that they were 696. William's own ship, named the Mora, the fastest of the fleet, had a lantern at the mast-head to serve as a signal to her consorts, a vane above the lantern to show the direction of the wind, and on the prow a bronze figure of a child with bow and arrow aiming for England. When dawn was breaking the Mora found herself alone, having outsailed all the others. A sailor sent to the mast-head reported that he saw nothing but sky and sea. The duke cast anchor, told his companions not to lose heart, and cheered them and himself with a mighty breakfast, accompanied with copious draughts of wine. On a second journey to the mast-head the sailor reported that he saw three or four ships; on a third, that the whole fleet were in sight and approaching rapidly. By nine o'clock in the morning, September 28, 1066, the fleet was all assembled off the coast of Sussex, a few miles north-east of Beachy Head, and the landing, absolutely unopposed, was effected without difficulty on the long flat shore of Pevensey, in sight of the ruins of Roman Anderida.

The most notable incident of the landing, if true, is the well-known story of William's fall. It is said that he, being first to spring to land, stumbled and fell with both his hands on the shore, that all round him raised a cry: "A bad omen is that," but he with a loud voice said: "Lords, by the splendour of God, I have taken seizin of this land with my two hands. No property was ever let go without a challenge. Now all that is here is ours." From Pevensey the army marched eastward to Hastings (a distance of about

* Wace (ed. Malet, p. 60), who gives the number on his father's report.

fifteen miles), and there entrenched themselves in a strong camp with high earthen ramparts, fosse and palisades. They also began to ravage the country for some miles round Hastings, a fact which is attested both by the entries in Domesday Book and by a picture in the Bayeux Tapestry, "Here a house is being burnt." The tidings of William's landing, however swiftly carried to York, can hardly have reached Harold before October 1. They, of course, necessitated another forced march back to London, so rapidly had the shuttle to fly backwards and forwards in the loom of war. Harold reached London probably about October 6, and waited there for a short week, expecting the arrival of the troops whom he summoned from all quarters for the defence of the country. This summons seems to have been well responded to from the home counties and East Anglia; and some fighters came, we are told, from Lincoln and Yorkshire. But Edwin and Morkere, the Earls of Mercia and Northumbria, are accused of not having rallied as they should have done to the support of the king, who had saved them from utter destruction at the hands of Hardrada. The accusation which comes to us on the authority of so well-informed and generally so impartial an historian as Florence of Worcester, is one which cannot be passed over in silence. At the same time it is but fair to observe that the troops of the two northern earls had suffered severely at Fulford, and that there was very little time to collect new levies and bring them into the field from Northumberland and Cheshire before October 14. The impression left on one's mind by the conduct of these two young earls, is rather one of inefficiency than of deliberate treachery. At the same time it must be admitted that when Harold broke with Tostig, perhaps also with his sister Edith, and allied himself with the house of Leofric, he adopted a policy which brought him little help abroad or happiness at home.

On October 12—after a hasty visit to Waltham where he had built a great minster in honour of the Holy Rood—Harold marched southward and took up a position on the last spur of a low range of Sussex hills, about seven miles to the north-west of Hastings. He is said to have been earnestly entreated by his younger brother, Gyrth, Earl of East Anglia, to adopt a more cautious line of policy, to anticipate William's ravages of Sussex and Surrey by ravaging them himself, and to force the Norman to advance through a wasted land and attack him in the strong position of London. The advice would seem to have been wise; and surely a fortnight's delay would have given Harold a better fighting instrument than the hasty levies which reinforced the war-wearied and march-wearied men of Stamford Bridge. But Harold was exasperated by the ravages which William had already begun in the country round Sussex. He patriotically refused to imitate those ravages in counties which had ever shown a special affection for him and for his father's house. There are also some slight indications that he somewhat under-rated the strength of William's army, and hoped by a sudden stroke like that at Stamford Bridge to sweep it into the sea.

However this may be, on the morning of Saturday, October 14, Harold's army was drawn up in line on the ridge now crowned by the abbey and town of Battle, and William's army, having marched forth that morning from Hastings, confronted them on the hill which now bears the name of Telham. As for the battlefield itself, the chronicler, as we have seen, calls it "the Hoar Apple Tree"; one Norman historian, Orderic, calls it Senlac or Epiton, but it will probably always be best known by the name which is, of course, only approximately correct, the battlefield of Hastings. There is no evidence that there was even a village there when the battle was fought. The position of Harold's army was on a hill of moderate height, 260 feet above the sea level, so surrounded by narrow valleys, which might almost be called ravines, as to make it singularly difficult of approach by cavalry. In order to render it yet more secure against such an attack, Harold had, according to one writer,* strengthened it by a fence or palisade as well as by a fosse drawn, perhaps somewhat lower down, right across the field.

As to the numbers engaged on each side we have no information that is worth anything, only absurd and exaggerated estimates, especially on the part of the Norman writers concerning the size of the English army. As a mere conjecture, founded on the dimensions of the battlefield, there is something plausible in the suggestion† of 10,000 to 15,000 as the number

* Wace, author of the Roman de Rou. The question of the existence of this "palisade" has been discussed at great length by Mr. Round who denies, and by Mr. Archer and Miss Norgate who affirm, its existence (see English Historical Review, vol. ix., 1894). The question remains full of difficulty, the doubt being whether to attach most weight to the obscure utterance of one writer or to the silence of many. The conclusion to which the present writer is disposed to come is that there was some sort of hastily constructed fence, meant as a protection against cavalry, but that in the actual battle, which was waged chiefly between opposing bodies of infantry, it played an unimportant part and may have been soon thrust out of the way, as much by the defenders as by the assailants of the position.

† Made by Baring, Eng. Hist. Rev., vol. xx., 1905.

of William's soldiers, and the same or a little less for those of Harold. There cannot be much doubt that the quality of the invading troops was superior to that of the defenders. William's men were Normans, trained and seasoned by twenty years of fighting, supplemented by brave adventurers, with whom war was probably a regular profession, drawn from all parts of France. The backbone of Harold's army was doubtless his bodyguard of house-carls, terribly thinned by the fierce fight at Stamford Bridge, and these were reinforced by the peasants of the fyrd, brave men but little used to arms and hastily summoned from the neighbouring counties. Still they had the advantage, such as it was, of standing on the defensive in a position which had evidently been chosen with considerable military skill.

The chief weapon of the Normans was the sword, of the English the great two-handed battle-axe, the use of which was borrowed from their Danish antagonists. Both sides seem to have been armed with lances, and the best troops in both armies were clothed in long coats of mail, which were wanting, however, to the peasants of the English fyrd. The long kite-shaped shield, covering the greater part of the person, was carried by both nations, but the English were perhaps superior in the defensive tactics of the shield-wall, formed by men standing close together, shoulder to shoulder, and locking their shields into what the classically educated Norman writers called a testudo. On the other hand, William was evidently much the stronger in archers and in cavalry, and it was this superiority which eventually won for him the victory. The Normans fought of course under the standard blessed by the Pope, the Saxons under the well-known Dragon-banner of Wessex, and another which was perhaps of Harold's own devising and which bore the likeness of a full-armed fighting man. On the English side we hear of no leaders besides Harold and his two brothers, Gyrth, Earl of East Anglia, and Leofwine, Earl of Essex and Kent, both of whom seem to have fallen early in the battle. The lack of a strong lieutenant, who could have taken the direction of the defence when the king fell, had probably something to do with the issue of the fight. On the Norman side, as we might expect, the names of many leaders are given us, but we need only notice here William's half-brother, Odo, Bishop of Bayeux (son of the tanner's daughter), who salved his episcopal conscience by fighting with a heavy mace instead of with a sword, thus hoping to avoid the actual shedding of blood; Count Eustace of Boulogne, the hero of the flight from Dover; and William

Fitz-Osbern, the faithful friend of the Norman duke as his father had been before him.

We may pass over the account of the messages which are said to have been exchanged between the two rival chiefs, including a proposition by Duke William that, to save the effusion of Christian blood, they should settle their differences by single combat; and we may also pass over the story of the diverse ways in which the two armies spent the night before the battle, the English in song and revelry, crying "Wassail" and "Drink to me"; the Normans in confessing their sins and receiving absolution from the numerous priests who accompanied the army. Thus we come to the morning of Saturday, October 14, at nine A.M., when, as before said, the two armies stood fronting one another in battle array. As to the positions of the various divisions of the English army, we have no sufficient indication, except that we are told that the men of Kent claimed the right to march in the van, and strike the first blow in the battle, and that the Londoners made a similar claim to guard the person of the king, being grouped round his standard which was planted in the centre of the ridge. As to William's army, we are told that he put in his first line his archers (apparently light armed), in his second his mail-clad infantry, and in a third, behind them all, he ranged his cavalry. Moreover, there was in each of these lines another threefold division according to nationalities: the Normans in the centre, the Bretons on the left, and the Frenchmen (the men from the central regions of France) on the right.

The prelude to the battle was a romantic incident which showed that the day of chivalry had dawned. A minstrel—or as one narrator calls him, an actor—named Taillefer craved of Duke William the boon of striking the first blow. He had sung on the march some staves of the great Song of Roland, describing the death of that hero and of Olivier in the gorge of Roncesvalles, and now he pranced forth before the duke—

On the rough edge of battle ere it joined.

He took his lance by the butt-end as if it had been a truncheon, threw it in the air and caught it by the head. Three times he did this and then he hurled it into the hostile ranks and wounded an Englishman. Then, after repeating this performance with his sword, while the amazed English looked on as at a feat of conjuring, he set spurs to his horse and galloped fiercely towards the ranks of the foe. One Englishman he sorely wounded and one he slew, and then a cloud of darts and javelins was hurled at him and the bold minstrel fell down dead.

For six hours the battle which was now joined raged with nearly equal fortune on both sides. No doubt the first rank of light-armed archers discharged their missiles, and the mailed foot-soldiers pressed forward to take advantage of any impression which they may have made on the hostile ranks; but also (if we may trust the Tapestry) even at this early period of the battle the cavalry were charging (uphill, of course) and dashing themselves against the English shield-wall. So far, on the whole, they dashed themselves in vain, though already thus early in the fight Gyrth and Leofwine seem to have fallen. At length the Norman horsemen, recoiling from a fruitless charge, tumbled into a fosse, ever after known as the Malfosse, which they had scarcely noticed in their advance, and rolled over and over in dire confusion, hundreds of them lying a crushed and helpless mass on the plain. Some of the English who were pursuing shared the same fate; and one of the most spirited pictures in the Tapestry shows how "Here the English and French fell together." This disaster had very nearly proved the ruin of the invading army, for the large body of varlets or camp followers stationed in the rear to guard the harness, or stores and baggage of the troops, seeing what had befallen their masters, were about to quit the field in headlong flight, and such a movement might well have spread panic through the ranks of the army. But then Bishop Odo of Bayeux, wielding his big mace, and with a coat of mail over his alb, shouted out words of encouragement and reproof, and stayed the panic of the varlets. About the same time apparently, and under the influence of the same panic-fear, a rumour spread through the ranks that William himself was slain. He had indeed three horses killed under him in the long and dreadful struggle, but, as far as we know, he received no wound at any time, and now lifting up the nose-piece of his helmet he showed his full face to his followers whose confidence was at once restored.

As has been said, for six hours the battle hung doubtful. From three o'clock onwards victory began to incline to the Norman side, chiefly owing to two manœuvres, the credit of both of which is assigned to William personally. In the first place, finding himself otherwise unable to break the terrible shield-wall, he took a hint from the disaster of the Malfosse itself, and ordered his followers to feign flight. After men have long stood on the defensive, galled by missiles from afar, the temptation to believe that the victory is won and that they may charge a flying foe is doubtless immense. At any rate Harold's troops yielded to it, apparently more than once, and each time when pursuers and pursued had reached the plain, the Normans turned and their cavalry encircled and destroyed numbers of the English. The other manœuvre was, we are told, an order given to the archers to shoot high up into the sky, so that their arrows might fall from on high on some unshielded part of their enemies' persons. Perhaps we have here another illustration of the fact that, for a conflict with missile weapons, it is not all gain to occupy a position on a hill. This is what the Scots learned to their cost in 1402 at Homildon Hill and the English in 1881 at Majuba. At any rate it seems to have been by this change of tactics that the decisive blow was struck. It was by an arrow falling from on high that Harold's right eye was pierced. The wound was mortal and the king fell to the ground. Whatever life may have been left in him was extinguished by four Norman knights (one of them the hateful Eustace of Boulogne) who not only slew but mutilated their fallen foe.

The English seem still to have fought on for some time after the death of their king, but without purpose or discipline. The Normans were not disposed to give quarter, and apparently the greater number of the mail-clad house-carls fell where they had been fighting. The lighter-armed men of the fyrd fled, and, according to one account, their pursuers followed them into a part of the field where, from the broken nature of the ground and the abundance of ditches, their own ranks—they were evidently mounted warriors—fell into some confusion, and seeing this the fugitives made a rally. Owing probably to the fading light William and his comrades believed this to be a movement of fresh troops brought up against them. They halted, and Eustace of Boulogne counselled retreat, but a blow between the shoulders dealt suddenly from behind caused him to fall to the ground, while William pressed on undaunted and found that the victory was indeed his, and in the old Saxon phrase the Normans "held the place of slaughter." The Norman duke caused his Pope-blessed standard to be planted on the brow of the hill in the same place where Harold's banner had floated. After rendering thanks to God for his great victory, he ordered his supper to be prepared on the battlefield in the midst of the thousands of corpses of both armies, whom the survivors all through the following Sunday were busily engaged in burying, or in removing from the field that they might be carried to their homes for burial.

The body of Harold himself, grievously disfigured, but recognised, according to a well-known story, by his lady-love, "Edith with the swan's neck," is said to have been given by the Conqueror to William Malet, a nobleman half Norman and half English, and a kinsman of the house of Leofric, with instructions that it should be buried under a great cairn on the coast of that Sussex which he had vainly professed to guard. According to one story, Gytha, Godwine's widow, vainly offered to buy her son's body back from his foe at the price of his weight in gold; but it is probable that William before long relented and allowed the body of his fallen rival to be disinterred and buried with befitting solemnity in the great minster of the Holy Rood at Waltham.

William himself, in fulfilment of a vow made on the eve of the contest, founded on the field of slaughter a stately abbey which bore the name of Battle, and in which masses were long said for the repose of the souls of those who had fallen in the fight, whether conquerors or conquered. The building of the abbey with all its dependencies must have done much to alter the face of the battlefield; and now for near four centuries the abbey itself has been hidden and changed by the manor house reared within its precincts, in Tudor style, by the family to whom it was granted on the suppression of the monasteries. Change upon change has since befallen the noble dwelling-house which still bears the name of Battle Abbey; and its gardens and groves, its tall yew hedges and terraced lawns, though all most beautiful, make it hard to reconstruct with the mind's eye the eleventh century aspect of "the place of slaughter." Only the well-ascertained site of the high altar of the Abbey Church on the crest of the hill enables us to say with certainty, in the language of the Bayeux Tapestry—

HIC HAROLD REX INTERFECTUS EST.

With the battle of Hastings ends the story of England as ruled by Anglo-Saxon kings. The causes of the change, so full of meaning for all future years, which transferred the English crown from the race of Cerdic to the race of Rollo, cannot be dwelt upon here: perhaps some of them have been sufficiently indicated in the course of the preceding narrative. It is enough to say that a great and grievous transformation had come over the Anglo-Saxon character since the days of Oswald and even since the days of Alfred. The splendid dawn of English and especially of Northumbrian Christianity in the seventh century had been early obscured. The nation had lost some of the virtues of heathendom and had not retained all that it had acquired of the virtues of Christianity. Of its political incapacity the whole course of its history during the last century before the conquest is sufficient evidence; and it is probably a symptom of the same general decay that for two centuries after the death of Alfred no writer or thinker of any eminence, with the doubtful exceptions of Dunstan and Elfric, appears among his countrymen. A tendency to swinish self-indulgence, and the sins of the flesh in some of their most degrading forms, had marred the national character. There was still in it much good metal, but if the Anglo-Saxon was to do anything worth doing in the world, it was necessary that it should be passed through the fire and hammered on the anvil. The fire, the anvil and the hammer were about to be supplied with unsparing hand by the Norman conquerors.

APPENDIX—AUTHORITIES

All that portion of archæological science which deals with prehistoric man is of recent origin, and the conclusions arrived at as to our own island, even by the most careful inquirers, must be accepted provisionally, as liable to much modification by the labours of future students. Meanwhile the results generally accepted by scholars may be found well stated by Professor BOYD DAWKINS (Early Man in Britain, 1880), by Dr. JOHN BEDDOE (The Races of Britain, 1885), and by the Rev. Canon GREENWELL and GEO. ROLLESTON (British Barrows, 1877). All these authors deal chiefly with the results of excavation in the caves and sepulchral barrows of Britain. The measurement of the skulls disinterred from thence and the character of the vessels found in proximity to the bodies, are the chief criteria by which they decide on the racial character of the occupants. Professor JOHN RHYS (The Early Ethnology of the British Isles, 1890, and Celtic Britain, 2nd edit., 1884) approaches the subject of British ethnology rather from the side of early traditions and the evidence, somewhat meagre and unsatisfactory, of Celtic annalists, but with much help from philology.

Passing from the consideration of prehistoric man to the notices of Britain furnished by the writers of classical antiquity we come first to the Greek and Roman geographers. The chief Greek writers are Strabo and Ptolemy. STRABO, who was a native of Asia Minor, lived at the Christian era, and may be considered a slightly younger contemporary of Augustus. His colossal work on geography was written in his old age, and was probably finished about A.D. 19. Though he was an extensive traveller, he never visited Britain: his knowledge of our island seems to be chiefly derived from Cæsar, and he is altogether wrong as to its geographical position, believing it to lie alongside of the coast of Gaul from the Pyrenees to the mouths of the Rhine. He imagined Ireland to be entirely north of Britain.

PTOLEMY, who was a native of Egypt, was a contemporary of the

Antonine emperors, and probably wrote about A.D. 150. He was essentially an astronomical geographer, whose object was to fix the latitude and longitude of every place of which he took note. His industry was extraordinary, and his scientific conceptions were somewhat in advance of his age; but owing to the inaccurate information upon which he had often to rely, his results are sometimes very far from correct. Thus, though he gets England and Ireland almost into their true position, correcting the errors of Strabo concerning them, he pulls Scotland so far round to the east that it is at right angles to England, and its northernmost point almost touches Denmark.

PLINY, who was born in A.D. 23 and perished in the great eruption of Vesuvius in A.D. 79, is the only Latin geographer who tells us much about Britain, and his descriptions do not add much to our knowledge, but relate chiefly to natural history and to the cultivation of the soil.

For the Roman conquest of Britain our chief authorities are, of course, CÆSAR and TACITUS. The former, in the fourth and fifth books of his history of the Gallic War, describes in a few brief, soldier-like sentences the incidents of his two invasions, hardly attempting to conceal their ill-success. The latter, in the fourteenth book of his Annals, gives us the story of the insurrection of the Britons under Boudicca and its suppression by Suetonius Paulinus. An earlier book in the same series undoubtedly gave the history of the conquest of Britain under Claudius, but this is unfortunately lost. He gives us, however, in his Life of Agricola, a pretty full account of the events which signalised the command of his father-in-law, Julius Agricola (A.D. 78–84), and a slight notice of some events which occurred under his predecessors. Unfortunately Tacitus, superb as he is in delineation of character and scornful summaries of palace intrigues, fails grievously as a military historian, which happens to be his chief function when he is concerned with the history of Britain. Mommsen (bk. viii., chap. 5) says: "A worse narrative than that of Tacitus concerning this war (Paulinus against Boudicca) is hardly to be found even in this most unmilitary of authors."

To make up for the loss of the earlier books of Tacitus's Annals we have the history of DION CASSIUS, a Greek rhetorician who wrote his Roman History about A.D. 222. Though a useful compiler, Dion is, of course, no contemporary authority for the conquest of Britain under Claudius. Such as he is, however, we have to depend on him almost entirely for our knowledge of that event.

After we lose the guidance of Tacitus, our information as to Roman Britain becomes excessively meagre. Even the work of Dion Cassius after A.D. 54 is lost in the original, and only exists for us in an epitome—a tolerably full one, it must be admitted—made in the twelfth century by XIPHILINUS, an ignorant and careless monk of Constantinople. In addition to this, however, we receive a feeble and flickering light from the collection of memoirs called the HISTORIA AUGUSTA. This book, the result of the joint labours of some five or six authors whose very names are a subject of controversy, relates in clumsy and uncritical fashion the chief events in the lives of the Roman emperors during the second and third centuries. Poor as is the performance of these authors, and though they were probably separated by an interval of one or two centuries from the events which they record, we have reason to be grateful to them for the information which they supply to us, especially as to our two most illustrious conquerors, Hadrian and Severus. For the reign of the latter emperor we may also glean a few facts from the work of the Greek historian HERODIAN.

The story of the imperial pretenders, Carausius and Allectus, and of the suppression of their independent royalty, is told in a certain fashion by two panegyrists, called MAMERTINUS and EUMENIUS, in their orations before the triumphant emperors; but it is hard to extract solid history out of their windy rhetoric.

A historian to whom we owe much, and should doubtless owe far more if a perverse literary fate had not deprived us of nearly half of his work, is the life-guardsman AMMIANUS MARCELLINUS, who lived in the latter half of the fourth century and wrote the history of the Roman empire from A.D. 99 to 378. As it is, possessing only those books which tell of the years from 353 to 378, we derive from him some valuable information as to the British campaigns of the elder Theodosius. If we possessed the earlier books of his history, we should almost certainly know much more than we do as to the appearance of Roman Britain in the second century and the mode of life of its native inhabitants, for Ammianus is fond of showing off his geographical knowledge, and resembles Herodotus in the interest which he takes in the manners and customs of half-civilised races. His Latin style—he was a Syrian Greek by birth—is extraordinarily affected and often obscure, but for all that, few literary events could be more gratifying to the historical student than the recovery of the lost books of Ammianus.

For the social, military and religious life of the Romans in Britain an invaluable source of information is contained in the inscriptions which are collected in the seventh volume of the Corpus Inscriptionum Latinarum (Berlin, 1873). Many of the most important will be found in the Lapidarium Septentrionale, edited by Dr. Bruce (Newcastle-on-Tyne, 1875). Inscriptions discovered more recently must be looked for in the volumes of the Ephemeris Epigraphica, published by the Academie der Wissenschaften at Berlin, or in the Archæological Journal and the proceedings of local antiquarian societies.

OROSIUS, a disciple of St. Augustine, has done something to lighten the darkness which hangs over the end of Roman rule in Britain. In the last book of his Histories, which were meant to show that the calamities of the empire were not due to the introduction of Christianity, he tells us with some little detail the story of the military revolt of the year 406, of which we also learn some details from the Greek historian Zosimus. A chronicler who generally bears the name of another friend of St. Augustine's, PROSPER TIRO, but who was evidently a theological opponent of that saint, and whose personality is really unknown, inserts in his Chronicle two all-important dates for the Roman evacuation of Britain and for the Saxon invasions. The contemporary poet, CLAUDIAN, writing in 403, also gives us in a few lines some important information as to the former event. This is practically the last trustworthy notice as to our island that we find in the works of any classical writer. Henceforth our history for many centuries is written for us entirely by ecclesiastics, and this must be the modern historian's excuse for the strongly ecclesiastical colour which he is obliged to give even to a political narrative. One such ecclesiastical authority is The Life of Germanus by the presbyter CONSTANTIUS, as has been previously said. This Life has suffered much from later interpolations. See an elaborate analysis of it by Levison in the Neues Archiv, vol. xxix.

The next writer who lifts any portion of the pall which hides the history of our island in the fifth and sixth centuries is GILDAS, the author of the Liber Querulus "concerning the ruin of Britain." Rightly is the book called querulous, for it is one long drawn out lamentation over the barbarities of the Saxon invaders and the irreligion of the Britons which had brought this ruin upon them. If Gildas, who wrote probably between 540 and 560, had chosen to tell us simply all that he had seen or heard from men of the preceding generation concerning Saxon raids and

Cymric resistance, his work would have been one of the corner-stones of English history. As it is, we have to be thankful for the few facts that he imparts to us between sob and sob over the wickedness of the world. A critical edition of this author by Mommsen will be found in vol. xiii. of the Auctores Antiquissimi in the Monumenta Germaniæ Historica. An excellent edition with notes by the Rev. Hugh Williams, Professor of Church History at the Theological College, Bala, is now in course of publication for the Hon. Society of Cymmrodorion.

More perplexing, but fuller of matter, good, bad and indifferent, is the work of the much later Welsh ecclesiastic, NENNIUS, who lived about two centuries and a half after Gildas. This author exhibits a degree of ignorance and puzzle-headedness which gives one a very unfavourable idea of the intellectual condition of a Welsh monastery about the year 800. His chronology is wildly incorrect, and he intermingles with solemn history stories of dragons and enchanters worthy of the Arabian Nights; but he has inserted into the middle of his book extracts from the work of a much earlier author (probably a Northumbrian Celt living under Anglian rule) who described the contests of English and Welsh between 547 and 679. This part of the book (to be found in chapters 57 to 65 of Nennius) has probably a real historic value. It is important to note that it is in this portion that the name of King Arthur is found. As already mentioned (p. 100) we are much indebted to the labours of Prof. Zimmer (Nennius Vindicatus) with reference to this important but most provoking writer.

Turning from the Welsh to the English authorities we come to the illustrious name of BEDE, the greatest scholar of his age and the best historian whom any European country produced in the early Middle Ages. His main work, the Historia Ecclesiastica, was finished in the year 731, about four years before his death. There is an excellent edition of this book and of some of the smaller historical works of Bede by the Rev. Charles Plummer (2 vols.: Oxford, 1896). The historical importance of this work begins with its account of the conversion of England to Christianity; and, for all the events of the seventh century and the early part of the eighth, it is priceless. As to the events which marked the Roman occupation of Britain, Bede probably had no other sources of information than those which we also possess. For the two centuries of darkness between the departure of the last Roman soldier and the arrival of the first Roman missionary he had evidently very scanty sources to draw from, and in fact he springs, almost at one bound, from the year 450 to 596.

For the closing years of the seventh century we have another valuable authority in the Life of Wilfrid, written by his contemporary, EDDIUS (Historians of the Church of York, edited by J. Raine, Rolls Series): and this is the more important as, for some reason or other, Bede shows sometimes a curious reticence as to Wilfrid's career. There is a very careful comparison of the two narratives, that of Bede and that of Eddius, by Mr. B. W. Wells in the sixth volume of the English Historical Review (1891), pp. 535–50. His conclusions are not favourable to Eddius's veracity.

In the eighth century, after we have lost the invaluable guidance of Bede, we may derive some help from the letters of two great Churchmen, BONIFACE and ALCUIN, both published in Monumenta Germaniæ Historica (Epistolae, vols. iii. and iv., 1892 and 1895).

For the whole period from the Saxon invasion onwards we rely with increasing confidence on the great historical document, or collection of documents, which is sometimes called the Anglo-Saxon Chronicle, but which, following Freeman's example, we generally designate by the simple but sufficient name of The Chronicle (Plummer, 2 vols., 1892). The reason for introducing the notice of it here is that, according to the opinion of its latest editor, we arrive, in the ninth century, at the time of the first compilation of this work, so all-important for the students of our national history. If he is right in thinking that the impulse toward the commencement of this great undertaking was given by King Alfred—a belief which seems to be shared by Mr. Stevenson, the editor of Asser—it cannot have begun to assume its present shape till near the year 900. Some materials, however, for the building of such an edifice must have been gradually accumulating for at least two centuries; in what shape, of what kind, of what degree of historical trustworthiness, we shall, perhaps, never be able to determine. There were probably rhythmical pedigrees of the kings and some stories of their exploits handed down through generations of minstrels; and, at any rate since the introduction of Christianity, some simple annals such as that to which Bede alludes when he says that 634, the year of the reign of two apostate Northumbrian kings, was, "by those who compute the times of kings," taken away from them and included in the reign of their pious successor Oswald. This hypothesis, however, will not help us much when we come to consider how Alfred's literary friends could recover accurate dates and details of events during the preceding 150 years of darkness, and we must probably admit that for that period there may have been a good deal of imaginative chronology of the kind suggested by Lappenberg, as already stated on p. 87. Thus all this earlier portion of the Chronicle has to be used with caution, and we dare not lay any great stress upon the historical character of its statements; only let not its authority be unduly decried, seeing that for a good part of the road it is the only light that we have.

Even after we emerge into the fuller light of the seventh century, and when we have no reason to doubt the truly historical character of the Chronicle, we cannot award it the praise of minute accuracy in matters of chronology. Continually historians have found it necessary to correct its dates by one, two, or three years; and even the foundation date of Egbert's accession, which used to be given on the authority of the Chronicle to 800, has had to be shifted to 802.

The Chronicle, if begun under the influence of Alfred (probably at Winchester), was continued in various monasteries on somewhat independent lines, and thus, as its latest editor points out, "instead of saying that the Anglo-Saxon Chronicle is contained in seven MSS., it would be truer to say that those MSS. contain four Anglo-Saxon Chronicles." These are represented by the four chief MSS. which are now known to scholars by the four letters A, C, D, E. The first of these MSS. is at Corpus Christi College, Cambridge, the second and third in the British Museum, and the fourth in the Bodleian Library at Oxford. Very briefly stated, the distinguishing characteristics of these four MSS. are as follows:—

A (sometimes marked by an Anglo-Saxon letter in order to distinguish it from a later and unimportant manuscript to which also that initial has been given) is also called, from its former owner, Archbishop Parker's manuscript, or the Winchester Chronicle. There can be little doubt that this manuscript was originally a native of Winchester, and began to be compiled there in Alfred's reign. A Winchester book it continued till the year 1001, after which it seems to have been transferred to Christ Church, Canterbury, where it was probably lying at the time of the suppression of the monasteries. This manuscript, in many respects the most valuable of all, ends with the year 1070.

C is associated on good authority with the monastery of Abingdon. "Its language [says Professor Earle] is of the most ripe and polished kind, marking the culmination of Saxon literature." It closes in 1066, but a short postscript has been added in the Northumbrian dialect. One important feature in this manuscript is its inclusion of what is called "The

Mercian Register," describing the great deeds of the Lady of Mercia from 902 to 924. In the next century it is distinguished by the hostile tone which it adopts towards Earl Godwine and his family.

D, which is generally called the Worcester Chronicle, but which seems to have a closer connexion with Evesham, is, in its present shape, a late compilation, none of it probably being of earlier date than 1100. It seems to be closely allied to C, but differs from that manuscript by its friendlier attitude towards Godwine. It is the only version which gives us any account of the battle of Hastings. It ends thirteen years after the Conquest.

E, the Laud manuscript or Peterborough Chronicle, is of great importance, inasmuch as it alone continues the history down to so late a date as 1154, and its great variety of style makes it a leading authority for the history of the English language. In its present shape it is emphatically a book of the Abbey of Peterborough, and loses no opportunity of glorifying that religious house. It probably owes its origin to a disastrous fire which happened at Peterborough in 1116, in which all the muniments of the abbey perished. A manuscript akin to D seems to have been then brought thither from some other monastery, and this copy of it, with sundry interpolations, has been made to replace the perished Chronicle. A and E are the two Chronicles which Plummer and his predecessor Earle have chosen as the corner-stones of their editions of the Anglo-Saxon Chronicles, but passages are inserted from C and D where these authorities give us important variations.

For the personal history of Alfred the Great and some information as to the events of his reign, we have the very important treatise by his contemporary, ASSER, De Rebus Gestis Aelfredi (Stevenson, 1904). Asser was a Welsh ecclesiastic, belonging to the diocese of St. Davids, who came about the year 880 to the court of King Alfred, seeking protection from the tyranny of his native sovereigns, sons of Rhodri Mawr. That protection was freely accorded, and the king, perceiving Asser to be a learned man, stipulated that he should spend at least half of every year in the land of the Saxons. Eventually he became bishop of Sherborne, and no doubt ceased altogether to reside in Wales. He died apparently in 910, about ten years after his patron. Asser's Life of King Alfred which ends practically with the year 887, giving no account of the last thirteen years of his reign, is a very inartistic work, containing annalistic notices, taken apparently from the Chronicle, strangely jumbled up with those interesting personal details as to the character and habits of the great king which give it in our eyes all its value. It has been singularly unfortunate in its transmission, since the only copy of which we have any certain knowledge perished in the great fire at the Cottonian Library in 1731. Happily, it had been already printed three times, but unfortunately those three editions all contained several large interpolations made by its first editor, Archbishop Parker, from a mistaken desire to round off its information by extracts from other authors. Partly owing to these interpolations, its genuineness has been subjected to severe attacks, which have sometimes seemed likely to be successful. Its character, however, has been triumphantly vindicated by its latest editor, Mr. W. H. Stevenson, who has succeeded in separating the original text of the Life from the interpolations of its editors, and thus presenting it with all its naïve charm, often also, it must be admitted, with all its provoking verbiage and obscurity, to the lovers of the greatest Anglo-Saxon king. In the same volume Mr. Stevenson has printed the Annals of St. Neot's, which were formerly, without justification, ascribed to Asser, and from which some of the worst interpolations into his real work were derived. It is an important testimony to the authentic character of Asser's work that large extracts have been made from it by so judicious a compiler as Florence of Worcester.

For the reconstruction of English history in the tenth century our materials are very unsatisfactory. The impulse given by Alfred to the composition of the Chronicle seems to have soon exhausted itself, and for fifty years after the death of his son (925 to 975) it is, as Earle has said, "wonderfully meagre: a charge which is often unreasonably alleged against these Chronicles in the most undiscriminating manner, but which may be justified here by a comparison with the historical literature of two earlier generations." Its aridity is in some degree atoned for by the ballads, such as that on the battle of Brunanburh, which are inserted at intervals in its pages; but with all the poetic interest attaching to these pieces they can hardly be considered a satisfactory substitute for history. In these circumstances we have to be thankful for such help as can be derived from biographies of the saints; especially from the nearly contemporary Life of Dunstan, by an anonymous Saxon priest who is known only by his initial B. (Memorials of St. Dunstan, edited by Stubbs, Rolls Series), and the similar anonymous but contemporary Life of Oswald, Archbishop of York (Historians of the Church of York, edited by J. Raine, Rolls Series).

The later lives of Dunstan, by Adelard, Osbern and Eadmer (all included in Stubbs's Memorials of St. Dunstan), soon fade off into legend, and must be used with caution.

We ought to have been greatly helped at this period by the work of ETHELWEARD the historian (Monumenta Historica Britannica, Petrie, 1848), who was of royal descent, was apparently for a time Ealdorman of Wessex, and wrote near the end of the tenth century. Unfortunately the basis of his work seems to have been the Chronicle itself, and when he has any additional facts to communicate, his style is so pompously obscure that it is difficult to make out what he means. In default, therefore, of adequate contemporary authorities, the historian is obliged to lean more than he has yet done on the compiling historians who wrote in the century which followed the Norman Conquest. Of these, happily, there is a goodly number, and they are on the whole very favourable specimens of their class.

(1) FLORENCE OF WORCESTER (edited by B. Thorpe, English Historical Society, 1848–49), a monk of whom we know nothing save that he died in 1118, having earned a high reputation for acuteness and industry, took as the staple of his narrative the work of an Irish monk named Marianus Scotus, who was settled at Mainz and composed a World-Chronicle reaching down to the year 1082. With the material thus furnished him Florence interwove extracts specially relating to English history from Bede, Asser and the Chroniclers, bringing down his recital to 1117, the year preceding his death. His work was almost entirely that of a compiler, but it was conscientiously and thoroughly done, and its chief value for us is that though his story approaches most nearly to that told in the Worcester Chronicle (D), it is not a mere transcript of that work, and he evidently had access to some manuscript of the Chronicle which is now lost. The important position which he holds in relation to Asser has already been described.

(2) Some important facts concerning Northumbrian history may be gleaned from the ill-arranged pages of SYMEON OF DURHAM (edited by T. Arnold, Rolls Series, 2 vols., 1882–85). This author, who was born a few years before the Conquest, became a monk at Durham about the year 1085, and spent probably the rest of his life by the tomb of St. Cuthbert. Soon after 1104 he wrote a History of the Church of Durham, which supplies some valuable information not to be found elsewhere, as to the history of events in the north of England during the thirty years following the Danish invasion of 875. In his old age Symeon began, but apparently

did not finish, a History of the Kings, which in its present state is a piece of patchwork put together from various sources, and in its chaotic condition corresponds only too closely with the reality of Northumbrian history during that dismal period. Its chief value for the historian is that it incorporates an old Northumbrian Chronicle by an anonymous writer (perhaps called Gesta veterum Northanhymbrorum) describing the chief events which happened in that part of the country from the end of Bede's history to the accession of Egbert (731–802). For a full discussion of the materials used by Symeon in this work the reader is referred to Mr. Arnold's preface and to Stubbs's preface to Roger Hoveden. It cannot be said that even his explanations make the matter very clear. An interesting tract, De Obsessione Dunelmi, which has been attributed on insufficient evidence to this author, is bound up with his works.

(3) HENRY OF HUNTINGDON (edited by T. Arnold, Rolls Series, 1879) was born about eighteen years after the Conquest and died soon after the accession of Henry II. He was an archdeacon in the diocese of Lincoln, and composed at the request of his bishop a History of the English, of which various editions were published in his lifetime, the first probably about 1130, and the last soon after 1154. Henry relies chiefly on the Peterborough Chronicle, but he seems also to have possessed some other manuscript, of which he occasionally gives indications. Unfortunately he relies not only on manuscripts and Chronicles, but also to a large extent on his own imagination. From materials not much ampler than those which we possess, he is fond of constructing a rhetorical narrative with many details, for which it is almost certain that he had no authority. Occasionally there seems reason to believe that he is repeating popular traditions or fragments of popular songs, but upon the whole it is safer not to rely greatly on his facts, where these are not corroborated by other historians.

(4) A much greater historian than Henry was his slightly younger contemporary, WILLIAM OF MALMESBURY (edited by Stubbs, Rolls Series, 2 vols., 1887–89), who was probably born about 1095 and died, or at any rate discontinued his literary labours, soon after 1142. For an elaborate discussion of these dates see Bishop Stubbs's preface. As he remarks, William "deliberately set himself forward as the successor of the Venerable Bede: and it is seldom that an aspirant of this sort came so near as he did to the realisation of his pretensions." His most important work for our purpose is the Gesta Regum, but from his Gesta

Pontificum (Hamilton, Rolls Series, 1870) some facts relating to civil history may be gleaned. He is especially minute in all points connected with his own monastery of Malmesbury and with that of Glastonbury, in which he seems to have been for some time a guest. He has a wide outlook over continental affairs, and though he has been convicted of many inaccuracies and is unfortunately not sufficiently careful as to the authenticity of the documents quoted by him, we must admit his claim to be considered a really great historian. The Gesta Regum became at once a popular and standard history, and was the source from which a crowd of followers made abundant quotations.

(5) A great patron of learned men, and especially of historians, was Robert, Earl of Gloucester, natural son of Henry I. To him William of Malmesbury dedicated his chief historical works, and it was from materials contained in his library that GEOFFREY GAIMAR (edited by Hardy and Martin, Rolls Series, 2 vols., 1888–89) wrote his Estorie des Engles. Scarcely anything is known about the author, except that he wrote before 1147, the date of the Earl of Gloucester's death, and that he was probably an ecclesiastic and a Norman. His history is a rhymed chronicle in early French, and is to a large extent based on the English Chronicle; a proof that he understood Anglo-Saxon, though it was not his native tongue. He evidently, however, had access to other sources of information now closed to us, and this gives his Estorie a certain value, notwithstanding the author's occasional tendency to glide off into unhistorical romance, as for instance in the long and legendary story which he tells about Edgar's marriage with Elgiva. His geographical indications are sometimes worthy of special notice.

For sixty years after 982 the fortunes of England were so closely intertwined with those of Denmark and Norway that it is impossible wholly to overlook the contributions which Scandinavian authors have made to our national history. These consist chiefly of the great collection of Icelandic Sagas popularly known as the Heimskringla, and formerly made accessible to the English reader only by LAING'S Sea-Kings of Norway, now in much completer form in the Saga Library of MORRIS and MAGNUSSON. Three volumes of the Heimskringla have been published: the fourth is still to appear. For a full and exhaustive account, however, of the rich Dano-Icelandic literature of which the so-called Heimskringla is only a portion, we must turn to the noble work of VIGFUSSON and POWELL, the Corpus Poeticum Boreale (two vols., Oxford, 1883), and to Vigfusson's Prolegomena to the Sturlunga Saga (Oxford, 1879). It is shown by these authors that while the name of Snorri Sturlason is rightly venerated as that of the chief literary preserver of these sagas, an earlier Icelandic scholar named Ari, born in the year after the Norman Conquest, was the first to bring them into some sort of relation with exact chronological history. The narratives seem to be wonderfully true in feeling but often false in fact. Probably a good deal of rather tedious critical work has yet to be done before the Heimskringla can be definitely and safely correlated with the Saxon Chronicle, but we may safely go to that collection of sagas and to the literature of which it forms part, the true Iliad and Odyssey of the Scandinavian peoples, for a picture of the manner of life, the characters and the ideals of those Danish and Norwegian sea-rovers who were the terror of Angle and Saxon, but from whom we ourselves are largely descended.

For the reign of Canute and his sons we are sometimes placed under obligation by the author of the Encomium Emmæ (Monumenta Germaniæ Historica, vol. xix., 1866), a panegyric on the widow of Ethelred and Canute, written apparently by an ecclesiastic of Bruges, who had shared her bounty when she was living in exile. The author sometimes deviates in the most extraordinary way from historic truth, but he seems to have been well acquainted with the facts, though he dishonestly concealed them to please his patroness.

With the extinction of the Danish dynasty and the revival of West Saxon royalty we enter upon a new period, in which our historical literature assumes a controversial character which it has not hitherto possessed. In previous centuries there has been no practical danger in speaking of The Chronicle, the amount of matter common to the various copies being so large and the divergencies between them so comparatively unimportant. Now, however, it is necessary to speak of The Chronicles in the plural, since they often give us absolutely different versions of the same event. The Abingdon Chronicle, as before remarked, is hostile to Godwine, while Worcester (or Evesham) and Peterborough generally favour his cause. Winchester is almost silent for this period. There is a nearly contemporary Life of Edward the Confessor in Latin by an unknown author (printed at the end of the volume, Lives of Edward the Confessor, in the Rolls Series, 1858), from which some noteworthy facts may be collected, but the value of the work is lessened by the writer's evident determination to praise to the uttermost Godwine and all his family, in order to recommend himself to Edward's widow Edith, daughter of Godwine, to whom this Vita Edwardi Regis is dedicated. In comparison with his wife's family the king himself comes off rather poorly.

The life of the Confessor was soon caught up into the region of hagiological romance, and loses historical value accordingly. It does not seem possible to build any solid conclusions on the Vita Edwardi Regis by Aelred, itself borrowed from the twelfth-century biographer Osbert, still less on the curious and interesting Estoire de Seint Ædward le Rei, a French poem written about 1245 and dedicated to Eleanor, queen of Henry III. (Lives of Edward the Confessor).

*****

The Norman historians, who now of course become of first-rate importance for the history, are fully described in the second volume. It will be sufficient here to mention the names of the most important: WILLIAM OF POITIERS, WILLIAM OF JUMIÈGES (both contemporaries of the Conqueror), ORDERICUS VITALIS (a generation later) and WILLIAM WACE, author of two French metrical Chronicles, the Roman de Brut and the Roman de Rou. The latter poem describes with much detail and some poetic power the events of the Norman invasion of England, but its author wrote about a century after the event, and the degree of reliance which may be placed on his statements, where not supported by more strictly contemporary authority, is still a subject of debate among historians. Editions by Pluquet (1826) and Andresen (1877–79) are mentioned with commendation, but the most convenient edition for an English student is that prepared by Sir Alexander Malet with a tolerably close translation of Pluquet's text into English rhyme (London, 1860).

The other all-important document for the story of the Conquest, the BAYEUX TAPESTRY, has been reproduced in facsimile, with a valuable illustrative commentary, by F. R. Fowke (London, 1875, reprinted in abridged form in the Ex Libris Series, 1898). Discussing the date and origin of this celebrated work, he rejects the traditional connexion of the Tapestry with Queen Matilda, but believes it to be strictly contemporary with the Conquest, having been "probably ordered for his cathedral by Bishop Odo and made by Norman work-people at Bayeux." Refer also to Freeman's Norman Conquest, vol. iii., note A, for a discussion of the authority of the Tapestry.

*****

Of the Welsh authorities for this period contained in this volume the present writer cannot speak with confidence. The chief appear to be (1) the Annales Cambriæ, supposed to have been compiled in the year 954 and afterwards continued to 1288.

(2) The Brut y Tywysogion, or Chronicle of the Princes, which begins in 680 and ends with 1282. It is thought to be based on a Latin chronicle written in the middle of the twelfth century by a Pembrokeshire monk named Caradog of Llancarvan.

(3) The Brut y Saesson, or Chronicle of the Saxons (800–1382), seems to be chiefly founded on the last-named work, but with some additions from English sources; of no great value, at any rate for pre-Conquest history.

It is to be wished that some scholar would carefully sift the Welsh chronicles and poems, and tell us what are the solid historical facts that may be gathered from their pages.

*****

Without attempting to give a list, however imperfect, of modern books dealing with the early history of England, it may be permitted to mention a few of the chief land-marks.

The history of Roman Britain has yet to be written. Every year excavations, inscriptions, coins add a little to our knowledge of these tantalisingly obscure centuries. Perhaps the best short sketches to which the student can be referred are the chapter on Britain in MOMMSEN'S Provinces of the Roman Empire (translated by Dickson: London, 1886), and a similar chapter in EMIL HÜBNER'S Römische Herrschaft in West Europa (Berlin, 1890). Both these scholars are complete masters of all that epigraphy has to tell concerning the Roman occupation of Britain. In the early chapters of various volumes of the Victoria County History of England, Mr. F. HAVERFIELD is bringing the Roman archæology of the counties there described thoroughly up to date. It is to be hoped that these may all before long be combined by him into one great work on Britannia Romana.

For Anglo-Saxon history perhaps LAPPENBERG'S Geschichte

von England (translated by B. Thorpe: London, 1881) is still the most trustworthy guide; but the Making of England and the Conquest of England by JOHN RICHARD GREEN have all the characteristic charm of that author's historical work; perhaps also it should be said, his characteristic tendency to translate a brilliant hypothesis into historical fact. The truly monumental history of The Norman Conquest by E. A. FREEMAN will assuredly always remain the great quarry from which all later builders will hew their blocks for building. Even those who differ most strongly from his conclusions must bear witness to his unwearied industry and single-minded desire for historical accuracy, whether he always compassed it or not. One of Freeman's antagonists, C. H. PEARSON, offers some useful suggestions in his History of England during the Early and Middle Ages; and the same author's Historical Maps of England during the First Thirteen Centuries contain an immense amount of carefully collected geographical material, and deserve to be more widely known than they are at the present time. Another doughty combatant, J. H. ROUND, in Feudal England (London, 1895), has set himself to demolish Professor Freeman's theories as to the battle of Hastings and some other matters.

SIR JAMES RAMSAY'S Foundations of England (1898) is an extremely careful digest of all the authorities bearing on the subject.

W. BRIGHT'S Early English Church History, C. F. KEARY'S Vikings in Western Christendom and C. PLUMMER'S Life and Times of Alfred the Great are all helpful books.

Where English and Scottish history touch one another the works of E. W. ROBERTSON, Scotland under Her Early Kings and Historical Essays; W. F. SKENE, Celtic Scotland, and ANDREW LANG, History of Scotland, will be found useful, and should be consulted in order to see the arguments of the champions of Scottish independence.

For the history of institutions reference should be made to Bishop STUBBS (Constitutional History); F. W. MAITLAND (Domesday Book and Beyond); H. M. CHADWICK (Studies on Anglo-Saxon Institutions); J. M. KEMBLE (The Saxons in England); F. PALGRAVE (The Rise and Progress of the English Commonwealth); H. C. COOTE (The Romans of Britain—worth studying, with distrust, as an extreme statement of the survival of Roman customs in Britain); F. SEEBOHM (The English Village Community); and P. VINOGRADOFF (Villainage in England, The Growth of the Manor and an essay on "Folkland" in the English Historical Review for 1893, which has been generally accepted as containing the true explanation of that much-discussed term of Anglo-Saxon law).

A good edition of the Anglo-Saxon Laws was prepared in 1840 by BENJAMIN THORPE and published by the Record Commission. A more complete edition, with full commentary, was made by REINHOLD SCHMID and published in Leipzig in 1858. Even this is now being surpassed by the work of FELIX LIEBERMANN (Halle, 1898–1903), who has published an excellent text, but whose commentary on the laws has yet to appear. For the charters and other similar documents of the Anglo-Saxon kings we may refer to KEMBLE'S Codex Diplomaticus (6 vols., 1839–48); BIRCH'S Cartularium Saxonicum (3 vols., 1885–93), and HADDAN and STUBBS'S Councils (3 vols., 1869–78), which are splendid collections of this kind of material for the historical student. As convenient manuals, Diplomatarium Anglicum Aevi Saxonici by BENJAMIN THORPE (1845); STUBBS'S Select Charters (1895), and EARLE'S Handbook to the Land Charters, will be found useful.

For a much more detailed list of authorities than can here be given the reader is referred to the excellent manual on The Sources and Literature of English History by Dr. CHARLES GROSS of Harvard University (1900).

Made in the USA
Las Vegas, NV
23 November 2024

12491211R00277